THE POLICE IN INDIA

M.B. Chande

ATLANTIC

PUBLISHERS & DISTRIBUTORS (P) LTD

Published by
ATLANTIC
PUBLISHERS & DISTRIBUTORS (P) LTD
7/22, Ansari Road, Darya Ganj, New Delhi-110002
Phones : +91-11-40775252, 40775214, 23273880, 23275880
Fax: +91-11-23285873
Web: www.atlanticbooks.com
E-mail: orders@atlanticbooks.com

Printed & bound in India by Atlantic Print Services

Dedicated to

My late Parents

and

Mr. K.F. Rustamji,

Padma Vibhushan

Foreword

It gives me immense pleasure to write "FOREWORD" to this book "The Police in India." It will be unjust to the author, as well as the work, to call it a mere history of the Police in India. In fact, it is far more than that. The initial chapters of this book trod through the arena of Sociology, Anthropology, Psychology — individual, social and mob, public administration and so on, focussing on the intimate relationship of the Police with the society, and its sustained well-being. It does not contain the stories of Police intelligence or investigation. On the other hand, it is replete with the history of the entire Police organisations, their functions in the changed circumstances, the drawbacks, and their causative factors, and the suggestions regarding the measures to improve them. The writer of this work is not an outsider watching objectively the working, and the functioning of the Police from a remote corner. He has himself served with the Police department for more than three decades in different capacities — from top to bottom — not only in the States of C.P. and Berar (erstwhile Madhya Pradesh), Maharashtra, but also with the Government of India; and also in different branches including the prestigious branch in-charge of the security of the Prime Minister and the V.V.I.Ps. There may be very small number of police officers, having such a varied and wide experience in different branches as M.B. Chande had. Over and above, it must be said that he did not work in these departments and branches mechanically, but kept his eyes and mind open, wherever he worked. It is from the pen of such a person having comprehensive knowledge of the various facets of the department, that this critical appreciation of the police working has emerged. His criticism is not merely for the sake of criticism, but it is the words coming from a person, who worked with his heart and soul in that department. The remedies, he has suggested, are not rooted merely in imagination of an objectivist, but it is an outcome of deep thinking, and versatile experience of a man, who was so intimately connected with the department, and the society.

Since time immemorial, maintenance of law and order and the dispensation of justice have been the functions discharged by the sovereign directly. Even today, they continue to be the functions of the sovereign. Political thoughts (Theories), and jurisprudence have undergone tremendous changes during the century, but the basic concept of Police and the Judiciary remained almost the same.

The theoretical part apart, the assumption of the adjective "welfare" by the State, has given rise to lot of misconceptions in the political thinking, so much so, that some people think that the sole function of the State is the welfare of the people; and with this background, they think that protection of the society is its subsidiary function. We also hear the loose talk that India should not spend so much on its defence, and divert the part of its defence expenditure towards the welfare activities. In their budgets the governments always categorise the expenditure as "plan" and "non-plan" expenditure. Unfortunate part thereof is that the expenditure on Police and Administration of Justice has been categorised as non-plan expenditure. And it is now, the settled policy that plan expenditure gets preference over the non-plan expenditure. That is why, we hear from all the quarters that the funds required for reforms in Police and Administration of Justice are not coming in adequate quantity. The author very strongly advocates for a positive change in this apathetic attitude of the Government.

The graded decadence in administrative control has resulted in disturbed conditions throughout the country; and criminal, anti-social and anti-national propensities have grown uncontrolled over the years with the consequence that people have lost faith in the Police.

During the pre-independence period, the role of the police in maintaining law and order was very simple. They were accountable to the Government, and to no one else. Theoretically, their loyalty was to the Government only. Government and the State were not two different agencies. They were expected to stand behind the Government like a rock, and protect it. They were not required to do anything special for the protection of the society, as their awe and fear were sufficient enough to cause a deterrent effect on the behavioural pattern of the anti-social elements of the society. Moreover, this function, they discharged without any blemish.

But with the advent of the Independence, even the conceptual complexion of the police functioning changed, and that too revolutionarily. The difference came to be drawn between "Government" and the "State". Loyalty came to be attached to the "State" and not to the "Government". Now, the Police are expected to be loyal to the "State" irrespective of the Government. Naturally, they have to assume the role of the protectors, and friends of the society.

Apart from this altered outlook, there have been tremendous changes in the society—qualitatively as well as quantitatively. The five decades after the Independence brought sweeping changes in the society, some of them were good; and some were not good. With the quantitative spread of education, social awareness has considerably increased. Awe and fear of the Police have completely disappeared. Social reforms, which occupied the back benches during the freedom struggle, came to the forefront after the Independence; thereby giving rise to sharp conflicts between different castes, classes and masses *etc.*, tearing as under the fabric that kept all Indians together. Communal tensions became the order of the day. Industrial progress actuated conflicts between enterprise and labour. Tensions between landlords and the landless took a serious turn. In short, the society, which was quiet and peaceful, has become defiant and turbulent. The turbulence has to be attributed to internal as well as external circumstances, some of them may be within or without the control of the Government. As a sequel to these factors, the functions of the Police have not only expanded, but also become more intricate and complex, and very important as they are the instruments of social defence.

The author has critically appreciated all such changes; and concluded that apart from being poorly paid, the Police were not well-equipped in all the aspects of their working, so that they could accommodate and adjust themselves with these changes in the society. Not only the Police failed, but also the Government of the day, which manned the state, failed to be receptive to these changes. In fact, each qualitative change in the society created the new arena of jurisprudence and law. Industrial development required altogether a new set of jurisprudence to cope with these changes. Student's unrest necessitated still different branch of jurisprudence, while social reforms warranted altogether a different type of jurisprudence. However, though the fields of legislation changed, the Police and the Police alone remained the law enforcement agency. This eventuated in the opening of different branches in the Police department. The author has dealt with this problem in a lucid manner. He has critically appreciated each change and has suggested the necessary remedies. The Assam Rifles, Central Reserve Police Force, Indo-Tibetan Border Police, Border Security Force, Railway Protection Force, Rapid Action Force *etc.*, are illustrative of the function-wise different branches, that have sprouted in the recent past.

The most important point, that M.B. Chande has dealt with, is regarding the discipline in the Police department. In fact, it is the cardinal principle of the entire Police Force. It is this aspect and conduct that the Police department makes itself felt differently from others; so also, it is this quality which makes a policeman mentally alert and tough enabling him to face confidently any eventual situation. Chande, who is of the strictest rectitude, and the disciplinarian of the old order, has definitely a cause to lament, and rightly too, about the falling standard of the police discipline. Discipline and loyalty are not only interconnected, but also inextricably twined. Though, he does not expect loyalty to a person, he does insist upon the loyalty only to the lawful authority on which it is built the whole edifice. He does not tolerate a policeman running away to save his life when people are in difficulties. Though, the Police are human beings tending to be vulnerable to various temptations, he wants them to be aloof from them, only because the society has employed them for its sustained protection and well-being and, therefore, policemen should be incorruptible; and feel proud for protecting the society. This particular aspect, the higher-ups in the police hierarchy, have to imbibe in the police personnel inclusive of the senior most cadres.

The author has dealt with another aspect, which is very important from the social or national point of view. It is regarding the supersonic speed of the legislative activities. It has been a common experience that laws have been enacted during the last five decades with tremendous pace, and it goes to the root of legislative wisdom. Though, in theory one may accept the proposition that the democratic government has to be receptive to the public pulse, it has to be borne in mind that the receptivity has to be rational and scientific. Legislatures are meant to enact the legislation, because there is a demand for it. Law is, no doubt, a means to achieve certain end. But it is, in fact, not the only means. There is no society in this world which has reformed itself by law. But unfortunately, there is a strong misunderstanding, prevailing today, that the enactment of legislation will remove the drawback, for which the law is ordained. Unfortunately, it is not so. There are many decrepit or current legislations on the statute books, which for one reason or the other, either mal-implemented, or mis-implemented or not implemented. In majority of cases, these laws are to be enforced or administered by the Police. Ultimately, it is the Police who come into disrepute, because of mal, mis or non-implementation of these laws; although there may be some other agencies responsible for this. But ultimately, it is the Police who are to be blamed for the failure, and even motives are attributed to them, thereby tarnishing or damaging the fair reputation of the institution.

Take for example the social reforms. It can be said, with authority, that society cannot be reformed by law alone. Our Constitution enacted Article 17, abolishing untouchability. We are implementing that Constitutional Mandate for more than four decades. Has untouchability been completely abolished today? The emphatic answer is "No". The reasons for the failure have to be searched out, and the search will show that there are so many correlated circumstances or factors which have blunted the sharpness of the edge of untouchability during the last five decades. However, the objective is yet to be achieved. Social behaviour is always bound by customs, traditions, mores *etc.*, which the society has inherited from the past generations. These cumulatively create such barriers which cannot be removed merely by a stroke of pen. It is the society which has to understand, and appreciate that these customary barriers are becoming impediments in their progress. This can be achieved more by education and human relationship, than by law. In short, whenever there is a cleavage between the institutional morality, and the social morality (or the ethical concept of morality of the society), the law is bound to fail. This happened in the case of Bombay Prohibition Act, and of Child Marriage Restraint Act. And the fate of the Dowry Prohibition Act does not appear to be far different than these unfortunate and infructuous legislations. Legislative wisdom, therefore, requires that before it enacts any social legislation, the legislature has to see whether it can provide sufficient machinery, and agency for implementing the same, and whether the Government has the will, as well as power, to implement the legislation in its real spirit. It is this sanity which will ultimately make the legislation either fruitful or fruitless; and save the Police from social ridicule and stigma.

The author has also advocated that in view of the degeneracy of moral standards of the society there is an urgent need for the reclassification of offences, their evidential relevancy, and the entailing quantum of punishment in order to impose the necessary checks against the ambivalence of human nature tending to break the most elementary rules designed to protect their fellow citizens, and make it possible for them to lead a good and peaceful life, free from any kind of molestation by others.

Last but not the least, the author has candidly dwelt upon the political interference with the day-to-day Police administration. Now, it is not a secret that the day-to-day working of the police is hampered, and at times nullified not only due to political interference, but also interference from other sources. Such a state of affairs has been established by the '*HAVALA KAND*'. The very fact that the investigation was lying dead before the investigating authorities for years, amply showed that political interference was responsible for it. The Supreme Court was moved in the matter by the people, and after the removal of interference and inhibitions, the investigating machinery found the culprits within months. That the Apex Court had to go to the extent of asking the Central Bureau of Investigation (C.B.I.)

to report directly the progress of the investigation to it (and not even to the Prime Minister, who is in-charge of the C.B.I.) reveals the magnitude and intensity, as also the vulnerability of law enforcement on account of such interferences. This aspect is now taking the shape of national debate — One does not know about the final outcome of this debate. But there is a loose talk, that the C.B.I. should be made an autonomous body. "Atonomy", in itself, is a loose term. Morever, "Autonomy" postulates separate entity. The concept of sovereignty does not permit the Police department to acquire a separate entity of its own.

Police will be called upon to deal effectively, efficiently and impartially the brewing turmoil and arrest the increasing tendency of the people to commit crime, and resort to violence. With the changing political conditions it will be dangerous for the society to permit its Police Forces to drift haphazardly from one policy to another or to allow expediency, either political or social, to override constitutional principles-cum-mandates. The Police Service, being the dominant organisation and capable enough to create or destroy the happiness of the community, should be scrupulously maintained at as high a level as possible, and their basic attitudinal change is absolutely necessary so as to prove their *bona fides*, their worth, trustworthiness, honesty, and above all probity. Their living and service conditions also require substantial improvement by the Government.

The satisfactory solution of this vexed and virulent problem of politico-criminal nexus-cum-interference has to be rationalistic. Discipline is the best preventive medicine. Imposition of self-restraint by all the police personnel while discharging their duties only in accordance with the lawful provisions would go a long way in removing this malady; but it could not be achieved without public support and co-operation; and for that the policemen are expected to be thoroughly incorruptible.

The author has said much about the fall in moral standards of the society, and corruption. Although, there may not be an instant medicine to overcome this disease, looking to the cultural heritage of this great country, one tends to be optimistic, and feels that a consensus could be arrived at in the near future.

The author has done a lot of laudable research on the subject. Evidently, his ardent objective is to usher in the operational existence of a really worthy, reliable, humane, efficient, and honest Police Force, free from any kind of interference from any quarter; and competent and capable enough in the lawful and unbiased discharge of their functions enjoined on them by the law of the land. This book should mark as very unique in the entire range of Police literature, and could prove to be a good guide to the public at large. I hope that the people at the helms of affairs would do well to read this and contribute to the national good.

Justice M.S. Ratnaparkhi (Retd,)
Bombay High Court, Nagpur.

Preface

I retired in 1976, after 39 years of Police Service in all its branches, including the security of the V.V.I.Ps.

In 1993 my book, "Shree Ram Janma Bhoomi" was published in Nagpur. During 1994-95 my another book, "A Concise Encyclopaedia of Indian History" was published by M/s Atlantic Publishers and Distributors, New Delhi.

During service, as also after retirement, I have engaged myself in deeply studying the mores and motivations of men, high or low, and belonging to various shades of opinion, trade; and different and divergent social, political, communal and ethnic groups of people prevalent in India. This study was specifically conducted to find out the realistic role of police functionaries, the Criminal Justice System and the reciprocal response of the public in the maintenance of law and order, public peace and tranquillity; and their efforts in containing criminal, anti-social and anti-national elements threatening the well-being of the society and the country.

The conclusion of this critical study is horrifying. It revealed that criminal, anti-national and anti-social propensities have grown faster than the population over the years, and the Criminal Justice System along with its police functionaries has nearly collapsed. In consequence, people lost faith in either. The most dominant factor responsible for such a state of affairs is the all penetrative and pervasive monster of "CORRUPTION" which has eroded most of the good qualities of the society, and its various components. All people have been victimised, and affected by corruption in one form or the other, and it did not exclude their moral conduct, the politicians who administer the country, and the social workers guiding the community. The political corruption has been of the worst type, for its multi-dimensional potentials have already generated far-reaching consequences of evil nature.

Misgovernance coupled with ineffective and partisan administrative control has thrust the community on the brink of anarchial conditions, which threaten to aggravate further and ruin the social and community order together with the peace and tranquillity. Police, as the only law enforcing agency in the country, will be called upon to deal effectively, efficiently and impartially the brewing turmoil, and save the country from further ruin. Therefore, people have a right to know all about their "POLICE", whom they have engaged, on the basis of contractual theory for the protection of their life, property, person, honour, and the maintenance of law and order, and the prevention and detection of crime and criminals. Imbued by this dutiful feeling I have ventured this composition under the title, "THE POLICE IN INDIA" with my frank expressions, based generally on my knowledge, and experience of the department, the community and the society. This book is not a "POLICE JARGON". The contents are as truthful and realistic as ever, though to some they may tend to offend; and in that eventuality I would earnestly urge them to indulge in some self-introspection.

I have attempted to cover comprehensively all facets of Police work, the Criminal Justice System, the causative factors of their success and failure and suggested some remedial measures. Various subjects in different headings have been presented in this book to make the readers specifically aware of the organisation, and the particular aspects of crime in its various manifestations, the contributing factors which overweigh either the success or failure of the Police in their mission of maintenance of law and order, prevention and detection of crime and criminals, *inter alia*, the various impediments, both legal and public, which the police are required to face in their day-to-day working; and all these are in their proper perspectives, providing the necessary framework in which improvement can be made in the future.

There is no doubt that the nucleus of the present system of policing was laid down by the British Government, and the development and expansion that took place during the pre-Independence era was the anxiety of the British Raj which would help the Indian people to live in peace, but would also doubly ensure the continuance of the British Rule in India. Paradoxically, the attitude of the post-Independence Government is not very much different. The fact that the British ruled the country for over one hundred years and gave peace, tranquillity and law and order to the citizens shows that the administration was patently and willfully efficient, although there was negligible corruption.

After Independence "Crime" remains one of the most intractable problem that faces the Government, and vast expenditure on the welfare state, and a higher standard of living have not brought us any nearer a solution. Alongside the progress and development of the country, crime continues to increase in all its manifestations, but the worst of it is the unbridled rise in the incidence of violence, juvenile delinquency, and economic offences. The old theory of Criminology that poverty breeds, broods and fosters crime is now no longer relevant in the society as some of the rich and elite are committing "white-collar" crimes in their avaricious race to acquire more and more wealth, and speed money by adopting anti-social, anti-national, and dubious methods. Relatively, the emoluments and service-cum-living conditions of Police have remained appallingly poor and unsatisfactory.

Today crimes are as complicated and complex as the conditions of life in which they occur, and in majority of the cases their investigation is also a complicated business. Science has been brought into police work from both sides — the criminal and the police. With the advance of industrial civilisation and the great and growing aggregation of population in expanding towns and cities, not only have the incentives and opportunities for crimes multiplied, but also new and increasingly sophisticated types of crimes are being committed. Modern conditions have given rise to organised crimes on an international scale under the political protection of mafia gangs, and their gangsters. In this democratic country elections are rigged by the rampant use of muscle and money power, and victory is secured, nay many times bought, and at times on gunpoint. Most of the voters are uneducated and poor, and their price is not much, and those of the elite class have mostly played truant during the election process. Leaders having criminal records get elected, and some of them hold ministerial posts.

Notwithstanding that the war against crime starts with the police, and they are intrinsically concerned with all its operations, the police alone cannot fight crime efficiently. The police form only a part of our Criminal Justice System, which comprises legislators, judges, lawyers, scientists, prison administration, but the most important of them all is the public. No investigation, however, efficiently done even with the aid of science, can be successful without public co-operation and assistance. Hence, it has to be ensured that all parts of our Criminal Justice System operate in unison, co-operation and play the supplementary and complementary role in the protection of the society, and the community, instead of taking diametrically opposite stand.

Policemen existed since times immemorial. They are found almost everywhere in the world and in every climate — cold, hot or temperate. But whatever the temperature, the policeman must always remain cool, courteous and impartial, and keep his uniform buttoned up for almost 24 hours during his service period. No country has been able to do away with police as they are the necessary checks against the ambivalence of human nature, which makes men to live in society, but want to exercise their wits breaking the most elementary rules designed to protect their fellow citizens' life, person and property and to maintain order in the society. The aim of the Government, as expressed in its criminal laws, is to safeguard its own existence, to maintain order, and make it possible for all citizens to lead a good and peaceful life, free from any kind of molestation by others, in spite of the fact that men are basically good, but laws are still needed to keep down the few desperate men in the society.

Today the picture of the police force is frightening. The members of the force no longer constitute a homogenous body for the common goal of the efficient police organisation and its administration, but they are overpowered by castes, class and creedal discriminations, and prejudices in their discriminatory enforcement of the various laws of the land. Now, unlike the past, the force does not work with the ideal, "one for all and all for one", as the composition of the force itself is based on castes, class and that has totally changed its entire complexion due to political interference, adversely affecting police efficiency, competency, reliability, probity, integrity, and obedience of superiors' orders.

Several Police Commissions, both of the Centre and the States were set up with a view to improve the all-round tone of police administration, working efficiency and service-cum-living conditions. During the last 48 years police forces in the country have been undergoing rapid changes as a result of altering society. The last two decades have been a period of experiments, and change for the police as a result of the various recommendations of the Law Commissions, and National and State Police Commissions. Most people would like the Police Service both to be efficient and humane. It is emphasised that the ability of the police to fulfil their functions would always depend on public approval. Some of the changes have been good, some of them have not gone far enough, and most of them have been pending for a long time as a direct result of politics in law enforcement. But lamentably, none of them have ameliorated the service-cum-living conditions of the police in general, and the constabulary in particular, or at least alleviated their grievances.

On comparing the pre and post-Independence scenario of the country, a dismal and disdainful picture emerges. The by-product of Independence is the change in the social taboos, and customs, generally morals and mores have been adversely affected, and vice and dishonesty have replaced virtue and probity in all spheres of the life. The administrative awe and fear have almost disappeared. In consequence, there is nowhere peace and public order. Laws meant to regulate the community are not only disrespected, but also flagrantly and wantonly violated by the law makers themselves.

There is terrorism, small or big, in almost all the States of the Union. The law and order problems of Jammu and Kashmir, Punjab and the North-eastern regions are stupendous, and they together threaten the very integration of the country. With the internal assistance of the terrorist, and insurgent elements Pakistan has imposed a proxy war on India, and the killing-spree of innocent people is unabated.

We have a turn down in the economy, we have increasingly high rate of unemployment, we see crime of violence increasing, almost without any check. We encounter everywhere political, communal, castes, class, creedal and language hostility. Our society has become like a molecule full of internal tensions held in a precarious balance by a criss-cross of group alignment. In consequence, the functions of the police are expanding and growing in importance. As an instrument of social defence no society can disown the police, or do without them. The nexus between the mafia hierarchy, politicians, and the police is the most formidable of the law enforcement problems of the future. Government efforts to scuttle and override the recommendations of Vohra Committee have been frustrated by the intervening directions of the Supreme Court. Indeed, the point has been reached in which the underworld can commit crime with ease anywhere, any time and buy immunity from police action. Policemen are passing through a disturbing phase and time. Ethical and political mandates run counter to each other, and the resultant situation has undermined the established traditions of honesty and loyalty. For all these, policemen rightly feel that they have been mucked about a lot. A partisan and demoralised police administration cannot function as the bulwark of law, order and social stability.

It is apparent, as also natural, that Police cannot remain as they are when the national environment is fast changing, may be to the detriment or benefit of the community or the society. Changes in the last 48 years have altered the shape and complexion of the society, nor is the devastating "FORCE" of these changes yet spent, perhaps, it may boomerang as the cycle of reaction has not started, and it may take some more years for completion, and undoubtedly there is going to be many more alterations before the society finally settles down in the near future. Therefore, the sort of police which the new society will have is of paramount importance, when one obviously notices the present conceptual trend of the society about the police:

> The society use the police as a scapegoat for its neurotic attitude towards crime. Public expect the policeman to be human and yet in-human. They employ him to administer the law, and yet ask him to waive it. They resent him when he enforces the law in their own case yet demand his dismissal when he does not elsewhere. They offer him bribes yet denounce his corruption. They admire violence, even against the society, but condemn the police for using force to contain it. They ask for crime to be eradicated but only by the use of "SPORTING METHODS."

Our Criminal Justice System has almost collapsed. Militant organisations like Naxalites, Maoist Communist Centre in Bihar, Peoples' War Group in Andhra Pradesh, the United Liberation Front and Bodo in Assam are running parallel administration. They have let loose a reign of terror. Failing to get justice through the government agencies, more and more villagers are approaching these organisations for justice. In these areas the police have ceased to function. We must take note of the fact that in rural areas unrest has been growing, and consolidating in different regions of the country. The ineffectiveness of policing account for emergence of private *senas* — bodies among Hindus and Muslims, landlords and land-less peasants, and they are armed to the teeth for protection. Still worse, they are mostly anti-national, anti-social and criminal gangs in our communalised and castiest conditions now prevalent in the country.

It is dangerous for the society to allow the police to drift haphazardly from one policy to another, or to allow expediency, either political or social, to override the "PRINCIPLES". For, the Police Service is one of the three dominant organisations which can create or destroy the happiness of the community. Whatever lessening of standards is accepted, in police it is of paramount importance that they should be scrupulously maintained at as high a level as possible. The basic attitudinal change in the police is absolutely necessary in their efforts to prove their *bona fides*, their worth, trustworthiness, and above all their integrity.

For the Government and the society, the point to be determined for the police is the degree of functional independence. How much the police today should be insulated against any outside interference to enable them to discharge their primary responsibilities without any fear or favour. And also to whom the police are finally accountable? Is it to the political party in power, to the electorates or to the legislators? The importance of functional independence of the police has been recognised even by the Supreme Court, and it is the statutory powers of the police to investigate into a cognizable offence, and that it cannot be interfered with even by the judiciary subject to (Section 491 of the Code of Criminal Procedure, 1956) only Article 226(1) of the Constitution to give direction in the nature of "*habeas corpus*". Therefore, no one can override, circumscribe, and circumvent the provisions of the Code, which has given the necessary powers to the police, and for that matter, the police are not the servants of any Government in the limited sense that the Government cannot order the method and manner of performance of the various acts committed to the police by the laws. When the requisite conditions in the specified provisions of laws are present the police are under a statutory duty to function in accordance with the mandates of the legislature. They have no other option open, and this is their functional independence, which is confined to the ambit of law. Therefore, at the time of recruitment, each policeman, high or low, is required to take the "OATH OF ALLEGIANCE" to the Constitution of India, and not to any other authority or political party in power.

Every political party has blamed all other political parties of misusing and abusing police to promote the party's interests in the process of retaining power. The police leadership itself has not raised its voice. As the impoverished police-leadership has not been able to: (a) protect the organisational interests, and (b) insulate the political interference at various levels down the organisation, functionaries at all levels developed a co-lateral alliance, out of concern for survival — a constable and a head-constable with a *sarpanch*, sub-inspector and inspector with a M.L.A., and all other higher ranks with M.P., matching the equation between the Director General with the Chief Minister of the ruling political party.

Discontent within the police force and indiscipline among the rank and file have been growing rapidly over the years. Subordinates have not only disobeyed the legitimate orders of their superiors, but also manhandled them, because the superior officers have failed to maintain their dignity and decorum for various personal reasons. The number of public complaints against the police is growing every day; and corruption among the police has touched a new height, and worst is that it has become co-operative. Relations between the public and police have considerably worsened. Frequent countrywide strikes by the Police had taken place, and the Army had to be called to disarm the striking police. Partisan attitude of politicians has decimated the functional neutrality of the police. The nexus between the politicians, gangsters, and the police has cancerously affected the well-being of the community.

The immunity that is wanted for the police is mainly against political contamination, and the preservation of their impartial functional independence. While political leadership could immensely help tone up Police Service by refraining from partisan interference, the accountability of the Police in our democratic society will continue to remain a problem, unless the leaders in public service themselves are able to grasp the responsibility assigned to them under the law, and show the correct response to the democratic aspirations of the people at large by their exemplary and selfless behaviour, conduct and probity like their ancestral generations, bearing in mind that they are the representatives of the people and along with them all services are answerable only to the sovereign people.

The Police have failed to think about the future in terms of social equity and justice. Their thinking would profit if they were to come out of their shell and concern themselves with their essential role, and human relations. Continued deprivation amidst plenty of failures in the redressal of their grievances bred widespread militancy and belligerence. A police administration that has so far failed in its task to ensure justice has been by-passed. Policemen failed to be stern and authoritative to the criminal, and anti-social elements. Therefore, the Police have to restore and once again achieve their previous reputation of an efficient instrument of the country for containing crime and criminals and maintaining law, order and tranquillity. They have to perceptibly behave, and prove that they are the friends of the law-abiding and dreaded foes of the law-breaking elements of the society; and then alone they would be able to acquire the long yearned sympathy, love, affection and respect from the people. They have to achieve this ideal purpose as spelt out by the United Nations Organisation. "As a law enforcement officer my fundamental duty is to serve the mankind, to safeguard life and property and protect the innocent against deception, the weak against oppression or intimidation, and peaceful against violence and disorder; and to respect constitutional rights of all men to liberty, equality and justice." And then, reciprocally, public will take the much-long awaited and needed steps to alleviate or redress police grievances, and ameliorate their conditions of service, pay structure *etc.*, and render the police the requisite respect for which they are clamouring over the years.

I express my most sincere and heartfelt gratitude to the authors of various books, periodicals, and newspapers, from the treasures of which, I have drawn extensively to compose the present book. This will ever remain my unredeemable debt.

I tender an advance apology for any mistake that might have cropped up inadvertently in this book.

I am grateful to M/s Shiva Agencies and Ameya Computers, Nagpur for processing in perfection the voluminous manuscript of 1,000 pages, and the printer and publisher for producing this book within a short period of time.

My wife, Radha's immeasurable assistance is beyond redemption.

In veneration, I dedicate this book to my late parents, and K.F. Rustamji, Padma Vibhushan (the founder Director General, Border Security Force), who inculcated in me the values of righteous thinking and right actions without fear or favour, and all these cumulatively helped me in all the trials and tribulations of life.

In gratitude, I pay my glaring tributes and homage by laying wreaths to commemorate the gallant deeds of all those innumerable brave colleagues, who sacrificed their lives to protect the country, community and the society.

M.B. Chande

Contents

1
Society

No person can even slightly visualise the various ramifications, and difficulties faced by the Police Forces in India while discharging their multi-farious, and multi-dimensional duties unless he acquires some basic knowledge regarding the most intricate nature of the Indian society and all its components, its national government *vis-a-vis* the police administration, and the Criminal Justice System in relation to the fundamental principles as envisaged in the science of sociology. It is really interesting to find that the socio-political atmosphere, and the allied environments largely fit into the various rudiments of sociology. Therefore, before actually dealing with the theme, "Police Role in India", it is considered expedient to portray the prevalent socio-political scenario in the country as manifested in that science.

1. Evolution of Child and Role of Family Environments

The child is the nucleus of the nation. The social circumstances preceding the birth of a child, lay down to a great extent the kind of life it is to lead. The parents' courtship and the marital relation, the customs, and the circumstances concerning pregnancy and birth; and the whole system of cultural practices surrounding the family are absolutely important for the child's growth. The technique of parental care affects its chances of being born and of being healthy.

Direct socialisation begins only after birth. Everyone is born with defined capacities, and certain inherent, and instinctive urge which provides firmer ground for analysis of human behaviour. If human needs are not satisfied it leads to tension until it encounters a stimulus capable of relieving the tension. The urge is, thus, a dynamic force behind any behaviour and it provides the starting point for the process of socialisation. The limitation of capability can be overcome by the development of socialisation, inherent in the process of learning through imitation, suggestion, identification and language. In the process of socialisation of a child the role of the family is the greatest. Throughout life an individual remains under direct, as well as indirect influence of his family. It is the family which controls and directs him, gives expression to his personality, and consequently governs his life. Family decides his life status, and teaches him norm of social life and to distinguish between good and bad; justifiable and unjustifiable; virtue and vice; holy and evil; social and anti-social; and development with or without criminal propensities.

The environments in which the child is brought up plays an equally important role in the process of his socialisation. The suggestibility of the child is greater than that of the adult, because in childhood it is devoid of maturity and reason. The suggestibility of an individual decreases with the increase in his maturity, and mental level. The child gets his first lesson in co-operation, tolerance, self-sacrifice, love and affection in the family environments which often influence his growth. Generally, it is found that a person is the total product of the family—good or bad. An important factor in juvenile delinquency is bad or vicious family environment. The relationship between the parents and, the child is one of the constraint due to the older age of the parents enabling them to command obedience from the child.

The school is the other important agency of socialisation as in the school the child gets his education eventuating in moulding his ideas and attitudes. A good education can make the child a good citizen, while the bad education can turn him into a criminal. A well-planned system of education can produce good socialised citizens. The persons with whom the child associates also play an equally important role in moulding the future of the child.

2. Family

Family is an universal institution found in every age and every society, and it is the fulfilment of the divine mandates of reproduction through sexual relationship between a man and a woman; and it is the nucleus of the human society, the habitation. With the developments of human societies the institution of marriage has been legally accepted and come to stay. In other words it is the recognised mating institution. The directive characteristic; (and yet, distinctive) of marriage, parental obligation, and nibbling relation make a family the primary institutional cell for a society. The whole social structure is built on family unit. It is in the family that the child learns the meaning of social responsibility, and the necessity for co-operation. In it the child develops his basic attitudes and ideals. Family system has always demandedly denounced, deterred and prevented promiscuity a few decades ago. But of late this benign system is showing signs of erosion, affecting the building up and bringing up the child — the nucleus of the nation. For the smooth functioning of the family life a system of reciprocal relationship, duties and responsibilities among its various members was satisfactorily developed, and maintained by the society. But from the recent past the most important function of rearing the child has been taken over by other agencies which has resulted in laxity in looking after the child by its parents; and it is particularly more where there is no joint family in existence.

The modern family is beset with many serious problems which have already affected the upbringing of the child. They can be generalised:

1. Laxity and variety in marital and sex relation thereby encouraging premarital or extra-marital sex relationship.
2. Equality of relationship between man and woman and the personal ego arising out of this relation.
3. Decrease in the importance of blood relationship resulting in the constitution of a family comprising husband, wife and their children.
4. Disorganisation of a joint family system.
5. Increase in divorces resulting in family disorganisation.
6. Instability.

"Thus the modern family, in comparison with the ancient and medieval family, has become weak and unstable."

3. Marriage

Every young couple aspires for an ideal marital life. There is nothing wrong in it if this aspiration is devoid of fastidiousness. Psychoanalytic and Pornographic literature including "the blue films" have already affected the ancient ideals and values of sex relationship. These days much importance is being given to the gratification of sexual desire, or even lust; and a growing tendency to declare variety in sexual relationship; not only desirable, but also necessary, and natural is unfortunately noticed. Marriages are now performed on this rickety base (and they are not solemnised) of romantic love; with the result that a large percentage of such marriages have been either seriously frustrated or broken. Frequency of family conflict and strive have disturbed the peace of the family, destroyed the faith in one another, and removed the sense of psychological security. The ultimate sufferer is this nucleus of the nation — Child.

Mores, customs and conventions which considerably regulate conjugal relationship are maintained spiritually in a family life which basically controls the individual. Significance, importance and values of rights and duties are the product of family life. Respect for the elders and sympathy for the young are lessons of a family which hold good in almost every healthy society. Every family has to try and achieve, and also ensure that the children should give up bad habits, and in their stead adopt good habits so that they become genuinely real and dependable possession of the society; and such a possession that can maintain and enhance the glory of the nation. Thus, family is a divine factory to produce best and honourable citizens for the nation. Is it not the moot question that how many families have fulfilled this mandatory objective of the community to which they belong?

Unfortunately, today among the young boys and girls there is a strong, almost terrifying desire for a perfect marriage out of heaven. This vision of the perfect marriage entertained by these youngsters is for the most part conventionalised and stereotyped as to be grotesque. In their would be partner they want beautiful characteristics, unmitigated love, devotion and fidelity plus comradeship and complete self-expression. They want to make sure that marriage is giving them everything, including a big dowry, they expect, and that is stifling no part of their personality. They forget that there are natural shortcomings of any human relationship. They fail to see the reality of marriage, and when they fail, they put the blame on their parents instead of upon the excessive and naive demands they make upon marriage. Before two persons unite by marriage bond they must be able to sink themselves in the creation of a new unit bigger than either of them. They must be ready to accept their relationship as the permanent framework of their life. Today marriage is decreasingly considered as sacrament, and increasingly as a civil contract.

4. Environment and Heredity

Environments are those forces, situation or stimuli that affect the individual from outside, and it is the physical world external to the individuals. Heredity is the transmission of genetic characteristics from parents to the offspring, and these hereditary traits are innate and they are present at the birth. It is obvious that both heredity and environment influence individual behaviour, but their relative influence is almost equal during the growth of the child. Research led to the conclusion that children of professional parents have the I.Q. (intelligence quotient) of 116; those semi-professionals and managerial classes 112; clerical skilled, skilled traders and retail business 107.5 semi-skilled and minor clerical occupations and business 105; slightly skilled 98; and finally the children of labourers, rural and urban farmers 96. Even if the intelligence difference is there, it is not to be attributed to hereditary or racial difference alone, as the factor of differential environment cannot be ignored. The influence of differential training, experience home, life, social opportunity, economic disadvantages *etc.*, definitely have their consequential influence in the matter of the growth of the child. Heredity has a limiting influence on personality developments. We see evidence of this in the child, whose inherited mental capacity is not restricted as to make it impossible for him to become a fully participating member of the society, and also to organise his personality. There is incessant reaction between heredity and environment. They are inseparable and heredity is particularly made actual with an environment. All the needed qualities and life are in the heredity, whereas all evolution of qualities depend on the environments, and both are contributory, complementary and supplementary to each other.

5. Racial Prejudice is not Inborn

The child is not born with a prejudice or bias of any kind. We often mark that children, in their own, frequently playing with the children of other races without any prejudice or discriminations, which are the result of socio-politico inculcations of beliefs and attitudes and which take firm hold through the process of the entire growth of the child. To all intents and purposes the young child undoubtedly starts his life without any bias or prejudice and during the pre-school years seems almost incapable of fixing hostility upon every group as a whole, which indubiously, and unfortunately is traceable to the process of socialisation where "*Mine*" becomes identified with "*Ours*" and the child is taught to consider the members of his group superior to other in every field. He learns to differentiate and rate others in terms of superiority-inferiority values, and thus develops attachment and loyalty only to those who share his prejudices. Group prejudice, thus, is not born, but learnt out of someone's teaching and finally acquired. The most effective method of eradicating prejudice is proper education for the realisation that race prejudices have so far done no good to the society and resulted only in creating social disharmony. But can it be done in India? The attempts of the various State Governments to enhance the statutory reservation of 50 per cent in scholastic, governmental and semi-governmental institutions as stipulated by the Supreme Court to a 69 per cent in Tamil Nadu, 81 per cent in Andhra Pradesh *etc.* will surely reverse the process of harmonisation when the child will attain the age of maturity, as his intelligence, talent and capacity would be subordinated to political will, and he would be divested of all opportunities for settlement in life through fair competition, which is the major factor responsible for building the nation.

6. Culture

By birth child is a biological entity. It acquires idealistic culture through socialisation, habits, thoughts and heritage. The development of culture is a continuous process through traits of accumulation, diffusion, accommodation, cross fertilisation, adulteration and stimulation. Culture thoroughly influences a child during the period of his growth and often he does not require any external force to keep himself in conformity with social requirements. His culture directs and confines his behaviour, limits his goal and measures his rewards. His culture gets into his mind, and shutters his vision so that he sees what he is supposed to see, dreams what he is expected to dream, and hungers for what he is trained to hunger. Culture has provided the many checks on the individual, and the unethical behaviour of a human being. Culture, in essence, is the design and perception, the composite of guiding values, and ideals in order to regulate the behaviour of the people in all aspects.

From the start, the responses of child are conditioned by the cultural factors and forces. First his parents, then his family members; later the neighbourhood, and then the whole society comes forward to initiate him in the culture which has filtered to the parents, and subsequently to the society through all past generations. Culture is the most important unifying factor amongst the hoard of other factors and forces which come together to form the vast complex-cell-society of men. In it, they merged the needs and desires of men and the channels of integration. Human personality is multi-faceted and requires an uniform development of all its aspects, for otherwise deformed or maladjusted being would considerably increase to shatter the social organisation of Indian culture, which is the realm of final evaluation of all Indians, irrespective of their race, religion, caste and social status; and the whole and composite Indian culture must be interpreted, and scrupulously enforced as such by the family, the society, community and finally the State without any differentiation or discrimination. Children, brought out through such cultural process, when they come of age, are sure to solve the present tangle of all-round diversity in the country, where there will not be any Hindu, Muslim, Christian, Parsi, Buddhist, Jain, Sikh *etc.*, but each and every component of the Indian culture and its society will be, '*Indian*' and, '*Indian*' alone.

7. Individual and Community

Individual: What is Individuality? In a sociological sense it is an attribute which reveals the members of a group of more than merely a member.

The more he depends on the strength of a character as a member of a society more is the degree in which he possesses individuality, strength of a character being understood as a dependence of judgement, initiative and even power of discrimination. Individuality of a person is expressed in a society. But both individual and individuality being different from each other, should not be confused, for individuality, is something given and to be depended upon; whereas individualism, bereft of social fabric, loses its face and becomes egoism. Undoubtedly, individual and society are interdependent, and without one the other cannot exist; but in spite of this we find many social tensions and an individual is found defying his social order, and even challenging that. It is due to various reasons, such as, opposing interests, jealousies, mal-adjustments, repression, and exploitation. Since, social integration has not been completed, total harmony, and homogeneous society is impossible; because the society has failed to step in, to achieve this national objective, though heterogeneity between different social units may be necessary for their cultural identification.

Community: Individual is necessary for social institution, whereas community is mandatory for the former's existence. Therefore, a community is a collection of individuals united by certain relations or modes of behaviour involving common usages, traditions, customs, procedures authority and mutual aid, which differentiate and mark them off from others (MacIver, Page, Giddings, Ginsberg, Cooley and G.D.H. Cole). "Community" as a word has been derived from two Latin words — "Com" meaning together and "Mints" meaning serve. Thus community means "Serve together". The science of sociology defines community: "A complex of social life, which includes a number of human beings living together under conditions of relationship; bound together by a common, however, constantly changing stock of conventions, customs and traditions and conscious to great extent of common social objects and interest." (Lundberg, Manahelm, Bogardus and G.D.H. Cole). The following elements are the characteristics of a community:

1. Group of People.
2. Locality: territorial area.

3. Feeling of oneness: We belong to a certain group of individuals.
4. Permanency of life in a definite place.
5. Naturality: since an individual is born in a community, which is not made or created by any act of will, but is natural.
6. Likeness of language, customs, traditions, sentiments, mores *etc.*, so as to form a culture of people living within a narrow territorial radius, and having a common way of life. In essence, it is the name of the structure of all social relationship — direct or indirect; organised or unorganised; conscious or unconscious; co-operative or occasionally antagonistic.

8. Rural and Urban Communities

Rural: In India about 85 per cent of the people live in 5,75,721 villages which play an important part in our social set-up. The village community is strongly conservative as far as its customs and traditions are concerned. The joint family system is no longer the peculiar characteristic of the village community as nuclear families are gradually taking its place. Retrospectively the Indian villages were an ideal democracy, and all their needs were generally fulfilled by their inhabitants. In the long history of this country, the Indian society retained its strength by integration and organisation as long as the villages were well-knit, and organised, but the percolation of the political, and industrial dirt, and their consequential evil effects, made the village community to disintegrate, although it is being made to believe by these agencies themselves that these new changes are for the benefit, upliftment, and upgradation of the material, industrial and political standards of Indian village life, and the villagers are in better harmony with the changed temper of our rural life which is being strengthened instead of disintegrated. Experience has proved this propaganda as mostly false and politically motivated. Due to disorganised village life a large number of educated village people are migrating to urban areas for settlement and it has lopsided the self-sufficiency of the village life.

Urban: The urban population with its different culture, occupations and the consequent differences and differentiations of the status of the people presents the appearance of a heterogeneous community, which has considerably weakened the solidarity of relations between individual members of the urban community, but on the other hand it has mobilised the lives of the people for their multiple urban affairs. The city is an environment created by society in which for the purpose of community living many aspects of natural environments are modified or entirely eliminated, whereas under rural conditions, social attitudes, and social institutions present characteristic differences from those developed within the cities. In the past several decades community life was very simple, but recently it discernibly changed through shedding of their homogeneous structural bonds of affinity, and feeling of collective welfare. In consequence both the rural and urban societies have become heterogeneous in all their aspects.

9. Social Tolerance

Due to co-related and yet, multiple reasons, the life in small communities demands almost total conformity from the individuals, who are subjected to greater degree of social vigilance, for the enforcement of codes and customs. However, the overcrowding of the cities have already had derogatory effect and influence on the social stratification. In urban communities "impersonality of social relations" is manifestly perceived. The most striking feature of the social aspect of the Urban life is its impersonality, because the people in the cities do not regard affectionately other persons. They love materials in preference to human beings. Every other thing including service in urban society is evaluated in terms of cash, and sale-purchase bargain. Money and cash govern the behaviour of urban man, who plays the subsidiary role due to, too much emphasis on ostentation. In urban community there is a lack of neighbourly feeling, resulting in increase in conflicts and unhealthy competitions.

10. Association, Institution and Language

Association: Like community, an association does not grow spontaneously as they are formed with certain objects. They are created by men volunteering to satisfy certain motives. Rules and regulations have to be framed to run a particular association for the universal obedience of its members. No association is formed without an aim, which being to seek the appropriate solution for a certain problem, and ultimately that is his identity. Any member of the association acting contrary to the rules or regulations is necessarily expelled from the membership, and this eventual action results against the critical members also. Even then an association has to exist in the community as its fraction and not as a whole, because it does not embrace the totality of ends or purpose of the entire community having its natural growth.

Institution: Institutions are the means of controlling individuals, their collective activities, and satisfying their needs. Inherently, it has more functions or proceedings which were formed on the basis of customs and dogmas and it is more stable than other means of social control. Every institution has some rules which were must be compulsorily obeyed by the individuals. Certain institutions are as old as the history of civilisation, such as the institution of marriage. Such an institution has social recognition behind it; it is the product of the social behaviour of human being; and it is relatively enduring. Institutions have manifest and latent functions; the former ones are deliberately recognised, whereas the latter are unrecognised or unauthorised of consequences. Institution is an unified pattern of diverse ways of human behaviour and action. It provides rules of social control, which individual accepts readily by way of habit. Institution provides definite role of status to individual through the various political parties *vis-a-vis* the government; and liberate the human energies contained in individual to play the subtle and respective role. Had there been no institution of marriage, there could have been social anarchy, because marriages provide a smooth way of fulfillment of the natural instinct of blind sexual urge.

Language: "Language is a system of arbitrary social symbols used to express communicable thoughts and feelings and enables the members of a social group or speech community to interact and to co-operate" (Charles Winnick). It is a medium of oral expression and helps in bringing human beings nearer and closer to each other. Man is in possession of natural society, and to understand his fellows and, to be understood by them, men were impelled to the production of language. The desire to communicate was the main cause of language making. Language is an evolutionary process. Different people belong to different societies or in some cases of the same society speak different languages. In consequence, language has played a very vital and significant role in the growth, development, and advancement of human society, which has got superiority over animal society only due to language and power of speech and understanding.

It helps expression of personality, preservation of culture, communication of ideas, easy social contacts and finally the increase of knowledge. Language, therefore, is a social creation. Although it helps expression of personality, in India it has become problematic. There are as many 179 languages, and 872 dialects. The Constitution of the Republic of India has recognised the following 18 important languages: 1. Hindi. 2. Marathi. 3. Bengali. 4. Punjabi. 5. Telugu. 6. Tamil 7. Gujarati. 8. Malayalam. 9. Kannada. 10. Sanskrit 11. Urdu. 12. Sindhi. 13. Assamese. 14. Oriya. 15. Bhojpuri. 16. Kashmiri. 17. Manipuri, and 18. Konkani.

These languages belong to the family of Indo-Aryan, Dravidian and Sino-Tibetan-Aryan.

In the remote past there was linguistic unity in India, as at one time or the other, either Sanskrit or *Prakrit* was the only language of the masses, as well as the classes; and all state businesses were transacted in that language alone. But as the time passed, and social set-up became more and more complex difficulties arose. During the Mughal rule Urdu or Persian was the state language, when hardly 2 per cent of total Indian population could speak or write in these languages. Though English was spoken hardly by 5 per cent of the total Indian population, it had become the official language in the British regime. After freedom in 1947, it was realised that English should not remain the national language, and it was rationally replaced by Hindi through the Constitution. But instead of cementing the various linguistic groups, Hindi is proving a great hindrance and stumbling block in this national cause. In this country each important language has a rich cultural heritage, and its supporters put forth their respective claim of their language for acceptance as national language. The concept of composite India has not developed, and regionalism, provincialism and allied feelings continue to dominate over nationalism. The Southern and Eastern States feel that English should continue to be the national language, because they are afraid that the introduction of Hindi as national language will be domination of North over the South. Thus, language has become a factor contributing more to disunity rather than to unity of India.

2
Control of Society

1. Society

Human being is a social animal and therefore, he cannot live without an organisation, which has the cumulative capacity to satisfy their needs. The collectivity which human beings have created during the long course of their evolution is their society. In a society there ought to be found a definite order of natural behaviour and relationship of the individuals, which is as old as their existence. Some of these relations are simple and some are complex; some are permanent; and some are temporary. Although it is a taxing problem to analyse the relationship between the individual and the society, it is absolutely necessary to understand and rigidly follow the extent of social control over the individuals and the individual's right to defy social order. In a society there is interdependence between the individuals, who while living in the society, solve their social problems which face them from time to time, and eventually they contribute social progress and also its retardation on account of the chain of actions and reactions resulted by different tasks, likings and dislikings; ideas and expectations; religions and communities; castes; creeds; custom and usage; vice and virtues; good and bad behaviour; evils; prejudices and selfishness; and various other naturally diverse duties and non-duties. Society's benefit lies only in co-operative association of the individuals. Finally, the evolution of the society is dependent on the ethics of values, and mores of the people, because ultimately society is only a web of intimately intricate social relationship.

The society lives, works and develops under the sovereignty of the State, as these two entities are inseparable. It is the responsibility of the State to enact benevolent and benign laws for the society, and its components, and in the democratic country like India, the politicians whom the society has chartered to lead it, form the State. For this purpose the individuals should completely merge themselves in the society, which should regulate their conduct and behaviour. If the society fails to exercise its powers the result shall be that due to their selfish nature, the individuals will quarrel with one another, and the whole social order will be completely disturbed. Individual and his groups both combine to form a unit of the society representing them. A responsible individual is an abstraction unknown to experience, because society and individual do not denote separate phenomenon, but are simply collective and distributive aspects of the same thing.

2. Spatial or Natural Group

Castes, class, tribes and hordes are important social institutions which play an important part in our social life. Caste is endogamous, whereas class is exogamous. Caste is a larger social group than class. The latter may be matrilineal or patrilineal. They are part of our social set-up, although each one has a definite role to play, and at the same time none of them can be dispossessed with.

Thus society and individuals are inseparable. Society is a constant growth. It is not the handiwork of God, and unsafe to believe that God-sent society for the individuals. In the process of evolution, individual, family, community and institution contributed a lot of their might to support the ardent desire of the family to lead a peaceful and honourable life for the protection of its members from external and internal attacks. Religious ethos of each and every family proved a contributing and cementing factor in the establishment of the ultimate strength of a good and virtuous society.

3. Socialisation and Social Order

The process of socialisation starts and begins to work long before the child is born. Human society is not an external phenomenon, but solely exists in the minds of its members. The human infant comes into the world as a biological organism with animal needs. He is gradually moulded into social being, as he learns social ways of acting and feeling. Without this process of moulding, the society could not continue to exist itself, nor could culture exist, nor could the individual become a person. This process of building or moulding human beings is recognised as "Socialisation" although it is very slow and consists of many steps or stages, such as imitation, suggestion, identification language. It helps in the development of the self through the elementary medium of elders, equals, education, and environments. Social order is maintained largely by socialisation. Unless the individuals behave in accordance with the norms of the society, it is going to disintegrate. To sum up, socialisation is the process in which an individual develops into a functioning member of the society. A person with socialised attitudes would not do any work which is socially harmful. He would put human welfare above the individual gain and human values above all these. Socialisation intends for the development of the human brain, body, attitude, behaviour and mannerism and it certainly inducts the individual into the social and cultural world; and it is through this process that the human beings find their fullfilment within the society. Socialisation also prunes individualism and the concomitant egoism. The child, is thus, inducted into the society as a good and ethical adolescent.

4. Social Process

(a) Social Interaction: An adolescent is a social cultural being and society is both natural and necessary for human beings, who cannot live in isolation. People live in various groups and associations. As members of these groups, they act and behave in a certain manner. The behaviour of each individual is affected by the behaviour of others, because interaction is the essence of social life. Behaviour system grows out of social interaction through which men interpenetrate the minds of others. Social interaction is the entire range of social relationships. Social contacts may be positive as well as negative. Without social processes it shall not be possible for the society to move forward and progress, which cumulatively modifies human behaviour, conflict, co-operation and competition. Social interaction consists of those mutual influences that individuals and groups have on one another in their attempt to solve problems, and in their strivings towards goal. Thus, it is the general process where by two or more persons are in meaningful contact, as a result of which their behaviour is modified, however, slightly.

Society is a web of social relationships, which is developed through mutual behaviour, and intercourse between the various members of the society — males and females, children, young and old men. Even then the various groups in the society are always undergoing strains of mutual conflict, competition, co-operation, and synthesis or other activities, which together constitute social interaction.

(b) Basic Conditions of Social Interaction: They can be divided under two categories: 1. Social Contact, 2. Communication.

The former has its origin in the mutual response between the various groups of individuals. Social contact can be positive and as well as negative. Positive social contacts tend to precipitate matters towards benevolence, co-operation, mutual understanding and assimilation. Negative social contacts create hatred, disregard of each other resulting in conflict. These interactions form the ground from which culture arises, and also they ensure the continued existence of culture; and together they form the essential pre-requisite for the understanding of social relationship.

(c) Forms of Social Processes: There are four forms of social processes:

1. Competition 2. Conflict 3. Accommodation or Co-operation, and 4. Assimilation.

(d) Competition and Conflicts: Both are basic processes that are disintegrative in nature. Both are the forms of non-co-operation and opposition. Competition is always impersonal unlike conflict-struggle which is always personal. Competition never ends, and it is an universal action in every class of the society. Competition takes four main forms: 1. Economic 2. Cultural 3. Social, and 4. Racial. It increases the efficiency of persons, groups and society, but at the same time it has to be ensured that it is fair, healthy and controlled; otherwise the results would be harmful to the society. It may be importantly noted that competition gradually changes into rivalry, which in turn results into conflict. There are bound to be differences of opinion in a society on important matters among the various individuals and their groups. The differences can be due to personal or collective reasons. It is due to this basic phenomenon that the conflict arises and develops. The principles for existence through struggle, and eventual 'survival of the fittest' are the main causes of conflicts. Co-operative conflicts occur among the groups within a society or between two societies, such as riots, communal upheavals, religious persecutions, and as such it is more harmful to the society than personal conflict which arises on account of various motives, every hostility, trust betrayal, and several elements. Because individuals are separate organs, they can agree as well as disagree or differ from each other. They have certain aims which they wish to exclusively attain for themselves eventually resulting in the frequency of conflicts in the society. So that insensate conflicts should not destroy the social fabric, the state machinery will have to be very vigilant, and active in curbing such tendencies.

(e) Accommodation or Co-operation: No society can develop, much less progress, when conflicts exist and dominate the normal behaviour of the social groups. Accommodation or co-operation is the most pervasive, and continuous of the social processes; and it is an integrating activity. Co-operation is the joint activity in the pursuit of common good or shared rewards; and it is an universal phenomenon. Even among the lowest animals, such as the ants and bees, co-operation is evident for their survival. All the progress that mankind has made in the various fields is to be attributed to the co-operating spirit of the people. Co-operation builds up group solidarity. Accommodation may be coordinate or subordinate. The former is on the footing of equality, whereas the latter is on the basis of disparity in status. In a multi-religious society of India toleration is the best form of accommodation, in which there is no settlement of difference; but there is the avoidance of over-conflict. In toleration no concession is made by any of the contesting groups; and there is no change in the basic policy. The co-existence of the multi-religious communities in India is only and solely possible on account of toleration, which politicians call, '*Secularism*'. The most common form of accommodation is the establishment and recognition of the order of super-ordination and subordination for effectively controlling recalcitrant attitudes. The organisation in any society is the result of such a type of accommodation. In a family the relationship amongst parents and children is based in terms of super-ordination, and subordination. In the larger groupings, whether social, political, economic, or even religious, the relationships are fixed on the same base. Similarly, in a democratic order there are leaders, and followers — those who give orders and those who obey them. The bureaucratic spiral is based on this principle. When individuals accept this position as matter of fact, accommodation will reach the state of perfection, which is essential for social harmony, as it is based neither exclusively on love, nor exclusively on hatred but is a synthetic and palatable mixture of both love and hatred.

*(f) **Assimilation:*** It is the process of interpenetration and fussion in which persons and their groups acquire the memories, sentiments and attitudes of other persons or groups; and by showing their experiences and history are incorporated with them in a crucial life. It is a slow process and gradually passes through different stages before the final stage comes, and therefore, it is evolutionary in essence. Being both social and psychological process, it helps in the promotion of cultural unity, mainly in the multi-religious, and racial country like India. The causes responsible for promoting assimilation are toleration, social contacts, cultural similarity, equal economic standard and social activities. The "*Shree Ram Janma Bhoomi tangle*" can be conveniently solved with full amity and accord only, without political, intervention on the basis of these factors.

*(g) **Interaction:*** Society is a constellation of groups, organisations, institutional agencies, collectiveness, and ecological entities so inter-related, and weaved that it operates as an inter-connected system. In society persons are bound together and dependent on each other in a system of inter-relationships, that combine to constitute a total functional structure. But the continuity in the instrumental unity is at times broken down to some degree due to anomalous antagonism leading to slight contradiction and confusion thereby eventuating the social deterioration and disintegration. In many societies there is "Strain towards consistency" which indicates the process of integration capable enough of harmonising the relationship of integration, and unification of the various structural components of society for proper organisation. At the same time it may be noted that integration does not involve similarity of various structural facts, but the tendency or inclination to accept the presence of certain

values as common, for promotion is necessary in this process. The aim of integration is to maintain a harmonious, and active relationship between the various structural components of the society. It not only keeps the society on going, but also imparts a meaning and purpose to the lives of individuals so that they feel themselves to be a part of the comprehensible, and harmonious social life. Integration is a difficult process, as it is faced with various difficulties:

1. The complexity of society makes it difficult to co-ordinate all the structural parts and to associate all the humans to meet their behaviour smoothly.
2. Cultural heterogeneity is another difficulty in the way of integration as people in the society belong to many ethnic and racial origins and are marked by class, religious and occupational differentiations.
3. Rapidity of social changes also presents great difficulty in integration.

New changes are introduced on an unprecedented role. Numerous cultural lags have produced stress and strains in the inter-related parts of the social web with the consequence that the individual finds himself in a state of bewildered society. In a social structure every group, individual, institution as well as association is required to perform certain specified functions. The social structure of a society is very much complex, and complicated. If it becomes elastic or malleable it will create social disharmony. On the other hand, if it becomes too rigid it will create many lags and might even create social stratification. Moral laws, etiquette, religion, education, and above all governments are all parts of the complex mechanism by which a social structure exists and persists.

(h) Social Organisation: The existence of unanimity among the members of the society is the main feature of social organisation. When a society accepts certain system unanimously that system lasts. On the contrary it tends to disintegrate, and results into group conflicts arising out of social tensions. Recently, in our complex and heterogeneous social system, conflicts have increased, and they led to more and more group tensions in all the spheres including families, industry, politics, government and also religious and ethnic institutions. There is confusion amongst the general individuals today about what is appropriate. Thus, the individual finds himself confronted by situations in which he is forced to become uncertain of his own role, and that of others. He is not only compelled to make choices but can also feel no certainty that he has chosen correctly. The overall result is disappointment and frustration. Therefore, social control on the individual has become the fundamental basis for maintaining harmonious relationship in a heterogeneous society in order to make it harmoniously homogeneous. This will acquire perpetuate unity in diversity.

5. Control of Society

(a) Social Control: It is a process by which the individual is made group responsive and by which social organisation is built and maintained. Society, in order to exist and progress, exercises controls over its members. The means of social control have been changing from time to time. In primitive societies, customs and traditions were employed for controlling individuals and groups. In middle ages, the Church (the institution of religion) had the greatest authority. With the passage of time, the authority of Church diminished, and the power shifted from it to the king, and to the State in democracy. With the march of technical advancement, control of social life passed on to a large number of economic, social, political and religious associations. For smooth and harmonious working of society it is essential that the society should function with certain norms and standards. Those, who try to violate them, or even dishonour them, should be made to realise their mistake and at the same time guarantee its non-repetition. This realisation-cum-control is quite different from control through force, customs, folk ways and mores. Public opinion, religion and morality are the dominant methods of social control. An individual is susceptible to the control by fear by God, family-reputation, social boycott and finally the penal laws of the State, when he thinks of doing any ethical, social or individual delinquency. These instinctive apprehensions of an individual initially refrain him from committing any such delinquency, but when the controls mentioned above are loosened or subordinated by his dominant unethical attitudes, he is prone to commit delinquency, and when his one wrong-doing escapes action by the society he repeats it until punished by the society.

A society must have harmony and order. Unless the individuals live up to, prescribed norms of conduct and unless their self-seeking impulses are subjugated to the welfare of the whole, it would be quite difficult to maintain effectively the social organisation itself. Social control is an influence exercised by society, as the group is in a better position to exercise controls over the individual than a single being, and such an influence is exercised for promoting the welfare of the society as a whole. The basic idea is to impel the individual to act in the interest of others rather than in accordance with his selfish motives. Social control is exercised for some specific end, or aim in view; and they are always the welfare of the society. In this type of social control from "within", the individual makes an attempt to guide his own behaviour in accordance with some previously developed ideals, goals or purpose. The essence of self-control is that it is the result of one's own realisation or feeling, little influenced by other's authority. Social control from "without" is exercised respectively by religion, morality, family reputation, ideology, custom, education, personality, folk ways, mores, public opinion, suggestions, and finally the law of the land. The chief aim of social control is to bring out conformity, solidarity, and continuity of a particular group of society. It will maintain the old order, establish social unity, regulate and control individual behaviour, provide social sanction, and ultimately check cultural moral adjustments.

(b) Control by Folk Ways, Mores, Customs and Habits

Folk Ways: They are the product of natural forces which men instinctively set in motion. They are instructive ways which are developed out of experience; and are handed down by traditions and admit of no exception or variation; and yet they change to meet new conditions. They are also the recognised ways of behaviour which arise automatically within a group to meet the problem of social living. They are those unconscious collective modes of behaviour that are believed to ensure the growth, and survival of the group. They are hereditary, and passed on from one generation to another as the most valuable treasure, and property of the ancestors. But they are of a more general and wider character than customs, and they cover all those modes of behaviour in spontaneous usages, which are not included in the term, "Customs", which though are related to the survival and growth of the group. Folk ways are not made obligatory by the group but are sanctioned internally; whereas customs are normative, and have great social significance.

Mores: Mores of people and groups regulate social behaviour and therefore, they are regulator of human behaviour. When the elements of truth and right are developed into doctrines of welfare, the folk ways are raised to the plane of "Mores", which term is derived from the Latin word "Mos", which stands for customs; and just as customs cannot be violated by any individual, so mores can also not be infringed without incurring severe punishment. There is a great feeling of horror about violating mores as they encompass directly the fundamental needs of the society, which is regulated in its behaviour on pain of group coercion. Therefore, mores determine much of our individual behaviour. They both control and forbid, behaviour and forbid it. They are forever moulding and restraining tendency of every individual, and they form the basis of the instrument of conduct. By conforming to the mores the individual gains identification with fellows and maintains those social bonds which are essential for satisfactory living. They are, therefore, the guidelines of solidarity as they are capable to hold the members of a particular group together. Mores are obeyed by some people in order to win the praise or reward; others obey them because of fear of social boycott, imposition of fine or physical punishment, including loss of life. The non-acceptance of mores marks out one as a social rebel and fit object for ostracism.

Mores are conducive to social welfare, but they also can prove harmful if they are not retained by a group after they have outlived their utility or usefulness because of changed conditions. In civilised societies mores tend to take the form of law. But in a complex society, folk ways and mores are not sufficient by themselves to provide social control for a society and, therefore, in such societies some special political organisation becomes necessary. Internal forces of public opinion are weak enough to ensure order in such complex society. And it becomes necessary for some enforcement agency to impose conformity through the mores, upon all members of the group. Since the mores of different groups are widely divergent, their force diminishes in those large societies where diverse groups are brought together. People in the rural communities are more obedient to them, and respect them more than their urban counterparts.

Customs and Habits: The question about the origin of custom is obscure and complicated. Many customs arose to satisfy the fundamental needs of man, especially more connected with his self-preservation tendency, sex life, procreation and the like. Some of the reforms, learnt by imitating other people, and many of them came as adjustments by changing situation or circumstances. Many customs still remain though their usefulness has long ceased to exist. They are obeyed more spontaneously because they grow slowly. They are the strongest ties or bonds in building for us social order.

All customs are not irrational. There are some customs and practices adopted by men which cannot be justified on any utilisation or ethical ground. The root of the difficulty is the modern minds consider only those acts rational which can logically be proved. But some acts which cannot be proved on logical grounds, can be justified on psychological or social grounds. Customs and traditions are group-accepted teachings of conduct that have become well-established, that are taken for granted, and that are passed along from one generation to other. The society has also to follow mandatorily the established customs which are very deeply rooted and well-knit in our social, economic and political fabric.

Habit: But custom is different from habit, which is an individual phenomenon. Habit is learnt; it reduces drudgery, economises energy and saves the needless expenditure of thought. One can, have good as well as bad habits. Good habits are to be continued, whereas bad habits should be stopped. Custom is a social phenomenon, and is formed on the basis of habits which by repetition becomes the basis of the order of social behaviour. Customs are the long established usages of the people and are not merely prevailing habits, but also rule more of actions. These rules are supported on emotional grounds and sided by two sets of forces:

1. Emotional or the sentimental positions attached to a custom.
2. Condemnation by its breach. Habits also precede and create customs, which regulate social life and they being repository of social heritage and traditions, universally mould personality and automatically and willingly seek obedience. To ensure the obedience of customs, *vis-a-vis* folk ways and mores, recourse to law has to be taken for social benefit.

6. Control by Public Opinion

After the 18th century the world witnessed the rise of democracy in place of monarchy and oligarchy. With the establishment of a democratic system, the importance of public opinion also kept on increasing. Generally, what passes on for opinion are really beliefs about controversial points, topics, one's own impressions, sentiments or prejudices. Then again public opinion is concerned on matters of public importance and not of a particular group of people. It is for the social welfare and is arrived at after careful thought. It is the tentative or deliberative adjustment of the public to a certain situation. It is the logical view of things, but it may not necessarily be true or even rational. It is the co-operative product of the interaction of human minds. It is also related to a particular age or times; and it is to be evaluated in the context of a particular situation. Since the culture of a society influences public opinion, it has a cultural base; and inversely, any public opinion is the cumulative result of expression of their views, a correlated and homogeneous agency to convey these expressions is the pre-requisite of a democratic set up; and since all cannot go to express their views causing confusion worst confounded, they authorise a person to convey, and express their feelings and eventually lead them.

7. Leaders

The influence of public opinion as a means of social control is very great and consequently effective. For fear of ridicule and criticism by the public, individuals do not indulge in anti-social activities. Today it is noticed that the society is moulded and even changed due to audio-visual propaganda which eventually forms the public opinion. Thereforc, it is imperative and equally essential that those, interested in forming public opinion, and are vested by the people to lead them, should have an ideal code of conduct and should actually, and always behave accordingly for the good of the people, who are prone to stimulate them. This principle is prominently manifested in "Bhagwad Gita." On the same analogy it applies to the family head. Ethical and benevolent education of individuals will be to reinforce an impenetrated base of a good society, which should perpetually watch and at the same time effectively ensure that the delegated leadership does not go astray and become delinquent. The society must find out democratic means and methodology to remove such leaders and their party and unshackle itself from the clutches of such parasitic leadership. If the media (Press etc.) is impartial, and honest it can be fairly understood that public opinion will be sound, healthy and impartial, and at the same time it will serve to improve an irresistible and effective deterrent on the erring leadership. Unlike in the past, the leaders and their parties have almost ceased to remain and exist ethically healthy, for it is being organised on sectional, communal and racial basis, rather than for the national interest.

8. Leadership and Personality

Leadership has played an important role in the human history since the early times. The historians have glorified heroes in battles and valued the importance of their deeds for the future generations. Leadership is required or needed in all societies. Leader is one who controls and conducts behaviour and attitude of his followers. The role of politicians, statesmen and emperors have received considerable attention in the imperial history. A leader is made by the society and for its benefit he exists; as such he must possess vitality, endurance, persuasiveness and decisiveness. Leadership is a function which endeavours to achieve, maintain and strengthen the nation through a particular organisation. Leader is something more than a citizen or a common man and enables to rouse the blood of the latter, and possesses enough strength to mobilise citizens as a united and spirited group. Rise and fall of a nation entirely depends on the action of the leaders. The leadership can be tratist or situationist. Leadership is not a personality trait. It is a way of relating ones self to others; and it assumes to those who take account of others in ways that facilitate group life, and group cohesion.

9. Leadership and Power

Leader's power is the ability to determine the behaviour of others in accordance with one's wishes despite opposition; because in every society power is very urgently needed for social interaction. Leadership depends upon the individual, the followers and the social conditions. Leadership is affected by conditions or situations to which power is occasionally blind, and in consequence it goes from the leader downward. The leader who, leads a mob must follow it. Generally, speaking leadership functions are related to goal achievement, strengthening and maintenance of the group. Thus, his functions are:

1. The determination of objective. 2. The manipulation of means. 3. The control of the instrumentality of action, and 4. The stimulation of co-ordinated action.

The leader enjoys prestige and in consequence great authority and power in the group; but he has to incur number of costs for his popularisation. He cannot afford to be selfish and self-centered. He necessarily has to build up a pious or holy reputation, maintain it and live by it, because his followers always stimulate him. A corrupt leader will undoubtedly encourage and protect corruption, which is subsequently followed by the members of his group. Likewise will be the result, when the leader is of a dubious character lacking integrity, probity and honesty of purpose. Therefore, people must choose a person as their leader whose conduct is beyond any shadow of doubt; and once having done so, they have to be constantly on his watch in order to ensure ethical behaviour of their leaders. This has become more relevant in the present context of our leadership, who have been frequently accused of corruption and dishonesty of all types and at all stages. According to the "*Laissez Faire Technique*" authoritarian leadership has to be discarded in a democratic country. In India it has already damaged, eroded and eventually prevented the development of a right tradition of leadership.

10. Crowd

In a general sense social interaction is a collective behaviour. When two or more persons behave in the same way, the resultant must be both the cause and effect for forming a crowd. Collective behaviour has a great potential, and it may act as an agent of flexibility and as a fore-runner of a social change, because a crowd is sentimentally emotional, less rational and prone to be more destructive. The members of the crowd show a very poor sense of responsibility, because when panic or hatred seizes then they do the most dastard and insane acts which are never to be anticipated, although for the commission of their acts they may repent subsequently. The crowd conducts itself like boiling milk, and in order to avoid its spilling from the pot on the oven, it is either to be removed from the oven or the fire-cum-energy is to be quenched. The leader, through various methods, brings his following crowd to the highest pitch of fury and if he fails to take timely action to douse peoples' anger which has gripped them, the crowd goes beyond the control of the leader, and only police force, sometimes even excessive, can alone control them; and failure of either has witnessed catastrophic results in the loss of human life and their property. Only a potential leader, who has an unimpeachable reputation can control the crowd effectively, but such leadership has become scarce, if not extinct, and almost not be found; and the unpalatable task of crowd control has fallen on the law enforcing agencies, which again adopt a partisan attitude if the agitation is initiated or sponsored by the ruling political party or its government. We have for instance the "Bandhs" by the State governments of West Bengal, Tamil Nadu, Bihar, Karnataka, Uttar Pradesh and others. In the "Bandhs" sponsored by the State Government the entire law and order enforcing agency, and the bureaucracy become docile and mute spectators to the abnormal behaviour of a crowd agitating for any rational or irrational grievances. The September (1994) 17/18 incident at the Allahabad High Court is the concrete example manifesting the irresponsible and yet, ostensibly democratic conduct of the State Government of Uttar Pradesh! To seek justice, the Supreme Court had to interfere, intervene and order the probe by the Director General of the Central Bureau of Investigation, only because the prestige of the judiciary was either brushed or jeopardised. Can this most exceptional course be adopted always and maintenance of law and order, peace and tranquillity for the common man be ensured and secured? Only the citizens have to fathom out the remedy for the collective causes leading to such lawless behaviour akin to the primitive society, and to eliminate them along with those who are prone to behave in this fashion, if at all democracy in India has to survive though striving.

11. Gherao

In political parlance, to make somebody immobile and pegged in order to coerce him to concede to the demands, whether rational or irrational of the agitators has been accepted and recognised as the normal method of expression of their feelings or yearnings. All the politicians follow it without any exception along with their proteges. Even the Parliament and State Legislative Assemblies, without any exception are not devoid of such instances of demonstrations, because the politicians have given sanctity to such frivolous democratic methods of agitation. They purposely become oblivious of the import of the definitions of "Restraint and Constraint" as enunciated in the Indian Penal Code. To the woes of the law enforcing agencies, the judiciary has also given a cold shoulder! There are innumerable instances of "Gherao" which had resulted in considerable disturbances of public peace and tranquillity, and loss of human life and property, and yet "Gherao" is considered to be the most innocuous methodology, and demonstration of unrest, both individually and in public.

12. Causative Factors

Ever since the Independence of the country in 1947, a growing tendency has been noticed to fully violate the laws of the land. It has become a demonstration of pride, prestige or privilege in this independent country, because it is being advocated that the country has achieved political freedom from the alien power only through such "methods of disobedience of law." Very few persons unfortunately consider or realise today that such behaviour does not sanction the sanctity of the law of land made by the people themselves. Every action is taken keeping the political gain in view. There is no other consideration than this.

In conformity with this ideal, political leaders generally resent, and strongly protest against the action taking agencies, hardly realising that such illegalities have been repeated with redoubled zeal and without any constraints or apprehension of the course of the law, as seldom it is encouraged to be taken; and mostly pruned. This phenomenon of breach of laws and the inaction of the law enforcing agencies, particularly in the offences against the society, is peculiar only to Indian conditions; whereas in the Western countries stringent action against the offender is taken. Traffic and crowd control offences are the most glaring instances of understanding the present replete breach of law in the country. Even educated people behave in such a fashion as to impress on the law enforcing agencies that they are sacrosanct because they are masters. Unfortunate is the officer, who errs in taking action in consonance with constitutional pledge taken by him for the enforcement of the laws of the land when he donned the uniform! Independence was achieved by such a movement that had "Disobedience of the law of the alien regime" as its base. The participants of this movement, who have now become the law makers, or their generations seem to have not forgotten their lessons of the past even in the post-independent period of their chosen government.

The "Action taken Report" submitted by the Government to the Parliament during its 1994 sessions is the most patent; but not the singular instance of protecting offenders, who were responsible in the "Security Scam" involving over rupees one thousand crores of loss of the tax payers' money in our educated society. Inversely was the conduct four decades ago of the uneducated aboriginals, who ran several miles to the police station with the murderer along with the dead body, and the weapon of murder. Is this behavioural change justified? Has it benefited the society? Have the cultural ethos, and morality of the country been converted into bathos or gone into oblivion? OR IS IT THE NEMESIS OF INDEPENDENCE OR SOCIO-POLITICAL DEMAGOGY?

3

Control of Law

1. Law

If all the restraints and constraints to be imposed from "within or without" fail to exercise social control, it is the law of the land that can improve and ensure control on delinquent individuals or their society. Early societies depended upon informal means of social control, but as societies grew in size, and complexity, they were compelled to formulate rules and regulations which defined the required type of behaviour and specified the penalties to be imposed upon those who violate them. Law makers and law enforcing agencies are authorised bodies; and in the democratic country like India the ultimate authority is the people, who give themselves various laws through the Constitution of the Republic of India. This authority of law defines clearly rights, duties, as well as punishments for their violations. When the society becomes delinquent, it becomes obvious that the informal means of social control are no longer sufficient to maintain social order and harmony. Security of life and property make formalisation of rules necessary. Law, while defining anti-individual, and anti-social actions, exercises the only powerful influence upon the behaviour of the people of the modern complex societies, including India.

Law is explicitly and deliberately made by the definite power of the State, which is the duly constituted authority by the society. It is the offspring of mind directing to aims which are far above the actual practice of the society. Law reforms the customs and abolishes those which are out of the tune with the changing conditions. It generally deals with matters which are vital to the life of the society. Law and customs are supplement and complement to each other. Activities which are performed unanimously are now consciously formulated by law. Law, divorced from custom, is bound to become artificial, and naturally it would not be seriously observed and obeyed by the people. Therefore, laws are the general conditions of human activities prescribed by the State for its members; it is the product of conscious thought, planning and deliberate formulation; it is definite, clear and precise; it applies equally to all without exception in identical circumstances, and its violation is followed by penalties determined by the authority of the State. This is the "Rule of Common Law". In view of the various ramifications and dimensions of law engulfing an individual preceding its birth, and following its death, the society has to doubly ensure that the law is enacted by a proper law-making authority through its elected legislators.

2. Legislature

It is the most important and effective agency for the formulation and expression of public opinion. The State today has entered in every individual's life. It not only determines through legislation the social structure, but also our beliefs and opinion. It has, therefore, become the most powerful instrument of social control; and to defy it against social interest, code and conduct, and behaviour is not only difficult but more or less impossible. Therefore, the society should elect such legislators, who have an ideal and ethical behaviour, and follow that code of conduct for the betterment and larger interest of the society, which has chartered them for their representation. The delinquent legislators should be outright discarded or rejected by the society, and shown the way they deserve through the election of worthy legislators.

India is a vast country in which there are many customs which are outdated; and currently not acceptable to the majority of the people. But since these serve the aspirations of few selfish people, they wish to retain such customs at all costs. This has resulted in many clashes between the laws, and the customs, and when the law attacks customs it has to depend very largely on the precarious sanction of force. The people are forced to obey the law as against the custom. This forced obedience creates a force resistance which generally endangers the authority of law and eventually breaks the cohesive social fabric. A law which is opposed to customs lacks the ground-cum-foundation which is essential to its effective operation and enforcement. Ultimately, the law must carry with it the sanction and sanctity of public approval. It must operate with and not against the forces of social change. But for a healthy society it is very imperative that the conflicts between the customs, and laws are reduced to the bare minimum in case the total absence of conflict cannot be achieved. Keeping this cardinal principle in view, the legislators have to make every effort to ensure that only such laws should be made as not to endanger the custom law-accord, and both go together hand in glove. Rising above personal prejudices, and party affiliations the legislators should strive to frame only those laws which do not jeopardise or contradict the inherent feelings of the general masses keeping at bay their electoral strategy.

3. Explanation of Crime

The Criminal and the Law: Paradoxically crime is inevitable in any human society since some violation or the other of any code of conduct prescribed for the members of a society is bound to occur owing to the decreasing ethical values of the components of the society. There is no society that is not confronted with the problem of criminality. Its form changes, the acts thus characterised are not the same everywhere and always. There have been men who have behaved in such a way as to draw upon themselves penal repression. What is normal, simply is the existence of criminality, provided that it attains, and does not exceed, for each special type, a certain level, although occasionally abnormal rise in this level, may be witnessed. To classify crime among the phenomena of normal sociology is not to say merely that it is inevitable, although regrettable phenomenon, due to the incorrigible wickedness of men, it is to affirm that it is a factor of public health, an integral part of all healthy societies. It is also a curious fact of life that crime, something horrible itself, should provide so much relief, and recreation to many when written about in fiction or portrayed in movies or on television. Of late, the number of such films have considerably increased, and in almost 95 per cent cases there is no film in which crime, murder, rape, smuggling, gambling *etc.*, are not exhibited. In the last two years the incidence of crime has been continuously on the rise and every year it has surpassed the figure of the previous year.

Each and every individual is a social animal, and he must live in a community. Therefore, while leading a community life he is required to obey the community rules which are formulated for the welfare of the entire society. These rules make the functioning of community life smooth and enable every member of the community to understand what is socially permissible or prohibitive. Therefore, technically "Crime" is any deviation from or any violation of, any well-established social law, eventuating in posing a danger to social harmony and stability. Thus, the society enunciates "Crime", and whosoever commits it is a "criminal". This very concept of crime has been defined in Penal Codes as an act which is punishable under any of the laws in force for the time being, because social awareness often does not go hand in hand with social control of crime, does not thereby lead to the diminution of crime. The function of criminal law is to preserve public order, and decency, to protect citizens from what is offensive or injurious and to provide sufficient safeguards against exploitation and corruption of others, particularly of those who are young, weak in body or mind, inexperienced, or in a state of physical, official or economic dependence. At the same time it is not the function of the law to intervene in the private lives of citizens or to seek to enforce any particular pattern of behaviour farther than is necessary to carry out the above purposes.

True, that in most traditional crimes there is the common element of immorality, and the harmful nature of the acts constituting crime (theft, murder, and rape *etc.*). But there are various other offences in which there is no immorality in the traditional sense, known as, *"Mala in prohibita"* and, on the other hand, there are many acts which are not crimes despite the element of immorality being present in the accepted sense. What conduct should be made punishable under the Criminal Law depends not only on the question whether the conduct is moral or immoral, but also on the considerations of the possibility of its implementations through the legal machinery like the police. As regards the moral quality of an act, the question arises as to who is to determine it? Should it be the law giving body in a society or should it be judged with reference to the hypothetical "average" persons of the society? Is it possible to divide morality into two compartments of public and private morality or leave private morality untouched by law? Any act which is beyond the tolerance of the society, as reflected through an ordinary person, should be the concern of criminal law, and there should be no theoretical limits to the State power against immorality.

Surely, the legislators should ask whether the general morality is based upon ignorance, superstition or misunderstanding, where there is a false conception that those who practice what they condemn are in other way more dangerous or hostile to the society, and their evil consequences are well-understood. The most opportune time has come to use criminal law, in order to sustain public morality by making any harmful feeling, independently of its repercussions on the general moral code, criminal, as it has become increasingly difficult, say, almost impossible to have an integrated society, because the whole moral fabric of the society has started fast disintegrating.

Apart from the issue that the State is justified in tackling those activities through criminal law, which essentially pertain to private morality, the problem should also be looked into from a practical angle. Even, if it is conceded that the State has no theoretical limits to prevent and punish immorality, the more pertinent point is to evaluate the practical limits of the State in the area. Surely it is one thing to make an activity criminal, but quite a different thing to enforce it. It is a common knowledge that many offences, for all practical purposes, are confined to the Statute Books, and the laws are not enforced because there is no will to enforce them or the criminal law machinery is inadequate, inefficient, incompetent, complacent, and finally unsuitable to enforce them. The Sharda Act, the Anti-dowry Act, Anti-untouchability Act, the Prevention of Corruption Act, for instance, have proved to be almost futile attempts to change the attitudes of people in social areas, where criminal law's potential is next to nothing.

Laws have accumulated because the mores have been inadequate, weak and inconsistent, and because the laws have not had the support of the mores they have been relatively ineffective as a means of control. Lack of effective enforcement of criminal laws dealing with offences, particularly against the society, have created problem both for the law as well as for the person whose conduct comes within the prescribed category. It has resulted in contempt and cynicism towards the laws in general, because the condemnation of the prohibited conduct is only in word, and not in deed. The hypocrisy inherent in such a situation. "These laws are unenforced because we want to continue our conduct, and unrepealed because we want to preserve our morals". But the impact on the deviant of this criminalisation of his behaviour transcends any actual experience of official reaction. Even when he is not publicly identified, and officially dealt with, he is only too aware that his behaviour is legally proscribed, as well as socially disapproved and in consequence he has become a law-breaker to commit offences with impunity, and eventually, he is made a hardened criminal, and a burden on the society. It is, therefore, imperative that criminal law should act with zeal in order to provide the most appropriate and effective machinery to cure the intended evil, and this will be in conformity with the adage, "A stitch in time saves nine."

4. Classification of Criminals

Generally, criminals can be classified into four categories: (1) Insane criminals, (2) Habitual criminals, (3) Criminal by passion, and (4) Occasional criminals. The habitual criminal, through showing activistic tendencies is also influenced by social and physical environments. Criminals by passion are otherwise fit but commit the criminal act due to impulse, anger, jealously and feel repentant subsequently. The occasional criminal commits acts of criminality when a chance is offered to him. Some criminologists consider another category of criminal — "Born Criminal" who commits acts of crime due to congenital reasons, but the author is unable to subscribe fully to this view, because experience has shown that mostly geographical, psychological, economic and environmental factors are the most dominant ones to actuate a person to commit an offence. The consciousness of an infant is a blank sheet capable of receiving any impression. The environment, all inclusive, such as economic, social, psychological and emotional, fill the blank sheet of the consciousness with diverse impressions, and in the process the value system and the behavioural pattern of the individual take shape. It was believed at one time that poverty breeds crime. This is, of course, true to a large extent in India, as penury and want are positive incentives to committing theft, and such individuals, even the want is no more, still exhibit criminal tendencies as a matter of habit. It is found while examining what human activity normally consists of: To begin with, a human being receives external stimuli through his sense organs like the eye, the ear, the sense of touch, and so on. This external information gets transmitted to the brain where it is processed. The brain is the processor of human computer. After the processing, when the decision has been arrived at as to what is to be done, the effector mechanism in the shape of muscular activity comes into play. It is obvious, therefore, that the aberrant behaviour of man, socially and morally, is attributable to the socio-economic environments, which generate crime including mass psychology. The majority of murderers and notorious thieves began as delinquent children, and the true seminary of crime must be sought for upon each public square or each crossroads of our towns.

5. Reaction to Crime — Punitive Approach

Punitive Reaction: Reactions to crime have been different at different stages and even in various societies. The society regards the criminal as basically a bad and dangerous sort of a person and wants to inflict punishment on the offender in order to protect the society from his onslaughts, although it is not denied that the criminal became a victim of circumstances and a product of various factors within the community and society. There is yet, another aspect — preventive, in which instead of focussing attention on particular offenders, the conditions responsible for crime causation are eliminated. It should, however, be understood that these three approaches are not mutually exclusive. Not only do they overlap with each other, sometimes they may co-exist as parts of the overall system in a society. The rationalism of punishment may be divided into two classes, based on retributive and utilitarian theories.

6. Retribution Theory

It aims at restoring the social balance disturbed by the offender. The offender should receive as much pain and suffering as inflicted by him on his victim to assuage the angry sentiments of the victim and the community. Retaliation fulfils a religious mission of punishing the offenders, it re-establishes the social harmony affected by the offence, and the offender's guilt is believed to be washed away through suffering. Judicial punishments can never be used merely as a means to promote some other good for the criminal himself or for the society, but instead, it must in all cases be imposed on him only on the ground that he has committed a crime, for a human being can never be manipulated merely as a means to the purposes of someone else and can never be confused with the objects of the law of things. If legal justice perishes, then it is no longer worthwhile for men to remain alive in this country. Such a punishment reflects denunciation of the criminal, and his act by the society. The penal system should be so designed as to ensure that offenders atone by suffering for their offences, and their sufferings should be of the same magnitude as that of their victims, but this basic concept has lost too much of its ground in the context of modern, and more enlightened views on the functional values of the penal laws.

7. Utilitarian Theory

Punishment should be such that it must serve as an instrument of reducing crimes either by deterring the offender and others from doing similar acts in future or it should prevent the commission of offences by incapacitating the offenders, in case reformation of the offenders is not feasible by their own conduct. This is essential because punishment acts as a deterrent both to the offender and the community. It is assumed that as in day-to-day life the infliction of pain or its apprehension keeps people away from certain proscribed behaviour, the same purpose is served by punishment in relation to conduct forbidden by law. It is reported that crimes are almost unknown in Saudi Arabia, and it is a common sight in towns where people leave their shops open unattended even while they are away from them for some time, because of drastic punishments.

8. Fines

Fines as an additional or alternative form of punishment have been increasingly favoured by the law as well as judicial authorities. They are singularly more appropriate in offences relating to traffic, employment of persons unauthorised by law, violation of laws regarding manufacture or distribution of goods. They are frequently imposed in relation to property crimes like embezzlement, fraud, theft, violation of lottery and gambling laws and minor offences like loitering, and disorderly conduct. The imposition of fine may be made in four different ways as provided in the Penal Code. It is the sole punishment for certain offences and the limit of maximum fine has been laid down, in certain offences it is an alternative punishment, but the amount is limited, in offences where it is imperative to impose fine in addition to some other punishment, and in offences where it is obligatory to impose fine but no particular pecuniary limit is laid down. According to Section 64 of the Indian Penal Code, in many cases courts award imprisonment in default of fine.

9. Forfeiture and Confiscation of Property

Forfeiture of property which is the subject matter of the offence is a possible mode of punishment under the Indian Penal Code in certain circumstances (Sections 125, 126, 127 and 169 of the Code — just as waging war against any Asiatic power in alliance with the Government of India, committing depredation on territories of power at peace with the Government of India and public servant unlawfully buying or bidding for property).

But forfeiture of the whole of the property of the criminal is not possible according to the present law. The Law Commission is of the view that this harsh punishment, which will fall not only on the criminal but on his dependent family, is not to be commended. It is obvious that the Commission does not appear to have applied its mind to the problem in depth. Such a punishment is called for in cases of smugglers and black-marketeers, where *prima facie* the source of income or property acquired by the offender may be illegal. (Smugglers and Foreign Exchange Manipulators, Forfeiture of Property Act, 1976). As regards hardships to the family of the offender, the same is caused in varying degrees by all forms of punishments. It was argued that in a welfare country like India the hardship caused to the family can be mitigated by the Government with some kind of financial aid, and as such in the Indian Penal Code Bill of 1972, this type of punishment has been retained.

10. Imprisonment

Imprisonment in its pure and simple form is a kind of punitive reaction, its object being primarily to deprive the offender of his liberty, which is the most serious damage which can be caused to a human being, only next to deprivation of life by death sentence. Imprisonment, as a form of punishment recently got prominence as a result of the decreasing use of the capital punishment and transportation. The most serious thing which happens to the prisoner is the stigma arising out of a prison term as he faces difficulty in getting accepted once again in the society. In the past three decades, prisoners often felt quite justifiably that the real punishment began after they left the prison. But now the position is different in view of the debased moral values of the various components of the society. There are several instances in which the released convict is garlanded, and taken out in procession by his stooges with the result that he becomes the hero of the society, and this preferential treatment to him eventuates in his being idealised by others. He is now, no more considered to be a renegade by the decadent society.

11. Capital Punishment

It has been one of those subjects of human concern, which has given rise to an endless debate without producing any conclusion. To abolish or not to abolish is the problem which has been faced by many countries. In India, although the problem has been engaging Government and public attention over the years, it is still there on the Statute Books, though its use has been sparingly made, and there is a growing tendency to restrict its use to grave offences committed under aggravating circumstances. The capital punishment is confined by the Code only to the following six main offences:

1. Treason — waging war against the Government of India (Section 121), abatement of mutiny (Section 122).
2. Perjury resulting in conviction and death of an innocent person (Section 194),
3. Murder (Sections 302 and 303),
4. Abatement of suicide of a minor or insane person (Section 305).

5. Attempted murder by a life convict (Section 307, Clause 2), and
6. Dacoity with murder.

The Law Commission in its 35th report thus concluded :

"Having regard, however, to the conditions in India, to the variety of the social upbringing of its inhabitants, to the disparity in the level of morality, and the education in the country, to the vastness of its area, to the diversity of its population and to the paramount need for maintaining law and order in the country at the present juncture, India cannot risk the abolition of capital punishment. On a consideration of all the issues involved, the Commission is of the opinion that capital punishment should be retained in the present state of the country." Now capital punishment is on the Statute Book, but to use it rarely seems to be the best compromise adopted by the courts.

12. Evolution of Punitive Reaction

The sentence of law is to be moral sentiment of the people in relation to any offence, what a seal is to a hot wax. It converts into a permanent final judgement what might otherwise be transient sentiment. The mere general suspicion or knowledge that a man has done something dishonest may never be brought out to a point, and the disapprobation existed by it may in time pass away, but the fact that he has been convicted and punished for a certain offence stamps an indelible mark upon him for life. The criminal law thus proceeds upon the principle that it is morally right to hate criminals, and it confirms and justifies that sentiment by inflicting upon criminals' punishments which express it. This close alliance between criminal law, and moral sentiment is always healthy and advantageous to the community.

13. Can Present Criminal Justice System Contain Crimes and Criminals?

Almost 50 per cent of the crimes committed are not reported to the police, mostly because people by now, have come to the conclusion, that no useful purpose would be served by reporting to the police, whose lethargic, apathetic attitude is the main contributing factor for this belief. Property offences which initially appear to be difficult, even if reported to the Police stations, are scarcely registered and, therefore, the question of their investigation does not arise. Those offences, which fortunately get registered, are unfortunately not investigated vigourously. Detection of offences is a chance, and does not exhibit the skill of the investigating officer, and his pursuance. The discretionary powers given to the police with regard to investigation of cases have rendered the police machinery corrupt, and as such no justice can be expected from them. Cases which are registered mostly end in undetected as far as the property offences are concerned. In offences against persons, the percentage of conviction is much lower than as was in the past and those ending in conviction do not create a prohibitive influence on the would be criminals or repeaters on account of the lenient punishment awarded by the courts.

Unfortunately, we have reached a stage whereby the anti-socials and criminals are neither afraid of the laws which have been enacted to control and contain crime and criminals, nor are they afraid of the law-enforcement agency on account of its inertia, and corrupt behaviour. The people look with starry eyes helpless to find out a suitable agency for the redressal of their grievances. In desperation, they have chosen to enroll the assistance of politicians. Therefore, unless there is weightage of political support or money, no grievance generally is likely to be redressed. Cumulatively, people are made to react seriously to such a situation and they take law in their hands, resulting in heinous offences like murders, attempted murder, loot, arson or the like. The system of administration of justice has totally failed in the country due to various reasons discussed at appropriate places in this book. Succinctly, the delayed trials, lenient punishments, and the treating of the culprit, innocent until the prosecution convincingly proves the charge, are the main features for this dismal failure.

People now want a reclassification of crimes regarding the "burden of proof". In offences against society, morality, and nation, now the burden of proof should shift on to the accused himself to prove that he did not commit the crime. People also want that the evaluation of the evidence tendered should be realistic and the punishment awarded should be rigorous enough to ensure a deterring effect on persons prone to commit crimes or having criminal propensities. There is no control of law which has totally failed to contain crime and criminals and the anti-social activities of the aberrant members of the society.

Similarly, in all the departments of the Government, the local bodies and semi-government undertakings, unlike the past, people have a unique experience. All lawful as well as unlawful requirements of the people are not fulfilled until there is a political support or liberal payment of bribe money. Criminal as well as civil justice to the public has now become anathema. People now think, to publicly humiliate, and beat the public servants, is the only remedy left with them to set things right.

4

National State and Social Disorganisation

1. Theory

The imperial State of the ancient past was the first type of the State which had emerged from the primitive patriarchal conditions, and became the justifiable part of the government authority in operations. A number of factors influenced its formation and growth. Kingship, religion, war and political consciousness with awareness were the most powerful forces behind the formation of the national state. Now, only the political consciousness is the most dominant factor in forming the national state in a democratic country, which India ostensibly is. In conformity with the wishes of the people of India, we have chosen to be governed by a democratic type of a state and through it to maintain law and order, peace and tranquillity, irrespective of the fact of our belonging to various religious faiths. The most important function of the State is to superintend and control the citizens and to punish them for the accepted and the recognised wrongs perpetrated by them; besides their general amelioration and emancipation. The State has become a moral and ethical institution. Prevention and detection of crime and the punishment of offenders tops the list of priorities of the functions of a State. People have accorded it only as the right of compelling obedience from the citizens. The national state has established a suitable government as an institution through which the State effectively carries out its obligatory functions politically entailed upon it.

2. Importance of Political Parties

Political parties have become adjuncts of the government. They are the instruments whereby candidates are nominated or elected. Though, they are not official organisations created by the State, they are nevertheless, quasi-official in the sense that State sanctions, regulates and permits them to offer candidates for public office. The ultimate aim of any political party is to come in power and keep control of the government in its hand.

The number of political parties in a State varies from one to many. In a two-party system like England or America, the advantage of the system is its capacity to present more clearly issues and fewer candidates and avoidance of a multiplicity of position on issues, and a wide number of candidates. The losing party in this system serves as an effective opposition. In the multiple party system government changes rapidly, as voters are bewildered by a number of viewpoints presented by multiple candidates. The merger of five political parties into Janata Dal failed to give any stability to the Indian party system. Contrived defections and counter-defections continue giving scope for political corruption of a wider range. The political parties in India are personality-centered rather than policy-centered, and are religion-oriented. The Indian National Congress has also split up into more than two parties due to personal ego, pride and prejudices. At present more than 30 parties operate at the national and state levels. Many a times inner cliques or rings, or caucuses develop. The political party which has been chartered by the people to act as a link between the people and their government has now become the media for the politicians to gain an occupation, and try to be permanent on it, amass money and hand over it to his next of kin. He ceased to play his role for the betterment, and larger interest of the people who had allowed him to lead them.

3. Pressure Groups

They play a vital part and role in the government's working process as they seek to promote interest of their members through external inducements. It is never a political group which initially seeks to compete political power, and eventually replaces the existing government, though it may possess political character for the sake of expediency and eventuality. A pressure group is an association of persons with a common interest, who try to influence the government actions in legislations, administrative procedures or political decisions. The instances are of the Muslim

League and its allied organisations, which have influenced the government to such an extent as to violate the fundamental principles of the "Rule of common law and equality of law" cited in the Constitution of the Republic of India by compelling the government to give the Muslims a preferential treatment in respect of all the Muslim personal behaviours and relationship to *Shariyat*. Another current instance can be vividly seen in the various states which are vying with each other to raise the quota of reservations in academic and administrative units from 50 per cent stipulated by the Supreme Court to 82 per cent eventuating in flagrant violation of the judicial sacrament. All these actions of the pressure groups are discordant with the national state and its unity, which has been seconded to political expediency, and exigency. In the Indian political system pressure groups play all pervasive, and conspicuously important role in the political process as a whole through elections. At different levels of electoral processes, in nomination, canvassing and campaigning, these groups take cudgels on behalf of their favourites, and get them a coveted place in the legislature; and later in the cabinet. They have a sizeable block of voters in their favour and pockets and they also contribute to the financial sinews of the party concerned. The members elected with the support of the pressure groups are compelled to do their biddings with far greater strength and surety than the bidding of their party. The pressure groups make use of all their resources and persuasive forms to procure political decisions, and administrative actions of their choice. They also influence public opinion through mass media at their disposal. In Indian democracy, their role is seemingly greater than in a totalitarian government. Seshan, the present Election Commissioner has pointedly brought to the notice of the people the mal-engineering in fair and peaceful elections, and the dire need to thwart this tendency in a bid to its elimination or decimation.

4. Social Significance of Religion

Prior to the advent of what may be called the age of the reason, religion had been the chief supporter of the moral, and spiritual values of life. Some ultra-materialistic thinkers have proposed that moral values of life are the customs of the purely materialistic life of man — his economical and social life, and his psychological being. True morality arises out of understanding that the whole cosmos, of which we are only a fractional part, is maintained in an orderly way. The material life of man may erect the upper super-structure of social morality upon the foundation of universal order, but is beyond its power to alter or substitute that basic order by one and his own creation. To say that morality is wholly created or constituted, material aspects of life would be tantamount to consider the human life as an isolated event outside the general order of this eventful universe. Religion may have become politically detestable due to the various exploitations done by human beings, who themselves are responsible in eschewing the consideration of the social significance of religion in human life; and its conduct must be in conformity or harmony with that cosmic order.

Modern man has not discovered a more firmer ground on which he can base the morality of mankind. The fear of the State, community or immediate neighbourhood and the vigilance of his own family members may force a man to conform to the established modern patterns. But he can deviate easily, provided he becomes sure that his conduct would remain undiscovered. There is no inner binding to a man devoid of religion, which invoked the inner necessity of moral values, and which claimed that all one's conduct, apparent or hidden, are under close observation of some supernatural being and that the true value of religion lies in this aspect of religion which is the most important from the sociological point of view. The sense of good and bad may be connected directly or indirectly with the historical process of society. What is good today may be considered bad tomorrow, but this fact does not diminish or negate the necessity of isolation of good from evil. Both morality and religion are inter-connected. Morality prepares the way for the perpetuation of religious beliefs. Whereas religion reinforces morality with its supernatural sanctions. Morality concerns itself with the entire life of the masses that is with the motives, and thoughts no less than with his actions. Acts which are not illegal may still be regarded as immoral. The falsehood, ingratitude and meanness are all immoral though not always illegal. As long as man does not cause injury to someone else by telling a lie, he is not doing anything illegal. The domain of morality is one of voluntary self-determination, whereas the law operates in the area of obligatory actions. An act is illegal because law declares it to be so. Law can prescribe external acts, but it cannot dictate morality. Law is based upon expediency.

The ethical appeal is always to the individual's own sense of what is right or wrong, in the last resort always to his sense of what is good or evil. It can disdainfully be seen that this superhold of morality on human beings for regulating their conduct and behaviour is loosing its moorings, and that too at a very fast pace with a gloomy picture for the posterity.

5. Social Disorganisation

The functions of every group are determined in an organised society, which is always dynamic and not static. These functions of the various groups in India could not remain the same at all the times. As time passed the functions of one group were transferred to another, and that was not conducive to any precise definition of the function of the various groups which eventuated into disorganisation. Now, the functions of family, state, castes, creeds, and other groups, are dependent not on the choice of their selection, but on the opportunities made available to human beings by the State, which has increasingly made them dependent on it for their subsistence, and even survival. Thus, a lack of system in the mutual relationship of persons, their respective status and functions, social values, mores and institutions is perceptible, and the social disorganisation has been set in, thereby disintegrating the common thread holding the social webs. In the past four decades, our social order was simple and social pressures and tensions were bearable. With this condition of the society, there were no strains or tensions on the social equilibrium. Now, our society has become very complex, intricate and complicated in which each individual is working under some sort of a strain and these strains and tensions have evidently disturbed the social equilibrium to a considerable extent.

6. Fight for Power Out in Open

In the past for nearly four decades law, order, peace and tranquillity existed throughout the country, but the recent political history has been noticeably volatile. Almost, the entire nation has been the site of significant controversies that have profoundly influenced the political discourse, and events in the country. The unprecedented mobilisation mounted by the "*Hindutva*" forces to unrest control of the Babri Masjid in Ayodhya and the ensuing debate over secular and communal identities, the conflicts over job reservations, completely side-tracking intellectual capabilities, expression of "*Dalit*" assertions are all centered in the country's politics irrespective of the party ideology. Assertions of communal and caste claims have been drawn more deeply into politics and statecrafts. These have mostly resulted in democratic changes in voting preferences, a part that is symptomatic of the peoples' disenchantment with successive political regimes since the landmark election of 1967. Political instability was always threatening in the various states. Part of the explanation lies in the collapse of the values of the Congress Party, and the singular failure of the State Government to tackle specific problems of economic, and social justice and pay adequate attention to the slow rates of growth and limited industrialisation. Equally important is the social transformation set-in motion by changes in the political economy and the agricultural politics. Some of these changes have unmistakably benefited the backward castes and classes, who persistently went on demanding a commensurate share of the political and bureaucratic power, which is marked by the stiff resistance of the upper and middle castes and their refusal or apathy to accept the political consequences of the new order resulting in economic change. From 1957, the domination of upper and middle castes was challenged by the backward castes after Babasaheb Ambedkar embraced *Buddhism*, and the latter continued to use their newly-gained and generated politico-economic power and their natural strength to question the monopoly of the upper, and middle castes over the structure of powers, which the former had all the while dominated. This challenge, unfortunately, was political and not social from the outset. The pursuit of power, material interest and the consequential gains had generally taken place on the basis of social solidarities of castes, rather than those of classes. Seldom has backward class politics pursued the themes of class injustice or redistribution of material resources in the society. Upper and middle castes' domination was denounced, there was no attempt to come to grips with the issues of principles of social transformation which the downtrodden often raises.

Various backward caste alliances forged since 1970 were mainly concerned with alteration in the power structure. Arguments about equality, the removal of injustice were less; and the sharing of privileges and making politics the circuit of privileges was more incisive. One consequence of all this is a noticeable increase in the social mobility of backward castes and classes in economy and the government. The shrinking of privileges is hotly contested by upper and middle castes without creedal or racial discriminations, and it has become the economic phenomenon. Naturally, reservations beyond 50 per cent, as stipulated by the Supreme Court, is being protested against by upper and middle castes as their posterity has no future at all. Thus, an open opposition between upper, middle and lower castes and classes has aggravated beyond the restitution of social harmony. Underlying the dissatisfaction of these two formations, and the emergence of the third alternative has now interpellated a powerful social force which is the coalition of all backward castes and classes and *Dalits*; rendering solution to the question of dominance and privilege politically open; and then society which is already disorganised is fraught with inherent and internecine consequences of conflicts in the next few years. The minority community of Muslims will effectively tilt the fulcrum of the political balance, but not without the discord of the national unity and integration. And this is the prevalent scene of our "National State" can we all remedy it? No! only the posterity has the answer to this riddle.

7. Retrospective Introspection

Like all, the civilisations of the world, in India, too the society has always remained the most importantly dominant factor in building the nation, acquiring and maintaining its progress; and stabilising its glory. Therefore, a critical study of the society has become imperative in order to clearly understand the various factors, in which social experiences function in developing, maturing, nurturing, repressing human beings through their interpersonal stimulations, social relationship and various forms which have affected them, and whenever they continue to affect.

The Indian society is the conglomeration, and as well, the gross product of the various religious faiths, which from time to time existed in India. From about 3000 years a highly organised society was developed with a very good standard of morality. All the evidence points to a high degree of standardisation and organisation implying strong centralisation with full controls over production, distribution, and an efficient system of taxation. In essence, the picture is one of the rigid and highly ordered bureaucratic machine, capable of organising and distributing surplus wealth and defending it, but little conducive to the political liberty of the individual. More or less the society represented very perfect adjustments of human life to specific environment that could have only resulted from years of special efforts. And it has endured it, it is already specifically *Hindusthani* and forms the basis of the modern Indian culture in all its aspects, both mundane and spiritual. In due course of time the differentiation between higher and lower classes based on status became rigid. Their functions became stratified into castes based on the occupations followed by their members. The priests became professionals. The warriors became the fighter class or caste. It was by this process of evolution that the *Brahmins*, *Kshatriyas*, *Vaishyas* and *Sudras* came into being. Strict rules of endogamy and exogamy were established, but with occasional relaxations. These classes or castes of society were called the four "*Varnas*".

Caste system developed further as different occupations were taken over by different castes. As time passed by the caste system became more rigid. However, the interchanging of castes also existed depending on the merits of the behaviour and achievements of people. The caste system became an essential part of the society in latter *Vedic* Period (for about 4,000 years ago). As stated by Hrislay, "castes came to be recognised as a collection of families or groups of families bearing a common name, which usually denotes, or is associated with a mythical ancestor, human or divine; preferring to follow the same calling and regarded by those who are competent to give an opinion on forming a single homogeneous community". The duties of the four "*varnas*" traditionally remained the same from generation to generation. The very fact that the institution of castes survived over 3000 years is a clear proof of the services which it must have rendered to the *Hindusthani* society in different periods of history and it is this caste system in its original benign form, which in a way was largely responsible for the preservation of *Hindusthani* culture, which could not be conquered by the invaders belonging to other religions, although paradoxically they conquered the *Hindusthani* territory. The only reason was, that the system was based on economic principles of division of labour, which ensured efficiency excellence and perfection in production. It provided social insurance and promoted social service activities and was responsible for preserving the purity of blood amongst various groups. In a nutshell, the concept of the organic unity and interdependence ran through the whole caste system, and each unit formed a part of the whole. While none was allowed to remain in want, each was under an obligation, as long as he was able to contribute his share of labour according to his capacity and for the benefit of the whole society. Thus, was the ancient tradition preserved, social tranquillity safeguarded, civic and economic welfare secured; and individual happiness and contentment were promoted with some or practically no political intervention or interference. Later on parochial interest of those who were supposed to lead the society eroded this sound system, and its national fabric, and the caste system, as it stands today, has done more harm than good, and is described as, "The most disastrous and blighting human institution." It is also anti-national as caste prejudices and caste feuds had always dominated our history. Currently, it has shown symptoms of future group conflicts as a result of political interference or intervention, not for their general amelioration but to reap advantage of their bulk votes in the electoral process.

While *Hinduism* was largely accepted by the people of India with the sound basis of several centuries, *Jainism* was followed by 8th century B.C. after the death of Mahavir in about 468 B.C. the flowering faith began to dwindle, although it spread in all parts of India. The Muslim invasion of India in about 712

A.D. was the major factor which contributed to its total decline in those days.

Before the advent of *Buddhism* in India (487 B.C.) the *Hindu* society based on *Vedic* ideology lost its former glory and many kinds of abuses and superstitions had crept up into it. The *Vedic* Hindu religion presented a confusing mass of ideals and things, which was beyond the comprehensions of the common man. The *Vedic-Hindu* religion, with its lofty ideas and ideals of God, soul, salvation and creation of the world was merely a rattle, which did not satisfy the inner yearnings of the people, who wanted a simpler religion, as could be understood by the people, and could be made by them a part and parcel of their lives. It was in this atmosphere that *Buddhism* made its appearance in the country. The phenomenal growth of *Buddhism* in the country was due to (a) simplicity of teaching of Buddha, (b) simple philosophy of life with a simple code of conduct not requiring the employment of priests, and expenditure of money, and (c) *Buddhism* did not believe in any caste system.

Royal patronage under Ashoka (273 B.C.); Kanishka (78 A.D.); and Harsha (606 A.D.), and the absence of a rival religion, as Islam and Christianity were yet to invade India, gave a tremendous impetus and boost to popularise and extend *Buddhism*. In the time of Kanishka, the *Buddhism* had split up to *Mahayanism* and *Hinayanism*. The religion of Buddha started in one corner of India, and spread mostly throughout the Asian countries. In the later centuries, *Buddhism* diminished in India as its principle of "*Ahimsa*" did not appeal to the royal heads in the face of Muslim invasion, and its methods of coercive conversion and finally, the Muslim conquest of India from the 7th to the 18th century gave a death blow to *Buddhism*. However, it was revived by Dr Babasaheb Ambedkar, in October 1956, when he embraced *Buddhism* with the only and sole aim to emancipate and ameliorate the downtrodden societies of this country. Dr Babasaheb Ambedkar never envisaged the present tactics of the various political parties to appease the members of Scheduled Castes, Scheduled Tribes, Backward Classes and Muslim minority community in order to gain political mileage through their "Vote Bank" and the driving of the permanent wedge between the unity of upper, middle; and lower strata of the Indian society, a grotesque but not pragmatic picture of every day life in this country. This is leading to internecine group conflicts.

The invasion of the Northwestern India, including Punjab by Persia (518 B.C. to 335 B.C.); by Greek under Alexander (330 B.C.); by Sakas, Pahlavas, the Kushans (1st century B.C. to 358 A.D.) and by Huns under Tormana (515 A.D.) did not materially harm the nation, for the invaders were either driven away or they subsequently got themselves assimilated and Indianised by treating India, and its culture as their own. The whole of India emerged as a big nation and remained integrated as such until 712 A.D. when Muslims invaded, and finally conquered the whole country. Their rule of over 1000 years in the country multiplied their population through the process of reproduction and conversion, and a new faith — Muslim Religion got deeply entrenched in the body polity of the country. To combat Muslim fundamentalism Guru Nanak, followed by other nine *Gurus*, and particularly Guru Govind Singh, founded and fostered the *Khalsa Panth* (Sikh) which was initially the "Armed Hand" of the Hindu society in order to protect the Hindus from the atrocities perpetrated by the ruling Muslims, who were unprecedently repressive (1464 -1802 A.D.). With the termination of Muslim rule in India in about 1757 A.D. and the subsequent conquest of the whole of India by the British Imperial Power, the Christianity, yet another faith or religion, got embedded in the soil of this country. Like Muslims, Christian population was also multiplied by procreation and conversions.

Thus, the country was governed by the Hindus (inclusive of *Buddhism*, *Jainism* and *Sikhism*) by the tenets of *Shastras*, *Upanishads*, *Sutra* and *Puranas*. *Manusmriti* discusses in details about the observance of moral laws and duties which are the most virtuous and pious behaviour (*Dharma*) of the individual being. There is clear mention of the four "*Varnas*" classes as the components of Indian society, and in addition they contained implicit, and as well explicit instructions about the duties to be performed by the individuals of each "*Varna*" in order to achieve and perpetuate the well-being of the society as a whole. The Hindu sages and philosophers have also discussed at length the pertinent duties and responsibilities of each of the four "*Varnas*" of the composite Hindu Society with a clear warning that even a fractional deviation from the prescribed duties could lead the individual, the society and ultimately the nation to harm. Lord Krishna and his *Bhagwad Gita* are the foremost and worldwide acclaimed (about 3,000 B.C.). Kautilya's *Arthashastr*a (330 B.C.) lays down the duties of the ruler and the people to make an ideal society; besides he has usefully and at length discussed the economic, social and political life of an individual *vis-a-vis* the society and the nation.

In the Mughal period the tenets of Quran, and the philosophical writtings of scholars like Amir Khusro, Abul Fazl and a host of others had inspired the general behavioural pattern mostly of the Muslims. Likewise the Bible and the various Christian philosophers have influenced the Christian community.

It was not until the 16th century that clear-cut distinction was made between the State and the Society and more weightage was given to the "Rule of Common Law" rather than "Rule of Religion" for governance of the nation and its subjects. Several writers like Hobbes, and Machiavelli, who propounded a clear-cut distinction between the State and society comprising individuals, discovered the principles which go to make an ideal State and society. Another Scholar Sir Thomas More in his "Utopia", published in 1515 A.D. dealt with the everyday social problems, thereby depicting an ideal social order, which meant to serve as an example to others to be emulated. He presented a picture of an ideal life as a way of pointing out what actually an individual should be. This philosophy was deeply embedded in the soil of Europe, the ruling powers of which had almost politically conquered the entire world. By that time throughout the Western countries Herbert Spencer's theory of the organic evolution of society was displaced by the psychological interpretations of social life. By the beginning of the 20th century More Dongal, G. Wallace and Hobhouse in England and Ward Giddings and Dewey in America tried to interpret social evolution in psychological terms. Durkheim was the first modern thinker, who emphasised on the reality of the society. He laid stress on the social facts and provided a separate ground to sociology from that of psychology, and asserted that social facts are external and exercise constraint and ultimately, inconsequence, the society. Imbued by this philosophy of sociology, the British rulers, and their administrators of this country gave a new impetus, direction and dimension to the Indian citizens to mould themselves according to the present Indian society. As a means to achieve the ends, the study of sociology was started in India in 1919, but it was in 1930, that its study as a separate discipline was recognised. Since then many individuals and thinkers have contributed to the growth of society. During the British regime no cohesive Indian society could be established, the only reason being, "Divide and Rule Policy" adopted by the British Government for perpetuating their rule in this country. The Indian society was never allowed to exist as a whole and a composite entity. It was purposefully divided into various segments, and the most important and politically predominant among them are: Hindu society, Muslim society and the Christian society and since 1976 the Sikh society.

During the pre-Independence period from about 1880 to 1947, our integrated Indian society, although very short-lived, could be formed due to strenuous efforts of the leaders belonging to all castes and creeds. After India had achieved Independence in 1947, it was hoped that one homogeneous Indian society could be moulded to form an integrated and strong India, but the anticipation has been not only aborted but also belied by vested interests of the politicians, and in consequence the present state of affairs of the Indian society is being witnessed. To all intent and purposes no such Indian society is extant. On the contrary the entire Indian society has been divided and sub-divided into various ethnic, religious, linguistic and political groups; and consequently the whole of Indian society stands disintegrated.

The Indian society now has become more heterogeneous than in the past and there is no common thread of affection or affinity between the warring factions of the various castes and classes. It is latent that the entire Indian society is on the brink of a socio-political volcano; and it is nobody's guess as to when and with what potency it is going to erupt, although there are obvious indications signalling castes, classes conflicts in the near future when the youths of any caste, creed or religion, is bound to come to the streets after suffering the pangs of hunger caused by deprivation of the means of livelihood. There is every possibility that these conflicts may lead to large-scale disturbances, and an universal increase in the incidence of crime against person, property, society and even the nation as has been witnessed in Jammu and Kashmir, Punjab, Assam, the North Eastern regions, Uttar Pradesh, Bihar, Orissa and in some other states. Already the entire police force of the country has come into the dock and charges of general apathy, inefficiency, corruption, lack of honesty to duty, probity, partisan attitude, sycophancy, and the domination of political interference by the proteges of the rulers; which cumulatively have reduced to nullity their past reputation of "THE EFFICIENT FORCE" and the "FRIEND OF THE SOCIETY" of which the older generation of police was proud. Who else is to be blamed for this state of affairs? From where honest, sincere, and conscious police officers and men and the bureaucrats are to be procured? Are the present set of laws, both criminal and evidence, sufficient enough for the revival of the previous good reputation of the POLICE? Several such allied or correlated phenomena have been tried to be dealt with in the forging Chapters.

5
The Genesis of Police

From the *Vedic* period, the changing pattern of the Governments, notwithstanding the protection of life and property of the people have been the cardinal functions of the State. The administration of criminal justice and the structure of internal security system have been inextricably linked with the broad stream of religion, ethics and political institution. Therefore, the term "Police" broadly connotes the purposeful maintenance of public order; and protection of persons and property from the hazards of public accidents and the commission of unlawful acts. It specially applies to a body of officers, both civil and military, charged with the maintenance of public order and safety; and enforcement of the laws of the land, including the prevention and detection of crime.

1. The Concept of '*Danda*' and Origin of Police

There is ample evidence of a security organisation in the Harappan civilisation. The Indian merchants had established colonies in the far-flung parts of the then known world and undertook prolonged maritime journeys. They had evidently employed security guards to ensure smooth trading ventures. The townships unearthed in the Indus basin, and other sites of the contemporary civilisation give fairly a clear picture of the social, political and religious life of the people. They had also drawn up elaborate arrangements for internal security as the two rows of the houses have been identified to be military barracks for accommodating regular army detachments intended for the defence of the city. An interesting Harappan seal shows the figure of a man holding a stick which has now been interpreted as portraying *Dandadhar.* It seems that this is the first pictorial representation of a "Policeman".

The early "*Vedic Samhitas*" elaborately illustrate the insecure living conditions of the pastoral *Vedic* community who constantly beseeched the celestial deities to protect them and their material belongings, not only from natural calamities but also from human marauders. The "*Vedas*" and the "*Brahmanas*" are replete with prayers on this score. There is hardly any crime which was not known then, on account of which the *Vedic* people lived restless and were nightmarish at times. Similar living conditions have also been portrayed in the Buddhist and Jain canonical literature. The "*Jatak*" stories have detailed accounts of robbers having regular settlements and frequently looting the merchandise and decapitating the merchants. These insecure conditions rendered so imperatively that the merchants had arranged their own guards and security men for their own security and protection.

During the Mauryan period, the agrarian population was drifting towards towns. Some of these uprooted people took to crime and threatened the city elite. According to the *Arthasastra* of Kautilya, the then administration was forced to advise the imposition of stringent curfew from about two and a half hours from dark, since there were professional thieves in operation. Such a crime situation was required to be tackled through the police officers, garrison commanders' soldiers, and security agents, who served as detectives.

Danda which symbolised the coercive power of the State, was adequately buttressed by moral and spiritual applications. It was never arbitrary or ruthless; and at the same time, it was the first basic postulation responsible for the birth of a police system. The later "*Vedic*" and "*Smriti*" texts, the Buddhist and Jain religions scriptures, besides the great epics of the *Ramayana* and the *Mahabharata*, adequately mention the protection of the subject as the most important and basic duty of the king. The concept of *Danda* was the most important political idea propounded by the Indian thinkers. The primary meaning of *Danda* is rod or staff. Traditionally the staff or sceptre has been an emblem of command or authority. In a broader sense, it was an abstract idea symbolising cosmic force and was, like so many Hindu ideas, personified and given a concrete form. *Danda* the symbol of the right to punish — is *Dharma* itself for a king in his functions as a dispenser of justice, and was considered his most righteous duty, and an unavoidable obligation towards his subject; and therefore *Danda* became an important adjunct to royal office.

2. '*Dandaniti*' of Kautilya

Kautilya, who canonised an elaborate system of policing and laid down several grades of bureaucracy, could rightly be called the father of the modern concept of Police. It is apparent that the traditions set by him were followed throughout in the history all over India, except those certain new designations were evolved after the advent of Kusanas, who brought with them the system of posting military commanders/officers as governors or heads of various states/departments. *Dandaniti* propounded by Kautilya in *Arthasastra* was the science of dealing with crimes *vis-a-vis* the punishments to be given to criminals; and then, *Danda* became the essence of the Government.

Manu emphasised the *Arthasastra* ideal as the supreme authority of *Danda* by raising it to the level of the foremost political expedient, as well as a divine institution. This view is justified by the function of *Danda* in ensuring individual security in respect of person, property; as well as, the stability of the social order. The epics consider the concept of *Danda* as the upholder of *Dharma* — duty, the prime and most righteous of the King, who was the protector of the people. The awe resulting in the protection given by *Danda* ensured the safety of the people and preserved the sense, "This is mine" for, prevention, treachery or deception; and destruction of the weak by the strong ultimately the coercive factor of *Danda* was elevated to a science and eventually it became the art of governance or the government itself. All these important and cardinal functions of the State including the security, and protection of the people, and maintenance of law and order were carried out by the police.

The Maurya had organised a highly competent, effective and centralised administration system in an era of primitive road communication, thick and impregnable jungles, unconquered mountains and uninhabitated valleys infested by robbers, *dacoits* and violent tribes, and that was done through effective police system. The Mauryan states were autocratic police states, and their functions were political, economic, social and at times religious, and it affected almost all the aspects of human life and allegedly infringed on the privacy of man from the time of conception to cremation.

Though the police had functioned in a rudimentary fashion since the *Vedic* period, the credit for creating a separate agency of police with the specific powers of administration, implementation and enforcement of laws and regulations, and for the prevention of crimes, their investigation, and the prosecution of criminals goes to Kautilya. From the law enforcing agency to a complicated espionage and counter-espionage system, the control of border traffic, smuggling and immigration; custom and revenue investigation, an effective vigilance department, including political, and military intelligence Kautilya had left nothing to chance. Therefore, the view held by Western scholars that the "Indian Police system" is the creation of the British rule in India is totally false. It is interesting to note that even today *Danda* — Baton is used as an insignia to denote the highest police authority, and is worn on shoulder-straps by the Inspector General of Police and above in each and every police force of the country.

3. Earlier Police Organisation

The policing system of Kautilya was on two distinct lines, *i.e.*, civilian departments entrusted with police powers and a cadre of regular police officers. He had conferred police powers on almost all the departments which had public dealings. He had ensured that the intervention of the State in all matters concerning administration was total. The cadre of regular police officers comprised of the rural and urban branches, which functioned on similar lines. The hardcore was composed of three-tier system; namely:

1. essentially for the rural areas — *Pradesta*,
2. for urban area — *Nagarka*, and
3. at the top of rural and urban areas — *Sthamikas*.

The most junior rank was the *Gopaa*. Police headquarters were located in the capital with representative police officers in all principle centres and important villages. These were stationed in the midst of 800 villages (*Sthaniya*), 400 villages (*Mukha*); 200 villages *(Kharavatas)*; and 10 villages (*Sangrahana*).

Samaharta was a senior officer of the Central Government and variously characterised as Home Minister, Finance Minister, and the Administrator headed by the law and order machinery with a countrywide jurisdiction. The suppression of crime and maintenance of law and order was his ultimate responsibility. He had a several competent secret agents to report on criminals, and anti-social elements, including dishonest official. He asserted the royal writ. The officers concerned with the maintenance of law and order, investigation of criminal cases and the punishment of criminal worked under him.

4. Deputation of Police Officers

The officers of the police department were deputed to do the following jobs for the State. Their nomenclatures and functions have been given against each of them:

(i) *Pradesta*: Revenue collection and defence by means of an elaborate police organisation were their chief functions. The king maintained a chain of communication between the Central Government and the rural officers. They served in an area of five to ten villages. They had investigative and punitive powers.

(ii) *Grambhartaka, Gramika, Gramakuta*: These were village police officers, and they were invested with executive powers, such as, banishing of thief or adulterer from the village, compensating for every loss of property suffered by each resident of the village.

(iii) *Nagarakas*: They were the urban police and their charter of duties covered almost all facets of town life, including the land survey and census operation. In a way *Nagaraka* was the head of the city police.

(iv) *Antapala*: He was the frontier officer, who commanded the border check post, where he controlled the entry of men and goods into and out of the country. He issued passes to incoming traders, stamped their goods, and after charging them for comfortable use of roads allowed them to proceed further. None were allowed to enter or leave the State without securing a passport from him on payment of the prescribed fees.

(v) *Sansthadhyaksa and Panyadhaksa*: They controlled the markets and traders to ensure that the customers were not cheated by the manipulation of weights and measures and adulteration of consumer goods, the prices of which were also controlled by them.

(vi) *Ganika Dhyaksa*: He controlled the institution of prostitution and gambling dens. (Even in the modern Government, law relating to immoral traffic in women, and prostitution are enforced by the police.)

(vii) There were secret service agents for the collection of internal, as well as, external intelligence and spying, espionage, and counter-espionage system was brought to perfection by Kautilya. Anti-corruption departments also functioned in order to check the malpractices of officials, as they were vested with wide powers. This system ensured to punish *malafide* and prejudicial arrests and seizures; interference with legal and *bona fide* activities of the people; misbehaviour of policemen and their dereliction of duties. For the purposes of police, the smallest unit village, was autonomous. What we find today about the various functions of the police, were already implemented by Kautilya, who is the primogenitor of the modern police system of the whole world, and the rules and regulations made by him were the precursor of the Indian Police Act of 1861, which the British Government had enacted; and for that matter, the entire criminal and social laws of India, which are enforced today, derive their roots from the *Arthasastra* of Kautilya, with *mutatis mutandis* changes, suitable to the present socio-political; socio-religious, and socio-economic conditions.

5. Constitutional Obligation of Subject

Kautilya had not only placed the responsibility of 'watch and ward' on the Central and district administration for the prevention of crime, but also had laid down that the people in the rural and urban areas, were by and large, answerable to the crimes committed within their areas, as they were required to give information to the State officials about suspected persons, and suspicious occurrences tending to have criminal linkages etc.

6. Changes in the Organisation of Police Role

After Ashoka, Kusanas were the link between Mauryans and their distant, but brilliant successors, Gupta and they sought to perfect the administrative machinery by intermingling the traditions of India and the political ideas, which they inherited from the Central Asia. The change in the designations/ nomenclature to *Maha Dandanayaka* and *Dandanayaka* did not divest the bureaucrats of their police functions. Military, police and judicial functions were given to them. The officers were the compatriots or close relations of the rulers. The combination of civil, military, judicial and criminal powers was necessiated in view of the stiff resistance which the Kusana invaders encountered in India. During the Gupta period, more or less a similar pattern of policing was adopted. The judiciary and the police continued to be the important agencies of the State administration. With the passage of time the police responsibility widened, and different organisations had to be necessarily created in order to implement effectively the law and order system and bring criminals to justice. But the most important duty of the police remained the same — investigating crimes, arresting criminals, producing them in the court of law under chains and later implement the orders of the court. The police were invested with the function of modern jail or prison department. In the early centuries of the Christian Era, there were varied and diversified nomenclatures for police personnel. *Manu's* police were divided into two functional departments, namely, the criminal investigation department, and the law and order wing. As of today, the criminal investigation department was sub-divided into two units — one for collection of criminal intelligence and investigation of crimes and the other: 'Special Branch' for collecting intelligence for the security of important dignitaries, prevention and prosecution of economic offences and undertaking espionage. *Manu* had suggested extensive use of the secret agents and agent provocateurs. Their activities were of secret and confidential nature due to their method of recruitment, elaborate training and their result-oriented performance. During the time of Harsha *Yamacetis* (women police) also existed.

7. Village Autonomy

The villages in ancient India have enjoyed autonomy since the *Vedic* period, and the system was hardly disturbed by the rulers seeking to establish imperial authority in India.

The Mauryas, who carried their interference in public life to the minutest details allowed the autonomous status of the village communities to exist, and they adequately safeguarded their efficient functioning. This system continued during the following centuries with almost negligible changes. Almost every Government had established police posts at vantage and vulnerable points in the countryside, including the frontiers with specific charter of duties. The crime-prone areas were especially guarded by armed police contingents, and a proper 'watch and ward' including vigilance was not only maintained, but also ensured through continuous patrolling combined with intensive combing. The village police also helped in the realisation of the State revenue.

8. Effects of Police System

Thus, the principles of internal security, the moral and ethical responsibilities of the rulers, and the system of policing developed in ancient town and villages, and they were sufficiently followed and improved by successive Hindu Kings, as they were suitably advocated by the then prevailing legal canons. The standard of maintenance of law and order was high, but it depended largely on the severity with which the evil doers were treated. Mutilation or maiming was a common punishment and death penalty was frequently awarded, even for such minor misconduct as evasion of taxes, damaging a sacred tree, obstructing a royal procession and like other sundries. It was the general 'Awe' of the administration that was responsible for maintaining law and order, peace and tranquillity and thwarted criminal and anti-social acts of the perpetrators in the face of repeated alien invasions of the country year after year. The normal life of the subjects was not disturbed, and they lived in fearless amity, and with open doors for which the police system was singularly responsible.

6

The Evolution of Police in Medieval India

1. *Arthasastra* of Kautilya — Traditions

The 'Arthasastra' of Kautilya can justly be called a treatise on Criminal Justice System. It is replete with amazingly lucid details concerning:

(i) Exhaustive anti-corruption and surveillance machinery to keep a check against misuse of power and authority by officers and punishments meted out to the erring officers.

(ii) Precise definitions of robbery, theft, defamation, assault, culpable homicide not amounting to murder, murder and punishment for these, and other offences like rape, homosexuality, bestiality, sodomy *etc*.

Some chapters in the *Arthasastra* read like a manual for the police in modern times. A detailed guideline has been given for every act of crime and where and whom to look for as suspicious persons while investigating various types of crimes or what type of circumstantial evidence and *modus operandi* may lead to successful detection. So also detailed instructions have been given as to the manner in which inquest should be held in a case of unnatural death. There is accurate description of a dead body in order to recognise whether the death was by suffocation, by hanging (homicidal or suicidal), by drowning, by various types of poisoning, or whether the victim was killed with sticks or ropes or thrown down and thereby killed, and so on.

The above are the few of the umpteen instances from which it is possible to know how elaborately and intelligently Kautilya had thought and written about criminal jurisprudence to deal with crime and criminals, and their punishments. His sole objective was to ensure the general benefit of the State, the society, the subjects, the rulers and their security and safety. Undoubtedly Kautilya had laid very strong foundation of the policing system in India, and it stood the test of the times for several centuries after him. That was the era when throughout India there were Hindu rulers, who had administrative heritage of Mauryans, and for them the well-being of their subjects was the first priority. In later periods, it seems that the cardinal duty towards the citizens was either relegated to second position or neglected on account of unstable conditions due to centrally weak administration, and the consequential revolts eventuating the breakdown of the kingdoms.

The ancient police system in India was based upon the principle of local responsibility and mutual co-operation. In the village, which formed the basic unit of administration, security and peace was a matter of collective responsibility and shared by every resident of the village. One of the village leaders, known as the *Gramneta* or the village watchman was responsible to protect the village from criminals, while the body corporate of village was bound to make good the loss due to crime committed within the village limits, except in cases where they were able to trace offenders, and recover the goods or succeeded in fixing the responsibility for the crime upon neighbouring villages (*Sukra-Niti-Sar*). This practice made each villager alert, and watchful and compelled him to ensure that he did not commit any crime, nor allowed anyone to do alike; and thus, the social responsive conduct was amicably imbibed in the subjects. With the growth of larger kingdoms stringent laws came to be framed for the detection, and punishment of the criminals, and that led to the expansion of the police department in the various periods of history. Succinctly, they are mentioned below.

2. Period of 320-548 A.D.

The highly centralised nature of the polity of Mauryan period had given way to a fairly decentralised administrative structure during the Gupta period (320-540 A.D.). The king, helped by the crown prince, continued to be at the apex of the administration. The other princes were appointed as viceroys of the province, *(Desha* or *Bhukti)* into which the kingdom was divided. The province in turn was sub-divided into a number of districts *(Pradesha* or *Vishaya),* each district having its own administrative officers. The officer-in-charge of province *(Kumarmatya)* or of a district *(Ayukta)* wielded the real powers at the local level. Barring this insignificant difference between the Mauryan administration and that of the Guptas, there is no indication of a major change in the Police System, both in the urban or in rural areas. This system of criminal police administration continued for the next three centuries.

3. Period of 700-1200 A.D.

Starting from the '*Arthasastra to Sukra Niti*' written towards the end of the medieval period, and covering a span of nearly 1500 years, the following basic principles of criminal jurisprudence, then followed, can be briefly identified. Firstly, the fountain head of the justice was the king or the ruler who, in turn, was to be guided by the rules of justice as laid down by the '*Dharmasastras*'. The interpretation of such rules or edicts were to be guided by customs, traditions, usages and conventions of those times. Secondly, the trying authority was to be assisted either by jurors or by a council. In the third place, offences were defined in fairly clear terms and so were their respective and impending punishments. Fourthly, rules of procedures for conducting the trial were also laid down in meticulous details. It was imperative that cases were to be tried as soon as possible, and without least delay, evidence was to be recorded in presence of both the parties, cases were not to be finalised on the basis of only one type of evidence — oral or documentary or circumstantial but needed adequate corroborative proof. Cases were to be taken up for trial in order of priority in point of time, and also depending on the gravity or seriousness of the offence committed and finally, the judges were completely prohibited from having any private communication whatsoever with either party during the pendency of the trial. This was the general pattern of policing throughout India having several hundred principalities or rulers before the Muslims established their imperial authority in this country.

4. Period of 1200-1757 A.D.

During the Muslim invasions of the country and their consequential regimes in several parts of India, people suffered heavy losses, both of persons and property on account of the depravities committed by the rulers, whose rule was characterised by continuous bloodshed, intrigues and internal disorders, and total disregard to the dispensation of justice mainly to the Hindu population. Moreover, the "Muslim laws" coupled with the capricious orders of the religious heads (*Kazis*) were the prime factors which controlled the policing, and judicial factors; and judicial system in the states under their subjugation or occupation. During this period the entire country had come under the domination of Islamic rule. It is not difficult to imagine that the entire fabric of civil administration was torn as under and whole country was plunged in an era of constant turmoil, whatever distinction there was during the earlier era between the civilian and military functionaries got totally blurred and distorted. During the period of wars, conquests, mass coercive religious conversion, and rebellions were mostly practiced.

5. '*Thana*' '*Thanedar*', '*Foujdar*' and '*Kotwal*'

It was the usual practice of these rulers to establish houses or *chowkies* in different strategic areas for the maintenance of internal order in the conquered territory. The '*Thanedars*' had under them garrison of troops and they were more in the nature of military command post of martial law administrators than a civil post to look after the safety, security and well-being of the habitants. Moreover, such centres of powers, having been manned by aliens, could never be expected to have rapport with the rural population. Throughout this period, and at least till about the 18th century, Muslim rule preserved its character of foreign conquest in the whole of India. The Viceroys and other principal officers came and went without taking any real interest in the life and well-being of the inhabitants of the area under their charge.

Being preoccupied with conquest and collection of revenue, the Mughals were only marginally involved in the detailed administration of the countryside. Outside the urban areas, therefore, the maintenance of law and order, and the administration of justice remained by and large, in the hands of Zamindars, many of whom became '*Foujdars*' of empire. But this change in the office was more formal than real; because they functioned as "Contractors" of general administration.

Village level administration of criminal justice, though badly shaken and mauled during this period, maintained its, basic character as a preserver and sustainer of peace in a limited sense; and its ancient pattern could not be entirely uprooted. There was a council of village elders (Panchayat) presided over by the village headman which was the practice prevalent during the Mauryan era. The Panchayat managed the affairs of the village, including settlement of disputes, arrangements for watch and ward *etc.*

After the disintegration of the Turks-Afghan rule, the Afghan ruler Sher Shah Suri (1530-1560) effectively organised different branches of administrative system including the police. He continued the traditional principle of local responsibility, and held the village headman responsible for the safety of the area within their villages. An official organisation of police was also created, under a '*Foujdar*', who was the principal police officer and also the commandant of the local army; and '*Kotwal*' was the head of the city police in urban areas. They together enforced public morals and the former was the head of the criminal court of the province. The police organisation of the Mughals had shaped out of the vestiges of the police system of Sher Shah Suri. In the rural areas, the village watchmen continued to be responsible for police duties, but they were brought under the control of Zamindars, who were required to maintain their own police establishments. The hierarchical structure of the criminal justice administration during the Mughal rule in India was of the '*Foujdar*' and the '*Kotwal*'. The '*Foujdar*' was the Chief Executive for ensuring peace and security in the province of his charge with the help of a contingent of military troops through which, if necessary, he could enforce the will of the Emperor or his *Subedar*. The province was sub-divided into suitable districts for which he could set up '*Thanas*' (Police Stations) covering a group of villages, each such '*thana*' was placed under a '*Thanedar*' for proper policing of the rural areas. In the cities '*Kotwal*' was put in-charge of police functions. It was during the time of Akbar that the city administration was streamlined and all important cities and towns were placed under the direct charge of the '*Kotwal*'. The Maratha and Rajput rulers also followed this system. The provincial *Kotwal* was the in-charge of the capital city of the province. Besides his duty as the chief of the city police, the '*Kotwal*' was required to perform a host of duties for the municipal administration in the city and also as a censor of morals of its *habitats*. The administration of the district headquarters' town was also in the hands of an officer having the same designation of '*Kotwal*'. '*Kotwal*' enjoyed the position of a Magistrate for criminal cases. The '*Kotwal*' was expected to engage the citizens in a pledge of reciprocal assistance and to bind them to a common participation of weal and woe and to know each and every incident involving or suspecting to have involved criminal acts, or even behaviour against person, property and the State. Thus '*Kotwal*' was the ubiquitous and most trustworthy and efficient officer of the Emperor. They were Muslim by religion. It is interesting to note that even today the designations of '*Foujdar*', '*Kotwal*' and '*Thanedar*' are in vogue for the purposes of police functions.

During the Muslim rule, the Zamindars were made bereft of their power and authority to administer justice as a consequence of the assumption of authority by the Muslim *Foujdars* appointed by the royal court, but the fact remains that the Zamindars as a clan, barring a few exceptions, did not prove their mettle in curbing crime or lawlessness. Each such species was busy feeding himself, and whatever strength a Zamindar could acquire by maintaining his muscle men, was used more for ensuring collection of his revenue and oppressing the *ryots*. Seldom, if ever, was such right used for the safety and security of the common man.

With the disintegration of the imperial authority of the Mughals, there was a complete breakdown of the police system and it was to this legacy that the East India Company succeeded as "*Diwans*" in Bengal in 1765. By this time, the East India Company had also strengthened its political power and stability in the country in the provinces of Madras and Bombay, and it took upon it to bring about improvement in the policing system of the provinces under their domain as they reasonably anticipated and creditably achieved the British conquest of the entire India in the century to follow. The East India Company endeavoured to repair the centuries old Kautilya's policing system, and the administration of justice which were disarrayed or left in a dilapidated condition during the Muslim regime of India from about 712 A.D. to 1757 A.D.

7

Development of Police under East India Company (1757—1857)

1. Control of India

Starting from their trading settlements in Bombay, Calcutta and Madras, the British gradually, but finally assumed control over the country, and succeeded in establishing their domain. After the battle of Plassey (1757) and Buxar (1764), it became evident that the British Rule in India was lasting for centuries to come. The East India Company started with a initial advantage as they had favourably acquired the levers of power about a century before when the English merchants had started their apprenticeship in criminal justice administration in the territories of their occupation. In 1765, on the acquisition of the *Diwani* in Bengal, the British found that it was necessary to take certain minimum measures for the safety and welfare of the people, who had by then come under their control. Extortion and oppression existed unchecked throughout all grades of officials responsible for maintenance of law and order. Village headmen and Zamindars harboured offenders in return for a share of the booty. As a result, there was a very large increase in the number of *dacoities*, robberies and other organised crimes. By 1761, the East India Company placed itself firmly in Bengal, but prudence dictated the minimum necessary interference with the existing machinery of administration of the *Nawabs* of Bengal. Crime and violation of public order had assumed a critical proportion necessitating urgent remedial measures and action. Therefore, by a Regulation of 1772, criminal courts were established for each district of Bengal at his instance. In 1774, Warren Hastings observed that the founding of these courts was giving encouragement to criminals, since the standard of evidence demanded, made punishment difficult. Numerous gangs of *dacoits* were infesting the provinces, and he found that they had the protection of the Zamindars and other Local Officials. He proposed, therefore, to restore the posts of *Foujdars* (since abolished in the past regime) for controlling crime. Zamindars were required to assist the *Foujdars*, the ancient system of village Police responsible to the Zamindars was pressed into operation. These arrangements were not found satisfactory and in 1781, all the *Foujdars* were withdrawn. Violent crime and *dacoities* continued to thrive and Cornwallis, the then Governor General of Bengal, took the administration of Criminal Justice out of the hands of Deputy Governor, who was a native Zamindar, and established four councils of Circuit. A statutory measure was to remove the control of the Police from the Zamindars and create posts of Magistrates of districts. Each district was divided into police jurisdiction under the charge of supervising officer called *Darogah*. The charge of a *Darogah* was about 20 to 30 square miles — He had under him 20 to 30 armed *Burkundales* and all the village watchmen were also under his control. In cities or towns the office of *Kotwal* was continued and each ward was placed in charge of a *Darogah*. These reforms did not lead to any appreciable improvement in the situation. *Dacoities* and robberies were very frequent, and there was no check on the oppression of the people by subordinate officials low or high.

2. Regulations for the Police of the Collectorships of Bengal, Bihar and Orissa

It should be remembered that the British commenced their administration in the country previously from Bengal. Calcutta being their Capital and, therefore, all measures taken had emanated from Bengal and subsequently applied and implemented elsewhere in the Provinces of Bombay and Madras and their occupied territories. Cornwallis stands out in many respects as the innovator of our organised police administration. The principle measures introduced by him in this respect should, therefore, merit more than a passing reference. These were through his Regulation No. XXII of 1793 entitled, "Regulations for the Police of Collectorships of Bengal, Bihar and Orissa". The following were the important provisions:

(i) The Police in the country should be considered under the exclusive charge of the Government and who may be specially appointed to that trust. No Zamindar or landholder should maintain any police force or alike establishment.

(ii) If the complicity of Zamindars or landholders in committing crimes, or conniving them is proved, they should be compelled to make good the value of the property stolen or plundered.

(iii) Centrally situated police posts under the charge of *Darogah* or Superintendent with necessary officers under him to assist should be created in every district, and the area of operation should not exceed 10 square *cose* (About 30 square miles). The police posts and district should be numbered and named after the central place and these should not be changed without the sanction of the Governor General in Council.

(iv) *Darogahs* should be nominated by Magistrates, who were held responsible for selecting persons duly qualified for the trust. *Darogahs* were required to give personal security deposit of Rs. 1,000/- and surety bond by two creditable persons in Rs. 250/- each for his good conduct.

(v) Any complaint of murder, robbery, house-breaking, theft or other crime or offence, cognizable by the criminal courts, were required to be made to the *Darogah* at the jurisdictional police post. The *Darogah* was responsible to apprehend the offender, release him on bail with adequate and solvent surety and forward him to the Magistrate having jurisdiction within 24 hours.

(vi) The *Darogah* was empowered to arrest any person found in the act of committing a breach of peace, a notorious offender proving hazard in the commission of offences specified in the 9th Article of the said Regulation, such as a thief, robber, *dacoit*, murderer, all vagabond or suspected persons, who might be loitering about his jurisdiction without any ostensible means of subsistence or who could not give a satisfactory account of themselves or the alike. There were various other powers given to the *Darogah*, and they were on the same lines of a sub-inspector of police of today. Actually, Cornwallis had made the *Darogah* a very powerful instrument of administration for the East India Company, and through him law and order was maintained and peace and tranquillity secured. But at the same time, Cornwallis did not fail to include penal provision against a *Darogah* found guilty of corruption, extortion or oppression; and he ensured that the right type of person was invested with such wide powers by giving him a '*Sannad*' of office by the Magistrate under his signature and official seal and thereby prevent likely impersonation. This is like the identity card issued by the modern Government.

Regulation XXII of 1793 was slightly modified on 1st May 1793. It divided city areas into wards. All such *Darogahs* being under the City-*Kotwal*, were required to furnish a security of Rs. 5,000. The *Kotwals* and the *Darogahs* could not be removed without the sanction of the Government. The *Kotwal* was given the same powers as that of *Darogah*, enumerated above, and in addition, he was empowered to hold inquests in case of murder or unnatural death and record confessions of persons apprehended.

Cornwallis was, neither the first nor the last British Ruler in India, to display total lack of faith in the natives of the land and their institutions, especially in the area of criminal administration. In developing this attitude he was undoubtedly guided and influenced by the tenor or official minutes and proceedings. On top of these, the Collectors and the Magistrates continued their tirade against Zamindars, and other native institutions for their failure to curb crime and lawlessness. Cornwallis reacted by cutting off these native agencies altogether and by propping up the Company's European officers with enhanced powers and pay backed by a stipendiary necessary band of Bengalis and their minions. This predictably aroused an attitude of non-co-operation, if not open hostility, in the well-entrenched landed gentry. On the top of this, a sizeable number of Zamindari police and low-level policemen were discharged from service resulting in swelling the ranks of criminals. There was, therefore, a marked deterioration in the crime and public order situation in all the areas under British occupation. In order to stem the tide, the company had to protect its pride and once again invest many of the Zamindars with police powers in 1807.

In spite of the admitted failure of the measures introduced by Cornwallis, many of which had to be revoked or drastically modified during the next 20 years, the substance of his basic reforms surfaced once again after a lapse of about 60 years of experimentation in the British occupied India. Then in the wake of Police Commission of 1860, the Zamindars were finally divested of all their police powers, the *Thanedari* system was revived with stipendiary police officers vested with full responsibility of crime control and prevention. Control and superintendence over the police were strengthened and landlords lost control over village watchmen. In 1808, under Regulation X the post of Superintendent of Police, analogous to the later Inspector General of Police, was created. The object was to have an officer at the capital of the province who could co-ordinate the activities of district police authorities for the purpose of crime control and prevention of public disorder. This officer was accordingly made a justice of peace having concurrent, and, if necessary, overriding jurisdiction over magistrates. By the Police Act of 1861 (Act V of 1861) his nomenclature changed to that of Inspector General of Police, and he was entirely responsible for policing the whole province for which he was so appointed.

3. Bird Committee on Police

In 1808, House of Commons appointed Select Committee to enquire into the affairs of the East India Company. The report issued in 1812, extensively dwelt upon the state of crime and police particularly in Bengal. The general conditions throughout British India were not very much different. It admitted at the very outset that the establishment of efficient police was the object of the first importance. This was 'Bird Committee' which submitted its report in 1813. In substance it contained:

(i) Magisterial neglect at their police duties in favour of their revenue duties arising out of the union of the officers of Collector and Magistrate.

(ii) Want of intercourse between European and Indian Committees.

(iii) Jurisdiction and frequent transfer of district officers.

(iv) Sense of insecurity among *Darogahs* due to frequent dismissals and hence their tendency to acquire maximum spoils from their uncertain tenure.

(v) Criminal propensities of *chaukidars* or village watchmen.

(vi) The total wants of co-operation on the part of the people which acted as the greatest impediments to the success of the police operation.

(vii) Poor emoluments compelling the incumbents to compensate by other means of income.

The following remedial measures were suggested.

(i) Collector should cease to exercise magisterial function of control over the police and it should devolve on a separate officer to be called the joint magistrate.

(ii) Districts should be sub-divided into sub-divisions, in each of which a deputy magistrate should be posted with authority over the police.

(iii) Pay structure should be improved.

(iv) Village *chaukidari* system should be reorganised, the *chaukidars* should be better paid and the responsibility of village officers should be clearly defined and enforced.

Some of the recommendations of the Bird Committee were accepted and acted upon. The separation of police functions from revenue and judicial area was implemented and a District Superintendent of Police was provided for each district solely for supervision over the police. The organisational restructuring of the police and better salary conditions had to be languished for another 20 years and the regular police force was continued to be small and ineffective.

In 1844, there was a marked increase in the incidence of property offences with violence and once again it was advocated to unify the functions of the Collector, the Magistrate and police in the same functionary, *i.e.*, the District Magistrate (Fredeick Halliday) whereas Grant was strongly opposed to any such combination of powers in a single individual as repugnant to the principle of good administration. However, it was concluded that the Government had failed to provide a satisfactory system of policing with adequately paid force and it was a standing reproach of administration in British India. Halliday and Grant were the members of the Bird Committee. In the provinces of Bengal, Madras, Sind, Punjab and Bombay criminal administration were being hotly debated through the powerful minutes of Halliday and Grant between 1854 and 1857 on the lines mentioned above.

However, it was unanimously agreed that to render the police efficient, it must not be placed under independent authority. Although, the Collector should remain the political head and retain all powers and authority as Justice of the Peace and Magistrate, it was probably thought that the police cannot be organised, brought up to or kept in the requisite state of discipline unless it is commanded by the officer, who should give his whole individual time and energy exclusively to that object.

There was a growing demand that for securing efficiency, the police force should be placed under one command and unless there is uniformity of method of recruitment, training and discipline throughout the whole body, there would be no improvement in curbing crime and maintaining law and order. Those were the days when the police was entirely confined to each district under the Collector, and there was no general supervision whatsoever, there existed no regular communication from one district to another or to any central office on the several points of police business which so imperatively required co-ordination of thought and action. The then prevailing confusion was worst confounded, sign of growing discontent and unrest with consequential contempt, and hatred for British regime were surfacing, the law and order machinery had completely broken down or paralysed and crimes against property continued to be committed unabated. On the top of all these, the *Pendhari* and *Thagi* menace horrified the citizens, who were left without protection. All these factors cumulatively eventuated the War of Independence in 1857.

8

Police Developments during 1858 to 1900 Period

1. Effects of the War of Independence

The "War of Independence" of 1857 was won by the British. During the year 1857, there was lot of agitation in England against the continuation of the rule of the East India Company, whose main objective was profit and as such, it was pointed out that it could not be entrusted with the work of administration of the sub-continent like India. The British Government was equally blamed for having failed to discharge its obligations as it had the deciding voice in the affairs of the Company. Consequently, Government of India Act was passed in 1858, which declared that the Government of India was to be taken over by the Crown and the English East India Company was to be ended. The post of the Governor General was to be integrated in the post of the Viceroy, who was vested with all the powers of governance and administration. It forbade the employment of Indian revenues for military operations outside India without the consent of the Parliament, thereby consolidating the use of Indian revenue for the benefit of the citizens. A Darbar was held at Allahabad on 1st November 1858, and the 'Queen's Proclamation' for the assumption of the Government of India by the Crown was read. By virtue of this declaration the Crown was bound by the same obligation of duty which it owed to the British and the colonial people. By this declaration the Crown had undertaken to ensure that there was no discrimination in the matter of employment, administration and justice on the basis of caste or creed. The other declarations were irrelevant to the subject of police. Canning was the first Viceroy (1856-1862) of India. He had to face the problem of finance caused by a deficit of 36 million sterlings, and the War of Independence of 1857. It was expected of him by the British Government to put down the revolt by all sorts of repressive and reprehensible measures; but he continued the policy of pacification even at the risk of personal unpopularity. In his own words: "As long as I have my breath in my body, I will pursue no other policy than that which I have been following, not only for the reason of expediency and policy above stated but because it is just. I will not govern in anger. Justice and that as stern and inflexible as law and might can make it, I will deal out. But I will never allow an angry or indiscriminate act or word to proceed from the Government of India as long as I am responsible for it."

In 1861, the famous Indian Council Act was passed. This Act provided for the setting of legislation in the presidencies of Bombay, Madras and Calcutta and an extension of Viceroy's Executive Council by additional members for legislative purposes. By the law of 1861, Chartered High Councils were set up in place of Supreme Courts and *Adalats* for the East India Company. The Indian Penal Code, which was drafted by Macaulay in 1858, became the law after the necessary changes in it. It was followed by the Code of Criminal next year.

The severe famine of 1861 throughout North India ended with a mortality of 10 per cent of the population. In 1859 and 1860 large-scale disturbances were committed by armed bands of Indian *Santhals* in Bengal over a dispute between the European Indigo planters and the Bengal peasantry. The needed money for reform in the Police and Criminal Administration could not be earmarked in spite of imposition of new taxes on the people. When Canning was recalled in 1862, he handed over no debt, but credit in all the spheres of administration, and social as well as governmental obligation towards the Indian population, and he had done it without compunction, but in consonance with his aims and objectives he had consciously set for himself while taking over the post at the most vulnerable and critical juncture in the entire history of the British India. Even then in 1862, he was recalled and impeached by the Parliament, as obviously he failed to adopt oppressive measures against the Indian population according to the expectations of the British Government in order to avenge the "Mutiny" by Indian patriots.

2. Police Commission of 1860

In September 1859, Act XXIV of 1859 (The Madras Police Act) was passed by the Government of India and the broad principles enunciated in it were accepted for almost universal application throughout the country. The far-reaching developments in criminal administration had taken place in Sind after its conquest in 1843, and in Punjab after its annexation in 1849. In 1848, Governor of Bombay (Clerk) also took steps to tone up the policing of the province. The leading features of all these ameliorative measures were:

1. Police became a distinct department under the direct supervision of the Government, its members of all grades were divested of judicial functions and were under the exclusive control and management of their own officers.
2. The District Magistrate was to be kept fully and intimately informed and acquainted with the distributions and administration of the police. The police should execute all his lawful commands. But he will not interfere with the internal economy, and arrangements of the district corps for which its own officers were to be responsible.
3. The revival of the village police was also envisaged under the direct supervision of the district police, and disbandment or reduction of para-military police.

After the usual period of bureaucratic procrastination these changes were introduced between 1852 and 1855 in the teeth of opposition of District Magistrates. The superintendence of the police was vested with the District Superintendent of Police for his district, and the Inspector General of Police for the entire province to which he was, so appointed.

It was against these backdrops and the large-scale and *ad hoc* police proliferation of armed police units with mounting financial burdens, that the British Government made a distinct change in its perception of a really reformed police with a view to increase its efficiency in the era of prevention and detection of crime and their acceptability to the people in general and nearer to the base of the British Police. Therefore, the following three terms of references for the Police Commission, appointed on 17th August 1960, were made by the Government of India:

(a) To propose a new system of police applicable to India generally, whereby economy, and efficiency might be secured.

(b) To propose for publication of all available information regarding the best system of police administration.

(c) To collect the most complete, and comprehensive statistics obtainable, regarding the cost and establishment of the police of all kinds throughout India.

The Police Commission was tacitly instructed to adopt, as far as possible, and without detriment to the interest of the Government of British India, a unified system of police in the country and eventually. The Police Commission, *inter alia*, recommended that:

1. The police under each local government or administration should constitute one force and be under the officer to be styled Inspector General of Police in whom should be vested the control over the organisation, the responsibility of maintaining it in a state of efficiency by proper attention to its training, and discipline, internal economy and its general rearrangement through its own officers.
2. In the large districts there should also be a European Officer to assist the District Superintendent of Police.
3. The subordinate police force should be comprised of (a) Inspector of Police (European/Eurasian or native), (b) Head Constables, (c) Sergeants who would be subordinate to the Head Constables, and (d) Constables who should be divided into three grades of pay.
4. The force in each district should be divided into appropriate police sub-divisions.
5. The Head Constable was to be in-charge of police parties located at Station Houses.
6. Wherever practicable men of the police force should be enrolled from the province in which they serve.
7. Residential quarters should be provided at the cost of the State, and that accommodation of the families of the police should be discretional with the local government.

8. Suitable but inexpensive, uniforms should be provided for all grades of the police under each local Government and the uniforms should be furnished to all officers of police below the rank of Inspectors at the cost of the State.
9. Village watchman, being an ancient institution of India, it may not be desirable to dispense with it, though many of them may not be of the desirable category. In the existing conditions of the interior of the country, the organised police cannot be informed of all that occurs of public consequences, unless they have some tolerably reliable agency in the villages. The village watchman was just such a person: he was a man of the village but not enough an official to be alien or obnoxious to the villagers but only an official to be amenable to systems and reliable for duty on behalf of the police. Their remuneration was to be fixed by the District Officer, and they were to be under the orders of the organised police.

3. Police Act of 1861

A Bill was presented to the Legislative Council embodying more or less all the recommendations of the Commission and was enacted as Indian Police Act of 1861 (Act V of 1861). However, the Act did not come into force automatically in all the provinces since there was a provision in it, which stipulated that it would apply in any province only when so notified by the Governor General in Council. The Police Act was then introduced in Bengal — 1862, 1863, 1864 by stages in various districts (the province of Bengal comprised of present Bengal, Bihar, Orissa and Assam). The Act was gradually applied to other provinces except in the Presidency of Madras and Bombay and the Presidency Towns of Calcutta, Madras and Bombay. Madras Presidency continued with its Police Act of 1859; and devised an elaborate command structure on the lines suggested by the Police Act of 1861. The Bombay District Police Act VII of 1867 was promulgated with similar provisions. The District Officers were equated with District Magistrates for the overall supervision of the District Police Administration.

The tardy process of the implementation of the Indian Police Act of 1861, was largely due to the continued resistance from the ranks of the Civil Servants (District Magistrates). In fact, the Act was never extended to Bombay or to Sind. In Bombay Presidency no Inspector General was appointed till 1885. In spite of various impediments, both financial and administrative, the system of police organisation as envisaged in the Indian Police Act of 1861, began taking roots with a large measure of uniformity all over the country. The reorganisation introduced in 1861, was intended mainly to secure unity of action and identity system. But majority of the posts in the new scheme, including all highest officers, were given to the European officers of the Indian Army, and they continued to be filled from this source for some years. The supply of European officers from the Army for the police gradually dwindled and ultimately dried up almost completely. Then a system of filling all superior appointments by 'nomination' was introduced. But the better European youths preferred the Indian Civil Service for the post of District Magistrate. Quite naturally, being under officers of inferior calibre, the reputation and efficiency of the police did not improve, and an immediate remedy became essential.

4. Other Measures

In 1866, the Calcutta Police Act was enacted. By it, the administration of Police was entrusted to the Commissioner of Police, Calcutta. In Bombay, the office of the Police Commissioner had been abolished in 1860 on the ground that its existence "had produced friction in the administration" and the duties of the post were transferred to the Revenue Commissioner. This arrangement continued till 1881; and in 1885 an Inspector General of Police (Police Commissioner) was appointed as police administrator had become lax. The immediate administration of the Madras City Police was, subject to the authority of Inspector General of Police, vested in the Commissioner of Police and provisions of Act XXIV of 1869 were made applicable to him also.

Wherever there were civil disturbances, special Acts were passed. Such as the Bengal Military Police Act of 1892, and various alike provincial Acts for creating an organisation of para-military force for effective suppression of civil disturbances.

For similar reasons a separate detective department was formed to control the *Thagi* menace. In 1866, the first Railway Police was constituted and on the recommendations of the Railway Committee of 1882, the responsibility for the prevention, detection and prosecution of cases and maintenance of order on the railway platforms was entrusted to the Railway Police. The duty of watch and ward devolved on the railway administration.

In 1887, a system of competitive examination for higher appointments in the police was introduced mostly for Europeans, although it was felt at the same time to take in some Indians in the Superior Police Service. A few appointments in the rank of the Assistant Superintendent of Police were, therefore, thrown open to selected Inspectors, but it was rarely given effect to. For the reorganisation of village police, necessary steps were taken through suitable legislations between 1870 and 1883 in the various provinces of the country.

5. Major and Minor Acts

All the efforts of the British Government in India were specifically made to stabilise and consolidate their rule in the country after the Mutiny of 1857, and in a bid to do so the Government tried to introduce suitable measures for the improvement of the police force. It fully realised that an efficient police force was absolutely necessary to collect political, civil, military, and criminal intelligence, and that speedy and proper actions were taken to prevent and detect crime and prosecute the perpetrators and award them the suitable punishment. In order to streamline the administration of criminal justice, and present to the citizens of India a picture of benign and benevolent British Government through the medium of the 'Rule of Law', several laws were enacted covering all the aspects of human life from conception to cremation, and of the safety and security of the British Rule of India. The latter was the main concept of these ameliorative measures. The most important among these Acts are:

1. The Indian Penal Code, 1860 comprising 511 Sections dealing with all types of offences against State, all Armed Forces, the public tranquillity, the public servants, the election, contempt of lawful authority of public servants, for the evidences and public justice, coin and

Government stamps, weights and measures, public health, safety, convenience, decency and morals, religion, human body (from simple hurt to murder), wrongful restraint and confinement, criminal force and assault, sex, property including theft, extortion, robbery, dacoity *etc.*, misappropriation, cheating and breach of trust, fraudulent deeds and dispositions of property, mischief, trespass, documents and property frauds (forgery *etc.*), currency notes and bank notes, contract of service, marriage including adultery, defamation, intimidation, insult and annoyance, and finally attempt to commit any offence involving imprisonment. The precise definition of acts and omissions constituting an offence with the nature and quantum of the punishment to be awarded was elaborately indicated. While structuring the import of this Act, the religious sentiments of all citizens were taken into consideration. In a way this Act was the product of the *Arthasastra* of Kautilya, and suitably modified to the then prevailing circumstances—religious, social, political and administrative.

2. The Code of Criminal Procedure was enacted in 1898. In this Act the procedure to be adopted by trial courts for dispensation of justice (both civil and criminal) was minutely codified.
3. The Indian Evidence Act was passed in 1872. It depicted the quality and quantum of the evidence required to prove or disprove facts comprising the ingredients of the offences. Both the criminal, and civil proceedings were brought in its ambit.

In addition, 'Police Regulations' were framed in each Province throughout the country governing the conduct, training, discipline, dereliction of duty, and the resultant punishment to be meted out to the delinquent. By the implementation of these regulations, a reasonably trained, disciplined and responsible body of police officers and men was provided to each province.

6. Effect of Remedial Measures

These remarkable measures in criminal justice administration resulted in the people's growing awareness about the menace of organised criminal gangs (mainly dacoits). This menace was also recognised by the 'Rulers', as a major factor eroding the confidence of the community in the efficiency of the administration as a whole. Hence, countering this threat became a part of the state policy, and as such continued to receive concentrated attention. This was evident for the first time during the rule of Warren Hastings, followed by Cornwallis, Canning and others. The interest taken by Bentick and the commendable efforts of the sagacious and tenacious Colonel Sleeman led to the virtual extinction of the centuries old scourge of the *Thags* by about 1860.

In 1887, due to financial stringency, a substantial reduction was made in the police force resulting in increase in crime and general inefficiency. By 1900, it was manifest that the system introduced in 1860, had failed to remain efficient. The findings of the Committee appointed to fathom out the causes were:

"The extent to which the village police must co-operate with the regular police has been lost sight of, an attempt has almost everywhere been made to do all the police work through the officers of the department, that importance of the police work has been underestimated and responsible duties have ordinarily been entrusted to untrained, and uneducated officers recruited in the lowest ranks from the lower strata of the society. The supervision has been defective owing to the failure to appoint the staff contemplated by law, and to increase that staff with the growing necessity of administration, that the superior officers of the department have been insufficiently trained and have been allowed from various causes to get out of acquaintance and sympathy with the people and out of touch even with their subordinates, and that their sense of responsibility has been weakened by a degree of indifference never contemplated by the authors of 1860 system."

Therefore, in 1902, Viceroy Curzon ordered the formation of Indian Police Commission for the whole of India to make careful enquiries into the maladies of the Policing System of India, and suggest suitable measures for their overall improvement.

9

Police Commission of 1902, and Development of Police Force up to 1947

1. Necessity for Police Commission

In 1902, Curzon was the Viceroy of India. The reputation of the Police working noticed by him was:

"The police force is far from satisfactory, it is defective in training and organisation, it is inadequately staffed, it is generally regarded inefficient, corrupt and oppressive and finally it has utterly failed to secure the confidence and cordial co-operation of the people, for whom it seldom works with honesty and sincerity of purpose."

About crime in India, Prof H. Bailey made the following observations:

> "Crime in India is bewildering in its variety. The police must cope with a range of crime as diverse as any in the world. While people are vicious to one another in India in much the same ways that they are in the West, what distinguishes the Indian scene is the enormous variety of circumstances, within which crime becomes manifest. It is the richness of the soil, and geographical conditions that give to the Indian crime its incredible and fascinating heterogeneity. Only in a country which, is advancing in uneven stages, such crimes as cattle thievery, murder for witchcraft, *dacoity*, *etc.*, should continue to be committed."

How far was the police in India capable, and adequate to meet such a stupendous challenge and what were the various obstacles which the police faced while discharging its functions were the most important factors which the Police Commission of 1902, headed by A.H.L Fraser, Chief Commissioner of the Central Provinces, addressed to itself. The Commission made a comprehensive enquiry in the working of the police, recruitment and training, strengths, pay efficiency etc. It made several recommendations which were implemented in the different provinces and phases through a number of enactments, rules and regulations for the improvement of procedures in many matters.

2. Recommendations of the Commission

The Commission accepted the organisational set-up prescribed by the 1860 Police Commission and recommended that the post of Inspector General of Police should be filled by a selected District Magistrate, and the province should be divided into ranges, each range under a Deputy Inspector General of Police. In the district, in addition to the District Superintendent and Assistant Superintendent, a new rank of Deputy Superintendent of Police for Indians in the Provincial Police Service should be created whose status should be identical with that of Assistant Superintendent of Police. The jurisdiction of a Police Station should not exceed 150 square miles, and the officer-in-charge should be of the rank of a Sub-inspector. The Head Constable should function as a station writer, and not as an investigating officer. For dealing with tumult and local disturbances there should be armed Reserve Police in every district. For Bengal and Assam River police should be constituted under a separate superintendent, if necessary. There should be a Criminal Investigation Department in each province under a separate Deputy Inspector General for collecting and distributing information regarding criminals and organised crimes and for assisting in the investigation of complicated cases. The Deputy Inspector General should also hold the administrative charge of the Railway Police. A similar organisation under an experienced Inspector General of Police should be established for the whole of India.

Other recommendations related to Presidency police, village police, training, institutions, method of recruitment, syllabus for training, discipline, pay, emoluments and pension, conditions of service, prevention and investigation of crime, prosecution of cases, and supervision and relation between the magistracy and the police.

The Commission also postulated:

(i) That the police force should consist of (a) an European service to be recruited entirely in England (b) a provincial service to be recruited entirely in India. There should be an upper subordinate service consisting of Inspectors and Sub-inspectors, and lower subordinate service consisting of Head Constables and Constables.

(ii) That there should be a single Police Act for the whole of India.

(iii) That each district should be divided into circles consisting of 5 to 8 police stations, except in case of large towns, the area which should form a circle, and that an Inspector should be put in-charge of each circle to supervise the police work.

(iv) The strength of the police force was to be increased according to the yardstick fixed for that purpose.

(v) In the presidency towns there should be Commissioner of Police (under the Inspector General of Police or independently under the government), and he should retain much wider powers than were accorded to the District Superintendent of Police.

(vi) That the Provincial Training School should be established in every large province.

(vii) That the responsibility of the District Magistrate for the criminal administration of the district must be preserved, and that he should have authority over the police, but this authority should be of the nature of general control and direction and not detailed intervention.

(viii) That it was of paramount importance to develop and foster the existing village agency for police work.

The Commission observed that when the police organisation becomes perfect, and the force becomes effective for the performance of its detective duties, any necessity for the District Magistrate (generally called Collector) to take personal action in any case judicially brought before him ought to cease. In other words, a gradually decreasing role for the District Magistrate regarding Police administration was visualised.

The Commission also projected the principle that residential quarters should be provided for the police at the cost of the State. Another interesting observation of the Commission was that "no separate class of clerks, writers or ministerial officials shall be allowed in the police and that all duties connected with writing and accounts be performed by the enrolled men of the forces."

3. Police Record of Evidence

The recommendations of the 1860 Police Commission about the Station General Diary were maintained by this Commission also. The genesis of this diary may be seen:

> "The police should not be used as an agency for the record of any evidence, confession, inquest or the like, but a system of keeping faithful, accurate and minute diaries should be maintained. The diaries should specify, concisely but in detail, all duties in which any Police Officer may have been engaged, and every occurrence or information that may have required the attention of the Police within their respective ranges. All police officers engaged in any specific police duties, or detective duties should keep an accurate and minute diary of every step taken, and every information obtained in following the clue of evidence, such diaries should be police documents only, and be sent to the District Superintendent, but should be open to the inspection of District Magistrate."

It is unfortunate that the Commission did not recognise any meaningful and responsible role for the police for recording evidence of any kind. The denial of this role for the police in the documentation of evidence has had long range repercussion on the entire "Police Psyche" in the long years that followed. Provisions of the Criminal Procedure Code and Indian Evidence Act reflected the same attitude towards the police regarding documentation of evidence. Consequently, it turned out in practice that the police record of investigation, if at all used in courts, would not be in aid of the prosecution, but could be used by the defence counsel to point out inconsistencies between the police record, and the evidence recorded in the court. The mere existence of such contradictions is cited to demolish the prosecution case, without anyone bothering to examine how the contradictions came about and whether the police record is to be rejected totally as untruthful. (It is only, now that some interest and concern are being shown to look into this deficiency in our Criminal Justice System).

It was not necessary for the police to take cognizance of all offences committed in its jurisdiction. It was strictly forbidden by law to take cognizance of, or interfere with petty offences of any description, or otherwise interfere with the liberties or convenience of the people. Hasty arrests by the police were deprecated by the Commission. Under Section 157(b) of Code of Criminal Procedure, a discretion was given to the officer-in-charge of a police station to desist from taking cognizance of petty offences, this code also provided a schedule of offences, in which the police were required to take cognizance of offences committed in their jurisdiction.

4. Effects of the Commission's Recommendations

On the basis of these recommendations the entire police force of the country was reorganised in all the provinces within five years. The Indianisation of the Superior Police Service had started and the reservation of 50 per cent was maintained. Thirty per cent were to be recruited directly as Deputy Superintendents of Police and 20 per cent by promotion of posts for Indians in the Indian Police Cadre. This brought a perceptible change in the tone of police administration and raised the morale of the force, although the British Government was prone to distrust these Indian officers, who were seldom given independent command of a district. The erstwhile police administration of the '*Darogahs*' was ended and stern measures were taken to give substantial relief to the people from legendary "*Darogahs*" whose atrocious regime could be summarised:

> "They ruled their territory like little kings, their misdeeds were legion and always unpunished for who would have the temerity to report them to the Collector. The '*Darogahs*' Powers of harassment were enormous, they could have a person indicted for harbouring a bad character, or failing to assist an officer in arresting a criminal. Obtaining witness presented no problem to the *Darogah*. They were close to the people and were themselves willy and unscrupulous enough to meet the criminal on his own ground."

However, the positive contributions of the British Administration was to put the system of policing on a professional footing, with largely well-demarcated zones of responsibility — territorial and hierarchical, in bringing about a large measure of uniformity in the system of policing, procedure and practices. Regional variations were not quite marked for a vast and plural society like India.

On the negative side, however, the process of erosion of the community responsibility in policing, had begun during Mughal rule, which was further accentuated from the late 18th century. In a way, the Indian Police Act of 1861 marked the statutory culmination of this trend all over British India. The second negative feature was the delayed introduction of a professional police supervisory level, caused largely due to the persistent apprehension of the civil servants about dilution of their power base. Even introduction of a professional supervisory cadre became unavoidable. The latter's command structure was allowed to be diluted by bringing in a dual control to be exercised by the civilian magistrates. Flowing from this, the third negative aspect of the new system of policing was that the crucial public or community accountability of police was never allowed to take its root in India, and this was a marked departure from the police institution introduced by the Britishers in their own country, although that was the initial intention of the British Government in introducing the police reforms.

5. The Non-cooperation Movement and the Police

Currently with all these ameliorative measures for toning up the Police Administration the attitude of Viceroy Curzon, was to show his firm belief that Indians were lacking in all those qualities which made Englishmen good administrators. His lack of faith in governing through Indian officials or with their aid, his policy of reserving all higher posts for Englishmen by every possible means in his power and finally the partition of Bengal in 1905 gave a tremendous impetus and boosted the "Non-cooperation Movement" launched by the Indian National Congress under the stalwart leadership of Lokmanya Tilak, and after his death Mahatma Gandhi.

The period from 1914 to 1946 was a time of great stress and strain for the police department on account of two World Wars of 1914-18 and 1939-46, and the major political movements that took place, in particular the Non-cooperation Movement of 1920 and the Civil Disobedience Movement of 1930-31. The entire edifice of the British Administration was shaken to its foundation by the 'Quit India Movement' of 1942. Some hurried increase in the force was sanctioned to meet the situation. Fractional Indianisation of the superior police service had started, but still over 90 per cent of the officers were not of Indian origin. Frequent communal riots, political unrest culminating in large-scale disturbances and destruction of government property, and the communal carnage of 1946-47 on the eve of partition of the country created the most harassing situation for the police force throughout the country. The police was frequently engaged in quelling disturbances, or in dealing with political upheavals. The task of prevention and detection of crime was left with inefficient and insufficient subordinate police officers. Naturally, the standard of investigation became very low.

All these factors cumulatively kept the police force of the country much away from substantial improvement in policing of their jurisdiction, prevention and detection of crime, and rendering satisfactory criminal justice to the people, for their entire resources and energies were channelised to safeguard the British Imperial interest in India in the last bid to perpetuate their regime. All sorts of atrocities, which the institution of *Darogahs* had committed on the people in the past (described above) were allowed to be committed in innumerable places by the Europeans as well as native police officials in order to suppress the national uprising for freedom of India. In these nefarious acts, the British Government not only incited the police, but also actuated them to behave in this atrocious fashion for ensuring its own safety, stability and consolidation of regime in this sub-continent. All these eventuated in the total loss of goodwill of the people for the police, so much necessarily conducive for their willful co-operation in dealing with crimes and criminals and prevention and detection of offences. People still continue to believe that the police force is of the 'Alien Agency' and exists only for the benefit of the rulers, and as such is antagonistic for their protection and well-being. This appears to be the only reason why people have distanced themselves from the police and anathematised the entire organisation.

6. During Independence

In 1947, India became Independent, but the country itself was partitioned. This partition and subsequent industrialisation, urbanisation and developmental activities multiplied police functions and the resultant problems. After the attainment of Independence, all the European Officers left India. Since they constituted a very large proportion of superior services, there was a wide gap in the rank of these services, which had to be filled in by hurried promotions of subordinate Indian officers. In spite of this and because of the extra work put in by senior Indian officers, and the inherent capacity of the organisation, it was able to bear effectively the strains of the disturbances and succeeded in giving "skeleton" police service to the people.

With the advent of Independence, the Indian psyche underwent a transformation. Sovereignty, power, administrative control and direction were exercised by the people through their representatives belonging to various political parties, the number of which kept on increasing. A growing number of indigenous 'Teddy Boys' appeared, and the problem of 'rowdies' became guardedly acute. Crimes and vice dens kept on mushrooming. Rural areas were rapidly transformed into urban or semi-urban areas due to rapid and ill-planned growth of industries. Population increased rapidly resulting in worsening the problem of unemployment. Students' indiscipline increased. Expansion of industries led to growing unrest. And above all communal amity and harmony was torn asunder and disturbed eventuating in repeated communal disturbances. The use of force, including firing became the landmark of policing.

Such was the texture and complexion of the police that was made available to the people, who, failed to realise their own deteriorated moral values, disorganisation and disintegration of their social fabric and yet they expect the police to deliver the goods righteously to them. To all these maladies corruption was amicably aided both by the police and the people and a stage has now come, when the corruption has become all pervasive and dominant factor in the movement of police machinery for good or bad, lawful or unlawful. To improve the conduct and efficiency of the police is a stupendous and challenging task which the Government, *inter alia*, people will have to tackle so that its benign effect can be felt, and experienced by the public. Can it be done?

7. Reputation of the Present Police Structure and Organisation

Under the Constitution, police is a state subject and only residuary powers have been vested in the Centre. Under the residuary powers, the Centre controls the Central Bureau of Investigations, Intelligence Bureau, Central Reserve Police and various para-military forces recruited by it, and the police forces of the centrally administered territories. The items 'Police' and 'Police Order' are specifically included in the State List. Under Articles 256 and 257, the executive power of the State is subordinate to that of the Union. The Parliament is empowered to transfer any subject from the State List to the Concurrent List in the national interest (Article 353 of the Constitution). The Centre has a duty to protect the states from internal disturbances (Article 355 of the Constitution). There are certain other features of the Constitution which indicate that the Centre, if it desires, can intervene in the law and order problems of the States in certain situations. The only reason for assigning the subject of police to the States and not to the Centre is said to be that in a democratic set up it is considered to be more desirable that the law enforcement bodies should have roots in the localities they operate, because a police force brought out from outside may alienate the local people and it may not be easy for the police to act effectively in such a situation due to its ignorance of prevailing local conditions and intimacy with the public. Although, this is advocated to be the ostensible reason for such a position, the most important reason is that the State wants to have under its entire control the whole of the 'Police Machinery' for enforcing its will. As a corollary, the political party in power will assert to enforce its writ through the medium of the executive machinery of the police, rightly or wrongly. If the State Government, *inter alia,* the Chief Minister, is divested of this power, the government will become politically and potentially weak. When the government is taken over by any other political party, against which action was taken by the previous regime, the police officials taking that action are invariably victimised. The whole career of the police officer is jeopardised for no rhyme or reason. Actually, when such a situation arises, the police officials have no constitutional safeguards. Such a state of affairs, which unfortunately exists, by and large, fits in the description of the term "Police State" where the interests of the ruling party take preference to those of the general public, for whose benefit the Police Force is primarily and essentially created and paid from the taxes paid by the people. For example, British liberty does not depend and never has depended upon any particular form of police organisation. It depends upon the supremacy of the Parliament and on the rule of law. The British Police are national in character, and they are answerable to the law of the land and ultimately to the democratically elected Parliament. There is a growing concern and feeling in the public about the manner in which State Police functions. For instance, the Communist ministry in West Bengal, Coalition ministry in Kerala of Muslim League and Congress and the former Bharatiya Janata Party (BJP) in UP, the Janata Dal ministry of Laloo Prasad Yadav in Bihar, and the Mulayam Singh ministry in UP can be cited as classic examples to elucidate and elaborate this point in order to understand the predicament of the Police Force in coming to a decision of action or inaction. When such a situation is faced by the police the best course, taken by them is laxity in action or total inaction. The demolition of Muslim structure (Babri Mosque) at Ayodhya was the result of this confusion worst confounded and both the Central and the State Governments cannot eschew their responsibility for that malady, as both the governments had acted to draw political mileage by their communal behaviour, and betrayed the Secular Constitution of India. This diarchy is currently being faced by the State of Delhi where there is control of two governments having diametrically opposite political ideologies.

It is not a utopian dream that the Policeman should be the friend of the peace-keeper and the dreaded foe of the peace-breaker. All the advanced countries of the world have derived benefit and benevolence from such a police demeanour, of course, there are some exceptions in order to prove the dictum. In 1947, the country became really independent and democratic for the first time in the entire history, and all the vestiges of autocracy and its tyranny with the help of the police force have to be completely removed. The ideal purpose of police in a community can best be fulfilled and permanently adopted as described in the following words, which spell out the duties of law enforcement officers, as laid down in the International Code of Enforcement Ethics:

> "As a law enforcement officer, my fundamental duty is to serve mankind, to safeguard life and property, to protect the innocent against deception, the weak against oppression or intimidation, and peaceful against violence and disorder, and to respect constitutional rights of all men to liberty, equality and justice."

When and how can this be achieved?

10

General Police Structure and Organisation

1. Earlier Police System

In early times, police functions in India, were based upon the principle of collective responsibility of the population. This system well-suited the simple and agriculturist society of the country at that time. The Hindu kings did not disturb the pattern of collective security, on the other hand, they encouraged the participation of village community in the essential social obligations on their part. Majority problems of crime, law and order at that time were confined primarily to the limits of the village, and then it was possible to solve them, and that too within the community itself on the basis of the prevailing notions of equity and justice, which the people appreciated because of its inexpensiveness and dispatch.

The Muslim rulers, who followed, introduced the element of coercion and compulsion in the system, as they were always under the fear of reprisal at the hands of the vanquished kings, and the lurking suspicion and lack of faith in the loyalty of their subjects. Although, the indigenous village police system was retained by the alien rulers, including the British, it did not enjoy the same amount of trust, and confidence from the top as before. This obviously affected the prestige and dignity of the village functionaries. Consequently, dependence on military force had to be frequent, leading to bitterness and non-cooperative attitude on the part of the people, who had almost ceased to confide the police. Instead of the community responsibility being encouraged, autocratic or arbitrary enforcement of laws and governmental orders were increasingly practiced. The village functionaries, who approved of such methods came to ascendency, and those who tried to resist were eliminated by the rulers, resulting in the emergence of a new elite in the shape of Zamindars. As a result, the indigenous police system lost its democratic base. The orders of the rulers were ruthlessly and severely carried out and peace was maintained under the threat of dire consequences and with the ulterior motive and intention to acquire perpetuity of the alien reign, and collect the maximum revenue from the subjects. This pattern of police administration continued, almost unabated, until the enactment of the Government of India Act, 1935.

2. Organisation of the Police Under Police Act of 1861

Until the year 1860, when a Police Commission was set-up for the first time to find ways and means of bringing about reforms in the police organisation, the police was subjected to various experimentations which could not produce useful results. It continued to have a chequered career without a proper organisation, and was devoid of its own officers who could instill a sense of discipline in the personnel and guard their interest. As stated earlier the police was a mere instrument at the disposal of the chief revenue officers for enforced collection of revenue. On the basis of the recommendations of the Police Commission of 1860, the Police Act of 1861 was passed by the British Government, and this Act laid the foundation for the police set-up in the country, which continues till date without any major changes having taken place in its concept or organisational pattern in the intervening period. According to Section 4 of this Act, the administration of the Police throughout a general police district (in the case of the state) has been vested in the Inspector General of Police (now Director General), and his subordinates, such as Deputy Inspector General, Superintendent and Assistant or Deputy Superintendent of Police *etc.* This Section also provided that the administration of the police throughout the district shall be under the general control of the District Magistrate of that district. In accordance with this stipulation, the Superintendent of Police, though in-charge of the police administration, was to function under the general control, and direction of the District Magistrate. The concept of this provision in the Police Act of 1861 had its foundation in the 'Oriental Theory' which was evolved during the British regime, and that envisaged that there should be one officer in each unit of administration in whom all threads of administration would be collected and to whom the people would look for guidance in every field of activity. It was then agreed that, concentration of energy and effort in a single functionary and not their diffusion, was what Oriental people understood. Even after Independence in 1947, this system has not been changed by the Indian Government for the very reason of concentration of authority in one designation although, such a system has proved to be derogatory to the interest of maintenance of law and order and tranquillity, as the police do not normally acquire the powers to function independently under the statutes for the aforesaid purpose. Even after Independence and till date, the country adopted in its entirety the police organisational set-up that British rulers had introduced and nurtured for their own ends (and now for the benefit of the political parties forming the government). Incidentally, the British had in their own country abolished the magisterially controlled police as early as 1829, because of its inefficiency and corruption, when the famous Peet's Police was created which was commanded and controlled entirely by their own officers. The police in India has come in for scathing criticism several times for having continued the Mohamedan and British system of policing, though abominable and which by wonderful accidents is being considered to be the best system for the country which the present government has misgoverned. The widely accepted principles of jurisprudence are being sacrificed at the altar of vested interests of the politicians governing the country.

3. The Final Set-up

The final set-up which emerged had an Inspector General of Police (now Director General of Police) in each province for the direction and supervision of the police force, to be assisted by Deputy Inspector General of Police for carrying out the supervisory functions and working on territorial and functional basis. Territorially each province has been divided into ranges, each range is under the charge of a Deputy Inspector General. Similarly, functional Deputy Inspectors General were established to look after the auxiliary organisations throughout each province, such as, one for Criminal Investigation Department, another for Railways, Police Headquarters and so on. The provinces were divided into several districts, and the district police chief was called the Superintendent of Police, who was to be assisted by an Assistant Superintendent or Deputy Superintendent. Each district was further divided into sub-divisions, circles and police stations respectively officered by a Sub-divisional Police Officer, Circle Police Inspector, and Sub-inspector, and the last named is generally in-charge of a Police Station covering approximately an area of about 400 kms on an average and assisted by Assistant Sub-inspector, Head Constables and Constables. Thus, the nucleus of the police organisation is the police station, and on its efficiency, integrity and honesty depends the reputation of the entire police organisation, and therefore, to man a police station men of proven honesty, integrity and ability are absolutely necessary. It is a disdainful comment that very rarely such type of a police station, as is envisaged by the general public, is made available to the people, who by degrees have totally lost confidence in the entire police organisation, of whatever territory it belongs to. In consequence 'Police' have ceased to be the 'Friend' of the people and currently, they are being identified as 'Foes'.

4. Metropolitan Cities and Commissioner of Police

The system of police administration in the presidency towns of Bombay, Calcutta and Madras was different as the police worked directly under a Commissioner of Police without the magisterial control. The Commissioner of Police himself enjoys essential magisterial powers for the control or regulation of assemblies *etc.* The Commissioner of Police is the senior most police officer, but junior to the Director General of the State. Down the hierarchy, he has several Deputy Commissioners, Assistant Commissioners, Inspectors and Sub-inspectors for assisting him in policing the metropolitan town. Their officers are of the same rank and status as those of the district police, but the gazetted officers of and above the rank of Inspector have limited magisterial powers regarding control or regulating crowd or assemblies and dealing effectively with the criminal and rowdy elements of the society in their territorial jurisdiction. Here again the smallest, but the most important and significant unit, is the police station, and as in the rural areas, officers and men of probity and efficiency are required for the proper administration of criminal justice by ensuring effective and vigilant control over crime and criminals. Due to the urbanisation of population which have migrated from the rural areas in search of means of livelihood, enormous and unproportionate industrialisation and unbalanced pecuniary composition of the city society have resulted in a considerable increase in the criminal activities in cities requiring the creation of more commissionerates in the country. Now, any city that has crossed the ten lakhs population mark is being officered by a Commissioner of Police vested with the same powers as those enjoined upon the police officers of the presidency towns.

5. Prosecution Agency Before Independence

There were two separate agencies for the prosecution of cases set up by the police for trial in a court of law in the districts. In the lower courts (Magistrate's Courts) where no serious cases were heard, generally, the Police Prosecutor conducted the cases. In most provinces, these prosecutors were entirely a part of the police organisation, and worked under the Superintendent of Police of the district, where a Prosecutor Inspector was placed in-charge of this prosecution work, and he was of the rank of either a Sub-inspector or Inspector and was required to pass a special law examination, if he was not already a law graduate. In the sessions courts (judge's courts) where all the serious cases were heard, Public Prosecutor, who was an experienced lawyer from the local Bar, was generally appointed to prosecute police cases on terms of payment mutually agreed upon by him, and the government, who appointed him on the recommendations of the District Judge and District Magistrate, and the latter supervised his work. The Superintendent of Police had almost no voice in his appointment or replacement on the ground of independence of the prosecution agency.

State cases being heard in appeal and revision in the High Courts were looked after by the Government Advocates, who worked as Public Prosecutors, and were specially appointed by the government from the Bar.

6. Prosecution Agency after Independence

In order to improve the system of prosecution of police cases the Union Government, on the recommendations of Law

Commission and various State Police Commissions, warranted that police prosecutor at all levels must be law graduates, well-versed with the intricacies of law and procedure. This was also done in order to ensure the independence of the judiciary when the functions of the executive and judiciary were separated, and the entire judiciary system came directly within the purview of the State High Court. As a result, states drew up separate cadres of prosecuting officers recruited entirely from law graduates, and the separation of prosecution agency from the police organisation is now completely ensured. Sections 24 and 25 of the Criminal Procedure Code, 1973, stipulate that a Police Prosecutor shall be appointed by the State and Central Government for prosecution of their respective cases in the High Courts and Sessions Courts. He must be a lawyer with minimum of seven years practice at the Bar. For conducting cases in the High Courts the consent and advice of the High Courts concerned are obligatory. Depending on the prosecution workload in the district, Additional Prosecutors could be appointed out of the panel made by the District Magistrate with the concurrence of the District Sessions Judge.

As far as the Magistrate's court is concerned, one or more Assistant Police Prosecutors are appointed in each district by the government, but they should not be police officers. Various interpretations apply to this proviso. Some states have taken it to mean that the Assistant Public Prosecutor should be entirely detached from the police and should not even come under the Inspector General (now Director General). Others have taken it to mean that they should not be enrolled under the Police Act, and should not enjoy any police powers such as investigation, search, arrests *etc.* In the former interpretation, the Assistant Public Prosecutors have come under the District Magistrates, but in the latter case, they still work under the Superintendent of Police of the district. Supervision and co-ordination procedures are still being worked out for the assumption of the final stage. In few states Director of Prosecution as envisaged by Law Commission, has been appointed at the state level.

Section 25 makes a special provision that in a particular case, if a regular Assistant Public Prosecutor is not available, the District Magistrate can appoint even a police officer as

Assistant Public Prosecutor for that case, provided that he has not taken any part, whatsoever in the investigation of the case being heard in the court, and further that he is not below the rank of Inspector of Police. This new provision, in the Criminal Procedure Code, 1973, obviously aims at giving the police prosecuting agency a professional base, and it may be expected that non-law-graduates will be eliminated completely.

7. Criminal Investigation Department

The Criminal Investigation Branch with its concomitants, the Special Branch and the Crime Branch has been set up on the basis of recommendations of the All India Police Commission of 1902-1903, and in due course of time has much expanded and strengthened in all states. Because of the vast requirements of security and other correlated functions, some states will have to bifurcate the old department into two portions: one dealing entirely with security and intelligence and the other with investigation work and control of selected crime. Full-fledged organisations for vigilance and anti-corruption work, manned by selected officers, have also been created at the state level to keep a watchful eye on the ever-expanding government machinery with vast opportunities for corruption, collusion with undesirable elements and favouritism because of the invidious systems of checks and controls, inevitable in a welfare state. The heads of these special departments are the senior most officers of the police hierarchy but mostly they are under the disciplinary control of the Chief of the Police Organisation of the State.

8. Armed Police

One marked feature of the post-Independence period has been a vast expansion of the Armed Police, both at the Centre and at the States. A nucleus of the military type of police force existed even during the British rule. During World War II, Military Police Battalions were raised in the provinces for such duties as watch and ward at concentration camps, set up for persons suspected of having allegiance to Axis countries, guarding the line of communication systems and so on.

There were under the Centre some battalions of the present Central Reserve Police, then called the Crown Representative

Police, mainly to deal with any trouble in the Princely States of that time.

During the pre-Independence era Military Police and the Crown Representative Police were hardly ever used for normal police duties, and occasions, when they were deployed for law and order duties, were few and far between and their deployment created a frightening impression about them in the minds of general public, as their sight had the deterring effect on the law breakers. Paradoxically, since Independence, law and order problems have assumed stupendous proportions. Their frequency has been alarming and violence so great that the normal law and order forces have been completely outwitted. The State Police Forces have to depend entirely on the support of the Armed Police Battalions of the States or Central Government. Though, the undue prolification of Armed Police has divested the valuable funds, which could otherwise be spent on the reorganisation and improvement of essential police services for the people, but in the conditions prevailing in the country at the moment, the Armed Police Battalions have proved a boon in obviating an otherwise chaotic scene, although the required and necessary force used claimed many civilian lives. This practice brought disparagement to the local police force, and greatly lowered their estimation and morale, and ability to control crowd or effectively disperse the unruly mob. And as such at all levels it should be deprecated, as a growing tendency has been noticed with the local police forces, of shunning their responsibility by inviting the Armed Police to deal with any situation involving law and order and threatening the peace and tranquillity of the general public.

Armed Police Battalions which are called by different names in the various states, such as, Provincial Armed Constabulary in Uttar Pradesh (PAC), Rajasthan Armed Constabulary (RAC), Special Armed Police Force in Madhya Pradesh, Military Police in Bihar, Assam Rifles in Assam, Malabar Police in Tamil Nadu and so on, are in the nature of reserves at the disposal of the Police Chief of the State, who can direct them to act either on a requisition of the Range Officer, such as, Deputy Inspector General of Police or *suo motu* on his own appreciation of a particular situation. Generally, they could be called to deal with a major anti-*dacoity* operation, serious civil commotion, crowd control at the time of VIP visits, for duty at large fairs or festivals or any other law and order situation. Sometimes they are used for guarding the national borders and security duties in sensitive areas. They also can be deputed for duty in neighbouring states to assist the local police of that state on the orders of their own State Government. This is done on a reciprocal basis on the principle of regional co-operation.

These battalions are established under their respective Acts and Rules. Their organisation broadly speaking is, on the lines of an Armed Infantry Battalion, though their armament is more limited and sometimes specialised. Each battalion is commanded by a Commandant of the rank of Superintendent of Police, and it is subject to the control of the Inspector General and Deputy Inspector General concerned. A battalion has between four or six companies each of a hundred to one hundred and twenty men. Under the Commandant is the Assistant Commandant of the rank of Junior Superintendent of Police or Deputy Superintendent of Police. An officer of the rank of Deputy Superintendent of Police or Inspector of Police is placed in-charge of each company, which has four platoons each of about 35 men headed by an Inspector or Sub-inspector of Police. In this respect the system differs from State to State. In some states, the ranks of Inspector and Sub-inspector of the Armed battalion are termed as *Subedars* and *Jamadars* respectively. Each state has on an average 12 to 15 battalions or more in bigger states.

Para-military force under the direct control of the Central Government are Assam Rifles, Border Security Force, Central Industrial Security Force, Central Reserve Police Force, and Indo-Tibetan Border Police. They are deployed frequently to assist the State Police in the maintenance of law and order under Article 257A of the Constitution of the Republic of India. These are described elsewhere.

9. Wireless Section

All the district headquarters in a State, important sub-divisional headquarters and even police stations are connected with wireless communication, and there is also inter-communication between the various states, which is co-ordinated by the Central

Directorate under the Government of India. This organisation in each State is headed by a technical expert of the rank of a Deputy Inspector General or a Senior Superintendent of Police. He has under him a set of technicians and a number of wireless operators, who are mostly locally trained in the organisation itself. Similarly, well-equipped workshops exist for repair work of operating sets and their ancillary equipments. The radio section staff has put up very efficient control rooms in most of the important cities which have proved to be a boom in times of emergencies as well as daily operations of mobile patrols, traffic control and other incidents, which may look insignificant initially, but could lead to major flare up if not handled promptly in the early stages. These organisations have very successfully provided television coverages on various occasions for controlling big crowds during large fairs like Kumbha Mela. In most of the State's computers are in operation to aid crime detection and process various police statistics. Please also see Chapter 15 on Auxiliary Police.

10. Police Training Institutions

Efficient Police Training Institutions have existed in India eversince the British rule. After Independence the importance of good training for all ranks of the force has been very much stressed. Many new training institutions have been created for imparting initial and refreshing training in the states as well as Central Government Police Training Institutions. The Institutions, training Gazetted Officers and Sub-inspectors, are mostly known as Police Training Colleges. Those training lower ranks are termed as schools or just training centres. Assistant Superintendent of Police, after their initial training at the National Police Academy, have also to spend some period varying from one month to six months at the State Police Training College of their state to familiarise themselves with the local laws and conditions. The recruitment of State Police Forces is generally made beginning from the lowest grade, in the rank of Constables, Sub-inspectors, in some cases Inspectors and Deputy Superintendents of Police. Promotions are made in the next higher rank, *i.e.,* Constable → Head Constable → Assistant Sub-inspector → Sub-inspector → Inspector → Deputy

Superintendent of Police → and in rare cases Superintendent of Police. There are separate training schools for constables and head constables.

Under the charge of a Superintendent of Police or a Deputy Superintendent of Police, Senior Constables or Head Constables now undergo refresher training after some years of service or prior to their promotion to a higher grade. The Principal of the Police Training College, which trains Sub-inspectors and Gazetted Officers is a Senior Superintendent of Police or in some states a Deputy Inspector General of Police. Police Training Colleges also organise refresher, and promotion courses of various types in order to streamline the officers and their subordinates.

11. Miscellaneous Organisations

(a) Motor Transport: Most states have their own arrangements for repairs of Police Motor Transport for which they have set-up highly developed Motor Transport workshops, where all minor and major repairs are carried out most efficaciously, and at the same time ensure speedier, reliable and durable services. Police Constables are also trained here to become drivers or mechanics. A senior Foreman is usually in-charge of the workshop, and a workshop Superintendent or Superintendent of Police is in overall charge of the Transport Section. The Foreman has a number of mechanics under him. With increasing stress on mobility, police forces now have a sizeable fleet of motor vehicles of various descriptions but even then the required vehicles could not be provided by the government for paucity of funds to the detriment of police mobility required for tracing out criminals, and dealing with law and order situations.

(b) The Traffic Police: It forms an appreciable part of the Police Force, particularly in large cities. Special training is organised for the personnel drafted to this section of the police and officers are selected for their preference and aptitude for this work. The actual traffic control on the streets is done by police constables and head-constables, who are specially selected for their smartness, education and intelligence. As in a police station, their work is supervised by higher ranks. They have a distinctive uniform, usually of white colour to facilitate identification even during nocturnal hours. Thc Traffic Police in India is still primitive in its technique as compared to other modern developed countries, but the redeeming feature is that there are visible signs of awareness and a desire for modernisation, although public co-operation is usually wanting. Please also see Chapter 15 on Auxiliary Police.

(c) ***Railway Police:*** The Government Railway Police (G.R.P.), which is a part of the State Police and deals with crime control and detection in Railway premises, could not grow much because of the age-old dichotomy of financial control between the State Government and the Railway Administration. All proposals for improvement are stifled because neither of the two administrations wants to foot the bill. However, the Railway Administration has, during the past few years greatly improved their watch and ward system and has organised a regular all India force for the protection of the railway property called the "Railway Protection Force" (R.P.F.). The R.P.F. is under an officer of Inspector General of Police (now upgraded recently to the rank of Director General), who is drafted from the Police and works under the Railway Board. These are officers of the rank of Inspector General in each Railway to assist him. For this force a special enactment — "Railway Protection Force Act" has been brought on the Statute Book and the members of the force are governed by the provisions of that Act. Details of the forces have been given elsewhere in this book. Please also see Chapter 15 on Auxiliary Police.

(d) ***Forensic Science Laboratories:*** A new feature in the states is the establishment of Forensic Science Laboratories with separate sections for Chemistry, Biology, Physics, Ballistics, Hand Writing and Photography. Science has been brought prominently and unmistakably to the aid of investigation in the last few years. Clues left at the scene of occurrences or on the persons of victims and culprits can be examined scientifically in these laboratories to provide convincing and irrefutable and coherent evidence during investigation of crimes. These laboratories are under the charge of a Director, who is a scientist and works under the Police Chief of the State. His rank is more or less equivalent to that of Deputy Inspector General of Police. These laboratories are mostly manned by the scientists and the technicians of various sciences. Blood examination and grouping is also done here in order to clinch the guilt on the concerned perpetrator.

(e) ***Police Dogs:*** Police dogs also play an important part in investigation of crime and almost all states have police dogs very well-trained in tracing out the culprits, helping in patrolling, duties and guarding of buildings. However, due to unsuitable climatic conditions in many parts of the country, they have not proved as successful and useful in India as in some other countries. Please also see Chapter 15 on Auxiliary Police.

(f) ***Fire Services:*** The fire services in some states are a subsidiary to Police Department. In most of the places they are still under Municipal control but in many cities this work is being taken over by civic bodies. Their absorption in the Police Organisation does go to make for efficiency and smartness, but as a matter of principle it is debatable whether the Fire Services should remain outside the police. The only disadvantage discernible is that the fire services can be the target of the public frenzy in times when people are agitating against police action. In such cases, the work of public utility service can be very much hampered due to its close association with the police.

(g) ***Home Guards:*** Home Guards organisation have come into being only in recent years. They are to assist the police in its civic functions at the time of emergencies like natural calamities, wars, large-scale disturbances, elections *etc.*, and situation in which additional civil force is necessary to augment the existing strength of the unarmed police in order to enable them to cope up with the extraordinary and additional stress of duty which they are often required to perform. They are voluntary organisations which are kept in constant training and are called out only when there is an extreme necessity. In many states the organisation has spearheaded even to the rural areas and comprises of a Woman Wing also. Although it is an independent organisation, in a way it is subsidiary to the police department. The degree of dependence and control on and by the Police Department varies from State to State. Please also see Chapter 15 on Auxiliary Police.

(h) ***Indian Police Act of 1861:*** The Indian Police Act of 1861, conforms the basis of the organisation of the Police Department throughout the country, although a few states have Police Act of their own, but the provisions contained in them are in conformity with those of the Indian Police Act, 1861 with certain *mutatis mutandis* changes requiring some adjustments to

suit local conditions. The major laws enforced by the Police are also the same all over the country.

(i) Indian Police Service (IPS): The Indian Police Service, constituted under the All India Services Act, 1951, and framed under Article 312 of the Constitution provides the higher officer cadre for all the state forces. According to Indian Police Service (Appointment by Promotion) Regulations of 1955, 25 per cent of the Deputy Superintendents are eligible for promotion to the IPS cadre. The IPS officers are recruited, trained and organised on all India basis. This, by itself, brings about a cohesion and camaraderie so essential for the integration and common approach in administrative matters as provided in the Police Act of 1861. Under Section 4 of this Act the existing head of the Police Force in every state is the Director General of Police, who is responsible to the State Government for the administration of the police force throughout the State. He is required to advise the State Government on all police matters. He is responsible for the internal economy, equipment, training and discipline of the force. The Director General is not directly responsible for the actual handling of the law and order situation which are required to be dealt with at the district level by the Superintendent of Police under the control and direction of the District Magistrate, who for all practical purposes, decides the policies and procedure for handling of such situation. The Director General, in actual practice, functions only in an advisory capacity. This responsibility in fact, is circumscribed to the task of raising and training of police force to be placed at the disposal of the District Magistrate, who under the Police Act, is responsible for the success of criminal administration and maintenance of law and order in the district. Experience has proved that such a dual pattern of administration is conducive to controversial orders and subsequent actions under political pressure and ultimately the police administration is blamed without any fault, because when the law and order situation deteriorates on account of delayed or haphazard action, it is the police, who are physically required to handle the situation, which by the time they act, has already slipped out of the hands of the Police. The District Magistrates are generally hazy in gauging a law and order problem requiring immediate promulgation of the prohibitory order. Moreover, the

District Magistrates suffer from 'superiority complex' by virtue of their authority ordained under the Police Act. It is high time now that the police should be allowed to function independently without the control of the District Magistrate, who writes the "Annual Confidential Report" of their Superintendent of Police.

The 25 per cent promotional quota into IPS Cadre for the Deputy Superintendents of Police is very meagre, there is not only the necessity, but also a growing demand to raise it to 50 per cent in order to obliterate setting in of frustration, among them, as very limited promotions are made in that Cadre. The result is that time-tested, well-versed and experienced officers gradually lose interest in their work when promotional avenues are not open or made available to them, causing a great loss to the department. This is one of the reasons besides low emoluments, good candidates for recruitment, are not forthcoming.

The Senior Administrative set-up in states consists of the Director General, Inspector General, Deputy Inspector General, Superintendent, Assistant Superintendent and Deputy Superintendent of Police. Deputy Superintendents are of two categories. Some are directly recruited through competitive examinations by the State Public Service Commission, and the rest, the percentage varying from State to State, are promoted from the rank of Inspectors. They are assigned various departmental branches on the basis of the workload.

(j) ***District Police:*** Every state is divided into districts which form complete administrative units by themselves. The district police is headed by a Superintendent of Police. In larger districts, where the volume of work is heavy due to its size, population, and crime problems, there are one or two additional Superintendents for assistance by division of work and portfolios.

The district is divided into police sub-divisions and circles in order to help, share the workload and responsibility of the Superintendent of Police. The Sub-divisional Police Officer is of the rank of Assistant or Deputy Superintendent of Police, and the police circle is in-charge of an Inspector, known as Circle Inspector. The promotional prospects from one rank to the other are not satisfactory as normally 15 years' service the incumbent has to pass before he is considered fit for promotion, and provided his record of service makes him eligible for it.

The district police is divided into Civil and Armed Police. The Civil Police provides the staff for the police stations, outposts, district crime bureau, district special branch, traffic police, special investigating agency, motor transport, wireless *etc.* As regards the Armed Police, they are deployed for guards, escort duties and also provide the striking force in the event of an emergency.

(k) Police Station: Every district is divided into a number of police stations, depending on its size and population. The police station is the basic unit of police administration and the reporting centre for all crimes, both cognizable and non-cognizable, occurring in its jurisdiction. Under the Criminal Procedure Code, all crimes have to be recorded at the jurisdiction of the police station, detective and law and order matters are carried on from there. Other police functions are patrolling, surveillance, execution of warrants, service of processes, collection of information, and intelligence both political and criminal *etc.* The Officer-in-charge of a Police Station is known as Station Officer or Station House Officer who is either of the rank of a Sub-inspector or Inspector. There are city, as well as, rural police stations. Assistant Sub-inspectors, Head Constables and Constables, in varying numbers depending on the size of the police station and the volume of work assist the Police Station Officer in his work.

- *(i)* ***Out Post:*** The jurisdiction of a police station is generally large extending in an area of over 400 kms necessitating creation of outposts at suitable places, both in the cities and in the rural areas, and they are in-charge of a Sub-Inspector/Assistant Sub-Inspector of Police or Head Constable as required by their size and volume of work. The outpost staff of 4/5 constables is generally utilized for patrolling the beats.
- *(ii)* ***Village Policing:*** The Police system in the villages, from the ancient times, depended on the joint responsibility of the village. This was enforced through an elected or hereditary headman, who was assisted by one or more watchmen, remunerated by the village community. The village watchman kept a watch at night, took note of all arrivals, departures and observed all strangers, and reported suspicious strangers to the headman. They had

to detect culprits if a theft occurred in the village. If they failed to recover the stolen property, they were obliged to make up the loss so far as their means permitted and the remainder was levied on the whole village. This broad framework of village policing continued, with minor alteration to suit local needs during the British regime. Now-a-days village policing has almost become most ineffective and inefficient as the factor of 'joint responsibility' is not recognised by the Government due to various political reasons. The police authorities have almost no control, whatsoever on the village police, and in most states, they are under the control of the District Magistrates.

12. Home Department

The police comes under the administrative control of the Home Department, the Secretary of which belongs to the Indian Administrative Service (IAS). The Director General is expected to keep direct touch with the Home Minister through the Home Secretary. All proposals and reports relating to police department and allied matters, meant for the information/action of the government are channelised through the Home Secretary, who is the mouth-piece of the Home Minister. Legally, the Home Secretary has no executive authority of his own to exercise control over the police. He merely advises the Home Minister and then conveys the decisions of the Government on various matters of the police department through the Director General.

The Chief Secretary to the Government, who belongs to the IAS Cadre, plays a very positive role so far as the police department is concerned. Actually, he is the head of all services under the control of the State Government. Important service matters pertaining to police department are advised by the Chief Secretary to the Government, and all files relating to the police are channelised to the Home Minister by the Home Secretary through the Chief Secretary.

13. Relation with the Central Government

The Government of India Act of 1935 founded the real base for the separation of Central and Provincial Governments, and provided for a federal system of distribution of legislative powers between the Centre and the Provinces/States. Their lists were drawn up for this purpose: (1) Federal list, (2) Provincial list, and (3) Concurrent list. Police functions come under the Home Ministry, which was redesignated in August 1947 as the Ministry of Home Affairs. The main function of the Home Ministry is to deal with matters pertaining to maintenance of peace and public tranquillity within the country and matters pertaining to Centre-State relations. Although 'Police' is entirely a State subject, it has been included in the concurrent list. Likewise is the case with prison department. By virtue of the powers vested in the Home Department by the Constitution of India, the Home Ministry has taken several steps to improve the standard and efficiency of the Police Department by rendering such technical, and scientific assistance, and their training as would be useful in the investigation and detection of crimes, and thus, it has strengthened the State Police Forces. Details about such training institutions have been given separately.

Similarly to assist the armed branch of the police in reaching a higher standard of efficiency and performance, several training courses have been provided and organisations like the Central Police School of Weapons and Tactics at Indore (Madhya Pradesh) have been established. From time to time, depending on the availability of funds, (which is the last priority of the government as far as police is concerned) the Central Government has provided funds on various counts, such as, providing accommodation to lower staff, modernisation of technical facilities *etc.*, which acts to some extent as a morale booster to the State Police Department. All the same, signs of growing unrest due to poor salaries to all rank and file, including officers are discernible and it is no hidden truth that their emoluments are definitely below than those of other services. Police personnel are continuously on duty for varying hours, which, on several occasions, are extended beyond 18 hours a day. Many a times they are required to work all the 24 hours of the day without any respite and for several days without any relief.

The nature of their duties is hazardous and arduous and umpteen number of policemen have sacrificed their lives in the due performance of their duties. On account of some bad work done by some of the 'black sheep' among them the police generally, have lost sympathy of the public, who have also lost confidence in the former. Necessary steps by the Central Government are warranted to correct this anomalous position and improve the Police-Public relationship by improving the standard and efficiency of the police through proper recruitment and training. Only better salary and service conditions would be able to attract educated and well-behaved youths who would take pleasure and pride to enroll themselves in Police service, and without prejudice to anyone, willingly do the hazardous or onerous and yet, honourable duty, which is so essentially needed for the betterment of the degraded society, and the welfare of the state, and in consequence the Nation.

11
Central Government Unarmed Police Agencies

Succinctly, the following are the Central Government Unarmed Police Agencies:

1. Intelligence Bureau (IB)

The history of Intelligence Bureau during the British regime can be traced to a small group of officers and reliable network of the informers employed by Sir William Sleeman for the supervision of '*Thuggee*' organisation between 1830 and 1837. The '*Thuggs*' — secret gangs of criminals travelled in disguise, murdered helpless travellers, mostly by strangulation with a handkerchief or a scarf used as a noose. The success in the eradication of *Thuggee* menace was largely due to the employment of reliable informers.

The *Thuggee* and *Dakaiti* Department established by Sleeman in 1835, was in effect the Criminal Investigation Department concerned mainly with these two particular forms of crime. In 1877 under the charge of Colonel Hinderson, this department was given the additional duty of collecting secret and political intelligence, which the British Government badly required after the 1857 War of Independence. All the modern intelligence collecting organisations are a natural development from the old, but expanded functions of the *Thuggee* and *Dakaiti* Department. In April 1904, the new organisation with nomenclature of Central Criminal Intelligence Department came into being under Director, H.A. Staurt, who was the just incumbent to this post.

This department was instructed:

(a) To deal with special forms of crime, some of which have been rendered more difficult of suppression by the recent extension of railways and the increased use of the

Post Office and Telegraph by natives. To organise and supervise operations directed against criminal tribes, organised *dacoits* working over large areas, wandering gangs of criminals, note forgers, coiners, professional poisoners etc.

(b) To collect and test intelligence upon political matters, including social, religious and political movements not necessarily of criminal character.

(India Finance and Commerce letter No. 51 of 11 February 1904, 10R: L/P2J/6/670 file 493 of 1904)

In actual practice political intelligence work occupied the whole time of the department, and its functions in relation to special forms of crime were quietly dropped. For this reason after the First World War (1914-1918) the name of the department was changed to the Intelligence Bureau.

This new organisation was made directly responsible for the collection of information required by the Governor General personally, the Army, the Agent to the Governor General and his Political Agents, and the Governor of the neighbouring provinces regarding what is going on in the Northwest Frontier Province proper (Now gone to Pakistan), Tribal Territory, Afghanistan, Sinkiang, and the part of USSR (Russia) most adjacent to India. In addition, it was to provide intelligence regarding subversive activity connected with or directed by Communist International and the intrigues of Ghadar Party emanating from Moscow, and other places in Europe, and Afghanistan. In a nutshell, it collected all the intelligence regarding the anti-British Government activities and generally it was considered as the eyes and ears of the government.

By the Nineties, the intelligence system in India, both in its political and non-political spheres, had been well-organised, but the inauguration of the provincial autonomy in 1937 (of Indian leaders) brought about one important change. The police in each province came under the authority of the Minister of Home Affairs, who was responsible for day-to-day administration of law and order. At the same time, the Governor General had an overriding responsibility, and was empowered to intervene in certain emergencies. He, therefore, had his own sources of information independent of ministers. For this purpose, a Central Intelligence Officer (CIO) of the rank of Superintendent of Police, was seconded from the local police force in each province and was made responsible for reporting direct to the Director of Intelligence Bureau stationed in Delhi. The CIO was also required to make a careful study of the press, both English and Vernacular, to keep in touch with the political organisations. He was the eyes and ears of the Central Government in the period between the inauguration of provincial autonomy and the achievement of Independence.

The Second World War (1939-1946) added considerably to the work and responsibility of the various intelligence branches and considerable expansion of their strength was made, but the principles and methods remained the same. The entry of Japan into the arena of conflict, the activities of the Indian National Army (INA), Congress opposition to the war efforts, counter-intelligence activities, the 'Quit India' movement, all these events surpassed each other and the intelligence agency found its hands full.

After the achievement of Independence, T.G. Sanjeevi Pillai was appointed the first Director General, Intelligence Bureau. After a long tenure he was succeeded by B.N. Mullik, who left his mark not only on the Intelligence Bureau, but also on all aspects of police work and a whole generation of police officers. Independence brought serious problems, such as, invasion of Kashmir, integration of princely states, Hyderabad Police Action, Nagaland and Mizoram problem, Punjabi Subha and language agitations, communist uprising in Telengana (Andhra Pradesh), agitation over formation of linguistic states, Chinese incursion, communal and caste conflicts, terrorism, the Bangladesh development, the Ayodhya tangle *etc.* The organisation has grown with the passing years and continued to guide the national leaders away from catastrophe. It is also in-charge of foreign intelligence. It is supposed to be the most effective machinery in the maintenance of internal security of the country *vis-a-vis* the collection of the necessary intelligence.

But lately, a tendency to tailor intelligence for the ruling political party by some of the officers of the Intelligence Bureau is discernible, and all possible efforts are needed to curb it.

2. State Intelligence Agencies

The Police Commission of 1902-03 had suggested that the Provincial Criminal Investigation Department should be under the charge of a Deputy Inspector General of Police, who would also have under his control special Branch of political intelligence (with differences only in details). This is the general pattern of organisation followed throughout India. With the upgradation of the post of Inspector General of Police of a state to that of Director General, the Criminal Investigation Department is now headed by the Inspector General of Police in almost all the big states. It collects political as well as criminal intelligence concerning its State. It is required to furnish periodically all the political intelligence collected by it to the Intelligence Bureau. Thus, the Intelligence Bureau has in its possession all the intelligence collected by the states' intelligence agencies and its own officers, agencies and sources. The Intelligence Bureau very carefully scrutinises, sifts and siphons this information, and fully and promptly keeps the Government informed about all the political happenings in the country.

The Central Forensic Laboratories at Calcutta and Hyderabad, the three officers of the Examiner of Questioned Documents at Calcutta, Hyderabad and Shimla, and the two Detective Training Schools at Calcutta and Hyderabad were under the administrative control of the Intelligence Bureau before they were handed over for administration to the Central Bureau of Investigation in January, 1974.

3. Foreign Intelligence

Many of the security problems have international ramifications. They are aided, abated and sustained from outside the country. Admittedly, police have to face and eliminate these problems working within the country. Apart from security in the field of insurgency and terrorism, security in such area as Economic, Industry, Defence, Nuclear and other scientific know-how has assumed great importance. Almost all the countries of the world have felt the need to set-up a specialised agency to work outside the country, not in competition with the foreign office, but as a supplement to it. The common objects of such an Agency is to collect information, rcsearch and investigate into the background and send it to its Headquarters where it is analysed and communicated to higher authorities. Every country has such an Agency like the Central Intelligence Agency (CIA) of United States of America. While setting up such an Agency, countries have found it fit, to associate police officers with it. The role of the police in such an agency is well-understood.

Foreign affairs are handled by the Ministry of External Affairs. Its representatives are posted in various countries, on reciprocal basis, and they fulfil important national requirements.

4. Research and Analysis Wing (RAW)

This is yet another Central Government Intelligence Agency. It is headed by an officer of the rank of Director General of Police and it works directly under the Prime Minister. Mostly, its functions are to collect political intelligence and undertake such special enquiries as are directed by the Prime Minister. Intrinsically, it is the Prime Minister's intelligence branch.

5. Special Protection Group (SPG)

Since 1987, a new force with the nomenclature of Special Protection Group has been raised in order to cater and provide security needs to the Prime Minister, Ex-Prime Ministers and their families and various other important dignitaries. More or less it is a commando force, and its members are specially trained for that purpose. The members of this force have special service conditions and privileges.

6. Special Police Establishment (SPE) and Central Bureau of Investigation (CBI)

At an early stage of World War II, the Government of India realised that the vast increase in the expenditure for war efforts provided opportunities for manipulation and anti-social persons, both officials and non-officials, for indulging in bribery and corruption at the cost of the public and the Government. Therefore, to investigate offences connected with the transactions relating to war efforts an organisation known as the Special Police Establishment (SPE) was set-up by the Government of India in 1941. The functions of the SPE were to investigate cases of bribery and corruption in transactions which the war and supply departments of the Government of India were concerned with. The superintendence of this organisation was vested with the War Department. At the end of 1942, the activities of the SPE were extended to include cases of corruption on the Railways. In 1943, in order to overcome some legal difficulty, an ordinance was issued by the Government of India by which the Special Police Force for the investigation of certain offences committed in connection with the department of the Central Government, with powers to investigate such offences anywhere in British India, was constituted. Since, corruption went on unabated by the Central Government servants on 30th September 1946, the Delhi Special Police Establishment Act was passed, and the superintendence of the SPE was transferred to the Home Department of the Government of India. Its jurisdiction extends to all the Union Territories and it can also be extended to the states, with the consent of the State Government concerned.

In 1963, Economic Offences Wing was added to the SPE for dealing with cases of violation of Import & Export Control Act, and various other fiscal laws of the Central Government.

With passage of time generally corruption increased unbridled, and the SPE was required to investigate cases under the Prevention of Corruption Act, and violation of Import and Export Control Act, and other 16 Central Acts. A growing need was felt, for a Central Agency at the disposal of the Central Government, which would investigate not only cases of bribery and corruption but also cases of breaches of central fiscal laws, major frauds relating to the Government of India Departments, public joint stock companies, passport frauds, crimes on the highways, airlines and serious crimes committed by organised gangs or professional criminals and therefore. "The Central Bureau of Investigation" (CBI) was set-up by the Government of India on 1st April, 1963. The jurisdiction and powers of the SPE continued to remain as before.

The CBI was also entrusted the task of collection of intelligence relating to certain types of crimes, study of specialised forms of crimes of particular interest to the Government, or crimes having inter-state or international ramifications, or crimes of particular importance from the social point of view, the conduct of police research, and the co-ordination of laws.

The powers of SPE and CBI investigating officers are not exclusive but concurrent with those of the state police officers, and they are mainly to supplement the efforts of the latter. But in order to avoid duplication of investigation an administrative arrangement has been arrived at between the Central and the State Governments about the types of cases to be taken up by SPE and CBI.

Requisition by the State Government for initiating investigation by CBI into cases which substantially and eventually involve State Government employees is generally necessary. Now, the CBI/SPE is authorised to investigate offences under 19 different Sections and 55 Central Acts.

The CBI/SPE is headed by a senior IPS officer and most of the incumbents are drafted from various states on deputation. The CBI/SPE chief is of the rank of Director General.

7. Sardar Vallabhbhai Patel National Police Academy, Hyderabad

Indian Police Officers, until the country became Independent, received probationary training in their respective provincial training colleges. For the first time in 1948, the training of all India Police Service (IPS) probationers was centralised when the Central Police Training College (CPTC) was established at Mount Abu. Later, this institution was renamed in 1967 as the 'National Police Academy', and in 1974 "Sardar Vallabhbhai Patel National Police Academy." In 1975, the Academy was shifted to Hyderabad.

Initially, the CPTC confined its training to the IPS probationers' course up to 1960, when advance course was introduced for in-service training of the superintendents of police. In 1973, this programme was renamed as the senior officer's course. In 1979, another in-service course called the Top Management Development Programme, was introduced for officers of the rank of Deputy Inspectors General (DIG) of Police. A new wing for training of the trainers was added in 1982. Here, the purpose had been to provide training to State Police Service (SPS) officers, who are posted as trainers at the State Police Training Colleges and to separately conduct a Training Administration Course for IPS and SPS officers, who are posted as Principals and Vice-Principals in these colleges.

The Academy is headed by a Director who is an IPS officer of the rank of Director General of Police. Since 1965, the Academy has been organising a 9-month basic training course for sub-inspector cadets of the Central Bureau of Investigation.

8. Institution of Criminology and Forensic Science (ICFS)

In 1955, the UNESCO had organised a symposium in London and it unanimously felt that a systematic understanding of Criminology and Forensic Science was necessary for law enforcement officers and that the universities should be encouraged to include these disciplines in their curricula. The Government of India and the University Grants Commission agreed with the recommendations of the Forensic Science Advisory Committee, specially set-up by the Ministry of Home Affairs, to examine the need for inclusion of this subject for study at the university level, and that ultimately led to the establishment in 1972 of the Institute of Criminology and Forensic Science headed by a Director under the Ministry of Home Affairs, Government of India. The following are the objects of this institution:

1. To conduct in-service training through long-term professional courses ranging from 5 weeks to 18 months for scientific personnel from the various Forensic Science Laboratories.
2. Orientation and International courses for senior officers drawn from the various branches of the Criminal Justice Administration, *i.e.,* the judiciary, the police, the correctional services *etc.*, and other government departments.
3. To undertake research in the field of Criminology and Forensic Science.
4. To act as a reference body in the above fields for national as well as international institutions and provide information to workers engaged in studies in these fields.
5. To promote understanding and goodwill by providing facilities for training and research in these subjects to scholars from foreign countries.
6. To act as publishing centre for indigenous literature in the form of books, monographs, booklets, pamphlets,

journals and newsletters in Criminology and Forensic Science.

At present the ICFS runs 22 different courses, some of these being professional, orientational and international and they cover a wide range of subjects such as crime and justice, criminology, anti-social criminal behaviour, juvenile delinquency, crime control and police community relations, special course on prevention and control of drug abuse, criminology and forensic science, toxicology, chromatography, document examination, police photography, ballistics, scientific investigation of crimes *etc.* The main object of these courses is to cater to the needs of Criminal Justice System as a whole.

The ICFS had been reorganised as a Centre of Research leading to Ph.D. degree of many universities. Because of its high research component, the Planning Commission has enlisted it as a science and technology organisation. Officers from the Army, Navy and Airforce regularly participate in some of the newly structured courses.

9. National Crime Records Bureau (NCRB)

Crime records have always been vital to the police both for prevention and detection of crime. In order to improve the efficiency of the crime records various organisations were set-up. The first was the Central Fingerprint Bureau (CFPB) in 1956, then the Crime Research Section of the Central Bureau of Investigation in 1964, the Directorate of Co-ordination Police Computers (DCPC) in 1976, and finally the National Crime Records Bureau (NCRB) in 1986. All these were established to provide the crucial basic data on crime and criminals so that police working could become more systematic and efficient.

The recommendations of the National Police Commission (NPC) were accepted by the Government, and in consonance with these recommendations Crime Record Bureaus have been established at the Centre, and also at the State and district levels for more efficient collection and dissemination of crime-criminal information among the states/union territories. Thus, the CRBs receive, store, and furnish different types of data/information relevant to various requirements such as investigation, study of present scheme of court trials and procedures and sentencing policy, also on the conduct of the criminal, assessment of the effect of probation and correctional services, and also to facilitate scrutiny of the various environmental factors promoting deviant behaviour and criminality in society. Thus, the NCRB serves effectively the overall purposes of the Criminal Justice System as a whole under the control of the Ministry of Home Affairs, Government of India with the following objectives:

(a) To function as a clearing home of information on crime and criminals including those operating at national and international levels so as to assist the investigation and others in linking crimes to their perpetrators.

(b) To store, co-ordinate and disseminate information on inter-state and international criminals from and to respective states, national investigating agencies, courts and prosecutors in India without having to refer to the police station records.

(c) To collect and process crime statistics at national level.

(d) To receive from and supply data to penal and correctional agencies for their tasks of rehabilitation of criminals, their remand, parole, premature release *etc.*

(e) To co-ordinate, guide and assist the functioning of the State Crime Records Bureaus.

(f) To provide training facilities to the personnel of Crime Records Bureaus.

(g) To evaluate, develop and modernise Crime Records Bureaus.

In spite of the modernisation of crime records computerisation has had only a marginal impact on crime control. Though substantial data have been stored in computers, enquiries by investigating officers have been few, and even in these cases computer outputs did not really help investigators to solve their cases. On the whole the computerisation programme had suffered mainly on seven counts:

1. Lack of flow of adequate information/data from police stations upwards.
2. Inadequate updating of data.

3. Inadequate use of available data by the police investigating officers and others.
4. Non-availability/low quality of adequate data on police records.
5. Shortage of technical staff.
6. Lack of awareness, interest and faith in modern methods of crime detection, inclusive of crime processed information.
7. Computer in the NCRB have become worn out and outdated.

The NCRB publishes each year a report on 'Crime in India', since 1986.

Director General, a senior IPS officer heads the NCRB.

10. Bureau of Police Research and Development (BPR&D)

The Bureau of Police Research and Development (BPR&D) was established under the Ministry of Home Affairs, Government of India in August 1970 as a Central Police Organisation for promoting a speedy and systematic study of police problems in a changing society and bringing about rapid application of science and technology to the methods and techniques of the police in the country. Subsequently, in 1973, on the basis of the recommendations of the committee on police training (Gore Committee), a Directorate of Training was also created in the BPR&D, *inter alia* to aid, and advise the states/union territories on the training of police officers, evaluate the existing programmes, assess the future needs of police training *etc.*

In the same year, the Central Forensic Laboratories at Calcutta and Hyderabad, the three offices of the Government of Examiner of Questioned Documents at Calcutta, Hyderabad and Shimla and the two Detective Training Schools at Calcutta and Hyderabad were delinked from the Intelligence Bureau and placed under the administrative charge of the BPR&D. In January 1974, the third Detective Training School was established at Chandigarh and in 1978, the administrative control of the Forensic Science Laboratory was also transferred to BPR&D. But the Institute of Criminology and Forensic Science, Jhandewala, New Delhi, which functioned under this

Bureau became independent in 1976. The preparation of the All India Crime Statistics which was also the function of this Bureau was entrusted to a new organisation in January 1986 — National Crime Records Bureau.

The BPR&D has the following four broad divisions:

(a) Research and Publication Division under Director (R&D) who is an IPS officer of the rank of IGP.

(b) Development Division as above.

(c) Training Division under Director (R&D) who is also an IPS officer of the rank of IGP.

(d) Forensic Science Division under a senior forensic scientist designated as Director.

The BPR&D personnel are drawn from various services/ disciplines including police, scientists, technical experts and ministerial staff. Most of these incumbents are on deputation, although a certain number of them are permanently absorbed in the BPR&D.

The Development Division reviews the performance of various types of equipment used by the police forces in the country and also undertakes the developments of new equipment in various fields such as arms and ammunition, riot control equipment, traffic control equipment, police transports *etc.* It has developed a range of less lethal weapons for the police force, including plastic pellet system. Modified cartridges, 303 special police ammunition, 1.5"/38 mm Rubber Bullet 120 gms, and water canon *etc.*

The Training Division evaluates the existing police training programmes, assesses and co-ordinates the standards, improves training courses, training devices and new courses for exploring the future needs. It monitors the training programmes for the IPS officers (both within and outside the country), apart from arranging training programmes for foreign police officers in India, it organises symposium for the heads of Police Training institutions all over the country. All India seminars on, 'Police Community Relations' and the in-service training of the senior most IPS with 20 or more years service *etc.*

All possible efforts are made to bring about attitudinal changes on the part of the investigating officers and to foster greater reliance on the application of science and technology to criminal investigation, as also to eliminate any tendency for the use of "Third Degree Method".

The Research Division carries out Research of Studies on various subjects of interest and importance to the police forces in the country. It carries out various studies of practical utility on problems pertaining to police organisation and administration, crime and delinquency, enforcement of laws, security, law and order *etc.* It publishes two quarterly journals — *The Indian Police Journal,* and *The Police Research and Development Journal.* These journals are intended to disseminate information and ideas about the latest problems being faced by the police forces in the country and measures required to deal with them. It brings out a Documentation Bulletin regularly, relating to police science, forensic science, and criminology for use of the police institutions and forces of the country. It organises, each year, Police Science Congress.

12

Central Government Armed Police Forces

1. Assam Rifles

The force was originally raised in 1835 as Cachar Levy by Grange, a civilian in-charge of Nowgong district in Assam and initially conceived as an armed police unit to guard the settlements and tea estates against depredation by marauding tribals. Since then this force was gradually raised in status and evolved as follows:

Frontier Rifles	- 1883
Assam Military Police	- 1891
East Bengal and Assam Military Police	- 1913
Assam Rifles	- 1920

Their contribution towards the assimilation of the people of these tribal areas into the national mainstream is truly monumental. In the words of Dr Venier Elwin, once adviser to the Governor of Assam (untruncated) the achievements of the Force can be summarised:

> "The guardians of law and order, the pioneers of every advance into the interior, the guardians of our borders and above all, the friends of the hill people."

As parts of these inaccessible areas were brought under the control of the administration, the war like tribal inhabitants were progressively subdued, and pacified though not fully. The outposts established by the Force in the past, have now grown enormously such as, Aizawl, Lungleh, Kohima, Mokokchung, Tuensang, Hoflong, Cherrapunji, Tura and many other places. The official role of the Force is — Security of the North-Eastern Sector of the International border; Maintenance of law and order in the tribal areas of Arunachal Pradesh, Nagaland, Mizoram, Manipur and Tripura and counter-insurgency operations in these areas; Internal security of other areas only when the local police is unable to cope up with the situation.

*(a) **Military Expeditions:*** From its very inception the Force has been involved in various frontier and trans-frontier military expeditions carried out either singly or in conjunction with or under Army's operational control and they included Burma war, Bhutan war, as many as 20 encounters with various Naga Tribes during 1824-1879 period. In the First World War (1914-1918), some Battalions of the Force were deployed with Gorkha Battalions of the Indian Army in France, Egypt, Gallipoli, Mesopotamia, North Persia and North-West Frontiers of India. Because of the meritorious services rendered by the Force it was given the title of Assam Rifles. In the Second World War (1939-1946), the Force was mostly deployed in Burma following the invasion by Japan.

*(b) **Law and Order Duties:*** Some of the Battalions of the Force were sent to assist civil authorities of Arrah arid Patna in Bihar (1917), Dacca in East Bengal (1906-1908) in maintaining peace and order and Malabar in Madras Presidency to quell the Mopla rebels in 1924. In the post-Independence period the Assam Rifles Battalions were as busy as ever, especially in the North-East Frontier Areas (NEFA) when the administration was pushed up right up to the McMohan Line. After Independence some of the areas of NEFA became an arena of cessionists and insurgent activities, mostly in Nagaland, Mizoram, Manipur, Tripura, North Eastern Assam districts and the Assam Rifles Battalions were deployed to deal with that menace and suffer heavy casualties. It still continues to do so. The saga of great heroism and nursing patriotism of the Force was widely acclaimed during the 1962 Chinese Aggression when a large number of men and families lost their lives and many officers and their men were decorated for gallantry. Five Vir Chakras were awarded in 15 days. N.K. Rustomjee, ICS, who was for many years Adviser to the Governor of Assam described the bravery of the Force as under:

> "The Force was suddenly called upon to face the toughest challenge in its long and eventful career. They were attacked

> by overwhelming superior numbers at their solitary posts along the McMohan Line where they stood their guard bravely to defend the country's honour."

In 1950, Assam was rocked with severe earthquake. The succour given by the men of Assam Rifles is to-date remembered by the locals. In appreciation of the splendid work done by the Force, Jairamdas Daulatram, the then Governor of Assam paid tributes in the following words:

> "Probably no event brought-out the splendid qualities of the officers and men of Assam Rifles more prominently before the outside world than did the Great Earthquake of 1950. The Assam Rifles are essentially a force for maintaining law and order in NEFA, but they have transformed themselves more than once, and at no notice into an efficient military force playing a notable role in the wars to which India had to be a party. The Great Earthquake of 1950 showed that the Assam Rifles were not only an armed force for civil and military purposes, but they constituted a well-disciplined volunteer corps for the service of people at a time of grave danger and distress."

The force had undertaken five mountaineering expeditions at various altitudes up to 28,208 feet (climbing of Kanchenjunga peak). After repeated efforts a strategic post was established in October 1961 at the trijunction of India, China and Burma at Chaukan and Hpungan passes for administrative control and to check intrusion into Indian territory by foreign nationals. This post Vijaynagar is even today after 30 years, an air-maintained post since there is no road communication.

In 1989 two of its Battalions were sent to Sri Lanka as part of the Indian Peace Keeping Force under the operational control of the Army. It is also deployed in Jammu and Kashmir.

The Force is at present being commanded by an officer of the rank of Lt. General on deputation from the Army and designated as Director General Assam Rifles.

2. Central Reserve Police Force (CRPF)

In 1939, in a sleepy town of present Madhya Pradesh "Crown Representative Police" started functioning and primarily was employed to aid princely states in times of emergency arising out of *dacoity* or political situations. In early 1940-41, the Force provided detachments in various places of Central India such as Cherkhari, Mhow, Indore *etc.* Small contingents also took guard duties of political detenus of German and Italian origin at Deolali. In 1942, the force was deployed in Sind (Khaipur State) to deal with the '*Hur*' menace. During 1943-46 the Force was deployed for operations against dangerous *dacoits* in Central India, Baroda and Kishangarh states, Rewa, Pataudi, Dujona, Datia, Chavkhari, Nowgong, Loharu, Ratlam, Ajmer, Rampur and Rajkot areas. In 1947, the force took a leading part in the integration of Kathiawar states of Manawada, Bantwa, Sardargarh, Mongrel and Junagad.

The force had also the honour to take over viceregal guard duties at Delhi, where it came into limelight. Soon after Independence the force was entrusted with duties of guarding Western Borders, and had its detachments at Barmer, Godra, Jaisalmer, Jodhpur, and Kutch.

The force, under the Ministry of States, noticed in this tiny organisation the nucleus of what was to be in future the strong arm of the Centre for suppression of disturbances of all kinds. In 1949, the Central Reserve Police Bill was passed, and the Central Reserve Police Force (CRPF) was constituted as one of the armed forces of the Union for the purpose of utilisation in the internal security front, and its scope of duties was extended to all over the country. Simultaneously, the Government conferred certain powers under the Code of Criminal Procedure connected with the suppression of internal disturbances and restoration of order. The Force now came under the Home Ministry of the Government of India. In the succeeding years the demand on the force continued to increase and at present the force is approximately 1.20 lakhs distributed throughout the country, under the Director General, who is a senior officer of the Indian Police Service. The Force comprises people from all corners of the country working in total harmony, and unison, and presents a picture of secularism and national integration. It is today the most versatile force of the country. It has an admirable capacity efficiently to switch from one role to another, whether in dealing with insurgents and extremists, or in handling sensitive law, and order situations, and rendering aid to civil authorities in natural calamities.

From 1956 onwards the CRPF battalions were posted to Jammu & Kashmir and Nagalands and Assam on semi-permanent basis for law and order duties. The valiant action and sacrifice of the CRPF personnel at Hot Spring in Ladakh on 21st October 1959 against overwhelming strength of Chinese troops, and in Yunong Bridge while repulsing an attack mounted by Pakistan guerrillas enhanced the prestige of CRPF. The most crowning achievement of the Force had occurred on 4-9-1965 when a brigade attacked by Pakistan Army on the Sardar Port in Rann of Kutch was repulsed with 30 enemy soldiers dead. The Union Home Minister hailed this extraordinary achievement: "This battle will go down in the history of Indian Police, nay in the history of Military battles." The Force played a major part in guarding the nation's borders during the Indo-Pakistan wars, and on various occasions it worked under the operational command control of the Army in Punjab, Jammu & Kashmir, and the Northeastern Region in tackling terrorist insurgency. No general election was concluded in sensitive areas without its assistance. On 22-9-87 one battalion was airlifted to Sri Lanka to form a part of Indian Peace Keeping Force. After the Hot Spring incident every year, on 21st October a Memorial Day is observed, and commemoration ceremony held at the head quarters of each district throughout the country in order to pay respect and tribute to the departed police personnel of the soil. In this ceremony names of all those killed in action during the year are read and the police parade pays homage to them by reversing arms and laying wreaths.

In April 1989, a Mahila (Women) Battalion became operational to deal with women agitators and perform all the pertinent duties in connection with the maintenance of law and order and peace and tranquillity. In January 1988, the personnel of this Battalion were deployed in Sri Lanka.

With such a high tradition and efficiency in service, the force was stigmatised when in 1979 a few of the disgruntled elements of the Force revolted and struck work. Two hundred and fifty personnel were dismissed, and 558 awarded various punishments.

Director General, a senior IPS officer heads the force.

3. The Indo-Tibetan Border Police (ITBP)

The Indo-Tibetan Border Police (ITBP) was raised in 1962 in the wake of the Chinese aggression. Since, the ITBP has to operate exclusively in the Indo-Tibetan Border in the states of Jammu & Kashmir, Himachal Pradesh, and Uttar Pradesh covering a long international border of about 1200 kilometeres from Karakoram pass in Ladakh to Lipulekh pass at the trijunction of Indo-Tibet and Nepal border, personnel belonging to those regions are preferred for recruitment in the force as climatically and psychologically they are fully attuned to the area in view of their operational role. The ITBP work over the Line of Actual Control — the international border of India with foreign countries. The force undertakes both intelligence and armed police work in the shape of indoctrinating and training the local population in resistance within the border areas.

In September and October 1965 the force was deployed in Jammu & Kashmir Sector (Rajowri-Poonch).

Generally, the role of the ITBP is:

(a) To keep vigil on ingress routes and to prevent border violations in co-ordination with the security forces.

(b) To provide a sense of security to the population living on the border.

(c) To control trans-border traffic, crime (including smuggling), and unauthorised civilians ingress and egress in co-ordination with Intelligence Bureau.

(d) To provide protection and all facilities to the Intelligence Bureau to enable it to carry out its assigned tasks both during peace and war.

(e) To function under the operational control of the Army as may be required in sensitive areas.

(f) To function in a role similar to that of Border Security Force in a war situation.

The ITBP functions in most of the parts which are located at high mountains and altitude up to 18,000 feet, where there is little oxygen, practically no vegetation and the winter temperature often goes lower than 50 degrees celsius, therefore frequent rotation of battalions is done for rest and training. During

1987, the force was given additional responsibility for providing security to banks in Punjab. Keeping in view the deployment and difficult conditions of service in ITBP, the training has been kept to conform to the highest order to develop and practice special skills such as:

(i) Expertise of semi-automatic weapons.

(ii) Commando operations and tactical mission including improvisations in fields of explosives, their diffusion/neutralisation.

(iii) Rock climbing, mountaineering, skiing and snow craft.

(iv) 'Living on the land' including the knowledge survival techniques in snow-bound mountains and high altitudes.

(v) Meet the challenge of surprise attack and infiltration taking the advantage of terrain itself.

(vi) Carry out guerrilla role/stay behind role in case any part of Indian territory is overrun.

(vii) Carry complementary role to the Army on the outbreak of the hostilities after bearing the first onslaughts of the invading forces.

The ITBP was deployed in Sri Lanka (Ceylon) for providing security to the Indian High Commission in Colombo, and various other miscellaneous duties such as during General Election and law and order disturbances.

This combative force had the privilege of climbing atop the peak of the Mount Everest through Company Commander, Sonam Palzor, who was a member of Indian expedition in May 1984. It has also the rare distinction of conquering Mount Everest for the second time in May, 1996 under a severe blizzard after losing three men of the force.

The ITBP personnel, including officers, on an average have to spend more than 2/3 years of their service career in field duties and that too mostly at high altitudes. Therefore, environmental and psychological factors operate simultaneously and augment one another to affect health of the incumbents rendering them prone to suffer from hypoxies and other heart-ailments. In addition to the extremely low temperatures, the ITBP personnel are required to hazard the high velocity turbulent winds of varying speeds beyond 80 kilometres per hour. A terrible tragedy over took the ITBP post at Mana on the evening of 19-1-1968, when a strong blizzard in the form of a whirlwind struck the post, completely destroyed three buildings and buried to death under snow 20 personnel. The ITBP over the years has evolved the strategy of merging conventional and non-conventional techniques of warfare with the intent of imparting to the force a holding capacity at various levels, to delay and harass the enemy in its path and enable the Army to reach the most forward locations in strength as it is not possible to bind down large contingents of Army in these remote areas during normal times. The force is headed by the Director General (analogous to Lt. General). Most of the officers and men are either on deputation from Army/Police or many are ex-army personnel.

4. Border Security Force (BSF)

Origin: India has a land border of 15,200 kilometres with Pakistan, China, Nepal, Bhutan, Burma and Bangladesh and coastline of 7,517 kilometeres. The land border includes some riverine stretches also of this border. The BSF stands guard over 6,957 kilometres of land border, including 844 kilometres which is riverine. The border with Pakistan is 2,718 kilometres, with Bangladesh 4,239 and with Burma 288 kilometres.

The system of border vigilance, as inherited in 1947, consisted of the Police Force of bordering states guarding the border with the help of check posts and occasional patrolling. This system continued till the end of 1964, as the pressures on the border till then were not so great and the system of border security across the border, in Pakistan, was similar to ours. The concerned states of Rajasthan, Gujarat, Punjab, West Bengal and Uttar Pradesh attended to the patrolling of their respective border with the help of their own police force. Jammu & Kashmir had become live very early in 1949, and was thus a special area for vigilance by Army, the deployed units of paramilitary forces along under Army control.

Early in 1965 repeated Pakistani intrusions into the Rann of Kutch pointed to the need to restructure the border policing and Prime Minister Lal Bahadur Shastri decided to raise a centralised force for the border security. In May and June 1965, it was decided that the various State Armed Police Units manning the border of the country should be brought under the control of the Government of India with regional commands through a suitable central organisation for their immediate command and control. This contemplated new force was to discharge the duties of protecting life and property against depredations from across the border, prevent smuggling, infiltration and minor intrusions and to function under Army operational control when a major threat develops, and Army takes over. The Director General (equivalent to Lt. General of Army) was to head the force, and the onerous task of raising the force fell on K.F. Rustamji, the Inspector General of Police, Madhya Pradesh, who was specially selected for this purpose. Rustamji organised the work of the BSF headquarters in six directorates, each under the charge of an officer of the rank of Deputy Inspector General of Police/ Brigadier. To raise the force was a mammoth task but Rustamji most creditably accomplished it within a short span of time, and in terms of Article 356 of the Constitution, Central Government assumed direct responsibility for the security, of the country's enormous border. Border Security Force Act (47 of 1968), and rules postulate as under the role of BSF.

(a) Provides a sense of security among the people living in the border areas.
(b) Prevents trans-border crimes, unauthorised entry into and exit from the territory of India.
(c) Prevents smuggling or any other illegal activity.

The BSF Act states, "there shall be an armed force of the Union called the Border Security Force for ensuring the security of the border of India, and for matters connected therewith during hostilities. BSF men fight the enemy either by themselves or under the Army like any other armed forces of the Union which is also used for internal security duty.

(a) Indo-Pak War 1971: While Rustamji, with his foresight, imagination and confidence inspiring personality was grappling with the problems of standardisation of BSF organisation evolving a content of training which will neither be that of police nor the Army, but instead, would help to evolve a distinct personality for the BSF and establish an infrastructure that will cater to the needs of a growing force, the war was started on 3rd December

1971 by Pakistan. The immediate impact of the start of the war on the eastern side was Border Security Force involvement, not merely in holding ground but also deep penetration into East Pakistan together with *Muktibahini*, the latter seeking to liberate their country from the oppressive military regime of West Pakistan (In order to oppose the brutalities of the Pakistani Army People's Liberation Army — *Muktibahini* was already formed by the inhabitants). In respect of the advancing columns of the Army, BSF units often provided flank protection, defence of captured areas, and mopping up of stray Pakistani Army elements on the Western side, the BSF's role primarily was to hold ground against enemy attacks, both in Punjab and Jammu and Kashmir where the grit of the BSF was put to a severe and relentless test; and while withstanding the shock of the initial attack it fought some very gallant actions. In Rajasthan, BSF not only held grounds, it also made some notable advances. In the Rann of Kutch BSF personnel fought all by themselves and captured Chadbet, Naganpurkar, and Virwah from the enemy. BSF's contribution to victory was not achieved without suffering losses: 127 killed, 392 injured and 94 taken as prisoners of war. Announcing on December 16, 1971 in Parliament the surrender of East Pakistan Army, the Prime Minister paid glowing tributes to the Border Security Force for the role it played in this war.

The BSF is also deployed on internal security duties, combating extremists leading to their apprehension and seizure of arms and ammunition from them. As the objective is to make BSF the representative of the country as a whole, it is ensured that people from all states/regions are enrolled fairly and equitably on the basis of their population. The force has its own aeroplanes and its marine vessels. In the deserts of Rajasthan the force uses camels for its conveyance purposes of the personnel and for their requirements during their course of border patrolling. Some mountaineering expeditions (25,447 ft) were also successfully undertaken. In all BSF's work comprises — interception of intruders, apprehension of criminals such as smugglers and cattle lifters, and provision of security to villagers living on the borders against raids of criminals from across the border, particularly dacoits and kidnappers.

The Border Security Force, youngest of the forces of the country, has now emerged as a competent, and dependable force and is already stabilised as an Armed Force of the Union with a distinct personality, image and skill and possesses the requisite efficiency.

5. Railway Protection Force (RPF)

In 1854, Railways commenced its operations in India and the East Indian Railways employed certain staff designated as 'Police'. Seven years later, the Government of India too used the term 'Police' to denote its own force by enacting the Police Act of 1861, and deployed a contingent for the security of the railway with the owner companies bearing their upkeep. By 1882, as a result of the formal division of the Police Force deployed on the Railways into, 'Government Police' and 'Private (Company) Police', the Railway Companies directly assumed the responsibility of protection and security of their property, as well as the goods entrusted to them by public for carriage. For this, they appointed '*Chowkidars*' for various departments and placed them under the control of their local departmental heads. With the increase in the commercial traffic and consequential steep rise in the incidence of theft of goods entrusted to the railways for carriage, the '*Chowkidari*' system was reorganised after the First World War into, "Watch and Ward Organisation" under a single superior officer designated as Superintendent Watch and Ward — a system which continued up to 1954. Thus, for a full 100 years, though the force was used for providing security to the vital artery of national communication and economic progress, it did not have any legislative status. It was only on 29th August, 1957 that the Railway Protection Force Act (RPF Act) was enacted by the Parliament. For the maintenance of an effective and disciplined force, the RPF Act was modified by the Parliament *vide Act No. 60 of 1985* for the construction and maintenance of the force as an Armed Force of the Union. This was with a view to meet the emerging responsibilities which shall devolve on the force in the days to come and to make the force more efficient and effective instrument for discharging its responsibilities. The RPF has 95 per cent holding of arms.

A negligible number of women have also been inducted in the Force in big cities.

Duties and Powers: Section II of RPF Act 1985 lays down the following duties of the members of the force:

(i) Promptly to obey and execute all lawful orders issued by superior authority.
(ii) To protect and safeguard railway property.
(iii) To remove any obstruction in the movement of railway property.
(iv) To do any other act conducive to better protection and security of railway property.

Under Sections 12 and 13 of the RPF Act the RPF personnel can arrest without a warrant or on an order of a Magistrate any person causing obstruction in the discharge of his lawful duties; any person about to commit or suspected to have committed a cognizable offence relating to railway property; any person concealing himself within railway limits with a view to committing any cognizable offence relating to railway property; and any person committing or attempting to commit a cognizable offence involving imminent danger to the life of any person engaged in carrying on any work relating to railway property. For the investigation of such offences powers to search without warrant have been bestowed on officers of and above the rank of a *Naik*, in accordance with the provisions of the Code of Criminal Procedure.

Under the Railway Property (Unlawful Possession) Act the members of the Force have been empowered (Section 6) to arrest without a warrant any person concerned in an offence punishable under this Act, to investigate into such offence on the same lines as that of the Police Station Officer, and such enquiries made by the RPF Officers are deemed to be quasi-judicial proceedings within the meaning of Sections 193 and 228 of the Indian Penal Code (such powers of quasi-judicial proceedings are not given to the police). The offences are mostly relating to the unlawful possession of the railway property.

The RPF, being an Armed Force of the Union, has acquired certain powers under the Criminal Procedure Code (Section 131) for the dispersal of unlawful assemblies through its Gazetted Officer. Under the same code RPF officers and men cannot be prosecuted for their acts committed in the discharge of their official duties except with the previous sanction of the Central Government (Sections 45 and 197 (2) of Code of Criminal Procedure). The RPF personnel are regarded as Railway servants within the meaning of the Indian Railway Act, and as such they derive all the powers mentioned in the said Act which are necessary in the due discharge of their duties. There are various railway offences, petty or serious, for which RPF personnel have been empowered to arrest without a warrant the concerned offender.

The Force has considerably well-maintained the security of the vital artery of national communication and economic progress. It is headed by the Director General, who is generally an IPS officer.

6. Central Industrial Security Force (CISF)

For the protection of assets, prevention of loss, maintenance of security and watch over personnel of the various public sector undertakings, the Central Industrial Security Force (CISF) came into existence through Act No. 50 passed by the Parliament in 1968. It started with a modest beginning with about 2000 personnel and over the years, in order to meet the growing demands from the various industrial undertakings the CISF has a strength of about one lakh. It also provides fire protection to the industrial establishments through the fire wing, which has a training centre at Deoli (Rajasthan).

With a view to make the Force more effective and responsive to the needs of the undertakings, as also to extend its jurisdiction for the purpose of deployment for internal security duties in any part of the country, the Central Industrial Security Force Act (CISF Act), 1968 was amended in 1983 by the Parliament and the status and character of an armed force were bestowed on it. This is Act No. 14, which was subsequently amended by Act No. 20 of 1989, and it made the force even more effective. After declaring the CISF an Armed force of the Union, the Government had deployed the CISF for internal security duties, emergent law and order duties, election duties *etc.*, throughout the country.

In order to keep pace with the technological advancements in Industrial security, the technical wing of the force came into being in 1986. This wing is actively engaged in identifying the advanced security gadgets in and outside the country, creating awareness about their utility among the force personnel, the security managers, and senior executives of the undertakings and providing expert consultancy services to all concerned.

The CISF is under the Home Ministry and is engaged in performing the following duties:

(a) Ensuring effective security and protection of public sector undertakings, on specific demands.

(b) Providing fire safety cover to the public sector undertakings.

(c) Deploying the force for internal security, law and order duties in any part of the country, as and when ordered by the Indian Government (Ministry of Home Affairs).

(d) Modernising the Industrial Security and fire protection system by introducing scientific gadgets and providing export security consultancy services to the industrial undertakings.

In order to make the Force assertive and effective in the discharge of its duties, the CISF personnel have been given wide powers of arrest *etc.*, of a person concerned or reasonably suspected to have been concerned with any cognizable offence which relates to any property belonging to or in the possession of, any industrial undertaking, as the primary role of the CISF is to ensure protection and security of men, material, buildings, and installations vital to the industrial undertakings owned by the Government, both of the Central and the States.

It has created a special task force with commando trained personnel to meet any exigency that may arise. The Force collects intelligence in advance about disruptive activities of trade unions. The scope of protection and security of industries by CISF extends to a wide variety of undertakings such as:

(a) Space Centres, (b) Super Thermal Power Plants, (c) Major Ports, (d) Steel Plants, (e) Fertilizer Plants, (f) Coal Fields, (g) Ship Yards, (h) Oil Refineries, (i) Petrochemical Complex, (j) ONGC Installation, (k) Hydel-power projects *etc.* In terms of physical strength the force is deployed from Nagaland in East to Gujarat in the West, and from Kashmir in the North to Kerala in the South in over 200 industrial installations.

About 80 per cent of the incumbents are on deputation from the various state police forces and 20 per cent of vacancies are filled by absorptions of persons from various industrial undertakings. The CISF has its own training centres for imparting necessary training to its members. It is headed by senior IPS officer, who is designated as Director General of Central Industrial Security Force.

7. Rapid Action Force (RAF)

This is an extraordinary police force created in 1993 by the Central Government under the direct control of the Home Ministry for deployment in disturbed regions with a view to quell riots, which the local police, for some reason or the other, are unable to control effectively. As the name suggests, the members of this Force are specially trained to take quickest possible action immediately after their deployment with the sole object to restore peace and tranquillity *vis-a-vis* the normal living conditions of the people. More or less, RAF is a 'Commando force' which has excelled in its professional abilities after continuous and rigorous training, which enables them to be always in a state of efficient preparedness for dealing with any eventuality.

13

State Police Forces Part I

It may be remembered that prior to the 15th August 1947, there were about 665 Princely States, big or small, in the country. The rest of the Indian sub-continent was under the British regime. (The evolution of the Police Force under the British Regime has already been mentioned in earlier chapters). The Princely State Rulers, more or less, had adopted the same pattern of police organisation as was found in British India. Actually, all their top police officers were taken on deputation from the British India-Police cadre, and they had developed these forces on the British India Police Pattern, except some local nomenclatures in the designation of the Police Officers and personnel. However, the terms, '*Darogah*', '*Kotwal*', '*Foujdar*', '*Choukidars*', were functionally synonymous to Sub-Inspector, in British India. After Independence and during 1947 to 1957, *i.e.* before the reorganisation of states on linguistic basis, the Police Forces of the various Princely States were organised and they functioned as before. Obviously, they continued to maintain certain peculiarities, which lapsed when the reorganisation of the states on linguistic basis was completed in 1957. The various units were integrated forming a combined cadre in each hierarchical rank.

1. Imperial Police (IP) and Indian Police Service (IPS)

Prior to Independence superior Police Officers belonged to the Indian (Imperial) Police Force were appointed by the Secretary of State through competitive examinations. The first open competition for the service was held in England in June 1893, and 10 top candidates were appointed as Probationary Assistant Superintendent of Police. The number of candidates recruited in England during the next few years were:

Province	Year			
	1894	1895	1896	1897
Madras	3	2	3	2
Bombay	1	—	1	—
Bengal and Assam	2	2	2	2
Northwest Frontier Province and Orissa	1	2	1	2
Central Provinces	—	1	—	1
Total	7	7	7	7

These were covenanted services, and the incumbents wore shoulder badges of their provinces in which they were appointed, such as B.P. for Bengal Police *etc.*, from 1907 officers were directed to wear the letter I.P. on their epaulets to distinguish them from the Provincial Services Officers. The sanctioned strength of the I.P. Officers in British India was 743 in 1924 of which 77 (10 per cent) were Indians. In 1946, it was 721 of which 221 (30 per cent) were Indians. (*To Guard My People — The History of Indian Police* by Sir Percival Griffith (197), pp. 95-100 and 427). Thus, it will be apparent that the I.P. officers had formalised the Police Forces of the states, as well of most of the Princely States. The first batch of the Indian Police Service (IPS), who were synonymous to the Imperial Police were recruited in 1948 through competitive examinations under the Emergency Recruitment Scheme to fill up the vacancies caused by the departure of British and Muslim Officers after the partition of the sub-continent in 1947 and suspension of recruitment to I.P. The Provincial Police Service Officers and war service recruits were appointed to IPS. In 1951, the All India Services Act (Act LXI of 1951) was enacted and Rules were framed regarding the recruitment, training and conditions of service *etc.* Now, after appointment, the IPS Officers undergo the basic training course for a period of one year in the Sardar Vallabhbhai Patel National Police Academy, Hyderabad. In the 31 states of the Union, the total authorised strength of the IPS Officers was 3312 in 1991 (Source — Ministry of Home Affairs, Government of India), and this figure included the Provincial Service promotees.

2. Police Hierarchy

The head of the State Police is the Director General of the equivalent to the rank of Lt. General in the Army. He is assisted by some Inspectors General of Police and Deputy Inspectors General in the work of administration and supervision of the entire Police Force. Each district is in the charge of a Superintendent of Police. Down this hierarchical ladder there are Deputy Superintendent, Inspectors, Sub-inspectors, Assistant Sub-inspectors, Head Constables and Constables.

The force in each district has a 'Reserve Armed Force' to deal with emergencies such as disturbances and the like. In a way this is the Armed Wing of the Force, and it has special physical conditions for its recruitment and training. The routine work of policing, prevention and detection of crime, maintenance of law and order is done by the normal police. A separate department — Criminal Investigation Department exists to help the normal police in detection of special form of crimes and collection of cirminal intelligence. The Special Branch attached to this wing deals with political intelligence.

Recruitment for Constabulary is done in each district. The recruits are trained at various training centres established in each State. For the post of Sub-inspectors recruitment is done on the State level through competitive examination. After selection the candidates are trained in the Police Training College of that State. Depending on the work done Sub-inspectors are promoted to the rank of inspectors, who are promoted as Deputy Superintendents and Superintendents. Such departmental promotions are rare and are based on 'Proportionate quota system'.

However, there are rare instances in which a Sub-inspector of Police had retired as Deputy Inspector General of Police till 1950. A constable is promoted to the rank of Head Constable, who in turn, is promoted to the rank of Sub-inspector. The number of promotion on each cadre is so less that it does not serve as incentives to all ranks from Constables to Deputy Superintendents.

All the above is the general pattern of Police organisation in each State, and therefore, only peculiar features of each State Police Force have been mentioned against each of them. They are seriated alphabetically, along with their approximate strength.

3. Andhra Pradesh

In the erstwhile Hyderabad State of Nizam, Policing was performed by irregular troops called 'Aligal Pattern', 'Sibandi' peons and other village servants. In the trial of the accused and in bringing home the charges against them, all kinds of threats and torture were used. The 'Pargana Naibs' were armed with complete authority to arrest, liberate and punish these people. The village servants, in return for the police duties performed by them, held land free of assessment, and received a share of the yield from the villagers. The 'Sibandi' peons were paid Rs. 3/- per month from the land revenue of the village. In 1885, the Police Force was established in the city under the *Kotwal* (The present-day Police Commissioner is still referred to as *Kotwal*), The District Police was kept under the control of '*Muhtamin*' (Superintendent) assisted by *Ameen* (Inspector), *Jamadar* (Sub-Inspector), *Dafedar* (Head Constable) *etc.* This Force was to function in the '*Diwani*' territory which was directly administered by the Nizam. The areas which were under Zamindars known as *Jagirdars*, however, continued to be policed by the *Jagirdars* themselves.

By 1872-73, the head of the entire police administration of the State was called '*Sardar Muhtamin*' and apart from acting as the Head of the Police Force, he also acted as the Secretary to the Government for the Police Department. Soon this post was named Inspector General of Police. In 1912-13, the whole Police Force was reorganised by Henkins who was Inspector General for over 22 years from 1897, and the various independent Police functionaries like *Paigas*, *Jagirs* and *Samanthans* were ultimately brought under the control of Inspector General. As a result of the 'Police Action' in September 1948, the Nizam merged the Hyderabad State into Indian Union as Part 'B' State.

Immediately after the Police Action, the Communist mounted violent movement in the Telengana districts of Raichur, Nalgonda, Karimnagar, Medak, Adilabad *etc.* At the height of the trouble more than 11,000 officers and men from the various Police Forces of the neighbouring states of Madhya Pradesh, Madras and Bombay in addition to 26,000 strength of Hyderabad Armed Police combated the terrorists and partially succeeded in controlling terrorism. On Ist November 1956, the state of Hyderabad merged into neighbouring districts of Madras, Madhya Pradesh and Bombay on linguistic basis on the eve of Reorganisation of States. The Kannada speaking districts of the State merged into Karnataka, the Marathi speaking districts amalgamated with Maharashtra, and only the Telugu speaking districts were left to be policed by the Andhra Pradesh. Andhra Pradesh Police Commission was set up in 1983-84 in order to render the Force efficient. There is no separate Police Act for Andhra Pradesh where Indian Police Act of 1861 is applicable.

The Hyderabad City includes Secunderabad and like in all big cities, the head of the Police Force is the Commissioner.

According to 1991 census, the population of the State was 66,304,854 with about 32 lakhs Scheduled Tribes, and the area is 275,068 sq. km. There are about 750 women police in the State. Hyderabad is the capital. The strength of the Force is about 75,000.

4. Andaman and Nicobar Islands

The Union Territory was constituted on November 1, 1956. The islands are in two groups — Andaman and Nicobar. The majority of the population is of Indian origin and there are few hundred tribals. The Inspector General of Police is the head of the Police Force. As per 1991 census the population was 277,989 with about 22,000 Scheduled Tribes and the area of the state is 8249 Sq. kms. The capital is Port Blair. The strength is about 2,000.

5. Arunachal Pradesh

Government of India, Foreign and Political Department Notification of 1914 provided that the Assam Frontier Tracts Regulation of 1880 should extend to the hills inhabited by Abors, Miris, Mishmis, Singphos, Khamlies, Bhutias, Akas and Daflas. The three frontier tracts — Central and Eastern Section, Western Section and Lakhimpur Frontier Tract are collectively known as North East Frontier Tract. In 1921, these tracts were included in the 'Backward' tracts under Section 52 of the Government of India Act 1915/1919. From 1937 to 1943 by various administrative changes the new administrative unit was known as Tirap Frontier Tract. By alike various changes after Independence, a separate territory collectively known as North East Frontier Agency (NEFA) was formed by the integration of five divisions of — Kameng Frontier Division; Subansiri Frontier Division; Tirap Frontier Division; Siang Frontier Division; Lohit Frontier Division. The administration of this area, until then under control of the Ministry of External Affairs, was taken over by the Ministry of Home Affairs and in 1965 and in 1972 (21st January) the Territory (NEFA) was constituted into the Union Territory of Arunachal Pradesh under the provisions of Section 7 of the Northeastern Areas Reorganisation Act of 1971 and thus, it ceased to be a tribal area within the State of Assam. By gradual administrative process on February 20, 1987 this Union Territory became a full-fledged state of Arunachal Pradesh under a Governor with its own Legislative Assembly. The Police Force of the State is headed by Inspector General of Police. According to 1991 census the population was 858,392 with 5 lakhs Scheduled Tribes. Police strength is about 4,000 in an area of 83,743 Sq. km. The capital is Itanagar.

6. Assam

The Police Force of today is the result of a continuous process of development since the occupation of Assam by British in 1826. Under the Ahom Kings or even earlier to them there did not seem to be any organised Police Force. In 1885, Grange, the Civil Administrator of Nowgong District formed a small unit of 750 officers and men, and it was called as the 'Cachar Levy', which was mostly utilised for the protection of the estate owners. The 'Cachar Levy' was subsequently known as the 'Military Police of Assam' or the 'Frontier Police' and this was the origin of 'Assam Rifles' of today.

Till 1874, Assam formed administratively a part of the Province of Bengal, and in that year, it was constituted as independent unit under the Chief Commissioner. In 1876 the administration of the Police was conducted from the Provincial Head Quarters of Shillong. The Police at that time was divided into four branches — Frontier Police; Civil Police; Municipal Police; and Rural Police, in 1878 the Force was classified into two wings — Civil Police for the discharge of ordinary civil functions; and Frontier or Armed Police for quasi-military work.

The new Province of Eastern, Bengal and Assam was formed in 1905 and the Provincial Headquarters was shifted from Shillong to Dacca. The new Province of Assam came into existence in 1912. In 1917 the Military Police were named as Assam Rifles.

During the Second World War 1939-1946 there was a tremendous increase in incidental work of the Police Force and Policing of sensitive, problem-ridden and strategically located border states like Assam was a difficult proposition, and it continued to be so ever since the attainment of Independence following the partition of the country. The Sylhet district was transferred to East Pakistan and the capital was shifted from Dacca to Shillong. Several problems connected with the partition of the country kept the Police Force over busy from 1947 to 1950, and the Force proved inadequate for various complex problems.

The disturbed conditions at Naga Hills arising out of the activities of the followers of A.Z. Phizo claiming independence for the Nagas posed a new problem to the Assam Police in 1956, and the following years. The terrorist activities still continue.

In 1953 the administration of the Village Defence Organisation was taken over by the Police. With unflinching devotion to their duties the force faced the situation arising out of the unprovoked and treacherous Chinese aggression of 1962, and maintained the law and order in the State. In 1965, the Pakistanis mounted a novel aggression by sending in a planned manner large number of infiltrators to the State. The threat was very grave, and it tended to upset the communal harmony and the economic well-being as the infiltrators made a rush for the fertile cultivable land of the State. The Force was augmented to meet the situation. Threat by Pakistan infiltrators continued up to 1971, and subsequently, it was carried forward by the infiltration of Bangladesh and imposed sever strain on the Force.

Since the early sixties the people of Garo Hills and United Khasi and Jaintia Hills started an agitation demanding status of autonomy within the Union of India, and the Force had to tackle this turbulent situation. The Government finally recognised the logic in the demand for autonomy of the Hill people and created the State of Meghalaya with effect from 21st February 1973. Mizo Hills has also been carved out of the State of Assam to a Union Territory with effect from 21st February, 1972 terrorism still continues, if not unabated, off and on it erupts. Throughout the Force sustained many casualties.

The Force is headed by a Director General. The area of the State is 78,438 Sq. km. and the population was 22,294,562 with about 17 lakhs Scheduled Tribes, according to 1971 census as no census could be held after that. The capital is Guwahati. The strength is about 80,000.

7. Bihar

In 1765, the East India Company succeeded as the *Diwan* with the disintegration of the Imperial authority of the Mughals and by 1790 the Company took over the criminal administration of the State (It was a portion of Bengal, Bihar, Orissa and Assam).

Reorganisation of the Force took place in the same pattern as mentioned in earlier chapters. The Indian Police Commission, set up in 1902, made various recommendations for the overall improvement in the Force. On the basis of these recommendations the Bengal Police was reorganised in 1906 and Bihar and Orissa came to be constituted as a separate province in 1912. In 1936, Bihar was separated from Orissa. As a result of States' Reorganisation in 1956 the district of Purulia was transformed from Bihar to West Bengal. Bihar Military Police is the State Reserve Force. The Force is headed by the Director General. There are some women police in the State. According to 1991 census, the population was 86,338,853 with 60 lakhs Scheduled Tribes, and the area is 1,73,876 Sq. km. The capital is Patna. The strength is about 80,000.

8. Chandigarh (Union Territory)

The Union Territory of Chandigarh came into existence on November 1, 1966. It is the capital of both Haryana and Punjab. The Police Department was headed by the Senior Superintendent of Police, directly under the control of the Home Secretary of the Union Territory, who functioned also as an ex-officio Inspector

General of Police. In the year 1979, the post of Inspector General of Police was created.

The Police Force have very important tasks to perform, *i.e.*, looking after the security of the two Governors, two Chief Ministers, Council of Ministers of two States, and several important dignitaries, who happen to visit Chandigarh frequently. Recently, it was continued to be threatened by terrorist activists of Pakistanis and Khalistanis.

The area of the state is 114 Sq. km. and it had a population of 640,725 according to 1991 census. The capital is Chandigarh. The strength is about 4,000.

9. Dadra and Nagar Haveli (Union Territory)

The Dadra and Nagar Haveli was liberated from the Portuguese Rule on 2nd August 1954, and since then it is under the Government of India as an Union Territory. The Governor of Goa, Daman and Diu is the Administrator for Dadra and Nagar Haveli. The total population of Dadra and Nagar Haveli is about 1,40,000 having 80 per cent of the *Adivasi* population (Tribals). It consists of one district having an area of 491 Sq. km. The capital is Silvasa. The State has only one district having two police stations, namely Silvasa and Khanvel and is headed by Assistant Inspector General of Police, Daman and Diu and Dadra and Nagar Haveli. The strength is about 200.

10. Delhi (Union Territory)

Delhi, the country's capital, has a long history ever since 1237 A.D. of policing through the famed institution of the *Kotwal*. Organised form of policing was established by the British after the 1857 War of Independence. Till 1911, Delhi was the part of undivided Punjab. Then it was made enclave by taking out chunks of territory from Punjab, Uttar Pradesh, Rajasthan and it was created by the British, who wanted to shift their capital from Calcutta to Delhi, which was continuously the imperial city under many dynasties in the past centuries.

The first Commissioner of Delhi was appointed in 1912 and he was vested with the powers and functions of the Inspector General of Police. According to 1912 Gazette, Delhi district was under the control of the Deputy Inspector General of Police with its headquarters at Ambala. The Police Force in Delhi district was commanded by the Superintendent of Police. The strength of Delhi Police was 2 Inspectors, 27 Sub-inspectors and about 1000 Constables. The Rural Police was in the charge of two Inspectors with their headquarters at Sonepat and Ballabhgarh, there were 10 police stations under three *tehsils*.

The city of Delhi had three police stations. In 1946, the Delhi Police was reorganised in the wake of partition followed by a large influx of refugee population, widespread communal riots and high incidence of crime. On February 16, 1948, the first Inspector General of Police was appointed. The total strength of Delhi Police was increased to about 8000 with one Inspector General of Police and 8 Superintendents of Police by 1951. After the States Reorganisation in 1956, Delhi became a Union Territory with the Centre taking on the direct responsibility of its governance.

By 1961, the total strength of Delhi Police increased to 12,000 officers and men. As an entity it lacks an identity of its own tradition, for the simple reason that its officers never belonged to a single, separate cadre and have always been a part of a conglomerate cadre of deputationists. From 1989, efforts were made and measures were initiated to give the Delhi Police its own distinctive identity, and its personality to which all officers and men could relate emotionally.

The Delhi Police has made a conscious beginning to bring the women police in the forefront in various spheres of police activities.

In addition to 10,285 Home Guards, out of which 440 are women. The scheme of special Police Officers, introduced in 1985, has been operating with good success. Under this scheme, any able-bodied adult, who does not have a criminal background, is entitled to function as a Special Police Officer on honourary basis in order to patrol the streets, non-addiction, de-addiction camp, promote self-defence camps for young girls in the crusade against eve-teasing *etc*.

At present, the strength of Force is about 50,653 officers and men under the Commissioner of Police, who is of the rank of Inspector General of Police. According to 1991 census, the population comprised of 93,70,475 with an area of about 1,485 Sq. km.

11. Goa, Daman and Diu

The Portuguese settlements of Goa, Daman and Diu were merged with India as a centrally administered state on August 11, 1961. Goa achieved a separate statehood, and Daman and Diu were delinked from it. The Police Force of Goa, prior to its merger was of the nature of a para-military force of the Portuguese Government. After the merger Goa Police followed the Bombay Police Manual for its guidelines. The whole police force is headed by Inspector General of Police. The area of Goa comprised 3858 Sq. km. and that of Daman and Diu is 111 Sq. km, and the total population was over two lakhs with about 11,000 Scheduled Tribes as per census of 1991. The state capital is Panaji. The strength is about 3,000.

12. Gujarat

Gujarat had been a part of the great Empires of the Mauryas and the Guptas — up to the 13th century. Hindu Rulers maintained the indigenous Police System based on the *Arthasastra* of Kautilya. With the end of the 13th century Gujarat passed through the Muslim rule and evolved a synthesis of Hindu-Muslim culture along with their policing system.

Until the commencement of Independence in 1947, Gujarat was a part of bilingual Bombay State. On 1st May 1960, it was broken up into two states, namely Maharashtra and Gujarat on account of the Reorganisation of States. Several Princely States were also merged in the Gujarat State. The cities of Ahmedabad, Baroda, Surat and Rajkot have Commissioner of Police as the head of the City Police Force. The whole Police Force is headed by Director General of Police. The area of the State is 196,024 Sq. km. and population was 41,174,060 with about five lakhs Scheduled Tribes according to 1991 census. The state capital is Gandhinagar. The strength is about 63,000.

Haryana

Haryana Police began its history long back to the *Vedic* Ages. The Kurukshetra and *Mahabharata* was situated in Haryana. It remained as an adjunct to Delhi till 1857. When the British Rule crushed the rebellions of the Nawab of Jhajjar, Bahadurgarh, the Raja of Ballabhgarh and Rao Tula Rao of Rewari, the territories were handed over to the rulers of Patiala, Nabha and Jind. Later on Haryana was formed into a separate State on November 1, 1966.

Its area is 44,212 Sq. km. and the population was 16,317,715 according to 1991 census. The state capital is Chandigarh. The force is headed by a Director General. The strength is 30,000.

14. Himachal Pradesh

The State of Himachal Pradesh came into existence on April 15, 1948, following the integration of the Princely States of Chamba, Mandi, Suket, Sirmaur and 26 small hill states of Shimla Hills. Subsequently, Bilaspur State was also merged with Himachal Pradesh. Financial resources of these Princely States were not adequate enough to maintain regular Police Force and the existing Police Force had to perform several multifarious duties entirely unconnected with the police work. In the late thirties a common Police Force with a joint Police Adviser, who was an officer of the Indian Police, was created. A common training centre was started at Solan in Baghat State.

After the formation of the State in 1948, the Police Force was streamlined. A senior Superintendent of Police, who was a retired officer from Punjab, was appointed to head the Police administration in the State under the control of the Inspector General of Police for three States of Delhi, Himachal Pradesh and Ajmer. In 1953, a separate Inspector General of Police was appointed for Himachal Pradesh.

As a result of creation of a separate State of Haryana and the reorganisation of Punjab State in 1966, the districts of Kangra, Shimla, Kullu and Lahaul Spiti were transferred to Himachal Pradesh.

The Head of the Force is Director General. The area of the State is 55,673 Sq. km. As per 1991 census the population was about 52 lakhs, of which about two lakhs are Scheduled Tribes. The capital is Shimla. The strength is 12,000.

15. Jammu & Kashmir

The State of Jammu & Kashmir is distinct in many ways. Since ages, different cultures and religions streamed into the State, and it has acquired the distinction of harbouring three religions of the world in its three geographical regions of Jammu (Hindu), Kashmir Valley (Muslims) and Ladakh (Buddhists). In the past, these three religions had strived, and their followers co-existed with a degree of harmony, amity and tolerance until 1947, when Pakistan invaded it resulting in the total disruption of communal amity and harmony. Constitutionally also it is distinct from the rest of the Indian States due to the special status given to it in terms of Article 370 of the Constitution of the Republic of India.

More than three-forth of the State is mountainous and road transport is the main mode of communication. The railway head is at Jammu. Ladakh region, except for airlink, remains out of bounds for about six months as the Shrinagar-Leh road remains covered under metres of deep snow.

Kashmir signifies the crown of the country which has at the cost of thousands of lives been defended against foreign aggression and international mischievous action on several occasions in the post-Independence era. Three wars have been fought with Pakistan in 1947-48, 1965 and 1970-71. Though the military campaigns by Pakistan failed to force any change in the geography of the State after 1947, the attempts at creating conditions of instability in the State have continued unabated by Pakistan. It is proxy war in which methods of spying, subversion, sabotage and terrorism by well-trained armed bands have been continuously adopted by Pakistan through its Inter Service Intelligence (ISI) Wing. Heavy loss of life and destruction to property, both of the State and the public, is almost an everyday feature. There is neither law, nor order, there is no peace and tranquillity, but disorder and disturbance throughout the State.

All these features combined to demand a Police Force, which is professionally competent and committed to serve a cause which is greater than of routine policing. The Police Force has to be prepared, motivated and fully equipped to face the increasing and multi-dimensional challenges in the context of the present security scenario.

The Director General is at the apex of the Police Force. To what extent this Police Force has been moulded is significant from the sacrifices that police personnel have made since 1983, while facing the menace of terrorism and forces of disruption and disorder. At present they are virtually engaged in fighting a proxy war with Pakistan shoulder to shoulder with security forces to safeguard the unity and integrity of the country.

The area of the State is 222,236 Sq. km. Of this total area 1,21,000 Sq. km. is under the occupation of Pakistan and China. The population was about 80 lakhs with a Muslim majority of over 40 lakhs (1991 census). The State touches the international boundaries of Afghanistan, Russia (USSR), China, Pakistan and Tibet, and strategically it is not only important but also vulnerable and hence is the greatest need for perfect vigilance and policing. The State capital is Jammu during the winter and Srinagar during the Summer. The strength is 32,000.

16. Karnataka

From 1799, after the death of Tipu Sultan, the British introduced a resemblance of a police system for maintenance of law and order by training a small but selected body of infantry and cavalry men who were supplemented by the 'Kanda Char' — police peons. They were under the '*Dewan*' assisted by three Commissioners and '*Amildars*' in charge of 115 to 120) *talukas*. At that time the Bengal Regulation XX of 1817 was made applicable to the police. Late during 1866, the Indian Police Act of 1861 was made applicable to the district of Bangalore and Bangalore Town, and an officer from Madras was placed in charge of Bangalore district. This was the erstwhile princely State of Mysore. The general management of the Police was vested with the Deputy Commissioner and in the district and *Amildar* in the *talukas*, the latter had an Inspector under his command. After the rendition in 1881, the direction of Police was placed in the hands of the *Dewan* and the Deputy Commissioners. Thereafter, a Police Secretary was appointed to assist the *Dewan*. In 1885, the post of Police Secretary was abolished, and the post of the Inspector General of the Police was created. The police forces of Mysore and Bangalore had a police force of their own. The municipalities used to bear the expenditure pertaining to Bangalore Town Police and that of the Rural was met through the provincial funds. By 1894, the system changed, and the cost of the entire police was being met from provincial funds.

Between 1930-39 and in various stages the *Amildar* was divested of his control over *Taluka* police. The powers of the

Deputy Commissioner and the Superintendent were defined and the latter was given sufficient powers to have control over the force. The police set-up of Coorg was not well-organised under the Raja. By the application of Indian Police Act of 1861 a proper policing system was applied both to the Mysore and Coorg States.

The new State of Karnataka came into existence on November 1, 1956. The erstwhile State of Mysore with 10 districts, 4 districts from erstwhile State of Bombay, 3 districts from erstwhile State of Hyderabad, 1 district and 1 *Taluka* from erstwhile State of Madras and part of Coorg state were integrated into one unit. Consequently, the new State of Karnataka had five different police systems, Acts, Rules, Manuals and even uniforms when it was formed. In all these spheres uniformity was brought and by 1965 the entire force was reorganised. The State enacted the Police Act in 1963, and brought it into force with effect from April 2, 1965. The city of Bangalore has a Police Commissioner as the head of the city police.

There is a Water Front Police for North Kannada (North Kanara) district for patrolling through motor launches. There are also some women police officers and women in the organisation as and when required to be used. In addition, there is Industrial Security Force under a Deputy Inspector General of Police to look after the security of the growing State Public Undertakings.

Bangalore is the capital of the State. The Director General is the head of the State Police Force. The area is 191,791 Sq. km. with 44,817,398 population having about 19 lakhs Scheduled Tribes according to 1991 census. The strength is 50,000.

17. Kerala

The State of Kerala was formed in 1956 by merging the Princely States of Travancore and Cochin and the Malabar district of the former Madras Presidency, consequent upon the Reorganisation of States on linguistic basis. The Kerala Police Force also naturally evolved from the police forces of these three distinct regions. During the last 33 years, Kerala Police has crystallised a force with a single and common identity.

In 1809, in the Princely State of Travancore a force called '*Kaval*' (Guards) with a strength of 200 was instituted. In 1881, a Police Act, modelled on the Indian Police Act of 1861, was enacted and the force was reorganised. In Cochin, a rudimentary police set-up was established in 1812 with '*Dandedars*' and '*Darogahs*' but in 1835, they were substituted by '*Kotwals*'. This was merely a designation change, and the basic police function did not alter. In the Malabar region, which was a part of the Madras Presidency, a modicum of policing was started in 1800 with '*Kolkars*', '*Dafedars*' and '*Jamedars*' as police officers. In 1801, it was substituted by the Malabar Police. Malabar Special Police was instituted in 1912.

In the early days of Kerala, Anti-corruption Branch was taken out of the Police Department and formed into a separate department. Perhaps, Kerala is the singular State where the Anti-corruption Department has been completely separated from the Police Force. There are few women police also.

The Kerala Police Force is headed by a Director General. The area of the State is 38,863 Sq kms. and had a population of 29,011,237 persons with about three lakhs Scheduled Tribes according to 1991 census. The state capital is Trivendrum. The strength is 50,000.

18. Lakshadweep (**Union Territory**)

Former Lakshadweep, Minicoy and Amindivi group of costal islands in the Arabian Sea had been grouped into one administrative unit in November 1956, and since then it is recognised as a union territory. Only 10 islands, out of a total of 20 islands are inhabited. Till 1965, Police Officers and men working in the islands, were on deputation from the neighbouring States of Karnataka, Tamil Nadu and Kerala. The capital of the state was Calicut, though the islands lie 200 miles offshore of the country. In 1964, the capital was shifted to Kavarathy, one of the islands in this group. The first batch of policemen for this union territory was recruited in 1964. The Code of Criminal Procedure and the Indian Penal Code were applied to this territory with effect from 1-11-1967. A Superintendent of Police heads the Force. The Administrator of the State, who is an officer of the Indian Administrative Service, is the ex-officio head of the Police Force.

The area of the State is 32 Sq. km. and the population was 51,681 according to 1991 census. Out of this 38,173 were Muslims and known as '*Moplas*', who had revolted against the British Government in 1906-08. This rebellion was crushed down by the Assam Rifles-men deployed from Assam. The capital is Kavarthy. The strength is about 400.

14

State Police Forces Part II

1. Madhya Pradesh

Madhya Pradesh was formerly known as Central Provinces and Berar before the Independence of the country on 15th August 1947. The Government of the Central Provinces (Berar was subsequently added in about 1902 as acceded territory from the dominion of Nizam-Hyderabad in order to pay off the loan amount due to British Government of India) administered by the East India Company was transferred to the British Crown in 1858 when the East India Company was wounded up. As per the recommendations of the Police Commission of 1860, the Central Province was constituted as a separate administrative unit under a Chief Commissioner. The Province comprised Sauger and Narmada territories, and the Nagpur State together with certain other tracts acquired at various times. Lt. Col. H.D. Taylor, who was appointed as the first Inspector General of Police, organised purely a civil constabulary out of the Nagpur irregular Police Force, regular Zilla Police, Military Police and '*Sibandis*'. Contingents of cavalry regiments were incorporated in the Mulki horse to form a body of mounted police. At that time, there were a few police stations (Station Houses) and outposts in the charge of *Darogah*. The important landlords were held responsible for the maintenance of law and order within their areas. Through *Darogahs* the offenders were arrested and sent up for trials to courts. The *Darogah* used to receive 10 per cent of the value of the stolen property received by way of incentive. The Police Force was further organised and officered under the Inspector General of Police and sufficiently grew in strength with 135 station houses and 215 outposts *etc.* However, the writ of the new police did not run in 40,000 sq. miles of territory which lay entirely in the hands of Zamindars, who dispensed a sort of 'rude, rough and tardy' justice of their own, financial impediment being the major reason for uniform implementation of the new police system. Like the Zamindars, there were '*Malguzars*' (Landlords), who were legitimate masters of '*Kotwals*', had the sole responsibility, for the immediate report of all crimes and for prompt and efficient aid to the Police in making investigation and arrests. They were hereditary.

In 1864 several important changes were made in the organisation of the Police Force. Like other provinces in British India, reorganisation of the Police was affected on the basis of the recommendations of the Police Commission 1902.

Soon after Independence, the merger of 14 Princely States of Chhatisgarh Agency, with a area of 31,000 Sq. miles and population of 30 lakhs took place with the State of Madhya Pradesh. A Police Reorganisation Committee was appointed in 1951 in order to bring about uniformity in the various integrated forces.

The Madhya Bharat Union was formed in 1948, and it comprised of 25 Princely States. Vindhya Pradesh was the second union of Princely States, which was also formed in 1948 by the merger of 35 Princely States. Bhopal was another Princely State. All these states had IP officers on deputation from Madhya Pradesh as their heads in the rank of the Inspector General of Police. On 1st November 1956, all these Princely States were integrated with the State of Madhya Pradesh under one command. Uniformity in all spheres of Police working (including railway police) was an arduous task and under the most capable stewardship of stalwart K.F. Rustamji it was accomplished smoothly and within a short time.

The area of the State is 443,446 Sq. km. with 66,135,862 population having two lakhs Scheduled Tribes according to 1991 census. There are women police in the State. The Police Force is headed by a Director General. The capital is Bhopal. The strength is about 90,000.

2. Maharashtra

The history of the Police Force in Maharashtra is closely related to the development of Police Forces in other parts of the sub-continent. When the whole of India was under the Muslim

Rule of Aurangzeb (1658-1707), Maharashtra was ruled by the Maratha King Shivaji and after his death his heirs and the Peshwas. After the commencement of the British Rule in India in 1858, the Government of British India took various organisational steps to streamline the police force in order to improve the functional efficiency. While these experiments in the police as well as in other administrative branches of the Government were going as in Bengal and Madras Presidency, most of the area now constituting Maharashtra State, except Bombay, was independent of the British Rule. The defeat of the Maratha Forces (Peshwa) at Koregoen and Ashti and their subsequent surrender to the British on June 18, 1818, transferred the rule of the Maratha country to the British. The District Police Arrangements under the Marathas were practically identical with those that existed in the 17th century. Each village maintained its own watchmen under the direct control of the village headman (Patil), and remunerated their services with rent-free land as perquisites. The watchmen were assisted by groups or gangs of tribes such as *Ramoshis*, *Bhils*, who were attached to each village or group of villages and resided on the outskirts and they functioned under the control of Patil who was answerable to the Government for any crime committed in the jurisdiction of his village, so much so that, in the event of non-recovery of the stolen property the Patil had to compensate the loss to the victim. The delinquent village was forced to indemnify the owners by imposition of punitive fines specially in case of any disturbances committed in the village. '*Mamlatdar*' was an officer of the Government at each *Taluka* (*Tehsil*) and a sizeable force called '*Sibandi*' was given to him for deployment in the *Taluka* to meet out any exigency.

Under the rule of Bajirao II, the District Police system was modified by the appointment of '*Tapasnis*' (present-day Investigating Officer), who was charged with the responsibility of discovering and seizing offenders. These officers were independent of the *Mamlatdars*, and they were directly working under the Government (like the Central Bureau of Investigation of today). In urban areas Magisterial and police powers were vested with the '*Kotwal*', who also performed municipal duties and all those functions ascribed to '*Nagerka*' or Police Superintendent mentioned in the *Arthasastra* of Kautilya. The criminal justice of the Marathas, although was rough and ready, then British Government rightly diagnosed that this form of justice was best suited the country at that time and was better appreciated than the sophisticated system of the British. In order to control effectively popular out-breaks and disturbances arising out of anti-British Government agitation Auxiliary Police Forces, such as Khandesh Bhil Corps, Ahmadnagar Police Corps, Ratnagiri Rangers, Thane Rangers and Ghat Light Infantry were formed and those were the semi-military police of modern times.

In 1843 Sind was annexed and formed part of the Bombay Presidency. In 1890, the Bombay District Police Act was passed, and the District Police of Bombay Presidency were reorganised. A force mostly comprising Bhandaries was formed for the watch and ward of the Bombay city. In 1902, the Bombay City Police Act (IV), which consolidated the provisions of the prevailing enactments and vested the control of the police in the Commissioner, was passed.

On the basis of 1902 All India Police Commission, the Police Force of the Bombay Province was reorganised. Until partition of the country in 1947, the territorial jurisdiction of the Bombay Province Police Force was extended to Sind, Gujarat, Karnataka and the Maharashtra districts. Due to the partition of the country the territory of Sind was ceded to Pakistan, and eventually it came under the control of the Government of Pakistan. In 1948 several Princely States were merged in the Bombay Province. In 1951, the Bombay District Police Act of 1890, and the Bombay City Police Act of 1902 were repealed and in their place the Bombay Police Act (Act XXII of 1951) was promulgated. By this Act and the Rules formed thereunder, it was laid down that there should be one Police Force for the whole State of Bombay, and that administrative head of the entire Police department be the Inspector General of Police.

In May 1960, there occurred another reorganisation of states on linguistic basis, and it changed partially the arrangement made by the reorganisation of states on linguistic basis in 1956. Gujarat and Kannada speaking districts of the Bombay Province were taken out and two separate States of Gujarat and Karnataka were formed. It was also contemplated that the Bombay City should be a separate administrative entity under the Union Government, and the residue of Bombay Province, divested of this industrial city and a great source of revenue, should be formed and named 'Maharashtra'. To this newly formed State the five Marathi-speaking districts of the State of Hyderabad (Nizam) should be added. There was total agitation over the formation of a separate Bombay City State under the Union resulting in the death of more than 120 agitators due to police firing and eventually this idea had to be given up. On 1st May 1960, the existing State of Maharashtra was formed with all the Marathi speaking districts of Hyderabad, Madhya Pradesh and Bombay Provinces (States). In important cities there are few women police.

Bombay City Police: The evolution of the Police administration in Bombay kept pace with the growth of the city itself. Until the end of the 18th century the watch and ward duties were carried out by the Bombay Militia (Bhandaris). In 1812 first full-fledged Bombay Police Regulation came into force. The first half of the 19th century can be called the age of magistracy. This was the period when the police department was burdened with more civic and non-police duties and less its essential police functionary and the judiciary dominated the Bombay city police. The various stages in the evolution of the Bombay City Police system are marked by Regulations of 1812, 1827, 1834, 1856, 1860 and 1865. The Bombay Police Act of 1856 (Act XIII of 1856) forms an important landmark in the history of the Bombay Police as it was most comprehensive Police Act, and it created the post of the Commissioner of Police for Bombay city from November 1856. By the Municipal Act II of 1865, the Commissioner of Police became an independent officer solely responsible for police duties in the city.

Besides Bombay city there are Police Commissioners in Thane, Pune and Nagpur. They all are Inspectors General.

Port Police: The port of Bombay is considered as the gateway of India. The sea port zone consists of three police stations situated in about 75 sq. miles. This force functions under the Commissioner of Police.

The Maharashtra Police Force is headed by a Director General. The State capital is Mumbai (Bombay). The area of the State is 3,07,762 Sq. km. having its population 78,706,719 with about 60 lakhs Scheduled Tribes according to 1991 census. The strength is about 1,20,000.

3. Manipur

Manipur, formerly a Princely State, is associated with the *Mahabharata's* hero, Arjuna bearing uninterrupted history till AD 35. Then it was divided into seven principalities and one of them was occupied by Pakhangba, who established his dynasty which ruled the State till its integration to India in 1949. It became a Union Territory in 1957, and in January 1972 it became a full-fledged State.

It appears that Police existed since AD 35 when the institution of Court '*Chairap*' came into existence. Police as an organised institution, came to notice as late as during 1475 when King Kiyanba ruled. The main functions of the police were maintenance of peace, checking of infiltration of foreigners and regulate exports and imports of goods.

Women police known as '*Patch Pheida*" existed in 1709 and their main functions were to control female criminals, to guard the 'Nupi market' and to deal with cases involving females. During 1826-34 police received military training during the rule of Gamhir Singh and his successor kings. The British conquered Manipur in 1891 and the British converted Manipur Police into State Military Police (SMP) and formed the first battalion of Manipur Rifles. In 1907 under Churachand Maharaja, Manipur State Darbar was installed, and the Superintendent of the Police was appointed to head the Police administration. In January 1956 the post of Inspector General of Police was created. In 1988, the post of Director General of Police was created. Two battalions of Manipur Rifles have been absorbed in the Border Security Force.

Manipur has been in the grip of insurgents ever since its integration with the Indian Government soon after Independence, the aim being to free Manipur from the control of the Indian Government. Several secessionists and extremists organisations like the People's Liberation Army (PLA) and the People's

Revolutionary Party of Kangleipak (PREPAK) are operating linking up their activities with the terrorists from Mizoram, Nagaland and Tripura. Violent attacks are frequently made on non-Manipur Indians, who are killed in large numbers and their houses destroyed by setting them on fire. Banks are looted, with repeated incidences of kidnapping for ransom. Meiters are the majority community and the above-mentioned outlawed groups have been able to get their support in their drive against outsiders — '*Mavangs*'. Manipur is also involved in border disputes with Assam, Mizoram and Nagaland.

All these violent activities have to be combatted by the Police, and it is really an ordeal for them. The increase in the casualties among the Police Force is significant of their vulnerability as all odds are against them.

The Force is headed by a Director General. The State has an area of 22,327 Sq. km. and a population of 1,826,714 with four lakhs Scheduled Tribes according to 1991 census and a sizeable number of them are tribals. The capital is Imphal. The strength is 11,000.

It is interesting to note that Manipur subscribed to *Vaishnava* rites ever since 1714, and was traditionally a Hindu State. At the beginning of the century there was not a single Christian in Manipur but by 1991, the Christian population has risen to 421,702 due to the large-scale conversion from Hindus.

4. Meghalaya

Meghalaya, which comprises United Khasi-Jaintia Hills districts and Garo Hills district, was a part of the former Assam state when India attained Independence. Meghalaya was made a full-fledged State on 21st January 1972.

The criminal administration of the State is conducted in accordance with the provisions of the 'Rules for the Administration of Justice and Police' framed for the two original districts of United Khasi and Jaintia Hills. There is a two-tier system of criminal administration in Meghalaya, so also there are two types of police functioning in the State namely the 'Regular Police' and 'Rural Police'. The former functions under the Director General of Police in accordance with the normal criminal law of the country. The Rural Police consists of village authorities, such as, Sardars, Dalois, Pators, Lyngdohs, Nokmas *etc*. The Regular Police have no control over the Rural Police who function under day-to-day supervision and control of the Deputy Commissioner. The provisions of Section 25 of the Indian Evidence Act (No confession made to a police officer during the course of the investigation shall be proved against the person accused of any offence) and Section 26 (confession of accused while in police custody not to be proved against him) and Section 162 of the Code of Criminal Procedure (Statement made by any person to a Police Officer in the course of an investigation, if reduced to writing be signed by the person making it and it can be used as evidence) are not applicable to the Rural Police. The Rural Police are required to arrest all offenders and to repress all disorders and to keep watch over bad and suspicious characters, and for achieving this the village authorities can seek the help of the Deputy Commissioner. People are duty-bound to aid the police in the discharge of their duties and their failure to do so render them liable to pay such fine as is imposed by the village authorities.

Another feature of Khasi democracy is the participation of the entire population in recording policies, judicial decisions at their '*Darbar*' on the principle of decentralisation of powers. Each village has its own *Darbar*. It holds frequent sessions in which all male adults are required to attend. The *Darbar* functions as a Court of Justice by deciding criminal and civil cases and disputes, besides handling law and public administration. The *Darbar* is presided by 'Syiem' or Deputy Syiem.

Indian Police Act of 1861 is followed in this State. As there is no separate Police Manual for Meghalaya, the Assam Police Manual is followed. The capital is Shillong.

The area of the State is 22,489 Sq. kms. and the population was 1,760,625 of which Christians are 702,854 as per 1991 census. The Scheduled Tribes are about 11 lakhs. The strength is 8,000.

5. Mizoram

Mizo district of Assam became a Union Territory on 21st January 1972, and came to be known as Mizoram. With the signing of the Peace Accord by the Government of India on June 30 1986,

Mizoram was constituted into a separate State with effect from February 20, 1987.

In Mizoram, a rebellion demanding secession from India began in 1966. The insurgent Mizo Army under the leadership of the Mizo National Front (MNF), president Laldenga, operating from Burma and Bangladesh hide-outs, rapidly liberated almost the entire area, then a district of Assam, and held it for several days before massive Indian Army intervention gradually pushed them back. The situation has not been fully improved, as Police casualties continue to occur at the hands of terrorists. Ever since 1966 the main task of the police force had been constant operation against the insurgent elements. In this difficult task they have been assisted by the Central Reserve Police Force.

The Police Force is headed by a Director General. There is no separate Police Manual or Regulation, and Assam Police Manual is followed. The area of the State is 21,081 Sq. kms., and the population 686,217 according to 1991 census. Christians are 413,840, Scheduled Tribes are about five lakhs. The capital is Aizawl. The strength is about 4,000.

6. Nagaland

The Naga Hills and Tuensang Area (NHAT) was a district under the Assam State. It was a centrally administered area in 1957. Under the constant political pressure for an independent state, the State of Nagaland was formed on December 1, 1963. The Rules for administration of justice and police in Naga Hills District of 1937, regulate the working of the state police. The police in Naga Hills consists of (a) Regular Police subject to Police Act, 1861. (b) Assam Rifles subject to Act of 1920, and (c) Rural Police consisting of '*Manzadaras*', '*Goanburas*', Headman of Khel and other village authorities recognised as such by the Deputy Commissioner with their subordinate village authorities.

Under the provisions of Sections 3 to 6 of the above Rules, the Regular Police shall act only when required to do so by general or special order of Deputy Commissioner or the Superintendent of Police, or other officer duly authorised may assign to the force any portion of the duties of Police under the Police Act of 1861 in any locality. Section 7 of the said Rules lays down that the ordinary duties of Police shall be discharged by the *Manzadaras*, *Goanburas*, Headman of Khel *etc.*, who shall arrest criminals and suppress all disorders within their respective jurisdiction. Sections 8 to 10 of the Rules list the duties to be performed by the Rural Police, and they are the same as found elsewhere in the country from collection of intelligence, investigation, arrest to prosecution and maintenance of law and order.

Traditionally, every Naga village has a Village Council chosen from among the founder clans and the priest clans according to their respective customs. Thus, the regular police in Nagaland have only a limited sphere of functions, and it is not to act *suo motu*. However, the pattern of policing has greatly changed since it attained the statehood and application of almost all the sections of the Criminal Procedure Code that are required for the day to day police functions. Although this has widened the sphere of the function of the Regular Police, at the same time the administration of justice and police relating to the position of the Deputy Commissioner *vis-a-vis* the police remained unchanged. In consequence, this has led to somewhat confusing situation in which two sets of Rules, at times contradicting each other, are governing the working of the police in the State.

Director General of Police is the head of the Police Force of the State. The area of which is 16,579 Sq. km. and population was 1,215,573 of which Christians were 621,590 and 651,000 were Scheduled Tribes according to 1991 census. The State capital is Kohima. The strength is 16,000.

7. Orissa

Orissa State became a separate entity with statehood on 1st April 1936, before which portions of Orissa were a part of Bengal, then later Bihar. Some portions were with Madhya Pradesh and some were with Madras. In 1905, Sambalpur was added to Orissa as a part of Bengal till 1912. In 1912, separate Bihar and Orissa provinces were formed. In 1936, some portion of Madras — Ganjam and Koraput — were added to Orissa. In 1947, except Mayurbhanj all other feudatory (Princely) states were merged with Orissa and in 1949, Mayurbhanj also merged with Orissa.

Orissa had come under the invasion and occupation of different outsiders from time to time. Even it underwent the savages of Muslims, Marathas and subsequently the British. From 1515 to 1578 Orissa was ruled by Hindu Kings, from 1575 to 1592 the Muslims ruled Orissa, from 1592 to 1742 Mughals and from 1742 to 1751 the Marathas ruled Orissa until 1803, when the rulers of East India Company occupied Orissa. The rulers followed their own system of policing the country under their subjugation. However, it appears that the system of policing mentioned in the *Arthasastra* of Kautilya was more or less prevalent in Orissa, as suggested by the names '*Senapati, Dandapala*, *Durgapala* and *Anantpala*'. In early police system there was no clear distinction between police and military work. Policing in Orissa was a curious mixture of the various systems adopted by different rulers during their regime. The *Kotwals*, *Fouzdars*, *Darogahs*, *Chaukidars* or *Rahadars* and the Zamindars were the various nomenclatures used by the rulers for police officers. The village police system was invariably prevalent practically during each regime. The Zamindars or landlords of the villages were specially responsible for police duties in their respective jurisdictions and prevented crimes and detected criminals, and maintained law and order. The Britishers continued this system. It was only in 1860, after the appointment of the Police Commission and enactment of Indian Police Act of 1861, that conformity in the police force could be brought about. Thereafter, the Police Force of Orissa adopted the same pattern as was introduced in Bengal, Madras and Bombay Presidencies. The force was further streamlined with the implementation of the recommendations of 1902 Police Commission. In 1946, the Orissa Military Police was established and the Orissa Military Police Act was passed.

On 1st January 1948, the integration of 25 feudatory (princely) states, inhabited mostly by Scheduled Tribes, were not without bloody uprisings, due to activities of *Praja Mandals* launched by the subject against their oppressive rulers, and subsequently these uprisings were suppressed by some of the rulers against the Orissa Government consequent to the loss of their territories and powers. Therefore, there was a delayed recognition of the Police Force, during which process screening of officers and men, who were untrained and of poor standard, low paid and ill-equipped so as to fit into different police ranks and absorb them into Orissa Police was scrupulously done. The widespread communal riots in and around Rourkela, followed by state-wide student agitation in September 1964, and alike traumatic experience coming in succession revealed the utter inadequacies of the police force. Exclusively for proper intelligence work the post of Deputy Inspector General (Intelligence) was created in 1964.

Carrier Pigeon Service: After the World War II, the Orissa police had started the Carrier Pigeon Service in 1946 with headquarters in Cuttak by obtaining forty birds from the Indian Army. Gradually, it was spread to all the districts and even some police stations located in Hilly areas. More than 40 years have gone back, and a communication revolution has swept the country but the utility of 955 birds kept in 35 lofts has not diminished, and the pigeons still continue to be an important part of the State's communication network. From each of these 11 centres, on an average 400 messages in a year are sent and equal number received. For further details Chapter 15 on 'Auxiliary Police' please be seen.

The Force is headed by a Director General. The area of the state is 155,707 Sq. kms. with a population of 31,512,070 of which 5,915,067 belong to Scheduled Tribes as per 1991 census. The State capital is Bhubaneshwar. The strength is 35,000 approximately.

8. Pondicherry (Union Territory)

The French territory of Pondicherry consisting of Pondicherry, Karaikal was amalgamated with Yauman, Mahe and Nahuthara in order to form one administrative unit of Pondicherry under the control of the Union on 1st November 1954, following an agreement with the Government of France.

After the integration of the French Pondicherry, the existing police force, which was supplemented and placed under the control of the Inspector General of Police, on deputation from the State of Tamil Nadu where he worked as a Senior Superintendent of Police. Until 1963 police administration was carried out in accordance with the French Regulations. After the Indian laws were extended from 1st October 1963, the Indian Police Act of 1861 was introduced in order to streamline the police force. On June 1, 1967, the force was reorganised, consequent upon the introduction in 1966 of the Pondicherry Police Act (Act 6 of 1966).

The force is headed by an Inspector General of Police. The area of the State is 492 Sq. kms. having 789,416 as its population. The State capital is Pondicherry. The strength is 2,000 approximately.

9. Punjab

Ever since the *Mahabharat* (3,000 years) the region of Punjab had mostly remained turbulent with few and far in between interludes of peace. There were invasions after invasions by the Aliens — Greeks, Hunas, Kushans, Mughals, Afghans etc. Law and order could not be maintained and peace and tranquillity could not be preserved, for the administration had no time to look after the policing needs of the people as they were pre-occupied in military combats. However, according to local needs, a semblance of some type of police system was introduced, mostly under the command of the military. As in other parts of India, here also the village headman (*Lambardar*) and his *Chowkidars* or *Kotwals* looked after the watch and ward of the villagers and prevented crime, detected criminals and maintained law and order.

On the annexation of Punjab in 1849, by the British, a Police Force was organised on the lines of the Sind police. It consisted of a military preventive police and a civil detective force. In 1857, this force was largely increased as it comprised disbanded soldiers of the old Sikh Army of Maharaja Ranjit Singh. Police jurisdiction was co-terminus with revenue divisions. Police powers were vested with *Tehsildars*. The cities had watch and ward organisation financed by a Watch and Ward Taxing Committee. The force was reorganised on the basis of the recommendations made by the 1860 Police Commission, and the introduction of Indian Police Act of 1861. The Military Police, as a separate organisation, was abolished and a single homogeneous force of civil constabulary for the performance of day-to-day police functions was created under an Inspector General of Police. In 1869, the Railway Police was inaugurated to deal with crimes on the railways. The village police was remodelled. In each village one or more watchmen were appointed. After 5 or 6 watchmen a *Dafedar* was ascribed the work of supervision. They were under the village headmen or '*Lambardars*'. *Zaildars* and *Inamdars* were also appointed to supervise the work of *Lambardars*. On the basis of 1902 Police Commission, subsequent reorganisation was done. The police had to face political agitations, including terrorism during the freedom struggle of the country. The World War II during 1939-46 led to the reorganisation of police force and its arrangements in rank and file.

On the achievement of Independence in 1947, the partition of Punjab led to an unprecedented exodus and exchange of population of non-Muslims from the West Punjab and Muslims from the East Punjab to India and Pakistan. After the departure of Muslims and British Police officers, the remaining 30 per cent of the effective strength of Punjab Police was called upon to deal with a situation unknown to history. Guarding of Indo-Pakistan Border was additional duty that was foisted on the already depleted Police Force. Even then several contingents of this force were deployed for special duties outside the State.

On the integration of Patiala and East Punjab States Union (PEPSU) with the Punjab, a new State came into existence in 1956. The complexion of the State changed altogether. The urban population increased beyond all proportions and beyond the controlling capacity of the Police Force. In 1960 Police Commission under the chairmanship of Justice Mahajan looked into the requirements of the Police Force. But before consideration could take place, in October 1966, the Punjab State was bifurcated into Punjab and Haryana, and at the same time some area went to Himachal Pradesh. In 1981, the advent of terrorism due to Khalistan movement in the State totally changed the law and order scenario and on each dawn the terrorists crimes and related political activities occurred in an increasing proportion particularly in the incidence of murder, occasional looting and arson. In 1984, 'Operation Blue Star' was conducted to flush out the terrorists from the Golden Temple at

Amritsar, and the Army was required to be extensively deployed for combing up operation throughout the State. Now, the previous stage of policing through or with the aid of military contingents of the whole of the State of Punjab has come, and the civil police has almost lost its existence and identity.

The Punjab Police is passing through a very critical time and doing its best to control and contain the menace of terrorism, and in this national duty a large number of police officers and men have gallantly laid down their lives and most of the others are engaged in pitched battles with the terrorists. Since the main thrust of the activities of terrorists was felt in the border districts of Gurdaspur and Amritsar, a separate Border Range was created in 1988.

The police force is headed by a Director General. The State area is 50,357 Sq. km. with a population of 20,190,795 according to 1991 census. The work done by Director General K.P.S. Gill in containing terrorism in the State is not only laudable, but also unmatched in the annals of the entire history of the various police forces of the country. The State capital is Chandigarh. The strength is about 40,000.

10. Rajasthan

As a result of the historical forces which perpetuated feudal traditions with a despotic administration, each Princely State had its peculiar system of police administration, which was the most important arm of the government. The most pronounced influence on the criminal administration in the State was that of the prevailing feudalistic stratification of the society, *Jagirdars*, the feudal chiefs under the ruling princes exercised immense powers over the subjects. Except for a number of directly controlled police stations and outposts many station houses (police stations) and outposts were manned by '*Jagir Sawars*' of powerful and solvent *Jagirdars*, who therefore, were not strictly under the control of the police. The '*Jagir Bakshi*' awarded freely departmental punishments or even exonerated many a defaulters. Thus, a sizeable number of police personnel owed allegiance to the feudal chiefs rather than the police hierarchy. Due to unequal financial resources, disparate social structures and feudalistic traditions, different states had different modes of administration. Till the end of the 19th century, the Princely States, by and large, had antiquated police system *vis-a-vis* criminal justice and this indigenous system continued during the first quarter of the 20th century.

The '*Fouzdari*' system of criminal administration was in force till the 19th century. The police personnel were subordinate to *Fouzdar*, who invariably was controlled by *Tehsildar*. Policing in many Princely States was known as '*Ghata*' system. The *Chowkidari* system was prevalent in almost all major states of Rajasthan. In many states, the *Chowkidar* or Patel was paid out of the regular fund voluntarily contributed by villagers for an assured peaceful life and recovery of stolen or lost property. Therefore, the main emphasis was on recovery of stolen or lost property rather than punishing the criminals. However, progressive rulers of major states like Jaipur, Jodhpur, Bikaner etc., adopted measures which gradually transformed the feudalistic and repressive administrative machinery into a reasonably efficient and responsive system.

Rajasthan was born in 1950 as a result of integration of 22 Princely States and six 'Tikanas'. The integration of these states proceeded in seven phases starting from 18th March 1948 to November 1956, when the police hierarchy at different levels was graded together so as to form one composite homogeneous Police Force of Rajasthan doing away with the disjointed, untrained, badly led and equipped, illiterate and poorly paid police force. A unified police regulation was formed. It was necessary to give the State a well-equipped and fully motivated Armed Police to guard the long Indo-Pakistan Border of about 650 miles. During 1951-52, the Rajasthan Armed Constabulary (RAC) was raised in adequate number. The RAC gave reasonably good performance in guarding of the difficult and desert international border, and in the extermination of several *dacoit* gangs which ravaged the State from the hauling Sand-dunes from the North-West to the dreaded Chambal ravines in the South-East and the Pakistan Borders. A uniform State Police Service was formed in 1951, and the integration of other ranks belonging to the merged states was completed in 1952-53, and finally, uniformity in training and equipment and pay was achieved.

Abolition of the *Jagirdari* system and the rule of *jatts* received from the vested interests and influenced sections of the landed aristocracy owing allegiance to princely houses led to the formation of powerful *dacoit* gangs. Many *jagirdars*, free booters, ex-army personnel and petty landholders of Rajput-origin took to arms. There also are *dacoit* gangs operating from Indo-Pak Border. The *dacoity* menace has stretched over to Rajasthan, Madhya Pradesh and Uttar Pradesh borders seriously threatening the peace and law and order in the contiguous rural areas. Many dacoits have been liquidated and still an equal number continue their depredations.

In the tribal areas of the Udaipur Division inhabited by Bhils, Mewar Bhil Corps was raised in 1890 for the maintenance of law and order in the tribal areas. This force of 1,000 officers and the personnel was absorbed in the Rajasthan Armed Constabulary.

Police Camel Corps: Rajasthan is the first State in the country which provided its police with substantial number of camel *sawars* to combat the *dacoity* menace in desert areas and on the long Indo-Pakistan border. They are also used in the anti-smuggling operations from across the borders. But most of the camels are not state owned. At present the camels are maintained by constables of police stations and they are paid a fixed allowance. This is in contrast to the Border Security Force practice where camels are maintained at the cost of the government. Camel allowance for purchasing and maintaining camels is granted, but the camels are not owned by the government, but by individual members of the force.

The Indian Police Act of 1861 has been made applicable to the State since 1957. There are about 700 women police, mostly in urban areas. The head of the police force is Director General. The area of the State is 342,214 Sq. kms. and the population was 48,880,640 with 4,183,124 Scheduled Tribes according to 1991 census. The State capital is Jaipur. The strength is 52,000.

11. Sikkim

Sikkim was given a political shape in the 17th century by a Buddhist King titled Gyalpo. During the 18th and the 19th centuries Bhutanis and Gorkhalis poured into Sikkim and threatened to overcome the State. The Gyalpo approached the

British Government in India for help, and the latter came to his rescue. In 1861, Sikkim became protectorate of the British Government of India, and in 1950 the Government of India and its ruler Chogyal, who wanted an independent kingdom, faced political turmoil. During 1973-1975 there were uprisings against King Chogyal, and they ended in the merger of Sikkim into the Indian Union.

The Sikkim Police was first raised at Aritar, Rhenock, East Sikkim on 27th November 1897 as the trade route between India and Tibet was then via Jelepla, East Sikkim. After the merging of Sikkim into India there had been rapid expansion of the police force since 1975. The Indian Police Act of 1861 is in force. A few women police are also there.

The police force is headed by a Director General. The State area is 818 Sq. km. with a population of 403,612 having 73,623 Scheduled Tribes as per 1991 census. The State capital is Gangtok and strength is about 3,000.

12. Tamil Nadu

The basis of the early police system was the '*Kudikaval*' (*Kotwal* in other parts of contemporary India) or '*Stalakaval*' meaning in general terms 'Village watchman'. Dating from the time of the formation of village community, it represents a simple and effective device of a self-contained group of inhabitants protecting their lives and property from the aggression of hostile and jealous neighbours. Theft had been the common and the most dangerous form of crime in a primitive community, and should a theft occur in a village it was the duty of the '*Kudikavalagar*', the people's watchmen, to trace and recover the stolen property, and in the event of his failure to do so, to compensate the owner from his resources. This office of the village police was hereditary, and he was paid by contribution of grain at the time of harvest by all the villagers (in a way barter system).

In 1659, the East India Company had appointed a few watchmen to guard its commercial establishments in the Madras city, and the surrounding areas. After the Sepoy's Mutiny at Vellore in 1806, the English East India Company reorganised the Police administration in the occupied territory. In the same year, Superintendent of Police was appointed to head the force in Madras city. A part of the police force was paid from the Assessment Fund and the rest from the General Revenue of the Government. For administration of oath, officers were drawn from the Hindu, Muslim and *Harijan* communities. It is interesting to note that even from those days *Harijans* were being treated as members of a separate religion and not as forming part of the Hindu community by the English. Obviously, they had contrived this notion.

In 1828, a storm ravaged the coast of Madras city and they gallantly saved several lives and restored the inundated property. In recognition of their services nine medals were struck in silver with the names of the recipients engraved on these and awarded to the gallant policemen by the East Indian Company Government. Obviously, this medal was the fore-runner of the Police Medals of later days.

With the growth of British power in the State, there was a simultaneous increase in the Indian territories under British subjugation throughout the sub-continent. The remedial measures, for improving the police administration and dispensation of criminal justice implemented in the Madras Presidency, were also adopted in other parts of the country. The State Police Commission of 1828 and 1832 looked into the working of the police. A superintendent of police in each district was appointed as the head of the district police, but for all other administrative functions he was to work in collaboration and at times in consultation with the District Magistrate. In 1856, the City Police Act (Act XIII of 1856) was passed, and the first Commissioner of Police for the Madras city was appointed. Three years later, the Madras District Police Act was passed, and the administration of the police throughout the general police district was vested in the Inspector General of Police. The Commissioner of city police was also the justice of peace, though he was subject to departmental control of the Inspector General of Police. The recommendation of the 1860 and 1902 Indian Police Commissions were implemented. Thus, in the beginning of the 20th century the police force was established, but it failed to get a willing co-operation of the public on account of paucity of literate candidates for the force due to poor salary offered to them.

After the Independence in 1947, some contingents of the force were sent to the Hyderabad State during the 'Police Action'. The force, like other police in various states, had undergone reorganisation from time to time, and it is now reasonably in good shape.

A women police wing functions in Madras city and some urban areas. The force is headed by a Director General and the State has an area of 130,058 Sq. km. with a population of 55,638,318 in which 5,20,000 were Scheduled Tribes according to 1991 census. The State capital is Madras. The strength is 68,000 approximately.

13. Tripura

During the princely days in 1873, nine laws were decreed and the same included a Criminal Procedure Code and a police guide. Subsequently, a *Darbar* Proclamation ordained that in the absence of any law of its own, the corresponding law in force in British India shall also apply to Tripura. The Police Chief of Tripura was also responsible for collection of revenue. In 1905, Police and Revenue Departments were separated. It was integrated to India on 15th October 1949. In the year 1956, Tripura became a Union Territory and on January 21, 1972 it acquired statehood.

Till the early part of 1970, the force was single district entity under the command of a Superintendent of Police and the Chief Commissioner informally functioned as Inspector General of Police. In 1965, a full-time Inspector General in the grade of Deputy Inspector General, was appointed. With effect from February, 1987, the force is headed by a Director General of Police, who is also the ex-officio Commandant General, Tripura Home Guards.

Indian Police Act, 1861 is in force. Tripura Police Regulations include various provisions from the police regulations of West Bengal.

The area of the State is 10,491 Sq. km. and as per 1991 census the population was 2,744,827 having 583,920 Scheduled Tribes. The State capital is Agartala. The strength is 10,000.

14. Uttar Pradesh

Uttar Pradesh has a colourful history since *Vedic* age. The two great Epics *Ramayana* and *Mahabharata* featured the Royal family of Kosala and Hastinapur in Uttar Pradesh respectively. In the 6th century BC Uttar Pradesh was associated with *Buddhism* and *Jainism*. It came under the Mauryan Rule. In the medieval period it was ruled by Muslims. These two rulers assumed direct responsibility of maintaining law and order for urban areas, and the policing of the rural areas was left to the local chieftains and landlords assisted by, village headmen and *Chowkidars*. The *Kotwal*, *Darogah*, *Fouzdar*, *Dafedar*, and *Jamedar* were the designations usually given to the police officers. The responsibility to compensate the loss of the property stolen and subsequently not recovered was of the village police officials as they were held personally responsible for the prevention of crime and detection of criminals and maintenance of law and order in their jurisdiction. They were paid either by contribution of the villagers or through grant of land, free of assessment by the State.

The Uttar Pradesh Police established in 1861 under the British consequent to the 1860, Police Commission's recommendations and the enactment of the Indian Police Act, 1861, was renamed in 1876 as the Northwestern Provinces and Oudh Police. In 1902, after the Police Commission of that year, it was again renamed as the United Provinces Police and finally in 1954 it is called Uttar Pradesh Police after the merger of Princely States. The armed police of Uttar Pradesh is known as Provincial Armed Constabulary and it was deployed in 1949 in Hyderabad State.

The State of Uttar Pradesh is the largest state of the Union. It is a frontier state along the foothills of the Himalayas having common borders with Tibet and Nepal. Its area is 294,413 Sq. km. and its population was 138,760,417 with three lakhs Scheduled Tribes according to 1991 census. It has River Police also. There are some women police in cities and in important urban areas. The State capital is Lucknow. The head of the force is Director General. Commensurate with the size of the State, the force has outnumbered other states in strength of 1.53 lakhs.

The force has been often charged by the people and the judiciary for having failed to maintain law and order in the rural areas, contain depredation of *dacoits*, and lack of civil behaviour while dealing with the public. May be the society has produced such candidates for enlistment to the Uttar Pradesh Police!

15. West Bengal

It appears that the police system, that existed in ancient times in this region was based on *Arthasastra* of Kautilya, and it continued until the medieval period when Hindu Kings ruled the region. Almost from the 13th century Mughals, Pathans and Muslims ruled this region and with them they had implemented their own policing system. The Muslim empire was divided into *Subhas* (Provinces) which were composed of *Sarkars* (Districts) which were again sub-divided into *Parganas* or group of villages. The maintenance of law and order and the administration of justice were in the charge of '*Nazirs*', the *Diwan* being the highest judge in civil and criminal matters. The *Nazir's* principle agent was the *Fouzdar*, the commander of the local groups, and also the head of the District Police Administration. Under him in the cities there was *Kotwal* and in *parganas* '*Shigatdar*'. A city or town was divided into wards, each containing a *chowki* and patrolled by one horseman and 20 to 25 footmen for the purpose of patrolling the area. They were known '*Bargandar* and *Sipahis*'.

In 1765 Emperor Shah Alam II granted to the East India Company the *Divani* of Bengal, Bihar and Orissa. Since 1698, the East India Company had purchased the *Talukdari* rights in the adjoining land of present-day Calcutta, they acquired the usual responsibilities and powers in the matter of policing and criminal justice, and since then the criminal police administrations are being looked into, and controlled by the British. Since Calcutta was the seat of the Governor General of East India Company for almost one hundred and fifty years, whatever improvemental reorganisation of the police force took place, was initiated in this State and followed in other territories of the British domain in India. As the existing system for control of crime was wholly inefficient it resumed the superintendence of criminal justice throughout the country. In 1792, "Regulations for the police of the collectorships in Bengal, Bihar and Orissa" were passed and they became foundation of police law in Bengal and police force, as a separate entity, under the direct control of the Government was formed. In 1808 Superintendents of police were appointed and they were given concurrent criminal jurisdiction with district and city Magistrates. By Regulation XX of 1817, all the rules which had from time to time been enacted with regard to the duties of *Darogahs* and other police officers codified under 34 Sections, and after the recommendations of the Police Commission in 1860, were generally incorporated in the Indian Police Act of 1861. By 1858 the East India Company was transferred to the British Crown. The Indian Penal Code of 1860, the Indian Evidence Act of 1872 and the Code of Criminal Procedure of 1898 were enacted and brought into execution throughout British India and uniformity in policing and administration of criminal justice secured under an Inspector General of Police for each province.

In 1866, the Calcutta Police Act was enacted, and the post of Commissioner of Police for Calcutta city was created as the head of the city police and he was also appointed as Justice of Peace. In the same year Calcutta suburban's were excluded from the general police district of Bengal. The same year the Railway Police was constituted, and by 1882, the responsibility of prevention, detection, prosecution and maintenance of order on the railway platforms were entrusted to it. In 1870, the village *Chowkidari* Act was passed for the appointments, maintenance and dismissal of village *Chowkidars*, but the panchayats signally failed in their duty to make regular payments to *chawkidars*, and it was set right by the recommendations of 1902 Police Commission, based on the all-round recommendations of this Commission, the force was streamlined. During 1926-1943, several measures for the improvement of the efficiency of the force were taken. In 1943, the Bengal Police Regulations were formed and it substituted all the outdated regulations of the past.

Partition and After: Partition and Independence of the country in 1947, brought about far-reaching changes in the State of West Bengal touching various aspects of the life of the people and gave rise to many complicated problems in matters of administration of police of the State, at a time when the strength of the police officers was greatly depleted due to the departure of a large number of Muslims and British officers and vacancies in their ranks remained unfilled, and in between the 'Great Calcutta Killings' mutually by Hindus and Muslims took place. A large number of refugees migrated from East Pakistan (East Bengal) to West Bengal increasing many fold police problems. The Bengal Panchayat Act was formed in 1956. The duties of *Chowkidars* and *Dafedars* were defined and the cost of maintaining them was proportionally shared by the State Government and the various Panchayat Samitis. In 1960, another Police Commission under Justice K.C. Sen (Retd.) was appointed. The Police Commissioner of Bombay and Madras are under the administrative control of the Director General of Police of their respective states, but the Commissioner of Police of Calcutta functions independently and the Director General and the Inspector General of Police does not exercise any control over his working. There is River Police for riverine belts. There is a small women police, mostly in cities. There is Port Police.

The area of the State is 87,853 Sq. km. and the population was 67,982,732 according to 1991 census of which 30,70,672 were Scheduled Tribes. The capital of the State is Calcutta. The strength is about 58,000.

15

Auxiliary Police

1. Railway Police

The origin of the Railway Police lies in the memorandum of the 'Supreme Government' accompanying the resolution appointing the Indian Police Commission of 1860. While the 'Supreme Government' emphasised the need for a police force in each locality, an exception was made in the case of the Railway Police. The evolution of the Railway Police in India was peculiar in many ways. The main reason for this peculiarity was the growth of the Railway System, till lately under private enterprise. In 1866, the British Government had ordered the creation of Railway Police Force entirely at the disposal of the Agents so far as it was consistent with the laws in force. The administrative control of this force was vested both in the Agents and the Inspector General of Police of that State through which the railway line passes. This was rather a dual administrative system entailing controversial directions and the resultant action, with consequential diminution in the effective disciplinary control over the incumbents of the force. The cost of the maintenance of the force was met by the concerned Railway company subject to only one-fourth contribution made from the Government. Differences soon arose and the Government Railway Police (GRP) was sanctioned and their duties were confined mainly to passenger traffic. The Railway companies continued to maintain their own force — Watch and Ward Establishment, which was the predecessor of the Railway Protection Force of today. This force guarded the railway property.

On recommendation of the All India Police Commission of 1902-03, a separate railway police district was formed as the railway line runs through more than one district jurisdiction. As far as yardsticks, the Commission had recommended that the Superintendent of the Government Railway Police should not have more than a length of 1,500 miles in his charge. The jurisdiction of a police station should not exceed 100 miles, and the police strength should be such as to allow a head constable or a constable to travel in every passenger train that passed within its jurisdiction. The overall administration and supervisory control of the various railway districts in a State was to vest in the Deputy Inspector General of Police for Crime and Railway in order to acquire and maintain co-ordination and co-operation to combat crime and criminals. The Superintendent of Police of a Railway District does not come directly under the control of the District Magistrate, as is the case with the Superintendent of Police of a District in accordance with the provision of Section 4 of the Indian Police Act of 1861.

This old system has been adopted and presently a railway police district is divided into police circles, police stations and outposts. Normally, a railway police station does not exceed a length of 100 miles of the railway track, but in areas where there are law and order problems due to heavy traffic and high incidence of crime, police stations with smaller jurisdiction have been established. The expression 'Railway limits' includes all *ghats* and ferries, but lands acquired for block or residences for railway servants. The limits of station-yards are confined to railway lands lying between two distant signals of a railway station.

Indian Railways are the main arteries of the nation's inland transport. With their charismatic growth from 34-km in April 1853 (Bombay to Thane) to a countrywide network of over 7000 kms. Indian Railways are today Asia's largest and world's second largest system under a single management. The railway network is divided into 9 zones which are sub-divided into 54 divisions. Divisions are the basic operating units. The Railways carry approximately 12 million passengers and 90 million tonnes of goods a day and operate about 1400 trains, which pass through stations and sections vulnerable to crime. Further, deterioration in any crime and order situation anywhere in the country directly affects the Railways. Security on the Railways has, thus, proved to be a challenging task before the Government Railway Police and the Railway Protection Force, respectively, under the Home Ministry and the Railway Ministry.

Policing is a State subject. Maintenance of law and order and control of crime on the Railways are the main responsibilities of the State Governments. The Ministry of Railways share with the State Governments the cost of GRP both 'crime and order' on 50:50 basis though it has no control over the GRP. Against the approximate strength of the GRP of 40,000, the Railway Protection Force has a strength of 80,000 personnel, and the latter is responsible for protecting and safeguarding the booked consignments and the railway properties. This force was constituted under the Railway Protection Force Act of 1957, and it is an armed force of the Union.

That the incidence of crime on the passenger trains is assuring serious proportions is beyond any dispute. Added to this unwholesome situation are the anxious hours for the passengers when they pass through the terrorist-affected states of Jammu and Kashmir, Punjab, Uttar Pradesh, Bihar, Orissa, and Assam. Since crimes in the running trains are committed by criminals, cutting across jurisdiction of states, the investigating officers of the GRP are confronted with immeasurable difficulties in identification of criminals and recovery of properties. The difficulties of the ill-equipped GRP are all the more compounded by the fact that the GRP of most states are the dumping grounds of old and incompetent officers and men who are no match for quick footed railway criminals, and naturally the public has a feeling of 'nexus' between them. Naturally, passengers are reluctant, *inter alia*, for various reasons to report the crimes to the GRP. Generally there is lack of co-operation between the GRP and the RPF and also the local police. Moreover, anti-railway activities, such as, sitting demonstrations on the lines, 'Rail-Roko' agitation, often inspired by sectarian consideration, sabotage of railway lines, at times by terrorists, including Naxalites, have added sinister dimension to the GRP work on the law and order front. As of now, the work of the GRP throughout the country leaves much to be desired. The protection offered by the GRP to the travelling public in the face of the above threats is, thus, negligible and minimal. It is high time that the public, the Railway Administration, as also the Governments, both of the Centre and State, took proper stock of the disturbing trends and initiate such tangible measures as would guarantee the safety and security of the passengers and their properties while on the move in the trains.

2. Port Police

With a coastline of 5,600 kms., India possesses 11 operational major ports. Of them most important are Bombay, Calcutta, Madras, Kandla, Cochin, Tuticorin, Visakhapatnam, Mormugao, Paradeep and New Mangalore. The ports come under the Government of India, Ministry of Surface Transport. All major ports are administered by statutory autonomous Port Trusts. The Indian coastline is also served by 19 intermediate ports and about 250 minor ports, of which 152 are working ports. Ships of all kinds and conditions, and under all flags come to major ports to be docked, to discharge and receive cargo.

Every product of the earth, natural and artificial, is loaded and unloaded here. Traffic in and around the harbours is intensely congested and has to be regulated by the police. Long lines of trucks loaded with goods must be able to get to the ports without too much delay and good order must be maintained in the docks and piers. The traffic handled at major ports averages to about 200 million tonnes per year, and the number of ships that entered all the major ports for cargo operation is about 2,000. A free trade zone operates at Kandla Port ever since March 1965 in a 320 acres area near the port and provides for the establishment of small and medium industrial units and the requisite facilities for them. The township of Gandhidham has grown near Kandla on the Kutch coast.

Thieves and smugglers generally invade the area. Valuable goods and other property, belonging to the port, running in crores are stolen annually. They hover around the ports like water-rats and use small sailing crafts and are ravenously hungry for foreign merchandise. They go down the bay and steal from the ships anchored there. Those who make the big hauls of valuable goods are hardy, bold and daring men, most of whom are thoroughly reckless and brutal and are capable to stand up to kill or be killed. Apart from thefts and smuggling vices like gambling, prostitution, illicit sale of liquor and bootlegging and drug running are widely prevalent. Foreign sailors, to satisfy their sex hunger, are ready to pay any amount to touts and pimps. They also indulge in gambling.

Almost all ports are controlled by Dock labour unions. Here inter-union clashes and illegal strikes are common. In almost every port 50 per cent of the population subsist on pilferages and smuggling. The ports and their residential areas are virtually under the control of criminal gangs, who operate and thrive on pilferage, gambling, smuggling, keeping brothel and prostitution and money lending.

With a large number of unemployed people *mafia* gangs find it easy to employ them for their underworld and nefarious operations. Old gangs are busted by the police, but soon new gangs are formed. Bloody clashes amongst rival groups are frequent. The sound of gun-fire or bomb explosion breaks the silence of the night in various ports, and the following morning it would be a common sight to see some persons lying either dead or grievously injured. Often the police arrive so late at the scene of the crime, that the perpetrators escape detection and subsequent punishment, another reason being no body is prepared to give evidence against them under threat of dire consequences.

The functions of the Port Police are the prevention and detection of crime, including smuggling and drug running, maintenance of law and order, regulation of traffic within the port area and checking vices like gambling, bootlegging, smuggling *etc.* The police staffing pattern varies from port to port, but ordinarily a Deputy Superintendent of Police or a Superintendent of Police in big ports is in-charge of the policing duties and jurisdiction. The number of police stations also varies depending on the importance and area of the harbour. In some big ports a special staff under a senior police officer is usually deployed to deal with specialised crime, smuggling and vices within the port area. Since 1970, the Central Industrial Security Force (CISF) have been inducted into several major ports mainly for the purpose of safeguarding the property of the Port Trust. But duties connected with the prevention and detection of crime, investigation and prosecution of cases, and control of traffic, remain with the port police under the respective State Government.

3. River Police

In the riverine districts, having inner waterways, speed boats and other type of mechanised transport are provided to the police stations with separate specialised staff. They watch the movements of criminals, who use mainly country boats to cross the rivers and commit crimes in the neighbourhood. The Police use these boats for the purpose of checking criminals living within a mile of the river bank, intercept criminals using country boats and steam vessels, to which Indian Steam Navigation Act applies. Professional *dacoits* and smugglers have been found frequently using boats for the purpose of crossing and recrossing rivers before and after commission of crime. The river patrols become effective only when they operate in conjunction with land patrols.

In many parts of the country vast areas remain under water for days together or account of heavy floods, when the police are required to discharge manifold duties-cum-responsibilities, like rescuing of persons and property, conducting searches for missing persons, distribution of food to alleviate hardship and suffering and evacuation of persons from the submerged areas during the ravages of floods.

4. Home Guards

The genesis of the Home Guards organisation in India goes back to in 1946 when the Bombay city was rocked by series of communal riots and strikes. The organisation came into existence as an invaluable auxiliary to the police in the maintenance of peace and tranquillity when it was found impossible for the small body of police to meet the challenges of disorder and lawlessness. The Bombay experience created the realisation for the necessity for an organisation to play a supportive role to the police not only in the maintenance of law and order but helping in emergent and disaster situation. In the year 1959, Government of India asked all State Governments and Union territories to set-up similar organisations.

Home Guards are entrusted with the following duties:

1. Serve as an auxiliary to the police and generally help in maintaining internal security.

2. Help the community in any kind of emergency — civil or otherwise.
3. Provide essential services like motor transport, pioneer and engineering groups, fire brigades, nursing and first-aids, operation of water and power supply *etc*., through functional units.
4. Promote communal harmony and give assistance to the administration in protecting weaker sections of the society.
5. Participate in socio-economic and welfare activities, such as, adult education, health and hygiene development schemes *etc.*
6. To help in the Civil Defence of the country.

It has been laid down that at the time of recruitment one should be literate and be within the age group of 18 to 50 years. Home Guards may be males or females. To start with, the idea of Home Guards evoked considerable public enthusiasm and the organisation attracted volunteers from all sections of the society including doctors, engineers, educationist, lawyers *etc.* But interest started waning later on, mainly due to frequent calls and continuous deployment in some states affected their profession adversely. Various types of duties, other than those mentioned above, are required to be performed by Home Guards and they include regulation of crowds at fairs, festivals and other large gatherings, maintenance of provisions of essential supplies and services during strikes, control and regulation of traffic in the streets, election duties, anti-smuggling duties and allied such duty which the police are unable to perform due to their pre-occupations or paucity of staff for deployment. They also perform duties relating to the verification of ration cards, regulating queues at booking windows at railway stations, bus stands, guarding examination halls, and help in the defence of international borders along with the para-military forces.

Every State Government has enacted the Home Guards Act and Rules, there is no Central Act and Rules. Home Guards, when called out for training or duty have the same powers, privileges and protection as police officers. No prosecution can be instituted against Home Guards in respect of anything done by them in the due discharge of functions or duties, as they are deemed to be public servants within the meaning of Section 21 of the Indian Penal Code. However, their deployment is confined to their own state.

Home Guards are not standing whole time salaried organisation. They are paid allowances, the scale of which varies from state to state, when they are called on duty. They are provided with appointment certificates and free laid down uniform.

The Government of India has prescribed the strength of the Home Guards at 515,908 for the entire country, but as an economy measure 15 per cent reduction was imposed. The organisation is functioning throughout the country except Arunachal Pradesh and Kerala. There is one company of 110 men for each Community Development Block in the rural area and one company for every 25,000 of the population in urban area.

The leadership of Home Guards comes from diverse sources. In some states police officers not only head the organisation but they also command the district units. In some, the chief is a policeman, while the District Commandants are departmental officers, who have risen from the organisation itself or might be ex-army officers. Generally, the budget is shared 50:50 per cent basis by the Central and the State Governments.

5. Mounted Police

There are over 2,000 horses and about 2,500 Mounted policemen in the country. In spite of all-round mechanisation, the Mounted Police have their own utility which is not likely to be dispensed with. Mounted Police units have indeed a glorious history and a colourful record of achievements.

Police horses have been used on traffic patrol duties and police training institutions for training of cadets in the past. They are also used in ceremonial parades and public functions. They are used for escorting the President of India on all ceremonial occasions. They proved very effective to control crowd, but their use has been restricted considerably due to heavy brick-batting and use of bombs by unruly mobs.

6. Pigeons in Police Work

All vital information, maps, photographs, plans *etc.*, could be sent through the trained pigeons. They are valuable and indispensable in the army and this was fully recognised during the First and Second World Wars when thousands of trained pigeons were pressed into service, who gave illustrious performance in every mission. A booklet published by the Government of India in 1945 — "Indian Pigeons Service" mentions that 90,000 men were employed during World War I to handle pigeons, and during the World War II almost the same number of persons were engaged. Several birds have won the Coveted Victoria Cross and in the Hall of Fame in the USA birds are kept stuffed with legends of heroic deeds.

After the cessation of hostilities, Orissa Police (the only in the country) were quick enough to recognise the benefit of pigeons and a few pigeons together with outfit was obtained from the Army. In the absence of road communications to the police stations and villages, lack of telephone and wireless facilities and inaccessible areas due to dense forests, and hills full of carnivora, police stations in the interior could not keep contact with their district headquarters. As an experimental measure, the pigeon service was first introduced in the hilly district of Koraput. The results were soon found to be satisfactory and encouraging. The pigeon service was extended to all other 12 districts. At present it touches all corners of the State. The pigeon service is operating in all district headquarters, sub-divisional headquarters, outlying circle headquarters and police stations and their out posts. The Police Training College at Angul is also provided with a pigeon loft for imparting training to different ranks.

Wireless communication is always not effective and dependable as wireless messages fail to travel from a plain area to a place situated at higher altitudes. There is no guarantee of absolute secrecy in wireless messages as every wireless centre can intercept them. The pigeons are specially useful during natural calamities. During the devastating floods of 1955 and 1960 in Orissa when the entire communication network of the State broke down, the pigeon service was the only means of reaching urgent messages to the headquarters from the marooned and inaccessible area.

Over 40 years have gone by and communication revolution has swept the country, but over 1200 odd carrier pigeons are still operating in Orissa. They are lodged in 38 pigeon lofts scattered all over the State. The pigeon loft is constructed at a place having some nearby prominent landmarks, such as, a tall minaret, temple, church or a chimney so that it can easily locate the loft from a great distance while returning from long distance flights. From each of its 38 lofts, on an average, 400 messages in a year are sent and received.

There are three categories of pigeon messengers — 1. Static, Mobile, and 3. Boomerang. The static service is meant to carry one-way messages. When a police contingent moves out to interior places, they carry a few pigeons in portable baskets. Such pigeons are released daily with messages.

As the very name suggests, a boomerang moves only between two places. The boomerangs are sent with a message to a particular place several miles away from the loft, and they are expected to fly back after delivering the message, which is written on a slip of paper 3" * 4" in size (especially prepared for the purpose) in indelible ink. The paper is folded and rolled and finally inserted into a plastic container — known as Message Container which is about one and a half inch long and tied with a belt to the leg of the carrier pigeon. Each carrier pigeon has a number which is indicated in a small metal ring fixed to the leg. This is its identification. The pigeons are divided into groups, according to the directions in which they are sent. Around the leg of each bird there is a coloured plastic ring and the colour of the ring indicates the direction it is to be sent, each of the four colours standing to a particular direction.

The message is written in duplicate and sent through a select pair of birds — male and female. If a bird is sent alone il is probable that it would be romantically drawn to a bird of opposite sex on the passage. Another reason why a pair is dispatched is that if one bird meets a tragic consequence, the other one is likely to reach its destination. Carrier pigeons have an infallible memory, but in case one bird stays, the other one leads the way. At the destination the birds descend and settle on the "Boomerang Box" and the policeman on duty relieves it of the paper containing the message. After some rest and time they are flown back, with or without any message, and the homing instinct in these birds is so powerful that they have irresistible urge to return to their habitat before night fall.

Specially birds known as "Homers" are selected and trained very carefully for a long duration and with constant practice to fly over the to and fro destinations. These birds are endowed with an active homing instinct and gifted with more ability to fly long distances at a stretch. A homer is more spruce and streamlined in appearance with a brighter gleam in the eyes. Added by a pair of muscular wings, the homers can fly long distances and return to their loft without getting lost. The homer's navigational skill has been the subject of research both in India and the West, which is the homing pigeon original home, but so far it has remained one of the nature's mysteries.

Some scientists are of opinion that homer pigeon have at least two compasses. The best understood is the sun compass which they learn to use when young and use it when the sky is clear. But pigeons can also fly perfectly well on overcast days, indicating that sun is not their only means for orientation. Others say that the bird uses the earth's magnetic field for navigation or that they can see polarised light and hear very low frequency noises with the help of which they can fly back home.

As of date, the birds which have served the Orissa Police for five decades are fighting a losing battle with man and machine. And, as the country prepares to enter an era of high technical communication, the apathy towards all that is traditional grows even more greater. The Orissa Government does not seem to be much interested to continue their service, which was initiated, and availed of by only the Orissa Government in the country.

7. Dogs in Police Work

It seems highly probable that dogs have been used in England to track criminals for many decades — perhaps, even longer than any other country. The dog, owing to its ability to track by disturbances and smell is such a greater asset to the police in tracing criminals and narcotics *etc*. Training of dog is important, but the handler should be equally well-trained so that he can guide and direct his dog upon useful lines. The success of the dog mostly depends upon its handler who guides and controls it in almost every movement it makes, then alone the dog can be of valuable assistance. While the investigating officer examines in detail the scene of crime, the dog handler should be responsible in thoroughly searching the surrounding area. Doing this is not a matter of merely casting in two or three general directions, but first learning to take stock of the situation. The best team-handler and dog should not depend entirely on the fact that the dog is the best tracker and the most obedient. A police dog trails-exercises should be regularly arranged to test its power of observation, interpretation and intelligence of its handler. If a good dog has a bad handler success of the case cannot be achieved.

The use of dogs in police work has been adopted by almost all the modern police forces of the world. The first police dog appeared in India in the North West Frontier Province (now in Pakistan) as early as in 1941. Madras raised a Kennel in 1951 to be followed by Bihar in 1955. Since then dogs are being used in other states and by the para-military forces. To the credit of police dogs is the detection of a very large number of grave crimes, and they are increasingly used in crime detection work, although the climatic conditions of the country hamper their success.

There is a Standing Advisory Committee which co-ordinates the breeding, supply and training of police dogs throughout the country. It may be mentioned with pride that one police dog had succeeded in catching not less than 100 miscreants, and when the last miscreant was put on trial, the Presiding Judge observed:

> "I regret that the court cannot communicate its appreciation to this remarkable animal. If it were possible to promote police dogs for performance of duty, this dog should certainly be elevated in rank".

8. Traffic Police and Enforcement of Road Traffic Laws

To control traffic, enforcement of laws and regulations to facilitate orderly movements of traffic and action to prevent and investigate road accidents are primarily a police responsibility. Section 31 of the Police Act of 1861, stipulates that it is the duty of the police to keep order on public roads, streets, thoroughfares, *ghats*, landing places and all other places of public resort, and to regulate assemblies and processions *etc.*

The Wedgewood Committee examined the problems related to road traffic and its recommendations led to the legislation of the Motor Vehicle Act of 1939. This was the first comprehensive piece of legislation on the subject. This All-India Act has been amended several times to keep it up-to-date. It was repealed and replaced by the Motor Vehicle Act of 1988, which came into force with effect from July 1, 1989.

With rapid industrialisation, unprecedented mechanisation and larger concentration of population in cities and towns, the problem of traffic control over-shadows any other police regulatory task. The magnitude of the road traffic problem can be visualised from the fact that over 6000 people are killed annually in accident in nine metropolitan cities, and the number of accident victims involving teenaged, is steadily on the increase. This shifts the onus of responsibility for the accident from the victim's ignorance to the killer's aggressiveness. Heading the death list are pedestrians (45 per cent) followed by bicyclists and rickshaw drivers (34 per cent) and two wheelers (16 per cent). Only a meagre five per cent of accident victims are occupants of car, drivers or passengers. Many traffic experts testify that with the induction of more and more fast-moving cars, the frequency of hit and run deaths is on the rise. There are "unknown vehicles" most of which are suspected to be Marutis. However, the trucks are the main scourge followed by buses for having claimed several hundred lives.

The statistics below compiled by an expert group, "Accident Prevention and Trauma Care Management" at Trivendrum in 1987 reveal that over 40,000 people are killed every year in road accidents in India, that the accidents rate per 10,000 vehicles is over three times as high and fatality rate almost 15 times as high as those in the developed countries, and that in India, which has one per cent of the total number of vehicles in the world, accounts for 6 per cent of the road accidents.

Country	Accidents per 1,000 vehicles	Fatalities per 1,000 vehicles	Injuries per 1,000 vehicles
India	31.8	5.9	163
Britain	14.0	0.4	24
U.S.A.	12.2	0.3	25
Japan	9.8	0.2	18
France	8.7	0.4	50

Automobile accidents are caused due to many factors, "Negligence" being the most important, both of the operator and the victim. Many accidents can be prevented by proper enforcement of traffic laws and rules, better road conditions and education of the public, as also improving pedestrian facilities. Enforcement of traffic laws and rules should not be limited to punitive measures based on arrest and prosecution but should include such non-punitive as active and conspicuous patrol, warnings and traffic education right from the school level. Such measures are more liked and naturally welcome by the public, who extend the needed co-operation. Courtesy and at the same time firmness make a good traffic policeman, for which proper training courses and exercises have necessarily to be frequently taken. Mobile traffic patrols have been found to be very useful in controlling and regulating traffic. The roads in Indian cities have been planned almost a century before and they leave no scope for further width in order to accommodate the ever-increasing vehicular and pedestrian traffic on them on account of the constant increase in the population. Therefore, traffic control presents the most complex problem as reduction or dissipation of the vehicular and pedestrian traffic on such saturatedly crowded roads is almost impossible. While growing new cities or expanding the present ones this utmost and irremoveable difficulty should be first taken into consideration by the town planners. On most of the roads there are on either side commercial establishments and the owners or their customers park their vehicles on the roadside reducing the already narrow roads to almost zero breadth position for movement. People do not like separate vehicular parks and the needed co-operation in this regard is never extended by them to the police, if some ingenious officer thinks about such a scheme. At present, it appears that there are no visible signs of improvement in the situation, though the traffic police are striving their best to remedy this exasperating situation. Even cattle squat on the roads and hamper traffic movements.

In the metropolitan cities conditions for regulating traffic are much better, as several agencies are working for meeting the traffic requirements such as construction of broad roads and their maintenance, allotment of parking spaces, location of bus, rickshaw and taxi stands, bus stoppages, installation of traffic signals, proper lighting *etc.*

Regulation of traffic has two aspects: (1) Regulation of traffic inside the Municipal limits, and (2) Regulation of traffic on highways. While all cities in India have a separate traffic branch under the city police, the regulation of traffic on the highways is left to the local police stations concerned which do not have sufficient manpower and equipment to provide highway patrols. The police investigates all cases of road accidents, but these investigations are not thorough as with the increase in the road accidents, the police station strength does not increase with the consequential result that most of the offenders are untraced and go unpunished.

Those few cases, sent up for trial, either do not end in conviction or the punishment given by the courts is very trifle, even in fatal accidents, and, therefore, there is no deterring effect on traffic rules violators. The law of the land, in this regard, has to be amended with a view to impose heavy punishment to such offenders so as to ensure determent. It is the safety aspect for which the police are held responsible, while the causes which lead to lack of safety are the conduct and competence of road users and the role of other agencies whose performance is vital for effective management of traffic police, and each of them has to bear in mind the most important factor of human element.

The National Police Commission in their 7th report recommended that all major road accidents should be examined in detail through research and analysis to ensure that the defects in road engineering do not lead to accidents in future. They also recommended the establishment of a road safety cell headed by an engineer, who is an expert in Traffic engineering with members consisting of representatives from other departments and agencies, including the police. The Motor Vehicle Act of 1988, provided under Section 215, for the constitution of a National Road Safety Council at the Central, as also State level.

9. Police Wireless Communication

Use of wireless communication for police purposes linking a few states was started in 1946 and consolidated in 1949 by the establishment of the Director of Co-ordination (Police Wireless) and wireless links between Delhi and the headquarters of several states, which in turn were similarly linked with the headquarters of the district. These links operate in high frequency (HF) channels which facilitated transmission of messages through code signals. The next stage of improvement in this facility was in 1964 when very high frequency (VHF) channels were introduced and the headquarters in the districts were enabled to have communication of speech, as different from morse code messages, with subordinate units within the district. Control Rooms were established in important cities and linked with mobile patrol vans by VHF in the urban police wireless network. In this development, rest of the police stations have been connected by VHF with their respective district headquarters.

As an extension of the VHF network mentioned above, portable pocket sets have been supplied to police officers on patrol duties in most of the Commissionerate cities and in some major cities in order to acquire and ensure constant touch with the police stations or the Control Room and secure adequate and speedy response in an emergency. The growing needs of the communication system have mostly been met by the Government. In the next stage of expansion when the police sought frequencies in the Ultra High Range (UHR) and Micro Wave Band for having direct speech on multi-channel between the State Police Headquarters and the different units in the districts, they came across an objection from the Posts and Telegraphs (P and T) Department, who as a national carrier of all communications, have been insisting on providing this communication facility in the higher range from the P and T network itself without allowing a further expansion of the independent police wireless network. The microwave channels would certainly prove a great asset in the efficient supervision and control of police tasks, as has been permitted, as a special case in Tamil Nadu.

The National Police Commission recommended that the police should be allotted the necessary frequencies in the category of UHF and microwave range to facilitate the expansion of the police wireless set-up in different states in the interest of national security as well as police efficiency. This will co-ordinate and facilitate meshing with the P and T network at certain points which would enable the two systems help each other on a reciprocal basis in temporary failure situation.

Out of 399 districts in the country almost half are connected with teleprinters. The National Police Commission has recommended teleprinter coverage to all districts and the introduction of cryptographic machines for transmission of classified information.

The allotment of frequencies to the police even in the HF and VHF categories has not been up to their requirements, which are varied and their communication ranges are from a few hundred metres to thousands of kilometeres. The total number of static terminals are about 20,000, and the total holding of wireless sets of all types by the Centre and States have exceeded 60,000. At present there is acute shortage of frequencies and only a dozen additional HF frequencies have been allotted in the recent past against a demand of 209 HF frequencies. At present the Bharat Heavy Electrical Ltd., cater to the needs of the Police Department by providing wireless sets to it, but their number and efficiency are wanting improvements.

The expanding network of police wireless demands adequate number of properly trained personnel for operating different varieties of equipment. At present training of wireless personnel is arranged at the Central Police Radio Training Institution run by the Directorate of Co-ordination (Wireless) and a few other State Radio Centres. However, the total capacity of these centres is hardly 50 per cent of the overall requirements. The National Police Commission has recommended the augmentation of the present training facilities and setting up of a fully equipped Central Workshop at the headquarters of each State supplemented by regional workshops to take proper care of these sophisticated equipments.

10. Women Police

Women first entered the police force in India as early as 1938. Even prior to the Independence, a few provinces and Princely States had employed women in the police force. Delhi Police force was first to recruit policewomen on a regular basis with effect from 1948. The number of policewomen was practically negligible in other states until 1960s. Section 51(2) of the Code of Criminal Procedure stipulated that whenever it is necessary to cause a female to be searched, the search shall be made by another women with strict regard to decency. For this purpose, in the absence of policewomen, police officers hired women.

With the perceptible increase in the number of crimes against women, as well as by women, and difficulties to find hired women, more and more states started recruiting women police and even since 1970s the number of policewomen has grown rapidly, but today their strength is far from adequate. Earlier the response to the effort to recruit women in the police force, had, by and large, been lukewarm. A rough survey revealed that 60 per cent of candidates are from police families or having some connection with the latter.

Many women reject police work because of the round the clock schedule, the personal risk factor due to dangers inherent in the job, the exposure to the more sordid, seamy side of life, the semi-military pattern of operations and discipline. Of late, however, the situation has undergone a change and college educated unmarried girls from lower income groups and very few from middle income groups are showing eagerness to join. Even so, police women form hardly one per cent of the total police force in India, today.

There is a rapid increase in the crimes committed by women and in which women are victims. Demonstration in the streets by women were practically unknown before the Independence. Now-a-days, the greatest problem facing the police is to deal with women and children demonstrators in the public places.

Women act as carriers of contraband gold, narcotic drugs, wrist-watches and other valuable articles and often the small smuggled goods are concealed inside their private parts. Male Law enforcement officials find it a problem to search them effectively. Not infrequently when a woman is arrested, she becomes hysterical and does not hesitate to bring in false charges, for example outraging her modesty against the male police officer who arrested her. Male policemen engaged in law enforcement in brothels are often charged with free sex by the prostitutes.

In the enforcement phase of police work, policewomen are generally acceptable to women and children who have been victims of sexual offences. Women police officers find it easier to get leads about the offenders in such cases, which male officers have failed to get in interviews, because the victims feel more at ease with women police. Runaway constitutes an important segment of the delinquency picture, and in the case of runaway girls of nubile age group, of course, women police are indispensable. The very nature of a woman enables her to relate instinctively with a person in distress, and in the same way, she senses her maternal sympathy. In the enforcement of Immoral Traffic (Prevention) Act, the Juvenile Justice Act, Child Marriages Restraint Act and in cases of dowry deaths women police have proved extremely useful. Seemingly the public is not aware of the vast area of law enforcement where women police can be and have been effective. There are about 15,000 women police officers and other ranks at present in the country in the various states and the number falls too short of the requirement. Often when a policewoman is not available to a particular police station, she is procured from either the district headquarters or nearby police station by requisition. Recently, the Central Reserve Police Force (CRPF) and the Central Industrial Security Force (CISF) have formed women police units which have proved a great asset in the due discharge of their duties relating to crowds. Some of the states have also established police stations manned entirely by policewomen, for example, Kerala, Andhra Pradesh, Delhi, Orissa, and Madhya Pradesh. They handle reports where either a woman is a complainant or an offender. In the examination of female and juvenile witnesses' womenpolice have been found to be very useful. In demonstrations police women have a great calming effect on aggressive behaviour and elicitless violence and abuse than male policemen. The first women to be appointed in the Indian Police Service (IPS) was Kiran A. Bedi in 1972. Since then many women have joined the EPS and their successful participation in a common training programme with their male counterpart in the National Police Academy constituted a unique development in the history of police in India. Several women police officers are recipients of the gallantry awards. In the role of honour, Kiran Bedi tops the list, not only for police functions but also for the reforms she has brought about in the Tihar Jail (Delhi) as Inspector General of Prisons. For her singular reformative services she has been rewarded with the prestigious "MAGSAY SAY" award, which no police officer throughout the entire police forces of the world, has so far received.

16

System of Policing

1. Police Station and Station House Officer

Section 2(5) of the Criminal Procedure Code defines "Police Station", it is the old "*Thanedari*" police system introduced by Lord Cornwallis in 1793. It has, over the years, suffered from major defects, namely large and unwieldy jurisdictions, poor and inferior quality of officer-in-charge and inadequate strength.

A police station is the kingpin of the entire police edifice. For the bulk of citizens living in the country, whether living in a city or town, or in a remote village, it is at the level of the jurisdictional police station that the citizens are mostly in touch with the police and the police with the people. Citizens come to police station with their grievances or complaints against persons known or unknown, from whom they have suffered or apprehended injury or harm to their property or person. They lodge information or complaints. The public expectations from the police can only be fulfilled if the public are satisfied with the integrity, fortitude, professionalism, impartiality and promptness in the service rendered by the jurisdictional police station. Therefore any reform to strengthen policing, either in urban or rural areas, has to deal with the organisation, location and working of the police station.

Many police stations are vast and unwieldy in size and their areas are more than 350 square miles. Some police stations have an area of 1176 sq. miles catering to a population of 19 lakhs in some parts of the country. Some of the villages in rural areas have now grown into townships due to rapid urbanisation and industrialisation, but such unwieldy police stations have continued to remain in rural areas. Therefore, it is now necessary that every five years there should be a review of the areas and jurisdiction of police stations and they should not be required to cater to unmanageable police station units. Although the prevention and detection of crime remain the primary duties of the police, such duties, as are not concerned with crime and criminals, are also required to be performed by them. Such duties are connected with the personal safety and general welfare of the public and with the administration of a number of laws, regulations, administrative orders and the like. The number of laws, regulations *etc.*, which the police are required to enforce has grown rapidly over the years and the public, even the police cannot keep track with them. It is difficult to think of any department of the administration whose dealing with the public may not bring the police into action at one stage of the other.

Today crime can no longer be regarded as a mere anti-social activity of a comparatively small number of criminally disposed, or merely vicious individuals. The alarming growth in the volume of crimes and violence and its trends, particularly its extension to politicians and women is most dangerous characteristics. Political crimes, hitherto unknown to our criminal calendar, have appeared. The great and growing extent of crimes and violence today is not a temporary phenomenon and it has become a growing social malady. The pattern of crime is changing, and enlarging and police methods could not keep pace with these changes in crimes and with the clever brains responsible for them.

All these problems narrated above have to be tackled at the level of the police station itself. Therefore, police stations have to be strengthened and made effective, as also the integrity, professional competence and impartiality of its members have to be ensured. The staff has to be in strength commensurate with the volume of work in a number of areas, and exactly this is urgently wanting. A police station, to be effective, should be a compact unit. It is always due to want of timely and effective action at the level of police station that problems develop into major threats to public order.

The officer-in-charge of a Police Station defined under Section 2 of the Criminal Procedure Code, and commonly known as Station House Officer (SHO) is the cornerstone of the whole system. Superior police officers assume powers of the SHO for the purpose of investigation of crimes by virtue of Section 36 of the Criminal Procedure Code. The SHO wields enormous powers under most of the laws of the land. The outstanding duty of the SHO is to prevent and detect crime, but from the recent past it has been relegated to a discretionary status by the multifarious duties he is asked to perform by the Government. He must be in touch with all that happens in his jurisdiction, and keep the higher officers fully and constantly informed. He must maintain good relations with the magistracy and other officials, village headmen and people generally. He must know the criminals and their anti-social activities with a view to apprehend them or keep them in check by suitable measures. He has no disciplinary powers himself, and yet, he is expected to control his subordinates and goad them to action. This anomaly has to be corrected by giving the SHO suitable disciplinary powers to inflict minor punishments to his subordinates, who can be controlled most effectively only by this provision. As policemen lose incentive if the payment of reward is delayed they tend to become lethargic, apathetic, arrogant and disciplinary incorrigible if immediate punishment is not meted to them for their dereliction of duty. Generally, a Sub-inspector of police is the SHO, but according to the importance of certain police station an Inspector is put in-charge of that police station.

2. Urban Police

Our census described an urban area with a minimum population of 5,000, and it categorise all towns with a population of one lakh and over as cities. Section 8 of the Code of Criminal Procedure 1973 defines any city whose population exceeds one million as a metropolitan area. The problem of policing urban, rural and metropolitan areas are many times different, although universally police enforce the same laws of the land. In cities, there is concentration of population due to large scale movement of people from villages to cities, even from long distances, in search of employment. In addition, there is the existence of a large floating population, the presence of unplanned slums due to shortage of housing, all cumulatively increase anonymity. Sophisticated and special nature of crime, the prevalence of the large-scale racketing in drugs, wine and women, gambling and running of brothels and other vices in various forms seem to be accepted as unavoidable evils. Rapidly expanding slow and fast moving vehicles create serious traffic problems. There is presence of crowd everywhere and every minute gangsterism, labour and student unrest and inter-party clashes, public or political demonstrations in shape of processions and *bandhs* are mainly urban phenomenon entailing the rapid and frequent development of law and order problems.

Guarding of vital installations and providing security to MPs and MLAs residing in the area and visiting dignitaries is a major problem in urban areas. Providing protection to citizens against crime and criminals, day and night, requires adequate police arrangements, such as foot and mobile patrolling. Law and order problems arise frequently because of the activities of the various organised gangs or groups. Urban areas are characterised by much greater awareness of the rights of citizens. Cognizable cases must be registered and investigated promptly, and effective and timely preventive measures must be taken to ensure order. Public opinion is vocal and there is a vigilant and active press, and all these put pressure on the police for improved behaviour and better performance. To tackle all these complex and multi-faceted problems of the city, the Commissionerate Police System, in which the entire police force is placed under the charge of a single functionary — the Commissioner of Police, has been introduced in most of the Metropolitan cities. He is endowed with all the regulatory and licensing powers under various Acts which are normally exercised by the District Magistrate of the District. Besides, the powers of restraints under the Code of Criminal Procedure are also vested in the Commissioner. In the District Police system, the District Magistrate is in overall charge of the criminal administration of the district, and he is the final authority, legally speaking, in any matters affecting law and order. However, with the separation of the judiciary from the executive, the powers of the District Magistrate in respect of law and order and crime administration are now limited to the issue of prohibitory orders under section 144 of the Criminal Procedure Code of 1973 (including imposition of curfew) and to the security sections of the same Code. During the British regime the commissionerate system was introduced in Bombay, Calcutta, Madras, and now it has been extended to Delhi, Nagpur, Pune, Thane, Ahmedabad, Baroda, Hyderabad,

Trivandrum and Bangalore. Except in Calcutta, where the Commissioner of Police functions independently and is directly under the Home Department of the State, all Commissioners of Police function under the administrative control of their respective Inspector General/Director General. Various State Police Commissions and National Police Commissions have recommended that all cities having a population of 5 lakhs should have commissionerate police system, as what is needed is a police system capable of going into effective action at short notice, functioning under a well-organised professional police leadership directly responsible and accountable to the government, the legislative, the press and the public.

3. Village Police

There is ample evidence to conclude that there was a village police system for the compact social group of each village, even during the *Vedic* period, although it has undergone changes in respect of powers and duties with the changing pattern of the society. In ancient times every village was a self-administered unit. The Epic India marked the transition from village to urban life. Town of considerable importance like Mithila, Ayodhya, Hastinapur *etc.* sprung up. Epic kings, made laws, instituted courts and organised police and intelligence services and ensured internal order. Kings depended very largely on the information of their spies for the administration. The institution of village headmen continued, but more attention was given to the environs of the palace and in and around the growing towns. During later period (800 to 320 BC), the headmen exerted great influence and maintained peace in the village with the help of village watchmen. Each village constituted a petty Commonwealth, having a complete system of municipal police in which the regal, ecclesiastical and general interests were represented and respectively provided for. Each village, town, city and district were provided with officers of police with gradation of rank. The village policemen were paid by contributions from every inhabitant. During the Mughal period the police administration was mainly confined to the seat of their power. Being largely preoccupied with conquests and collection of revenue, the Mughals were only marginally involved in policing of villages.

Outside the urban pockets, the maintenance of law and order remained in the hands of Zamindars and big landlords, who exercised Police, Revenue and Magisterial functions.

The British retained the prevailing system of police in thc country-wide with a few minor changes. The Police Commissions of 1860 and 1902-03 expressed the conviction that the village police ought not to be separated from the village organisation and placed under the regular police. They recommended the strengthening of the position of village headman by (1) not subordinating him to the regular police force headed by the Superintendent of Police, (2) Placing him under the control of the District Magistrate, (3) giving him magisterial powers to try petty offences, and (4) having the village watchmen directly under him, so as not to subvert the system in its essential principles.

Section 40 of the Code of Criminal Procedure, 1973 imposed certain obligatory duties on the village headman, accountant (*Patwari*) watchman, every member of the village panchayat *etc.*, in the sphere of law enforcement. They are primarily responsible for communication of information about cognizable offences committed in their jurisdiction to the nearest Magistrate or the officer-in-charge of the police station. Guarding the village, patrolling for the purpose of prevention of crime, protection of the persons and property, reporting of unnatural deaths, guarding of corpse and its surroundings, assisting Magistrates in any inquest, removal of dead bodies to morgue, disposal of unidentified dead bodies, providing assistance to Magistrates and police officers during enquiry and investigation *etc.* are important aspects of the rural police work.

The village police systems, as existing in various states, are the outcome of historical developments. There is no uniformity in these systems, and they differ from state to state. After the Independence and the enactment of Panchayat Raj Act, the position altered radically. The Balwant Rai Mehta Committee excluded the law and order functions from the Panchayat Raj as it was felt and also experienced that in faction-ridden Panchayats, the elected *Sarpanches* are likely to use the police to further their own ends. Besides, an increase of inter-castes and inter-class feuds and violence and other forms of crime, affluence and decentralisation of power in the rural areas unleashed powerful crimogenic forces. Experience has shown that the crime problems in villages are no longer simple as compared to the pre-Independence days. Now-a-days all types of crimes are committed in rural areas, and they have become more intricate and complex eluding detection and subsequent punishment to the perpetrators.

The success of police operations in rural areas depends mainly upon prompt communication of information about a crime by the village functionaries and adequate and efficient staff of regular police to handle them. Most cognizable offences are suppressed, they are not reported to the police, nor the police register them, even if reported, police stations are not only few in number to serve the public but most inadequately staffed. Justice to the common man is not available or denied.

Our Criminal Justice System has completely collapsed. Militant organisations like Naxalite, Maoist Communist Centre (MCC) in Bihar and People's War Group (PWG) in Andhra Pradesh are increasingly enforcing an extra judicial system in the country-side, meeting out instant and brutal justice. In the country side of Assam, the United Liberation Front Army (ULFA) and BODO concentrated areas are running parallel administration. In these areas the writ of the government does not run. In Bihar the MCC is in full control of 9 districts — Gaya, Aurangabad, Chatra, Palamau, Jehanabad, Patna (rural), Nawadah, Hazaribagh and Giridih. It has let loose reign of terror. Failing to get justice through governmental agencies, more and more villagers are approaching the MCC's court for justice. The MCC extorts tolls from persons having money at gunpoints and hold up development activities to keep the region backward so that they could continue to exploit the wretched condition of the poor. The police have ceased to function, and the rule of law has disappeared completely.

The village watchmen have now fallen between two stools, namely, the magistracy and the Panchayat and the politicians combined. The police are hardly in the picture. Village watchmen are mostly engaged with the duties of the Panchayat administration and their contribution to police administration is almost nil.

Not only the system of rural policing has to be streamlined and made more effective, but the jurisdictions of the disproportionately large rural police stations should be made more compact and manageable. It is also an urgent necessity to augment the police station staff to handle crime and other problems surfacing after the Independence. At present for 675 of the urban population there is one policeman, whereas for 5,403 rural population there is one policeman. In terms of area, the ratio ranges from one police station for 7.9 Sq. kms. in the urban areas to one for 1,069 Sq. kms. in rural areas. Over the years, the villages in India have undergone vast changes. Crime has increased, sophisticated and new methods have been devised to commit then, law and order problems, new social legislations have multiplied. Accent on helping the weaker sections has increased. And all these factors have cumulatively increased the duties and responsibilities of the police, the strength of which continue to remain hopelessly inadequate.

We must take note of the fact that unrest in rural areas has been growing and consolidating in different regions. The ineffectiveness of policing account for emergence of private "*Senas*" (armies) among Hindus and Muslims, and also among landlords and landless peasants, armed to the teeth for protection. They are mostly anti-social and criminal gangs. Already in India there are too many guns around, both licensed and unlicensed in our communalised and castiest conditions. These private *senas* are utilised to eliminate anyone who stands in the way of our amoralities, of which there are endless variations, and undoubtedly this is a symptom of the gap left by the police. If this serious and disquieting development is to be reversed, the overall policing has to be strengthened.

The work of policing by its very nature entails constant interaction of the public with the police station and its staff. The powers vested in the SHO under the various laws of the land are enormous having very wide discretion and the execution of these powers has far-reaching effect on the fundamental and other rights of the citizens. The potential for corruption and abuse of power exist to a great degree with unending temptations and the eventuating opportunities. Therefore, it is imperative and equally important that adequate supervision is exercised over the working of police stations and this responsibility falls mainly upon all the supervisory officers of and above the rank of Sub-inspector and they can only do this work, provided they are of the strictest rectitude, and insulated from corruption-cum-temptation of whatever kind.

4. Police Patrol

Among many duties performed by the police, effective patrol remains the epitome of police service to the community. No police chief of any country in the world has questioned the absolute need of patrols, which are indispensable to acquire good criminal administration and control on crime and criminals.

While the police force to be at its best must always maintain more or less the essential features of a military establishment, the individual policeman on his beat is at once a soldier, watchman, detective, lawyer, judge, public censor of morals and general regulator of human conduct from spitting on the sidewalks to committing homicide, from giving the people free use of the public streets to the apprehension of criminals that come within the scope of his duties.

A policeman on patrol duty, whether in an urban or rural area, is the visible symbol of law and order. A signal from him brings fireman, ambulance and additional police. He carries heavy responsibilities, for protecting every house, shop, and office and properties of the people. He must always remember that citizens are sleeping beyond the dark windows, secure in the knowledge that they are safe, because the policeman on patrol is walking the beat. This is the status of the patrolman on beat duty and the confidence of the citizens reposed in him, but even a fraction of this is not true or applicable to a patrolman in this country, because other duties, having political considerations, usually take off a policeman from his patrol duty, and seconded to such work as would not be useful to the citizens, who contribute towards his emoluments and maintenance. The result? Citizens have always suffered, as also the reputation of the Police Force, which is unable to deliver the goods for which it has been raised by the taxpayers. In the European, American and Japanese cities the police administration puts the largest possible number of patrolmen in uniform in the streets at all times during day and night mainly for the prevention and detection of crime, regulating traffic and crowd in the streets.

The patrol officer is the direct representative of the police department. Developing contacts within the community, in his beat, is the foremost responsibility for the total police department. There must be rapport and meaningful interaction between the patrol officer and the people in his beat. He has to develop contacts with criminal ranks and vice operators, and at the same time ensure that he does not become a victim of the vices. He must, by his own conduct and behaviour, acquire enthusiastic support of the law-abiding segments of the society and frighten the law breakers. The patrolman has to ensure that all occurrences in his beat are promptly reported to the police station. These are the essential objectives of a patrolman, and the foundation stone of a good policing system, which ultimately brings a police station into good or bad repute for efficiency and police-public relationships.

The SHO has to survey very carefully his jurisdiction and prescribe the various beats to be patrolled by the available policemen and at the same time ensure that the whole beat area is kept under constant watch and observation by the patrolman for obtaining better results in combating crime and criminals and detect offences. There are various types/methods of patrol:

(i) *Foot Patrol*: It is the oldest and original type of police patrol, and its usefulness remains undisputed. It yields excellent results, far more satisfactory than mobile patrol. The method of foot patrol consists of fixed points, surveillance pickets. A foot patrol has a special value in maintaining good rapport with the public, obtaining better information and maintaining high degree of service to the people. If worked uninterrupted on proper lines, a foot patrolman will be an encyclopaedia of his beat.

(ii) *Automobile Patrol*: In recent years use of automobiles equipped with radio in patrol duty has been spectacular. It covers a large area, but one of the foremost rules to be adhered to is that the patrolmen in the vehicle should get out of it frequently, and move about at random in various directions, for some time maintaining the element of surprise in their movements.

(iii) *Horse Patrol*: They are used in big congregations to maintain law and order and to regulate easy flow of pedestrian traffic. The horse rider, on account of his elevated position, can see clearly the distant crowd. It is very seldom used, because at all places there are no police horses.

(iv) *Motorcycle Patrol*: It is primarily used in fair weather for control of vehicular traffic. Its use is restricted to cities and towns.

(v) *Bicycle Patrol*: These patrols are used in such places where automobiles cannot negotiate.

(vi) *Miscellaneous Patrols*: Plain Clothed Patrol, Fixed Point Patrol, Border Patrol, Highway Patrol, Harbour Patrol, Railway Patrol, Special Patrol and Air Patrol do not need any description as their names fully explain how they are deployed. When they are to be deployed will rest on the exigencies of the situation, which the SHO is required to monitor.

(vii) *Block Patrol (Nakabandi)*: In this form of patrol a large number of policemen are required to seal the entire area so as to prevent ingress or exgress through the block patrol without being noticed by the patrolmen on duty. When there is spurt in crime in a concentrated area this patrol is useful to catch the offenders, but if there is no element of surprise in the deployment of this form of patrol no useful results would accrue.

(viii) *Flying Squads*: It is a team of police consisting of a Sub-inspector and four to six constables, and head constables, moving in a vehicle fitted with a two-way radio equipments. It is at the disposal of the main control room which monitors its movements and directs it to reach the place of the crime about which the control room is informed. Actually, for all purposes it is a mobile police station for taking prompt action against crime and criminals.

5. Patrol Officer

The officer-in-charge of a patrol must be at least of the rank of a Sub-inspector and it is extremely important, and also essential because he is the first official of the law enforcement agency who comes into contact with the public, and how he acts in the performance of his duty, determines the attitude of the public towards him, the Police Department and the Government. It is also equally essential and important that the staff under him is properly trained in their duties and responsibilities. All of them should function without any prejudice or bias against particular class of the society, and under no circumstances, they should observe or be inclined to racial, social, economic, caste and creed discriminations.

Although patrol duties and the eventuating work is the foundation of good and successful police administration, on several occasions the patrolmen on duty are withdrawn and asked to function other various jobs, most of which relate to "bandobast duties" on the visit of VIPs or law and order. If they are withdrawn for the latter exigency, for days together they perform it and actually no beat is served by a police patrol. The patrol duty remains a theoretical conception only in the Police Manuals with the consequential sufferance of the citizens, who contribute to the police budgets, and as such they are denied their constitutional right of police protection. The cause of this malady is often argued to be dearth or paucity of policemen, which no doubt is the real one, and yet, the Government has done precious little to correct this malady by augmenting the requisite police strength in each police station, as it rightly feels that Police Department does not earn revenue for the Government.

But the Government and the public fail to realise that a good, efficient and impartial police system will alone be capable of ensuring the safety of the country and its citizens.

6. Informers in Police Work

The success of the police department in detecting and controlling crime and its prevention to a large extent, depends on the use of reliable informers. In the first place their identity is a closely kept secret which is never divulged to any senior police officer, or for that matter, to anybody even the courts. Every police officer has his own circle of informers, whom he has cultivated over a period of years.

Police informers, as distinct from "informants", are usually people of unsavoury character and associate with criminals, anti-socials and other law-breakers. Whatever their character originality, mixing constantly with anti-socials must eventually make them tainted. Informers are not pleasant to handle, but often produce excellent results. In his contact with the criminal classes, the policeman must be ever on the alert to locate and cultivate the person, male or female, who has information to give. Usually, information will not be volunteered unless appropriate inducement is given, and he must weigh carefully its value against the privilege or advancement sought.

Informers can be divided into three groups:

1. Those who inform occasionally,
2. The habituals, and
3. The purveyor of information on a professional basis.

Occasional informers are those people who may bear a grudge or for high motives because of their sense of duty or a public-spirited desire to help the police, or those seeking the proclaimed reward. As a general rule, occasional informers, having divulged their information, rarely come in contact with police again. However, the manner in which police handles their confidence influences their future co-operation and assistance.

The habitual informer is usually motivated by gain, but not always of money. He or she, is usually a law-breaker and seeks to trade information for special privileges. In this area and activity, we encounter gangsters, gamblers, drug-peddlers, prostitutes, liquor vendors and carriers of any other vicious trade. They always prove a valuable source of information.

The professional informer is usually a hardened criminal, recently released from jail or a criminal on bail, who is quite capable of dodging the police. He often attempts to sell bogus information.

The cultivation of informers is a very difficult task. When dealing with suspects the selection of informers is a very difficult task and not all suspects can be used as informers. After the initial contact some favour or inducement should be shown to them and on results payment can be made to them and not on promises. "Secret Service Fund" is specially made available to the Police Department out of which payments are made for the information given. The payment is sometimes very high depending on the nature of information furnished. Promises, threats or undue pressure will often produce a desire to give false information.

Influences which usually induce people to inform on others are emotions such as hatred, jealousy, greed, or a desire for revenge. More practical reasons are a desire to bargain for the right to continue illegal activities, to avoid penal action for a crime committed by the informer, to ingratiate and occasionally on a higher plane, to repay a good turn done to him by a policeman. A dishonest informer, when short of money will often sell bogus information. In assessing his values and motives there is no substitute for police experience.

At all times policemen must be conscious of the need to protect the informer, not only from his associates and acquaintances but also from unwanted police attention. To be of use to the police he has to consort with known criminals and cannot hope to escape police surveillance. In dealing with informers' absolute secrecy as to their identity and activities should be maintained. If the informer is exposed, the police may not only lose a source of information but could as well be responsible for loosing the informer's life. Therefore, the police must ensure fool-proof protection to informers. No matter what the cost, policemen must keep their word to the informers. Under no circumstances should they be employed in any area of activity where they may be accepted as police, and at all times they should be kept outside the normal scope of police work. Except in very rare instances, where informers hold high position politically or otherwise, senior policemen should use junior members to make actual contact with informers. Under no circumstances should an informer be permitted to call the policeman's office or home, and they should always meet at the previously and frequently changing selected place to avoid detection. An informer must never be utilised as a prosecution witness. Code names should always be used, both for the nature of information and its giver.

An informer, committing criminal or anti-social acts should never be allowed to escape action by the police, and the sense of "Sacrosanct" should never be allowed to touch the mind of the informer. If an informer is paid out of "Secret Service Fund" it is advisable to obtain his receipt, provided he is willing to give, and there should be no compulsion in this regard. The "Secret Service Fund" is beyond the scope of audit by any agency and this provision has been made to maintain the requisite and necessary utmost secrecy.

Many a times under-cover operatives, both serving policemen as well as known criminals are used with good results, and there is nothing unusual about this method, as it has proved very useful, all over the world, in the capture and elimination of criminals worked for a large number of felonies and who had, on innumerable occasions, eluded police detection. And such was the practice advocated by Acharya Chanakya during his period. Serving in-cognito police personnel have often proved to be extremely useful in fishing out information against people of any status after their induction in the latter's domestic lives. They could be deployed for political as well as criminal intelligence.

17
Policeman in Making

1. Recruitment

No Police Force, throughout the world, however, equipped with sophisticated gadgets, can claim perfection without proper training of only the deserving recruits, who have aptitude, pleasure and pride for police functions. Therefore, a great care has to be taken before a person is recruited to the force while verifying his antecedents and testing his physical and mental capabilities. In order to recruit deserving candidates the Government of India had constituted "Gore Committee" in 1972 to make an exhaustive enquiry on "Police Training" and suggest and recommend ways and means with a view to securing proper recruits, enlist and train them as the efficiency of the force was greatly depleted. To quote the report of the Committee: "The nature of the police role in a democracy requires that the members should be selected impartially. They should be administratively competent, politically neutral, and imbued with the spirit of selfless service. A police officer enjoys vast powers under the law and exercises wide discretion. The recruitment procedures should, therefore, be so devised that they are free from political, personal or corruptive influence. The need for objectivity in selection cannot but be over-emphasised. It is pointed out that there is a deliberate strategy of political parties injecting into the police system through channels of recruitment at different levels, young men who are strongly committed to the ideologies of political parties and could be expected to influence from within, the functioning of the police system to conform to these ideologies. In the last two decades, instead of weeding out such persons, there is a preponderance of them, as Government had given prominence to the 52 per cent reservation and quota system based on cast and class. Orders are received directly from the ministers to recruit their recommended candidates, and failure to comply with such instructions, any directive, ended in privations to the disobedient officer. The result is that the police efficiency, competency, reliability, honesty, probity and integrity and all other qualifications of a good policeman have been eroded to the point of their extinction. It is absolutely necessary that the police administration *vis-a-vis* the government must engage in a responsible recruitment programme to select only the deserving candidates, who are available in hundreds even in the classes and castes belonging to the "Reserved Categories".

Today, the picture of the force is frightening. The members of the force, no longer constitute a homogeneous body for the common goal of efficient police administration, but they are overpowered by caste and class and creedal prejudices and hatred, which become manifest in their discriminatory enforcement of law and maintenance of public peace and tranquillity. The Governments, both of the Centre and the State, are fully aware of this police administrative malady, and had requested the National Police Commission to study this problem and suggest ways and means for correction. The National Police Commission recommended that much attention is needed in the recruitment of police in all ranks, free from communal, castes and political prejudice so that they can render impartial service to the public. Every right-thinking person is fully aware how important it is for policemen not even to be suspected of any bias, although it is a part of our society where social, communal, political prejudices are common, which have continuously harmed the development and progress of the Nation in all the spheres. Can it be remedied under the present policy of appeasement of Government? Perhaps, "No" until each and every citizen of this country is treated on parity irrespective of his caste, creed and political affiliations.

The police hierarchy in states consists of the following in descending order:

1. Director General of Police,
2. Inspector General of Police,
3. Deputy Inspector General of Police,
4. Superintendent of Police,
5. Assistant Superintendent of Police,

6. Deputy Superintendent of Police,
7. Inspector of Police/Subedar,
8. Sub-inspector of Police,
9. Sergeant,
10. Head Constable/Havildar,
11. Naik,
12. Lance Naik, and
13. Constables

As one descends this hierarchy ladder the strength of the cadre increases in number. Constables stand first in relation to their number in the force and as such maximum care has to be taken while recruiting them, because an unworthy constable would always pose a potential danger in jeopardising the force in view of his numerical strength. Absolute confidence and obedience of lawful orders are necessary from each member of the force, if the force has to function efficiently. A weak coupling in the chain of command would tend to degenerate the competency of the force. Instances are not wanting, on the other hand they are so many, in which the constabulary had refused to obey lawful orders of their supervisors, and on the top of it subjected them to face enquiries on trumped up charges, and the Government had no hesitation to support this disobedient element of the force. The result is that political exigency and expediency have subverted the discipline *vis-a-vis* efficiency of the force.

All posts from the Director General to the Assistant Superintendent of Police are held by the Indian Police Service Officers (IPS). Recruitment to IPS is done through the Union Public Service Commission and appointments regulated according to the available vacancies in the State Police Cadres and Central Police Organisations. Examination to IPS are held annually and regulated under the provisions of the All India Services Act, 1951 (Act LXI 1951), and Rules framed regulating the recruitment, appointment and training and conditions of service. They are required to undergo a training for 12/15 months at the National Police Academy, Hyderabad and practical field training in the various functional areas of the district police administration of the districts of their posting.

Recruitment and appointment to the other ranks from Deputy Superintendent of Police to Sub-inspector of Police is regulated by the State Government, and there is negligible differences in the rules of recruitment and appointment in various states, more or less they conform to the same pattern. The largest number of recruitments takes place in the rank of the constabulary which constitute a large majority of the staff and form the foundation and base for the entire police structure/ edifice, and therefore, any attempt at meaningful efficiency has necessarily to start at this level only.

The pre-Independence Police Force was of the British Government and for the security of that Government. The force worked with the ideal, "One for all and all for one", and in composition it was homogeneous. Rank and file was not divided. Orders were scrupulously and willingly obeyed. The mentality of the force was devoid of caste, class, religion and politics and their loyalty to the government was traditionally unflinching, which no one could erode. Investigations and intelligence reports were not affected by any bias and they depicted the true picture of a case and correct appraisal of any situation. Based on these reports the Government adopted its functional strategy. With such hard-core discipline, loyalty, integrity and probity of the force, the British could succeed in ruling the country for one and a half century through a very small number of police personnel. For instance today a *tahsil* police station has about 100 policemen, when until the Independence the same police station had hardly 10/15 and yet, the police administration was commended by the public irrespective of political opposition, because detection was good, offenders were promptly arrested and punished, law and order, and peace and tranquillity were maintained and above all the members of the force had no caste or class prejudices. Their only bias was that they were pro-British, when the security of the British Empire was in jeopardy.

Post-independence picture, particularly after 1965, of the police force is in contrast with that of pre-independence. Now the composition of the force itself is based upon caste, class and religion and that has totally changed its complexion. The policeman displays apathy/lethargy in taking action against criminals. His zeal and energy have almost dissipated, tending him to be remiss in the due discharge of his duties; class, caste and communal consideration affect his actions, which are not impartial; his intelligence reports are tainted, they are not true to the core, depending on the class/caste he belongs to, he conceals or exaggerates facts with the consequence of faulty assessment of a situation by his superiors, and above all his investigations are extremely faulty due to his vested interests — monetarily or politically. And now all kinds of corruption are rampant among policemen, irrespective of the rank. He is now a foe of the public and his behaviour totally is in contrast with that of his previous generation. Reason: There is a preponderance of undeserving recruits in the force and, therefore, it is all the more necessary to enlist qualitatively better candidates only keeping in view the well-being of the reputation of the force.

2. Training

The need for systematic training is now recognised by every major police in the world, and not one of them is without its training schools and colleges. The best extensive arrangements to meet the need are found in England, United States, Germany, France, Canada, Australia and Japan. The training of policemen at all stages should receive increasing attention, although how thoroughly and how long a recruit should be trained before being let loose on the public has been a difficult question to settle, but all the same he should be trained till such time as both the recruit and the instructor become confident enough to the extent of recruit's capability for discharging his duties. Training is a conscious effort to improve and increase knowledge, skill and aptitude of an individual in a desired direction. The object of training is not only to develop professional skill of an individual for the performance of duties in the assigned job, but also to improve his capacity for shouldering greater responsibilities. There is paramount need and importance of training at different levels in the police organisation for improving efficiency and quality of police service. Unfortunately, however, though the crucial and transforming role of training in the police organisation is acknowledged by one and all, there has hardly been any meaningful endeavour to expand and improve the scope and quality of the police training in India.

The Committee on Police Training set up by the Government of India under the chairmanship of MS. Gore (1971), reviewed the existing training facilities in different training institutions and came to the conclusion that police training has been neglected over the years and training arrangements, except in some Central Organisations, are unsatisfactory qualitatively as well as quantitatively. The most important reason, for such a continued existing situation, is the lack of conviction about the value of training on the part of police authorities as well as of the Government at the Centre and in the States. During their training period, recruits are withdrawn and posted out for duties such as elections, communal riots and other co-related exigency in order to muster the needed policemen due to their insufficient strength in districts. Often the result is that the required training is not imparted, and untrained or insufficiently trained policemen are commissioned to district work, and naturally they continue to remain ineffective and inefficient. In training the personal qualities of a good policeman are taught to the recruits. They are: "A policeman needs tact, wide knowledge of human nature, a cool and unprejudiced mind, courage, incorruptibility, keen observation and willingly ready to act on his own initiative." Given adequate knowledge of the practical side of his work, the policeman will be able to discharge his duties fairly well to the satisfaction of all, himself, his superiors and the public. Three objectives are to be achieved during training, namely: (1) to teach the recruit the legal, technical and practical sides of police work, (2) to encourage personal qualities which go to make a good policeman, and (3) to give the recruit a frame, reference and opportunity in which to fit his career and emerge out a good policeman. Sub-inspectors and Constables constituting the cutting edge of the police administration need greatest emphasis and attention during their training.

3. Constable's Training

Constables constitute about 80 per cent of the total police force of the country, and they are the most frequently visible police officers, generally the first to come in contact with the people. The members of the public form their impression of the police force by the manner in which a street constable performs his duties. Police force can only become popular not because the head of the department is capable and detectives are efficient but the constables on patrol duty are alert, active and competent and know their legal and constitutional position in the society. Therefore, sufficiently literate and having good I.Q. (intelligence quotient) candidates should only be recruited and accordingly trained. The percentage of illiterate incumbents should be made to deplete to the point of extinction while selecting candidates. Actually, the Criminal Procedure Code and the Police Act give powers to a constable to effect arrests without warrant. His other duties, like beat duties, shadowing of suspects, collection of intelligence regarding crime and criminal and political activities require exercise of judgement and imagination. Generally, constables spend 49 per cent of their time on duties which require initiative, exercise of discretion and judgement, and also interaction with the public. They spend 37 per cent of their time on duties which are similar in nature, but do not involve interaction with the public and only 14 per cent on duties which are mechanical in nature and under the command and supervision of superior officers, when they are expected to implicitly obey the instructions, directions and orders of their superior officers. Although, it is true that well-educated recruits after proper training can become good police constables, they tend to inject an element of indiscipline in the hierarchical police set-up, because of inadequate promotional opportunities they become frustrated and disgruntled. Normally, a constable takes 14 to 15 years of service to be promoted as Head Constable and by the time he retires at the age of 58 years he is hardly confirmed as Sub-inspector. The ratio of promotion is one Police Head Constable to 15 Police Constables and one Sub-inspector to 125 constables. Therefore, the remedy would be to revise promotional structure in the police organisation so as to permit quicker upward promotional flow from the rank of constable.

Even after a constable joins the service it will be desirable to offer him opportunities to further improve his educational standards, and there should be no pretence of teaching wherever such classes are held. At present, very little organised efforts are made in the Indian Police to further improve the educational standards of the constabulary after they join the service.

Through training the policemen should be taught that there is no qualification so indispensable to them as a perfect command of temper and the greatest stress should be laid on duties of police to help and befriend the common and the poor people.

4. Refresher Courses

Constables, after their initial post-entry training, receive no further useful training in their service career. Refresher courses for a scanty period are held in almost all the states, and while the constables are seconded for study to Refresher Courses, they are often withdrawn in preference to law and order duties. These courses should be utilised to find out bright and promising constables, who can do well in more important and intricate assignments. It is absolutely necessary that young constables are posted at police stations officered by competent and well-motivated and incorruptible Sub-inspectors, who are reputed for their efficiency and integrity, because from the very inception of their service they will learn all that is good and eschew all that is bad for a policeman and enable them to build up their own moral as well as departmental character. Unfortunately, adequate care is not taken by many Superintendents of Police in the matter of posting of immature constables, and the results are often very disastrous. Instead of learning basic police work the young constables tend to get in the rut and absorb some of the vices that beset the police work in the field.

5. Training of Sub-Inspectors

Like the training of the constabulary, proper training of Sub-Inspectors also is of great importance because the Sub-inspector of Police occupies a pivotal position in the police organisation. Actually, almost all statutes of the country have empowered him to take cognizance of offences, and it is through him the laws of the land are enforced and criminal justice administered. As the officer-in-charge of the police station, he is the king-pin of all police actions, preventive, detective and regulatory in his own jurisdiction. The work of a Sub-Inspector of Police is difficult and daunting and demands from the officer physical courage, and stamina, as well as sagacity and a high degree of mental alertness. Very often in tense and fast-moving situations he has to take quick and on the spot decisions. It is often experienced that Law Officers on the firing line often have only minutes, even seconds, to make decisions that perplex experienced judges for weeks, and therefore, training of Sub-Inspectors must be extensive and thorough, and he has to be trained to work under abnormal conditions without any respite for long duration and much against his physical durability and at the same time with full mental control and ice-cooled composure.

He has to train his observations, like a photo lense and memory like a computer. His power of reception and retention of a particular subject should be of high order. The old view that in the police profession requisite experience could be gained by merely being on the job is not only fallacious but also dangerous because failure of an officer to display correct initiative and discretion at a crucial stage can have far-reaching consequences and unhappy law and order situation. He should be well-versed with the elementary knowledge of all the religions in the country, as such a knowledge would help him in solving communally prone situations arising out of multi-religious followings.

During training the cadet Sub-Inspector should be taught the technique of thorough and systematic investigation of cases with the assistance of scientific aids and abhorrence of extra-legal methods. There are instances of young Sub-Inspectors adopting third degree methods, resulting in the death of the suspects in police custody. Since recruitment of university graduates will tend to bring in well-educated persons of competence and character and are expected to provide qualitatively better type of service to the people at police station level, in almost all the states the minimum qualification for recruitment in the rank of Sub-Inspector, in both the armed and unarmed branches, should be graduation.

In states, the quality of instructors posted to the training centres is mostly poor. They have become the dumping grounds of unwilling and even of corrupt officers. In some places, they do not get any special allowance and suffer from acute accommodation problems. Since, the success of training depends almost entirely on the quality of instructors, well-qualified in the art of teaching and motivated police officers should be posted to training centres in order to avoid a ritual where unwilling and ill-equipped instructors perform the rites of training and drilling to unwilling trainees. No worthwhile improvement in the training of the officers is feasible and training will continue to be a ritual unless capable and conscious officers are brought into training institutions.

In training schools a sincere and all out attempt should be made to effect an attitudinal transformation of the officers so that they develop the right attitude towards the public, never forgetting that they are servants and not the master of the community which defrays them. These are the ethical tenets of police service taught and inculcated during the training. All these are not imbibed by all the Police Sub-Inspectors, may be some less, some more. In only few cases, good leadership of superior officers has imbued Sub-inspectors and enabled them to become Police Officers of high moral, acumen and professional abilities. And, yet in a large number of cases the same training standard converted these young Police Sub-Inspectors into inept imbeciles. The fault does not lie with the training but with the quality of candidates selected and also with the selectors who have neglected the interest of the society and nation in preference to their vested interests of whatever form and origin. This is the sole reason why the all-round quality of police work-cum-efficiency has deteriorated in the last three decades, and public remain totally unsatisfied and fathoms away from befriending the police, giving them the required co-operation and assistance, much less appreciation, because the servant has now become master.

6. Practical Training

On completion of basic training in the Police training colleges (the duration of the training varies from state to state from 12 months to 18 months), the Sub-Inspectors are attached for practical training in police stations and the offices of Circle Police Inspectors and during this phase many young officers, belonging to inferior pedigree degenerate and are gradually sucked into the vortex of police sub-culture. They are advised by police veterans to come to grips with brass tacks and follow questionable practices like keeping previous figures in view in registering cases, staging bogus encounters in *dacoity*-infested areas, catching hold of eyewitnesses who were nowhere near the scene of crime, *etc.*, if they want to succeed on the job and other vices. Here again, like constables, young Sub-inspectors should be posted under competent and carefully selected officers, who would take keen interest in imparting good training and hammer them into a model Police Sub-Inspector, totally honest and incorruptible to any form of allurement. The supervisory officers, of and above the rank of Deputy Superintendent should ensure by occasional contact with the young Sub-Inspectors, that their professional calibre, personal character and socio-national outlook are properly fabricated. One generation of good police officers would certainly create subsequent generation of good police officers and the tarnished image of police would soon be obliterated simultaneously gaining public recognition, appreciation, co-operation, sympathy and affection. This distant future has to be brought nearer by the all-round good behaviour of the serving policemen. When and how it will occur will depend on the governmental measures taken in this direction, and only an impartial and national government will be able to muster courage to weed out the undesirables so that those, sitting on the fence and are likely to turn bad, would be prevented by the deterrent action taken by such a government for whom nation precedes everything, even the political party in power. Public pressure has to be mounted in order to ensure that this utopia becomes a realisation.

If it is seen that a Sub-Inspector is not shaping well and has not the making of a good police officer, he should be discharged forthwith. In the police organisation there should be unwavering insistence on the principle that any doubt with reference to appointment or separation from service ethics must be resolved in favour of the organisation. The same attitude is also expected of the Government.

The basic training usually prepares an officer for the first few years of his service, but the policeman works in a changing society and there is nothing constant about the range and variety of police duties just as there is nothing constant about the pattern of crime or the hidden trends in the society that dispose men to crime. It is seen that field officers on completion of six to eight years of service tend to get narrow and cynical and require a break from departmental routine and an opportunity of reflection and readjustment of values. A refresher course of about 2/3 months period is held for such officers in order to acquaint them with new court-rulings and legislations and techniques of crime investigation and the paramount need for obtaining people's co-operation in dealing with police problems.

7. Stress Management

It is noticed that many police officers, particularly those operating at the police station level, are not able to cope with tremendous stress and strain and hectic pace of police work involving almost 18 hours a day working without any leave and at stretch for several years. Instances are not wanting when police officers have suffered from Angina, or such other type of heart trouble, in a few cases they become mental and physical wrecks. The stressful nature of the police work shatteringly affects the health and family lives of many officers and encourages alcoholism, prostitution, gambling, *etc.*, among them (may be it is obtained mostly without payment from anti-social elements). Scores of police officers in their forties suffer from cardiac and other nervous ailments. It is necessary to impart some sort of a brief training programme to combat the physically and mentally debilitating effect of the police work.

Thus, for effecting any real improvement in the police, there should be utmost stress on the training of police personnel, particularly of the ranks which come frequently in contact with the public. However, the cardinal fact has to be borne in mind by senior and supervisory officers that training can be effective provided the organisation has faith in it, and the organisational climate encourages the observance of precepts taught during the training. Big responsibility rests on supervisory officers to build up the congenial organisational influence by setting on exemplary behaviour themselves so that the junior officers would simulate them.

8. Role of Police Supervisors

The police is a hierarchical organisation with well-defined ranks and with considerable emphasis on discipline. Insistence on discipline is necessary because the police very often have to act in difficult and fast changing situations where orders emanating from above are to be carried out without demur by the rank and file. In many countries, the police organisation have been modelled on the pattern of the army. The militarisation has been considered necessary, because just as the army fights against the external enemies, the police have to wage a relentless war against the enemies of public within the country. In India, the police have army badges, the uniform and the weapons have also been patterned after the infantry by the British Government and after the Independence they have been adopted without any significant change. This para-military character of the police with its over emphasis on authoritarian command structure and close control and supervision has generated an organisational climate in which there is greater concern for how the work is done instead of what is done and why it is done. However, it is increasingly felt that this old, if not obsolescent structure and form of the police organisation, are not able to respond properly to the challenges and complexities of crime control and order maintenance in the modern societies. Now, the time has come to carefully consider if it is necessary to give up the para-military heritage of the police for a more humanistic, professional and service-oriented organisation. In this task of transforming the police organisation, the police supervisors will have to play the most important role of change-agents.

9. Group Central Leadership

Generally supervision has been defined: "Adaptive and relative human transactional process used by one member of the organisation on other of a subordinate level to direct their behaviour towards the accomplishment or organisational goals and fulfilment of personal needs." Police supervision is thus essentially a good directed process. For exercising beneficial influence on the output and motivation of their assigned groups the police supervisors will not only have to function as seniors who just issue orders, but also as leaders who can well influence and wield the subordinates to an integrated operating unit, and lead them to reach the goals of the organisation. For the complex and challenging work of today, the old authoritarian approach has to be given up in favour of the group-central leadership.

In police work there will be inevitable situations, like riots and natural calamities, where the police supervisors will issue orders which must be properly and willingly carried out down the command spiral. Time will not permit, to the detriment of the situation, prolonged discussions, or seeking advise/opinion of others. But in normal circumstances, for dealing with the complex problems of crime control and order maintenance there is considerable scope for discussions and consultations with colleges and subordinates.

Empirical research findings indicate that the group-central leadership with its reliance on participative strategies is more effective than the autocratic leadership in holding the group together and in improving the subordinates' job satisfaction and their productivity on the task. Good supervisors are those who show in a variety of ways that the individual subordinate is important to them and they understand and appreciate him on and off the job. A successful police leader will be able to promote internal cohesion by emphasising before his subordinates the goals of the organisation and at the same time treating them like human beings by recognising and fulfilling their rightful individual needs. He should always be able to generate achievement motivation among his subordinates.

One of the first and equally important task for supervisory officers will be the restructuring of the police organisation in order to make it more flexible in the light of the problems at hand. For generating ideas and for the purpose of planning, an atmosphere of equals should be created so that there is freedom of fearless and free exchange of ideas and the inspired sense of participation in the subordinates. This loosening of hierarchical relationship, once the process of planning has been completed, can be tightened in order to ensure better implementation. The supervisory officers should seek to develop a system for first obtaining, and then supplying his subordinates' information to do the job more easily. The job has to be made more meaningful and interesting so that it increases the efficiency of the personnel. In order to satisfactorily accomplish job tasks, the supervisory officers should ensure that all reasonable facilities are made available to the subordinates before they are dispatched to their assignments, which should invariably be time-bound. As the police task cannot be outlined from above there is a dire need for co-ordination and consultation among the subordinates, and the greater flow of communication and information from subordinates to their supervisory officers should not only be encouraged but also ensured.

10. Discipline

The supervisors will have to bear in mind that discipline is not a negative force, and it is an important constructive leadership tool for enforcing compliance with the established rules of conduct.

The success of the supervisor will depend on his ability to maintain proper discipline in the organisation. To ignore rules and conduct is to encourage delinquency. Minor infractions, if not checked, are bound to lead to major ones, and the supervisor has to bear in mind that it is the certainty of reaction and not the severity which will deter irresponsible behaviour on the part of the members of the force. Disciplinary action by supervisory officers may be punitive or non-punitive. The former is seldom constructive, but is at times and under certain situations, imperative and has a salutary effect on all members of the force. However, formal act of punishment leaves behind a trail of bitterness or ill-will in minds of the defaulting officers, who seldom acknowledge their delinquency. However, whenever feasible counselling is to be preferred to the formal act of punishment for achievement of rectitude. Discipline, if imposed in an impersonal and impartial way, would tend to minimise feelings of bitterness, provided it is imposed in a fair, open and consistent manner. Inconsistent, partial and unexpected discipline leads to confusion and anxiety.

11. Personal Development

The supervisor has also a major responsibility towards personal developments. Instead of looking only at his own individual development, he must see that his subordinates also develop in a manner that they contribute to the organisational goal. He must motivate his subordinates by his personal conduct to learn the required skills which will enable them to function in a more efficient and effective manner. Regrettably there is considerable depletion in the number of such supervisory officers in the police force of today. The superior is a developer of human resources, and as such, it is imperative for him to create conditions in the organisation that will encourage this learning process by the subordinates. Nothing contributes more to job satisfaction and morale as a sincere interest in employees' development. Achievement is never possible except against specific, limited and clearly defined targets in service institutions. The supervisor has to define target, set priorities and deadlines in that order, and then make his subordinates accountable for results.

12. Tomorrow's Police

Therefore, increased professionalisation should be the hallmark of each and every rank of the force, who should strive to develop himself thoroughly, and acquire the richness of experience and self-confidence on which effective performance depends. As a professional he should be able to exercise constructively his discretion under the laws of the land based on a tangible body of knowledge. The old concept of a police officer as a "Renaissance Man" who once, when he fixes on his badge, becomes magically able to perform any job to which he is assigned, regardless of training, interest or personality style, must go. His professionalisation activities should be inter-related with the work, and while discharging his police functions he will endeavour to solve willingly problems confronted by the public, and without any expectation of reward or pecuniary benefits. He will ever remain alert to his duty call. He should bear in mind that his means of livelihood, and the maintenance of his family are contributed by the public, who are taxed by the government to raise the force. He is the servant of the people and certainly not their master. He has to function resolutely and not partially, and without any sort of bias. He has to be incorruptible to all pressures and allurements, and service before self will be his moto. These are the frugally minimum expectations about him of the people, but they have been belied generally by his own species. It will be the task of the supervisory officers to bring about a positive change in the current behavioural pattern of the subordinate officers, and for that only their own behaviour would be able to guide, influence and secure the desired organisational goal — willing and active public co-operation in fighting the battle against crime and criminals and anti-socials. Can this optimism be transformed into reality? Only the future generations of policemen has the solution to solve this riddle, and unless the attitudinal change is brought about by the Government, public will continue to be unhappily pessimistic. Public pressure on the Government constituted by their elected representatives can alone deliver the needed solution to this ever-eluding problem, and it is none other than "qualitative recruitment without any kind of consideration of each and every rank of the organisation and continuous public service-oriented training. For that considerable improvement in emoluments, and better service and living conditions of the constabulary would be equally essential".

18

Powers, Duties, Accountability and Conduct

1. Power and Duties

Power is an emotive word, particularly in relation to Police. It suggests a right to punish at will, free from effective control. The Police has no such power. The power and duties of the police are stipulated in the Indian Penal Code, Criminal Procedure Code, Police Act, 1861, Indian Evidence Act and various other statutes enacted by the Parliament and State Legislatures, the Constitution of India, and judicial decisions. Delegation of powers and duties to different ranks is spelt out in Police Manuals or Police Regulations and Government Instructions issued separately from time to time. The development of the Police has always been conditioned by two conflicting needs: one to maintain order and protect people, the other to ensure that police do not act unreasonably or oppressively. The Police are, like other citizens, answerable to the general law of the land, nor do they have special immunities. A law-breaking policeman is prosecuted and punished just like anyone else. The only power the police possess is the power to inconvenience by bringing people before the courts, and even then the police cannot use that power improperly or unlawfully or unfairly. The laws of the land dog the policeman at all stages of his career, and even then some of his class is involved in some crime or the other.

Offences under all statutes, including Indian Penal Code have been divided into two categories: Cognizable and non-cognizable. In the former the police are directly responsible to take immediate action on a complaint, which must be registered and investigated. The police have no inherent power to investigate in non-cognizable offences except with magisterial permission. Over the years, a large number of offences has been listed as cognizable, expanding the duties and responsibilities of the police. Apart from the traditional forms of crimes relating to the protection of human body and property, offences against the state and public tranquillity in the recent years, there has been a growth in the incidence of social and economic offences. Crime of violence has increased, civil disorders have become fairly common, and the growing complexity and mechanisation of society has made necessary a considerable expansion of legislation. An expansion that has contributed towards a deterioration in the relationship between the public and the authority. With the per capita increase in wealth of the people crime rate has also increased and belied sociologists, who propounded that elimination of poverty would bring a decrease in crime. The entire community is affected by crime-virus. Almost any kind of public demonstration or public dispute, now-a-days, is liable to degenerate into disorders. There is a disturbing willingness to use unconstitutional, and often violent methods to further sectional interests or to impose opinions or policies on others. The paramount problem facing the police is to balance the preservation of constitutional rights of freedom of speech, expression and freedom to assemble for organised protest guaranteed under Article 19 of the Constitution, with the duty to protect lives and property. This is not an easy balance to attain, but it is essential that it be reached in order to strengthen democracy.

Our society has been plagued, over the years, by a steadily increasing number of communal and caste riots. Most disquieting features in these riots are the large-scale involvement of *mafia* gangs, and the use of fire arms and explosives mostly unlicensed by the rioters, threatening the very survival of our democracy. The most obvious way to deter a communal rioter is to ensure that he believes that his involvement in a riot will be followed inevitably by a punishment, but this rarely happens, on account of the policy of appeasement generally adopted by the Government.

Terrorist and secessionist activities and political crimes, such as, murders, kidnappings, assassination, *etc.*, hitherto unknown to our criminal calendar, have enlarged the duties and responsibilities of the police. To these may be added trafficking in narcotic drugs and gun-running which have assumed very serious problems in recent years. Their impact on the society has been very great. Laws and Regulations now flow in a ceaseless stream from Parliament and State Legislatures and Government departments, and they are so large that the public, and even, the police cannot keep track of them.

No police force, however, efficient, can discharge its multifarious duties satisfactorily without the support and co-operation of the public. While, whatever scanty public support and co-operation may be available in cases which provide a sense of public outrage, such as, murder or rape, violence against women or children, *dacoity*, robbery *etc.*, attempts to enforce controversial laws, which people for one reason or another, do not think as morally wrong, provoke reaction ranging from pointed criticism to physical resistance. Gambling, black marketing, pornography, illicit distillation and sale of liquor, bootlegging, exhibition of blue film, prostitution, smuggling of grains to rationing areas, traffic offences, come under this category. In these cases the offenders often buy immunity by corrupting the police or bringing pressure on them through politicians. Thus, the police are criticised both for enforcing laws and for failing to enforce them. Moreover, prosecution in these cases can be lengthy and expensive, and even if successful, the penalties are usually no more than a light tax on these profitable trades.

There is considerable scope for exercise of discretion at various stages in the exercise of police powers. Often the police have been charged with corruption, abuse and misuse of power in the discharge of their duties, which thrives where the police leadership is lukewarm in combating the evils or political pressure is brought on them for being lethargic and apathetic when dealing with such anti-social elements. The ceaseless expansion of police functions has enlarged the responsibilities of the police, and given them more and more duties and added power. It must be kept in mind that as the political struggle becomes more and more acute and intense, the police, as the guardians of the established system of the Government, will be the first object of attack. An effective safeguard against any abuse of authority or arrogation of powers would be for the police that whatever they do, they must do under the provisions of the law, and remain throughout subject to its sanctions.

Security of VIPs is the responsibility of the Police. The VIPs are innumeral, from President of India down to an elected member of the gram panchayat, private businessman, or even a cinema star and the list is unending. This work is so much, and so heavy that the police have no time to attend to the complaints of the people, investigate them thoroughly and prosecute the offenders. Invariably the investigations are slip-shod, and faulty, loopholes or lacunae are either corruptly created or the result of their being handled by inefficient or incompetent officers, and at times under direction of a superior authority, either administrative or political. The overall consequence is that generally the offenders escape punishment adding to the already existing chaotic conditions in the country.

2. Police Discretion in Law Enforcement

Criminal offences fall in two categories *Maluminse* (an evil in itself) and *Malum Prohibitium* (evil because prohibited). Murder, *dacoity*, robbery, and rape *etc*., are examples of offences which fall into the first category, and police can tackle them assuming that public support is available. But any attempt to enforce some laws falling into the second category often causes resentment among the public ranging from criticism to physical resistance.

Preventive powers of police are stipulated under Chapter X (Maintenance of Public Order and Tranquillity), and XI (Preventive action of the police) of the Criminal Procedure Code, 1973. In the dispersal of unlawful assemblies the police have wide discretionary power to disperse an unlawful assembly from persuasion to firing. It is the policeman on spot, who decides what measures are necessary, but the use of minimum force is emphasised by the law. Enforcement officers have hardly minutes, even seconds to make decision what type of minimum force would be required to disperse the unruly crowd, and such a decision is not easy to take, as a wrong decision would worsen the situation substantially. At the same time hesitant use of force makes subsequent control of mob more difficult resulting in more severe, and at times irreparable damage.

In the investigation and prosecution of offences there is enough scope of misuse and abuse of discretionary powers in the registration of offences, arrests, search, seizures, grant of bail, detention, examination and interrogation of witnesses and suspects and submission of charge sheets. Complaints are often made about non-registration of cognizable offences, the registration of which are mandatory under the law, minimisation of offences like treating a murder case as a case of suicide or natural death, arrest of innocent persons on false charges, torture of suspects to extort confessions *etc.* Discretionary power does not envisage in the notorious encounter deaths.

Many of the social legislations fall under the category of "Malum Prohibitium", and for one reason or the other, the people do not feel strongly about them or do not think of them as morally wrong. Enforcement of such laws is regarded by some people without enthusiasm or even down right hostility. It is hardly sensible to expect the Police to put thousands of violators of traffic rules, and regulations, daily before courts, which would only increase the back-log of cases awaiting trial for several years. Even if such cases end in conviction, penalties are usually a small fine. There is acute shortage of Police manpower and consequently the Police must have some scale of priorities in law enforcement. Section 157(b) of the Criminal Procedure Code, 1973, provides that, "when it appears to the officer-in-charge of a police station that there is not sufficient ground for entering in investigation, he shall not investigate the case". The sole object of the legislation is to prevent officers from wasting their time and energy in chasing trivial cases, and concentrate on serious ones. The more important thing is that the Police should be left to fight against real crime instead of going into conflicts with fundamentally law-abiding members of the public, on whose cooperation they must rely in the performance of their day-to-day duty.

Due to the strictures by the Commissions of Enquiry and Courts for misuse or abuse of discretionary powers on the ground of lack of evidence or impropriety of action, often police officers on the spot, become more confused, timid and hesitant to use their discretionary power in dealing with mob violence lest they might be criticised both for using their discretionary powers, and for failing to do so. The inevitable result is that crime is given an opportunity to foster and spread. Sometime back, a decision was taken by a High Court that to ask an accused person to give his specimen handwriting, fingerprints, palm or foot prints, tantamounts to compelling him to be a witness against himself as it infringes Article 20(3) of the Constitution. A full Bench of the Supreme Court of India had upset this ruling. This is one of the several classic examples how the Judiciary impedes law enforcement. Police must be more free. Crime is a stark reality and court decisions should be just as starkly realistic.

The latitude allowed the police officer involved is not fixed by any guidelines. There is no better school or training which would substitute experience. The situation of a police officer is in contrast with that of a judge sitting in his chamber, as all the time he needs, to come to a decision is at his disposal. He may even adjourn the court. A policeman has to decide on the spot of the movement his actions, he has no one to consult, except his experience, and he is in the midst of hurly burly and violence and riot. If a Magistrate makes a mistake it is construed as an error of judgement or, at the most, the spirit of law not interpreted correctly. A decorous appeal is preferred and a higher court reverses his order. Does he lose his job, is his salary docked, is he disciplined, or does he suffer mentally or financially? No, with the policemen what a difference! If he makes a mistake, woe betide him. People forget the proverb "To err is human" and do not care to find out if the mistake of a policeman is not motivated by his self-interest. He is liable to disciplinary action, involving suspension, the least, and possibly dismissal from service. He is liable to a civil suit for damages which may run him financially a beggar along with his family. The unfortunate policeman is, often a convenient scapegoat between the devil and the deep sea. Obviously, there is no question that the police on occasions make errors. But should a criminal go free because the policeman has blundered? And should the criminal be allowed to menace the society and continue his criminal activities unabatedly?

Lakhs of cases are pending in the courts, some for more than five years, acquittals are high and bail for repeaters is easy. Criminals are let loose to prey upon society. The public are demanding from the police to use rough and ready methods to curtail crime, or keep it under control as to stop violence in the streets. A major part of the misuse and abuse of discretionary powers is based upon ineptitude of our legal institutions in fulfilling the elementary end of any legal order, *i.e.,* to keep the peace.

The policeman's position in society can be analysed: The public use the police as a scape-goat for its neurotic attitude towards crime. We expect him to be human and yet in-human. We employ him to administer the law and yet ask him to waive it. We resent him when he enforces the law in our own case, yet demand his dismissal when he does not elsewhere. We offer him bribes, yet denounce his corruption. We admire violence, even against the society itself, but condemn force by the police on our behalf. We ask for crime to be eradicated, but only by the use of "Sporting Methods"

3. Police Accountability

In a wider sense, the accountability of the Police in a democracy, which, idealistically speaking, stands for the government of the people, by the people and for the people, and is to every member of the society whom the profession professes to serve. Indeed the concept of accountability to the member of the public at large is particularly significant for the members of the Police Service whose activities cover, rather impinge upon, many facets of individual's life and his relationship with others. And, to that extent it can be said to provide the police both a test and opportunity to prove their *bona fide*, their worth and utility. The fact that the propriety of police action and behaviour in recent times came into serious question and criticism makes the public sceptical about their *bona fide* utility.

The National Police Commission (May 1981) in its VIII report has spelt out three spheres of police accountability. They are: (1) Police are accountable to the people, (2) Their accountability to law, and (3) The Police functionaries are accountable to the organisation. To examine the issue from the last point, there is no question or doubt that policemen are duly answerable to their departmental heads, and the command hierarchy for the only and simple reason that it is a disciplined body and it must function as such as one unit without any divisible tendencies.

At the senior most level the Director/Inspector General of Police in the states is answerable both to the Home Minister and the Chief Minister of the State. It is also in a way the measure of direct accountability of the police that an officer-in-charge of a police station, or a Superintendent of Police of a district or an Inspector General of Police in a State is many times transferred to satisfy what could euphemistically be termed as the popular urge for justice. Such action, involving the suspension of officers, has often taken place. Regarding accountability to law, the frequent commissioning of judicial enquiries into incidents by the Police, statutory magisterial enquiries into all cases of death in police custody, besides the constant judicial supervision of the executive functions of the Police are sufficient enough to show that Police are certainly accountable to the law and rules of the land. From the point of view of the police, the question is what role the law of the land lays down for them, or what is the precise Constitutional provision of the police in our federal democracy?

The point to be determined for the police is the degree of functional independence. How much the police of today be insulated against any outside interference to enable to discharge their primary responsibilities without any fear or favour? Viewed from the other side, it is also a question of considerable importance in the sense that all public services in a democracy are ultimately accountable to the elected representatives of the people. The Police, being a public service, have to be guided, and moulded by what role is thought or considered appropriate of them in a democratic set-up. It is indeed, a moot point in the life of the nation as to how much of a citizen's life should be controlled or rather over viewed by the police? Since the expanding role of the police has been accepted in our country and by the society, it has to be suffered by the citizens for the sake of greater good. It is only just to think of and devise means for exercising necessary democratic control over such a police system. The point should be well-taken when increasingly strong demand is made to institutionalise even the right of the electorate to recall their elected representatives for arrogating the ultimate supremacy of the people in a democracy.

Although no precise definition of the Constitutional role of the police is found in any of the statutes, the preamble of Police Act, 1861, has recognised the Police as an efficient instrument for the prevention and detection of crime. Everyone is obliged to maintain that whatever be the circumstances or reasons, the police in India till today have not out-grown the role assigned to them more than a hundred years ago. Myriad statements have been made that the role of the police has changed after the Independence, but the duty of enforcing law and preventing crime is only a by-product of the main function of the police, mostly acting as a peace-force to maintain and uphold the Constitutional rights of the people. One can only wish this to be officially accepted and recorded in the statutes. It is a long felt and much-lamented need that the law of the land clearly lays down what role the police should play in the decided changed socio-political life of the nation. That will remove considerable misgivings, clarify un-warranted expectation and strengthen the police machinery for the job it is meant to perform.

Within the allotted sphere of functions, which to all intents and purposes, should signify only the prevention and detection of crime. The importance of functional independence of the police has been recognised even by the Supreme Court. The statutory powers of the police to investigate into the circumstances of any alleged cognizable offence cannot be interfered with even by the highest judiciary, subject to only (Section 491 of the Criminal Procedure Code, 1956, since amended). Article 226(1) of the Constitution to give direction in the nature of *Habeas Corpus*. Even the District Magistrate, who is given statutory power under Section 4 of the Police Act of 1861 to have general control and give direction to the police cannot interfere with the police investigation as he cannot override provisions of the Criminal Procedure Code, nor can the rules made under the Police Act override the Criminal Procedure Code.

On the same analogy, cognizance of an offence, investigation, arrest, prosecution and trial proceed in accordance with the law and are not susceptible to any ministerial interference. There is no room (authority) for any magisterial interplay in the investigation of criminal offences. The police are not the servants of the State Government in the sense that Government can order the method and manner of performance of the various acts committed to police by law, and when the requisite conditions in the specified provisions of law are present, the police are under a statutory duty to function in accordance with the mandate of the legislature, and they have no other option open. On the whole, the legal position emerges that the police have complete functional independence in the investigation of cases, and also enjoy considerable independence of action in matter of dispersal of unlawful assemblies and maintenance of public order, having concurrent powers along with the magistracy, and in a progressive Police Force such independence should not only be preserved but enhanced to make the force more effective and responsible. Such were also the findings of the Working Group set up by the Administrative Reforms Commission. Therefore, Section 4 of the Police Act, 1861 be suitably amended, and the century old general control of the District Magistrate should be removed, if the concept of police accountability in a democratic society is really to gain ground and stand the test of practical validity.

The working group of the Administrative Reforms Commission has also recommended that the legal status of police ought to be manifestly impartial and uninfluenced by external pressures, for much of the time a policeman is not acting under orders and must rely on his discretion based on the knowledge of the law. This consideration applies with particular force to police activities which are sometimes described "quasi-judicial" such as enquiries with regard to suspected offences, the arrest of persons and the decision to prosecute. In matters of this kind it is really in the public interest that a police officer should be answerable only to his superiors in the force, and, to the court when that matter may come before it.

In practical administrative terms, a feeling of being ultimately responsible to the State Legislature or Parliament runs through the entire fabric of public services including their political bosses. Therefore, the primary or the privatal force moving the wheels of administration in a democratic form of the government comes from the political heads, who are elected by the people, who are unquestionably sovereign in a democracy.

The immunity that is wanted for the Police is mainly against political contamination and preservation of their functional independence. While the political leadership could immensely help tone up the public services like the police by refraining from partisan interference, the accountability of the police in a democratic society will continue to remain a problem unless the leaders in public service themselves are able to grasp the responsibility assigned to them under the law and show the correct response to the democratic aspirations of the people at large by their exemplary selfless behaviour, conduct and probity bearing in mind that they are the representatives of the people and along with them all services are answerable only to the people.

4. Police Leadership

"There are no bad soldiers, only bad commanders". This conviction guided Napoleon in all his successful military campaigns. An efficient organisation can be crippled by an incompetent leader as a superb army by a poor general. Leadership is something which manifests itself in the attitude of a person, something which has the power of influencing the thoughts and life of others if not commanding them, without the leader consciously trying to influence or command them. Frequent failure of Police during a crisis in many parts of the country, including Delhi, has demonstrated that leadership in the police force is the greatest single factor for efficient or poor performance of duty. In the handling of disturbances leadership of high order is needed. The leader has to take decision at the spur of the moment, and he has to be firm in order to save lives, in order to ensure that the situation does not drift into a chaos, or much bigger breakdown. The main defect that appears in the handling of situation during a crisis is that when the time comes to operate there is inaction, and a defensive mentality, and above all due to lack of training, loss of cohesion, and morale in assaulting units. When men have their tails down, there can be no confidence in the higher command. An officer has at his disposal human material, what he can make of it will depend entirely on his firm guidance, and a clear lead. Inaction and defensive mentality, are criminal in any officer, however, senior.

There should be throughout complete mutual confidence and good-will amongst all ranks deployed — pulling together as one great team for the successful operation of the situation.

Efficient leadership is not achieved merely by issuing orders and instructions. The leader himself sets an example, leadership is an aggregate which results from all that a leader does, says and thinks. When leadership is effective, its outgrowth and by-products are sound discipline and good organisational spirit. Discipline within ensures stability under stress and strain. Leadership is a relationship, and means the process of attaining willing co-operation from the subordinates in the performance of a given task. Inspiration is the essence of leadership. Loyalty is a principle ingredient — loyalty to all subordinates, to their own seniors, and to the objectives of the organisation.

"Leaders are born and not made" has been a generally accepted statement throughout the ages, but there is now a general agreement that leadership can be learnt. It depends partly on aptitude, that is, something innate, and partly on circumstances, environment and training, which cumulatively would create a leader of outstanding merit.

Our police structure is a legacy of the British rule, and the administration functioned strictly on the basis of hierarchy. The ethos of the administration was a bureaucratic one. Politicians or political parties, did not interfere in running the administration. Police leadership functioned efficiently till the last days of the Raj. Then tale is no small of leaders of the police forces, who had been suspended or forced to retire when they were found wanting and quite up to the task that had to be done, and public interest always prevailed. On the achievement of the Independence, the old colonial system was interjected by new element — politician and political parties. The concept of neutrality and impartial functioning became the first victim. Senior police officers got increasingly aligned with politicians. Alternatively, they withdrew in a shell, and did the minimum expected of them.

Over the last 48 years the police have received much buffeting at the hands of the politicians. The police leadership was ceased to function effectively due to day-to-day political influence, political control in police functioning, corruption and indiscipline within the rank and file. The result is that even when a riot is taking place, there is no guarantee that the officers will lead from front or that men will have the confidence that officers will give correct orders and protect them from *bona fide* mistakes. Administrative progress and efficient and impartial law enforcement became increasingly difficult when senior officers exercised power by lobbying, by string-pulling, by insinuating, by forming cliques and cohort and secret intrigues. Feelings of jealousy towards colleagues or superiors in office aspiring to rise to a higher rank are then encouraged. Man-management requires that while efficient and impartial officers should be given adequate protection, there should be no hesitation to discipline the wayward, and the intransigent. But the greatest handicaps found by the police today are political patronage and partisan politics.

In various States there are a regrettable proportion of delinquents in police ranks, among them men who have been reinstated after having been dismissed on serious charges with the inevitable consequence of indiscipline, and the various disabilities which bring this in its train. Police recruitment, discipline and promotion are subject to various external influence, mostly political. All these things tend to neutralise the efficiency of police leadership. If only it were possible to remove the police from the control of politicians as those of the British Police System, many of the shortcomings of our police would disappear, and relations between the police, and the public vastly improved.

Speaking about moral courage to say "No Sir" we rarely came across a police chief during the Emergency rule who refused to carry out illegal verbal orders of political executives. Leadership, man-management are interdependent, but without good leadership there cannot be high morale or good management. A lament increasingly heard throughout the country, is the poverty of our leadership at every level of administration, national leadership not excluded. There has been a galloping and consistent erosion of moral values, and a perceptible decline in moral standards among the various constituents of the society. It has affected the police and army as well. Service pride and self-discipline nurtured over the years are no longer valid. This has deeply affected the police administration and struck at the very root of the leadership.

Where senior police hierarchy is motivated solely by considerations of personal aggrandisement of who can get what, when, where and how, and take shelter behind politicians for self-interest, sacrificing the interest of the force, loyalty of men towards their superiors takes a back seat. Frequent police strikes, assaults and manhandling of senior police officers by their subordinates and desertion of senior police officers by their subordinates in the midst of riots, refusal to open fire on the rampaging armed mob engaged in looting and arson or refusal to make arrest when directed to do so, favouring, one party against another in a conflict situation, *etc.*, have crippled the police administration.

Mushroom growth of senior assignments, in recent years, have subverted command, control and discipline. Infighting between senior police officers, for power and pelf, has been growing rapidly and spilled from the police corridors into the streets. The nexus between politicians, gangsters and police is the most formidable law enforcement problems of the future.

It is difficult to say what can be done to bring into being at one time impartial and efficient police force out of the chaos which we have reviewed. But perhaps, the most intractable, and from the police point of view, the most damaging factor is the complete failure of the police leadership. The role of the police leadership is fast changing as new developments are taking place both inside the police organisation and outside in its task-environment. Discontent within the force and indiscipline within the rank and file have been growing rapidly. The volume of public complaints against the police is increasing steadily, and relations between the police and public are worsening almost every day. The police leadership must stand up manfully and fight every adverse influence, political or executive. An army of sheeps led by a lion can win a war, but an army of lions led by a sheep cannot.

5. Principles of Police Conduct

The following principles of police conduct have to be observed if the Police Force is to be competent and honoured by the public:

1. Police must bear faithful allegiance to the Constitution of India and respect and uphold the rights of citizens as guaranteed by it under any circumstances and while doing so they should immunise and insulate themselves to all kinds of pressure or temptations.
2. Police should enforce the law firmly, fully and impartially without fear and favour, malice or vindictiveness.
3. Police should recognise and respect the limitations of their functions *vis-a-vis* powers. They should not usurp or seem to usurp the functions of the judiciary and sit in judgement on cases, nor should they avenge the individuals and punish the guilty by adopting illegal methods.
4. When the application of force is necessary or inevitable in securing the observance of law, or in maintaining order, only the absolute minimum required in the circumstances should be used.
5. The primary duty of the Police is to prevent crime and disorder and the police must recognise that the test of their efficiency is the absence of both, and not the visible evidence of police action in dealing with them. At the same time they should, under no circumstances, burke registration of crimes and their investigations.
6. The police must recognise that they are members of the public, with the only difference that in the interest of the community and on its behalf they are employed on payment by the citizens of the country to give full time attention to duties which are normally incumbent on every citizen to perform.
7. The police should realise that efficient performance of their duties will depend to the extent of ready co-operation they receive from the public. This, in turn, will depend on their ability to secure public approval for their conduct and action, and to earn and retain public respect and the ensuing confidence. The extent to which they succeed in obtaining public confidence *vis-a-vis* co-operation will reduce proportionately the necessity of the use of physical force or compulsion in the discharge of their functions.

8. The police should be sympathetic and considerate to all people and should be constantly mindful of their welfare. They should always be ready to offer individual service and friendship and render necessary assistance to all without regard to their wealth or social standing.
9. The police shall always place duty before self, should remain calm and good humoured character be there danger or provocation and should be ready to sacrifice their lives in protecting those of others. They should be steadfast, but not stubborn and gracefully amenable to correction.
10. The police should always be courteous and well-humoured, they should be dependable and unattached, they should possess dignity and courage and should cultivate character and the trust of the people.
11. Integrity of the highest order is the fundamental basis of the prestige of the police. Recognising this, the police must keep their private lives scrupulously clean, develop self-restraint, and be truthful and honest in thought and deed, in both personal and official life, so that the public may regard them as exemplary citizens. This applies to other services too.
12. The police should realise that they can enhance their utility to the administration, and the country by maintaining a high standard of discipline, unstinted obedience according to the Constitutional Mandates and superiors, loyalty to the Force and twenty-four hours preparedness.

19

Crowd-control

1. Crowd

A "crowd" is an assembly conjugated into a close body without order, but at the same time it should be borne in mind that crowds do not always collect for agitation. At the same time, the police has to keep in mind that a crowd, although innocent in origin, nature or purpose, can become an unruly mob without a warning, a mob, in turn, can generate rioting. It is difficult to determine at what time the innocent crowd becomes a mob, and, therefore, it is imperative for a policeman to be always vigilant and ready for action to deal with and control an unruly mob, especially in towns and cities, where local leadership is divested of their hold due to the enormity of the spread of the population without rapport of any kind amongst the localities of their habitation. No two crowds are similar and each presents different problems. The most striking peculiarity of a crowd is that whoever, be the individual that composes it, however different be the mode of life, their occupations, their character, or their intelligence, they exhibit considerable homogeneity in their thought and action. The common stimulus in any subject or situation which produces some degree of psychological tensions in the members of the crowd. This tension which each person feels takes on a circular character whereby it is spontaneously transmitted to every member almost simultaneously.

Crowds have been generally classified due to collective behaviour into:

1. *Casual Crowd*: It is shortlived, loosely organised at a very low-level and motivated by the attraction of the moment. They do not have a common interest or purpose, and they do not follow any leader.
2. *Conventual Crowd*: It is one whose activities are directed by conventual rules or exceptions. The behaviour of this type is less spontaneous than that of the Casual Crowd, and is subject to the influence of cultural expectancies.

3. *Active or Aggressive Crowd*: It acts towards a definite goal. There is, in this form, a mark subordination of the individual's wishes to the demand and objectives of the group, the people work under positive leadership and strong emotions, and are engaged in some kind of aggressive action.

   This type of crowd is most dangerous and difficult to control and handle by the law enforcement agencies.

4. *Expressive Crowd*: It has no clearly defined goal, or one may say, paradoxically, that its goal is expression for its own sake.

5. *Communal (Religion) Crowd*: People of the same religion or faith coming together for the sake of some religious rites to be performed or discourses *etc.*

India is the only and the biggest country in the world, where people professing all the major religions of the world inhabit. They are Hindus, Muslims, Christians, Parsees, Sikhs, Buddhists and Jains. Under the Constitution of India all religions are treated equally, providing freedom of worship for all communities. There are religious congregations like the "Kumbh Mela" where 25 lakhs or even more people assemble during the fair. These festivals are unique from the police angle since the problems of crowd control and traffic always presented by the congregations impelled by religious fervour, have few parallels in the world. Such crowds are multi-facets in their composition and behavioural pattern.

The problems are further complicated by the presence of a large number of criminals from the various parts of the country as they are afforded a ready opportunity to commit crimes ranging from pilferages to abduction or kidnapping of children and women. Their identification is almost not possible in spite of the fact that a semblance of a police officer or two are deputed to watch their activities by the various police forces of the country. Always these festivals are vulnerable to communal riots, warranting extraordinary precautions and vigilance by the police on duty. Rumour mongering worsens the communally prone situation in such crowds.

2. Freedom of Speech, Assembly and Public Order

Traditionally, in India ever since the partition of Bengal (1905) and subsequently during the Civil Disobedience Movement against the British Government lakhs of people participated in meetings and processions organised by political leaders to ventilate their grievances against the Government. These demonstrations were banned by the Government, and religious meetings and processions, which often resulted in communal riots, were regulated under the law. None can doubt that Independence brought about a marked change in the character of our society. India entered the turbulent period with social defences still aligned to the conditions of pre-Independence period. Freedom of speech and expression, and freedom of assembly guaranteed under Article 19 of the Constitution let loose all restraints, millions of people, who were subdued and not allowed to express themselves during the British Raj became vocal, many times vituperative, vitriolic and demanding.

Millions of people are packed explosively in slums, refugees arrived in large numbers, large-scale industrialisation has taken place, working-class consciousness has been influencing and dominating the simple economically motivated protests of earlier times. Instead of being dedicated to increase production, trade unions are launching strikes, political parties have multiplied, and there is active rivalry among them. At the same time, the numbers of scholastic institutions with their student population have enormously increased coupled up with growing indiscipline. Dissatisfactions of various types, due to price increase, shortages, frustration, corruption in high places, deaths in police custody, and growing incidence of police torture, and above all the feeling, nay conviction, that the Government does not consider any matter quickly unless there is a recourse to direct action, have surfaced in the post-Independence period. All these have created conditions in which public demonstrations in shape of public meetings, processions, *bandhs* and *morchas* have been growing alarmingly. Almost any kind of public demonstration, now-a-days, is liable to degenerate into disorder. There have been a large number of serious disturbances in the country, including communal riots arising out of public meetings, processions and

bandhs and many of them have left their mark in case-law and the reports of various Commissions of Enquiry.

3. Fundamental Rights

Free society must preserve the rights of freedom of speech or expression *vis-a-vis* freedom to assemble for organised protest against those who would suppress them, and those who would abuse them. The Constitution of India has granted protection of certain rights regarding freedom of speech under Article 20, and under Articles 25 to 28 has granted freedom of religion. Public order is often jeopardised by the behaviour or conduct of the public while exercising these fundamental rights. In these situations the paramount problem facing police officials is to balance the preservation of these Constitutional rights with the duty to protect lives and property. This is not an easy balance to obtain, but it is essential that it be reached in order to strengthen democracy. In this category there are various demonstrations, primarily among them are: Religious Demonstrations, Demonstrations by Government Servants, Industrial Workers, Students, and demonstrations connected with elections. Subject to the orders for the maintenance of public peace and control of traffic, the public have a right to the use of public streets and thoroughfares for procession with music and generally no restrictions arise, except, in communally prone pockets, where the rival religious groups object to the playing of music near places of worship, and this has to be regulated under Section 30 of the Police Act. In the use of loudspeakers, although allowed under a licence or a permit, the organisers never care, and purposely violate the legal restrictions imposed by the police to such an extent that they tune the loudspeakers to their maximum pitch and at any hour and for any duration with utter disregard to the discomfiture of the inhabitants of the locality. The organisers totally become oblivious of the basic fact that they would certainly be irritated if they are subjected to a similar treatment by others. While preserving the fundamental civic right they themselves violate it. More than regulation by the police, personal restraints in such matters would go a long way in maintaining amity and the resultant peace and order.

Various law courts have held that there is no fundamental right for anyone to hold meetings in Government, or industrial premises as the fundamental right with regard to the protection of the individual's property is infringed by such demonstrations. When public meetings, are held within the campus of an educational institution police must not interfere with them, unless their assistance is called for by the educational authorities. If, however, the students hold public meetings and take out processions outside the campus they become the members of the public and, therefore, are liable to all consequences and repercussions of police action like ordinary citizens. Election propaganda takes the shape of speeches delivered at public meetings and processions are taken out for influencing citizens in the interests of the candidates. Police are required to protect such election meetings or processions, or demonstrations against disturbances caused by opposing parties or groups. The responsibility for keeping order at meetings on private premises is that of the promoters and organisers. Sometimes police are called upon for assistance, but their role remains essentially a secondary one as until the possibility or apprehension of the commission of any cognizable offence, police remain inactive. The primary object for which roads, streets, and thoroughfares exist is passage. There is no such thing as a right of the public to hold meetings on the roads, streets and thoroughfares. Two things are to be considered before any public meeting is allowed on such public places of passage. *First*, whether the assembly is likely to interfere with the right of passage, and *secondly*, whether the assembly is likely to endanger public peace and tranquillity. There is no private right of any individual to make use of any public place for holding public meetings. The duty of the police is to vindicate public right, and not to facilitate abuse of the streets or thoroughfares by any individual.

The words, "Public Meetings" do not find place in the chapter of individual rights guaranteed under the Constitution, but it forms a part of the rights available to Indian citizens under Article 19. The word, "Public" means as of belonging to the people, pertaining to a community or nation, and the word "Meeting" means a gathering or assembly of persons convened for the conduction of some business. And such a gathering in public place is entitled to be recognised as, "Public Meeting" or "Public Assembly". To a "Public Place", the public have or permitted to have access whether on payment or otherwise. In this country the use of a place as of right has been held to be determinative principle. Section 3 of the Prevention of Seditious Meetings Act, 1911 defines the expression, "Public Meeting" to mean "a meeting which is open to the public or class or a portion of the public", and it further says that, "the meeting may be a public meeting notwithstanding that it is held in a private place or notwithstanding that admissions thereto are restricted by ticket or otherwise".

4. Regulation of Public Meetings and Demonstrations

A procession is only an assembly in motion, an assembly that intends to go from one place to another, or to a place and back or may even go round a place. When an assembly becomes a procession, even if it is not on public road, streets, or thoroughfare, it would be subject to control under sub-section (2) of Section 30 of the Police Act, 1861. There is nothing in the Constitution to show that the right to take out any procession is guaranteed as a fundamental right. What is guaranteed is to assemble peacefully, but without arm and the said right is also subject to such reasonable restrictions as may be imposed in the interest of public order. It is open to the Magistrate under the above referred Section to give any order that may be necessary to prevent obstruction of public thoroughfare or breach of the peace.

Throughout the country lawful demonstrations, in shape of public meetings and processions have been employed by various groups in the exercise of the constitutionally protected rights of freedom of speech and expression, freedom of assembly, and freedom of religion guaranteed under Articles 19 and 25. In this country, political, religious, trade union and election meetings and processions have often led to disturbances, which had their devastating repercussions throughout the country claiming a very heavy toll of life and property, year after year many people are killed or grievously injured during disturbances. There are legislative provisions to ensure public order during public meetings and processions, and yet, demonstrations and agitations have become an inevitable part of democratic practices with the conviction that the police must not be used as a pretext to suppress views hostile or unfavourable to the Government.

A vitally important role, in the prevention of disorder in public meetings, and processions, is played by the police. They are the final responsibility and when disturbances occur, more than other the police are blamed for lethargy, apathy or inaction. The police alone can assess the situation at first hand and, in the light of that assessment take appropriate preventive measures. The great use of the police is to prevent any mischief in the bud, and to interfere as early as possible before it breaks out into any kind of disturbances. The override duty of the police to preserve the peace and tranquillity and maintain law and order has consistently been recognised by the people and courts. And yet, police interference with meetings, processions, and other assemblies in public places has not infrequently, given rise to controversy. By and large, police practice has been to avoid interfering with public meetings as far as possible. To every person engaged in law enforcement, the challenge is not only to preserve and protect the freedom guaranteed to our citizens under the Constitution, but also to protect each citizen in the enjoyment of his freedom from those who seek to destroy it by criminal means. Some people will regard some laws as unjust and other people will regard other laws, or even the same laws as unjust, and at the same time they conveniently forget that mobs have no regard for any law. The police are not privileged to take sides or to discriminate among laws. Their job, however unpalatable it may be, is to uphold all laws.

Preventive magisterial jurisdiction provided in Chapter VIII of the Criminal Procedure Code, 1973, constitutes a powerful adjunct to executive authority, salutary when used in moderation. This "Preventive Justice" consists in obliging persons, whom there is possible ground to suspect of future misbehaviour, to stipulate with and give full assurance to the public, that such offences as apprehended shall not happen, by binding pledges or securities for keeping the peace or for their good behaviour. In addition to these provisions, Magistrates can turn to the law of preventive detention to prevent very severe disorder.

Notwithstanding varied and plentiful legal and administrative means available to maintain public order, the policeman on the spot plays the most important role. His attitude and performance and discretion allowed to him become accentuated when issues like freedom of assembly or freedom of speech are involved. A policeman, by his very appointment is, by law, charged with the solemn duty of seeing that peace is preserved at any cost. He has the difficult task of applying the Criminal Law, while at the same time recognising the "extra legal" concept of the right of public meeting. The performance of this task demands almost superhuman qualities of tolerance, impartially and courtesy, and above all, the rigidity to enforce the laws meant to achieve the maintenance of public peace and tranquillity, without compromising under political or sectarian pressures.

5. Industrial Disputes

An "Industrial Dispute" is defined in the Industrial Dispute Act of 1947 as "any dispute or difference between employees and employers, or between workmen and workmen, which is connected with the employment or non-employment or the terms of employment or with the conditions of labour, of any person".

This Act provides several agencies like works committees, conciliation officers, Board of Conciliation, Courts of Inquiry, Labour Courts, and Tribunals to resolve a variety of industrial disputes. But in the perception of the labour, the formal and legal exercises before such bodies are viewed, are time consuming and cumbersome, where the management is at an advantage with assistance and advice of legal experts and can also afford a prolonged legal battle without any financial difficulty. This circumstance makes the labour feel that they have a better alternative to secure their objectives quickly by coercive and pressure tactics in the form of strikes and other demonstrations and agitations supported by muscle power. The multiplicity of trade unions also induces minority groups to adopt militant postures to secure bargaining powers which may not be available to them on their own strength. Industrial disputes have, therefore, tended to become focal points for trial of strength between the labour and the management and also between the labour unions.

Labour unrest following strikes and lock outs has also tended to result in violence, ultimately affecting the maintenance of public order in the locality concerned. When the industrial dispute crosses the limits of democratic and accepted legal form and gets into areas of violence and breaches of public order, it immediately attracts police attention under the law, and the police are required to intervene for effective maintenance of law and order. Maintenance of order accompanied by quick and effective prevention of crime, particularly crimes involving violence, in a conflict situation is very necessary for removing the elements of coercion and pressure from conflict atmosphere.

When cognizable crimes are committed they should be registered and promptly investigated. Picketing is regarded as a legitimate part and tactic of trade union activity in a strike situation so long as it is confined to verbal persuasion, and appeal to workers to stay away from work. But when picketing is accompanied by violence, obstruction, intimidation or overt interference, it becomes cognizable offence punishable under the Criminal Law (Amendment) Act, 1935 and the police have to deal with picketers under this law.

Gheraos generate considerable tensions in industrial disputes and are increasingly resorted to by striking workers, particularly when strikes are prolonged, and the contending parties do not show any inclination to compromise. Various courts hold that *gherao* is physical blockade, and is punishable for wrongful restraint and wrongful confinement as they endanger personal safety and liberty. When such cases are reported, the police are duty-bound to register them and to rescue the person '*gheraoed*' and to ensure his liberty and safety. Since such cases are cognizable offences the police shall register criminal cases and arrest the offenders involved.

Sit-in-strikes are always resorted to when the workers lay down tools while actually working inside the factory during a shift. While their continued presence within the factory premises during their shift period may not by itself provide ground for police intervention or action in the strike situation, the refusal of such workers to leave the factory premises even after their shift period is over should be deemed a criminal trespass, as held by the Supreme Court, and they should be dealt with by the police under Section 447 Indian Penal Code which is a cognizable offence.

Recruitment of new workers in a prolonged strike situation often leads to labour unrest when the striking workers oppose the management to the recruitment of new workers in an attempt to break the strike. While it must be recognised that any person whether a new recruit or an old worker, has the right to seek opportunity for doing work of his choice, but any action taken by the police to give protection to new recruits for exercising this right in a strike situation might amount to undue police intervention or interference in favour of the management to break the strikes. The consensus is that when the management try to bring new recruits police action should not be in the nature of giving them individual protection to enter the factory, but should be confined to action under the law if and when specific offences get committed in the confrontation that might ensue between the striking workers and the new recruits.

Blockading egress and ingress of goods from and to a factory generate considerable tension in industrial disputes. Law courts have held that the employer's right to remove the finished goods from the factory cannot be restrained under any circumstances even if an industrial dispute is pending, or if there has been a closure or lock-out of the factory. Forcible obstruction to the removable of such goods is an offence under the penal law, and it is the duty of the police to take prompt action to avert such a situation and give redress against such unlawful obstructions. Police action in such cases should not be in the nature of preventive or protective action, but should be related to specific offences, if and when they occur in the nature of such machinery or equipment and the obstruction thereto by the striking workers.

Strikes and lock outs in a public utility sector is defined in Section 2(a) of the Industrial Disputes Act, 1947, and are subjected to more restraints than applicable to strikes or lock-outs in other industrial establishments. When the maintenance of essential services like communication, transport, supply of electricity or water *etc.* is threatened by an impending strike by the workers, Government usually resorts to a special law or ordinance for totally prohibiting a strike in the services concerned.

Then, in such a situation police action would be: (1) preventive action against organisers of strike, (2) prompt registration of cases arising from cognizable offences, and arrest of offenders, (3) giving protection to loyal workers, and (4) giving protection to fresh recruits or the personnel drawn from other units like Army, Home Guards, Territorial Units, *etc.*, for the performance of essential jobs. The primary objective before the police in such situation is to keep the essential services going and they should not hesitate to take whatever action is permissible under the law to secure the objective.

An efficient service organisation — the Central Industrial Security Force (CISF) has been created by the Central Government under the Central Industrial Security Force Act, 1968. The superintendence of this force vests with the Central Government.

As the law stands today, there is no bar on security staff employed in private sector undertakings becoming members of trade unions. A very serious situation arises when the security staff come under the influence of striking unions. In such cases management can reasonably ask for police assistance to protect their property against theft, mischief or criminal trespass.

Use of musclemen and gangsters by the striking unions has become a normal phenomenon in industrial disputes. They are used to beat up managerial executives and loyal workers, attack their homes and molest their women folk. Strong police action is needed to curb these anti-social activities. Not infrequently musclemen are used to terrorise striking workers to break the strike. In all such cases police must interfere and intervene to maintain law and order.

Collation and evaluation of intelligence by the police before or during a strike or lock out is very important as timely knowledge of the activities of organisers and strikers help the police to anticipate crisis situations, and be adequately prepared to deal with them.

Every large industry should have a well-planned strike scheme, prepared in consultation with the police, occasionally rehearsed, revised and put into operation as soon as the situation demands it. Police has to show a high degree of impartiality and fairness and ensure that their conduct is regulated by these two principles when dealing with a strike situation.

20

Castes and Communal Conflicts

1. Castes Conflicts

According to 1991 census, out of the total population of India of about 90 crores, there are about 14 crores of people who belong to the Scheduled Castes, Scheduled Tribes and other Backward classes, and the Muslim population is about 20 crores. There are about 10 crores of Christians in this country. Sikhs, Buddhists and Jains are included in the Hindu population.

Traditionally, there are four castes in Hindu society, which is the largest in India. They are: *Brahmin*, *Kshatriya*, *Vaishya* and *Sudra*, an arrangement of hereditary groups in the social hierarchy. This division of the Hindu society, according to *Bhagwad Gita*, is on the basis of trades and professions — *Varna*. In the past this division gave Hindu society stability, cohesiveness and self-sufficiency, but since about 100 years it also led to exploitation of large section of the population, the denial of many rights to them, and produced a static community which became fragmented with the emergence of numerous sub-castes under each caste. The pride and dignity of labour were seconded to parochial and sectarian interests and people did not care for the entailing fissiparous tendencies which have jeopardised the national integrity and the homogeneity of the Indian citizens. Outside the pale of castes the 'Avarnas' of whom there are about 14 crores in the country and are known as, Scheduled Castes, Backward Classes and Scheduled Tribes. The lowest order of the Hindu society comprises mostly of untouchables, out-castes, depressed classes — and clubbed as "Harijans", who have been excluded from the Hindu social order altogether over centuries, but more, since the last 100 years. Besides the Hindu society, the other communities such as Muslims, Sikhs and Christians are also sharply divided and developed modified caste-based social structure such as *Sunnis*, *Shias*, *Ahmadiyas etc*. in Muslim community, *Akalis*, *Nirankaris*, *Radha Soamis* of Beas *etc.*, in the Sikh community, and Roman Catholics and Protestants in the Christian community, although they preach equality and brotherhood of men.

Castes conflicts are endemic, and several times epidemic in our country and for that matter no religion is free from it. Castes conflicts between upper and lower castes of *Rajputs*, *Bhumihars*, *Yadavas*, *Kahars*, *Kurmis*, *Harijans* in Bihar, Dravida Munnmetra Kazhagam (DMK) in Tamil Nadu consisting of a group of castes which are anti-*Brahmins*, *Kammas*, *Kapus* and *Reddys* in Andhra Pradesh, and infighting between them is not unknown. In the *Vanniyar* dominated districts of Tamil Nadu the *Vanniyar Sangam* had demanded 20 per cent exclusive reservation in the government services. All these castes and sub-castes dominate the entire area of their occupation and exercise a decisive influence on the political complexion of that area.

In Karnataka, the *Lingayats* and *Vokkalingas* are still fending. In Kerala the Nairs, Izhavas, Muslim League, Christians and Hindu affiliated Bharatiya Janata Party with their respective ties to Congress, Socialists, Communists and Marxists are locked in struggles. In Maharashtra caste tensions are endemic in rural areas. There are 57 groups among the Scheduled Castes in Maharashtra. Of course, the *Mahars*, *Chamars* and *Mangs* constitute 90 per cent of the total Scheduled Caste population. Out of 53 per cent, 36 per cent *Mahars* had been converted to Buddhism under the leadership of Dr B.R. Ambedkar in October 1956 at Nagpur. *Mahars* voiced their resentment against the upper class domination — mostly of *Deshmukhs* and *Marathas* since 1956 and occasionally this strained relationship resulted in riots, loot and arson causing injury to property and person. These resentments ceased to be vociferous and often ended in bloody clashes. There was large-scale violence during the *Marathwada* agitation in 1977-78 when a total of 277 villages had been involved and affected. Scheduled Castes residing in 169 villages were attacked. Police had to resort to firing to control the situation.

In Bihar, a total of 16,743 incidents of atrocities on *Harijans* were reported in the first eleven months of 1981 as against 13,746 cascs in 1980, 13,426 in 1979 and 15,053 cases in 1978.

They indicate a growing tendency to attack *Harijans*. Inter-caste feuds have turned the State of Bihar into a killing field. Recurring clashes between different castes, raping of women and setting fire to *Harijan* hutments have become a way of life in Bihar. On 29th May 1987, a mob of 700 *Yadavas*, all armed with lethal weapons descended on two settlements like locusts on the foot of Umga Hills in Aurangabad district in Bihar, and butchered to death several *Harijans*, including women and children. The marauders were all *Yadavas* belonging to Maoist Communist Court (MCC) group and committed this dastardly crime as a measure of retaliation against the *Rajput* landlords. Hate and revenge are manifested in this case. In the killing fields of rural Bihar, the emotions take on an extreme manifestation. Hate fuels a killing, revenge fuels another in retaliation. Somewhere in this vicious cycle, the killing acquire caste, colours and turn into full-fledged estate battles.

2. Untouchability

Leaders like Mahatma Gandhi, Jotiba Fule, Dayanand Saraswati, Professor Ranga and several others in almost all the states of the country fought throughout their lives against the practice of untouchability and had expressed that "if untouchability stays, Hindusthan goes". Article 17 of the Indian Constitution abolished "Untouchability and its practice in any form". The Untouchability (Offence) Act, amended in 1976 and renamed as Protection of Civil Rights Act with a number of additional provisions providing stringent punishment for repeated offences and making all offences under the Act cognizable and non-compoundable have not been folly enforced, or wherever, and whenever they were enforced lethargy and apathy of law enforcement agency was the real cause of their half-hearted implementation. It is argued that, most of the officers of the law enforcement agency, belong to upper castes. The provisions of this Act are not impartial, as for the sake of politics, the balance of justice has been purposefully turned in favour of the "Untouchables", who are prone to commit similar offences against their upper caste brothers who have no ready remedy, and the malicious malaise and malady of a caste-ridden Hindu society continued unabated, with many-fold increase in rancorous estrangements in their relationship eventuating in distancing the required amity and accord among the various sections of the Hindu society. Government has done precious little to carve a homogeneous *Hindusthani* society and purposefully allowed the discordant tendencies to grow for political gains in the shape of bulk votes and vote banks. According to the figures released by "Crime in India (1990)" published by the Ministry of Home Affairs Government of India, 10,068 cases of rape were reported in 1990 as against 9,752 cases in 1989. The increase in such diabolic crimes was particularly noticed in Madhya Pradesh (2302), Uttar Pradesh (1541), Bihar (1005), Maharashtra (875), Rajasthan (740) and West Bengal (501) when compared with 1990 figures. In the succeeding years upward trend in such crimes continued.

3. Reservation Policy

The first Backward Class Commission was constituted on 29th July 1953 under the chairmanship of Kakasaheb Kalelker, who questioned the very logic behind reservations, saying "I am definitely against reservation in the government services for any community for the simple reason that the services are not meant for the servants, but they are meant for the society as a whole" but finally he conceded to the policy of reservation, not on account of his conscience, but duly subdued by his political brotherhood. Dr B.R. Ambedkar recommended reservation for a period of 10 years beginning from the inception of the Constitution of India on 26th January 1950, and the amelioration of the living and educational conditions of all the downtroddens, but for political exigencies, the party in power, extended the reservation each time by 10 years and now a stage, for the permanency of reservation has reached.

In Gujarat, Rane Commission submitted its report in 1981, which the Government of Gujarat accepted in a modified form and its announcement gave verbal ammunition to the anti-reservations, because the Rane Commission had categorically stated that family income and occupation, and not caste should be the sole criteria for determining social and educational backwardness for reservations. It stressed that identification of backward classes in terms of caste would only perpetuate the evil of caste systems and the accrued discriminations. But Solanki Government predictably did the opposite of what the Commission had recommended and plumped for the more politically advantageous, the retention of only the caste criteria.

The first anti-reservation stirs in 1961 in Gujarat left 40 dead, and property to the tune of several crores burnt in course of 100 furious days. The bloody five months anti-reservation movement in 1985 had taken a toll of 335 lives, injury to 904 persons, destruction of 5323 houses and establishments and property losses of over fifty crores. It left the people frightened, government shaken and social fabric in the state of Gujarat totally ruined. Long duration of curfew resulted in business losses of around Rs. 2,500 crores. Chief Minister Madhav Solanki was thrown out of the chair. In Bihar the eternal class and caste cauldron, the anti-reservation agitation consumed over five crores rupees worth of property, many lives, and ultimately Karpoori Thakur was forced to resign. Violent anti-reservation agitation in Bihar, Gujarat heartened pitting neighbour against neighbour and friend against friend. There were *lathi* charges, teargassing, police firings and umpteen inevitable deaths.

The Mandal Commission submitted its report to the President in 1980. This was the report that the ruling Congress Party and the opposition were afraid even of discussing honestly in the Parliament, leave aside implementing it, Mandal Commission Report remained the main rallying point for the Backward Classes movement and the bugbear of the upper castes organising anti-reservation movements in various parts of the country.

During the Primeministership of V.P. Singh, the recommendations of the Mandal Commission were being considered in 1992-93, and the mere move to implement them caused wide-spread disturbances and self-immolations of tens of students particularly in Delhi, Bihar, and a few North Indian states. Property worth several crores was destroyed. Ultimately, the move was withdrawn, and a reference was made to the Supreme Court for a decision. The Supreme Court ruled that 50 per cent reservation to Scheduled Castes and Scheduled Tribes and other Backward Classes should be given and accordingly implemented. At the same time, it ruled that creamy layers in such castes and classes should not be given the benefit of reservation, as their financial position has not only improved, but also become superior to others. And, yet the Government of Tamil Nadu has granted 69 per cent reservation.

Muslims are also aspiring and claiming reservation proportionate to their population. As much as 8 per cent reservation is being considered by the Government of Uttar Pradesh. The Congress Government at the Centre has also been contemplating to grant proportionate reservation to the Muslim Community. Some other State Governments may be contemplating in a similar manner. The basic idea behind this contemplation is the political strategy for acquiring the bulk votes of the Muslim Community, which is largely poor and uneducated. In case Muslims are granted proportionate reservation by any government, whether of the State or Centre, the Christians are bound to agitate for this facility and Hindus, who are not favoured by the reservation quota, would feel offended and further discriminated as the number of jobs in the government services or its undertakings, which were left for Hindu candidates would be made over to the Muslim and Christian candidates in that proportional number. This will bring and breed ill-feelings, and hatred and further estrange in particular Hindu-Muslim relationship. Agitation by either is bound to follow culminating in communal riots almost throughout the country.

The Bharatiya Janata Party (BJP) is in favour of reservation on the principle of "economic backwardness" irrespective of caste or creed and without any discrimination on religious or caste basis. From now onwards over a period of 10 years, most of the middle-class population will become economically backward on account of the deprivation of service facilities to them in preference to the candidates belonging to Scheduled Castes, Scheduled Tribes and Other Backward classes, irrespective of the fact that the general eligibility of the former is many more times better than the latter. This has already created hatred among these classes of the Indian society. Reservation policy, not only in giving jobs in the government and semi-government undertakings, but also admissions to all academic institutions, including vocational and professionals has considerably widened the existing gap with increased animosity and the seeds of caste and class conflicts have already been impregnated deeply in the body polity of the Indian society, and it may erupt like a volcano when the pangs of hunger of the youths, deprived of means of livelihood, would compel them to take to streets and cause disturbances, including loot and arson.

Reservation quota is more than 50 per cent in various states and in Tamil Nadu it has been made 69 per cent in contravention of the ruling of the Supreme Court. There are glaring instances in which admissions to vocational or professional institutions have been denied to a candidate not belonging to the "Reservation Category" even if he has received 85 per cent or over marks, whereas the one of the "Reservation Category" is favoured easily with the admission in the academic and professional institutions even his percentage of marks is abominably and dismally low. The system of reservation has degenerated to such an extent that one mark out of 900 was enough to get Laxmikant Dhurve, a tribal boy from Balaghat district, a seat in an engineering college in 1995 when the cut-off marks for the general category for students for an engineering seat was 540. What sort of engineer would this boy make when year after year he will be given admission to a higher class because no teacher would be willing to fail him?

It is now almost half a century since Independence, and yet the clamour for reservation has not only subsided but has increased both vertically and laterally to the point that it has become practically impossible for a lad from the so-called upper caste to get into the mainstream of medicine, engineering or technology. The paradoxical truth is that many of such students, belonging to the reservation category have either dropped out of their academic institutions because it was unable for them to keep pace with the standards of teaching. Those, somehow get cleared through extraneous methods, are detested and derided by the general public. What will happen if Muslims are given proportionate reservations in that there will be an accentuation of castes and communal conflicts in a society already afflicted with them. Should religious or caste division be accentuated and given an antagonistic turn? The demand for reservation for Muslims has been articulated by Sitaram Kesri, a Cabinet

Minister in the Government of India, and is blatantly intended to canvass Muslim votes, and it is hoped that the Muslim themselves will see it as such. On account of this policy of the Government a permanent wedge has been driven in the amity of budding youngmen, and a sense of deep frustration, and despondency made them restive and belligerent towards the members of the "Reservation Category". This is obviously not a healthy sign for the Nation, as the presence of existing animus and simmering wrath are bound to erupt like a volcano disintegrating the Nation. Although already late, the disquieting situation can be retrieved by giving uniform treatment to all in such matters, where intelligence, efficiency, and capability should be the sole criteria-cum-consideration. Already our public servants are collaborators in corruption and nepotism, directly or indirectly, and instead of serving the people, who pay their emoluments, they take pleasure and pride in harassing the public. This anomaly has to be corrected if disintegration of India is to be averted in not far distant future.

There are obvious indications that every caste or class is fighting the other caste or class and many undemocratic forces are at work almost everywhere in the country, but particularly in the rural areas, which are reflecting the caste oppression, class domination, religious bigotry, and the politics of the gun. The illicit manufacture of guns and explosives, thanks to the direct and indirect involvement of politicians, and their wide circulation has complicated the matters. More and more castes and classes are resorting to guns and explosives to achieve their goals. The Indian democracy has to be saved from the war of castes and classes and the country be freed from anarchial conditions by removing reservations, which the young generation of the country considers an "*Anathema*". The only feasibly amenable solution is reservation for economically backward classes, irrespective of their caste or creed.

The Police has completely failed on account of the Government policy to ensure the rule of law, especially in the countryside. Complaints from the *Harijans*, downtroddens, and the poor are not generally registered. Police take sides of the class or caste to which they belong, and this has brought cleavage among the members of the force, which no longer has remained a homogeneous unit, and their performance, efficiency, and competency have already been impaired. Against the ensuing violence, people started defending themselves by turning towards the militant extremist groups. Rulers rarely intervene. An elected representative feels his responsibility to his family and when it goes further, to his caste or class, much more strongly than his responsibility to the society as a whole.

4. Communal Conflicts and Legal Provisions

Background: Hindu-Muslim antagonism can be ascribed to a complex set of factors going back to the Muslim invasions in 712 A.D. and Aurangzeb and British encouragement of Muslim separations for their own ends during the imperial rule. Partition of the sub-continent of India was the logical culmination of these historical events, and the post-1947 India, though seemingly secular, could not remain unaffected by them. Before the introduction of communal electorate in 1919 there was no Hindu-Muslim riots. But the communal electorate drove a wedge in the Hindu-Muslim amity and accord and vertically and inevitably divided them. Jinnah's speech at the All India Muslim League's Lahore Resolution in 1940 that the Hindu and Muslim could not co-exist in a United free India increased bitterness between the two communities. In addition, several factors are involved in Hindu-Muslim conflicts at a particular place and time, and their subsequent spread to other places. Causes of conflicts in dubiously have local variations but they are always a mixture of historical, religious, social, economic and political factors which often exploded into violence. These apart, urbanisation and overcrowding of towns and cities, ill-treatment of Hindus in the neighbouring Muslim countries and influx of Hindu refugees from these countries and their tales of woes and sufferings, instigation from foreign powers and administrative failure can be added. Communal writings and speeches, and spreading of false and exaggerated rumours, and irresponsible press reports incited communal violence. The most important developmental factor is the mixture of religion with politics.

Hindu-Muslim conflicts have become a bone of contention in the struggle for power and this, to a great extent, has vitiated the atmosphere for the promotion of communal harmony. In this situation intractable postures on the minority questions are often assumed by politicians of different views, depending on whether they are in power or in the opposition. Communal minded politicians, both Hindu and Muslim, have never left the gullible common citizens alone, whether they be Hindu or Muslim. Seeds of dissent are planted by exploiting deep religious traditions of both the communities, difference in their different religious practices and rituals are highlighted, and often it is shown that one is out to destroy the other.

The electoral process in the country instead of pulling down the boundary walls of community and religion, have unfortunately made them more pronounced with the political lexicon of post-independent India importing such patent obscenities of the "Vote bank". Each major communal incident results in the formation of Commission of Inquiry headed by a judge, yet no one is punished in a court of law. Too often, the offenders are protected by politicians in power. Police are prevented from making preventive arrests, and investigation of cases arising out of communal riots is not allowed to run its full course. Prosecution of cases in courts is withdrawn and convicted offenders are granted pardon in the hope of promoting communal harmony, but this has proved to be an illusory hope. The cause that resulted in the communal violence has been different in each case, the perpetrators have been different, and the nature of violence has also been different. One feature, however, has been identical, and that is the failure of the police to provide protection to the innocent community and the men, women and children killed during the riots.

Political expediency has brought the simmering, problem of communal to a boil. There are several impediments to the growth of national identity failing to prefer communal harmony. The Constitution of India provides that there shall be no State religion and that State shall treat all religions equally. But what has normally been allowed to happen in this country through all these years after the Independence is that politics has continued to seek its selfish advantage under the cloak of religion, and we have almost invariably chosen the path of compromise with so-called religious demands, with full awareness that the adopted course of compromise is detrimental to the cohesive integration of the nation as a whole.

We have so far failed to enact a Uniform Civil Code as ordained in Article 44 of the Constitution of India, and the recent direction of the Supreme Court in this connection has been brazenly flouted by giving assurances that no such Uniform Civil Code would be enacted against the wishes of the concerned population — Muslims. The Constitutional provision that laws should be uniform for the followers of all religious faiths has been blatantly violated when in 1986 the Muslim Women (Protection of Rights) Act removing the Muslim from the purview of Section 125 Criminal Procedure Code applicable to all Indians, irrespective of religion, castes, sects etc. This legislation was strongly opposed even by the eminent, scholarly and national Muslims. It segregated Muslim women from others in respect of payment of alimony and offended the basic principle of equality in the eyes of law. The consequences were the occurrence of large-scale communal riots in different parts of the country.

Legal Provisions: There are adequate legal provisions to prevent, avert and contain communal riots provided they are enforced in time, impartially, firmly and without any caste or creedal discrimination. They vary from preventive arrests up 151 of the Criminal Procedure Code to detention under the Preventive Detention Act or Maintenance of Internal Security Act. Actually, there is no dearth of such provisions under the existing laws, which are as stringent as effective in controlling and containing communal clashes. Prohibitory orders under Section 144, with curfew, if necessary, can also be imposed. In every police station, which is prone to communal disturbances, an up-to-date list of communal and anti-social elements is maintained with the intention to put them under preventive custody when the first sign of the impending trouble is discernible. Due to the promulgation of Section 144 Criminal Procedure Code entry of communal leaders, and assembly of persons in disturbed area can be prohibited, and curfew imposed to restrict movement of persons in the riot affected area. In some States legal provisions exist for the externment of criminals having previous convictions under certain specified offences and anti-social elements from the area affected or likely to be affected by riots and not to enter the area without proper permission of the authority making the order. Section 153-A, of the Indian Penal Code provides punishments to those promoting enmity between different groups on grounds of religion, race, place of birth, residence, language *etc*., and enhanced punishments if the offence is committed in any place of worship.

Making, publishing, or circulating any statement or report containing any rumour or alarming news with intent to create or promote or which is likely to create or promote, on grounds of religion, feelings of enmity, hatred or ill-will between different religious groups or castes or communities is punishable under Section 505 Indian Penal Code, and it also provides for enhanced punishment if the offence is committed in any place of worship, or in any assembly engaged in the performance of religious worship or religious ceremonies. Section 15 of Police Act, 1861 provides for stationing or quartering additional police in the disturbed area, and collection of punitive tax under Section 15A of the same Act from the aggressive community towards payment of compensation to the victims of riot. These provisions are rarely used, though they can prevent riots occurring again in the same area and have salutary effect in other riot-prone areas too. Political consideration has always weighed while taking recourse to this deterring provisions of law. A rioting mob engaged in assault, looting and arson is an unlawful assembly and can be dispersed by force, if necessary, by the police, Magistrates, and Central Armed Police Forces and Army under Sections 129 to 131 of the Criminal Procedure Code. Here "Force" includes all types of force including firing upon the mob which may result killing of some persons in the larger interest of the society, and no action would lie against the officer concerned in such an eventuality. *Lathi* charge and bursting of tear-gas shells are the preliminary methods for the dispersal of rioters before resorting to police firing, when it becomes apparent that the riotous mob cannot be dispersed by these or any other method. The bullets which the State Police Forces use are specially manufactured and contain less charge and are not deadly, but those used by the Central Armed Forces and the Army are deadly.

With such wide range provisions of law to prevent, control or contain riot, normally people feel that there should not be any occurrence of riots, and yet, riots take place. Playing of music before a mosque during prayer hours invariably ends in protest followed by communal riots, unless religious processions are properly regulated under Section 30 of Police Act of 1861. Not only conditions in the licence should be clearly spelt out and explained to the licensees, but they must be firmly enforced and this is hardly done for various reasons which are beyond the control of the local police officers on account of political intervention encouraging belligerent attitude of the licensees and the paucity of policemen. Only a large number of policemen on duty are easily able to enforce the conditions of licence, and such number is rarely available to the local police. Theoretically, it is emphasised that routes of procession should be clearly indicated in the licence so as to avoid Muslim locality, and mosques. Practically, it is not possible as Muslim and Hindu localities are often not segregated, more or less they are mixed localities and their places of worship contiguous. In such cases assistance of the leaders of either community would go a long way in maintaining law and order and peace and tranquillity but these days, such leaders, with honesty of purpose, are difficult to come across when the police approach them; their primary and preliminary consideration is to acquire political gain or mileage and police have to use them very tactfully and cautiously. Shouting of slogans, carrying of *lathis* and other weapons, placards, use of loudspeakers can also be prohibited, but to what degree and extent police can enforce such restrictions is not certain, and is a matter of debate. Several instances are on record when rigid enforcement of such prohibitory orders precipitated the situation and ended in the confrontation with the police force, causing more harm than the actual riot. Therefore, the spirit of the law, the available resources of the ensuing situation can alone avert a clash. Our police forces are to be trained, and tuned accordingly.

5. Tear Smoke (Gas) in Mob Dispersal

Water cannons are being used for decades but their limitations are obvious as water capacity can be exhausted within less than 10 minutes, and determined rioters may regroup and resume their activities once the danger has passed. Now-a-days tear-gas has become an essential part of the equipment of the modern police force in a country liable to civil unrest. It has been found useful for the following reasons: (1) It reaches the whole of the mob instead of only the front rank, (2) It can be used without compunction against passive resisters, including women, under circumstances in which the use of other form of force would be objectionable, (3) By its use police are not tired out, and a considerable saving in manpower can be affected, and (4) By causing every person in a gassed area to think of his own physical discomfort to the exclusion of everything else, tear-gas rapidly breaks up the common object of the mob. Communication between leaders and the mob is lessened causing the break in the unity of the mob before mass hysteria has taken its hold.

Prior to the use of tear-gas, or for that matter any force, it must be established that the mob has an avenue of escape, if not panic would result, stampede created, and several persons would sustain injuries, and even some die as had happened in Nagpur (Maharashtra) on 23rd November 1994 in which 114 people, young and old, women and children were trampled to death by peaceful demonstrators themselves, when police swung into action to disperse them. They belonged to the *Gowari* community. The whole area was strewn with corpses, and tarred streets changed their colour to red, because profuse blood that had spilled all over the area. Before police could realise their mistake, the most horrendous tragedy of the post-independent Jndia had occurred for which police alone were responsible. This is a classic example of lack of foresight of the police officers dealing with this crowd, which was peaceful throughout, and merely desired to see the Minister concerned to redress their grievances. It is said that this tragedy was radioed to the Chief Minister (Sharad Pawar), who did not consider it necessary to meet the aggrieved. Such a callous behaviour of the law' enforcement and administrative agencies has left the indelible stigma on the Government of Maharashtra. Only prudence could have averted it, and obviously, it was dismally lacking at all levels of the administration in this particular instance. A commission is enquiring into it.

6. Bias Attitude and Apathy of Party in Power

These are two of the several instances which show the discriminatory attitude of the Government, and to what extent the politicians belonging to the party in power can wreak vengeance or subdue the rioting mob. In the wake of the assassination of Indira Gandhi in 1984, the Congress proteges killed over 2,500 Sikhs in Delhi alone, where thousands of military and para-military forces are stationed, the highest administrative heads, including the President and the Prime Minister of India are quartered, and yet, loot and arson of property belonging to Sikhs had taken place. People did not sack such Government which remained the mute spectator of such gruesome atrocities only because, Indira Gandhi belonged to Congress Party, to which the Government also belonged. The Sikhs are not a majority community, and the perpetrators were not Muslims. Even after eleven years of these ghastly offences the offenders are not charge-sheeted, and so much time has lapsed that even if they are prosecuted as a token of deliverance of justice, there may be no chance of punishing them. And only it will be a farce.

Hindu-Muslim riots on an unprecedented scale ever since Independence occurred throughout the country in December 1992 and January 1993, following the demolition of a mosque structure at Ayodhya (Babri) and over 1,550 people were killed and majority of them were victims of police firing, and they were Muslims. Ceremoniously the government commemorated them by doling large sums of taxpayers money to their next of kin as compensation. These riots were engineered by Muslim and property worth several thousand crores of rupees mostly belonging to Hindus was either looted or set ablaze. Police officers, who took the required action in order to control the situation, were dubbed as communal and departmentally dealt with. Soon followed the blasts engineered by Pakistan Inter Services Agency (ISI) in Bombay claiming over 200 lives. Sharad Pawar, the then Defence Minister, stationed himself in Bombay itself for about a month and personally supervised the Army operations, as if the Army commanders were inefficient and incompetent to control the rioters. Sudhakar Naik, the Chief Minister of Maharashtra had to go. Such a conduct of politicians has made the laws and their enforcement agencies impotent and infructuous, but in this process they gained politically and the law enforcement agencies lost their honour, dignity and pride followed by the wreckage of "National Integration". For these politicians' votes are the main concern and criteria, not lives, not the torn and bleeding hearts that rioting often leaves behind. The course of event is repeated each time with chilling regularity. A wave of communal hatred sweeps over the land. Tensions mount and rumours are floated. Even the administration, and the police are communally or politically affected. Bands of youths set out for street control with systematic brutality, and they indulge in looting followed by arson and murder of innocent people. This is the normal pattern of communal riots, and they crunched the national pride and honour along with that of the subjects.

It is obvious that the government did not adopt a cogent and cohesive policy to nationally integrate the people of this country, but on the contrary purposefully and schemingly it manoeuvred fissiparous tendencies with the ulterior object of ensuring that its "Vote Bank" does not get numerically depleted. This has resulted in the Government's dismal failure in bringing steadfast communal harmony and castes amity.

7. Rise and Growth of *Mafia* Hierarchy

While analysing local developments since Independence it is found that there has been rapid growth of anti-social elements known as *Dadas* or *goondas*. Political and communal parties and groups have often utilised their services. It were these individuals who fanned the flames of riots and threw bricks, bottles, bombs and crackers and set fire to shops, public transport and cut off telecommunication lines. It were these individuals who first looted and urged others to do like-wise. These individuals distributed lethal weapons, before, during and after the riots. They are the main shock troops or commandos of the riotous mob and the mainstay of riots. The very availability of firearms and hand bombs account for their frequent use during riots, in the country, manufacture of fire arms and bombs has become a cottage industry and gun running from bordering countries is not uncommon. Thanks for the covert support of the politicians.

8. Trends in Communal Riots

Noticeable trends in communal riots — Hindu-Muslim are:

1. Growth of "fundamentalism" in both communities.
2. Both Hindu-Muslim organisations are growing in number, and are better organised than before, and blatantly communal.
3. Riots go on for weeks, sometimes for months, they recur after having stopped, and they stop only to regroup and start again.
4. Spread of communal violence in villages and industrial areas.
5. Greater use of unlicensed firearm, bombs, and other explosives.
6. A lot of participants in the riots tend to be rather young and armed.
7. Participation of anti-social elements in greater number due to encouragement, and support directly or indirectly of political parties and groups.
8. Instigation by foreign powers unfriendly to India.
9. Any deterioration in the position of Pakistani or Bangladeshi Hindus, has been quickly reflected in the worsening of Hindu-Muslim relations in India. Each new border incident has had repercussions or recrudescence on Muslim life in India.
10. Attacks on Hindu temples in Pakistan or Bangladesh or Muslim mosques anywhere in the world, including India, have contributed to communal riots in India.
11. Mass "Proselytisation" (conversion) of Hindus to Islam in India has often led to communal riots.

Almost everywhere the position of communalism unabashed the devil of men. The intensity of the communal hatred that erupted across the country was a brutal throwback to the days of partition of friends stabbing each other, of setting ablaze entire localities, of mothers with babies in arms, and pregnant women and babies being brutally shot or speared to death, of blood flowing down gutters in congested gullies, of carcasses strewn across streets. The blood that flowed down the narrow gullies in the communally affected towns stunned the conscience of the law-abiding, and saner elements of citizens, who could do precious little to checkmate such situations on account of the numerical majority of our Members of Parliament, who are more interested in protecting, and conserving their "Vote Bank" than the welfare of the Nation and its citizens.

The silver lining in the dark cloud accompanied by the relieving feature is that apart from these frequent outbursts, Hindus and Muslims in many of the riot-affected areas lived in the same locality, worked together, sent their children to the same schools and colleges, and sick and wounded to the same hospital. In the midst of carnage, voices of sanity could be heard from leaders and ordinary people of both the communities, not affected by narrow sectarian consideration. "Do not shed blood, donate blood instead". The appeal was to prominent' citizens to visit riot-hit areas, and set up blood donation camps so that the blood of Hindus, Muslims, Parsees, Christians and any citizen of this country, irrespective of his caste or creed should be usefully utilised to save the victims of the raging violence fighting for life. Such innumerable instances have occurred. A Hindu has sacrificed his life to save a Muslim, his hearth and home, and family, and similarly a Muslim has done. Is this the indication that Hindus and Muslims of this country cannot co-exist in full amity and accord? Does the animosity or rancour between the members of both the communities spring from hatred which was generated since the past several centuries, and does the hatred still linger in the hearts of the present generation? The sensible answers would be a big "NO". Then the only causative factors are the momentary incitements by some agency which considers ' 'Hindu-Muslim Accord and Amity" detrimental to its general interest. Given their own way, without any intervention or interference of any political or communal leaders, Hindus and Muslims can live amicably like real brothers of the same mother — INDIA, and provided that the political discriminations are totally removed and forever.

As the years roll by the conflicts become ghastlier and uglier, more and more persons are killed, the underworld is strengthened, and prepares for fresh bouts of rioting and politicians found the right occasion to build up a political base and increase their, "Vote Bank". What made matters worse is that Pakistan never missed, whenever there was the remotest chance, of creating distrust between the two communities and misguiding Muslims of India against Indian's "Secularism". Reportedly, Pakistan is funding fundamentalist Muslim Organisations to create internal unrest to destabilise India.

9. Dispersal of Riotous Mob

A riot is mob violence. It may consist of indiscriminate looting and arson and open attacks on rival communal groups. It may be organised or spontaneous. But always the one pervading element that is present in group violence that must be controlled by the law enforcement machinery, which comprises the police, and the magistracy or by military action, force is always subdued by greater force. In the working of the law enforcement machinery the powers and responsibilities of the police and magistracy are complementary, but where both the magistracy and police face any unlawful assembly together, the law requires that the police should act under the guidance and orders of the Magistrate in the said assembly for its dispersal, as by virtue of Section 4 of the Police Act of 1861, the police force in a district is placed under the District Magistrate for guidance, general control, and direction.

A hallmark of a police department is its emphasis on preventive law enforcement. In the control of riots, as in other cases of police responsibility, the most significant incidents are not those which occur, but which do not. Several principles guide in planning to prevent riots. Effective law enforcement envisages that the law must be enforced impartially and equitably for all people. There can be no select few, who receive preferential treatment, or a select group singles out for particularly harsh or unjust treatment. Our Constitution clearly defined that all men should receive equal treatment under the law, and none should be discriminated against on grounds of religion, caste, race *etc.* Every riot is brought about by previously existing factors. Whatever be the background, it should be apparent that the atmosphere which continues to a riotous situation develops over a period of time, and many factors are often involved. The most effective method of preventing a riot is to eliminate conditions which might lead to friction and misunderstanding and ultimately culminating into violence and lawlessness. Although the police can play an important, if not a leading role, in this function, it is important to ensure that the activities of police should never be a contributory cause for any kind of mob action and violence. But the paradox is that minority groups view the police with lack of confidence, and even animosity, and they prefer to turn over to politicians rather than police for guidance.

10. Military Aid to Civil Power

The responsibility of quelling riots and protection of life and property entirely rests with the State Government under the Constitution of India, which has included it in the concurrent list. Accordingly, the Central Government, generally as a supervisory authority and in case of unabated growth of violence as an overriding authority, enables its direct intervention, interference and situation demanding, involvement. When the developing situation makes it apparent that the State Police Forces are not adequate for the task, or for some reason or the other incapable to effectively control the situation, the civil authority may call in the Central Police Armed Forces (Para-military Forces), or the Army for assistance and the eventuating stage of calling these forces for assistance has to be decided by the State Government. The Ayodhya syndrome — the destruction of a Muslim structure at Ayodhya in December 1992, is a classic instance of the government apathy or lethargy, and the failure of the State as well as the Central Government to take timely measures and action. Instead, both the Central and the State Governments embroiled the Supreme Court in the picture in a bid to face it to solve the vexatious and ever eluding tangle of, "*Shree Ram Janma Bhoomi*". The Supreme Court was clever enough, though inordinately delayed, to return the ugly to the administrative heads. All these actions and inactions ended in colossal loss of life and property and above all the permanency in discordant behaviour and attitude of the Muslims as well as Hindus, and their relative estrangement. This euphemistic attitude of the administrative machinery and the judiciary has inextricably lop-sided the political balance in the country, and gave redoubled pace to the policy of appeasement of minority community.

The use of the Central Armed Police Forces and the Army in aid of civil power has been provided under Sections 129 and 131 of the Criminal Procedure Code formed by the British Government immediately after the War of Independence in 1857, and amended in 1973, as such situations were anticipated even then. But the only difference is that in the past such assistance was solicited in extremely rare cases and police dealt with the situation effectively, and now this assistance is required as frequently as possible, and in consequence reduced the police to executive impotency and nullity. This has emboldened the anti-social elements and insulated them, and now a situation has come to such a pass that brutal force is often required to disperse the unruly mob. When a Magistrate is present it is entirely his responsibility and discretion to decide how the Central Armed Forces or the Army should be used and in what manner to disperse the unlawful assembly. When the Armed Forces or the Army is called in aid of civil authority to quell riots, the civil authority retains full control and is responsible for all the actions taken, leaving to the Commissioned Officers of the Army the discretion to utilise the forces under his command in the best possible, way and to use such physical measures as and when necessary, provided he conforms to the rule that only the minimum force to attain a particular objective should be used. When the Magistrate present decides to use the Armed Forces or the Army, he may issue order in writing to the Commissioned Officer present accordingly, but the discretion to decide in what manner the necessary action should be taken for the dispersal of unlawful assembly, and the decision to arrest offenders should remain with the Commissioned Officer. As soon as the unlawful assembly has been dispersed, the Magistrate can ask the officer-in-charge of the Armed Forces or the Army to cease action. These forces can also be used for the maintenance of law and order even after the disturbances have been quelled during patrolling of the affected areas duly accompanied by a police officer or Magistrate to effect searches, arrests *etc*. While deploying the Armed Forces or the Army the cardinal principle, and most important too, that is to be borne in mind by the Commanding Officer is that as little force as possible should be used, and as little injury to person or property should be caused as may be consistent with the attainment of the objective of dispersal of unlawful assembly. The firing should be ordered in phases and in a controlled manner and directed only at the more volatile rioters or Section of them. The aim should be low, the shooting should be effective, and as far as possible incapacitating the mischief-monger (and not killing the enemy as in war) and immediate first aid to the injured should be given.

11. Survey of Communal Riots

Prevention and control of riots is a highly complex and demanding assignment and most important responsibility of law enforcement agency — the police, who have been subjected to serve criticism, for their omissions and commissions, in the handling of communal riots which have grown from year to year. A survey of riots during the last five decades disclosed the following salient features which should provide an answer to the questions — why police failed to prevent and contain communal riots?

1. Intelligence agency often failed to collect and communicate timely information before, during and after a riot resulting in the misdirected action of the local police.
2. Delay in taking preventive action, or taking preventive action against wrong persons.
3. Ineffective enforcement of all prohibitory orders, including the use of loudspeakers etc.
4. Delay of police and Magistrate reaching the scene with adequate strength of police force and such adequate police strength, in actual working, is rarely available due to the policy of the government to repeatedly turn down the demand of increase in the strength of the police.
5. Peace committees not formed and appointment of special police officers under Section 17 of Police Act not made in initial stages, police failed to locate infiltrators and keep them under close surveillance, censorship was not enforced and stock piling of lethal weapons, explosives, stones *etc.*, were not detected due to the failure of the police in searching places of worships.

6. Not all cognizable cases arising out of riot are registered and a large percentage of then, in which powerful anti-social elements, friendly to the party in power, was suppressed. Investigation of cases and their prosecution withdrawn.
7. Home guards deployed on duties proved useless as they were mostly untrained and lacked discipline. Moreover, they had vested interest in the locality and its inhabitants.
8. Mobilisation of available police force within the district often delayed considerably leaving the local police officer to deal with the initial fury of the riotous mob with his already depleted police force culminating in worsening the situation.
9. On account of improper training of policemen in dealing with riots, the effectiveness of police action was diluted.
10. Para-military Force, and the Army were not called in time due to several attributary factors affecting the political balance of the locality.
11. Inexperienced District Magistrates and Superintendents of Police hesitated to take timely action. Generally, they abdicated their powers and waited for instructions from their senior officers, and in the meantime, the mob swelled and the situation deteriorated. For this lethargy and apathy there is one convincing reason and it is the unwanted and unnecessary interferences and interventions of the ministerial authorities of the Government in power either directly by them or through their stooges, who render a helping hand in their electoral success.
12. The Magistrate and police generally hesitate to use force in the initial stage forgetting the adage. "Strike when it is hot". Their reluctance resulted in more rowdy and eventually a greater force was required to be used *to* quell disturbances. Weak magistrates and police officers afraid of a subsequent enquiry, vacillated to order use of force at the appropriate time or remained in hiding as cowards, and they hesitated to exercise their right of private defence in the protection of life and property which is their most important duty.

13. Infiltration within the police force of political cadres, breaking all rules of recruitments, infected the virus of communalism within the rank and file and impartiality of the police in law enforcement could not be ensured.
14. For various political expediencies no steps were taken to contain communal speeches and writings inciting communal hatred and ill-feeling.
15. The greatest handicaps were political patronage and partisan politics. Police were pressurised to deal with the rioters leniently. They were prevented from making arrest and registering cases against them.

The aftermath of a riot generally presented a familiar picture. After having advised the police to take firm action (And as publicly as possible, even telecommunication, radio and press media used with the portrait of the leader) against the law-breakers, the government switched to its policy of appeasement and offered them a free pardon. Order to impose collective or punitive fines, on the aggressive community, not issued to avoid confrontation in the Parliament and state legislatures. *Laws lapsed into disuse,* and the result is that communal riots had broken out at the same place within an interval of 2/3 years. This is clearly due to the fact those involved in the previous riot were not convicted and allowed to remain on bail while the cases against them pending in courts for several years and ultimately forgotten and important eyewitnesses either deceased or turned hostile under pressure of injury or reward.

Majority of the police force consists of constabulary, and they are the first to be on the scene to challenge the rioting mob. They should be given adequate in service training periodically to deal with the problem impartially and firmly. There are several instances in which a tough constable faced the fury of the mob single-handed, opened fire, and forced the mob to retreat. Seldom his services are recognised for the award of "Police Medal", where again politics has played an important part. This has discouraged such gallant behaviour of the constabulary.

The communal problem has been examined from every conceivable angle in the last five decades. The factors causing communal tensions, and clashes have been identified and suggestions made for remedial action in different spheres — political, social, economic and administrative. Preventive measures too have been spelt out in great details. Despite the voluminous reports of scores of Inquiry Commissions — Judicial and Administrative, and Minority Commission and discussions at the National Integration Council and debates in the Parliament and State Legislature, no tangible solution to this vex and recurring problem is found, probably the "Will" of the Government is lacking.

12. Illegal Gun Culture

Easy availability of fire arms and explosives threatens the internal security of the country. One of the major causes of reported carnages in India is that the total stock of firearms, both legal and illicit, with anti-social elements has multiplied several times, over the years. There are more firearms with private individuals. We have virtually permitted private arsenals to be built up in most of the districts all over the country for a rebellion against lawful authority. The situation is so serious that it calls for the cancellation of all existing arm licences, and then renewal for those who really need the arm, and not without any searching enquiries and scrutiny.

Apart from large-scale smuggling of weapons and explosives and gun-running from across the borders, hundreds of clandestine factories are operating in different parts of the country, manufacturing guns, pistols, revolvers and hand-grenades as a cottage industry. Many of these units are financed by politicians in power. Political power in Bihar flows from the barrels of a gun. In this State political parties depend more on firearms than on the support of people to win elections. Gaya and Nalanda districts of Bihar are the nerve centres of the illegal weapon trade, almost every village has a factory. Arms are available at a low price varying from Rs. 200 to Rs. 1,000.

Uttar Pradesh has the largest private arsenal of arms in the country. There is one licensed arm for a population of 200. Most incredible is the fact that a large number of licensed weapons were carbines, a weapon banned for private ownership in the country. The issue of arms licences in the State has been electric. Licence holders included infirm women over 60 years and men over 75 years of age, even some blind persons are reported to possess valid arm licences. Between 1980-85, a number of controversial leaders involved either in caste or political rivalries were able to secure licences. Government contracts can be secured at gun point mostly for civil works. Students are able to secure admissions in colleges, particularly in Uttar Pradesh and Bihar at gun point. Election are fought with fire-arms and rival candidates or elected candidates are killed. *Dacoities*, robberies, extortion, kidnapping or abduction for ransom are committed with free use of arms. Enmity between the persons or parties is settled by gun fire resulting in deaths. Criminal gangs on many occasions, have greater fire power than the police. Even murders by firearm are committed in the precincts of the courts, High Courts not excluded. The volume of crime with firearm is increasing.

Periodical drives against possession of illegal fire-arms have little effect when there is a much longer fresh inflow. The problem has to be tackled at the root. Extreme measures are needed to save the country from disasters. The murder rate per lakh of the population has risen by merely 70 per cent in the last 25 years all over the country. The continuous drift to lawlessness is apparent even to a lay person.

The entire Chambal-Gwalior region in Madhya Pradesh sits atop a volcano in the form of an enormous arsenal with even the number of licensed, privately-held fire-arms running in excess of weapons in police possessions. Taking the 85,000 licensed rifles, guns and pistols in the four districts of this *dacoity* infested region, together with the number of unlicensed fire-arms in private possession — estimated conservatively at around two lakhs means that the privately owned arsenal is vastly larger than the total stores of weapons of all police units in Madhya Pradesh. Datia, the smallest district of Madhya Pradesh with a population of 3.5 lakhs boasts of 28,000 licensed arms — roughly one weapon to 12 persons. Morena district where a rifle is virtually the status of symbol, accounts for 24,000 licences. This number is claimed by many to be much more. Morena district has the dubious distinction of possessing the largest number of *dacoits* in the Chambal ravines.

All the districts situated on either bank of the Chambal river, have a large number of licensed arms and still a larger number of unlicensed arms, estimation is not possible. People living in this region have succeeded in obtaining all India licences from Haryana often paying more than Rs. 4,000 as graft money for buying the favour.

And, of course, licensing of fire-arms has become a thriving industry. Right from the verification of antecedents of applicants by the police till the issue of a licence corruption is widespread. Many officers and political leaders are involved in it. The going rate for a licence varies from Rs. 4,000 to Rs. 10,000. Some licensed arm dealers are engaged in inter-state illegal arm trade in large scale. Most of these arms and their ammunition go into the hands of criminals.

Every ruling political party has systematically armed its cadres with firearms and hand-grenades to fight its opponents. Due to close rapport between gangsters and politicians, it became easy for the anti-social to acquire firearms, both licensed and unlicensed. Influential politicians have been helping anti-socials, and criminals in getting arm licences and thereby secure their loyalty and assistance during elections and on other occasions. During the last two decades there have been a sharp increase in the use of firearms, and explosives by the criminals in the commission of grave crimes like *dacoity*, murder and robbery.

Over the years, the use of firearms during communal and caste riots has been causing great anxiety to the police. Rioters are armed and fire on police from house tops and alleys. A much larger armed force is now required to arrest and disarm the rioters.

Pilferages of fire-arms from ordnance factories are by no means small, and they go into circulation clandestinely. Gun-running has already become a lucrative venture. Added to this is the menace of smuggling of weapons from across the country's extensive border. Our unfriendly countries have been systematically helping the insurgents and terrorists in Jammu & Kashmir, Punjab, Rajasthan, Gujarat, Uttar Pradesh, Bihar, West Bengal, all the States of the Northeastern Regions, Maharashtra, Andhra Pradesh, Tamil Nadu. Practically, the whole of India has been covered by these smugglers, who supply free or at fabulous prices sophisticated firearms, their ammunition and various explosive devices. The blasts in Bombay, Calcutta, Madras, Secunderabad, Hyderabad, Ahemadabad, and trains, and at various places in the States bordering Pakistan were engineered by Pakistani ISI and caused several hundred deaths and loss of property running into several thousand crores.

The menace of firearms has become a serious threat to the internal security of the country. The National Police Commission has dealt with this subject in 38th Chapter — Arms Act Fifth Report, and made several recommendations to improve the frightening situation prevalent in the country today. More than 12 years have passed, but very few of its recommendations have been implemented by the Government. Meanwhile, an explosive situation is developing in the country month by month. Unless checked in time right now, it is bound to lead, in no distant future, to civil war and anarchial conditions in most of the States. Government did not spell out its impediments for having failed to take stern action on all the recommendations of the National Police Commission. Not infrequently police have been blamed for their apathy/lethargy and corruption in taking stern action against the violators of the Indian Arms Act, and the Rules framed thereunder. Partially this allegation is not baseless. But police is not the singular culprit. They cannot dare to act on their own. Instances are not wanting when police did not recommend the grant of an arm-licence to a certain individual because of his criminal propensities or established record, and yet, the same person was granted an arm-licence because he could invoke political blessings at the highest level of the party forming the Government. The dumb-founded police, not surprisingly, adopted the stance of least resistance and become wiser to benefit themselves from such shady deals! The emboldened criminal browbeat the police. It is a political gain, but the greatest administrative loss. The pride and prestige of the police have been sunk by such political interferences.

Reminiscent of the British Rule were the days, when people dreaded to possess even a four-inch blade knife for fear of punishment, and now after 48 years of the Independence people are not afraid at all to manufacture illicit arms and ammunition and possess tonnes of unlicensed weaponry, and that is the test and difference of administrative control.

21
Students and Police

1. Generation Gap

The globe is the battlefield in the war between generations. The students and the youth represent the more aggressive and volatile generation up in arms against the establishment which they derisively call the government. The student population representing the elite section of the youth search for a new order, new set of values, and morals and expulsion of all, "Garbages" of the existing order. The older generation which controls the society have some sort of love-hate relationship with the youth, and more particularly with the student community. They want their offspring to accept the values practiced by them and emerge as social conformists. The spirit of turbulence and rebellion, the display of black flags in the street, the denigration of the older generation by the youth, into the non-conformist behaviour upsets the middle age, and the old who start disliking the young generation half realising the consequences of a society that dislikes its young people.

An Egyptian priest, almost 6,000 years ago wrote on the walls of a tomb:

> "Our earth is degenerate in the later days. There are signs the world is coming to an end because children no longer obey their parents".

Likewise, Socrates wrote about 2,400 years ago:

> "Children now love luxury, they have bad manners, contempt of authority, they show disrespect for elders and love chatter in place of exercise. Children no longer rise when elders enter the room. They contradict their parents, chatter before company, gobble up dainties at the table, cross their legs and tyranise over their teachers."

The confrontation between the society, and the students has a long chequered history, the university students have never been fully accepted as regular members of the society throughout its long history. The university came to India in 1857 during the British Rule, and the university graduates and under-graduates acquired some social respectability as they subsequently turned out to be the collaborators with the Britishers in managing the bureaucracy, and the various professions, including teaching, law and medicine. In a caste-ridden feudal Indian society these university products formed a special group of elite in the bureaucratic and social hierarchy. The universities soon started multiplying, and they turned out to be workshops of producing man-power for the government offices, and mercantile houses. In the over-populated country like India, the jobs could not keep pace with the number of graduates produced resulting in clamour for more jobs and those, unemployed, or without honourable means of earning their livelihood, became increasingly restive and pro-demonstrative.

2. Factors Influencing Students

The student movement represent a microcosm in the national political sense, adopting the same media of protest like the parent bodies, and more times making common cause with the parent bodies, and their various front organisations functioning among the working class, agricultural workers and various other professions. The students and youth also participate frequently in the political movements of the parent bodies, then bringing out a broad reconciliation between the students and the society; but opposing each other as various groups of students draw inspiration from different political parties. In the Western world the university and the society are distinct from each other, and the derisive forces of the society are not allowed to percolate into the university, this situation is in total contrast with that of our universities.

3. Disadvantages of Students

The Indian student has many other disadvantages to suffer. He has many legitimate reasons to complain about his living and working conditions including spiraling prices affecting the cost of education. There are frequent changes in the pattern of education, and even after 48 years of the Independence we have failed to acquire a fixed pattern of education, which the earlier generation had during the pre-Independence era. The low quality of teaching and the uninspired attitude of the over-burdened and often poorly qualified teachers, more preoccupied with the political intricacies and non-academic pursuits which preclude pride in identification with college community. The school leaver, in young and immature, has only few opportunities for the wholesome extra-curricular activities, and is disturbed by his own bleak and uncertain future of mounting unemployment among the educated caused by non-availability of job-oriented and purposive motivated education. To add to it, in our country where a substantial voters are uneducated, the students, who are more educated than their parents, to some extent justifiably display more responsibility and awareness of social and political problem and feel that they have some solution to offer to today's problem. Thus, the unrest among the students often reflects wider national tensions, the local politicians playing exploitative and instigative roles. The Indian students mostly depend on their parents for the conclusion of their education as there is no facility to "earn and learn". He is caught in a cauldron of deprivation, frustration, and resentment against the social/ government neglect. He can thus be turned into action without much provocation, and his behaviour is marked with turbulence and rebellion. The idiom of expression of his protest is through clashes with police or sections of public, and attack on teachers and invigilators in examinations, the matrix of negotiations being generally *gheraos* and demonstrations.

4. Student Community Relationship

The relationship between the student community and the society, to a large extent, governs the attitude of the students towards the Government in general and the police in particular, as the latter is the executive arm of the Government. The university students, who contribute disproportionately to the informed public opinion, and from where ranks will come for tomorrow's social and political leaders, are conscious of being part of this unique social stratum as they play an unusually important role in the day-to-day political and social developments of the country, understandably, they adopt an elitist attitude towards the police tempered with the surroundings in which they live. Generally, as a class they, are cynical and suspicious about the police, and are inclined to doubt its honesty, impartiality and freedom from political control. Far from conceiving the police as an agency possessing integrity, dedication and a sincere desire to help the citizen in distress, they are quite willing and prepared to believe the worst in respect of police rudeness, discourtesy, and physical abuse, which to a larger extent, is the result of behaviour of some of the members of the force. Such instances, though exceptional, the students conceived them universal. The students have already developed this impression about the police by the time he is in the process of matriculation — a boy of hardly 17 years. The girl students are no exception to such impressions of the police.

5. Student Contact with Police

The students contact with the police can be broadly grouped with that of citizen with an anxiety about his safety. His evaluation of the police, particularly relating to police behaviour, corruption and favouritism, his contact with the police during public disorder, both as a participant and as a spectator, and his general familiarity and knowledge regarding police duties, accountability, salary structure and working conditions. The most unpleasant relationship between the groups arise during public disorder where at both groups are pitched against one another. A large number of students has seen police using *lathi* or bursting tearsmoke shells either as a member of the demonstrating group or as a spectator. Some of them had also the experience of use of firearms by the police. They are prepared to accept these incidents or events as necessary provided they are made to believe that police are justified in what they do, and this belief is most difficult to penetrate their conception, and rectify their preconceived ideas about police. The student community as a whole considers demonstrations and agitations necessary and proper to secure their legitimate demands, and even a minor interference by police is in their mind on extension of political interference. The modality of protest actions adopted by the militants among the students, however, do not conform with the law of the land, and the visible symbols of the Government including the police, transport bus, and telephone exchanges generally become their targets notwithstanding the issue involved.

The anatomy of student agitation and the police reaction to the same vary from situation to situation and place to place. The student groups consider the police as the main obstacle in realising their own demands and making their voice heard at the policy-making level. The policemen on the other hand feel over-burdened and perplexed while dealing with the student situations. A survey of a number of agitations and police response bring out certain interesting features as under:

1. The demands of students could be academic or non-academic and the chances of confrontation in the latter category are lower.
2. Resentment of students against entry of police into university campus or scholastic institutions, particularly into hostels is almost universal and confrontation over this issue causes sympathy of the entire student population, though in varying degrees.
3. Confrontation between the students and their institutional authorities over academic issues changes direction on police due to police intervention when called upon to control the unruly students.
4. The non-academic issues have a high potentiality of student police confrontation — the highest point being a grievance against the police itself during which the police loses its role of an uneasy referee to that of a loathed party. Some of these non-academic demands of the students may be attributed towards the police itself, its behaviour, regulation of traffic, failure to arrest or investigate and inability to maintain neutrality in the event of a clash between two warring groups of students. In such instance the students give a call for '*hartal*' or '*gherao*' etc., in order to draw the attention of public to their grievances, and for no reason or rhyme, the police and student willy-nilly get pitched against one another.
5. The educational institutions have been utilised on several occasions as sanctuaries of political revolutionaries, and also that of anti-social youths, in most cases without the knowledge of the general student population of

those institutions. This situation, besides compromising the sanctity of the campus, also makes rule operation difficult, thus, endangering the safety and security of the society as a whole.

6. Police administrative promptitude in handling student grievances and agitations is directly relatable to the proximity of the scene of occurrence to the seat of policy-making. Student agitations at the state headquarters are dealt with more promptly and effectively than those at district, sub-divisional, *tahsil* or police station headquarters. The administrative hierarchy at these levels hardly inspires confidence of the students, and these administrators, therefore, are compelled to resort to more punitive than persuasive measures to control situations. The lack of sufficient force in such places has a demoralising effect on the confidence of the officers at lower formations to deal with the students.
7. Formation of students' union even in small towns and rural areas on account of pluralities of scholastic institutions and their consequential rival groups, always prepared for combat with one another on any issue, however, insignificant it may be. Thus, in effect, a small group with militant propensities, will dominate the sobre one, though not particularly excelling in games, sports, dramatics, academics, and succeeds in directing the student behaviour in campus; and its confrontation with the establishment arrogates to itself the total leadership of the student community.

The police responses to various student grievances and street action also vary according to situations. The police personnel as a whole prefer the presence of a superior police officer while dealing with student groups. The presence of a senior police or magisterial officer has often normalised tensions and solved the problem of the agitating students as they are in a preferable position to contact the higher levels of the governmental hierarchy. Prompt redressal of genuine grievances of students has always been of help, as students as a group display considerable understanding of their immediate surroundings, and the limitations of the other social groups.

Use of force against vast body of students has the potentiality of escalation of the situation further and snowballing it into a major confrontation engulfing the various sections of the society. The police also views it as a confrontation between the younger generation, and the force that represent the establishment, rather than of confrontation between the students and the police as such. The police authorities and personnel view the student community as one of their critic groups and, therefore, treat the students with great circumspection. They are conscious of their groups and potentialities, who often succeed in collecting individual problems of law infringements and put the police in the defensive, even in glaring instances of violation of law by individual members of the group. The reactions of the police vary locale to locale and situation to situation, sometimes with dignified forbearance, sometimes with an attitude of patronage, and some other times with irritation and resentment. The student community enjoys much wider base than the police as all sections of the citizens are one way or the other connected or interrelated with it. In a confrontation between the students and the police, the vocal sections of the society and the middle class as a whole are more concerned, responsive and indulgent to the student view point than the legal niceties, and the functional necessities of law enforcing agencies. The situation weighs more favourably towards the students in a democracy, where the student community as an elite section of the society play an important role. The police gets isolated and this isolation sometimes finds expression in a near sadistic manner, contact points causing irritants resulting in more often than not avoidable confrontations. The basic hiatus, however, stems from the fact that the police do not want to permit the students to operate as a special group in the eyes of law as against the desire of the students to sustain their privileged position in the society. The police credibility for impartial enforcement of law is not, however, buttressed with bright image of its own, making itself open to critical and evaluating judgement by a discriminating group like the students. A rapprochement between the two groups is possible only by proper understanding of each other's role, and place in the society, improved truthful image of the police and better appreciation of their own civic role by students.

22

Policing Tribal Society

1. Tribal Societies

India has the record largest tribal population in the world, next to Africa. There are 630 tribes which are sub-divided into groups and spread over the length and breadth of the country. The tribes differ considerably from one another in race, language and culture and in their myths. There are tribes living in the remotest corners of the country in a primitive stage, and in abject poverty. The social values, customs, culture and beliefs of the tribals govern their family life, marriage, rituals, festivals, community living, moral codes which are not only quite different from those of the non-tribals, but they vary from tribe to tribe, and differences can also be noticed among the various groups within the same tribe. There are tribal societies, where marriage by elopement or kidnapping is prevalent, and they have institutions where young boys and girls of nubile age are expected to stay at night, which naturally results in promiscuous sex, but this has social sanction. Some of the tribes believe in certain superstitions and their practices, like witchcraft, sorcery, human sacrifice, *bhanamati etc*. Some of the above cases are criminal offences and punishable under the Indian Penal Code elsewhere in the country. But the tribals do not consider them to be criminal offences according to the value system in prevalence in their society. The tribals do not consider violation of many of the forest, excise and prohibition laws as offences punishable under the law in other parts of the country.

While the main features of law enforcement are same everywhere, differences in the pattern of policing are bound to occur in tribal areas due to the terrain, topographical conditions, road communications, their distinct culture, customs and the tribal customary laws in force, evolved over centuries. They always believed in a much simpler and more personal and humane administration, free from legal technicalities. Many customs prevalent among different tribal societies contravene established laws, rules and regulations. Their customary laws are handed over from generation to generation, and are still unwritten, but such a system is more responsive to their social needs. The tribal welfare councils are providing cheap and quick justice with simpler procedures based on the principles of natural justice without exploitation by the lawyers. In civil and criminal matters and registration and transfer of property they have evolved simpler regulations.

The Constitution of India provided certain provisions of autonomy in the administration of Hill Areas; and these provisions are included in the Sixth Schedule to the Constitution, and they protect the people of the Hills from the domination of the more advanced people of the plains. A sort of regional autonomy has thus emerged out of the above provisions enabling the tribals:

(a) To safeguard the ways of life,
(b) To participate in the political life of the country and the administration of their own areas, and
(c) To develop themselves according to their own generation and tradition.

Accordingly their land, forests, social organisation and systems of justice became the sole subject of their own autonomous administration along with aspects of economic developments. The latter is, however, the joint responsibility of the States, and the Autonomous Bodies of different tribal societies.

Some provisions of the customary laws contravene letter and spirit, the provisions of the normal laws of the country. The tribals have their own conception of crime and punishment and this factor must be kept in mind while enforcing criminal law and justice in tribal areas. There is different type of Criminal Justice Systems prevalent in Arunachal Pradesh, Hill districts of Assam, Meghalaya, Nagaland, Manipur, Mizoram and Tripura, where the tribals of India are mostly concentrated.

2. Arunachal Pradesh

Civil and criminal justice in Arunachal Pradesh is administered under the Assam Frontiers (Administration and Justice)

Regulation, 1945. There are three tiers of criminal courts under this Regulation, namely, (1) Deputy Commissioner, (2) Assistant Commissioner, and (3) Village Authority (Rule 15). Members of Village Council are chosen by the villagers according to their traditional method and from these members the Deputy Commissioner appoints such persons as he may consider desirable to be members of such Village Councils. Village authorities, may under Rule 19, try cases involving theft; mischief, excluding mischief by fire or explosive substances; simple hurt; criminal trespass, house trespass and assault or using criminal force. Rule 20 empowers a village authority to impose a fine not exceeding Rs. 50, and award payment in restitution or compensation. Village authorities try all cases in open *Darbars* in the presence of at least three independent witnesses, besides the complainant and the accused, and their proceedings are not required to be reduced to writing. There is also no preliminary enquiry by the police. Proceedings before the Assistant Deputy Commissioner are to be recorded in writing. Appeals lie from the decision of the village authority to the Assistant Commissioner and from an original decision of an Assistant Commissioner to the Deputy Commissioner. Appeals lie to the High Court against sentence of three years imprisonment or upwards. An Assistant Commissioner may also try case *de novo* even when such case has been earlier disposed of by a village authority. Village authorities may try all suits, without limit of value, where both parties are indigenous or agreeable and the cases are not submitted to arbitration. Courts higher than the village courts follow the spirit of Civil Procedure Code, 1908 in civil cases; and the principles of Criminal Procedure Code, 1973 in criminal cases. Appellate hierarchy is the same as in criminal cases. Though according to 1945 Regulation, a Village Council authorised to dispose of only petty criminal cases, yet the Government has issued an administrative instruction that all cases involving criminal liability, including heinous offences other than those against the State, will be dealt with by Village Councils, provided restitution or award of compensation to the injured party is considered as sufficient deterrent and accepted as such by the clans concerned. This instruction has, however, no statutory basis. Arunachal Pradesh has 11 districts, 17 police stations and 61 outposts.

3. Hill Districts of Assam

North Cachar Hills District of Assam is an Autonomous District under the Sixth Schedule to the Constitution and the North Cachar Hills Autonomous District (Administration of Judicial) Rules, 1955 regulate the judicial system. The provisions of these rules are exactly on the same lines as those of the United Khasi Jaintia Hills, and the three-tier system is prevalent. In Kanbi Anglong, the 1937 Rules of Administration of Justice and Police are still in force.

4. Meghalaya

After the formation of Meghalaya, the State adopted the following laws by an order:

(a) Rule for the Administration of Justice and Police in the Khasi-Jaintia Hills, 1937.

(b) The United Khasi Jaintia Hills Autonomous District (Administration of Justice) Rules, 1953.

(c) The Khasi Siemship (Administration of Justice) Order, 1950.

(d) Rules for the Administration of Justice and Police in the Garo Hills District, 1937.

(e) The Garo Hills Autonomous District (Administration of Justice) Rules, 1953.

(f) Assam High Court (Jurisdiction over the District Council) Order, 1954.

The districts being autonomous have their own set of rules in conformity with their district traditions and customs.

The criminal administration in the State of Meghalaya is conducted in accordance with the provisions of the "Rules for the Administration of Justice and Police" framed separately for the two original districts of Garo Hills, and the United Khasi Jaintia Hills. These rules provide similar procedures for the dispensation of Criminal Justice. While the "spirit" of the Criminal Procedure Code is observed in the administration of Criminal Justice, the actual work is carried out in accordance with the local rules, having the force and as well sanction of the customary laws. Criminal Procedure Code is applicable only in municipal areas.

There is two-tier system of criminal administration in Meghalaya. There are two types of police functioning in the state, *viz.,* the Regular Police and the Rural Police. The former functions under the control of the Director General/Inspector General of Police in accordance with the normal criminal law of the country. The State Police Department functions throughout the geographical area of the State and is responsible for maintaining law and order and internal security, and enforcement of all laws framed by the Parliament and State Legislature. The State is divided into five police districts. At the district level the Deputy Commissioners exercise powers of the Superintendent of Police and the Assistant Commissioners exercise the powers of Sub-Divisional Police Officer, and they are governed by the Police Act of 1861.

The Rural Police consist of village authorities such as *Sardars, Dalois, Pators, Lyngdohs*, and *Nokmen etc.* The Regular Police have no control over the Rural Police, who function under day-to-day supervision and control of the local authority subject to the overall control of the Deputy Commissioner. The provisions of Sections 25 and 26 of the Evidence Act and Section 162 of the Criminal Procedure Code are not applicable to the Rural Police (In-admissibility of confession before a police officer and statement made before a police officer — admissibility of). The duties of the Rural Police are the same as are found in other parts of the country. People are duty-bound to aid the Rural Police in the discharge of their duties, and their failure to do so renders then liable to pay fine which can be imposed by the village authorities.

Another feature of Khasi democracy is the participation of the entire population in moulding policies, judicial decisions at their *Darbars* on the principle of decentralisation of powers. Each village has its own *Darbar*. It holds frequent sessions in which all male adults are required to attend. The *Darbar* functions as a court of justice by deciding criminal and civil cases and judicial disputes, besides handling law and public administration. The *Darbar* is presided by SYIEM or a deputy

SYIEM, who normally first attempts for reconciliation without bringing the parties to trial. The Khasi State takes the form of a confederation the federing units owing allegiance to the SYIEM, Meghalaya has five police districts with 31 police stations. The SYIEM's moral duty is to keep alive the unity of the State.

5. Nagaland

According to the Rules for Administration of Justice and Police in Naga Hills District, 1937, which after creation of Nagaland State in 1962 have been continued over the entire State. The police in Naga Hills consist of:

1. Regular police subject to Police Act of 1861;
2. Assam Rifles subject to Act 1920; and
3. Rural Police consisting of *Manzadars*, *Gaonburas*, *Chiefs*, *Headmen* of *Khel,* and other village authorities recognised as such by the Deputy Commissioners with their subordinate village authorities.

The same Rules vest the control of the police in Deputy Commissioners acting under the order of the Governor, and in such other officers as the Governor may from time to time appoint.

Under the provisions of Sections 3 to 6 of the above Rules the Regular Police shall act only when required to do so by general or special order of the Deputy Commissioner or the Superintendent of Police, or other officer duly authorised may assign to force any portion of the duties of police under the Police Act of 1861. Under Sections 8 to 10 of the same Rules the village officials of the Rural Police are empowered to function as ordinary police elsewhere in the country.

Traditionally, every Naga village has a village Council chosen from among the founder clans, and the priest clans according to their respective customary manner.

It may appear that the Regular Police in Nagaland have only a limited sphere of function, and that it is not to act *suo motu*. However, the pattern of actual police working has greatly changed since the creation of the State in 1962. Although the sphere of the functions of Regular Police has been considerably widened after 1962 by the application of practically all

Sections of the Code of Criminal Procedure, the rules for the Administration of Justice and Police relating to the position of Deputy Commissioner *vis-a-vis* the police remain unchanged. This leads to a somewhat confusing situation in which two sets of rules, at times contradicting each other, are governing the working of the police in the State.

Nagaland is divided into eight police districts with 36 police stations. The Nagaland Armed Police are mainly deployed to man the various border observation posts. The Assam Rifles is specially raised to deal with the problem of insurgency in Nagaland.

6. Manipur

The Manipur (Village Authorities in Hills Areas) Act, 1956 was passed (modifying the provisions of 1947 Regulation) by the Parliament providing for administration of criminal justice in hill villages of Manipur. Under this Act a village authority for each village has been constituted to deal with administration of criminal justice and maintenance of law and order. It has powers to arrest persons without orders from a Magistrate or without a warrant in large number of cases mentioned under Section 16(b) of the Act. Section 20 of the Act defines the jurisdiction of the village courts, which have concurrent jurisdiction with that of the criminal court within the local units of whose jurisdiction the village is situated in respect of various offences of petty nature, such as, under the Cattle Trespass Act, Police Act *etc*. Under the Indian Penal Code offences of petty nature and thefts in which the value of the stolen property does not exceed Rs. 200 come within the cognizance of the village courts. While trying these cases the village court can impose fines of not more than Rs. 200 or in default imprisonment not exceeding a term of one month. Thus, an elaborate justice system has been evolved under this Act providing speedy justice in large number of cases which generally and frequently occur in villages, without delay and with full participation of the villagers themselves. At the same time the customary law of the tribal has been protected and they have the freedom to decide the cases and suits in accordance with the customary law. Manipur is divided into eight police districts with 52 police stations.

7. Mizoram

Prior to British annexation of Lushai Hills, each village had its own Chief, who ruled over the area under his control practically as an absolute monarch. All powers, administrative as well as judicial, were vested in the Chief, who tried cases with the help of council of elders, called "Upos". They did not very much interfere with the system of administration of justice. This system was permitted for all offences except the grave cases like murder and rape, which had to be reported to the Superintendent of Police. The maximum fine, which could be imposed in those days, was Rs. 40. The British followed the policy that there should be no interference in this system, and at the same time it was ensured that no glaring injustice was manifested.

Upon the formation of the Mizo District under the Sixth Schedule to the Constitution, the Chiefs rights were abolished under the Assam Lushai Hills District (Acquisition of Chiefs Rights) Act, 1954 upon payment of compensation determined under that Act. Simultaneously, the Lushai Hills District (Village Councils) Act, 1953 was passed by the Lushai Hills District Council. The village council consists of elected and nominated members, which vary with the number of houses in a particular village. One-third of the members are nominated and the rest are elected.

Under the Lushai Hills Autonomous District (Administration of Justice) Rules, 1953 the Village Courts are the lowest courts dealing with suits and cases between parties, being Scheduled Tribes, and at least three members of the Council are required to try these cases or suits. The Village Council can hear all cases of civil and miscellaneous nature falling within the purview of village or tribal laws and customs, and also offences of petty nature, but cannot try any case involving an obligatory punishment of imprisonment under the Indian Penal Code. As a corollary, a Village Council cannot impose sentence of imprisonment. It can impose fine up to Rs. 50. It can award payment of restitution or compensation in accordance with the customary law.

The next higher court is the Subordinate District Council Court. This court has original jurisdiction in all suits and cases in which both the parties are not from the same village. But its jurisdiction is limited to cases in which both parties or persons belong to Scheduled Tribes. It cannot try certain excepted categories of suits and cases which are to be tried by the courts of the Deputy Commissioner and his Assistants. The subordinate District Council Court will also hear appeals from decisions of the Village Court.

Appeal from the Subordinate District Council Court lies to the District Council Court which will sit in a bench of not less than two judicial officers. Appeal from District Council Court lies with the Guwahati High Court.

The Civil Procedure Code and the Criminal Procedure Code are not applicable as such, but the courts have to follow the spirits of the Codes, in their proceedings. Lawyers are not allowed to appear in these courts, except with the special sanction of the Administrator of Mizoram, which is not normally allowed.

It seems to be very incongruous to have two simultaneous and parallel centres of judicial authorities, and it appears that the Village Councils have been divested of their importance and they exist on the sufferance of the people. Mizoram is divided into three police districts with 29 police stations.

8. Tripura

In Tripura, under the Tripura Tribal Areas Autonomous District Council Act, 1979 which applies only to certain selected predominantly tribal villages, provisions have been made to form Village Councils which shall have power to try civil suits, and criminal cases up to certain limits. The value of the civil suit should not exceed Rs. 1,000 and they should relate to money due on contract, recovery of property, compensation for wrongfully taking or injuring any property and damages caused by cattle trespass. The criminal case may relate to such offences in which the mandatory punishment does not exceed six months, and as such they are petty in nature and effect. Appeal lies to the District Judge. These Districts and Village Councils are constituted under a State Act. The administration of justice through tribal village authority has evolved naturally out of conditions of tribal life and commands ready allegiance from the people, who are more willing to co-operate with their own and traditionally established institutions and they have survived the test of time through long usage and convention, yet, it is a matter of anxious consideration as to how far the prevalent disintegration of the traditional tribal apparatus in the State has contributed to the existing disorder, and it is only due to the fact that the fabric of tribal life has also been weakened. Poor conditions of police stations, and jail buildings encouraged extremist elements to attack them, set prisoners free and take over arms and ammunition after killing the guards. Police personnel posted in this region, particularly at the middle and lower levels, are of poor standard and not adequately trained for anti-insurgency measures, recruitment of sub-standard personnel, and posting of lower calibre of senior officers have adversely affected the efficiency of the police. There is urgent need to increase the number of police stations to control infiltration and insurgency activities on the international borders. Tripura is divided into three districts with 45 police stations.

Insurgency has become the most serious problem of Mizoram, Nagaland, bordering areas of Tripura and Manipur. The security forces and the Army are deployed in division strength to deal with the activities of insurgents. The problem has to be tackled ultimately by the local police in eliminating the extremist elements and winning over the local population. The use of Army for day-to-day policing has to be deprecated. The intelligence machinery is extremely weak. Infiltration of Bangladesh subjects is a major problem. The international border is being policed by the BSF, Assam Rifles, and the Army. Smuggling has assumed serious proportion, particularly in Manipur, and the connivance of politicians, and the police is the major cause for this malady. The insurgents are reported to be organising smuggling to finance their underground activities. It devolves mainly on the BSF and Assam Rifles to tackle the problem effectively. Corruption is widespread at every level of administration. Large funds allotted by the Central Government are misappropriated. Politicians are reported to have financed the activities of the extremist elements by diverting funds from out of Central Governments contribution to keep the insurgency activities alive. Unfortunately, the bureaucrats could not prevent this type of misappropriation of Central Government funds, and have rendered themselves vulnerable to public criticism. Corruption free police officers are rare and honest among them are seemingly victimised, and strengthening of anti-corruption measures is the dire need of the hour.

23

Police and Human Rights

1. United Nations Declaration

The issue of Human Rights has not always been understood in the same perspective, or accepted or fulfilled at the same level of appreciation throughout the history of mankind. Philosophers like Manu, Socrates, Plato, Mahatma Gandhi and several others were the products of their times. Adolf Hitler's genocide stemming from racial prejudices was the last straw, and the shock treatment given by him during the World War II brought the final outcome of the upheaval in the formation of the United Nations Declaration of Human Rights in the year 1948, without a single dissent.

This Declaration recognised the dignity of human beings, who is born free and entitled to all rights and freedoms of man, without distinctions of race, colour, sex, language, religion or other differences of origin. It postulates that everyone has the "right to life, liberty, and security of persons." A specific right following from this declaration is the recognition of all human-beings everywhere as persons before the law, with equal rights and equal protection of the law. The concept of "rule of law, due process, fair trial" are backed by this declaration. The Government of India, as a signatory to the Resolution of the United Nations on the Declaration of Human Rights, ensured that practically all the human rights envisaged in the Declaration have been embodied in the Constitution of the Republic of India — Chapters III and IV, subsequently referred to in this chapter.

2. Police and Human Rights

The truth that human personality is inviolable and that all human beings, whatever their rank or status in society be, have a right to live with dignity is the fundamental principle underlying all laws concerned with human rights in any free democratic society. India shares the belief with all the nations, who are parties to the

Universal Declaration of Human Rights. The founding fathers of the Constitution attached great importance to human rights and accorded them a high place in the Constitution. In the words of Dr Radhakrishnan the guarantor of fundamental rights was "a pledge to our own people and a pact with the civilised world". The police, therefore, have a vital role to play in protecting the human rights of our citizens and in bringing violators to book.

3. Human Rights in Constitution

The fundamental rights in Part III of the Constitution fall into certain broad categories. Articles 14 to 16 guarantee different aspects of the right of equality. Article 17 abolishes untouchability and forbids its practice in any form. Article 19 guarantees basic freedom such as freedom of speech and expression, freedom of assembly, freedom to form associations and customs, freedom of residence and freedom to carry on any profession or business. Article 20 provides constitutional guarantees against retrospective criminal laws, double jeopardy, and self-incrimination. Article 21 guarantees that no person shall be deprived of his life or personal liberty except according to the procedure established by law. Certain safeguards in respect of arrest and detention of persons are provided by Article 22. For example, every person who is arrested must be informed of the grounds of such arrest, must not be denied the right to consult and defended by a lawyer or legal practitioner of his choice, and must be produced before the Magistrate within 24 hours of such arrest. However, these provisions do not apply to those detained under the preventive detention laws. Traffic in human-beings and forced labour is prohibited by Articles 23 and 24. Article 25 guarantees freedom of conscience and religions to citizens and non-citizens alike.

The founding fathers of the Constitution were fully conscious that for the meaningful enjoyment of fundamental rights, which are in the nature of civil and political rights of every citizen of India, should be assured of proper nutrition, health, education and employment and the means to improve his standard of living. These goals were articulated by them in Part IV of the Constitution which lays down the Directive Principles of the State Policy. In substance they are in the nature of social and economical rights. Although Directive Principles are not enforceable by any court, they are "nevertheless fundamental in the governance of the country, and it shall be the duty of the State to apply these principles in making laws." (Article 37) Fundamental rights and the directive principles together form the conscience of the Constitution.

4. The Role of the Police

Law and order are essential to civilised existence. In a lawless society, where violence predominates, human rights, be they civil, criminal, political, social or economic and religious, of individuals and of group are likely to be trampled on or at the very least ignored. Thus maintenance of law and order, whether in identifying or investigating any criminal activity or in controlling civil unrest, is clearly the primary task of the police force. The police are one of the chief instruments in creating and maintaining an environment of peace and order within which legitimate individual and group ends may be pursued.

The role of the police in ensuring the protection of human rights does not end there. They have two other vital roles to play, one, a police force has a duty under the law to bring law-breakers and offenders to book. In other words to use their initiative where so empowered by law to stop or prevent human rights violations occurring in the society. Secondly, to examine their own methods and behaviour and to ensure that the protectors of human rights are not its major violators.

Police have lamentably failed in giving due protection to the untouchables as envisaged in the Untouchability (Offences) Act, 1965 because they banned the registration of offences and prosecution of offenders under this Act. They also failed to protect the health of young children and prevent their exploitation by their working in mines, factories or other hazardous employments because police did not put criminal process in motion against the employers, and the parents of such children, who collude to break the pertinent laws. The constitutional safeguards against trade in human-being remains an empty slogan in the face of the persistent and notorious failure of the police to initiate criminal proceedings to eradicate this evil under the concerned laws, like the Suppressions of Immoral Traffic in Women and

Girls. Bride burning, dowry death and other offences arising out of the Dowry Prohibition Act could certainly be reduced if the police were more keen and prompt in taking steps which would prevent such occurrences. The shameful phenomenon of bonded labour will persist if the police are apathetic, lethargic and also reluctant to bring to book the perpetrators of this crime by enforcing the provisions of the relevant Act — Bonded Labour System (Abolition) Act.

One of the aims of any civilised law-abiding society is to ensure that the law-abiding are protected and the guilty punished. A society where the guilty, especially the affluent and well-connected, go scot free and flaunt their acquittal in the face of indigent innocents who are convicted is resented as an unjust one. Such a state of affairs is bound to breed a large number of mal-contents whose anger and frustrations inevitably lead to attempts to overthrow the system, and at the same time generate a myriad tensions and conflicts. The police have an important preventive role in situations which can lead to infractions of law and order and may also later on endanger public peace and security. The failure to punish the guilty who committed heinous crimes during the 1984 anti-Sikh riots generated deep resentment and gave rise to an acute sense of injustice amongst the victims of the crimes and their families. Such a situation had also occurred in 1948 after the assassination of Mahatma Gandhi by Nathuram Godse, when the *Brahmins* were molested. The 1984 anti-Sikh riots were fueled and fanned after the assassination of Indira Gandhi by her Sikh bodyguards. In either case the perpetrators were Congress proteges, the motive was vengeance against the community of the offender, and this Government belonged to the Congress party. The police under pressure from the Government did precious little to protect the life and property of the innocents, whom providence gave birth in their respective communities. Was it their fault or of the Government — or was it a symbolic and patent failure of the police to remain neutral and impartial in giving human right protections to the innocent victims when they were conveniently in a position to give? Can such a force, which has no independent existence in relation to their duties of law enforcement has a right to survive and claim that their duty is to protect human rights, or is it a police force belonging to an autocratic government in the democratic country like India? Or are they raised at the expense of taxpayers money to protect only the chosen few who belong to the political party forming the government? The sovereign public has to answer all these questions, and they can remedy it through their superlative power of ballot paper. When human rights are violated by the Government such as indicated above, no action is taken, whereas the relative policeman is prosecuted for human rights violation when his acts exceed the powers given to him under the law.

5. Police Violations of Human Rights

Violations of human rights by the police occur partly because of the functions they have to perform and their manner of performance. The nature of their work brings them face to face with human rights issues, particularly and more frequently with the basic human rights of life and liberty. Regrettably these basic rights are rarely respected and are frequently trampled upon by the custodians of law and order, may be on their own initiative or under instruction/connivance of their superiors including the Government as was the case with the two instances quoted above. Police torture and use of third-degree methods are human rights violations involving protection against self-incrimination. The constitutional obligation to inform a person of the grounds of his arrest and produce him before the nearest Magistrate within 24 hours of his arrest are flouted with impunity. It is a notorious fact that the euphemistic label of police encounter is both a device and a disguise for eliminating people whom the police regard as hardened criminals, and whose prosecution and conviction according to the law of the land are well-nigh impossible because of serious and unending difficulties in securing evidence of witnesses, who refuse to testify truthfully as a result of intimidation followed by imminent danger to their life and property. Another reason is the strict requirements of criminal legal system which places the burden of proof on the prosecution and insist that the offence with which a person is charged is established beyond reasonable doubts, perhaps, courts expect the presence of eye-witness in each and every case. Perpetrators, generally commit offences in solitary places and take enough precaution that nobody has witnessed their criminal act. Circumstantial evidence, unless corroborated by independent witnesses, is not taken into consideration by our judges. The criminal is set at liberty to tease with greater ferocity the public with impunity by his criminal behaviour and acts; the indigent victim, and the police both look starry-eyed at the criminal who has managed his liberty and thus escaped punishment. This is the major reason that crimes against property, person and the society have been rising unabated since the last three decades, and the police organisation has become almost defunct as far as the prevention and detection of crimes are concerned.

6. Fundamental Freedom of Expression and Assembly Endangered

Other casualties at the hands of the police are freedom of expression, freedom of association and freedom of assembly, whose importance is beyond the comprehension of many members of the police force. This becomes strikingly obvious in the manner in which peaceful protest marches and demonstrations are handled. The protesters are regarded as potential criminals rather than as citizens entitled to exercise their fundamental rights. Political meetings where there is vitriolic, strong or trenchant criticism of the Government, Prime Minister, Chief Minister or any other minister for that matter, are broken up, if necessary by use of force, and the speakers are arrested either under orders of the Government in order to teach the protesters a lesson, or to the mind of the Commanding Officers of the force such criticism is subservient and, therefore a crime. By and large, the police, under pressure from their high command, ostensibly pose inability to distinguish between utterances which are incitements to crime and violence and speeches which articulate disapproval, protest and condemnation of the Government and the public functionaries of the day. Police either fail or are not taught to appreciate and hospitably accommodate the capacious content of freedom of expression guaranteed by our Constitution. The Government is to be equally blamed for this misconception as laws have been framed requiring prior permission in the form of a licence or a suitable certificate from the police authorities even before a dramatic performance is staged. When public utterances are made by any party in opposition police take action or is made to take action, whereas the same utterances by the party in power will be applauded by the police. This discrimination, impartiality and disparity in police action have violated a number of times human rights regarding freedom of expression.

7. Equality under the Law

Equality of treatment is another human right which is very difficult for the police to respect in their actual work. Unconstitutional commands from their supervisors, both official and political, are the order of the day and constitute serious professional/occupational hazards for a policeman who musters courage to defy them. Should he resist arbitrary and illegal orders, it is certain that he will be transferred and not unlikely that he may lose his job. It is safe and more convenient for an average policeman to yield to pressure, and oblige the accuser or the accused in accordance with the commands received by him. Respect for the rule of law is conspicuously absent. Such becomes the mentality of the majority policemen of all ranks.

Partisan role of the police is often noticeable by the public, and they are generally in communal or political riots. The very atmosphere of the police station, and its work culture breeds arbitrariness. The pace and quality of investigations differ widely depending upon whether the complainant or the victim of the crime is well-placed in life or politically well-connected. Respect for human dignity is non-existent. It is unthinkable for a woman of ordinary means to go unaccompanied to a police station to register a complaint against her landlord or employer, because it would be fortunate if she is not molested and gets away with a few vulgar and derisive remarks. It is the common experience of a poor worker or a landless labourer, who has the impudence to complain against his employer or the village landlord to find himself severely reprimanded for such temerity and should he persist, rough handling and beating are not uncommon occurrences. How does one cope with this depressing phenomenon?

8. Causes of Police Failure

For this disturbing state of affairs police alone cannot be blamed. Partially it is true that the police were a colonial force used by the British as much to crush political dissent and punish freedom fighters as to combat crime. The hang-over of this colonial mentality actually has disappeared, but the Government and its political party portray such a picture of the police in order to camouflage their unconstitutional activities. The root cause of the malaise is that the police have been used differently by different administrations. There has been excessive politicisation of the police force which will indulge inasmuch lawlessness as the Government of the day wishes, and when it does not wish, it tolerates the anti-constitutional activities of its one-time collaborator. Another cause is the source of recruitment. Persons who are drawn to the police force are generally from those segments of the society which entertain strong prejudices of caste and religion. Having witnessed the discrimination and the accompanying unfairness and cruelty as a daily routine in their immediate surroundings, the average policeman at the time of joining the force does not have such sensitivity to basic human rights. Above all, he has received no training or education worth the name which would help him to overcome these handicaps. Another reason is the obsession of the police zeal for securing convictions rather than imbued with a desire for assuring that justice is done. And in that zeal, the propriety and the legality of the means employed are totally overlooked, probably because there is tacit acceptance of them right from the top to the bottom level of the police force. One cynical voice which is constantly and customarily heard is that you cannot get at the criminal, especially, the sophisticated one in this modern age of technology by invoking the principles of the 'Sermon on the Mount', after all a criminal is not a gentleman but a stark criminal as he has harmed a law-abiding person, and for his acts of criminality he must be punished, if not by the court, by the police, and this is the expectation of the public also. The most disturbing feature is that the general run of the community also shares this trend of thought, especially when the crime committed is a sensational one or the persons involved are hard-core and tough offenders.

Here again when the offenders are under political cover or shield, the police reverse their mentality and take recourse to the protection of human rights. All the three — the political party in power, the criminal and the police are benefited, either in kind or cash, but the society, by and large, suffers irreparably. It is also true that there has been a general decline in social values with regard to fundamental freedoms when it comes to combating crime. Then, can such a state of affairs be remedied?

9. Probable Remedies

Frankly, there is no simple or magic solution for these all pervading ills. But if certain measures are implemented earnestly they may help in bringing about a qualitative change in the attitudinal approach of the police to human rights. In the first and foremost place politicisation and takeover of the police force by political bosses must be ruthlessly eliminated. Nothing has contributed more to the demoralisation of the police force than the manipulation by politicians and the power-wielders. Nothing has shattered the fair name and the credibility of the police more than its subservience and willingness to carry out illegal orders. Nothing has emboldened the police to violate the rule of law and indulge in lawlessness at the assurance of official patronage and political protection. It must be drilled into every policeman that his primary loyalty is to the Constitution and the laws whose obedient servant he must be at all times. There is little realisation among the police that not only are they entitled to disregard illegal orders but they could be held criminally liable if they executed an order which was patently illegal and criminal in nature. The order giver should be entitled to more severe punishment than the order executor.

Next, there must be radical improvement in the service conditions of the police force and the treatment meted out to them by the establishment. Urgent attention is required to better their working and living conditions which are very unsatisfactory. Do not expect the police to be incorruptible and law abiding if their pay and benefits are woefully inadequate to make both ends meet. It is difficult for the police to be civil or civilised if they are ill-treated. There must be public acknowledgement of their honesty and devotion to service whenever one comes across it.

The workload of the police has increased substantially, thanks to the added burden of providing security to VIPs' and coping with demonstrations and agitations, all of which are not non-violent. It is not realised that the police are over stretched, and this aspect was never considered seriously. Unfortunately, for the Government, police high commands and public there is a growing tendency to take subordinate police for granted till the occurrence of serious police unrest or a mini-mutiny, which had been in some states; but there is enough dormant hostility in almost all the forces of the country, and that made them basically apathetic, lethargic and irresponsible to their call of duty. They merely work as mercenaries — a body without life, a nucleus without cell, and just they work because they are goaded to work and find opportunities to make money, other than their emoluments.

There is crying need for proper comprehensive education of all the police personnel at all levels, and in all the aspects of police work. Promotional avenues should be considerably increased. Every police person must be made to grasp the basic principle that ends do not justify means and also to understand that insistence of the observance of the principles of human rights is a moral injunction which has an abiding validity, as also vitality.

With firm will and determination of all — the public, police and the Government, we can reform our police force, and will see the emergence of the ideal law-abiding policeman with a sensitive conscience for human rights, who is a friend, philosopher and guide of every person, however low or humble. It may be explained that assured progress is the realisation of Utopia.

24

Police *vis-a-vis* Social Defence and Changing Society

1. Social Defence

The terms "Social Defence" is subject to a variety of interpretation, in ordinary parlance protection of the society against crime. The old-age idea was that society could best be protected by inflicting in-human torture and severe punishment on offenders. Thus, the history of crime and punishment is replete with harrowing tales of brutal torture and inhuman treatment meted to offenders. Even for a petty theft or a trivial offence, the offender had to undergo barbarous punishment and stern repression. He used to be often dragged in the streets, maimed and even beaten to death. The ultimate aim of such extreme severity of punishment was to ensure, at any cost, the protection of the society. Social defence came to be synonymous with intimidation and stern repression, and as such it implied as the forceful protection of the society at the expense of the individual. Various earlier writers on criminology held the view that any measure needed to protect society was perfectly justified with the characteristic features of the principle of social defence; and that the society has an inherent right to punish the individual for his crime in the larger interest of the community. Although man has the right of self-defence, he handed over this inherent right to society by virtue of the social contract.

In fact the traditional notion of the greater good of the greater number finds its echo in the original objective of the term "Social Defence", that protection of the society is more important than the protection of individual, and hence the justification of repressive measures. In contrast to this ideology, and in course of time, this age, old notion has undergone a change and now it has been realised that the collective good can be achieved only with the welfare of the individual. In its modern connotation, social defence is a reaction against retributive system, and has acquired new dimensions which imply new conception of the struggle against crime and delinquency. The modern penal policy is based on the essential premise that, since crime is a social fact and human act, the process of dealing with crime is not completed once the offence has been legally defined and a penalty imposed by law. Now crime is understood to be a social and individual phenomenon and the need to prevent its commission or repetition by adopting an attitude conducive to the reconciliation and reformation of the criminal followed by rehabilitation and reintegration of offenders. It is a new movement which has acquired a new dimension in promoting certain specific reforms in the entire Criminal Justice System, including judiciary, police, prison, and other institutional and non-institutional correctional services. Social defence encourages not only the protection of the individual but also aims at establishing a system which is designed to ameliorate both society and the individual, thus providing for the attainment of social harmony. It seeks to ensure that the offender receives appropriate treatment within the existing framework. This principle is largely based on the substitution of treatment for retributive punishment. It is necessary to make room for punishment in a national system of social defence subject to the condition that the individual and society are harmoniously inter-related for the social well-being of all. Copious examples of this principle are available in our great epics and scriptures where there is an emphasis to adhere to the principle that punishment must correspond to the nature and severity of the offence. The judge had the discretion to award a greater or lesser punishment than that prescribed for the offence. Latitude to first offenders have always been shown while prescribing punishment for them. Such a lenient treatment was possible until the 19th century when the society was realistically and practically moral. Subsequent impact of politico-economic conditions caused degeneration in the morals and mores of the individuals comprising the society, and threatened its well-being at the hands of few individuals having criminal propensities. Therefore, the 19th century attitude was more in favour of repressive system of punishment which did not consider the offender as an individual, and the criminal offence was regarded as an abstract of legal entity and unhealthy to the well-being of the society. However, there was a movement in favour of the individualisation of penalties and it made a significant contribution to the legislative development of the current century. It also included prison reforms and special care and treatment for juvenile delinquents. But the defence of society was gradually downgraded in preference to the defence of individual.

The social defence movement gathered momentum since the beginning of the 20th century; and that led to the innovation of number of treatment methods for offenders. It is now realised that the criminal and not the crime is to be punished and the punishment must be regulated solely by the consideration of social defence. Prisons are no longer places for detention of criminals only, but they have acquired a new dimension as therapeutic centres to reform the personality and behaviour pattern of the prisoners. Now in accordance with the contemporary correctional practices prison stands mainly for three principles in the treatment process: (1) separation of prisoners according to sex, age, and criminal status; (2) classification, and (3) individualisation, the sole aim being the ultimate rehabilitation of offenders back to the society. Since the French Revolution which involved three basic human problems — liberty, equality and fraternity, humanitarian movement started all over Europe and other countries, the idea of basic human rights that any human being must have, even in prison, stirred the human mind all over the world. As a result, the International Penal and Penitentiary Commission including members of all countries of Europe, America and Japan was set up in 1870. After functioning for about 75 years and giving an humanitarian outlook to the penitentiary problem, it was transferred to the Economic and Social Council of United Nations. In 1958 standard minimum rules for the treatment of prisoners were passed, and implemented in all the signatory countries. Since then the Social Defence Section at the United Nations has been taking stock of the various social defence situations in different countries of the world.

In accordance with the Constitution of India, all the subjects of social defence fall within the jurisdiction of the State

Governments. Planning for social defence in India started during the Second Plan period. At the State level, the implementing authorities are the Inspectors General of Prisons and Directors of Social Welfare, but the pattern differs from State to State. In order to co-ordinate the social defence programmes at the national level the Central Bureau of Correctional Services was established in 1961.

The impact of industrial developments and the concomitant activities in this country brought in their wake a plethora of problems, of which juvenile delinquency and prostitution are the most important, and they affected the society the worst. Therefore, they are dealt with separately in this book.

Prison is the oldest penal institution for detention of criminals. The age-old idea was to remove an undesirable person because of his criminal propensities from society for a particular period and to keep him in isolation in prison so that he might realise his guilt, repent and learn or mend his ways. This idea was based on the feeling that man committed a crime according to his free will and he had, therefore, to undergo physical and mental tortures in jail, and subsequently get reformed by the time he was released back to the society. In view of the rising trend of criminal activities and multiplication of criminals in the society, and the severity or brutality with which offences against persons and property are being committed now-a-days, it may be necessary to revert to the custodial role of the prisons as was in the past centuries. The people constituting the society, has to take a decision in the democratic country like India. But the experience is that with more stringent punishment, offenders tend to improve their character and the very thought of being incarcerated again deter them from the commission of criminal offences. This awe-inspiring notion of any penitentiary institution has become all the more necessary in the present-day situation when crimes escalated to an unprecedented height, whereas detections and convictions fall dismally low. Parole and probation are the ingredients of the correctional systems in vogue all over the world today, including India. They have been separately dealt with in this book.

The concept that a criminal is not born, but the environments in which a person is made to live and grow make him a criminal, is still held good everywhere throughout the world. Is it parental responsibility or obligation to feed, bring and educate the progeny, when parents have not enough money to have one-time frugal meal a day; perhaps, once in two to three days? Or is it the responsibility and duty of the State to provide them with the necessary wherewithal? These ever-eluding problems do not come within the scope of police function. The people and the Government have to solve them, although for the Government's failure involving violation of the relative fundamental principles of the Constitution no hue and cry is raised for the benefit of more than 40 per cent of the Indian population living below the poverty line.

2. Social Changes

After the Independence, all the conditions, political and social, have changed and, in these days are changing more rapidly than before. More important still, ideas have changed and are still changing. Ideas concerning political, economic and social rights and wrongs, and the problems of justice in relationship between the State and the individual, between social classes and group interest, have gone for a sea-change. Tensions have been set up between the Government and the different sections of population. Fundamental issues as the redistribution of wealth and abolition of all kinds of social, education, and other anomalies or privileges have left great impact on the society and there have been shifts in the balance of power between various segments of the society based on castes and classes, and religion. Political struggles with a view to grab power have become more intense. This has resulted in the emergence of extremist groups, of both right and left wings of politics. Some of these groups have introduced totalitarian forms of the government, and the police, as the impartial agent of the law, have invariably been the object of attack by such groups. Thus, the police face the problem as how to ensure its functional role of the impartial agent of the law and not the political party in power.

3. Diminution in Respect for Authority

It is beyond dispute that one great change has been diminution in respect for authority — lowest as well as highest; and men have learnt to resent control before they have learnt to control themselves. It has affected all those whose duty it is to uphold authority and enforce the Rule of Law. Social and Economic changes during the last four decades have benefited (may be illegally) to a vast number of persons by greatly improving their living standards. However, at the same time crime has increased to a new high, civil disorders have become fairly common place and the growing complexities and mechanisation of society have necessary expansion of legislation, and such an expansion that has contributed towards the unbridled deterioration in the relationship between the public and the authority and the crime preventive and detective situation in the country.

Almost any kind of public demonstration or public dispute now-a-days is liable to degenerate into disorder. There is a disturbing willingness to use unconstitutional and often violent methods to further sectional interest or to impose opinions or policies on others. The pattern of forcing demands by mass or mob actions, outside the laws and courts have rapidly changed and spread like tentacles. There is now hardly any facet of our society that has not been assaulted, and none is immune from assault, by the prevalent pattern of lawlessness. When frustrated protests degenerate into violence and violence into counter violence, it is liberty-cum-law and order suffers in the long-run, because police/authority feel obliged to intensify their measures of law enforcement. Freedom and fundamental rights of people have been jeopardised by such lawless behaviour, but unhappily does not seem to be widely understood by the people. Free speech, raised in protest is the life-blood of democracy, yet the freer the speech the more likely it is to incite and inflame its audience to violence. But violence can kill democracy, for if given rein it will destroy the democracy that licensed it, while to curb its freedom itself may have to be restricted, and democracy thus impaled on the other horn of the dilemma. The paramount problem facing the police is to balance the preservation of the Constitutional rights with the duty to protect lives and property. This is not an easy balance to attain, but it is essentially imperative that it be reached in order to strengthen democracy. It is an ironical fact that soon after the Independence, opposing trends contrarily pointing towards success and failure, have often overlapped in time and space; the best and the worst have lived in each other's shadow. Gangsters have infiltrated into trade unions and political parties and have close links with political groups at various levels. They made nonsense of the law enforcement machinery due to their influences and power they exercised.

The conditions prevailing in the industrial belts have given rise to the growth of two parallel societies. One amassing huge fortunes, built palatial houses, own vehicles at the cost of workers and using their money power to keep all and sundry under their influence. The other consisting of workers, living mostly in slum, continued their existence in perpetual misery. Most of them are victims of gambling, alcoholism and sexual vices. Their children grow up to swell the ranks of criminals. Business rivalry has often led to the hiring of gangsters for the extermination of rivals. This phenomenon is prevalent in the metropolitan cities, where contract killings are arranged in increasing number. Real estate is an area where the use of criminal gangs is widely prevalent. Landlords employ gangsters to evict tenants because of the complete failure of our legal systems, resulting in the growth of "parallel justice" system which readily acquires the desired goal. A few of the administrators are the underworld's hardcore criminals. The changing pattern of the society has been changing the nature of underworld activities in big cities. Criminalisation of politics has helped the growth and expansion of illegal business activities of the underworld. Smuggling and gun-running, girl running from across the border have been rampant. Hundreds of brothels, call girl rackets, liquor, gambling dens, narcotic dens, male prostitution are mushrooming in almost all big cities. These criminals have developed a parallel economy and financial reserves which the Government do not possess. During election the political parties draw their requirements from these financial reserves. Inter-gang rivalry led to street fighting, even in court premises with guns and bombs leaving men dead or wounded. Policemen rarely interfered. They either take sides or remain in hiding. They appear at the scene to collect dead bodies for sending them to morgue and injured to hospital, which are not even spared of this ghastly crime.

Unplanned growth of slums have become a cancer of city life, where crime and vice are widespread and pervade almost every member of the slumdweller's family, and the police are required to keep constant watch on them, only on paper, for they have no men enough to perform this hazardous duty. Policing of city requires a more effective type of police administration, because of efficient and quick action of the criminals; with the existing inadequate manpower, and equipment, and poor quality of personnel it is almost impossible.

4. Political and Agrarian Development

Most disappointing has been the political development in which political parties became increasingly selfish, and corrupt and split by factionalism and fomented caste and class struggles. In place of national unity, caste, class, religious, tribal and linguistic bodies multiplied. Violence spread from the field of politics to the depth of the society — agrarian, caste and class relation, inter-communal relation, student and teacher relation, family affairs, employee and employer relation, police and public relation, took a very heavy toll of life, property and values. The national character meanwhile, underwent contortion. We keep on wailing that 'liberty growing and law and order declining'.

It was politics in the sense of narrow ambition for power and the parochial loyalties of small men threatened national unity and political order. Ambitions and corrupt practices catered to and nurtured parochial loyalties and selfish economic demands, and even instigated violence to achieve their objectives. There is sharp rise in corruption and criminality amongst politicians, many of whom with a record of criminal offences and various anti-social acts from the backstage and entered the political stream as MPs and MLAs. A direct result of this is the phenomenal rise of gangsterism and *mafia* rule, and growing nexus between politicians and gangsters. These developments destroyed orderly rule, paralysed the Rule of Law, balkanised the political system, and above all threatened the survival of the democracy.

Weak rulers and the growth of powerful *mafia* hierarchy offered a continuing spectacle of violent lawlessness, brutality and virtual butchery. Protection has to be bought. The law lapsed into universal disuse, and the police were not allowed to enforce the law impartially, fairly and firmly to meet the challenge of disorder. Against this backdrop it is irresponsible to talk of police failure in dealing with communal, caste and political violence, for violence had been a normal feature in our election. Every election from Parliament down to the gram panchayat, and municipal corporation is a witness to massive rigging, booth capturing, assaults and murders of opposite candidates, indiscriminate bombing and firing by armed mobs in the presence of the police, to scare away voters. Doors are chained from outside by political cadres and gangsters, who keep watch preventing voters from proceeding to polling booths.

Complaints against gangsters are not registered by police, and complainants who ventured to report, are threatened by the police and asked to seek redress elsewhere. The police are prevented from taking action against the gangsters because the latter have been fighting shoulder to shoulder with the politicians at the poll to ensure and snatch victory. In some areas the policemen become an extension of the political leaders and the underworld. The law-keepers and law-breakers are perceived inextricably linked with the underworld.

More than 80 per cent of the Indian population live in villages notwithstanding rapid industrialisation and urbanisation of the country. Agriculture continues to remain the most important source of income in the countryside. After the Independence many land reform legislations were enacted to benefit the landless poor, mostly Scheduled Castes and Scheduled Tribes, who had been living under abject poverty, exploited by rich landlords over the centuries. The failure of the Government to provide a proper forum which could have resolved the difficulties arising from the implementation of the land reforms promptly has resulted in heavy litigations involving tens of thousands of cases which have dragged for years with the end nowhere in sight. Most of the landlords belonged to one or the other political party. In the process the poor contenders, who had longingly hoped for a better and happier future have got themselves entangled in harassing in-terminable court cases.

Conflicts between the landowners and landless peasantry are increasing in number and viciousness. *Harijans* who form the bulk of the landless peasants are attacked and killed, and their women raped, and their hutments set on fire. The partisan paltry police force either failed or could not protect the victims. Private army, formed on caste and class basis and composed of musclemen and criminals all armed with licensed or unlicensed firearms, have increased in recent years to fight with the peasantry who ventured to go against their employers, who are landowners and upper-caste; spread of Naxalite movement is the direct result, for the poor peasants are now no longer prepared to tolerate their age-old exploitation and atrocities committed on their women.

5. Student Unrest

British left us with 20 universities. Today we have over 180 universities and innumerable colleges spread over in the rural areas; there are over 5,000 colleges mushrooming in the country. Politics has played havoc in our educational institutions. All student unions are politicised and operate at a political level. Elections to student's unions are fought with guns and bombs. Admission to universities are forced at gun point or paying heavy capitation fee. The value of intelligence and calibre has receded. Eve-teasing and molestation of women students and even sex abuses, on the campus are not uncommon. Vice Chancellors and teachers are beaten and confined for long hours and even killed. Police are often called to maintain order inside the campus. Please see a separate chapter on this subject.

6. Crime

With the rapid growth of industrialisation and urbanisation of population in cities and towns, new and increasingly sophisticated crimes have appeared. A disturbing development has been the increasing number of political crimes hitherto unknown in our criminal calendar. Many crimes have international ramifications. Boundaries have burst, no longer crimes are codified within the borders of one or a group of adjacent societies. Criminals have brought science in their perpetrations. Crimes by women and against women are rapidly increasing. More and more women are coming to streets to earn their livelihood, and the basic concepts of the Indian family life that the woman's place is in the home has become invalid. Juveniles are increasingly involved in all forms of crime. Virtue has been replaced by repleted vices in the society, only a fragment of the former is discernible. Castes, class and communal clashes have considerably increased in the last years. Bootlegging, smuggling of narcotics and other costly items of luxury, prostitution and gambling have many-fold increased and threatening the very existence of a virtuous society. The total impact of crimes against public safety, both of a person and property and morals of the society is terrific. They affected not only the victims but also the very roots of the social order and create conditions which engender various other forms of crimes. Here the victim does not feel wronged, for he lacks the intended social control of the larger society, he attunes to the sub-culture of the group to which he belongs. By the process of differential association with a delinquent sub-group the victim learns to accept such crimes as a way of life, and this makes his/her reclamation and eventual rehabilitation the more difficult, and he generally continues to be a recidivist.

Post-Independent period witnessed communal disturbances almost with monotonous regularity from one part of the country to another. The number of persons killed and injured during riots kept on increasing from year to year; of the major causes, politics of religion and instigation to fundamental communal organisations by Pakistan played very significant role in sustaining communal riots tearing apart the social fabric of the society.

India's North-east states, Punjab and Jammu and Kashmir have lived in the shadow of insurgency and terrorism. Murder, extortion, rape, arson, kidnapping and hijacking of aircrafts in flight, have posed serious threat to the country's security and defence apart from causing social tension and conflicts of many kinds. Smuggling and gun-running and infiltration of foreign nationals into India are matters of grave concern. The problem is further complicated when we take into consideration the encouragement and financial support provided by Pakistan to the insurgents and terrorists organisations operating in the country. More than 50 per cent of the policemen are locked up in the enforcement and anti-insurgency and anti-terrorist measures. Army troops have to be deployed in pockets of resistance and as normal laws were found in inadequate special laws like 'TADA' had to be enacted. [Terrorist and Disruptive (Prevention) Act].

7. Social Legislation

To achieve a Welfare State there has been, over the years, constant multiplication of social welfare legislations, and they seem to thrive like bacteria in a laboratory culture. The law moves with the main current of the society that it regulates. Each society has its own values, necessarily reflected in the ends that the legal order seeks to further. Law is the cement which holds society together, without it society would go to pieces. The law is much more active agent in social evolution at this turning point of the process of change. The conception of the proper functioning of the law is to preserve public order and decency, to protect citizens from what is offensive or injurious; and to provide sufficient safeguards against exploitation and corruption of others, particularly those who are young, weak in body and mind, inexperienced or in a state of physical, official or economic dependence.

No society will respect laws unless they are definite, consistent and equitable, and further the law will be fairly and equally enforced by all and against all and that infractions will be justly and expeditiously punished. The current multiplicity of laws, their constant amendments and their interpretations by courts perplex common man, encourage misleading arguments and drive policemen to despair.

We have many laws which the people cannot be made to obey them and at the same time not enforceable in practice. Prohibition, pornography, gambling, brothel keeping, unconventional sexual practices, polygamy, giving and taking of dowry, child marriage, trafficking in drugs, gambling in race tracks and sports events *etc.*, some of them falling in this category. Severe penalties in some of these cases have not been able to suppress them, because the people, for one reason or the other, do not consider them to be offences, but on the contrary they like them as means of human recreation. The incentive to oppose or corrupt the police has greatly increased due to this attitude of the people. Moreover, those who oppose do not abandon their opposition when the laws reach the Statute Book;

they redirect it against the police. However, illogical, or unfair, we must accept this as a fact of life.

8. Politics

Politics has not infrequently affected the framing of laws. Voice of dissent of those in opposition is ignored and laws are passed with the support of the majority in power. More often than not, failing to impose policies or opinions in the Parliament, and in State Legislatures, politicians in the opposition instigated the people to demonstrate in the streets. One of the curious and equally abominable developments of politics is the combination of law-makers and law-breakers — those in Government making laws and those in the opposition breaking them in the streets. The social will of untouchability could not be curbed by the legislation of "Prevention of Untouchability Act" and contrarily the upper caste imposed a social boycott on the entire *Harijan* population which refuse to come under their sway. The police often aided the upper castes having been heavily bribed, and involved the *Harijans* in false cases. In various instances the police officials were *Harijans* themselves! All anti-social activities have the strength enough to generate copious money as majority of the population do not feel bad about them, and moreover, some consider them to be the need of life, and hence necessary evils allowed or claimed to be practised by them despite the fact of legislations declaring them illegal or unlawful. This corrupted segment of the society vigorously corrupts the law enforcement agency with the ulterior motive of seeking paid connivance at their prohibited activities. Police in spite of resistance from a fragment of the force, cannot remain aloof from corruption as their human nature overwhelms their dutiful obligations. Vice super imposes virtue, which ultimately is being replaced by vice if such a state of affairs is allowed to be continued. The greatest source of friction between the police and the public arises from law enforcement. Generally, people feel no obligation to respect the law and no legal responsibility to obey it.

As the new laws pour out, the problem is to draw the line in each case between what the police must do, ought to do, can ignore and those they must not do. "Police discretion" has now become a major source of corruption, as the judiciary has always criticised the police, both for enforcing the laws and for failing to enforce them, may be at the instance or at the insinuation of others, politicians not excluded.

Full enforcement of our present laws is physically impossible, and as a result the police have developed a discretion in the registration and investigation of cases and prosecution of offenders. This discretion formed an area of great power, and has contributed to abuse of power and corruption.

9. Expanding Role of Police

The role of the policeman in our society, today, goes far beyond the duties of enforcing the laws, *vis-a-vis* the prosecution of law breakers. Modern day computers would be taxed to process the thousands of special services regulated, or unregulated, performed for the public by policemen every day. The Government servants strike in most of the States lasting for several days engaged the police providing security all-round, running convoys, distributing milk, removing garbage, delivering letters, reaching milk to hospital, helping the commercial establishments in the conduction of their business, providing police drivers to public transport, clerks to courts enabling them to function; and even posting cases and dealing with remand applications. (Maharashtra State Government Employees Strike lasted for 55 days in 1971-72). Too many issues are passed to the police when there is no other agency to "Carry the Can". The Police stand in the vanguard as a bulwark preserving the peace, protecting life and property, and making possible social changes within the democratic framework.

10. What Police Should Do?

The strength of the police is fathoms lower than the actual requirements of their multifarious duties. The age-old patterns of traditional preventive and detective measures in the fight against crime and criminals have become irrelevant now and they need to be improved continually. Scientific methods of investigations, as permissible under the law, should be adopted, and no deviation from this principle should be allowed at any cost, whatever may be the consequences. The fair, impartial, just and equitable enforcement of laws has to be ensured by all policemen, who should be made to obey only the Constitutional commands emanating from superiors and the Government as envisaged in the pledge they have taken at the time of their recruitment — obedience only of all lawful and Constitutional orders. While doing so they should bear in mind that they are not the servants of any political party in power, but of the public and the Government duly constituted through the process of election. All complaints reported at the police stations must be registered, prompt and painstaking investigation made and the offenders sent to courts for trial as the distance between the crime and the courts is often the distance between law and justice. A large part of the work of the police is carried on under the observation of the public, and often independent press, both of them are free to comment and criticise as they feel inclined. No police force can carry out duties with satisfaction to itself, the public and the Government without the help of the public and the press. The public and the press must be satisfied that the police are acting impartially within the powers constitutionally and lawfully conferred upon them and that they give reasonable information about their actions. This is a cardinal principle. Any criticism must be taken sportingly in order to sift its contents and correct the wrong done as to err is human. The police has a right to demand that the path they must tread should be clearly designed to lead to a just result for the community for whom they act, as well as for the accused. The policeman knows as much about crime and investigation as anyone else and his view should be heard by the public and the Government. It may be the verdict of the minority, but our system of justice is too important to be left to anyone section of the society — politicians, lawyers, judges or police. It should be the concern of all. Police by virtue of their association both with law-abiding and law-breaking segments of the society, possess singularly unique social experience, which unfortunately they are seldom allowed to sift and share with other agencies in the larger interest of the society. Police is of and for the community, which should take advantage of their experience in the maintenance of law and order. Today, public distrust and enmity or hostility of the police are very great. Lack of co-operation from the public is a major handicap. Several attempts have been made to study the "Public Image of the

Police". These surveys revealed a number of important factors as regards to the worsening of police-public relations. Partisan law enforcement and political interference in the day-to-day working of the police are mainly responsible for the loss of public confidence and respect for the police. Seemingly, no effort to scuttle this political influence and insulate the police from it has been made by the Government, and public is also aware of it, but they failed to react to this dangerous attitude.

Today the police force is divided into two camps — one unscrupulous and indisciplined, power loving, disloyal to the police hierarchy, brutal and corrupt; and the other, numerically a very small percentage, impartial, fair, disciplined, loyal, honest and humane. It is the former category of policemen who are mostly involved in cases of torture and other illegalities committed at the behest of the politicians in power. *Illustrations*: Communist rule in Kerala in 1950; Emergency rule in 1975-76 and Left Front rule in West Bengal in the last two decades. While one section of the police force arrest criminals and bring them to police station, the other section of the force allows them to escape. Political parties, over the years, have been successful to win, as many policemen as possible, over to their own way of thinking and acting. They have not allowed the police to stand firm at the middle and enforce the laws without fear or favour. They have pulled and pushed policemen to their side by coaxing, harassing, and, of course, transfers to buy loyalty. There was no saviour for them. Police has to remain buffer and maintain the precarious balance between the welfare of the society and the political party in power; between control and uncontrolled violence, and constitutional and unlawful orders from whatever source they may emanate. The rise and growth of political policemen have completely blunted the sharp cutting police instrument for carrying out illegal orders, mostly oral and seldom written, and sustaining the undemocratic rule of the politicians.

There has been serious inroads of communalism and casteism into the law enforcement machinery. Prevention and control of communal or caste riots have become extremely difficult because of the contamination of these elements within the force. In several states ministers are themselves involved in instigating communal and caste riots while sermonising the police to deal firmly with them, when things go wrong they blame the police and, as a face saving device, transfer or suspend the officer. The phenomenal rise in gangsterism and *mafia* rule in collusion with politicians in power has been a matter of grave concern, the police force has been inextricably linked with the underworld. When the police make out a case against a criminal with their witnesses, there are so many politicians to be sworn in for defence. Failure of this strategy is remedied by the Government of the party in power by withdrawing the case, "In Public Interest". Public never objected to this strategy. Cases against smugglers and gun-runners also meet similar fate, giving good leverage to proximity with them, and the ensuing corruption of the force.

11. Future of the Police

We have turned down in the economy, we have increasingly high rates of unemployment, we see a resurgence of Naxalites and rapid deterioration of law, and order and at the same time unbridled increase in insurgency, and terrorist activities; we see crimes of violence increasing faster than our population; we see hostilities between landowners and landless peasants, between Hindus and Muslims, between caste Hindus and *Harijans*, between tribals and non-tribals, and growing rivalries between different political parties and groups. We see corruption, indiscipline and discontent in the police force, and we see a Criminal Justice System that people perceive is not working at all and failed to provide protection to life and property; and we see the growth of the parallel extra legal, if not actually illegal system of grievances redressal through the *mafia* hierarchy growing rapidly in connivance with politicians and police, from year to year. There has been a steady increase in smuggling and gun-running across the borders and illegal manufacturing of firearms and bombs, mushrooming as a cottage industry, in different parts of the country. We see the volume of public complaints against the police is increasing steadily and relations between the public and police worsening almost every day.

Our society is like a molecule full of internal tensions held in a precarious balance by a criss-cross of group alignment. The functions of the police are unexpectedly growing in expansion and importance. As an instrument of social defence no society can disown its police or do without them. The nexus between the *mafia* hierarchy, politicians and police is the most formidable of the law enforcement problems of the future. Indeed, the point has been reached in which the underworld can commit crime anywhere and anytime with ease and buy immunity from police or even judicial action. Policemen are passing through a disturbing time. Frequent changes of the governments have led to frequent changes in politics which run counter, at times contrary. Successive governments effected radical changes in the police hierarchy and these changes undermined established traditions and old loyalties. For all that, policemen feel they have been mucked about a lot.

A partisan and demoralised police administration with unscrupulous and with "Yes Sir" leadership cannot work in a democracy as the bulwark of law and order and social stability. In our rapidly changing society it is of paramount importance that the standards of the police service and their leadership must be maintained at the highest level and without any outside intrusion, because police service is the only dominant organisation of civil administration for assuring and ensuring and actually maintaining internal security and peace; and which can create or destroy the happiness of the community and the integrated existence of the society. The task is as stupendous as hazardous. It is the biggest challenge posed to the police — how, when and where to harness the rapid strides of anti-social and criminal activities of the perpetrators. Can the desultory police force depleted in strength and moral conduct accept and face this challenge? The stakes are very high; and they are the amicable relationship between the public and police eventuating in an accord and co-operation and restoration of peoples' confidence in the entire police machinery that it is the police of and for the good of the people. The master-servant attitude has to be replaced by ties of friendship; and all these will depend on how a policeman conducts himself!

25

Weaker Sections of Society

1. Weaker Sections

The phrase, "Weaker sections of the people" has been used in Article 46 of the Constitution of India, in one of the Directive Principles of State Policy, to promote with special care the educational and economic interests of the weaker sections. The Scheduled Castes and Scheduled Tribes have been particularly named, and the State is directed to protect them from injustice and exploitation. The intention of the Constitution-makers is obvious that many other sections of the society, who are vulnerable socially, educationally, and economically, would be covered by the term, "weaker sections of the people". The Constitution itself provides for special care, and attention to the problems of women and children as well as the minorities. In addition, the physically and mentally handicapped and the economically disadvantaged sections among the rural folk as also the slum dwellers in towns will equally qualify to be covered under the term weaker sections of the society, to a greater or less degree. The Constitution in the preamble envisages justice, economic and political, special care and attention to these weaker sections. These are the Constitutional Mandates, but politics have sacrilegiously changed the import of the Constitution to suit their ends and preserve their 'Vote Bank', as now only the welfare of Scheduled Castes and Scheduled Tribes and Other Backward Classes constituting about 52 per cent of the Indian population is mainly considered for special care. The police are the designated arm of the State, entrusted with the protective responsibility of State itself, as stemming from the social contract theory. That is why the objectives of the police have been identified as the 'protection of the life, property and rights of citizens'. And in ensuring protection to these rights, the police have a vital role to play, by way of upholding the Constitutional provisions and in enforcing the conceived laws of the land, to which only, in the final analysis, they are accountable as servants of the people.

The weaker sections of the society suffer from some qualitative infirmities arising from lack of educational standards, economic opportunities, social status, suitable places of habitation and appropriate occupational opportunities. Since police is the law enforcing authority, it is imperative for them to go all out to facilitate their legitimate enjoyment of their rights and privileges without fear of exploitation.

2. Caste-class Impact on Society

Caste has been considered a fundamental unit of social structure in India, it has played a unique roll in the socio-economic life of the people over the ages. But what is rather unfortunate is the unwelcome resurgence of caste behaviour in the current political contest too, in the regional and national levels. Caste stratification and its impact is primarily exhibited in the Hindu society, but at least some of its endogenous influences and socio-economic disabilities are found also among other faiths like Buddhists, Sikhs, Christians and Muslims, on the basis of their original caste-origin, although all these faiths officially disown any such discrimination. Class is a slightly different concept. It refers to an individual's position in broader social hierarchy and is determined by the education, occupation, income and wealth, as well as family affiliation. But class to a larger extend overlaps caste in India, when we talk of weaker sections, though class-wise they are spread over all castes, they predominate among the Scheduled Castes and Tribes, and that is why they have been specially mentioned in Article 46 of the Constitution. Hence the framers of the Constitution felt special need for the protection of their Civil Rights, and for reservations in the matter of educational and job opportunities for them. But ostensibly politicians have made a world difference between what has been laid down and what obtains in practice.

The only means for effective social change in this direction would be social acceptance and it is more important than law or executive orders. It is because, social acceptance has not yet become the norm in India, principles enshrined in the

Constitution have to be enforced by the police. Moreover, what we see exhibit day in and day out in all aspects of our life that the caste system is stronger today than it was when India became Independent. Prior to Independence Scheduled Castes, generally known as *Harijans* (as pronounced by Mahatma Gandhi) were socially badly treated and economically exploited by upper castes and they were expected to stay well away as untouchable and not pollute them. Hence Dr B.R. Ambedkar spear-headed the movement for equality, temple entry and abolition of untouchability. This was followed by the Abolition of Untouchability Act, 1955. There are also substantial executive provisions for the uplift of these under-privileged citizens. But whether the intended benefits of the law and the executive orders really reach the beneficiaries is often to question on account of the absence of wide-ranging social acceptance and broad-based education. The service delivery officials and the enforcing authorities themselves are not free from bias and related faults. It is in such situation the police role in this context is important and has to be analysed.

3. Protection of Civil Rights Act, 1955—Problem of Enforcement

The advent of freedom and a reasonable spread of education, among the Scheduled Castes and Scheduled Tribes (SC and ST) side by side with the demonstrations of political process, has led to an emergence, among these many suffering people, of a fair degree of realisation of human rights and dignity of human rights. But the resentment on the other side of Caste-Hindus-landlords and other society leaders, to this normal exercise of their lawful rights by the educated SC-ST young people led them to treat these as grave provocations, resulting in many sporadic incidents of clashes, some of them involving arson, loot and murder all over in India. It is generally seen that the worst sufferers are the SC-ST people themselves, because their resources are not adequate for continued legal battle in courts, particularly because, most of them are landless labourers, who depend on Caste Hindu landlords of their village for their livelihood. With the elevation of their political status, the hand and glove relationship between SC, ST and Caste-Hindus of the Indian population was permanently torn asunder; and the amity and accord were lost forever. And in this churning process SC, ST and Other Backward Classes (OBC) have emerged a potential force, strong enough to tilt the balance of power, and now a stage has come where in all political parties clamour and strive the hardest to gain their support. They do not leave any stone unturned and are prone to adopt any strategy to fulfil their objective. Thus, the SC, ST and OBC factions of the Indian population have become a judge in the tug-of-war game of the various political parties in India. This vicissitude brought envy to the minority communities. There is also a potent danger to their existing amity. As the years roll by, the population of Caste Hindus would be decreasing in view of the family planning adopted by them. Inversely, the population of the SC, ST and OBC would be on the increase. By this practice of reservation of seats in educational institutions, and jobs in services, their social acceptance is itself endangered. Bitterness in their relationship on an increasing degree would be the result. There are little chances of homogeneous Indian society, unless politicians change their priorities regarding reservations, which should be only available to the economically weaker sections of the society as envisaged in the Constitution of India; or else face a dreadful situation in the coming years.

There is considerable unhappiness among the *Harijans* about the ineffective enforcement of the Prevention of Untouchability Act. Not all cases under the Act get reported and not all witnesses give evidence without fear or favour, with the result that only a small percentage of the cases end in conviction. Evidence is always tainted in order to support the complainant by the witnesses of his class, and to absolve or exonerate the accused by the defence witnesses belonging to the class of the accused. In either case, the evidence is so stereotyped and distorted that it is extremely difficult for the police to sift it, and come to a conclusion. For fear of blame or criticism, the police record verbatim whatever is said by the witnesses, either in favour or against the complainant, and leave to the court the work of washing dirty linens. This is the only reason, why there is a very low percentage of conviction. Inclusion of right to work in respect of all citizens in the fundamental rights guaranteed under the Constitution appears to be the only remedy to improve the currently estranged relationship in various classes of the society, and ending jealousy among them. A major concern in this context would naturally be an all-out device for effective service delivery to the weaker sections, particularly to the very young and vulnerable age group of 10 to 17 years among them. If such a programme is successful, it will purposefully prevent juvenile delinquency, so widely prevalent among the weaker sections and the urban areas, and constitute a major step towards police crime prevention through effective social defence. When it comes to the protection of rights of SC, ST and OBC the administration, and the police have been known to be inclined to act against the interest of the weaker sections, not only because of the influence of social, economic and political power, but also on account of an existing natural bias among these operatives which determine the use of their discrimination. Even police officers belonging to the weaker sections failed to protect the victim because they themselves were victimised by corruption at the hands of the oppressors. The discrimination to take action conformed on the police has always been used in such a biased manner that the victim belonging to the weaker section is hardly protected, corruption is the major cause as the victim is invariably poor and the culprit affluent, or fairly richer than the victim. Police should always react to the complaint in the most impartial manner; and if in any set of circumstances, the prevalent knife-edge balance of the advantage of discretion is to be tilted in anybody's favour, it should be for the benefit of the weaker section.

After all the other side can command all the conveniences, including the best legal talent, and other varied influences to buy its liberty from the clutches of law. Police have to strive in this direction that the weaker sections may be able to secure at least a medium of legal justice, approximating to minimum social justice.

According to Article 335 of the Constitution, while administrative standards are maintained on one side, and no room is given among those preferred persons for bias or reverse bias on the other side, reasonable representation, at all levels of the police organisation should be given to those candidates, who are really good and stand the test of selection in all respects. Unfortunately, it is not done. Entry in the police in either bought or influenced by political parties of those, who do not deserve any consideration as they no longer remain weaker section. While ruling that creamy layers of this section of the society should be deprived of the right of reservation, the Supreme Court may have this constitutional provision in mind.

4. Is Reservation A Helping Hand?

No one would disagree that those, who have for generations being downtrodden as a result of social taboos and related oppressive practices as regards availability of education, and job opportunities, should certainly be helped to reach an equitable standard now, and would support, and equally honour the provisions for reservations for Scheduled Castes and Scheduled Tribes and Other Backward Classes as contemplated by Articles 15 and 16 of the Constitution subject to the condition of Article 335 that such reservation should be consistent with the maintenance of efficiency in administration. Experience is the other way. This directive principle has been flouted, and efficiency has been allowed to drop at the bottom level. No one works, as now there is no barometer to gauge efficiency, for everyone has, for one reason or the other, become inefficient. Promotion to inefficient incumbents on the basis of reservation has, more or less, become a guarantee. Police are not an exception to this state of affairs.

Among the SC, ST and OBC often distortions arise because of only the relatively better off people socially, educationally, and economically cornering most of the benefits generation after generation, while their poor and uneducated compatriots, either do not know about these benefits, or are unable to take necessary steps to obtain them. When some of them finally do get around to claim them, they are done out of a good proportion of the benefits, by unscrupulous manipulators or corrupt public servants. A few police officers at all levels know this background and, therefore, they failed in taking steps to prevent untoward developments, where possible and take appropriate action where incidents of harassment and corrupt practices do emerge.

5. Women as Weaker Section

The International Alliance of Women considers the victimisation of women one of the most critical and pressing problem facing women around the globe today, and it called on the United Nations to promote equitable laws in all countries of the world as between men and women and fair treatment of women by the society in general, and the Criminal Justice System in particular. In India, victimisation of women is much more common as domestic violence, arising out of lack of education, presence of tradition and social expectation; not to mention the absence of equality in practice as against law and obviously in physical prowess. In India, the Constitution guarantees equality of status and proscribes discrimination as between men and women. But realising the inferiority of physical strength and the pressure of social tradition, the Constitution also provides for special protection for prevention of women exploitation. However, in actual practice, this does not seem to work and fallaciously, particularly on the domestic scene, in remote villages.

Quite a number of young married women die of burn in the kitchen, in what are recorded as unnatural deaths by the police, very few of them are really accidents. A large number are established as suicides, or obviously brought about as a result of persistent harassment by the husband and the in-laws. Dowry demands and related harassment are an inescapable part of the Indian domestic scene, substantially concomitant with arranged marriages. Dowry, when it first emerged, must have been intended as an endowment to enable the girl to settle down in some comfort in her new house. But in due course it has turned into a purchase price, and an instrument of oppression, may be, initially rash promises are made by girl's parents beyond their capacity, and subsequently they were tend to go on giving, under pressure, or mental agony or physical torture. Finally, a breaking point is reached, when the girl decides to end her life. Sometimes these natural deaths turn out into murders too. In these the unscrupulous in-laws, wantonly murder the girl, as a prelude to a new marriage, and a fresh dowry adventure. Education and employment for independence, as well as equal share in the parental property, could minimise such untoward developments. Even so the presence of tradition and fear of stigma, quite often exert undue compulsions even on the educated woman, as it happened some years ago in the case of a woman doctor of Tirupur, who committed suicide unable to bear the persistent harassment for dowry.

Women's associations have been very active on this front and considerably successful too. As a result of their efforts a new section in the Indian Penal Code (498A) has been introduced making it an offence for the husband or the in-laws to treat a young wife with cruelty — physical or mental. The law also postulates that no evidence other than the young woman's statement, or suicide confirmed by the injury, or circumstances, is necessary to prove it, within a period of seven years of the marriage. The provisions of the Dowry Prohibition Act and the Rape laws have also been considerably tightened up by the efforts of these women organisations.

Unfortunately in India, even since 20th centuries, a female child is always considered a burden on the family. Immediately, after the birth of a female child many parents killed it. The main reason was that in those turbulent days of foreign invaders, the safety and protection of a female child were always in jeopardy. In order to save from being molested or in any manner dishonoured, parents preferred to kill her. In several instances young girls committed suicide by self-immolation in order to save their chastity from Muslim invaders. Mass consigning to fire by several Rajput girls for the protection of their honour was prevalent during the Muslim occupation of India. This sacrifice was called "*Johar*". "*Sati*" was another form of female sacrifice in which a widow was compelled to torch herself alive along with the dead body of her husband lying on the funeral pyre. Gradually, conditions changed. During the British Regime "*Sati*" was banned and any attempt at that or insinuation or abatement was made a penal offence. In recent years, the invention of Sonography in medical science has given another tool in the hands of parents who cause abortion no sooner it is known to them that the woman has conceived a female child, and accordingly the foetus is destroyed, thanks to many unscrupulous medical practitioners. This process is known "AMNIOCENTESIS" and a new law controlling this process has been enacted. The treatment of women in India is somewhat in the nature of paradox. Women are honoured as mother goddess as "*Shakty*" — power, and elected even as Prime Minister, but when it comes to equal treatment at home this is conspicuously by its absence on a large front.

The increasing awareness of their equality and rights by women, and their free movement as equal in the work environment, away from the old masculine protective mantel at home is probably responsible for the increase in the number of rape cases. Eve-teasing and a variety of methods of dishonouring a woman are engineered by the masculine society of the country. Such offences are rarely reported to the police. People do not have guts enough to deal with such miscreants, who are emboldened to continue with their mischievous practices, almost with impunity; judiciary demands evidence for conviction; and unfortunately evidence cannot be secured due to the non-cooperative and apathetic attitude of the people. Women have now no protection from the society, which was their honourable privilege three decades ago. Even custodial rapes are committed. The quantum of punishment in cases of rape has been increased from two years to 10 years, the maximum may go up to life imprisonment. Police have streamlined the procedures to deal with these cases as well as dowry deaths and domestic violence, and their registration, investigation and disposal is as prompt as never before.

6. Children as Victim of Crime and Abuse

In a society, children are the treasurable assets and must be protected and looked after with care and cherished as such. That is the State responsibility in various advance countries. But in India 80 out of 1000 children die as infants. Of the rest too, quite a large number are insufficiently provided and inadequately cared and fed, with the result that a large percentage of them become victims of neglect, delinquency and abuse, which in due course led to crime and hardcore criminals, for which the foundation is laid when children start playing truant and absent themselves from schools. Neither the parents nor the school authorities take trouble to find out why the child has absented from his scholastic lesson. While on the subject, it is relevant to recall that the children of World are entitled to the following Universal Charter of Rights, conceived in 1966:

1. To affection, love and understanding.
2. To adequate nutrition and medical care.

3. To free education, with a name and nationality.
4. To special care if handicapped.
5. To be among the first to receive relief in case of disaster.
6. To develop individual abilities and become a useful member of the society.
7. To be brought up in an atmosphere of peace, and spirit of human brotherhood.
8. To enjoy all these rights regardless of race, colour, sex, religion, national or social origins.

These are special rights that the children enjoy, in addition to all other Human Rights.

But unfortunately in India, of the children below 14 years, who constitute a third of the country's 95 crores, a good percentage do not get a fair deal. This situation is not alone among the families of 40 per cent of India's population, who live below the poverty line, but also from other families, who should have known better and could afford more. The kind of ill-treatment that children get is directed more against the female sex and begins even before birth, as already mentioned. In many communities, particularly in rural areas, girl children of tender ages do not get a fair deal as regards food, health care and education and many of them die young. This is probably responsible for the lower proportion of women to men in India, compared to other countries. At least, where matters like this patently come to notice, the police should take appropriate action by bringing it to the notice of the concerned authorities, even if no cognizable crime is involved. But this is not done, more or less, at all. More generally among the poor families, young children are counted as a pair of hands, girls to work on household chores, boys to go out on petty jobs to earn money to supplement the family income.

At a certain stage, many children who do not get a fair deal, by and large, take to streets. Many of these children take to pilferages, peddling of narcotic drugs, liquor and the allied vices, even pimps soliciting prostitution. They are also sexually abused. Both passive and active sodomy is common. The Juvenile Justice Act, 1986 purports to give justice to such children. Police have failed in the majority of cases to deal appropriately and compassionately with the different streams of children, for many of them are not specially trained and equipped accordingly. The police has generally failed to realise that this purposeful method of social defence will ultimately control major crime as it has been established all over the world that substantial percentage of the habitual and professional criminals have invariably had a history of juvenile delinquency, recorded or unrecorded (Please see a separate chapter on Juvenile Delinquency). The police, as the major and far-flung agency of the Criminal Justice System, has a special responsibility all along the line, to deal with preventive social defence, as well as correctional social defence, in a discerning and compassionate manner. The violence and variety of crimes repeatedly shown in the film have created, though unobtrusively, almost a permanent impact on the children of tender age who have idealised a potent criminal as their "Hero". They practice the film methods; and the impression created by them rarely can be obliterated. For reasons best known to the Government, no limitations are put on showing such type of violence, including rape, drinking, gambling, gold and narcotic smuggling and armed combats *etc.*, which have now become an integrated part of any film, if there is no other theme liked by the people. The obvious conclusion is the degeneration in social moral standards, old values of virtue have diminished giving place to rampant dishonesty in every sphere of life, both domestic and public. Can such a society prosper? What the police can do in such circumstances? They watch as mute spectators and suffer the stigma — Bad Police. The public and the Government forget their correctional role, because they have found the offender — the Police. Such is the paradox of these democratic institutions!

7. Other Weaker Sections

The group of physically and mentally handicapped persons is the one that first should come to the mind of police. The bulk of these persons are, not really responsible for their handicapped situation, and society has surely an obligation to look after them. A two per cent reservation in jobs has been provided by the Government for them. The police should always be ready to give a helping hand, so as to enable them to face life and carry on without feeling unwanted, and at the same time, not having pointed attention drawn to their handicaps, and that way psychologically upsetting them.

That segment of the society may be considered weak, and might need help, in some form or the other, are the socially, educationally backward classes. The Constitution did envisage some help being given to them, but did not specify it. Many States have taken measures to help them by providing educational reservation and preferential job opportunities. However, these measures are cried to be insufficient. According to Mandal Commission Recommendations, the National Front Government had announced 27 per cent job reservation for these classes, and a possible 5 to 10 per cent side by side, on consideration of economic deserts. This had led to a widespread student agitation as backlash. Now a stage is on the anvil where in those, not belonging to Scheduled Castes and Scheduled Tribes and other Backward Classes, could be considered as economically and educationally weaker section of the society on account of the greatest preferential treatment given to SC, ST and OBC population. It is with the greatest difficulty that this group is able to secure admission to scholastic institutions and jobs in service.

8. Side Effects of Reservation Policy

The Constitution envisaged the phenomenon of reservation only as a transitional measure. The period of reservation has been extended from time to time, and one does not know how long these reservations would continue. Politically motivated and *ad hoc* measures have necessarily created distortion and problem in their implementation. For instance recruiting people who are far below average, still after giving full consideration for their background, will not be in accordance with the healthy proviso of Article 335 of the Constitution which envisages fair standard of efficiency in the administration. In the area of promotion also acute problem has arisen. Obviously placing a person, who has just completed his probation of two years over the heads of a set of continuously efficient people awaiting promotion after completing long years of service, is scarcely the right way to ensure efficiency and contentment in the organisation. Frustration, indiscipline and fall of standards have been permanently founded in the police hierarchy. Reservation have divided the society; and Police cannot be an exception to this situation. To maintain discipline has become a problem. There are officers and men who belong to reservation and non-reservation categories even in a small unit of an outpost of three to four men. Who will issue orders and who will obey them have remained unsolved questions? Always pro or anti-reservation stance is taken. Each category blames the other for any failure in an assignment. The police who have been assigned the job to give protection to the weaker sections of the society have themselves become weaker and diluted in their discipline, performance and efficiency. By crossing parameters, politicians have suspended the operation of Article 335 of the Constitution — fair standards of efficiency in the administration; and retrograde the country's progress by 47 years on account of their wrong policies.

Assessments of economic level of the family for grant of quota positions have always presented a problem in our country where black money is rampant and income certificates can easily be purchased. No level reasonable qualifying income has been prescribed by the Government and there is no full proof system by which, attempts at cheating may be firmly eschewed. The economic criterion should not only be prescribed for the open forward classes, but should also be superimposed, after a period, in all other reservations. The police duty in this context of all these, is to protect and assist in the enjoyment of these rights where deserved, and to help restoring their rights, when these are infringed by unfair practices. In a truly democratic society, all weaker sections of the community have to be guaranteed their Constitutional Rights and due protection by the police; and the police should do so in the larger public interest. Political will and public support should provide the backing for all police actions, which regrettably are conspicuously absent.

9. Slum dwellers

There is no town or city, big or small, where slums do not exist. A floor space of about 80 square feet (10 × 8 feet) is the usual grand and fortunate housing for slum dwellers. This one room serves as a kitchen, bed room, and living room for two to eight members of the family. Toilets are conspicuously not provided, and all excretions of excreta are performed in the open and uncovered places by both males and females alike. They may be sarcastically called 'ablutions'. These slums are over-crowded and resemble "rabit warren" and the slum dwellers are totally deprived of privacy worth the name. A slum constitutes the most important and persistent problem of urban life, and has become cancerous. It is the chief source of crime and delinquency. Economically, there is a constant struggle in a slum for survival due to ignorance, unemployment, under-employment, and low wages. Functionally, a slum provides cheap labour to the cities' economically better population, paradoxically slums have become lifelines of the urban population.

It is almost impossible to avoid rubbing shoulders with pimps, prostitutes, thieves, gamblers, smugglers and criminals — the large class of desperate and depraved live in the slum areas. They are a jumble of men, women and animals, trades and occupations, morals, immorals, and vices, and above all misery and nursery of diseases. Here criminals and anti-socials are born, grown, flourished and harboured, and stolen property concealed, illicit distillation, bootlegging, drug peddling, gambling, prostitution, sex abuse rampantly take place; and there is no vice which is not commonly prevalent here.

A common phenomenon of the growing towns undergoing urbanisation and industrialisation is the demographic imbalance, whereby there is a preponderance of males, who migrate from their villages leaving their families behind. This leads to an absence of normal family life, and creating a situation where there is a great demand for female companionship, thus contributing greatly to such problems as concubinage and prostitution. Children witness sex activity anywhere they peep as there is no privacy and premature acquaintance with sex matters become unavoidable for them.

In places, where women migrated from rural area to urban area centres with their husbands and children should have a stabilising influence on the social and moral life of the family. But this is not always the case with females residing in small habitations. In most cases, both the father and mother go to work leaving their minor children behind with the result that they grow up along with delinquent children.

The growth of slum areas scattered all over, haphazard mass migration of population from rural areas and breakdown of family and social life, resulted in high incidence of criminality, such as, juvenile delinquency, prostitution, trafficking in women, illicit distillation and sale of liquor, sale of drugs, organised gambling, pilferages, receiving and selling of stolen property *etc.* The list is almost never-ending. There is not a crime which is not committed here. Group conflicts due to growth of heterogeneous population in slum frequently burst into riots. Every petty dispute over withdrawal of water from a roadside tap or sharing profits from gambling often end in riots, if the police were not alert to scotch the disputes at the initial stage. *Goondaism* becomes a serious problem. The *goondas* mostly live in slums and take active part in looting, arson, molestation of women, whenever any kind of disturbances take place. They keep on waiting for such opportunities. In normal times they lend money at very high rates of interest to workers and forcefully recoup from them all the money that has become due together with accrued interest, if they have to escape from further torture by the *goondas* or their gangmates.

The important work of collection of intelligence within the slum areas have been often relegated by the police. Criminals are born and bred in these areas, and form the mainstay during political and communal disturbances and also during elections. There is considerable concealment or minimisation of crimes. The public avoid reporting crimes to the police and whenever any report is made, the latter avoid registration of cases reported to them. There is no question of investigation and prosecution of the offenders; criminality in slum areas is allowed to thrive either with immunity or impunity.

10. Police Image

India is a plural society, in which all the various components of the society should reasonably integrate themselves into a larger community, free of discrimination and contributing to the total national solidarity. Unfortunately, the National State of India, wherein plurality has become accentuated by the social disparity of the caste system, illiteracy and economic backwardness of the one-third of the population living well below the poverty line, has not yet been effectively integrated, for one divisive reason or the other, politics having played a dominant role. It is against such a background police have been asked to give protection to the weaker section of the society. The police in India is a well-knit organisation, attuned to the objective protection of society through social control, social defence and social service. The undermanned, over-worked, over-looked, inadequately equipped and ill-paid police organisations in the country have done reasonably well in the conduct of ten massive general elections maintaining the essence of public peace and order and in ensuring reasonable justice delivery though at times partisan on account of political intervention and other pressure. Still their image is not good at all; for improvement of their image, they have to shed apathy, lethargy, partiality for one reason or the other and corruptibility. For them protection of weaker section of the society is the last priority, as they have no enough time to attend to this extra work when their hands are more than full with '*bandobast*' duties mostly in relation to movements of their political bosses and their proteges. A time has come when the public, and the Government should take reformist, and revised view of the situation and create a special police force only for the protection of the weaker sections of the society at each police station level, so that this special force will be able to concentrate fully on the job assigned to them — the protection of Weaker Sections of the society.

26
Juvenile Delinquency

1. Dimensions of Juvenile Delinquency

The most important aspect of this subject is that in every age it has been regarded as a problem peculiar to the contemporary society, while the fact is that like adult criminal behaviour it has always existed in some form or the other, and there is no apparent reason to expect that it will not remain so in the future. This phenomenon has a two-dimensional basis. Firstly, the violation of any code of conduct, whether for adults or for young persons, is inevitable. Secondly, the definition of juvenile delinquency as deviant child behaviour itself depends upon the norms laid down by the society; in other words by the elders, and clash of values due to generation gap is bound to occur. An Egyptian priest almost 6,000 years ago wrote on the walls of a tomb:

(i) "Our earth is degenerate in those later days. There are signs that the world is coming to an end because children no longer obey their parents."

(ii) Socrates wrote about 2,400 years ago, "Children now love luxury, they have bad manners, contempt of authority, they show disrespect for elders, and love chatter in place of exercise, children no longer rise when elders enter the room. They contradict their parents, chatter before company, gobble up dainties at the table, cross their legs, and tyranise over their teachers".

The above two quotations evidently confirm the basic fact that the deviant behaviour of children has posed problems from times immemorial, and what has changed is only the nature and definitions of the behaviour considered undesirable. (*Journal of Criminal Law, Criminology and Police Science, 1956*). Then what should construe juvenile delinquency? It is not easy to give a precise definition of juvenile delinquency. One hurdle is similar to that while defining crime in general, *i.e.*, the choice between the social and legal definitions.

Another aspect of the definition problem is that quite frequently the statutes defining the various delinquent Acts are vague in terms of their contents, which is contrary to the basic principle of criminal law as expressed through the Latin expression, "*Nullum Crimen lege*" — no crime without law. Laws defining crimes should not be vague since the citizens must be able to know with a fair amount of certainty the acts which are proscribed for them. In this context the definition of juvenile delinquency may differ from country to country in view of their social taboos and living conditions. This vagueness in the definitions is defended on the ground that what applies in relation to criminal statutes is not relevant in the delinquency laws since the latter are not created to punish the juveniles but to protect and reform them.

2. Juvenile Delinquency Laws

They are characterised by the feature that they proscribe many acts which are regarded as non-criminals or even socially acceptable if indulged in by adults, like drinking or smoking. Some of the acts proscribed for children would be torts if committed by adults (such as frequenting public places like railway yard aimlessly without criminal intention). In the Western countries there is a great variety of acts declared by law to be acts of juvenile delinquency starting from indecent or immoral conduct and ending in petty criminal offence. It is a big list which includes begging and habitually remaining truant from school, and with it we, in India, are not concerned. The extension of the concept of juvenile delinquency to extremely wide limits has drawn criticism on the ground that it is neither necessary nor desirable to use police and courts in "Private matters" which can be better tackled by the families themselves. The issue was discussed by the Second United Nations Congress on the Prevention of Crime and the Treatment of offenders held in August 1960 in London. The Congress was of the opinion that the problem of juvenile delinquency should not be unnecessarily inflated. It recommended: (a) that the meaning of the term juvenile delinquency should be restricted as far as possible to violation of the criminal law, and (b) that even for protection, specific offences which would penalise small irregularities, or maladjusted behaviour of minors but for which adults would not be prosecuted.

3. Indian Concept of Juvenile Delinquency

In India the definition of juvenile delinquency presents no problem. The concept is confined to the violation of the ordinary penal law of the country so far as the jurisdiction of the court is concerned. The Children Act of 1960, for instance, defines a delinquent child as a child, who has been found to have committed an offence (Section 2 of the Act). Child under this Act means a boy under 16 years of age and a girl under 18 years. Children Act differs from state to state marginally, but the general import is almost the same. In these Acts separate provisions have been laid down for neglected and uncontrollable children. They are dealt with by the Child Welfare Boards, and not by Juvenile Courts (Section 4 of the Act). In Section 2 neglected child has been defined by the Act as a child who,

(i) is found begging; or

(ii) is found without having any home or settled place of abode or any ostensible means of subsistence or is found destitute, whether he is an orphan or not; or

(iii) has a parent or guardian who is unfit to exercise or does not exercise proper care or control over the child; or

(iv) Lives in brothel or with a prostitute or frequently goes to any place used for the purposes of prostitution, or is found to associate with any prostitute or any other persons, who leads an immoral, drunken or depraved life. Uncontrollable children are to be dealt with in the same way as neglected children under Section 17 of the Act. Delinquency is the only area which gives jurisdiction to the Children Courts in India. Secondly, the Indian definition has been given more briefly and clearly and that the content of delinquency is the same as that of adult offences.

4. Nature and Extent of Juvenile Delinquency

To point out that juvenile delinquency is on the unbridled increase in India is to state the obvious. What is probably more interesting and useful to understand the rate at which delinquency is continuing to rise and the type of crimes in which it is manifested in a higher degree than in others. Also it is significant to find out the patterns of juvenile delinquency in terms of differentials based on age, sex and religions. A critical study of the figures of juvenile delinquency from 1960 to 1995 in the country presents the following facts for consideration of all, including the law enforcing agency:

1. Juvenile delinquency, as manifested the world-over is essentially the problem of male children.
2. Most of the offenders apprehended in the last decade were connected with offences involving violence to the human body, and the numbers of murders was quite substantial.
3. The highest number of arrests were made for the offences of prohibition, gambling, and theft in that order.
4. The juveniles apprehended were in the age group of 10 to 21 years.
5. Socio-economic, religious, and education backgrounds were the essential factors for the conversion to delinquency of normally brought up child up to the age of 10 years.
6. Influence of school-mates — bad company,
7. Defective surroundings,
8. Absence of recreation,
9. Influence of community.

   Institutions like cinemas, newspapers, Doordarshan, present day motion pictures *etc.*, glorify sex, smuggling, bootlegging, violence, rape and various other forms of anti-social acts like gambling, drinking, smoking, pilfering, and methods of earning easy money for acquiring spontaneous richness. A continuous vision of such pictures makes the child susceptible to simulation of these acts. Even the Government Media of T.V. is not excluded. When elders see them, their children cannot be prevented from seeing them. This will also apply to pornographic literature or blue films.
10. Generally parents pay scant attention to children in order to know everything about them. Inversely in many

families too much love, care and attention are bestowed on the child and its initial delinquency is not properly dealt with and generally condoned.

11. Nucleus families. Parents are over busy in their pursuits of life for a living and their children are neglected as there is no elder person in the family to supervise and correct the aberrant behaviour of the child.
12. Broken families,
13. Criminal parents,
14. Social customs,
15. Disorganised society with diminution of moral values.
16. Unemployment of parents.
17. Increase in the number of female delinquents, most of whom take up to prostitution either willingly or coerced into the profession due to pecuniary circumstances. (Please see a separate chapter on Prostitution).

5. Prevention of Juvenile Delinquency

In affluent countries prevention in this sense includes the efforts to improve family relationships, better adjustments in schools, provision of education and recreation designed to produce useful and upright citizens and work, medicine and psychiatry. In our country, afflicted with mass poverty, the limitation of preventive programmes, experienced elsewhere are bound to manifest themselves more severely. Though the preventive programmes do not pertain exclusively to the juvenile delinquents, they are obviously more relevant and useful in the context of young persons in view of the fact that the chances of a person turning criminal after reaching a certain age, when the values and attitudes are more or less fixed, are somewhat lower than in the case of persons of immature age and understanding. Generally aberration resulting in delinquency is noticed in the age group of 10 to 15, both for male and female children. Therefore, forestalling the criminal behaviour by taking advance action in terms of individual and environmental adjustments can be the only measure to prevent juvenile delinquency; but it is easier to propound than to act in the poverty-stricken country of ours, where almost 60 per cent of the people live below the "Poverty line". But it is possible to timely identify potential delinquents and take action against them under the provisions of law, as psychiatric services are rarely available in the country for the simple reason of their being costly; and, therefore, beyond the pale of the common family of the delinquent. It is difficult to evaluate the existing child guidance centres (Available in negligible number) as a crime prevention agency. Shall we judge it in terms of its success with the juvenile recidivists, or shall we hold that its role is relatively simple and earliest beginnings of behaviour problems? Shall we measure its success as to the period of treatment and how long the duration of the "Cure" would last? The concept of success, both subjective and relative has to be seen from the angle of the children themselves, the policemen, parents, teachers, and all others associated with the reformation of the child, as statistics are extremely misleading, and prepared for better presentation of the performance of the dealing institutions.

6. Education and Recreation

In the 45 years of Independence we have not developed a new value system in which the school would be a force working against the discrimination, and rejection experienced by pupils drawn from the lower classes of all the extant faiths in the country. We have not made the school an instrument for fostering work attitudes, self-esteem and job skills to improve the employability of graduates of schools in deprived areas and finally we have failed to providing school experiences designed to improve the self-image of delinquency-prone children. The popular belief regarding the efficacy of recreational programmes has not found support in a number of studies. Being a good athlete is no deterrent at all to delinquency. Experiences through team play recreation have no significant carry-over to general character traits or conduct patterns. Even highly organised recreational activities do not absorb enough of the energy or time of the child to at least appreciably decrease his opportunities to engage in delinquency; on the contrary a play group may itself help to stimulate its members to illegal activities engaged in for fun after the games are over when there are delinquent members in the group. Many of the recreational programmes do not reach the deserving children. Where children have come to enjoy their delinquencies as games, so commonly the case, the thrills thus provided are usually greater than those which organised recreations can provide. If a child is disposed to law violation because of the influence of the family and neighborhood, his early training, his personality distortions or his attitudes towards an authority, it will require the greatest efforts through the correct and proper education based on morals and mores in order to convert him into a good and law-abiding citizen, and even community programmes would prove abortive in acquiring the desired effect mentioned above.

7. Juvenile Courts

Juvenile offenders have always had a different type of response from the criminal law system of most of the societies as compared to adult or grown-up offenders. This has been reflected in the concept of responsibility for the prohibited acts in case of young and mature violators of law, the obvious reasons being that persons of very young age do not possess sufficient maturity to understand the nature and consequences of their acts and it would be unjust to deal with them in the same manner as those who do not have similar disabilities. In India there is no criminal responsibility for children up to seven years of age. The concept of separate courts, institutions and procedures for juvenile offenders is quite a recent one. The juvenile courts came into existence with their own distinct philosophy incorporating various reforms on the basis of new theories of human behaviour, and the motivating force which created them was the concern for children and not of punishing them for every proscribed behaviour. Whether the juvenile courts fulfilled the role of parents in cases where it was needed is a different and debatable issue which has been raised quite recently, but the assumptions made regarding the role of these courts lead to a very special type of procedure and practice in them. The salient features are:

1. Separate hearing for children's cases only in those offences which are not punishable with death or life imprisonment (Section 27 of the Code of Criminal Procedure, 1973).

2. Informal hearing of a very simple nature resembling somewhat in the nature of conference taking place between the judge, the probation officer, the social worker, the child and the parents. The issue is to find out why the delinquent had committed the offence. The reports of the probation officer assumes great significance in this context (Sections 19, 20 and 23 of the Children Act, 1960).
3. Private hearing at the discretion of the court.
4. Protection against legal consequences and stigma with a provision of no disqualification to be attached to child delinquent due to conviction in a juvenile court (Section 25, Children Act, 1960).
5. Only one appeal against the order of conviction shall lie to the Session Court, whose decision shall be final
6. The juvenile courts are criminal courts, and not of civil nature.

8. Disposal of Cases of Delinquent and Neglected Children

Section 21 of the Children Act, 1960 enables the Juvenile Courts to pass the following order for dealing with the juvenile delinquents:

1. The child may be allowed to go home after advice or admonition.
2. The child may be released on probation under the care of any parent, guardian or other fit persons on their executing a bond for well-being, and good behaviour of the child for a period not exceeding three years.
3. The child may be sent to a special school (created under Section 10 of the Act) to remain there till he ceases to be child or for a period of at least three years if the offender is a boy above the age of 16 years.

9. Evaluation

The ideal which is best to set should be to find out what the child is, physically, mentally, morally and then if it is learnt that he is treading the path that leads to criminality, to take him in charge, not so much to punish as to reform, not to degrade but to uplift, not to crush but to develop, not to make him a criminal, but a Worthy Citizen. When the Government deliberately became inactive or apathetic to stop mass copying in scholastic institutions for petty political gains (like Uttar Pradesh and Bihar *etc.*); when the Government failed to consider merit in preference to caste and class discriminations, both for academic and service admissions; when the urchins are being continuously used to achieve some parochial and political gains, it could be nothing but sure anachronic waste of national human wealth; besides, it will anathematise the national integrity of an incoherent society.

27

Prostitution

1. Prostitution System How Introduced?

Prostitution is prevalent in all the societies in some form or the other; and it may be open or clandestine. For that matter even variable adultery may be termed as prostitution as it does not have the sanction of the society. As there are female prostitutes in India, there are male prostitutes in affluent countries of the Western World. Prostitution is based on sexual relationship of either sex. A prostitute has some relationship with her/his customers, and the prostitutes are of various types depending on the active or passive participations of the customers. Prostitution is a public order offence; besides, it is a commercial occupation for those who adopt it and is based upon the moral standard of the society. Paradoxically, unlike any other occupation, prostitution is generally looked upon with disdain by the society on account of the "Sex vice" involved in this trade. For that matter every trade earns bread for the person indulging in it. Society has been made amenable to acknowledge political corruption, social corruption, corruption in the services, dishonesty, cheating and various other anti-social crimes as a way of life in this country now in 1995, when the society abhorred these criminals and outcaste them three decades before. The same society does not now feel bad about these offenders. This very society which had stigmatised prostitution in the past centuries do the same even now when its social good ethos has been converted by its components themselves into bathos, and they do not want to show even compunction for themselves; and compassion for the poor women following the trade of prostitution for their subsistence. On the contrary these very persons often used them for the satisfaction of their sexual lust; often culminating into incest or carnal offences.

2. Sex Vice

Sex instinct is a natural human instinct, and great attraction between the opposite sexes. When male and female develop intimacy, there are positive chances of turning that affinity into love, and when that leads to marriage, which is a socially sanctioned institution for mating and hence moral, it does not constitute "Sex Vice" or illegitimate intercourse. Extra-marital or pre-marital sexual intercourse has been regarded illegitimate since several centuries in India, although it may be permissible in various other countries of the world, with which this chapter is not concerned, as the author is writing on the Indian conditions of this profession. The uncontrolled sex instinct, preferably termed as lust, has resulted into many social problems and sex-disorganisation. But at the same time suppression of this natural instinct results in sex vices and the attendant injurious activities and as such it should neither be suppressed unnecessarily, nor left uncontrolled. When sexual relationship is healthy or normal it is not objected by the society as it is devoid of obscenity. It is, however, perverted relationship that results in sex vices, and seemingly is not tolerated by the society. In India, according to information available there are practically no male prostitutes. However, a large number of persons although in most cases unreported, have taken to the vice of sodomy — both active and passive. The eunuchs noticed particularly in North India, are a product of the Muslim rule in the country. Muslim rulers had maintained several hundred women in their *harems* and they needed sexually impotent guards for their watch and security and for the obvious reasons of keeping these women away from sexual relationship with their guards the latter were castrated as a safety valve. Political prostitutes were in the pay-roll of the government ever since the ancient period, and they are employed for a cause and definite purpose. There are homosexuals and lesbians; and in the countries of the West, including America, their society is contemplating to legalise this type of sexual relationship. Therefore, this chapter mostly deals with women prostitution.

3. The Attitude of the Society towards Prostitution

It very much depends on whether the prostitute makes any discrimination among the customers, if her income has any social advantage or disadvantage and if her sex role has some links with others socially acceptable roles. But on the whole, in most of the societies' prostitution is condemned because it quite often creates law and order problem, and degrades women's respect. A woman prostitute demands money for her subsistence by selling her body; and in the process she loses social esteem. This is the concern, both of the society, and the Government, to fathom out the causative factors compelling a woman to take to the life of vice and continue in such despicable profession till death. Does she do so voluntarily for satisfying her sexual urge, or is she lured or forced into the body profession by circumstances within or without her control? She, as a member of the society, has every right to ask this pertinent question and seek a satisfactory and honourable solution to ward off herself from this vice. Who helps her to extricate from this wretched profession? Really no one dares. Her life is a drudgery and even she is forced to submit herself for sexual intercourse much against her will, she remains the most unfortunate soul, who is deprived of the remedy contemplated by Section 376 of the Indian Penal Code, (The offence of Rape) only because she has previously sold her body, and is considered to be a bad character. Therefore, a woman alone could not be condemned for committing "Sex vice", as sexual intercourse culminating in promiscuity is the need of both the sexes. Prostitution as a specific class is actuated in the various secret services for fishing out information, and morally it does come under the ambit of this vice, though there may be extenuating circumstances not to condemn it. Therefore, it cannot be answered either in affirmative or negative whether prostitution is "Sex vice", as the circumstances leading to prostitution would differ from instance to instance, and as one may look at it. Even then it may be possible to generalise prostitution for the sake of a legal definition and the efforts both of the society and the Government to contain it in a reasonable proportion considering its utility to the needy components of the society.

4. Prostitution Defined

With the divergent views of the various components of the society and the extant sex taboo, it is extremely difficult to attempt a precise definition of prostitution, the meaning of which may not be universally acceptable with consequential defects in its lawful enforcement. Generally, it may be construed as "Sexual intercourse on a promiscuous and mercenary basis with emotional indifference". (Clinard). H. Benjamin is of the view that a prostitute is one who agrees to have sexual intercourse with a person, who is not her husband, who offers her money for engaging her in the intercourse which may be extra coital. In other words it is permissible adultery, and the woman may be called a concubine if she restricts her flesh trade to one person only. In the past 75 years such a practice had the sanction of the society and keeping a concubine was not looked down upon; but on the contrary it was considered prestigious. The then existing laws permitted the hereditary rights to the progeny out of this extra-marital relationship; and that was the fashion of the day when polygamy was a prevalent taboo. In those days, the number of prostitutes was very low; and they were particularly meant for the needy persons. The definition by G.R. Scott has wider perception:

> "A prostitute is an individual who for some kind of reward or some other type of personal satisfaction and a part or full-time profession engages in normal or abnormal sexual intercourse with various persons who may be of the same sex or of the opposite sex to be the prostitute."

Thus, prostitution is a sexual profession, like any other profession in which there is bargain of "give and take", and in this there is the bargain of offering or receiving of body for sexual intercourse or on hire or without hire. Elliot Merill concludes that "Prostitution is an illicit sex union on a promiscuous and mercenary basis with accompanying emotional indifference".

Definitions by Hennigues, B.Z. Goldberg, Kingsley Davis and various criminologists could be concluded thus: Prostitution is any sexual act which is habitually performed by an individual with other individual of his own or opposite sex for a consideration which is non-sexual in which emotional involvement may or may not be present. In common parlance prostitute is one who abandons herself to many men, it may be for pecuniary gain or even it may be for mere sexual pleasure without receiving any form of consideration either in money or kind. Prostitution generally includes all feminine acts that women use in pursuing ends that require men as intermediaries. But all the same the essence of prostitution would be motive which determines whether a sexual union is prostitutional or not.

5. Legal Definition of Prostitution

The legal definition as enunciated in the Supervision of Immoral Traffic in Women and Girls Act, 1956 is:

> "A female who offers her body for promiscuous sexual intercourse for hire, whether in money or kind."

Thus all the above discussions make it amply clear that usually prostitution is sexual intercourse which is allowed by a woman (willingly not in all cases?) to the opposite sex for money consideration or for some other kind of favour; and in it a woman sells her body.

One may ask a pertinent question. It is this that a legally married woman and a prostitute both indulge in sexual intercourse with their male partner, who takes care of their subsistence. In either case the woman receives consideration. One may also argue that in case of a married woman the natural mandate of procreation would be fulfilled; but when contraceptives are used, or surgical aid is taken, there would be no progeny. Therefore, the only dominant difference in these two kinds of sexual relations is that in the case of a married woman sexual intercourse has been accepted by the society as normal ethics of mating with the intention of reproduction — the inherent motive of the creator. This may also be true in relation to a concubine. Whereas in the case of a prostitute this social ethical sanction is conspicuously absent. Even the introduction of Bigamous Marriage Act by the Government could not bridle the sexy persons in indulging in extra-marital sexual relationship. Moreover, indulgence in sex is not public and in extra-coital relationship the participants ensure utmost secrecy due to the apprehension of social boycott about three decades ago. But since then the views of the society have become too liberal, and the sex aberrant is now not condemned to social expulsion. The pornographic literature and the blue films, so abundantly available, actuate individuals in sexual indulgence, and if the wife is unable to satisfy the husband, for some reason or the other, the husband is prone to be a sex aberrant. The same phenomenon is applicable to a wife. In such a situation, if the institution of prostitution does not exist, the honour of a woman will be in great jeopardy. It is a prostitute who serves as an outlet to sexy aberrants or delinquents and to considerable extent thwarts a woman being dishonoured; and therefore, instead of condemnation by the society, she needs a helping hand, both of the society, and of the Government for her reformation and retrieval to the society in case she has been coerced into this flesh trade.

6. Does a Woman Willingly Submit to Prostitution?

As far as the Indian Woman Society is concerned there may be singular instance in which a woman may opt voluntarily to indulge in prostitution as a business to earn bread for her subsistence in thc absence of a bread earning job. It is the inherent desire of every Indian woman to establish a happily wedded life and have children and a home in its real sense. Therefore, it becomes the impelling duty of the society, as well as of the Government, to make available to every nubile woman such a job as would enable her to earn sufficient enough to maintain her livelihood. Although this onerous duty was discharged by the society several centuries in the past, paradoxically, prostitution took roots in that period itself and with the passage of each century its number increased many-folds. The study of the history reveals that before the 7th century A.D. prostitution had a social sanction, and in almost every town there was prostitute in a brothel and she was not considered venal, but on the contrary the society recognised her to be a necessary social appendage. From the 7th century onwards thousands of mixed castes were created on account of connection of women with men of lower castes. The *Sudras* and the untouchables were divided into countless sub-castes. The number of castes increased on account of the nature of the economy in which the people could not move from one place to another. Slavery also existed and slaves were required to do unclean work such as cleaning of latrines and the like. Female slaves satisfied sexual lust of their masters. That was the time of Muslim invasion of India. From 700 A.D. to

1857, Muslims ruled the country and before 1757 A.D., when the British took charge of the affairs of the country, several low Hindu women were dishonoured and the Hindu society refused to take them back within its fold and it neglected them and made them to fight and fend for themselves. A large number of them was drawn into prostitution mostly against their wishes. Once a prostitute, she became a class of her own business to be followed by the subsequent female generations on account of their being continuously renounced by the society. From the 5th century A.D. Tantric religion with all its mystic forms and evil practices was widely accepted and in the 7th century it was universally acclaimed. As only this form of worship was open to women and *Sudras*, they took up to Tantrism, in which its followers openly observed socially disapproved practices. The use of wine, flesh, meat, and coition under certain prescribed conditions of the discipline could be made without secrecy in appropriate places and times. In a very short period of time the lower hierarchy of the four *varnas* adopted to this type of cult (*vajrayan*) with amazing speed and popularity. The erotic figures on the temples of Khajuraho (Madhya Pradesh), Konark (Orissa) and Modera in Gujarat speak of the stronghold taken by this form of worship on the general population. The system of "*Devdasi*" — offering of nubile women in the services of God is an offshoot of this cult and such damsels often satisfied the lust of the temple priests, who never wanted them to lead the honourable life of a woman. Because of licentious or lascivious behaviour of the people from the upper strata of society prostitution could not be curbed; the continuous strifes between the warring powers for over one thousand years gave the business of prostitution a helping hand and a woman once coerced into immoral sexual relationship continued to be a prostitute till her death and her female progeny was sequestered with the same trade although in numerous cases much against her will. The position of a female child of a prostitute these days also is not very much different than that of the previous generations. No one would like to marry the daughter of a prostitute on account of the stigma; and in spite of all her good intentions, capacity, body contours and learning she is coerced by the society to step into the flesh trade of her ancestors.

7. Forms of Prostitution

Prostitutes are of different types, and forms, though it is believed by a common man that a prostitute is a woman who sells her body while sitting at one place where her customers can visit her. The following are the ways by which prostitution is practised:

(i) Common Prostitutes: It is very old form in which growing young girls are lured or forcibly carried away and kept in the brothels. Generally, the old and trained prostitutes keep an eye on beautiful girls of low-class families with the help of their punters and purchase them from their guardians with the intention of using them as prostitutes when they reach puberty. In some cases such types of girls are kidnapped. These brothel keepers ensure that there is a constant supply of young girls for their brothels and what method they adopt to achieve this goal, is nobody's guess. Once these girls are brought into the brothels hardly, they escape from this drudgery. The brothel keeper receives high price from the customer, when the girl is subjected to her first intercourse immediately, she reaches puberty. This is the reason that the brothel keepers prowl for their victims in various places. These girls are provided only food and clothing and scanty money. Rest of the money of their earnings is kept by the brothel keepers. These girls are exploited for the purpose of prostitution, almost coerced to sell their body much against their will. Such prostitutes have no social respect, and they end their life in the profession itself. Once in the den they are not accepted by the society.

(ii) Religious Prostitutes: These are the girls who are lured to the temples in the name of the religion-mysticism. Generally they are called "*Devdasis*", "*Basvi*", "*Murli*", "*Jogathi*" *etc*., respectively in Kerala, Telangana, Maharashtra and Karnataka. Their primary duty is to sing and dance before the gods on ceremonial occasions and subsequently their youth is always exploited. The girls are generally tendered to the temple for the fulfilment of some vow of their parents, relatives or guardians. They are mostly exploited for the satisfaction of the lust of the temple authorities, and rarely they indulge in sexual relationship outside the temple ambit.

(iii) Hereditary Prostitutes: There are certain families in which the girls are traditionally trained from the early youth in the art of singing and dancing and when these girls grow as youth, they are handed down by the mother herself for prostitution to the pimps without any sense of shame or immorality. In such families the birth of a girl is a matter of great jubilation as she is positively a source of earning. In Goa and Sawantwadi they are called *Goumantak Marathas* and *Kolati*; in Andhra a *Basvi* and *Koyi*; in Bihar and U.P. *Nutts* and *Berias*. They generally keep to one man.

(iv) Hotel Prostitutes: These are the prostitutes which are kept by the hotel keepers for serving their customers, who need a girl during their stay in the hotel. Such girls do not reside in the hotels but live at their normal place of residence and called when need arises. They wish to live comfortable and easy life by selling their body, as the customers pay them sumptuously dependent on the sex attraction of the girl. Usually for these girls, prostitution is not the main but only secondary occupation. There are also "Call Girls" as they attend to the calls of the hotel proprietor, and satisfy the sexual needs of a customer. These girls are luxury loving and take to prostitution of their own accord only for the sake of earning good money and squandering it on luxury.

(v) Traditional Prostitutes: The prostitutes which were in the past and even at present are kept by the elite of the society as traditional prostitutes. These are required to entertain their masters on festive occasions, or when otherwise called to do so. They stay at the residence of the rich men and are always available; actually they are the paid servants of the rich men keeping them; and it is a contract. These people maintain them and also their children till they grow up. Generally, the erstwhile members of the royal families or landlords maintained a traditional group of prostitutes, who were destined to perform special services. They are called "*Kalavantins*; *Nityamaglis*; *Mangalmukhis*". Besides, some so-called religious "*ashramas*"; centres of *Pandas* and *Mahants* women devotees are exploited both by the *Sadhus* and the visitors (Social and Moral Hygiene Committee Report, p. 8).

(vi) Prostitutes belonging to Criminal Tribes and Backward Classes: Young girls are drawn from these classes and they are especially found in Northern India. Amongst these nomadic tribes prostitution is prevalent in terms of custom, and they prostitute their girl without any social disgrace.

(vii) Decentralised Prostitutes: As a result of the enforcement of Suppression of Immoral Traffic Act brothels are often liquidated. Consequently, prostitutes have been decentralised into the various parts of the cities where they independently carry out their profession.

(viii) Victims of Adverse Conditions: There are many women who are compelled to follow the profession of prostitution due to adverse social or economic conditions, such as:

(a) Poverty or unemployment — for the sake of earning a livelihood.

(b) Renounced young widows who are considered a burden to the family. In some cases the widows are forced to lead a life of chastity, which they find difficult, and ultimately falling a prey to seduction, adopt the profession of prostitution.

(c) Those who are recruited to the profession as a result of old maidenhood and enforced widowhood.

(d) Those ill-treated wives who lead a miserable life. When such young maidens leave the house they often fall a prey to anti-social element, and subsequently land themselves in the flesh trade.

(e) Unprotected or destitute young girls are often abducted by outsiders and exposed to lead an immoral life under all kinds of duress.

(f) Parents, guardians, including husbands force their girl relatives/wives to indulge in prostitution for the sake of supplementing their income.

(g) There are prostitutes who do not live in "*Kothas*" but do their business independently at home. These entertain customers and get money from them for selling body, often at the instance or connivance of their guardians. They do not openly pronounce themselves as prostitutes as their presence in the society or locality is resented because it is felt that they spoil the moral of the young girls of the locality.

(h) Those girls who take up to prostitution because of social or other compulsions — ill-treatment of stepmother/

father, poverty, lascivious behaviour of local landlords, money lenders, death of a husband leaving behind young widow with scant or no means of subsistence, ill-treated wives, abducted girls *etc.*, is yet another category of prostitution. In most of the such cases these women have no intention to take to prostitution but adopt the profession because of compelling circumstances.

8. Fashionable Prostitution

It is found that the society is replete with the following types of prostitutes.

(i) The Call Girls: The call girl is an independently operating prostitute, who lives a very comfortable life. She lives at a place of her usual residence from where she goes to her customers, or they visit her. They dress themselves in good tastes and try to maintain contacts with rich and influential people in different walks of life. These even collect secrets from them and pass on to their clients employing them for this mission. Because only few people can afford them on account of their high 'fees', they have very few sex contacts. They are even in a position to turn down a particular customer, who does not suit to their taste. Big cities are their field of operations.

(ii) Dance Hall Prostitutes: These are employed by dance hall owners, and they are in the age group of 15 to 45 years. Although they may not be very beautiful, they are fairly tolerable, and they dance with the males who come to dance after purchasing costly tickets, but their dancing period is of short duration. They operate in big cities. They are discos, cabaret and striptease dancers (Denuding).

(iii) Street Walker Prostitutes: They are the bottom ladder of prostitution and decent people object and resent very much to their peddling in the streets for soliciting customers at a very nominal fee. She is not attractive, and her only qualification is her womanhood. In simple word she is a "Whore".

(iv) Brothel Prostitutes: In many societies there are brothels which are visited by the customers. Whereas in many cases these are located in isolated places, in many other cases the houses of the prostitutes are the brothels. Some such houses are very elegant and cater to the affluent section of the society, educated youth, rich person who can afford to pay their fees. Their houses are always open to all types of persons.

(v) Fleabag Prostitutes: Their customers are skid row males and they are aging ones, unattractive and mostly alcoholic and suffer from venereal diseases. Their fees are very low and they leave the profession only after death.

(vi) Bar Prostitutes: They are not full time prostitutes but are interested in supplementing their income by prostitution. Many of them are already in some kind of a job but are forced to the flesh trade due to some financial stringency or emergency. They live at their usual place of residence but visit the bar when called upon to entertain the customers. This is also confined to towns.

(vii) Prostitution for Pleasure: School/college going girls taking to prostitution for the sake of pleasure and occasionally for money, is also not devoid of sex vice. This may also be called adolescent prostitution, the growth of which is an alarming feature in an affluent society.

9. Causes for Prostitution

Prostitution is not an isolated event. It is the gross product of several social, economic, psychological and pathological factors. The "Codes of Morality" have not been the same for all times. The institution of marriage, which is an authorised and sanctified form of alliance between the members of the opposite sexes, has with it rigid rules and cumbersome conventions resulting in invariably a section of the people being left out of wedlock or being induced to seek to pleasure of flesh illicitly. Hence, instances of extra or premarital alliance have become common features in the society. Due to internal causes like epidemics, and external causes like disastrous wars, populations have invariably left with unbalanced equation of sex thereby defeating the wholesome canon that one man should have one woman with religious and legal sanction. Male female ratio differs from community to community.

Besides the child marriages and marriages between parties with in-compatible characteristics, both of which lacking the cementing factors of love between the couples, and the unpopularity of widow marriages, as well as the present persisting costly marriages have been some of the foremost and patent social causes in addition to economic and sociological ones, directly or indirectly leading to the prevalence of individual immorality and subsequently of individual sexual promiscuity in many cases. And they are the victims of such vicious circumstances, who are allowed into, or desperately driven to the house of ill-fame — brothels, which are the centres of commercialised vice and traffic in women and young girls.

Further, there are various factors which have exerted to lower the position of women in the society. The double standard of morality requires a woman to be pure and chaste, but gives freedom to a man for his sexual indulgence for satisfaction. Consequently, the unmarried motherhood ruins a woman's life; while it has no effect on the man. The society has come to such a pass of needing a unified code of behaviour, and a common standard of morality, both for men and women, but it should exclude free sex. Taking the above factors into account the following causes leading to prostitution can be enumerated:

(i) *Poverty:* Economic factors and neighbourhood.

(ii) *Religious customs:* Dedicating damsels to temples.

(iii) *Social customs:* The dowry system, child marriage, prohibition of widow remarriage, the system of polygamy, the dual system of morality and caste system, the bride price compels women to enter into sex promiscuity.

(iv) *Social conditions:* Rapid industrialisation resulting in acute shortage of living and housing accommodations force the industrial workers, as also office goers, to leave their wives in the rural areas. Consequently, in all the industrial and commercial centres there is an inequality in sexes resulting in increase of prostitution and subsequent spread of venereal diseases, and also late marriages for want of accommodations.

(v) Abundance of pornographic literature and blue films.

(vi) Ill-treatment of women in the family, compelling them to abandon family shelter.

(vii) *Kidnapping:* Young girls and innocent women are often seduced by lovers, procurers, employers or co-workers. Sometimes they are seduced under the promise of marriage and employment or removal from service.

(viii) *Unemployment:* Non-availability of means of subsistence.

(ix) *Unhealthy company and recreation:* Drinking, gambling, dance halls, sexy films, bad company *etc.* leading to moral disintegration of women.

(x) *Home conditions:* Broken homes, immoral character of parents, lack of affection during childhood, marital conflicts and maladjustments may lead to prostitution.

(xi) *Physiological conditions:* Feeble mindedness, unsatisfied sexual desires, lack of control or restraint on sexual impulses creating rebellious attitudes towards social norms and eventually such persons often seek resort to prostitution.

(xii) Lewd behaviour of an employer who threatens his female employees to submit to illicit sex under pain of removal from service-Philander.

(xiii) *Biological:* Some women are biologically so developed that they have great sex urge which can be satisfied, according to them, through prostitution. Sexually weak or impotent husbands eventuate his wife into prostitution.

10. Suppression of Immoral Traffic in Women and Girls Act, 1956

This Act was enacted in pursuance of the International Convention where India signed at New York on 19th May 1956. The sections of the Act mentioned below, to some extent, help in controlling prostitution:

(i) Punishment for keeping a brothel.

(ii) Punishment for living on the earnings of prostitution. Where any person is proved to be living with the company of a prostitute or has control over the movements of a prostitute or acts as a tout on behalf of a prostitute is presumed to be knowingly living on the earnings of a prostitute.

(iii) Procuring a woman or a girl for the sake of prostitution.

(iv) Detaining a woman or a girl in a premises where prostitution is carried on.

(v) Prostitution in the vicinity of public places.

(vi) Seduction of a woman or girl in custody.

In all these offences the maximum punishment is rigorous imprisonment for two years and a fine of Rs 2,000. Notwithstanding these punishments, this Act could not do much to prevent this trade in flesh. The detection of these offences is extremely difficult as no customer would go to a prostitute after giving information to the police. The judiciary requires strict proof on each count of the offence charged. To detect a case a punter is to be sent with marked currency to a brothel/ prostitute, and only after the recovery of the marked currency, the penal provisions of the Act could be invoked. Moreover, a nearer compromising position is contemplated to prove the ingredients of prostitution. It has made all the more difficult to find a person who is willing to go for prostitution in order to help police. A Gazetted Officer of the Police Department is authorised by law to take action under the Act. This Act, like most other Acts, has merely remained in the statute books and no neutrality or decrease in the incidence of this type of crime could be secured by the law enforcement agencies, and even the "Protective Homes" intended to give shelter to the needy women or girls, could not affect a positive influence in curbing prostitution. "Protective Home" is a correctional institution.

11. Conclusion

Since Independence several measures have been taken by the Government to ensure that the prostitution system is abolished or regulated through the medium of law. The population of the "Red Light" areas has increased considerably. The law enforcement agencies could not impose the necessary deterrent on the promoters of the flesh trade for reasons of ineptitude, apathy or corruption, laxity resulted by pressures from some dominant personality. The laws have many lacunas and as such the punishment can be avoided even if a provision of the law is violated. Nothing has been done to change the psychology of the society so that it at least accepts back in its fold those girls, who unwillingly had to become prostitutes. The naked exploitation of women continues unabated. There has been considerable demoralisation of women. Problem of illegal children, perverted sex behaviour, venereal diseases, alcoholism, law and order, (criminals often take refuge in brothels) squandering of wealth, gambling, smuggling and allied anti-social acts have increased at a galloping speed, and yet pressure was being brought on the Government to allow sex education in scholastic institutions through a regular subject of sexology. Thanks to the prudence shown by the Government, who did not include sexology as a subject in the curriculum. As it is, the "Door-Darshan" with its lewd advertisements have already unnecessarily increased children's curiosity and knowledge about sex and they have come to know almost everything about sex at a very premature age and their young minds have already been polluted. The national wealth of children has already been adversely affected. There is no aspect of life in which prostitution constructively contributes. It is all evil and profane but is continuing because of the disintegration of social ethics, and the money and muscle powers of certain dominant males. It has become an appendage of the society, and a seedling of criminality; and unless social ethics are established to its former purity, their gigantic growth cannot be pruned. There are innumerable instances of "Flesh Scams' and these would be repeated in greater numbers in case the society fails to take it seriously, for the disorganisation of the society has already been in process since the last two decades.

28

Probation and Parole

1. An Appraisal

In 1951, the United Nations Economic and Social Council Organisation (UNESCO) recommended the adoption and extension of probation system by all the countries as a major instrument of policy in the field of prevention of crime, and the treatment of offenders. At that time the only piece of Central Legislation reflecting probation philosophy was Section 562 of the Code of Criminal Procedure which gave direction to a criminal court to release a person, who was convicted of an offence punishable with imprisonment for not more than seven years, on probation of good behaviour or conduct by entering into a bond with or without sureties. This Section also provided that anyone convicted of theft, dishonest misappropriation, cheating or any offence under the Indian Penal Code with up to two years of imprisonment could be released after due admonitions. This Central Legislation extended the scope of the probation technique, as recommended by UNESCO, by enacting the comprehensive Act of 1958, "The Probation Offenders Act".

A critical evaluation of some of the provisions of the Act may be made in the light of the problems which have had to be faced due to judicial pronouncement or otherwise. The courts have used discretion contemplated by Section 3 of the Act, "release after due admonition" quite liberally. Many cases of theft and cheating were really not petty in nature and had reflected dangerous criminal propensities in the offender when he was released with mere admonition on probation, instead sent to jail under a term of imprisonment. The probation scheme has been extended almost through all the districts in the country. Instead of diminution, a spurt in such type of offences has been quite obvious in the last three decades, and the law enforcing agencies, have increasingly found it difficult to prevent, much less detect them, with the consequence that the society has suffered doubly, in that the offender could not be reformed and retrieved to the society as a good citizen and his being at large had the contaminating effect on the morally weaker sections of the society. In several instances such an offender had become senior in the art of crime and the leader of a dangerous gang, which multiplied without any deterrence. Instances are not wanting when, by and large, petty offenders had turned into desperadoes posing unmitigated hazard and menace to the society, and it has become very problematic how to contain them, even with the use of the provisions of Terrorist and Anti-destructive Act (TADA).

2. Objects of Probation and Parole

Probation and parole emerged as techniques to mitigate the consequences of severe punishment when imprisonment became the more common mode of penal sanction in place of transportation and capital punishment. Probation came into existence to save some selected types of persons from the rigours of punishment, even if found guilty by a court of law. Parole developed due to a number of factors operating independently of each other. Before transportation as a mode of punishment came to an end, the Government of United Kingdom sent the convicts to America and Australia from England, and the job of transportation was assigned to the ship-master or some contractor. After 1717, the British Government gave the contractor or ship-master "Property in the service" of the prisoner until expiration of his term.

Subsequently, the contractor or the ship-master sold the services to the highest bidder on arrival in the colonies, and the criminal became the indentured servant under a contract. In the process the prisoner was released subject to certain conditions. This has some similarity with the parole practice as developed subsequently. Of the factors which contributed to the growth of the technique were the English and Irish experiences with the ticket of leave system and the work of the 19th century American reformists (Frederick A. Moran — "*The origin of parole*" '*National Probation Association year book, 1941*'). This was done with the co operation of friends or other persons, who voluntarily stood sureties for the persons who, would have otherwise been sent to prisons.

The concept of probation may now be understood so that it may be distinguished from certain analogous techniques like the parole. Thus, probation in common parlance, means "submission of an offender while at liberty to a specified period of supervision by a special officer designated by the court". Therefore, probation order is not a punishment or a conviction order.

3. Position Under Indian Law

When any person is found guilty of having committed an offence not punishable with death or imprisonment for life, and the court by which the person is found guilty is of opinion, that having regard to the circumstances of the case including the nature of the offence and the character of the offender, it is expedient to release him on probation of good conduct, then notwithstanding anything contained in any other law for the time being in force, the court may instead of sentencing him at once to any punishment, direct that he may be released on his entering into a bond, with or without sureties, to appear and receive sentence when called upon during such period, not exceeding three years, as the court may direct, and in the meantime to keep the peace and be of good behaviour. It is further provided that when an order under sub-Section (1) is made, the court may, if it is of opinion that in the interests of the offender and of the public it is expedient to do so, in addition pass a supervisory order directing that the offender should remain under the supervision of a probation officer named in the order during such period, not being less than one year, as may be specified therein and may in such an order impose such conditions as it deems necessary for due supervision of the offender. (Probation Offender Act, 1958 Section 4). The sole intention of the legislature in passing probation laws is to give persons of a particular type a chance of reformation, which they would not get if sent to prisons. This type of persons are not hardened or dangerous criminals, but those who have committed offences under some momentary weakness of character or some tempting situation. By placing the offender on probation the court saves him from the stigma of jail life, and also from the contaminating influence of hardened criminals and prison inmates. Probation also serves another purpose, though of secondary importance, in eliminating overcrowding in the jails by keeping many offenders away from jails, and yet, under observations in the probation programmes. There is subtle difference between probation and suspended sentence. In the latter case the sentence of imprisonment or fine is pronounced, but the execution of it is suspended for a period, whereas in the former case the probationer offender does not know the exact punishment which would be enforced.

4. Selection of Offenders

The most important consideration is to apprise the risk involved to the society in releasing the offenders; and whether the risk is worth-taking in the context of the offender personality, and the community at large. To some extent the job is done by the legislature by laying down that the probation shall not be granted in some serious offences which are punishable with death or life imprisonment. The legislature has also laid down some guiding principles in the terms of the age of the offenders below 21 years of age thereby making probation more desirable in cases of younger offenders. Subsequent follow up through competent supervision of the probationers, and paroles is absolutely necessary. The report of the Probation Officer is of primary importance as an aid to the court for making the decision regarding the release on Probation. An ideal report should give information regarding family history and personal, social and economic factors of the offender, and a plan for the correctional treatment of the offender if the recommendation is for the grant of probation. The Probation Officer has to evaluate the personality of the offender, whereas the court has to make decision after taking into consideration the Probation Officer's report and the nature and circumstances of the offence.

5. Judicial Attitude

Sometimes the courts, it seems, have not really applied their mind to the question as to whether the offender deserved probation on the merit of the case and decisions have been focussed more attention on some question of technical nature. For instance, in some cases the question which arose for consideration was whether the age of the offender for the purpose of Section 6 of the Act was to be considered with reference to the date of the commission of the offence, or the date when the offender is convicted. A pick-pocket, a knifer, a house-breaker, a robber and cheat, a bootlegger, black-marketeer, food adulterer *etc.* and an offender committing anti-social offences have been invariably given the benefit of their age, and in several cases, courts placed them under probation. Experience has shown that these leniently dealt with offenders had turned into hardened criminals and posed a menace to the society. It is not possible to go up in appeal to the High Court or the Supreme Court in each and every such decision of the lower court. In the few cases in which appeals have been preferred the following are the contrasting observations of the lower and superior courts.

In a case of theft of Rs. 56 by the accused Abdul Qayum from the pocket of a person the trial court had given him six months rigorous imprisonment, and the probation order was refused in spite of the fact that the probation officer had recommended it. The trial court had observed that incidents of pick-pocketing were rampant, and it was just a stray chance that the accused was caught in this case. The appeal and revision petition having been rejected by the Patna High Court, the appellant finally came to the Supreme Court, which upheld the appeal and directed the trial court to place him on probation. The extreme liberty shown by the Supreme Court is obvious. The association of the accused with a seasoned pick-pocket, continuous rise in the incidence of pick-pocketing, the intensive training required for committing such type of offences before the offender embarks on his criminal career and the fragile chances of the offender being detected while on the job and his arrest are generally not very bright; all have failed to convince the Apex Court to maintain the sentence of six months rigorous imprisonment awarded by the trial court. These pick-pockets, although caught for the first time, their *modus operandi* would make it clear that this was not the first time they were pick-pocketing, and always they acted in little gangs and had always posed a problem both to the society and the police. Naturally many of the incidents of pickpocketing are not at all reported, and those reported end as undetected, almost in 95 per cent cases (1972-1-SSC-103).

Another case decided by Orissa High Court *(Jogi Nayak* v. *State,* A.I.R. 1965 — ORI. 106) shows even much more latitude to young offenders. In this case an accused, a young boy of 15 years was found guilty or robbery U/S 394 I.P.C. and sentenced to undergo rigorous imprisonment of one year. The boy had removed the jewellery from the body of a young girl after making her unconscious by inflicting grievous injuries to her. The trial court held that probation could not be granted since the offence was punishable with life imprisonment. The High Court released the accused on probation in view of the tender age. Almost similar stories are repeated when the accused dangerously stabs — "a junior member acting merely under the influence of their senior member." It is argued that the object of the Act is to prevent the conversion of youthful offenders into obdurate criminals as a result of their association with hardened criminals of mature age in case the youthful offenders are sentenced to undergo imprisonment in jail.

These are sample instances of the Judicial view. Whether the object of imprisonment is to cause incapacitation of the offender to commit crime, or it is to effect reformation of the offender, in any case short of imprisonment, is not going to deliver the goods. As an ordinary rule of prudence it can be stated that the short-term imprisonments should always be avoided as far as possible either by employing probation in the most appropriate and worthiest cases or some other alternative, but separate arrangement should be made to incarcerate offenders of tender age, for long terms. It must also be seen, while deciding the question of probation, as to what will be the effect of the particular decision on the morale of law enforcement officers, other offenders or prisoners, and on correctional staff. Each decision is likely to have an impact on many other persons and hence this injurious dimension must not be ignored. To treat the offender of a tender age leniently would be to differentiate the application of law as between responsible and irresponsible persons in favour of the former. The law should take its normal course; and if not allowed to do so, the result will be that an exception would be made in favour of an offender, merely because he is of tender age, or certain extenuating circumstances warrant it, and that amount to gross failure of justice. Here is an instance for consideration. A respectable merchant with fairly important business of poppy seeds was caught in possession of about 14 *maunds* of illicit poppy seeds with the obvious intention of smuggling, and the Orissa High Court gave due consideration to his "respectability" by awarding him lenient punishments (A.I.R. 1967-Ori. 54). In the other case a peculiar fact situation was involved in a case decided by the Rajasthan High Court *(Anand* v. *State* — A.I.R. 1967 Raj. 190) where one Ahamed and his friend were convicted for stealing an idol from a temple. In sentencing them to imprisonment and refusing them the benefit of probation, the High Court referred to the "explosive situation which could have triggered off a chain of reaction producing results which would have been more lamentable and far-reaching. This case has no place for leniency or grant of probation". In both the cases the interest of the society had to be protected before considering the interest of the individual against this background, more because the interests of the society were enormously dangerous. The Rajasthan High Court has considered something more which raises the problem of greater significance and complexity involving religious and communal passions, with consequential eruption of communal disturbances on large scale causing loss of life and property. Such erratic decisions failed to apply policy consideration in a different and unusual context.

An extreme example of public policy being considered in deciding the question of probation or imprisonment can be understood from an English case where an elderly woman of small means pleaded guilty of charge of smuggling out of England Pounds 85 (Exchange Control Act, 1947) to give medical treatment to her dying son in Italy. Trial court released her on probation, but the Superior Court directed her imprisonment. This was the case where due emphasis was given on the enforcement problem of the Act regulating country's economy resulting in great harshness to the old lady who did not have any criminal propensities (1949-2 ALL ER-705).

The problem of public policy assumed greater significance in the context of socio-economic or "white-collar crimes" and the choice of punitive sanctions in preference to rehabilitative ideal is obvious. No chances can be taken by the society with a man whose anti-social operations, disguised as a respectable behaviour, imperil numerous innocents. Secondly, the economic offences committed by white-collar criminals are unlikely to be discarded by gentle probationary processes. Neither casual provocations, nor motive against particular persons, but planned profit-making from number of consumers, furnishes the incentives not easily humanised by the therapeutic probationary measures. Similar views are expressed by Justice Krishna Iyer of Supreme Court [SSC 167: 1974 — SSC (Cri) 87], Therefore, it is not without significance that the Law Commission of India in its 47th report has recommended the exclusion of the Act to social and economic offences by suitable amendments: "We appreciate that the suggested amendment would be in apparent conflict with the current trends in sentencing. But ultimately, the justification of all sentencing is the protection of the society. There are occasions when the offender is so anti-social that his immediate and sometimes prolonged confinement is the best assurance of society's protection. The consideration of rehabilitation has to give way because of the paramount need for the protection of the society."

29

Insurgency and Terrorism

1. What is Insurgency and Terrorism?

Insurgency and Terrorism are not the same either semantically or conceptually. Yet, in recent years, they have been mentioned and discussed in the same breath. This is basically because the line separating the two has blurred lately and not only most of the emergent groups in recent years have made systematic use of terror to achieve their goal, a majority of the terrorist outfits in the world today are insurgents, irrespective of their different dictionary meaning. Insurgency is "rise in revolt against authority" whereas "Terrorism" means use of terror as a strategy or tool to achieve certain objective. Another significant difference between the two is that while an act of insurgency is always against political authority, terror could be used as a strategy either by a political authority or against it. Terrorism entails the threat or use of symbolic violent acts aimed at influencing political behaviour. Political terrorism is thus, a "systematic use of murder and destruction and the threat of murder and destruction to terrorise individuals, groups, communities or governments into conceding to the terrorists' political aims." It is importantly crucial for terrorists that people accept their perspective, if not by reason, by terror. On 9th December 1985 the United Nations General Assembly unanimously adopted a resolution condemning all acts of terrorism as criminal. Terrorism frequently occurs where there are no non-violent political alternatives, and the contributory causes highlighting the multi-dimensional nature of the phenomenon of insurgence and terrorism may be summarised:

1. Ethnic or religious conflicts, conflicts, hatred discrimination and oppression.
2. Socio-economic relative deprivation.

3. Perceived political inequalities, infringement of rights injustice or oppression.
4. Lack of adequate channels of peaceful demonstrations for the communication of protests, demands, grievances *etc.*
5. Existence of a tradition of violence, dissatisfaction, and popular turbulence.
6. The availability of a revolutionary leadership equipped with a potentially attractive ideology.
7. Weakness and ineptness of the government, police and judiciary.
8. Erosion of confidence in the regime, its values and initiations affecting all levels of population including the Government.
9. Deep division among governing elites and leadership groups.

It would be wrong to conceive that insurgency and terrorism are bereft of ideology. It is not always due to political reasons that terrorism gets a boost. Administrative failure, or the failure of governance also at times provides insurgents, and terrorist movement not only to set up their crusade but also to give it a rationale that helps them broaden their support base. Inept and inconsistent handling of insurgency and terrorism many a times resulted in escalation of such activities, but in a sudden flare up. It is sometimes weakness, and ineptness of the political leadership, and on the other occasions under/over reaction of such administrative agencies as police and security forces.

2. Post-Independence Scenario

The history of insurgency and terrorism in India dates back to the pre-Independence days, insurgency has a longer history than terrorism and the latter erupted and sprouted in modern times and the basic ideological force of nationalism is conspicuously missing. In spite of the fact that the nationalist movement in India led by Mahatma Gandhi, was largely peaceful and non-violent, political scenario since Independence has been dogged persistently by violent upheavals, the country not only had to face the challenge of insurgency in the North-East, it also had to tackle the use of political terror from the very beginning.

However, the advent of terrorism in the more prevalent sense of the term is identified with aggravation of the Punjab problems and rise of "Khalistan" terrorism in the 1965.

The communist-led violence in the Telangana region of Andhra Pradesh in the late 40s and early 50s, and subsequent Naxalite movement in the late 60s also employed political terror as a tool. The People's War Group operating in Andhra Pradesh has also employed similar tactics. Claiming to be fighting for the rights of the have-nots, and the downtrodden, the Marxist (or Communist) "revolutionaries" use terror as a crucial act, and at times, potent weapon against the rich and the landlords. These insurgencies and terrorism of North-East, Punjab and the Kashmir valley have assumed dangerous proportion, and threatened the very integration of the political unity of India.

3. Insurgency in the North-East

It is not possible to understand the insurgency of this region unless one learns its topography and geography. North-East is not a homogeneous region, 2.55 lakhs of square kms of this region constituting 7.7 per cent of the country's total land are divided into seven states (Arunachal Pradesh, Manipur, Assam, Tripura, Meghalaya, Nagaland and Mizoram), and contains as per the 1991 census about 4 lakhs people representing about 5 per cent of the country's total population.

The Scheduled Tribes (ST) population form about 23 per cent of the population in the region compared to about 9 per cent for all India. The ST population form a majority only in four states — Meghalaya (82 per cent), Nagaland (85 per cent), Arunachal Pradesh (71 per cent) and Mizoram (95 per cent). It is in a minority in Assam (about 12 per cent), Manipur (29 per cent) and Tripura (30 per cent). The region is reported to have 209 Scheduled Tribes. This low-density region has uneven density population. The average of 104 persons per square km. has as low as 8 persons in Arunachal Pradesh. Apart from the ethnic and religious diversity, there is an amazing multiplicity of languages, dialects used in the region. They number 420 out of a total of 1632 in the whole country, while the non-tribal population in the region resembles Indian social stratification, the tribal societies are, by and large, egalitarian, despite a degree of ranking. The tribal societies have sustained themselves in hostile surroundings with the self-help, self-reliance and community spirit. This spirit had not faded away.

The college, and indeed roots of insurgency in this region is as varied as its socio-cultural-spectrum. Nationalist Socialist Council of Nagaland (NSCN), Tribal National Volunteers (TNV), Peoples Liberation Army (PLA), Mizo National Front (MNF), Peoples Revolutionary Party of Kangleipk (PRPAK), Kangleipk Communist Party (KCP), United Liberation Front of Assam (ULFA) are some of the familiar names with insurgency in this region. One of the interesting aspects of insurgency in this region is that over four decades since the Independence of India have seen emergence and fading away of a number of insurgent groups. In fact, fading out of groups have given birth to newer groups. The two familiar explanations "foreign hand" and "under development" though not entirely without substance, appear only to be contributory, and not the main factor on closer scrutiny. "Foreign hand" appeared only to take advantage of the existing rebellious and insurgent situation, and "under developed" was used by the insurgent to elicit popular support. The roots of insurgency in this region, which began with Nagaland and later spread to other areas of the region are infact partly political and mostly economical, socio-cultural — a combination of the two. The British administration, which annexed and merged autonomous societies of the Nagas, Mizos and other North-Eastern Tribals with the Indian Raj followed the policy of least possible interference. But while in political sphere their interference was minimal, they introduced changes in the social sphere, and it was the missionary, not the administrator, who was the main harbinger of the change.

Aside from the fact that soon after Independence, Nagas under Phizo raised the banner of rebellion against the Indian Union and gave impetus to insurgency by forming a parallel government; the simmering insurgency in the region, in fact is gradual and steady spread across the whole of the North-East regions for over four decades since the Independence, has been attributed to political, administrative and strategic mismanagement arising out of misunderstanding on both sides towards each other — Government and the people. Regarding the Naga insurgency the government of India took political initiative in 1947 on its own to reach a nine-point agreement with the Naga leader, Phizo to check his demand for secession. The agreement envisaged that the existing arrangement would continue for ten years, after which the Nagas would be asked whether they wished the agreement to be extended for a further period or a new agreement drawn up regarding their future. As their agreement was not specific to indicate the independence of the Nagas beyond ten years, the Nagas interpreted it to mean that they could be independent after that period. In consequence the Nagas boycotted the first General Election in 1951 and gave an overwhelming 99 per cent mandate in favour of the independence and separation from India. This elicited strong armed response by the Government of India. The affairs of this region were soft-pedaled and have been badly handled by the political operators and bureaucrats making insurgency and terrorism an endemic problem for the region.

Political mismanagement and bureaucratic insensitiveness have together aggravated local discontent into armed insurgency into Mizos, the Meities and the Assamese (ULFA) causing manifold casualties in later years, the main cause being the disregard shown by the administrators to the continuation of Autonomous Council and District Council which were the supra-tribal centres in the process of articulation within a national society. The ethnic mosaic in the region has usually led to socio-economic grievances being politically viewed, and find violent expressions in acts of insurgency and terrorism with the feeling that the political regime in New Delhi is unsympathetic with them. Equally important contributory factors are the equations of land and forest rights and changes in the agrarian relations. There is a hiatus between the perception of the tribal committees and those of the various organs of state regarding the rights of the tribal people in the land and forests. The agrarian economy of this region has to a marked degree come under the control of the dominant market mechanism monopolised by the non-tribal merchants and traders from outside the region. This has aggravated exploitation and resulted in inequity. Violence has been the natural reaction.

Some of the recent violent movements in the region, with or without insurgency as their objective and terror as their tool, have their political wrangles and mismanagement of leaders at the Centre and in the States. The Bodoland movement and activities of United Liberation Front of Assam (ULFA) are two examples. The Bodoland movement which owned its origin both to the mismanagement by the leaders in Assam, and political brinkmanship of the leaders of the Centre to keep the Assam Gana Parishad (AGP) Government on the tenterhooks, has been violent at times, but it has neither been an insurgent nor a terrorist movement. The ULFA is a highly organised insurgent outfit and has used terror effectively to extract money from businessmen, traders, tea companies and even well to do professionals to keep its military and civil wings running successfully. Even though local ruffians have used ULFA, it has been successful in preparing a sympathetic base for itself among local population in upper Assam and far in the Brahmaputra valley.

Insurgency in this region is linked to the question of ethnic identity that has found expression in the demand for political autonomy subsequently leading to independence due to insensitive approach of the ruling elites at the Centre, and the States. Further the process of their integration in the national mainstream has released forces that have led to not only economic exploitation of the people of the area, but have also resulted in altering social economy of the region. The inhospitable terrain has aided insurgency strategically claiming lives of hundreds of police and para-military and Army personnel. The presence of hostile neighbours will sustain it for a long period in future also.

4. Terrorism in Punjab

It is to be borne in mind for understanding contemporary terrorism in Punjab the lead given by Punjab in extremism, more or less insurgency during the Indian National Movement. It is obvious that its soil contains seeds of extremism. This does not make terrorist politics during the national movement comparable with terrorism in the State today. The pre-Independence extremism was against the alien rule, whereas the current insurgency and terrorism are against the constitutionally established Government of India. Not only the context, the nature of terrorist politics, but also the scale of operation of the terrorists have changed.

The roots of terrorism in Punjab have been a curious mixture of factors — political, economic, social, religious and above all external interference by Pakistan — the most hostile country. The texts of the Punjab problem trace its origin when some Sikhs made representation to Cripps Mission before the Independence for an independent state of Sikhs. Then the demand was, however, dropped as the politics of accommodation followed by the Indian National Congress was able to convince the Akali Dal, the Sikh theocratic party advocating a separate Sikh State, to join the nation-building process along with it. But its inability to secure power in competitive electoral politics since Independence resulted in the demand for Punjabi Subha, a Sikh majority state within the Indian Union. But when even after the division of the State in 1966 into Punjab and Haryana (Hindi speaking) it would not guarantee power to itself, Akali Dal increasingly appealed to the Sikh Religious sentiments and highlighted Punjabi and in that process it kept stiffening its stand and acquiring more and more militant posture and started magnifying grievances. Anandpur Sahib resolution of the Akali Dal gives ample proof of confusion existing in Akali thinking regarding their political grievances, and all grievances were not powerful enough to attract more and more people to it. In the process from greater autonomy for Punjab within the Indian Constitutional framework the demand has now moved to creation of Khalistan, a Sikh theocratic State.

In the race for political power in Punjab, the Akali Dal was constrained to its ideology to appeal to a particular section of the society — Sikhs and articulate their grievances in a particular manner. It had inherent limitation in finding universal acceptance even within the State and the Dal leadership seemed clearly aware of this. Its aggressive posture on issues relating to Punjab and its political strategies since Independence clearly reflected this awareness. But the strategies resulting from this awareness even after having the Punjab divided into Punjabi speaking state (Punjab) and Hindi speaking state (Haryana) following an intense agitation for Punjabi Subha, led the Dal and the State into a political maze where it has got deeply caught into the politics of terrorism.

But Akali Dal's sectarian and negative politics is not the only factor responsible for the vice and spread of terrorism in Punjab. The counter-politics of the Congress to checkmate the Akali Dal in the race of power has greatly contributed to the present mess. One of the strategies adopted by the Congress was to win over influential Akali Dal leaders whenever the Akali seemed to be growing in influence. Some stalwart Akalis joined the Congress in 1948 and 1956. They may or may not have accepted Congress ideology, but they certainly carried their outlook with them, they even functioned as separate group. Their flirtations with the Shiromani Prabandhak Committee (SPC) elections created a sense of threat among the Akalis, which also played a role in their rising militancy.

The Congress always took advantage of the factionalism in the Akali ranks, which militants have used this as one of the grievances. Further the policy of destabilising the non-Congress governments pursued by the Congress since 1967 gave the Akalis, who thrice formed the Government in the State, a pretext to express their alienation from the national mainstream. However, the real abetment to extremist politics in Punjab was given by the Congress during the Emergency year of 1975-76, when the Congress Government in the State courted the communal elements among the Sikhs, during the Janata Party Rule. When the Congress leaders in the State worked hard to destabilise the Akali-Janata Government in Punjab, and after its come back in 1980, when the Home Minister-Chief Minister row gave tremendous boost to militants. Sant Jarnail Singh Bhindranwale was allowed to become a powerful leader in the 80s and dictated term in Punjab politics with his armed followers killing anyone at will till he was killed during the operation Blue Star, was a creation of this type of politics during this period. Even after Bhindranwale organised his killer gangs, and made the Golden Temple in Amritsar, one of the holiest Sikh shrines, as his operational headquarters, time and again a 'Nelson's eye' was turned towards him and his activities — the monster was deliberately allowed to grow in power and strength. Thus the operation Blue Star became a painful necessity, but instead of solving the problem it complicated it further. Nor did it hurt the Sikh religious psyche, it also resulted in such painful incidents as assassination of Indira Gandhi — the Prime Minister by her own Sikh guard with consequential anti-Sikh riots all over the country and gave Sikh terrorism a further boost.

The non-implementation of the Rajiv-Longowal accord and consequent failure and dismissal of the Barnala government gave the terrorist, further pretext to muster support on the ground that the Central Government was not serious about the grievances of the Sikhs and Punjab problem has been of familiar confusion and purposelessness aiding and abetting the cause of terrorism further. Thus, the problem of terrorism in Punjab is basically political that has condemnably thwarted its flourishing economic advance.

5. Strategies

Strategies of the terrorists and counter strategies adopted by the Government and its agencies to tackle terrorism in Punjab have been succinctly given below: Politics of terrorism in Punjab developed its roots during the latter part of 70s, but its shadow started looming over the State only in the 80s. Till 1982, terrorists struck at select targets, which included members of the police and administration, media persons writing against them, members of other sects — non-Sikhs, prominent Sikhs chiding and criticising them for their brutal ways and anti-social activities, prominent members of other political parties and so on. To finance their gangs they looted banks. Arms were either supplied to them by hostile country like Pakistan or purchased by them from any available source. Except for the firing on Nirankari procession, which in fact proved to be the politics of gun, they did not indulge in man-killing till in the first half of 1983. Massacre of bus passengers, chosen selectively by their faith in September 1983, was the first of their acts to spread mass terror. After that there was no end to the commission of such dastardly acts, most of them were seemingly indiscriminate acts, but they were calculated acts committed for a particular strategic purpose. Their targets were not restricted to Punjab alone, the terrorists came as far as Delhi, struck at will and returned safely in the panic that followed. And once Bhindranwale and his cult got firmly entrenched within the Golden Temple Complex, the killing at his bidding became a legendary act. It was for example, widely reported that devout Sikhs coming to pay obeisance to the '*Sant*' were asked to pick up a slip from a container which carried the name and address of the person. They were ordered to kill that person. Those refusing to comply with were given a plain slip to write their name and address and put in the container, to be eliminated shortly, Bhindranwale's extermination during the operation Blue Star in June 1984 put an end to this practice, but terrorism continued unabated in Punjab. Bhindranwale could have a great sentimental appeal on the Sikh masses over religious issues as they reverred him as "*Sant*" — "*Guru*". The assassination of General A.D. Vaidya after his retirement in Pune (Chief of Army Staff at the time of the Blue Star) definitely showed the reach of the terrorists and the impunity with which they could strike.

The response of State is most important in containing the cancerous growth of terrorism. Very recently a firm approach has at least been able to limit it to a level it can be tackled by the law and order machinery. The case of Punjab terrorism required even more tactful handling for three reasons: (1) a dangerous mix of religion and politics, (2) demand for separation from the Union of India, and (3) bordering State to the hostile neighbour of Pakistan, who helped the terrorists in all possible ways, and incited them to commit more gruesome actions.

On the contrary, people running the affairs of State in India chose to ride the tiger of terrorism for political expediency, realising fully well that the tiger may turn into a Frankenstenian blood hungry monster. There were several occasions when the rise of Bhindranwale could have been effectively checked and completely curbed down, but he was let off the hook on political interference. Similarly, there were several occasions since 1970s to hammer out a political settlement of the issue, on each occasion political considerations prevented a settlement. Likewise, partisan considerations always came in the way of evolving a national consensus on the real or perceived grievances of Punjab.

It must be pointed out here that neither the Police nor the security forces can bring about a solution to the problem of terrorism. Their efficient handling of the problem can merely thwart the terrorists campaign, and give the impression of firmness, with which the State proposes to tackle the law and order aspect of it. But this can only be a temporary deterrent, and only if effectively used. Too much use of political considerations, may not defuse the explosive of insurgent terrorism.

The Government of India has floundered in Punjab on both counts — political and administrative. Instead of quickly, efficiently and effectively dousing the fire of insurgent terrorism with a well thought out political initiative based on national consensus, politics was used to keep fire simmering, rather ablaze. Political considerations thwarted effective administrative measures as well. All these cumulatively encouraged the hostile neighbour Pakistan to wage a proxy war against India through the medium of insurgent terrorism. If parochial and as well partisan considerations are kept in the background, local administration, both civil and police is best suited to tackle the problem, and they may succeed in preventing future murders of innocent persons. Already several thousands of innocent persons have been killed by them.

6. Terrorism in Jammu and Kashmir

Kashmir valley was once a paradise. The issue of insurgency and terrorism in the Kashmir valley is different from both, the North-East and Punjab. There is the common factor of foreign land, which in the case of Punjab and Kashmir is one country — Pakistan, but that is where the similarity ends. The problem in Kashmir goes back to the portion of the sub-continent following decolonisation in 1947. The Maharaja Harisingh of Jammu and Kashmir, a Hindu (Dogra) king ruling an overwhelming Muslim population, took his time to decide accession to India or Pakistan. Taking advantage of this indecision, Pakistan laid its claim on the State on the ground of its demographic composition, and sent in tribal raiders, who almost reached Srinagar. It is then the Maharaja hastily decided to accede to India, and the Indian Army was flown and it pushed back the raiders and saved Srinagar.

The local population led by Sheikh Abdullah and Volunteers of his Muslim Conference, later re-christened National Conference, helped the Indian Army. However, the issue in the meantime was taken to the United Nations Organisation, and a cease fire was imposed leaving a large area under Pakistan occupation. This virtual division between India and Pakistan made Kashmir into a disputed territory and resulted in divided loyalties in the Valley — Muslims are pro-Pakistan whereas Hindus are pro-India. The political and administrative circles of both the countries believe that unless a firm grip is kept on the Valley it will slip out of hand. On the other hand, it gave foreign power a substantive presence in Kashmir as both India and Pakistan had applied their diplomacy, and used their foreign policy to acquire the area under each other's control. They in fact, fought three wars since 1948, Kashmir being a major question in each.

But the root of insurgency, terror and current political crisis in the Kashmir valley is as much in Punjab's policy of subversion as in Indian policy in Kashmir since the Independence. The Indian attitude to Kashmir and Kashmiris have fluctuated between overindulgence, rather appeasement, to suspicion. It is equally true that Kashmiris have also had ambivalent attitude towards India, the help of the population on this side of the Line of Actual Control (LAC) to Indian troops in 1948, 1965 and 1971 Indo-Pak wars notwithstanding. It has varied from re-affirmations of accession to India, to a quiet acceptance of the Indian presence to "we have acceded to India but —" attitude to hostility towards Indian Colonialism, to rebellion. The ambivalence on both sides, and failure of the Indian elite to develop cementing bond before integrative process could begin, has led to the mess that Kashmir is now.

Each of the leaders since the Independence, including Pandit Jawaharlal Nehru, followed a policy of appeasement on one hand, and in order to hasten the integrative process attempted to bring Kashmir closer to New Delhi, on the other. It led to the undermining of local political processes. So, Bakshi Ghulam Mohammed was propped up against a Sheikh Abdullah in the 50s. And even when the Sheikh was finally reinstated by Indira Gandhi two decades later after protracted negotiations, she did not take long to dismiss the Government led by Sheikh's son Farooq, when he began hobnobbing with the opposition for a place for himself in the national politics. It mattered little whether Farooq Abdullah had much greater credibility than his brother-in-law G.M. Shah, who was propped up against him. Farooq Abdullah was not allowed to return to the Chair of Prime Minister (for Jammu and Kashmir alone the Chief Minister of a State is designated as Prime Minister), till he rubbed his heels before Rajiv Gandhi, the third generation of the Nehru family. And, that too in a coalition with Congress (I) — Indira Congress. The loss of creditability it caused under the volatile circumstance to both the coalition partners did not matter to those enacting this political drama between the families of Pandit Nehru, and Sheikh Abdullah, as if the rest of the population of Jammu and Kashmir were inanimate beings.

Mufti Mohammed Syeed, the then Home Minister during the Janata Dal rule in 1989 was himself in the Kashmir politics for long and served as Minister in more than one government, never realised that most of the Muslim population of the Kashmir valley was hostile, either overtly or cohortly, to the Government of India and at any time they are capable to escalate insurgency and terrorism in the Kashmir valley. When the Kashmir valley exploded in December 1989 following the abduction of Rubia, daughter of Home Minister Mufti Mohammed Syeed, it created shock waves for the whole nation. But this explosion was not sudden. It was not an eruption of a sleeping volcano — surcharged hostility with Indian Government, and in fact, it was quivering to erupt for some time and with sufficient force to suggest that the governmental handling of the Kashmir problem was faulty, lock, stock and barrel. Mufti Rubia was released from captivity by the militants only after securing the freedom of their dreaded colleagues from Indian prison. The same strategy was adopted by the militants several times after abducting, kidnapping high-level government servants and foreign tourists. Each time the Government of India knelt before militants and negatived anti-terrorist movement. The charges and counter charges of political parties were mere cover up, and meant to direct popular attention from the real issues.

Kashmir does not merely face terrorism. It is facing an urban guerrilla warfare. Support for the insurgents, both active and tacit, in the local population is substantial, and on the point of overwhelming. And those in the local population, who were sitting on the fence, were silenced by the might of the gun. Cinema halls showing Indian films were closed, even hoisting of the Indian National Flag was not permitted by the insurgents who almost led the administrative machinery to act according to their dictates. There was no question of defiance as the penalty was fatal. This made the task of the police and security personnel so much difficult. The intelligence, the backbone of counter insurgency operations, were rendered ineffective so much so, that some officers of the Intelligence Bureau, supposedly working under cover, were murdered with ease. This showed that the intelligence network of terrorists was far more organised and effective than that of Kashmir Government or of the Government of India. As a result, not only the security personnel were unable to differentiate between terrorists, collaborators, sympathisers, fence-sitters and so on, and they were compelled to use indiscriminate force, opening themselves to the charges of State terrorism and having drawn the attention of the world body on Human Rights.

Pakistan is virtually fighting a proxy war with India with the ulterior object to conquer and permanently annex to the territory of Pakistan the forcefully occupied portions of the Kashmir valley. The use of religion as a weapon, abundantly supported by the terrorist infiltration, in the Indian portion of Kashmir valley is being used to achieve its goal, which is not only meant to conquer a territory, but also to vindicate her position on the partition in general and Kashmir in particular. To enable Pakistan to secure this goal ISI — the Pakistani Intelligence Service has been specially established. Its work is to provide sophisticated arms and ammunition to Pakistani-trained insurgents, infiltrate them into the Indian territory, commit atrocities like murder, rape, loot and arson, mostly on the Hindu population, and create disturbed conditions and such terror-stricken atmosphere that Hindus should leave their abodes, or in default suffer death or disgrace. About three lakhs of Kashmiri Hindus have already left their hearth, land and fled to take refuge outside Kashmir. The Government of Kashmir or the Government of India could do precious little to protect and salvage the Kashmiris.

7. The Role of Security Forces

Even though India has a long experience of over 40 years of fighting insurgency, terrorism, the Government of India and its agencies do not seem to have worked out a policy or strategy to deal with the twin menace. Politically the record of the Indian State is mixed. Some insurgent group has been successfully assimilated in the national mainstream, the persistence of some old as well as sprouting of new extremist movements indicate both partisan politics and a lack of political will on the part of the ruling elite. The confusion at the political level is reflected at the administrative level too. The law and order machinery which is the first governmental agency to come face to face with the menace both as targets and agents of law has generally responded without a clear-cut policy. The resulting confusion is of two kinds. First, violence purported by insurgents/terrorists recognises no limits of law and has a large target. As a result, they can and do hit with relative impunity. The police, despite the notorious image earned during the years, are constrained by law. Though they do transgress limits of law time and again, it adds further to their insularity, ambivalence and incompetence. Moreover, they have been rendered helpless due to a lack of training and proper equipment.

The police and the security forces fight against insurgency and terrorism with the following relative disadvantages:

1. Insurgency and terrorism are a war against State, the police are not trained to tackle a war.
2. Insurgents and terrorists have sophisticated arms and proper training, whereas police do not possess that gun power.
3. Police do not have training in counter guerrilla tactics like insurgents and terrorists.
4. Police do not have public sympathy hence their intelligence machinery is greatly impaired.
5. Oft-and-on political interference hampers the role of security agencies.

6. Police and security forces cannot transgress the parameter of law when dealing with the insurgents and terrorists, who have no such qualms.

The pressure mounted by security forces has many times contained the growth of insurgency and terrorism, but the specific absence of full political backing to the police have repeatedly revived insurgent terrorist activities. Another area of counter-terrorist strategy with high degree of political interference is the hostage menace. Militants rely heavily on taking VIPs as hostages to force political regime to concede their demands particularly to secure the release of their colleagues, who are arrested by the police with great difficulty, in many cases with the martyrdom of their colleagues. The exchange or conceding their demands is entirely in the hands of the Government. Not invariably political decisions compromise the strategic considerations. The damage to the morale of the police following continuous hostage swapping certainly affected and that too adversely counter-insurgency operations. The choice regarding the force to be used to counter-terrorism is also a political decision, and the deployment of police, para-military forces or the Army is taken accordingly; and lamentably, all the three have been used in different contexts, in different situations and in different degrees. The degree of success achieved has also not been uniform. None seem to have absolute success under all circumstances. Insurgency is a mini-war and combating political terrorism presents a dilemma. The degree of fire power available with the insurgents has rendered the police ill-equipped and para-military agencies like the Border Security Force, and the Central Reserve Police Force. With intelligence branch in shamble, the security forces, including the police often face problems. Co-ordination between various intelligence agencies is conspicuously lacking, and the terrorists having superior intelligence organ have always had an upper hand, more because, the topography of their operational regions is better known to them than the security forces.

Militants also keep pressure on the police and the security forces by changing their targets and venue. By increasing their geographical sphere of activity the militants have succeeded in straining the resources of the security agencies. They also move from one area to another across state border full of dense forests and deserts if under sustained pressure. This cannot be checked even police have beefed up their intelligence network at the local level, and act before the militants consolidate. The task is as stupendous as hazardous, and lamentably police is the singular agency to combat terrorism and insurgency with all the odds against them.

A clear strategy that the militants not infrequently apply is to force the police or security forces to overreact. The degree of force used by the law and order machinery in a democratic society is always under close scrutiny. Violation of civil rights, even in respect of a terrorist, who has committed hundreds of murder, rape and arson, becomes not only a national but an international issue. No one takes into consideration the good intentions of the police or the security forces, and they are left all alone, and equally helpless in their battle against terrorists, as if they do so far their own domestic reasons. Even the media has denounced them. Pakistan as well as international lobbies of militants have successfully brought India under cloud internationally. In such an eventuality, the police and the security forces have been renounced by everyone, including their own employer — the Government and the delinquents among them have been left all alone, unprotected to face the penalty that may ensue. The overall result is that the police and the security agencies have become apathetic and lethargic for their dreaded and hazardous combat against insurgency and terrorism, the outlook of their assignment has no more remained national, and they work only as mercenaries. Without political support, and the dominant will of the Government to ruthlessly root out terrorism and insurgency from the Indian soil, the police and security personnel are incapable to combat this twin menace. The partisan and discriminative attitude of the Amnesty International towards India has enthused militants to carry on with their nefarious activities. Already thousands of innocent persons have been killed, an equal number of women molested and there is no estimation of the loss of property due to plunder and arson. How much such a situation should be allowed to continue would depend on the will of the public, and their elected Government!

30
Drug Abuse

1. Drugs-crime Relationship

Consumption of drugs apart from medical needs or in unnecessary quantities is defined as drug abuse. In its broadest sense it refers to the use, usually by self-administration of any drug in a manner that deviates from approved medical and social patterns within a given culture. Society, as also the law, is mostly primarily concerned with the psychotropic or mind affecting drug or the drugs that alter mood and affect human behaviour, thinking and emotion. Drugs that produce pleasure, relieve pain, and anxiety, induce sleep or combat fatigue also profoundly affect the human mind, conduct and behaviour, reduce moral restriction or inhibitions, increase in capacity for violence, and induce defiance of legal, moral and social behaviour. Drugs that affect the central nervous system remove the sense of shame that veils out anti-social propensities, and for some people abstain from forbidden action because they are ashamed or afraid of sinning them because their inclinations are good. Even those that have a predisposition to crime are nervous and hence often have to fortify their nerves, before embarking on forbidden acts, with the help of drugs that remove the inhibitory influence of the cerebral cortex and trigger the release of coarser and primitive influences and desires. Drugs like alcohol or LSD induce feelings of omnipotence and invulnerability in their takers; established moral barriers often crumble under the effect of these drugs, and religious teachings, and marital obligations assume lesser significance under their influence. The individual assumes a fight back and becomes an "old savage in new civilisation". All these are often wrongly, though conveniently interpreted as an increase in one's self-confidence or stimulation of one's libido by the drugs. Drugs and crimes are thus inextricably inter-linked inasmuch as that:

1. Crimes are often planned and committed under the influence of drugs.
2. Drugs embolden criminals in the preparation of crime, help removal of inhibitions and thus rationalise the commission of crimes.
3. Continued use or indulgence of drugs promote crimes, by permanently changing human nature and behaviour more so during the phase of withdrawal or intoxication or by producing insanity or moral degeneration in their users.
4. Compulsive dependence on a drug over a long period runs a person economically, physically and mentally leading to loss of employment, and dependence upon offences like thefts, forgery, falsification and embezzlement of funds, gambling *etc.*, in order to find money to buy drugs.
5. Driving offences.
6. Industrial accidents, of which an estimated 50 per cent occur under the influence of drugs.
7. Offences relating to trafficking or trading in drugs.

An enormous and ever-growing need for the addicting drugs aided indirectly by the various international and control measures, has given rise to a vast underground trade, a huge black-market, and an underworld of drug traffickers, to keep up the growing pace of supplying the clandestine requirement of millions of drug abusers spread all over the world.

Illicit trading in drugs not only involves purchasing a quantity of the pure drugs and processing of raw materials by specialists in the trade to get the finish products but also careful packing and transport of the products through trade routes spread over thousands of miles, and finally also establishing close contact with the underworld peddlers and other shady elements for selling them to individual customers or the abusers. It is a billion dollar business — a most perfect form of organised crime that involves not only the poppy opium cultivators or producers or the manufacturers of the drugs, but also the traders, transporters, whole-sellers, retailers, and more often than not is managed, and run by hardened criminals, well-acquainted with the dark and slippery ways of the underworld. From a criminologist point of view, trading in narcotic and drugs is a highly specialised form of crime in which there are no complaints, or the aggrieved party and the victims are mere accomplices to the criminals — the suppliers or the traffickers in the drugs. It is one of the most elusive form of crime, but gives very little scope to any scientific police investigation, and leaves very few clues, if any, to be gathered from the scene of the crime.

2. Drugs Abuse

The problem of drug abuse is as old as the civilisation itself. As far back as recorded history every society has possessed drugs and could bring about profound alterations of moral and feelings and also individuals who deviated or digressed from the established social norms with respect to time, amount and situation in which these drugs were consumed. The drugs that are commonly abused over the world are:

1. Alcohol.
2. Narcotics such as opium and its natural and synthetic derivatives like morphine, heroin and pethidine.
3. Stimulus such as the Amphetamine, Methamphet-amine and Dexamphetamine *etc.*
4. Coco-leaves and cocaine and its various by-products.
5. Canabis derivatives and products like *bhang, ganja, hashis, charas, majum, Thandai etc.*
6. Hypnotics and tranquillisers like the barbiturates and sleeping pills, mandrex, diazepam, and neprobarate, *etc.*
7. Hallucinogens, *i.e.,* LSD poyote each, pailocybin mushrooms, and some morning glory seeds.
8. Miscellaneous—the volatile inhalants like acetone, benzene glue sniffing, and the anaesthetics like other nitrous oxide *etc.*

3. Adverse Effects of the Drugs

Adverse effects of the drugs, whether on individual or the society are far-reaching and manifold inasmuch as their abuse or misuse in one form or the other may lead to —

(i) *Aggression* — Violence and crimes such as homicide and rape mostly occur with the abuse of alcohol, L.S.D. and the amphetamines.

(ii) *Amotivation* — mental degeneration and intellectual impairment leading to loss of initiative and drive as with cannabis and the opioids. These abusers swell the ranks of school dropouts and the jobless.

(iii) Loss of speed, skill and accuracy leading to accidents on the highways and in flights and industries. Driving the automobiles under the influence of alcohol and drunkenness in the pedestrians are believed to be responsible for over 50 per cent of all accidental deaths on the highways.

(iv) Absenteeism in duties and sluggishness at work leading to reduction in industrial production from loss of man-hours and days.

(v) Mental depression and confusion leading to suicide as with alcohol, barbiturates and the amphetamines. Suicides occur particularly during the abstinence or withdrawal phase of a drug, when the supply of the drug is drastically reduced.

(vi) Moral degradation leading to sexual perversion and experimentation with sex and homosexuality or impotency in a male as with alcohol, cocaine, opium and the barbiturates. It should be remembered that drugs including alcohol never act as aphrodisiac and the feeling of increased libido or sexual power if any in the taker is false. In fact-prolonged consumption of a drug like alcohol or opium may result only in loss of libido and impairment of sexual power leading ultimately to impotency. To put in the celebrated words of Shakespeare, on the effect of alcohol over sexual power, "it provokes the desire but takes away the performance."

(vii) Belligerence and quarrelsomeness leading to public nuisance including traffic violations and offensive behaviour, damage to property and indecent assault, or misconduct towards a member of the opposite sex.

(viii) Insanities such as mania, paranoia, hallucinations and delusions as with alcohol, amphetamines, LSD or cocaine. In fact, LSD may lead to frank insanity with feelings of omnipotence and aggression, and to relapse of the insane fits known as "flash backs" weeks or even months after its ingestion leading to violence and crimes including "running berserk".

(ix) Cruelty to relatives and dependents and the near and dear ones.

(x) Ruining oneself and family economically through continued indulgence and self-neglect.

(xi) Physician's negligence during surgical operations and delivery. A physician may be accused of the criminal charge of causing death of his patient by a rash and negligent act, if he was found to be under the influence of a drug or a drink or an inhalant anaesthetic like ether at the time when either the operation or delivery was in progress.

(xii) Transmission of a disease, the most dangerous or deadly one being the AIDS, through the infected needles used for injecting the drug as in cases of intravenous narcoticism.

(xiii) Degenerative changes and diseases affecting the vital and essential organs like, heart, lungs, liver, pancreas, brain and the peripheral nervous system.

(xiv) Developmental defects in the offsprings of mothers, who are addicted to the drugs.

(xv) Deaths — Death of a drug abuser may occur from:

  (a) Inanition and self-neglect and inter-current infection.

  (b) Accident or suicide while under the influence of or during the withdrawal phase of a drug.

  (c) Transmitted disease like AIDS or viral hepatitis as may occur in intravenous narcoticism.

  (d) Accidental or chance injection of a more potent and purer form or fatal dose of a drug.

  (e) Hypersensitivity reaction peculiar to the victim may occur even with an otherwise non-lethal dose of a drug.

  (f) Loss of earlier tolerance to a drug though prolonged abstinence.

  (g) By a "hot-shot" or an extra strong dose of a drug — a favourite way for the peddlers to do away with a troublesome drug taker.

4. Circumstances Leading to Initiation to Drug Abuse

The World Health Organisation (WHO) has listed the following circumstances as leading to the initiation of an individual to a drug:

(i) For gaining acceptance — peer pressure,
(ii) To express-assert independence, sometimes hostility,
(iii) To enjoy a kick or thrill or a novel or even a dangerous awareness,
(iv) To gain improved understanding, insight or creativity,
(v) To foster ease and relaxation,
(vi) To escape from an unpleasant life situation,
(vii) For self-exploration or transcendental pleasure,
(viii) For the treatment of symptom or a disease,
(ix) "Doping" by the athletes, to bolster their level of performance, and
(x) For the commission of crime.

5. Traditional Versus Emerging Pattern of Drug Abuse

While the traditional pattern of drug consumption was localised as to the drug type, occasion of use, age and sex of the user, community character and geographic distribution of use; of emerging pattern of indulgence in them is characterised by an increase in the number of drugs abused, increased indulgence outside traditional occasions, increased usage by youth and women, increased consumption by the upper strata of the society, and the use of hitherto-unfamiliar drug in a given area such as cannabis in the West, and alcohol in India. It is precisely this emerging drug consumption pattern, characterised by both vertical and horizontal spread of drug abuse, that has become a source of grave concern to sociologists, criminologists, physicians and the statesmen alike. Now, as never before, newer and newer synthetic drugs have found an increasing use, all drugs being abused all over the world aided by availability, social acceptance and social disorganisation, outside pressure, commercial considerations, and last but not the least by an unprecedented drug boom and jet-age mobility.

6. Drug Abuse — A Growing Menace

According to the WHO in 1985 an estimated 590 million people of the world took to drugs and of these 30 million all over the world, but mostly in rural areas of Africa, Asia, the Middle East and West Pacific and urban areas and North and South America and Europe used Marijuana; 5.6 million chewed coca-leaves, mainly in Latin America, 7.8 million, mostly in South and North America and Europe, were dependent on Cocaine; 2.3 million used the amphetamines. 1.70 million spread mostly over the rural areas of the Far and Middle East and South-east Asia, were addicted to Opium and 0.70 millions mostly in North America and Europe, were heroin users. Heroin addiction is rapidly increasing in India. In Bombay alone, 2,500 dependent persons were enumerated in 1983, 15,000 in 1984, and 80,000 in 1985, 3.4 million used barbiturates, sedatives and the tranquillisers, worldwide. The remainder used other narcotics and chemicals. Minor tranquillisers alone accounted for nearly 15 per cent of all medical prescriptions in USA. A large majority of persons were dependent on mixtures of either several drugs and the alcoholic beverages up to 1995, and the use has almost doubled.

As most of the World's heroin is produced in Asia's celebrated Golden Crescent in the Golden Triangle, abuse of heroin has reached alarming proportions in many countries of Asia, including India, Pakistan, Bangladesh, Sri Lanka, Burma, Macao, Hong Kong, Singapore and Thailand, and also in countries of the Middle East. Thus, Pakistan with no reported heroin addict in 1980 is estimated to have nearly a million of them now. Cannabis too grows freely in these areas and is widely abused. In Europe though cultivation of drugs is not so common their trafficking and consumption remains widespread, cannabis holding the lead followed by the abuse of heroin and cocaine.

Cocaine and Cannabis continue to be widely abused in USA and Canada. The most alarming development about cocaine abuse is the emergence of "Crack", which is a free-basing or smokable form of cocaine, is very fast acting and can be consumed without the risk of contracting the dreaded disease — AIDS. An estimated 4 to 5 million people in USA alone either sport cocaine or smoke crack. The small State of Columbia alone in South America has an estimated 0.6 million abusers of Cocaine and while in Latin America and the Caribbeans, cannabis is still the most widely abused drug, the widespread cultivation and easy availability of cocaine have resulted in rampant consumption and trafficking in the drug in these countries with resultant serious socio-economic and political repercussions.

A more recent estimate made by a team of experts from South Asian Association for Regional Co-operation (SAARC) countries meeting in a Dhaka symposium held in November 1992 on the prevalence of drug abuse amongst the youths reveals that, nearly 10 million people from the SAARC countries have already fallen victims to the drug, and there are an estimated 7 million drug addicts in India and another about 1 lakh in Sri Lanka. About 1.5 million people in Bangladesh abuse ganja, while a million more are addicted to the tranquillisers. Among the drug abusers in Bangladesh 70 per cent are youth's, a sizeable number of them being students from the universities and other educational institutions in big cities. The number of drug abusers in Nepal number about 50 thousands, most of them being heroin addicts.

7. Narcotics Trade and India

India was not on the drug traffickers' map until early 1980s. Her emergence as a major conduct for international drug-trafficking is a relatively recent development, and was brought about by a shift in the origin of the trade from the "Golden Triangle", the South East Asian tri-junction of Burma, Thailand and Laos to the "Golden Crescent", the vast stretch of poppy growing and processing land in South West Asia along the tribal dominated areas of Iran, Afghanistan and Pakistan, nearly two-thirds of which fall within the territory of Pakistan.

Because of her unique geographical location between these two opium producing areas, India was imperceptibly drawn into the vortex of highly lucrative drug trade, and is today a major link in the chain of international drug-trafficking. According to available reports 80 per cent of all heroin, the most dangerous of the narcotics, is now routed through India.

Pakistan being the main source of nearly 80 per cent of the drug smuggled through India. Thus, the narcotic trade has assumed alarming proportions. Not all the heroin passing through India, however, leaves the country and a part of it always finds its way into the local market and then to the Indian consumers through the drug peddlers, as spill-over effect of the trade, that has gone on increasing as tougher surveillance measures make it more and more difficult to send the drugs out of the country.

Thus, simultaneously with its being a major transit point for the drug trade, India has also become a centre for large-scale drug abuse involving heroin. However, because of its prohibitive price, a gram of pure heroin costing Rs. 250 or more, smack or brown sugar, an inexpensive adulterated form of heroin has become very popular. In 1980 hardly anyone knew of smack addicts of India. But now there are roughly, million abusers of this stuff in the country, Bombay and Delhi having over a lakh of them each. There are 10,000 child smack addicts in Delhi, mostly the street urchins and rag pickers. At least five people are reported to die every day in this country, because of drug addiction.

The smack addicts include a cross-section of all classes of people — taxi drivers, students, office-goers, vendors, shop assistants and professionals; students being the most vulnerable section of the society. According to a report of the Indian Council of Medical Research (ICMR) 33 per cent of boys and girls of Delhi University are victims of the drugs. As to the sex of the addicts, in public schools, the girls outnumbered the boys, their respective percentage being 50.3 and 33.3 respectively.

8. Drug Barons of Columbia

Columbia situated in the Andean Heights is a glaring example of how the drugs can damage the social fabric and political structure of a nation. The cocaine trafficking is a booming business in Columbia, and is controlled by well-organised cartels, of which Medellin Cartel if believed to be the most powerful. It sells cocaine by the tonnes and controls nearly 80 per cent of the US market earning a fabulous profit of 8 million dollars a year. According to former President Betancur, the traffickers represent an organisation greater than the State and have the money and muscle power to strike at targets whenever and wherever they want. Over the years the cartel has thus been responsible for deaths of hundreds of political leaders, law-enforcement officers, and anti-drug activists. Fortunately, situation in India is not that bad! All the same it is not under control.

9. Global Control of Drug Abuse

Nine intentional treaties formulated between 1912 and 1953 were, in 1961 amalgamated into and replaced by the Single

Convention of Narcotic Drug (Geneva) and further modified in 1972. This single Convention has a two-fold purpose, namely:

(i) To control and regulate the Licit supply and demand of the narcotics.

(ii) To formulate and enforce measures to prevent their illicit use.

The Agencies entrusted with these responsibilities are:

(i) The United Nations (a) Commission on Narcotic Drugs, (b) Division of Narcotic Drugs, (c) International Narcotic Control Board, (d) Convention of Psychiatric Substances, (e) United National Fund for Drug Abuse Control (UNFDAC), and (f) Central Laboratory at Geneva.

(ii) The World Health Organisation's Expert Committee on Drug Dependence, which assesses various substances submitted to it on the health and welfare of the communities and makes appropriate recommendations to the first two agencies listed above.

(iii) The Food and Agricultural Organisation's (FAO) Division of Narcotic Drugs, recommends and provides for crop substitution in order to reduce cultivation of the drugs.

(iv) The International Criminal Police Organisation (INTERPOL) with its General Secretariat Lyon — France, and National Central Offices in various countries.

The international efforts at control are coordinated and augmented at the national levels by the police forces, customs and excise officials of the member countries, and each country has enacted its own regulations aimed at controlling the drug trade. The aims and objects of the national laws are the same as the international treaties, and conventions, *i.e.,* controlling the abuse and channelising the production, processing and supply of the drugs only to the legitimate scientific and medical needs.

Regarding the latest Indian Law on the drugs, *i.e.,* the Narcotic Drugs and Psychotropic Substances Act of 1985, and its subsequent amendments, it may be said that this act lays down deterrent punishments against illegal cultivation and trafficking in the drugs and fulfils a long felt need in the area of anti-drug legislation in the country. While the enactment of this law does signify the Government's concern over the growing menace of drug abuse in the country, benefits to be derived from this piece of legislation will depend much upon how often and how effectively its provisions are implemented by the law enforcement machinery.

10. Dimensions of Smuggling

Smuggling of narcotics/drugs has assumed a dangerous proportion in the borders states of Jammu and Kashmir, Punjab, Rajasthan, Gujarat, Tarai regions of Uttar Pradesh bordering Nepal, Sikkim. Assam, West Bengal and all coastal states. The areas of operation by smugglers and their ramifications are almost India-wide that it is not possible for the skeleton and ill-equipped police force to keep a track of these offenders. Most of the seizers were the result of information leaked out by some sneaker due to gang rivalries. In a majority of the cases the sneaker is eliminated ruthlessly in order to prevent future squealing. The process of elimination not only serves as a great deterrent, but also it has a terrifying effect on the would be informers. The gangs generally adopt very clever ruses, and purchase the law enforcement agency for allowing a large part of the contraband to be smuggled away, and purposefully surrender a very small quantity of the contraband in order to obliterate suspicion on both — the law enforcement agency, and the smuggler gang. Sometimes to bring the rival gang in trouble, location of contraband is passed over to the police, who make a big publicity for having effected the seizers. Invariably dumped up contraband falls into the hands of the law enforcement agency, and there is no accused. If by chance the accused is caught, the judiciary frees him as police fail to prove conscious possession by him. Narcotics/drugs and gold, silver, precious stones and alike valuable goods like watches are exchanged in barter. In recent years arms and ammunition have been added to this list; and now most of the terrorist activities in India are directly or indirectly financed through these gangsters. Occasionally, they carry espionage for the hostile country. Through profuse corruption the law enforcement machinery has been made rickety and almost defunct. Those who are convicted bear a paltry fine or lenient jail sentence of a few months. Whilst the convict is in jail custody, his family is liberally supported by these gangs, who are scrupulously honest in this regard. Corruption is collectively co-operative, and since most members of the law enforcement have been financially benefited, smuggling is allowed to go on unabated and without any fear of reprimand or disciplinary action, as majority of the supervisory officers regularly receive the proportionate share of booty. Here again scrupulous honesty is observed.

The corrupted enforcement agency, unwieldy borders with hostile country like Pakistan, and difficult terrain cumulatively made the problem of smuggling and trade in narcotics/drugs fathoms away from control. The trend of according lenient punishment by the judiciary has further aggravated it. Unless the burden of proof of innocence is shifted on the accused, and the punishment to be meted out is made very stringent, including capital sentence, like most of the Muslim countries, by no chance this vicious trade can be controlled. To the already existing difficulties political patronage to the gang *vis-a-vis* their leaders have been added, eventually making it impossible to bridle these gangsters with a view to curb, if not stop, their activities, as now they operate openly under political cover or protection. Some of them are the elected representatives also. They also lend their money and muscle support to the politicians and make them win electoral battles.

The appearance of newer forms of combinations of drug abuse, along with newer groups of users and the pattern and spread of them are causing fast growing and serious health hazards and social problems that have been aptly likened by the World Health Organisation (WHO) to terrorism directed against the health and welfare of the entire human race. So ruthless and all out have been the offensive or NARCO-TERRORISM and so all pervasive the spread of such drugs, that right now, there appears to be no escape in sight for mankind from its catastrophic socio-economic consequences. Any police effort must, therefore, be supplemented or complemented by weaning away the addicts from their degrading and deadly habits and rehabilitating them in the society, but also at educating the masses and curing the socio-economic ills that lie deep into the roots of drug abuse problems.

31

Guarding International Boundaries and Infiltration

1. Guarding the International Boundary — Historical Background

Various articles have been incorporated in the United Nations Charter to ensure that the territorial integrity of a nation signified by its international boundary or ground is respected. But still the violations of international boundary take place even today. The following short resume of the foreign invasions is desired just to highlight the importance of guarding international boundary.

History of India is replete with instances of how the country has braved war after war with the invaders for having failed to safeguard the international boundary against foreign invasions. With the advent of Maurya Dynasty in 322 B.C., we find for the first time a huge empire springs into existence unifying the innumerable fragments of distracted India, Chandragupta Maurya had to secure the international boundary of *Hindusthan* and establish the empire after attacking the Macedonian officers in command of the garrison in the Indus basin after Alexander's death and destroyed them. Thereafter, it is the story of continuous invasions of India's international boundary one after another of foreign invaders. The campaigns of the Greeks, beginning with the invasions of Alexander in 327 B.C. the Parthians; the Bactrians; the Syrians, all in the Era before Christ; and the Sakas, the Kushans of the sept of Yuch-chi horde of nomads, the Huns, the Gurjars, the Pratiharas in the early years of A.D. up to the reign of King Harsha, and then the Mohammedan conquests of India bear rich-testimony to the fact that how a weak guarding of the international boundary had time and again endangered the territorial integrity of India.

2. India's International Boundary

As on today India is maintaining an unwieldy long length of international boundary of approximately 15,224 kms with its neighbouring states of Burma in the East; Pakistan and Afghanistan in the West; Bhutan and Nepal in the North, Bangladesh in the East and Ceylon in the south. Guarding of international border has become an issue of significantly great importance.

3. Indo-Chinese International Boundary

China and India have some 3,917 kms of common frontier — extending from North-East of Kashmir to the tripartite junction of India, Burma and China near Tolu pass in the East. The conflicting chain of approximately 50,000 sq. miles of territory at three places on this long international boundary, which indicates the unresolved dispute over the Mcmohan line has already resulted in one humiliating war for India and China. The seriousness of the dispute, which neither government would at first admit, finally came out in the open on the heels of the Chinese capture of Tibet in March 1959. The continuing border incidents took a serious turn, culminating on 20th October 1962, in a massive military invasion of India's northern frontier from Ladakh in the west to NEFA in the East. The war caused a heavy damage to India until China decided to unilaterally order ceasefire on 21st November 1962. The prospect of an early respectable solution of this conflict remained ever eluding after then and naturally imposing a heavy burden on the public exchequer for ensuring round the clock vigil of this long Sino-India boundary. A vast deployment of Indo-Tibetan Border Police is engaged in-inaccessible, snow-bound remote areas of this boundary to ensure the physical security of this long border in order to avoid another Chinese incursion into our territory.

4. Indo-Pak Boundary

India has to secure its 3,310 kms. long border with its most hostile neighbour of Pakistan. This international boundary is spread over to the States of Punjab (547 kms.), Rajasthan (1,035 kms.), Gujarat (512 kms.), and 1,216 kms. of Jammu and Kashmir, out of which only 200 kms is demarcated. The international boundary can be termed as still born. Almost immediately after this boundary was marked on the map, the Pakistan's invasion took place. The Pak-occupied Kashmir has encroached into a large chunk of our Kashmir, and the line at which the two warring countries of Pakistan and India have at present agreed to halt is termed as Line of Actual Control (LAC) which is treated as the *de facto* boundary. This LAC extends for 700 kms. and another 98 kms. stretches in the boundary in Sia-Chin glacier.

5. Jammu and Kashmir Boundary with Pakistan

The Himalayan Princely State of Jammu and Kashmir (J&K) before its accession in October 1947 to the Union of India bordered on the North by China (Sinkiang), the Soviet Union (Turkestan) and Afghanistan, on the West and slightly to the South by Pakistan; on the South by India and on the East by Tibet. In geographical term, the territory of the State of Jammu & Kashmir has four broad natural regions; the northern areas of Gilgit, Chitral and Baltistan with a predominantly Muslim population; the southern area consisting of Jammu with a predominantly (Dogra) Hindu population, and the province of Ladakh region stretched between the valley of Kashmir and Tibet with Buddhist population. But the configuration of the international boundary, and for that matter the entire identity of the State has undergone a vast change almost immediately after its accession to India. The tribesmen from the north-western boundary of India fully aided and armed by the Pakistani Government attacked Kashmir immediately after Stand Still Agreement the Maharaja of Kashmir had offered to enter with two Dominions — India and Pakistan as an interim measure on 15th August 1947. At the beginning all the efforts of India and the United Nations failed to persuade Pakistan to withdraw the raiders, and the Pak Army from Kashmir resulting in pillage, death and destruction of the population of the State. This wanton destruction led the Maharaja with no option but to accede to India and seek military and political intervention, thereby making it obligatory for the Government of India to defend its territory when Pakistan raiders continued to advance into the State. They occupied and annexed a large portion of the State in the Northwestern part, when on 1st January 1949 a ceasefire was effected in terms of part I of the Resolution of the United Nations of 13th August 1948. Since then the international boundary between Pakistan and the Indian state of J&K remained, *'de facto'* with the Cease Fire Line (CFL) or Line of Actual Control (LAC) being regarded as the boundary between the two countries. The entire CFL in J&K State of India is being guarded by the Indian Army, whereas the two warring countries are at constant loggerheads and despite the two wars of 1965 and 1971, the stalemate could not be resolved in the Pak-occupied Kashmir claimed by Pakistan as Azad Kashmir including the snow bound Sia-Chin glacier in the north-western tip of the country. The Indian Army with the Border Security Force (BSF) is guarding this boundary in the face of not only our hostile enemy but a very hostile weather and terrain as well. The brave security forces are maintaining a sleepless vigil over the snow-capped dizzy heights of the Himalayas, in the treacherous passes, in the forest and other areas contiguous to Pakistan round the clock for 365 days and nights a year.

6. Punjab (India) Punjab (Pakistan)

The entire international boundary with Pakistan is 547 kms. long. It is fully demarcated border with boundary pillars numbering from 1 to 4,292. The entire international border here is guarded by Border Security Force (BSF) with the present secessionist movement in the Punjab, and with the insurgents receiving active aid from the hostile enemy, has rendered the work of the force in the partly riverine, partly land border of the Punjab, extremely arduous.

7. Rajasthan/Punjab and Sind of Pakistan Boundary

The entire stretch of this boundary is 1,035 kms. in length with boundary pillars duly numbered. This tract of international boundary which traverses vast tracks of deserts is being manned by the Border Security Force with 'Camel' as their principal means of communication in the sandy desert area. Here the security forces face scorching heat, the sand-storm with acute scarcity of water and devegetation in the sea of sand.

8. Kutch-Sind Pak Boundary

The international boundary between the Kutch tracts of Gujarat in India and Sind Province of Pakistan stretches for a length of 512 kms. of which 104 kms. boundary has not been demarcated. This marshy creek and swampy Rann is being guarded by the Border Security Force in an environment that can be turned anything except congenial conditions for prolonged human living. Not a blade of grass grows here.

9. Indo-Bangladesh Boundary

Following the partition, Pakistan and India were involved in a lot of boundary dispute. In 1947 the Governor General appointed Bengal Boundary Commission under the Chairmanship of Sir Cyril Radcliffe to demarcate the boundary line between India and then East Bengal (ultimately came to be known as Bangladesh after its liberation in 1971). Radcliffe gave the decision on 12th August 1947. Subsequently, certain disputes arose out of the decisions concerning its interpretation and implementation. A committee was appointed in 1948 by an Inter Dominion Conference to report on the matter. This committee recommended the appointment of a tribunal, known as the Indo-Pakistan Boundary Dispute Tribunal with the honourable Algot Bagge, an ex-member of the Supreme Court of Sweden, as the chairman. The function of the Tribunal was to adjudge and finally settle the boundary disputes arising out of interpretations of the Radcliffe's award, and for demarcating the boundary. The Tribunal rendered its award after careful scrutiny of the existing evidence, and it involved re-adjustment of the boundaries and exchange of enclaves. There were four areas, two on the Western boundary, and two on the Eastern boundary of East Pakistan (now Bangladesh). In 1958 there was an agreement between India and Pakistan known as Noon-Nehru Pact which provided ground rules to settle every' dispute while demarcation work was on. This agreement also provided exchange of enclaves. There are 95 Bangladeshi enclaves in India, and 130 Indian Enclaves in Bangladesh. Following the Noon-Nehru agreement survey work began to demarcate the border dispute between East Pakistan (now Bangladesh) on one side and West Bengal, Assam and Tripura on the other (the states of Meghalaya and Mizoram adjoining Bangladesh were not in existence at that time). The total length of this international boundary line between India and Bangladesh is 4095.70 kms.

10. West Bengal-Bangladesh Border

West Bengal has got the largest international boundary with Bangladesh that runs for a stretch of 2216.70 kms. This whole border area is fully demarcated with boundary pillars numbering 1 to 1,000, except for a stretch of 78.5 kms. The international border stretches from the midstream of the deepest navigational channel in the river at the mouth of the sea in Sunderbans up to the area where river form international boundary, and then on the land border of Jhow Kuty BOP (Dubri) in Cooch Behar border area in the north, out of 2216.70 kms of the boundary. West Bengal maintains about 350 kms of riverine boundary in the river Padma in Murshidabad district and river Tehamati-Kalindi in the south 24-Parganas district. The entire boundary has a number of disputed areas and adverse possessions. Some of the disputes were sought to be resolved in a government level meeting between Governments of India and Bangladesh in the year 1947, but in the absence of ratification those disputes remained unsolved as yet.

Besides these disputed areas there are 130 Indian enclaves in Bangladesh and 95 Bangladeshi enclaves in India. These enclaves are small pockets of lands belonging to each other in each other's territory. Status of the citizens in these enclaves is accordingly coterminous with the status of the enclaves to which they belong. Despite some decisions about the exchange of these enclaves, some of the important enclaves like Dahagram, Angarpota, Berubari still exist as bone of contention between the two countries. Under the Noon-Nehru Pact, and also under Indira (Gandhi) Mujib Pact of 1974, half of the Berubari was to be given away to Bangladesh. It was also decided that Bangaladesh will get a corridor through "Tinbigha" areas of India between the Panbari Mouja on the one end and Angarpota and Dahargram enclave on the other. The total length and breadth of Tinbigha corridor in 178 metres by 85 metres. Dahargram and Angarpota is one complete complex of Bangladesh measuring 7.15 sq. miles. Since the matter was sensitive pertaining to parting of territory, the Indian population resisted their exchanges and filed suits against the Indian Government in the Supreme Court. In June 1990, the Supreme Court of India has given decision in favour of handing over the corridor to Bangladesh in exchange of half of Berubari, and the Government of West Bengal has also expressed its determination to implement the decision of the Supreme Court.

11. Assam-Bangladesh International Boundary

The original boundary of East Pakistan (now Bangladesh) with Assam has now been truncated into three parts of boundaries of Assam, Meghalaya, Cachar of Assam and Mizoram as a sequel to the carving out of the States which were not in existence at the time of creation of East Pakistan. Originally, Assam had common boundary with East Pakistan for 1,023 kms., but now the length of boundary with the three states of Assam, Mizoram and Meghalaya stands as follows:—

Assam	— Bangladesh	— 202 kms. out of which 0.3 km still undemarcated.
Meghalaya	— Bangladesh	— 443 kms. fully demarcated.
Mizoram	— Bangladesh	— 318 kms. out of which 8 kms. still remain undemarcated.

The border of Assam with Bangladesh starts from Ramraikuthy in the bordering areas of Cooch Behar in West Bengal where the boundary of West Bengal ends at Border Post (BP) 1,001. The Assam boundary is demarcated except for 03 km., with BP 1,102 to 1,107. Thereafter, Meghalaya has a boundary with Bangladesh fully demarcated with BP 1,071 to 1,338 for 443 kms. Cachar of Assam has BPs 1,338 to 1,397.

12. Tripura-Bangladesh Border

The State of Tripura in the south-eastern extremity with Bangladesh runs for 85 kms. out of which 36 kms. are still undemarcated.

13. Manning the Eastern International Boundary

The whole of India's international boundary with Bangladesh is being exclusively manned by the Border Security Force. The entire stretch of this border is plain except some portions of partly hilly terrain in Meghalaya and Cachar areas. Rest of this boundary is plain interspersed with mighty rivers like the Bhagirathi (near Farakka), Padma, Brahmaputra, Mahananda, Punarbhaba, Atreyi, Tangon, Mathabanga, Ichamati, Kalindi, Haribhanga, Raimangal and several other minor rivers and their tributaries. India's international boundary with Bangladesh is peculiar with the characteristics of its being fluid and non-existent due to the prevalence of identical ethnic groups living on both sides of the border. Added to this disadvantage are the difficulties of communication in remote areas of the border which becomes totally marshy and water-logged during monsoons for about 5 months a year, seriously hampering the movements of troops.

14. India's International Border with States other than Pakistan

Besides having common international border with its closest neighbours, *viz.*, China, Pakistan, Bangladesh, India maintenance fairly long international boundary with Nepal (1,752 kms.); Burma (1,458 kms.); Afghanistan (106 kms.) and Bhutan (587 kms).

The Island of Ceylon, which though not having a common boundary is still involved in a dispute over the possession of the tiny Island. 'Kachchativu' lying between India and Ceylon. The Government of Ceylon alleges that the agreement signed in 1921 between the Government of Madras and Ceylon regarding the demarcation line between the two countries in the Palk Straits and Gulf of Mannar has shown 'Kachchativu' belonging to Ceylon, whereas India denies this. Another unresolved issue between India and Ceylon concerns the limits of their respective territorial rights in the Palk Bay and Gulf of Mannar. India claims 12 miles as its territorial waters, whereas Ceylon claims 6 miles of its territorial water. Hence, India has got to pay attention to the guarding of its territorial water between the mainland of India and Ceylon, more so following the influx of Tamil refugees and LTTE insurgents to India.

15. Extent of Guarding International Boundary

An analysis of international boundary India is maintaining with its neighbour *vis-a-vis* the relations with those neighbouring countries signified the extent to which the Government through its police forces and Army has to exert to guard its international boundary, particularly with those countries with whom it has not been possible to maintain very cordial relations because of their hostility on one pretext or the other. The northern Himalayan border is at precipitous heights, some positions of which remain perpetually under snow. Guarding this border continuously throughout the varying seasons is most hazardous and equally arduous. Borders skirmish is almost a routine affair to these forces; likewise some of the areas of J&K are mostly clad with snow, and the security forces have to negotiate through difficult high passes to keep the line of Actual Control under constant surveillance. The entire J&K State having a common boundary with Pakistan is perpetually undergoing the turmoil Pakistan creates with its determination to annex Kashmir. Sia-Chin glacier witnesses frequent bouts of firing throughout the year. Determined efforts of Paki-infiltrators into Indian territory are very frequent and caused many casualties. The Central Reserve Police Force, the Indo-Tibetan Border Police, the Border Security Force, the Assam Rifles, Provincial Armed Constabulary of Uttar Pradesh and the Armed Police Forces of all the States having international boundaries are involved in guarding the territorial integrity of the country, and till date they have commendably ensured its protection. For the security of the Nation thousands of them have sacrificed their lives; and even now, under extremely hazardous conditions, with total disregard to their safety and life and no family life whatsoever, they zealously continue to discharge creditably the duties assigned to them. These are our valorous custodians of the international borders.

16. Infiltration — Factors Responsible

Infiltration of foreign nationals from the bordering countries into Indian territories can be attributed to the following causes:

(i) Political: Infiltrators are sent to destabilise the internal security as is the case of Pakistan sending armed infiltrators into Kashmir valley and Punjab. Pakistan allegedly send infiltrators to communal riot-prone areas. Infiltrators are also sent for the purposes of espionage and gun-running across the borders. Political insecurity also accounts for large-scale infiltration as happened in Bangladesh before and during Bangladesh war with West Pakistan in 1970-71. At that time hundreds of thousands of Bangladesh nationals fled to India for shelter and food.

*(ii) **Economic:*** Steady deterioration of economic conditions due to low income, meagre resources, presence of population, and people living below the poverty line force people to seek livelihood elsewhere. These conditions prevail in Bangladesh from where large-scale infiltrations into India are taking place. These conditions prevail in Nepal also from where Nepalese nationals are infiltrating into Indian territories in large number.

*(iii) **Religious persecution:*** Religious persecution account for minority community to flee the country and take shelter elsewhere. This happened in the case of Pakistan and Bangladesh — both Muslim countries — who persecuted their Hindu population compelling them to leave their countries. The mass forcible conversion of Chittagong Hills Tribes (CHT) after attacks on them by fundamental Muslim organisations and groups is a classic example.

*(iv) **Breakdown of law and order:*** After breakdown of law and order in a country people of that country migrate to neighbouring country for shelter, security and food. This happened in the case of East Pakistan-Bangladesh where large scale communal riots were engineered, and the minority communities, for want of protection, were forced to migrate to India.

17. Infiltrations From (East Pakistan) Bangladesh

There was mass exodus of Hindus in 1948 (4,19,018); 1950 (9,25,185); 1951 (4,77,186) and 1964 (6,67,125) when they entered West Bengal for food, and shelter from East Pakistan-Bangladesh. Between 1946 and 1970 July the total number of East Pakistani nationals received in West Bengal was 42,03,378. These are all official figures. Unofficial and yet, reliable sources put the figure to about one crore. There was total breakdown of law and order situation in East Pakistan-Bangladesh during this period. They cannot be categorised as refugees, because there is credible information that East Pakistan-Bangladesh had hatched a plot to foment unrest and anti-national activities in Assam, West Bengal, Manipur and Tripura, where infiltration is being encouraged. When there are over 300 million poverty stricken, people in India these so-called refugees cannot be provided means to earn their livelihood in India. There is rising social tension in the border areas for the competition for jobs; and if these illegal migrants are allowed to stay their problems will be mani-fold and against national interest.

There are five types of foreign nationals flowing into the northeastern region. While the Burmese are sneaking into Nagaland and Manipur, the Bangladeshis are flooding into Assam, West Bengal, Tripura and Mizoram. The percentage increase of the total population in 1961-1971 in Assam was 38.4. Due to disturbed conditions there was no census in 1981. Although the question of infiltration in Assam is not a new problem as its origin dates back to pre-partition days when a large number of Muslims from East Bengal were encouraged to migrate to Assam to cultivate fallow lands and provide labour in the construction of railway tracts and to tea gardens.

Broadly speaking, there are three types of foreign nationals in Assam, first, Muslims who infiltrated from former East Pakistan after partition, secondly, refugees or displaced persons who did not acquire Indian citizenship, and thirdly, Nepali insurgents. Lakhs of foreigners got themselves included in electoral rolls. There are about 3 lakhs of such persons whose citizenship is questionable. Tribunals were set to try these "aliens" but they were finally wound up under pressure from political parties, who profited from the block votes of these aliens.

In Tripura the 1981 census recorded that the total population of the State which was 15,56,342 in 1971 census increased to 20,53,058 in 1981. Frequent communal riots in East Pakistan-Bangladesh forced minority communities to migrate to Tripura. The number of migrants swelled when Buddhists Chakmas from Chittagong Hill Track (CHT) in hundreds of thousand left their home and hearth due to frequent attacks on the Chakma villages by the Bangladeshi Army, and the para-military forces supported by fundamentalist Muslim organisations, and groups who killed hundreds of them, raped their women folk and forcibly converted them to Islam. Reportedly in June 1993 over 56,000 Chakma refugees from CHT of Bangladesh took shelter in six evacuee camps in south Tripura.

18. Infiltration from Pakistan

On the Indo-Pakistan border there has been large scale infiltration of Pakistan Muslims into the districts of Ganganagar, Bikaner,

Jaisalmer and Badmer in Rajasthan, Patiala and Sangrur in Punjab and throughout the Kashmir valley. The sudden rise of Muslim population all over has become a matter of concern, and the root cause to lop side the communal equilibrium in these sensitive areas. Pakistani nationals have been found in Punjab going about disguised as Sikhs. Some of those killed in the Golden Temple during the operation Blue Star were subsequently identified as Pakistani nationals.

There is large-scale traffic of trained armed infiltration from Pakistan occupied Kashmir (POK). This has been going on into a steady stream. In recent years, foreign nationals, who have infiltrated in the Valley include war veterans from countries like Sudan, Iran, Bahrain, Afghanistan. They are mainly involved in inducing and motivating the local Muslim population for anti-national activities. The problem of checking infiltration from POK has been difficult because of the support the Jammu and Kashmir Liberation Front (JKLF) receives from the leaders of POK.

19. Dimensions of the Problem

On 12th February 1984, National Convention on infiltration of foreign nationals was held in Calcutta. It was inaugurated by Justice H.R. Khanna, formerly judge of the Supreme Court, Lt. General Jagjit Singh Arora (Retd.) presided over the inaugural session. Their convention was organised by Purbanchal Anti-Infiltration Committee and included delegates from Bihar, West Bengal, Tripura, Gujarat, Rajasthan, Jammu and Kashmir and Uttar Pradesh. The consensus was that several millions foreign nationals' who have illegally infiltrated into the Indian territory must be found out and deported as they were a great security hazard. It was further unanimously agreed that the names of such infiltrators, enlisted as voters should be removed from the voters list. Photo identity card to each citizen living in a 5 km. periphery should be given for the purposes of proper identification. These suggestions are really good, and if properly implemented they are bound to check infiltration considerably. But political will is hindering this good measure. Studies by various persons and organisations led them to assess that there are at least 14 million migrants, and their descendants have over-all settled in various parts of the country. People should be aware of this dangerous situation.

20. Crime and Criminality on the Border

The extensive Indian border is susceptible to activities of criminals, anti-socials, smugglers, peddlers of narcotic drugs, gun-runners, insurgents, terrorists, traffickers of women and girls, who operate on both sides of the international border. In all illegal activities villagers from both sides are deeply involved. Large scale easy infiltration accounts for the growing incidence of crime which flourishes under the umbrella of the underworld.

In 15 years of terrorist activities in Punjab Pakistan has played a vital role in encouraging smuggling of arms and ammunition, narcotic drugs and gold into India. The menace of smuggling and gun-running has been rampant in our Western borders with Pakistan since long. The borders of Gujarat and Rajasthan are also invariably used. Horses, camels, fishing boats have been frequently used by smugglers in areas where vehicles cannot be used. Smuggling of arms and ammunition from Pak-occupied Kashmir into India to Kashmir goes on all the year round, and their seizure by the police and security forces has been colossal. Many infiltrators caught on the borders have been laying down their arms which were given to them by Pakistani ISI for destabilising the country.

Wagha is the most important check post in Punjab on the Indo-Pakistan border through which thousands of travellers from and to Pakistan pass daily. There are substantial allegations that the security forces deployed on border protection duty were letting pass travellers on false vaccination and immunisation certificates and on forged passports. The Central Bureau of Investigation made certain arrests also and they found out that there was collusion of officers of customs, the Border Security Force, the Pakistan Rangers and the local police on both sides of the border. It was also revealed that security officials on both frontiers had evolved a time-tested chit system. If a person is crossing over from either India or Pakistan, he had to pay a certain sum of money to the border guards stationed in Pakistani or Indian borders. That was the fee (graft) taken for not opening the luggage. Porters and touts act as go between and all are important links in the vicious chain. Once a deal has been struck with a traveller either in India or Pakistan, a chit is given to the porter, who delivers it to the pre-assigned official on the other side, thereby ensuring a free passage. At the end of the day a tally of chits is made and collected amount is distributed equally.

Reportedly, a Pakistani or BSF Jawan charges anything between Rs. 100 to Rs. 200 for not opening the luggages. Very often, the border crosser has all his papers in order and has nothing to smuggle. But that does not mean anything to the customs officials who would still demand a share. The smugglers profit enormously out of this system. Narcotics, drugs, weapons of different make and kinds, ammunitions, electric goods, cameras, textile enter India freely in this way. Tea, coffee, medicine make up the counter traffic. No action worth the name to stop smuggling has been taken. People coming through at Wagha on legitimate business and genuine documents are harassed by the government officials of all departments concerned. It was reported that during the Burnala Ministry in Punjab Police stations were allegedly auctioned to assorted gangs of drug and gun-runners for as high as Rs. 50 lakhs. The problem is how to combat the twin menace of gun-running and drugs smuggling and to ensure a corruption free government, law enforcement agencies, police not excluded.

The problem of gun-running in our Eastern Frontier is practically insignificant compared to our Indo-Pak Western border. Smuggling of narcotics is also not very high compared to Indo-Pak border, but in recent years narcotics from Burma side into Mizoram, Manipur and Nagaland has been reported to be taking place. Secessionists and insurgents have smuggled arms from Bangladesh and Burma.

Smuggling of items like coffee, paddy, rice, sugar, salt, onion, textile, bicycles, clothes and yams, tea, diesel, steel utensils, cosmetics, medicines from West Bengal and Tripura to Bangladesh has come to stay. Smuggling is easy with large number of weekly markets within a few kilometer of the border. The most active link in the smuggling chain is along the border of Bangladesh comprises touts or the agents called "Bomb Police", Customs officials, Panchayats, businessmen and traders, security forces, local police as well as political leaders. Agents and touts are known as "Bomb Police" because they use crackers to warn or regulate the clandestine crossing of Bangladesh nationals into India. These touts comprising men and women, sit in the ragged stalls on both sides of the road that leads to the Indian territory from Bangladesh. The stalls are all sham. A forged passport, a false visa, is available in return for money. A passport can be had for Rs. 200.

Cattle lifting and trafficking in women and girls are the most profitable crimes which fetches very high price. A large number of Bangladesh women and girls are sold to brothels in Calcutta, Bombay, Delhi through touts and gangs on the border having a very wide network. The most alarming feature is the growing involvement of women, children in the clandestine business of smuggling. They sneak into the Indian territory in groups, make purchases and return to Bangladesh. Incidence of *dacoity* and robbery in Indian villages, by Bangladeshi criminals is very high, but seldom reported or registered by the police. Many factors are responsible which inhibit security forces from playing an important role in preventing infiltration and smuggling across the border.

21. Why Infiltration cannot be Prevented?

The reasons are many but some of the important reasons can be given hereunder:

1. In a large number of cases infiltration takes place with the help of political parties' intent on collecting block votes and support of Muslim organisations and groups operating on the Indian side of the border. Infiltration has always the blessings of ruling party, which facilitate not only back-door naturalisation but encouraged soft preventive measures by the police and security forces. Unscrupulous politicians manipulated electoral rolls, and votes are polled through large-scale impersonation.
2. There is a large scale movement of villagers from across the border from India, Pakistan and Bangladesh and *vice versa* as a matter of routine because of their generation old close relations or associations. Crossing of the border has become a matter of routine for them who never consider it to be illegal.
3. Over-stay of many foreign nationals coming to India with valid passport visa, and inability of the administration to trace out and deport them.

4. Infiltrators who use the same dress, speak the same language and follow the same customs used by the local people, can easily settle down unnoticed at places, police posts being far away or unmanned for long stretches.
5. Close proximity of villagers on both sides of the border, human activity in the shape of cultivation of land, cattle grazing in close adjacent areas of the border and ethnic affinity of local population and availability of infiltration routes — all these provide facilities for infiltration.
6. Riverine borders have imaginary zero line. A majority of boats ply without permits. The dry riverbeds are among the favourite routes of infiltrators and carriers of smuggled goods during the winter months.
7. There is "no man's zone" on either side of the border. Farmers on both the sides of the border are tiling the land up to the farthest point of the border, making control difficult.
8. Barbed wire fencing in many pockets have not been completed. On account of the extensive border it is bound to take 8 to 10 years more.
9. Villagers do not co-operate, and their assistance has to be made compulsory under the law; without which no security force will be effective.
10. Large-scale corruption among law enforcement agencies, including security forces, panchayats, local politicians and local police has helped infiltration and smuggling, and unless this is stopped no measure worth the name would be effective.

32

Police as the Agent of Law and not the Party in Power

1. Constitutional Responsibility of Police

According to the report of the Kerala Enquiry Committee of the Indian Constitution of Jurists, 1960 "The police are not the servants of the State Government in the sense that Government can order the method and manner of the performance of the various acts committed to the police by the law, and it is not open either to the police officer or to the Chief Minister to change the course of law". Thus, conceptually the position is quite explicit.

> "Although a Home Minister is in-charge of the police and police administration and answerable to Parliament about it, still he has no power to direct the police how should they exercise their statutory powers, duties or discretion. If the minister were to give orders about arrests, to arrest or not to arrest that would be the end of the rule of law". (Kapur Commission report on murder of Mahatma Gandhi).

Although the Constitutional responsibility of the Home Minister is to ensure that police exercise their powers properly and diligently, he is not entitled to issue to the police specific instruction as to the manner of exercise of their statutory powers. But for general ineptitude, inefficiency, want of skill or honesty the Minister is responsible for administrative supervision to the Parliament.

The Government of West Bengal through its Minister had issued instructions to the police of that State that no action should be taken by the police for "gheraoing" a person. The issuance of such orders were considered necessary when the workers of Jay Engineering Works "gheraoed" their manager *etc*. The Calcutta High Court held the above stated view that there is no law which authorises the State Government to issue directions to officers in-charge of maintenance of law and order not to enforce the law of the land, nor to direct them to enforce the law of the land upon certain conditions being fulfilled, and complied with (AIR 1968 Calcutta 402 V 53 C 84). "Gherao" means stop a person from his legitimate free movements and restrain or confine him to a particular place. This is a cognizable offence punishable under the Indian Penal Code, besides it is an infringement of the fundamental right of a citizen guaranteed under the Constitution of India — Freedom of Movement. Democracy does not mean or envisage the subordination of law of the land to political ends.

Police Act of 1861 (Act V) lays down in no uncertain terms that superintendence of the police throughout the State shall vest in the Director/Inspector General of Police. The Chief Minister or the Minister in-charge of police department has only the supervisory control, and they are, in a way political bosses. From Chief Minister to the police minister of the State Government, the MPs, MLAs, Zilla Parishad chief, municipal council chairman and member of Panchayat Samiti, Pradhans, *Sarpanch* of village panchayats, and other political workers belonging to the political party in power, draw power and, influence over the police and want the police officials to do things of their bidding to save their own interests or the interests of their constituencies, and such interests are too more selfish than general. Their pressure on the police takes a variety of forms, ranging from a promise of career advancement and preferential treatment in service matters if the demand is yielded to, and a threat of drastic penal action and disfavoured treatment in service matters if the pressure is resisted. While it is not possible to punish a police officer with statutory punishment under the Discipline and Appeal Rules without adequate grounds and following a prescribed procedure, it is very easy to subject him to administrative action by way of transfer, or suspension on the basis of an alleged complaint made by the politicians, and taken up for enquiry. While suspension acts as a great humiliating factor, a transfer acts as severe economic blow and disruption of the police officer's family, children education *etc*. The threat of transfer/suspension is the most patent weapon in the hands of the politicians to bend down the police to their will. These were also the observations embodied in the Second Report of the National Police Commission in August 1979.

The fault is, however, not all of one side. Just as politicians seem to use police for their purposes, so policemen seek to use politicians for their gains. Even top ranking IPS officers down to recent recruits often invite and rely upon political assistance of every form. It is sought as a means or instrument in securing appointment and promotion, as a shield against impending disciplinary action, and as a means of securing or avoiding transfer or assignment. Thus, the necessary basis for a mutually advantageous barter is provided. This practice has percolated to the lowest rank of the force — the constable. After taking over charge of a particular posting, the first and foremost consideration, these days, of a policeman is to win the confidence of the local political leader belonging to the ruling party, and this is the most important task for him too. All bureaucrats have been contaminated with this form of political appeasement, subjugation or favour mongering.

Several State Police Commissions have also referred to this malady of political interferences in day-to-day police work which has become a norm. Some of the extracts are:

1. "The greatest obstacle to efficient police administration flows from the domination of party politics under the State Administrators. Pressure is applied in varying degrees, and so often affects directly different branches of administration." (Kerala Police Reorganisation Committee, 1959)
2. "The evidence laid before the Commission has disclosed that members of the political parties, particularly of the ruling party, whether in the legislature, or outside, interfere considerably in the working of the police for unlawful ends". (The Punjab Police Commission 1961-62)
3. "We have been informed that political interference is another source of corruption. Allegations have been made before us that the politicians' resort to the device of securing the assistance of *goondas* and bad-characters who are given protection by the police. This protection is the result of influence exercised by the politicians upon policemen". (Delhi Police Commission, 1968).

4. "There have been instances where the Government has been accused of using police machinery for political end. There are also instances of individual politicians' interfering with the administration, and the work of the police". (Committee of Police Training appointed by the Government of India in 1972)

The Indian Institute of Public Opinion, New Delhi revealed in a study of "Image of Police in India" that: (1) political interference is seen by the public as a major factor contributing to the poor image of the police and manifests itself in the misuse and abuse of police powers and disregard of law by the police, (2) people consider political interference with police as a greater evil than even corruption, and (3) political interference appears more pronounced in rural areas than urban areas (National Police Commission Second Report, 1970).

The brazen manner in which the police were misused during the Emergency of 1975-77 to subvert lawful procedures and serve purely political ends have been reproduced in the Second Report of National Police Commission in August 1979. "Police was used and allowed themselves to be used for purposes some of which were, to say the least, questionable. Some police officers behaved as though they are not accountable at all to any public authority. The decisions to arrest and to release certain persons were entirely on political considerations which were intended to be favourable to the ruling party. Employing the police to the advantage of any political party is a sure source of subverting the rule of law. The Government may seriously consider the feasibility and desirability of insulating the police from the politics of the country and employ it scrupulously on duties for which alone it is by law intended. The policemen must also be made to realise that politicising by them is outside the sphere of their domain and the Government would take a very serious view of it."

What has emerged is that the concept of police being the agents of the law of the land has not been provided with a structure which will sustain it and as such the police have, willy-nilly become the agents of the political party in power. There have been serious suggestions that the police should function under the judiciary, albeit one does not know how this will happen. When legislative and executive powers are united in the same person, or in the same body of magistrates, there can be no liberty. Again there is no liberty if the judicial power is not separated from the legislative and executive powers. Where it joined with the executive power, the judge might behave with violence and oppression. If we sharpen our perception, it will dawn on us that placing the police under the judiciary is a remedy which might arguably prove worse than the malady. It would undoubtedly amount to making the judge the investigator, and the prosecutor also, and this would not be in keeping with the imperatives of the rule of law. Actually, it would amount to moving the wheels of history backwards to the days of despotic autocracy. For, the same patent arguments that were advanced in favour of separation of the judiciary from the executive, will now with greater vehemence be advanced against the subordination of police to the judiciary, and this very idea strikes a chilling and unwelcome note.

With the coming into force the Code of Criminal Procedure, 1973 from April, 1974, many States kept the prosecution under a newly-created post of Director of Prosecution, who in turn was placed under the Home Minister of the State Government, at the district level they placed it under the District Magistrate. Thus prosecution, in spite of this change, continues to be under the executive. This change became imperative due to the following conclusions arrived at by a Committee of International Commission of Jurists in the International Congress of Jurists held in New Delhi in January 1959. "The prosecuting functions necessary involve the exercise of restraint and a sense of fairness which cannot be comprehensively reduced to precise formulation. Although it is the common practice to vest in the executive the final responsibility for the conduct of prosecution, it is essential that the supreme prosecuting authority exercises his function in on independent capacity rather than in pursuance of instructions given by the executive". The Law Commission had also made similar recommendation, and added that the responsibility of the police, according to their charter of functions, stipulated in the laws of the land, is the prevention and detection of offences and as it is naturally anxious to secure convictions, over-zealous police officers keep back relevant witness. It may also be considered that as long as a criminal case is under investigation with the police, and has not been put up before a court of law for trial of the accused, anybody can criticise it in the press, on the platform or in legislature. But once that very case has been put up before a court of law, nobody can utter a word of criticism anywhere for fear of contempt of court. And since investigation is as sacred as court trial, one fails to understand why double standards are applied — one during police investigation, and the other to the court trial. In fact, both being judicial process, should be treated equally. That is not being done, could, perhaps, be ascribed to the fact that investigations are conducted by police officers, who are not considered to be so respectable (as judicial officers are), because after all they are responsible to the executive! This apprehension of the public is not without valid reasons as the police become the fiddle in the hands of the political party in power, and as long as police are not insulated from the onslaught of political interference. In order to salvage the neutrality of the police and improve its accountability to the public and the laws it is imminently imperative to ensure that police are the Agents only of the Law of the land, and not the party in power.

2. Political Misuse of Police

Looking back over the years that have rolled by since Independence, one is apt to question and doubt whether we have progressed well on the path of democracy and evolved smooth and successful working arrangements for the purposeful functioning of the three important wings of the democratic system — Legislature, Executive and Judiciary. The executive has two layers — the top layer constituted by the elected political leadership in Government, and the lower layer covering the career executives in the form of civil services, police and para-military police forces included. While steering the country towards the promised objective of the socialist welfare state for its hundreds of millions of people, the Government has to control and regulate in an increasing degree the conduct and business of different sections of the people through progressive legislation and other related measures. This has meant increasing exercise of power by the Government through its widely spread apparatus of the executive in several matters affecting the daily life of the citizens. The yester generation of politicians and the civil executives provided an atmosphere of dignity and sense of direction for the civil services to function honestly and efficiently with public interest constantly held in view. Passing years saw the entry of a large variety of people into the field of politics and increasing contact between the politicians and the executive at various levels in a variety of situations, including those caused by decreasing majorities in legislatures. Scope of exercise of power through the political leadership in the Government induced political functionaries outside the Government to take undue interest in the conduct of the Government affairs, and gradually the spectre of political interference appeared on the scene. In this process the police become specially vulnerable to interference from politicians because of the increased political advantage that could be readily reaped by misuse of police powers, and in consequence the quality of performance and efficiency was and continued to be adversely affected by such interference. There are innumerable complaints, and rightly too, of partisan performance of police owing to frequent interference and pressures from political, executive or other extraneous sources. After the natural disappearance of the enlightened political leadership, as years passed by, there was a qualitative change in the style of politics. The fervour of the freedom struggle and the concept of sacrifice faded out quickly, yielding place to new styles and norms of behaviour by politicians to whom politics became a career by itself to enrich themselves and their kith and kins. Prolonged one-party rule at the Centre and in the States for over 40 years coupled up with the natural desire of ruling party men to remain in positions of power resulted in the development of symbolic relationship between politicians on one hand, and the civil services the other. Vested interests grew on both sides. What started as a normal interaction between the politicians, and the services for the avowed objective of better administration with better awareness of public feelings and expectations, soon degenerated into different forms of intercession, intervention and interference with *malafide* objectives unconcerned with public interests.

Political parties believed in establishing their political pressure by continuously keeping up an agitational posture, and the manner in which they have functioned, particularly on the one of periodical elections involving the free use of musclemen and *goondas* to influence the attitude and conduct of sizeable sections of the electorates. The involvement of such people in political activity brings in its wake anti-social elements who exploit their proximity to politicians to gain protection from possible police action under the law. This nexus between unscrupulous elements among politicians and such anti-social elements particularly affected the enforcement of social and economic enactments such as those against prostitution, gambling, smuggling, black-marketing, hoardings, adulteration, prohibition *etc.*, whenever they involve politically influential accused. Arrests and release on bail of persons involved in such offences and their subsequent prosecution in court attract political attention. This also results, in most places, in a kind of link being established between the elected representatives and the Station House Officer in the day-to-day affairs of the police station in which local musclemen or *Dadas* frequently get involved. This link facilitates the practice of corruption, and other malpractices by the police and politicians acting in collusion with each other.

Consequent on the agitation posture is taken up by political parties in opposition, protests, demonstration, public meetings, processions, politically motivated strikes in the industrial sector, and even in the Government services, *dharnas*, *bandhs*, *gherao etc.*, have become a recurrent feature in political activity in the country. Police have been increasingly drawn into the resultant law and order situations and are expected by the ruling party to deal with all such situations with a political eye putting down political dissent with force with police assistance has become a tacitly accepted objective of the politically-oriented Government, both of the Centre and States. More and more time of the police was taken up with law and order work, which really meant dealing with street situations in a manner that would cause maximum satisfaction to the ruling party. In the process crime affecting citizens' safety of person and property got progressively relegated. Police got progressively nearer to the political party in power and correspondingly farther from the uncommitted general public of the country, since most of the law and order situations tended to have political overtones, the political party in power got habituated to taking a direct hand in directing and influencing the police action in such situations. All these have led to a considerable misuse of machinery at the behest of individual and groups in political circles. Police performance under the compulsion of such environments has consequently fallen far short of the requirements of the law of the land, and impartial performance of duties on several occasions.

3. Examples of Interference

Generally, the following are the frequent instances in which police have been misused:

1. Arrest or non-arrest of a person against whom a case is taken up for investigation by the police.
2. Deliberate handcuffing of a person in police custody to humiliate him.
3. Release or non-release on bail of arrested person.
4. Suppression of material evidence that becomes available during searches and investigation by police.
5. Inclusion or non-inclusion in the charge-sheet placed in court on conclusion of investigation.
6. Posting or non-posting of police force in an area of apprehended trouble to create an effect to the advantage of one party or the other.
7. Taking persons into preventive custody to immobilise them from agitating political activity in opposition to the political party in power.
8. Foisting false criminal cases against political functionaries for achieving political ends.
9. Discretionary enforcement of law while dealing with public order situations, with emphasis on severity and ruthlessness in regard to persons opposed to the ruling party.
10. Manoeuvring police intervention by exaggerating a non-cognizable offence or engineering a false complaint to gain advantage over another party in a situation which will be outside the domain of police action in the normal course.
11. Preparation of malicious and tendentious intelligence reports in favour of the ruling party and with the

ulterior motive and intention to facilitate action against the opponent.

12. Transfer or suspension of police officers, who decline to carry out unlawful orders or instruction of politicians belonging to the ruling party, and thus, subjecting them to pecuniary and domestic hardships, with the ulterior intention and object that others should not dare to follow suit. This has assured prompt obedience even of unlawful or unconstitutional orders.

Political interference eventuates not only from political functionaries in the Government, but also from others outside the Government, who are connected in any manner with different political parties, including the ruling party. Further, an individual's capacity to generate political pressure on the police is not necessarily linked with his personal association with a political party. It can operate through several links, which are forced by consideration of money, castes, community, regional affinity *etc.* The unhealthy influence and pressures that are brought to bear on the police do not always originate from political sources alone. Capitalists, industrialists, businessmen, landlords, and such others who form the richer and more influential sections of the society, have immense capacity to generate such pressures to operate at different levels in the police, either directly or indirectly through political sources and influence the course of police action.

4. Repercussions of Interference

Interference with the police system by extraneous sources, especially the politicians, encourages the police personnel to believe that their career advancement does not at all depend on the merits of their professional performance, but can be secured by curring favour with politicians who count politicising and hob-nobbing with the functionaries outside the police system appear very worthwhile in the estimate of an average police officer. Deliberate and sustained cultivation of a few individuals on the political plane takes up all the time of a number of police personnel to the detriment of the performance of their normal professional jobs to the satisfaction of the general public at large. This process has set the police system on the downward slope to decay and total ineffectiveness. Besides, it has damaged the control system and weakened the normal chain of command that has to operate efficiently if the discipline, and the health of the police system is to be maintained. Interference at the operational level in police units results in total by-passing of the supervisory officers in the hierarchy. Subordinate officers see in their everyday official life that their superior officers count little in the ultimate disposal of a matter which lies in the normal course within their official cognizance only. Decisions taken at for higher level in the Government, though politically tainted, are passed on for implementation to the operation level subverting the command hierarchy. This was strikingly seen in the situation arising from the policemen's stir in certain states in May-June 1979, and it was found that this protest was triggered off by an alleged incident in one state in which a police officer, as low as a police constable, was attempted to be victimised at the behest of a political functionary. A note was circulated by the Ministry of Home Affairs, Government of India in the especially summoned conference of the Chief Ministers of all the States with contents. "There is a feeling in all States that interference not only in the matter of postings and transfers, but also in the matter of arrests, investigations, filing of charge-sheets is widespread. The principal grievances of the policemen are that if there is any unwillingness to comply with unlawful or improper suggestions, the policeman concerned is harmed or humiliated. Chief Ministers should ensure that there is no unlawful interference in the exercise of statutory powers in the matter of postings and transfers, and the States should seek to restore leadership and effectiveness of the official hierarchy with a view to ensure that the requisite rapport between the officers and men is not further eroded." To what extent political interference has been permeated can best be understood by the fact that in several States executive instructions have been issued conforming a kind of supervisory and inspecting role on the subordinate executive magistrates *vis-a-vis* the police stations. Such instructions are in total contravention of the provisions of Section 3 of the Police Act, 1861 — "No person, officer or court shall be empowered by the State Government to supercede or control any police functionary."

To seek appointment in police service most candidates go to the political leaders of the party in power down from the *gram panchayat* member to the Chief Minister. At various stages huge money is exchanged, and entry into police service is secured; on having been recruited through corrupt methods, such type of incumbent's first priority, naturally would be, to recoup all the money so spent by him. From the initial stage of his service he starts corruption, and is backed by those who inducted him in the service.

5. Political Instability and Politicisation of Police

"The political system that our Constitution has given to our country is such that it contemplates parties with different political ideologies administering the affairs of the Centre and State Governments. It is necessary in the interest of the territorial, political, and economic integrity of the nation to ensure that factors which contribute to such integrity are forever and continuously strengthened and not impaired; one such factor, and a very important and decisive one is the body of public servants at various levels belonging to the different discipline and functioning in the States and at the Centre. If the basic unity and territorial integrity of the country is to be emphasised at the political level it is imperative to ensure that the officials at the decision-making levels are protected, insulated and immunised from threats or pressures so that they can function in a manner in which they are governed by one single consideration — the promotion of public well-being and upholding of the fundamentals to the Constitution and the Rule of Law. The Government ought to ensure this, if necessary, by providing adequate and effective safeguards to which the officials may turn if and when necessary against any actual or attempted threats by the political and/or administrative authorities to sway the officials from performance of their legitimate duties. If a recurrence of this type of subversion is to be prevented, the system must be overhauled with a view to strengthen it in a manner that the functionaries working the system do so in an atmosphere free from the fear of the consequences of their lawful actions, and in a spirit calculated to promote the integrity and welfare of the nation and the rule of law." The above were the observations of Shah Commission (Chapter XXIV) in its third and final report, dated 6th August 1978, while enquiring into the excesses by the Government in collusion with civil services, including the police during Emergency. In conclusion, the Commission was of the view that there should be complete professional independence to the police while investigating and preventing crime and controlling it and all departmental matters, and while insulating or immunising the police from extraneous influence or interference it is possible for the Government to exercise due control on them in accordance with the same principles as are applicable to the relationship between the superior courts and junior courts. Whatever instruction or orders are to be issued by the political bosses of the police, should be in writing as generally oral orders are issued and they cause considerable embarrassment to the field officers when the orders happen to require the commission of illegal, irregular, improper or unjust acts; although interaction between the police and the elected representatives of the public is necessary for bringing to the notice of the executive whatever information the elected representatives may have in which they find that flagrant injustice by the police has been done and in which corrective action is necessary. But at the same time, it should be ensured that such interaction does not lead to unauthorised interference as such with the performance of the police. Like the civil services there should be "code of conduct" for the members of the political parties either of the Government in power or the oppositions.

6. Declaration by Police Personnel at the Time of Appointment

The authority of the police under the law is strictly defined and they are personally liable for the consequence whenever they invoke them. Police play no part in determining guilt or punishment and their accountability to courts, both criminal and civil, to local police authorities, to Parliament, to public opinion is unsurpassed anywhere else in the world. In the legal and Constitutional framework in which society requires them to enforce the laws enacted by its elected representatives, the most essential weapons in their armoury are not fire-arms, water cannon, teargas, rubber bullets, *lathis*, *etc.*, but the confidence and support of the people on whose behalf they act. The confidence and support of the people entirely depend on their personal and collective integrity and in particular the Constitutional freedom from political interference in their operational role. In view of the above stated Constitutional and statutory role of the police at the time of appointment each police officer down from the rank of a constable to the Director/Inspector General of Police has to take the following oath:

> "I do swear/solemnly affirm that I will be faithful and bear true allegiance to India and to the Constitution of India as by law established, that as a member of the police in the State .... I will honestly, impartially and truly serve the people without favour or affection, malice or ill will, that I will to the best of my ability, skill and knowledge discharge, according to law, such functions and duties as may be entrusted to me as police officer, and in such a manner as to uphold and protect the dignity of citizen as proclaimed in the Constitution". And yet, this pledge is violated from time to time by various incumbents of the Police Department, either directly or indirectly and taking of the pledge has remained merely a formality. To honour this pledge police neutrality has to be assured and ensured by politicians, whether belonging to the political party in power or in the opposition.

7. Police Neutrality and Peoples' Police

(i) Police Neutrality: The police role is based on impartial enforcement of all laws. It is this impartiality in enforcement of laws which has been an article of faith with generations of policemen is often described as, "Police Neutrality". The course of neutrality, impartiality and independence in the discharge of duties by a police officer is very important and must be accepted as a way of life in a democracy. In our society dominated by religions, castes and politics, that are mostly based on religion and castes, the need for impartial law enforcement assumes the greatest significance.

A survey of the working of the police ever since Independence would show that the police, by and large have failed to act impartially and could be manipulated to serve the interest of the party in power against the public interest. Unfortunately, there has been rapid growth of pliable police leadership which is prepared to act in a manner to suit its interest. Of several such instances, the following two would suffice to bear the point : (1) After the assassination of Mahatma Gandhi by Nathuram Godse in January 1948, *Brahmins* were subjected to loot, arson, murder and other privations of a horrendous character. This was in 1948, when the country had just become Independent. Since Nathuram Godse was a *Brahmin*, population belonging to this caste was made the target by the proteges of Congress, which was the ruling party. (2) In October 1984, the Sikhs, men, women, children and their properties were subjected to similar horrendous privations. Over 2,500 Sikhs were brutally killed in Delhi alone, and all these barbarous acts were committed by the proteges of the Congress, which was the ruling party, because the assassin of Indira Gandhi was a Sikh. On either occasion, police had no guts to take action, much less deterring or severe in order to prevent the commission of such atrocities, in many instances, the Government advised the police to be docile. But all the same there was failure to provide protection to the innocent people, and in order to avenge, the perpetrators were allowed a free hand and adopt the "Law of the jungle". It is a long list when police used force unwarranted, or in excess of that was required, while dispersing peaceful agitators under covert instructions from their political bosses, or to please them with the report that the opposition has been taught a lesson or partially or fully broken. Such a behaviour of the police is not in conformity with the Principle of Neutrality, and are reminiscent of the days of the British Rule or of the "Direct Action" launched by Mohammed Ali Jinnah and Suhravardi immediately before partition against the innocent Hindu population of this country. Either, during assault or in retaliation, police were communally affected, but now in the "Secular, Democratic" country like India such discriminatory, behavioural pattern has absolutely no place in "Police Ethics and Code of Conduct", may it be in relation to the political party in power or opposition. The fault is not wholly of the politicians but equally of the caliber and character of senior police officers, who are guided by self-interest.

Police have nothing to do with "Social conflicts" but they have to enforce the law with complete neutrality and without any bias. The most important reason why police officers yield to politicians and avoid to act is that they are either corrupt or incompetent or have a shady character. Politicians have made rapid strides inside the police force and even communalism has infiltrated into police ranks. This is corrosive of discipline and eventually of impartiality and efficiency. Political interference makes the police bend the law and even break the law, so as to advance their ulterior purposes. Professionally, where does the police take their stand in the political battles that are being fought daily in the streets? Their position is vital centre. For every policeman there is only one side — the middle ground, which he has to hold firm and stand steadfastly, unwaverred against the forces of deadly division, and render impartial service to all the segments of the society. A criminal has no caste, creed, class or religion, he is just a stark criminal and a social cancer to be eliminated by the police. But politicians have pulled or pushed the police from their side and simply made them impotent. The search for a committed police leadership with every change in the politically-oriented Government has led to most evil and dangerous police conditions.

In 48 years of Independence the police are now in the process of disintegration. Immersed daily in partisan law enforcement and subjected constantly to political interference, the police have become unreliable instrument except for carrying out illegal oral orders of political masters. It is a matter of surprise that they have stood up so long and so well in spite of difficult conditions under which they work, maintaining somehow some degree of professionalism. Police neutrality forms the backbone of police credibility among people. Everybody now believes that police strayed considerably from their ideal and moto, some less, some more. The imminent imperative need to steer the police back to its ideal is being repeatedly voiced by the public, the police themselves and the Government of the party in power, but the last-named agency is not very much enthusiastic about bringing such a change in the interests of the politicians forming the Government.

(ii) People's Police: People wish that the police should be omnipresent, omniscient and omnipotent. Their job is not only to protect and help their fellow citizens, but also to protect their fellow citizens against the Government or any other authority when they act unlawfully or illegally. Their duty is to simply see that the law of the land is kept, and they must be free from fear and favour. A policeman has always been guided by two conflicting or contrasting needs, one to maintain order and to protect people, and the other to ensure that they themselves do not act unreasonably, apprehensively, unlawfully or illegally. The police cannot prevent the Parliament from making what law it wishes, but they ensure that the Government servants do not exceed their legal powers, thus preventing any tyranny which, to the private person, is the chief danger of the welfare state, while this may seem an unorthodox and possibly dangerous conception of a difficult task for the police, it is the pith and marrow of democratic way of life. It is an utopian dream, and the concept of "*Ram Raj*". The police function is the essence of a government because the basic task of any Government is to maintain internal order. If citizens are unable to go about their daily work in a safe and predictable manner, one should be forced to say that the Government has ceased to operate effectively.

In India over the last four decades all the conditions, economic, political and social have changed, and in these days are changing more rapidly than never before. More important still, ideas have changed, are still charging. Ideas of political, economic, social rights and wrongs and the problem of justice in the relationships between the State and the individual, between social classes, and between group interests. The changing structure of the society has left its profound impact on politics and social life of citizens and that has led to the emergence of extremist groups — on both the right and left wings politics. These groups seek to introduce totalitarian form of the Government. The overriding problem of the future is that of protection of police from political attack, our society is on the threshold of widespread violence as never before. Communal riots, terrorism, insurgency are increasing in numbers. Socio-economic conflicts are increasing, and the police are required to interfere and intervene to prevent fragmentation of our society and preserve our democratic way of life. Civil disorders have become fairly common place, and the growing complexity and mechanisation of the society has made necessary a considerable expansion of legislation — an expansion that has contributed towards a deterioration in the relationship between the Government and the governed.

In the police station, the policeman meets the complainant, the suspect and hardened criminal. In the hospital, he meets the victim of rape, the person fighting for life after being grievously injured by a criminal, the person who attempted to commit suicide, the doctor and the nurse charged with kidnapping a new-born baby. In brothels, he finds teenage girls brought after kidnapping or abduction and sold for prostitution. In hotels, he meets call girls. In the university campus, he meets students on rampage. In the factory, he meets workers and management fighting for their rights. In courts, he meets magistrates, judges and lawyers, who, by and large, are very critical of the police and believe they are corrupt, brutal and untrustworthy. In the under world, he meets criminals and gangsters and those evading the law. He seldom meets the public at their best and they seldom welcome him. To the public, he is the law, the interfering, intermingling, dangerous and source of trouble. He finds, his children are teased in schools because their father is in the police force. In spite of his ostensible functions as protector, he meets only those he is protecting them from, and the travesty is that, for him they have no sympathy much less love. This is the image of the "Peoples' Police", and the society all these years has not only neglected, but also disowned him. The public never tried to understand him, his problems, difficulties, incompatibilities for one reason or the other, may be his created or foisted on him, conditions of service under which he works, most inadequate and beggarly emoluments and living conditions, non-stop strenuous work and the resulting deterioration in health and physical conditions, and above all his widow and orphaned children on account of his being killed while protecting the life of others or their property. The public never supported him or rendered a helping hand in the due discharge of his multifarious duties, and mostly adopted hostile stance. The police service is the most dominant organisation which can create or destroy the happiness of the communities. The State, the public and his own hierarchy have illtreated a policeman. It is high time that the public and the State take immediate, remedial and suitable measures to affect an all-round improvement in the police organisations and make it the most efficient law enforcement agency for the overall benefit of the public and the Nation, for obviously, the police did not lag behind, and kept pace with the deterioration in social ethics.

7. Autonomy of Police

Every political party has blamed all other political parties of misusing and abusing the police to promote partisan interests in the process of retaining power. The police leadership itself has not raised its voice, and it failed to protect the organisational interests, insulate from the political interference at other levels down the organisation and functionaries at all levels. A demoralised and frustrated police itself has become partisan in all their functional spheres, and to say that police public relations are at their rock bottom would be an understatement, and they have become adversarial. In the end, the one singular threat to democracy is people tending to take law into their hands. Not ones, but many a time, many Chief Ministers openly asked people to do so. Political parties formalised their nexus with criminals, armed gangs, private armies and terrorist organisations. Police have lost their initiative in influencing public policy, and restoring a semblance of their image-cum-authority as the protectors and promoters of the Rule of law, first prerequisite for democracy and development.

Indian Police did contribute to with all the internal contradictions, limitations and political pressures, keeping our Republic intact. The Republic and the public have a vested interest in promoting autonomy and accountability and thus professionalism among police forces. The increasing relevance for the autonomy of police force, and its accountability to public arises from the fact that all political parties sitting in opposition, have blamed the party holding power, of misuse and abuse of police, using police more as an instrument of party, rather than allow it to perform its role as an instrument of State, accountable to law of the land. All political parties in India have not only operated as parties in opposition, but also experienced power, one time or the other, in some State or the other. Indeed, we have entered a phase now where members of the ruling party have started accusing their own partymen running the Government, of abusing police by using them to spy individuals, and defeating their own party candidates in election with the aid of police. It was in this context and background that the President of India openly advised the Government to call a halt to the practice of using police for partisan political ends. The Jain Commission, currently enquiring into the assassination of Rajiv Gandhi has with it information and counter-information that the Government of India, though warned about the threat to the life of Rajiv Gandhi, was either lethargic or apathetic in giving him the necessary security cover-up, and this dismal, perhaps, willful failure of the Government, cost his life. Weighing without bias all these factors, police autonomy and accountability are of critical significance to the well-being of democracy in India, while retaining governmental responsibility for over-seeing the police.

33
Relation of Police with Press and Public

1. Press

In all countries of well-regulated democratic governments a large part of the work of the police is carried on under the observation of the press which is free to comment and criticise as it feels inclined. There is a distinct advantage in this system that the police are always alert to their duties of law enforcement in the constitutional manner only. In a democracy it is the right of the citizens to know-how public servants conduct themselves in the discharge of their official duties. Public servants are public property, and this is the price to be paid in a democracy.

The first to notice about the relations between police and press is that they form a reciprocally influencing system. The public estimation of the police is influenced, to a great extent, by the manner and tone of press reporting and comment on public affairs, and public opinion, in turn, influences the tone and content of press reporting. General satisfaction on the part of the public is the best criterion of the quality of the police of any country. A hostile attitude of the press towards the police can handicap the latter in a number of ways.

2. Freedom of Press in India

During the British regime freedom of press did not exist, and publication of news was strictly controlled. Moreover, adverse comments against police did not have any impact on the rulers, who rarely paid any serious attention to such criticism in the press and the building up of good police — public relations, except in cases where the interest of the British Raj was involved. The importance of ensuring good relations between the public and the police received attention of our national leaders after Independence. Under the Indian Constitution there is no separate guarantee of the freedom of the press. It is implicit in the freedom of expression which is conferred on all citizens under Article 19(l)(a). The right to freedom of expression carries with it the right to publish and circulate one's idea, opinions and views with complete freedom by resorting to any available means of publication, subject to such restrictions as could be legitimately imposed under Clause (2) of Article 19.

The independence of the press guaranteed by Article 19 comprehends all aspects from the acquisition of all information to the dissemination of views and opinions. The importance of freedom of the press consists, besides the advancement of truth, science, morality, and arts in general, in its diffusion of liberal sentiments on the administration of the Government, its ready communication of thoughts between citizens, and its consequential promotion of union among them, whereby oppressive officers are shamed or compelled into more honourable and fair, and equally impartial modes of conducting public affairs.

3. Police Image in India

Public opinion of the police varies from country to country, in some countries police stand as the symbol of security and protection, while in some other countries the police are viewed as an object of terror and hatred. In India, public distrust of the police is very great, and the police have never enjoyed the same sort of love, respect and friendliness on the part of general public as have British Police, and they do not exercise latter's unquestioned authority. They do not have the same discipline and strict respect for the law as their counterparts in Britain. Of the specific reasons, the greatest handicaps to good police work are political patronage and partisan politics.

4. Relations Between Police, Public and Press

Relations between police, public and press in India have been a love-hate one, more of the latter. The citizens view the police as the strong arm of the State that harass and not befriends them. The police are feared by common man, misused by the powerful for their selfish ends, pilloried by the press and made a scapegoat by the party in power. Cordial police-public relationship, despite some successful experiments remained a dream, and this is something unprecedented in India and has to be attempted in a sincere and serious manner. The fact that public and press are interested in every aspect of police work, and the tone of press reporting and comments profoundly influence the public opinion. Today, there have been ceaseless expansion of police functions which has given them more and more duties and added power. The police have to enforce many regulations, orders and laws, which touch the public life at a number of points and have nothing to do with criminals and criminal activities. Traffic control and enforcement of social legislations are examples of this enlargement of police duties. The bulk of police dishonesty has always occurred in connection with regulation of traffic and enforcement of social legislations in which the police have a wide discretion in prosecuting. When we examine the prohibition of carrying more than two persons on a scooter or motorcycle under the Motor Vehicle Act, we find that no citizen, high or low, educated or uneducated, owning a car or not, is inclined to observe this law. On the contrary, he often violates it. Because to carry more than two persons in a hired transport is much more expensive than carrying them on his scooter or motorcycle. Sights of conveying four to five persons, even a baby child in the arm, on a scooter or a motorcycle are not infrequent. Purposeful and voluntary violation of this law suits the people as they are financially benefited. The police are caught in a vice, resulting in unending displeasure of the parties involved. To take action or not to take action, either of the party is displeased. So, while incurring displeasure policemen seek for pecuniary benefit which is readily offered and given. This is the bane of corrupted police machinery. Bereft of these discretionary powers, the police may entangle the public, who may suffer harassments and at times privations, for very petty or minor offences which are likely to be committed involuntarily by the people in their avocations. Thus, is the existence of the vicious circle. If people do not commit any infraction, there will be no contact with the police, corruption is incidental to the unlawful conduct of the people. The public and the Government have to realise that law is a journey which cannot be made to wait at one station. Laws for that matter, were introduced to condition society, but now law should change to suit the conditions of the society. Laws, which cannot be obeyed by the general public for one reason or other, should not have any place in the Statutes Book, no beneficial results would accrue if people voluntarily committed infractions and thereby damage the sanctity of law. Instances, such as the deliberate Constitutional violation by Indira Gandhi in her capacity as Prime Minister to suit the political and personal convenience in a bid to retain power during 1975-76 have always encouraged the general population to violate law. The leader is always imitated and followed. The same principle applies to charges of corruption by Prime Minister or the Chief Minister and their cabinet colleagues. The conspicuous absence of even symbolic honesty among such politicians has greatly enthused civil servants to remain corrupt. Corruption takes place, because it is tolerated at all levels. So pervasive it has become that people have now come to realise that without corruption their legitimate requirements would never be fulfilled. This is the administrative and social picture which the policemen witness day in and day out.

Moreover, in regard to certain police activities, notably, corruption and bribery, some of the examples are almost incredible, because of involvement in corruption and sharing the ill-gotten money with their subordinates by high-ranking officers. This was unthinkable in the days of the British regime and even still sixties. With poor integrity of politicians and public servants of every level of administration none may expect police to be angelic.

The ugliest and, most abominable aspect of this corruption is that it has become co-operative, both in collection from public transport operators, gamblers, smugglers and various vice-dens and payment to the rank and file. Several instances can be cited when public transport operators, even prostitutes, had observed strikes and created road blocks in protest of police harassment. However, such excesses can be minimised by an alert press.

5. Role of Press

The question of relations between the press and the police is much more complicated today than it was before the Independence. None of us is in doubt that the existing police-press relationship in India is far from satisfactory. It was expected after the Independence that the relationship between the police, public and the press would be congenial, but they were pitch-forked by several factors which had developed over the years. Of the specific reasons, the greatest handicaps to good police, public and the press relations are political influences in police work and partisan law enforcement. In a stable developed society where Parliament and State legislatures and the Executive are healthy and vibrant the functioning of the press is confined largely to its traditional role of reporting and interpreting events. But since these institutions have become defective or on the decline, a greater responsibility has devolved on an independent press to critically examine their deeds. Unfortunately, in India these most important institutions are packed with people of lesser integrity, nexus between politicians and criminal gangs has come to stay, corruption in the bureaucracy and even judiciary is frequently reported, and they have become ineffective, police brutality is considered passe and politics is sordid. In such a situation, an independent press plays a vital role of keeping India as open society, which is the only way it can be governed.

It needs to be mentioned that sectional loyalties surface very often, and when communal and caste disputes arise, the press has the vital duty of staying absolutely neutral. One of the worrying trends, however, is that sometimes newspapers ceased to become impartial observers and turned virtually active participants.

In a faction-ridden Indian society where sectional loyalties surface periodically, elections are rigged and violence during election has been a common feature, partisan law enforcement and abuse of power by the police have become endemic and the Army is being called frequently in aid of the civil administration, the press has to play a role of a watchdog to safeguard the rights of citizens against oppression and tyranny at the hands of State power.

Police have to establish a system of communication through which the authentic facts relating to crime and disorder can quickly be given to the press. Newspapers are entitled to all the legitimate news of the police, it has a right, under reasonable restrictions to have access to the police chief and to propound such enquiries as are reasonable and fair and are not impertinent, and not calculated to interfere with police in suppressing crime and pursuing criminals. It is seldom appreciated that in the intercourse between the police and the representatives of press there should be a happy medium in a free society, otherwise the newspapers are likely to publish distorted or contorted, or even false or exaggerated news which will cause great harm to the reputation of the police. Public interest in police matters is enormous and they have a right to know more about the police which they pay for. It must be remembered that the police and the press, in their own sphere, are watchdogs of public security and safety and their paths are parallel. Both as public servants assume sacred responsibilities. Both will exist as long as public has confidence in their impartial and comprehensively truthful behaviour. A time has come when both have to take a new look at their mutual problems and build a proper image. The neutrality of the press cannot be given up although several principal newspapers and journals have well-defined stances to favour a political party of their affiliation, may be they are financed by them. Criminalisation of politics has introduced a new dimension in police-public relation. Persons involved in crime get elected on party tickets and even become members of Cabinet. Co-operation of the people towards such a government and police, can hardly be forthcoming. We cannot blame the people for it. About the killing of over 2,500 Sikhs in Delhi during 1984 anti-Sikh riots public impression may be summed up. "Here is a force of over 50,000 strength that failed to protect law-abiding citizens and also failed to take action against the criminals, some of them politicians, involved in the ghastly incidents." Such ineffectiveness of police will never be able to draw any public sympathy or co-operation. This is a serious situation getting more serious day-by-day. Political parties have also to redraw their priorities if they want to serve the country and improve police-public relations. Various committees, commissions, and even the National Police Commission comprising eminent persons, whose competency, objectivity or loyalty to the country were unquestioned, have examined this aspect and their recommendations to achieve better police, press and public relations, though accepted by the Government, have not been implemented by it, and that is hindering good public-police relations.

According to present trends press is interested in publishing newsworthy stories, and failure of police is considered more newsworthy than its success. It is left to each press to adopt its own policy to inform the public and also to highlight public expectations. Press has its own representatives to collect information and materials which may be different from official versions. When divergent information of an event is given by the police to the press, people tend to accept press reports. Police will have to rethink in order to give information that is more accurate, without jeopardising their law enforcement duties of investigation of crimes. If all the newspapers should tomorrow begin a united effort to impress police efficiency by encouraging and also applauding honest men in the force, by demanding proper and lasting legislative reform, by separating good from the bad, by intelligent and impartial discussions of police and administration, by holding the minister in charge as well as the police chief to the strictest accountability for whatever is wrong, a new era is bound to begin in the working of police administration.

6. Police and Public Co-operation

Starting from a conceptional angle, the police in a Democratic Welfare State, function on behalf of the people to fulfil their priority needs of dealing with crime problem. Even during the pre-Independence era — British Raj, effective enforcement of laws could not be secured without the co-operation of the people. Under the law no search can be conducted, and seizures made unless there are at least two respectable and independent witnesses to attest these procedures. Even the inquest over a dead body has to be performed in the presence of five or more reputable and independent persons, and all these should belong to that locality. Imagine the situation when no witness is forthcoming an account of the non-cooperative attitude of the people, no investigation worth the name could be completed and dead body would lie without holding inquest on it, crime will be allowed to remain undetected, and criminals would be free to indulge repeatedly in their criminal activities, and safety to person and property would be perpetually endangered (Sections

100, 165, 174 of the Criminal Procedure Code). Public assistance is absolutely necessary, nay it has been made mandatory as per the provisions of Section 37 of the Code of Criminal Procedure:

> "Every person is bound to assist a Magistrate or police officer reasonably demanding his aid — (a) in the taking or preventing the escape of any person whom such Magistrate or police officer is authorised to arrest, (b) in the prevention or suppression of a breach of the peace, (c) in the prevention of any injury attempted to be committed to any railway, canal, telegraph or public property."

The legislators did not stop at this. Under Section 39 of the same Code, "every person, aware of the commission of, or of the intention of any other person to commit any offence punishable under any of the following Sections of the Indian Penal Code shall give information to police." These offences include offences against the State, public tranquillity and peace, illegal-gratification or bribery — giving and taking, adulteration of food and drugs, murder, attempted murder and offences affecting life and property, public servants, criminal breach of trust, mischief, house trespass and currency. It has also been laid down in the same Section that if there is some excuse for the person not to give the required information to the police, the burden of proving such excuse will lie on him. As a corollary he will have to prove the circumstance which prevented him from reporting the offence to the police. Similar mandatory provisions exist under Section 40 of the same Code. Under this section every officer employed in connection with the affairs of a village and every person residing in a village shall forthwith communicate to the nearest police station officer any information regarding: (a) the presence of any notorious receiver or vendor of stolen property in or near such village, (b) arrival or departure of a person reasonably suspected to be a *thug*, robber, escaped convict or proclaimed offender, (c) commission or intention to commit a non-bailable offence or any offence related to unlawful assembly, (d) occurrence of any sudden on unnatural or suspicious death, (e) commission or intention to commit any offence of murder, attempted murder, house-breaking, *dacoity*, forging currency *etc.*, and (f) any matter concerning the disturbances or likely disturbances of public peace, tranquillity or the safety of property or person.

Again under Section 38 of the same Code public are liable to assist in the execution of warrants. Under Section 43 of the same Code any private person may arrest or cause to be arrested any person who in his presence commits a non-bailable and cognizable offence or any proclaimed offender. In the dispersal of unlawful assembly public have to give necessary assistance to the police under Section 127 of the Criminal Procedure Code. Such wide powers were given to the people and all these obligations were imposed on them in 1860 itself when the Code of Criminal Procedure was enacted during the British regime. The same provisions are enforceable. The legislators relied on the people more than the police and that is why the mandatory provisions of witnessing police procedures by respectable and independent persons were enacted, the legislators distrusted the police from its inception, and it appears to have stemmed out due to the unlawful or illegal practices of some irresponsible policemen, who worked only for the administration and never for the good of the people, and while doing so, and in order to enable them to play the role of sycophants, they concocted documents and evidence, just to please their administrative and regal bosses, which are now substituted by the politicians and their party in power. Unfortunately, the same picture is exhibited even now. There are several occasions when no person other than a policeman is present anywhere near the scene of the offence, and yet the courts expect the police to produce an "eye witness" in support of the charge against the offenders. It has become extremely difficult to get respectable independent persons to attest police procedures, and police make their stooges to attest such procedures merely to satisfy the legal requirements. These trumped-up witnesses cannot stand the cross-examination in a court of law resulting in the acquittal of the case and strictures against the police, in spite of their best intentions to punish the guilty person and save the society from his depredation. Public squarely blame the police, conveniently forgetting the very fact that they have failed to fulfil their lawful and constitutional obligations in giving the necessary aid to the police. The remedy lies in prosecuting these members of the public, who have refused to come to the aid of the police as required by law, and while taking recourse to it, public will be further distanced and estranged from the police and their accord and co-operation would never be forthcoming, the blame could be apportioned to both. The laws are not realistic, and they are equally impracticable. With the basic distrust on a policeman, even of the rank of Director General of Police, while assessing evidence given before him, no police force in a democracy can function honourably and with pride, whereas any member of the public, of whatever low character he may be, is believed and trusted by the judiciary, because it has been ordained by the law of the land. This dishonourable and stigmatised image of police has to be changed, and wiped off in a democracy, for trust begets trust. This should be the first step taken both by the people and the Government, if necessary, by suitably amending the outdated law of 1860, in order to better police-public relations. There are several instances in which brutal murder, *dacoity*, arson or rape, though witnessed by tens of people, some of them advocates, doctors, engineers and of high social status, could not be prosecuted as no witness is forthcoming to testify against the offenders. Are such people dutiful to the Constitution? Do they honour it? Have they any concern or consideration for their fellow brothers, or the society to which they belong? If they behave adversely what moral right have they to blame the police for their non-cooperation with the public. These are the two sides of the same coin, and where reciprocity is either inherently missing or cannot be achieved, it will be non-sense to talk of "good police-public relation", such a talk will be as irresponsible as the behaviour of both the people and the police. It is not to advocate the cause in favour of the police, but at the same time it must be noted that this is a fact of life. Though late by almost 45 years after we have achieved Independence, a beginning has to be made in restructuring the law so that confidence of honesty is reposed in the police by the public through their elected representatives, accompanied by a very severe punishment to the delinquent policemen.

Contrarily is the position of offences arising out of political rivalries, or group or caste, class or religion conflicts. A large number of prototype witnesses are produced by either party, most of them concocted by even the rival party. Falsehood and fabrication of evidence are so replete that it is a task for the investigating officer to come to a truthful conclusion. Politicians have always engineered such evidence. Even with best efforts and intentions the impartial behaviour of a policeman is often assailed, and either of the parties accuse him of partisan attitude. Here again, cases are replete wherein politicians, even at the ministerial level, have harboured the real culprits and in order to dilute or diminish press criticism, sent up cases against innocent persons of their party on fabricated evidence. Thereby they have secured the protection of real culprits, so that they could be handy for further depredations, and silenced the press and public criticism. Those prosecuted are never convicted as the falsehood is exposed in law courts, strictures are passed, police is blamed, and the intended action against the delinquent policeman for his failure to sift evidence in a bid to come to a truthful conclusion, is thwarted by the same politicians, who had made the policeman a scapegoat. How such an abnormal and unlawful behaviour of politicians, who have taken the police for ride, could be conducive to better public-police relations? Who has gained, and who has suffered? It is for the law abiding citizens to find out.

7. Crime Problem and the Police

A comparative study of the crime figures with an interval of a decade showed a disproportionate increase in crime to population, negativing the excuse/argument that crime increased due to the population growth. The increasing crime rate and the trend towards violence and the heavy frauds affecting public economy are even more alarming and fear generating, and have declined peoples' confidence in the police and the Government. In dealing with the crime problem, the police has the primary responsibility and that responsibility could certainly not be adjudged in India today, as having been carried out to meaningful public satisfactions. Even the police response to calls for dealing with emergency needs of the public, including the vital preventive effort and immediate action on reported crime, is generally adjudged far below public expectations. Equally short of expectations is the standard of performance of the police in dealing with reported crime and in the matter of their investigations and disposals.

The basic police mission is the protection of life and property, and the rights of the people against the background of well-maintained public peace and order. And, therefore, apart from leadership calibre and motivated team response within the organisation, and the influence of money, muscle and political power in the environment, the basic sequence of peoples' expectations would be police perception, their performance in pursuance, and peoples' acceptance of it. All these will determine peoples' attitude to police and enhance the police image.

It is today an accepted axiom that nobody of police, anywhere in the world, can perform their functions effectively and to the perceived satisfaction of the people whom they serve, without the willing co-operation of the public. For one thing, in no country of the world, can the State itself provide police organisation with adequate strength and proportionate equipment to give full protection to all citizens. Such a protection has to be symbolic. In most advanced countries, the proportion of police strength to population in one to around 450. But in the States of India it is one policeman to about 1,000 population. The proportion is even less than this in many States. For another thing the quality of police service in all its aspects, will depend largely on the nature of public co-operation, that only the professionalised police are in a position to secure in the locality for the effective performance of their functions. Unless the victim, the witnesses and the people pull their might together, there will be no satisfactory achievement by the police. Where crime takes place, it is for the people to report them promptly. Many of them do not, and that interferes with police performance. May be this is because of unsatisfactory prior behaviour and performance of the police themselves reflecting adversely on the level of public confidence and co-operation. Similarly, preserving the scene of crime intact, and witnesses spontaneously coming forward to give evidence, voluntarily and fully, make all the difference in success and failure in police work relating to investigation and prosecution. Quick trials without adjournments by the judiciary would also go a long way in the increased input of good public-police relations as no witness would prefer repeatedly going to the court forsaking his profession, and as such he is encouraged to abstain from giving evidence. He will be obliged to obliterate his presence from the scene of offence. The best way he selects is to say that he is not a witness to the crime. The police, unfortunately seem to expect public co-operation as a matter of course and complain bitterly when they do not get it. But the people do not perceive it that way, unless they have worked hand in hand with the police on many occasions in the past, may be non-police duties, such as community projects, natural calamity *etc.*, so that the public can really get to understand the problem faced by the police from the policeman's angle. All the same, there is no getting away from the fact that in order to assuredly get effective and good police-community relations, it is the policeman, who has to get his perception right and his performance in line and take the first step to acquire public co-operation by his own behaviour, and performance, in an environment free from political and other pressures and incorruptible attitude to any form of allurement. Only with such all-round efforts by each member of the police fraternity meaningful public co-operation and accord will automatically come about, and there should be no reason why this dream cannot become a reality, provided both the public and the Government reciprocate by giving a helping hand to the mass of police organisations by implementing the recommendations of the National Police Commission (1978-81). After all, the will of the party in power could alone do it. Solitary involvement by the police to achieve this goal may take another five decades like the past, and the police would be continued to be stigmatised as the police of the politicians in power, and not of and for the people, who pay their emoluments through nose from hard earned money to secure protection to their life and property, and yet, unfortunately remain without it.

34

Complaints Against Police

1. General Survey

One of the fundamental requirements of good government in a democracy is to guard against excesses or omissions by the police in exercise of their wide powers in the discharge of their statutory duties, which cause injury, harm, annoyance or undue hardship to a citizen. Once the police are given adequate powers it is essential to ensure, that they keep to them. In law enforcement, ends never justify even a slightly dubious means. Whatever their origin or foundation it is essential that complaints against the police are investigated as speedily as possible, and those found guilty are removed from the force irrespective of their ranks. If complaints are impartially investigated, the department and its officers can clear themselves of unfounded charges made against them, and a greater degree of confidence and mutual respect is established between the police and the public. Impartial enquiries must never be sidetracked because a single policeman has power to do great harm to other people as well as to the reputation of the force. The maintenance of police morale does not depend on whitewash but on satisfying conception of policeman's place in the society.

Complaints against junior officers are generally enquired into by their immediate seniors, who submit their reports to the Superintendent of Police/Deputy Inspector General/Director General of Police for necessary action. But this is one-sided method as the relationship between various ranks of police hierarchy is so intimate that independent and impartial enquiry can only be made by an officer of the strictest rectitude, probity and integrity, and strangely enough, these days, such an officer is a rare product of the department. In each district, at the divisional or state headquarter a complaint cell exists, under the charge of the senior most officer. This cell studies the reports of the enquiry officers and takes necessary action against the defaulting police officer. Complaints are also made before the District Magistrate, Sub-divisional Magistrate, who after enquiry, forward their reports to the Superintendent of Police of that district for taking necessary action. In quite a number of cases parties have gone to courts with private criminal complaints against the police personnel for their alleged misconduct. The staff of a police station is most vulnerable, as it is they who come into contact with public, and naturally, they become the offending party.

The police misuse and abuse their powers and resort to brutality in a variety of situations like killing of suspects in false encounters and torture on prisoners in various forms of 'third-degree', grievous hurt or death caused while in police custody, involving innocent persons in false cases, suppression or minimisation of cognizable offences reported to them, *etc.*, most of these cases are due to politicisation of police, and growing nexus between politicians, anti-socials and police. Discretionary law enforcement is impregnated with seeds of corruption, and therefore, police administrators must take positive action to ensure equality of enforcement and to bring all perpetrators to justice, remove from the ranks all those who discriminate and ensure that every officer follows the guidelines laid down by the higher functionary and affirm that there is never an individual choice to enforce or not to enforce law. If senior police officers of supervisory ranks investigate complaints promptly and impartially and deal with the guilty offenders firmly, a greater degree of confidence and mutual respect can be established between the police and the public, but the supervisory officers will have to follow the dictum, "Practice before preach". There has been a growing demand that police misdemeanour should be a subject matter of a judicial probe, and this is because, public rarely come across a supervisory police officer, who has no extraneous intimacy with his subordinates for one reason or the other. The standard of police conduct is usually set by the senior officer at the supervisory level and it has been proved beyond any dispute that corruption and abuse of power have thrived where senior officers are themselves dishonest or they are lukewarm in checking corruption and abuse of powers within the rank and file. Complaints or corruption charges against police are enquired into by the State Vigilance and Anti-corruption organisations, and by the Central Bureau of Investigation, if senior police officers are involved.

Complaints against the police fall into the following main categories:

(1) Misconduct, (2) Misuse and abuse of power, (3) Burking and minimisation of offences, (4) Violence, and (5) Corruption.

2. Malpractices in Law Enforcement

There is no doubt that the police is the principle agency of law enforcement under the Constitution and various statutes, and they have been entrusted with the undoubted duty to bring predators to book without any fear or favour. And yet, in a democratic society wedded to the concept of rule of law, the laws and procedure adopted by the State for achieving this laudable objective have to conform to civilised standards. In their battle against crime and delinquency the State and its officers cannot, therefore, forsake the decency of good behaviour and have recourse to extra-legal, unconstitutional and brutish methods for the sake of detection of crime and criminals. No man or group is above the law, nor is any one beyond its protection. These truths apply equally to the Government.

Has there been proper balancing of the minimum human rights of the accused, and the demands of corporate good of the society, or are these weakness and inadequacies in our Criminal Justice System which need to be plugged to make the administration of criminal justice a more effective instrument of social defence against escalating crime and delinquency? Obviously, the answer must be in positive, but it has also to be admitted that there are quite a few handicaps in the working of the police which ought to be removed by reforming our somewhat outdated criminal laws. Rule of law requires an honest, devoted and dedicated band of public servants, who are both capable and willing to carry out the behests of the law. The principles of police conduct lay down, "The police are essentially a law enforcing agency. They should not question the propriety or necessity of any duly enacted law. They should enforce the law firmly and impartially without fear or favour, malice or vindictiveness". And so the United Nations Code of Conduct prescribed for Law enforcement officials is: "Law enforcement officials shall respect the law and the present Code. They shall also, to the best of their capability prevent and vigorously oppose any violation of them."

3. Legal Handicaps of Police in India

Indeed, consistent with the principle of the rule of law, and the tenets of accusatorial system of jurisprudence, the Constitution of India and the laws of our land have also guaranteed certain basic rights, and procedural safeguards even in favour of the violators of the law. To mention a few:

1. Presumption of innocence in favour of the accused and burden of proving guilt lies with the prosecution. (Chapter VII Indian Evidence Act).
2. Inadmissibility of statements and confessions before the police (Section 162 Criminal Procedure Code, and Section 25 of Indian Evidence Act).
3. Arrest of an offender not on mere suspicion, but on reasonable suspicion (Section 41 of Criminal Procedure Code and Article 21 of the Constitution).
4. Search of a place only on reasonable grounds and prior recording reasons thereof (Section 165 Criminal Procedure Code).
5. Production of the accused person within 24 hours of the arrest before a Magistrate, exclusive of the time taken for the journey from the place of arrest to Magistrate's courts. (Sections 56, 57 of Criminal Procedure Code, and Article 22(2) of the Constitution).
6. Guarantee against retrospective penal legislation, double jeopardy and self-incrimination. (Article 20(1), (2) and (3) of the Constitution).

It is true that the endorsements of these rights make detection of crime difficult. The extent of damage caused by the wrong-doer may tend to create a sense of righteous indignation amongst the law enforcement agencies of the State, and at times, a certain amount of undue zeal to bring the offenders to justice at any cost may unconsciously motivate or induce them to adopt malpractice.

Section 26 of the Indian Evidence Act stipulates that, "Confession of accused while in the custody of police not to be proved against him", unless it be made in the immediate presence of a Magistrate. There are thousands of remote places in the country where police go for investigation, and there is no Magistrate stationed there by the State. The police are helpless to bring the offender before justice, nor is it possible for the State to station thousands of Magistrates in such places. The impracticability of these provisions encourages a criminal to escape punishment and inversely enough, the policemen to adopt malpractices to bring the criminal before justice in the larger interest of the society. If both the police and Magistrate go together for investigation of each and every case, which is neither feasible nor legal in view of the separation of the executive and judiciary as per Constitutional mandates, a great injustice may eventuate if both in collusion with each other, decide to implicate and involve an innocent person with ulterior corrupt motives. Section 27 of the same Act directs that, "No confession made by an accused to a police officer while in custody of the police should be proved against him unless the information given by the accused relates distinctly to the fact thereby discovered." If Sections 26 and 27 are juxtaposed they are anomalous to each other, making investigation by police more difficult and intricate. Under such legal provisions, which are all favourable to the accused, the police become more helpless. At the same time, Section 27 only applies to a police officer, and not any other agency. Right from the inception the legislators are convinced that police is not an honourable or respectable agency to be trusted in the matter of use of such statements, and on that basis alone, no accused should be held guilty of the offence charged. In such a situation the police come in a quandary, and come out of this predicament by adopting the following malpractices:

1. Padding and concoction,
2. Illegal detentions,
3. Planting of property, and
4. Use of third-degree methods in eliciting information, or confession from suspect or accused.

Indeed, this is the most notorious single factor which has brought disgrace to the police. The problem has become so grave that apart from quite a few suspensions, dismissals and convictions of defaulting officers, a few of them had to be sentenced either to long-term imprisonment or imprisonment for life or even with sentences of death. This matter has become so serious in several countries of the world that even the United Nations had to be concerned about this abuse of official power and the world body had to issue a declaration known as, "Declaration on the Protection of All Persons from Being Subjected to Torture and other cruel, Inhuman or Degrading Treatment or Punishment" to counter such malpractices. But the law-abiding elements of the society are inextricably allowed to suffer on account of the continuous depredations of these criminals, who are not normal citizens as they have criminal propensities.

Non-registrations or minimisation of complaints, interpolations in first-information reports and other record, putting up false cases and incorrect registration are other malpractices which are also adopted by the police when vested interests make a profitable bargain.

4. Causes of Malpractice

The following are the important reasons which tend a policeman to have recourse to malpractices:

1. Too much emphasis on statistics for judging the efficiency of officers.
2. Over-zealousness on the part of investigating officers in relation to serial No. 1 above.
3. Malice, ill-will or hostility towards an individual or a section of a community.
4. Dishonesty, selfish motives or other corrupt practices.
5. Adverse working conditions or over work.
6. Lack of training, equipments and forensic science facilities.
7. Laziness.
8. Lack of uptodate knowledge of law and the case laws.
9. Lack of public co-operation and support.

10. Legal handicaps elaborated above.
11. Too high, unreal and unfeasible standard of evidence demanded by the judiciary. The distrust of the police and the evidence they produce often operate a vicious circle as has been pointed out by Justice Krishna Iyer, in *Inder Singh's* case: "Judicial quest for perfect proof often accounts for police presentation of full-proof concoction.......No we must be realists".

For the decimation or elimination of all these malpractices it is absolutely necessary to follow the old adage, "Trust begets trust" and make a beginning by overriding Section 25 of the Indian Evidence Act and Section 162 of the Criminal Procedure Code to make voluntary confession and statements to police in course of investigation as admissible evidence under the law. If a police officer is never trusted, he will continue to remain unworthy and a little more trust in the police will surely make them into a responsible force deserving of confidence of the public, the Bar and the Courts.

Those related to judicial functions, advocate that non-ethical practices should be scrupulously eschewed by the police, as the harm that can be caused by following such practices is far greater than the benefit that may accrue. It is no duty of the police to bypass the law, they act under the law and not in derogation of it. But they fail to understand that when criminals go on escaping and their number increases, the society as a whole, is in jeopardy, and men, women, children and their property are at the mercy of the perpetrators. These days no one is safe, criminal elements in the society are preponderous and they have irrevocably, as at present, affected the country socially, economically, politically and ethically. The public have to prevail on their elected representatives to consider the prevailing lawless conditions in the country, and bring out the much-needed amendment of that law at the earliest, as the very laws which were designed about 150 years ago to protect the law-abiding citizens have often thwarted or hindered the efforts of scrupulously honest policemen, of which they are many, to apprehend wanted criminals and punish them through judiciary. The remedy lies in systematic and scientific modernisation of the law and its course from time to time, and making the legal system fit to cope effectively with the needs and circumstances of the living present.

5. Violence by Police

Everybody, apart from the police, is concerned with the frequent use of violence by the police. The law provides for the use of force when such use is necessary for the protection of the society. Under the right of private defence of property or person the use of force by any individual is ordained lawful. Police use force mostly for the protection of others and on very rare occasion for their protection. If the "Right of Private Defence" is abrogated their will be lawlessness and "Might is Right" rule in the country, the weaker will be preyed by the stronger, and law will be displaced by anarchy. Force is quelled by a greater force, and for the maintenance of public peace and order and tranquillity and the rule of law the legislators have vested in the police the power to use adequate force and certainly not more than necessary to compel the submission to the rule of law-by-law-breakers.

Increasingly, the disturbing truth is that politico-criminal nexus is responsible for use of violence by the police, as an instrument of administrative policy. For too many people, in for too many different situations, are on the edge of violence, after Independence, with guns with their finger on trigger. The old drill of the police of warning, teargassing and lathi charging in dispersal of riotous mob ceased to be effective.

After the Independence the Nation entered the most turbulent period in Indian history, perhaps, like the one witnessed during Muslim invasion in the 8th century, and onwards. Its causes — social, political, communal, economic, educational, class and caste riots, public disorder and violent crimes become the normal feature of everyday life. Police stations, Legislative Councils, Assemblies and even Parliament have been often besieged; Government offices, public transport vehicles, railway trains, tracks and banks were attacked, and shops looted or set ablaze by armed mob. Essential services and the amenities given by them are disturbed, even hospitals are not spared. Armed criminals with the support of politicians captured polling booths, looted polling boxes and killed rival candidates during the election, enabling criminally inclined politicians to win an easy victory and enter the most sacred body either of Legislative Assembly or Parliament. Judges, including of High Court, were attacked and killed. Almost any kind of public demonstration turned as violent as furious, and many persons, including a large number of policemen were either injured or killed in the line of duty. The public indifference to the battles being fought in the streets in almost every community in the country has been a serious development and the police, day in and day out, are bearing the brunt of the attacks. Peaceful "bandhs" calls given by political parties either in power or opposition did not remain peaceful and party cadres armed with lethal weapons fought in the streets. The clear and inevitable result of this situation is that the violence of law-breakers is opposed and controlled by the violence of the police, perhaps, allegedly with greater ferocity like opening of fire in self-defence or in the defence of the life and property of the law-abiding citizens, whose protective duty has been lawfully entrusted to the police and in the process, besides the criminals, some innocent persons might have been killed.

The growth of private armies (*Sennas*) formed, in the country side, on castes and class basis, with the blessings of politicians encouraged large-scale violence in the society. These private armies include ex-convicts, criminals, and anti-socials, all armed with either licensed or unlicensed firearm resorted to violence during various land disputes, or class or caste rivalry during elections. People in villages sleep with loaded guns by their side to resist attacks. The Government failed to control the circulation of unlicensed arms, and explosives, and took no action to ban these illegal private armies.

There can be no doubt that the control and circulation of these fire-arms would go a long way towards checking violence, the great difficulty encountered by the police is to disarm the armed hoodlums, who vastly outnumber the police. The problem of violent crime is, in large part, a problem of crimes committed by gangsters who are flourishing with the support of politicians and their parties. Explosions of high intensity bombs killed hundreds and injured thousands in the last decade.

The next major problem confronted by the police is the disappearance of the fear of law, if not respect for it, which is an important element for the maintenance of law and order. The deterrent effect of swift, sure and just punishment has been lost, because of the gross delay in the trial of cases. Lakhs of cases are pending in various courts. Those, who are involved in heinous crimes are not punished promptly because of endless procedural delays. Bail, even for repeaters is easier. When the policeman finds that he can get no support to enforce the law against a criminal and in such volatile situations, the temptation is very great to resort to force, which impartially measured against the one used by the violators of law, would be perceptibly less.

A policeman has the right to use force to disarm, subdue and arrest the violent criminals and policemen can go on indefinitely supplying examples in which a great deal of force had to be used in performing their jobs, and in the process thousands of policemen are being killed every year. Apprehension of criminals is extremely difficult because of the scarcity of witnesses and the support the criminals get from politicians and political groups; variations in the administration setting to introduce variations in the use of violence by the police have worsened the situation. Policemen use violence legally, because they are pressurised to do so by the politicians, political groups, and even by the Government.

Failing to deal with insurgents and terrorists by legal methods like registration of cases, investigation, arrest and prosecution for want of witnesses to give evidence (witness never come forward for fear of their life, as many witnesses have been killed or dismembered) and reluctance of judges to convict, the police, in the terrorist-prone areas, are allegedly killing suspects in "fake" encounters. In addition, the police are being pressurised by the politicians to beat up and even kill their rivals. The standards of police conduct are usually set by the Government. When the Government itself is involved in law breaking how do public expect the police to be angelic.

In India, the use of violence by the police is both an occupational prerogative and a necessity. Police are compelled much against their will, to use violence as the only measure adequate for control and apprehension in the presence of counter-violence in the due discharge of their duties. Speaking about abuse of human rights by the police, a leading journalist wrote in a tone of high moral indignation. "What protagonists of human rights often overlook and ignore is that the terrorist violates human rights with far less qualms than the police and security forces. Since democracy essentially thrives on the Rule of law their first killings are aimed at crippling the legal system. Accordingly, they make a special target of judges, politicians, policemen and also their families. Terrorists are anti-social and disruptive elements, their activities are criminal in nature". And therefore, it is all the more necessary for the Government, public and police to bring them to book and achieve their total elimination, if not instant eradication.

6. Torture in Police Custody

Torture and violence have been identified with the police in India ever since the *Vedic* Age (2,000 to 1,400 B.C.). The ordeals of water, fire and single combat dual were considered legal methods to sneeze out the truth. Distress or promise in whatever form was also used to squeal out the truth, as truth is never readily secured. Manu who originated law of this country and Kautilya who propounded his "*Arthasastra*" emphasised the necessity of torture to protect the society from the hands of criminals and evil-doers, who menaced the well-being of the society. Tortures like burning of limbs, mutilating of limbs, tearing by wild animals, trampling to death by elephants or bulls, *etc.*, were prevalent until the Buddhist powerful kings began ruling the country. After Asoka embraced Buddhism, the brutality in torture gradually decreased, and the age of humanitarianism and the administration of justice had become correspondingly imbued with humanitarian ideals (BC 320-300 A.D.). Torture in any form was prohibited and special favour was shown to prisoners who happened to be old or women. As and when Buddhism started its declining influence, torture became prevalent. From 712 A.D. to 1857 there was Muslim rule in the country. Muslim rulers took a savage pleasure in witnessing torture with greater cruelty and ferocity, and they administered criminal justice on the basis of religion and creedal discrimination. Actually there was no Criminal Justice System. The "*Shariat*" laws — (Islamic law) was in force. The Indian Penal Code enacted by the British in 1860 after assumption of power, abolished the "*Shariat*" law and gradually evolved order from chaos. By and large, the British were fair and legal, but in the interest of the British Raj, they encouraged brutality and "Third Degree" against terrorists, revolutionaries or anti-British elements and used special powers and extra-legal methods. Their only aim was to consolidate and perpetuate the British empire in India.

7. Causes of Torture

The main reason for the growth of torture is the investigating officer's over-zealousness either of his own or prompted and connived by superiors to secure conviction since conviction is considered to be the yardstick to assess the merit of an investigating officer. The craze of conviction became so much rampant that system of investigation itself underwent a reverse process. Investigating officer commenced his investigation with the accused, or suspect, and from him worked his way to the witnesses, who are sometimes surprised to find how much they are supposed to know. Here came tutoring of witnesses to fill in the gaps in evidence. To extract information from the suspect or accused various forms of torture, contrived by an investigating officer, were adopted.

8. Post-Independence Position

After the Independence, in order to protect prisoners against severity of treatment, in our Constitution a number of safeguards and considerable restriction on law enforcement officials have been provided. However, as the years rolled by, there was no perceptible change in the Police operation, and in fact, the practice of torture became more pronounced in recent years due to the vested interests utilising the police for their personal and party ends by the politicians forming the Government. The basic concept of democracy changed the duties, responsibilities and ethos of the police. Police brutality was seemingly condemned, but at the same time the police have been used and misused to deal with various conflicts which arose as the gap between rising expectations and their fulfilment widened. The police have been used as the strong arm of thc administration, charged with the main duty of keeping a political party in power. The police have been badly politicised and misused for partisan ends. The current social scene in the country is pregnant with violence of different varieties. With so much violence around, and this does not exclude our political, religious and social leaders, the police which are just a micro section of the same society, cannot be any different.

9. United Nations Declaration

On 9th December 1975 the United Nations General Assembly adopted a 'declaration' on the protection of all persons from being subjected to torture, and other cruel in-human or degrading treatment or punishment. India is a signatory to this 'declaration', which consists of 12 Articles which mainly conform to the definition of torture, thereby aiming to prevent it, if not stop it.

> "For the purpose of this declaration torture means any act by which severe pain or suffering, whether physical or mental, is intentionally inflicted by or at the instigation of a public official or a person for such purposes as obtaining from him or a third person information or confession, punishing him for an act which he has committed or is supposed of having committed or intimidating him or other persons. It does not include pain or suffering arising only from, inherent in or incidental to lawful sanctions to the extent consistent with the standard minimum rules for the treatment of prisoners. Torture constitutes an aggravated and deliberate form of cruel, inhuman or degrading treatment or punishment." (Article 1)

And in conclusion Article 12 postulates:

> "Any statement which is established to have been made as a result of torture or other cruel, in-human or degrading treatment or punishment may not be invoked as evidence against the person concerned or against any other person in any proceedings."

Magistrates police and the government medical officers cooperate with each other, and they try to cover up tortures in police custody. Magistrates and the government medical officers are pressurised to record the police version of events and accounts of torture are rarely recorded.

10. Compensation to Victims and Private Suits

Successive Indian Governments have persistently resisted all attempts to establish right to monetary compensation for wrongful actions by their officials. They have argued that the State is not liable for the acts of their officers when discharging "Sovereign Functions". They have also failed to act on the 1956 Law Commissions Recommendations that State's liability should be the rule and "Sovereign Immunity" the exception. Moreover, the Government has made an express reservation to Article 9 of the "ICCPR" by stating that, "there is no enforceable right to compensate persons claiming to be victims of unlawful arrest or detention against the State". As a result, Indian courts have traditionally been reluctant to award compensation to victim of human rights violations. The position, has however, improved since 1980. In the 1981 Bhagalpur (Bihar) blinding case, the Supreme Court held that the State is liable for acts of its servants when they acted beyond their authority and now many courts are awarding monetary compensation to the victims. Civil suits and private criminal cases are also filed.

But "torture" did not stop, or its use reduced. With the increase of torture in different forms, many persons are killed in "fake" encounters with the police. During the Naxalite movement in West Bengal in 1970, and during the Emergency period of 1975 we came across torture in several forms administered by police. Faced with the increasing incidence of *dacoity*, loot and arsons in various parts of the country, particularly in the terrorist-prone areas, figure of death in false encounters rose from one to several hundreds. In revenge terrorists killed an equal number of policemen. The blinding of 30 alleged criminals in Bhagalpur (Bihar) is still fresh in the mind of the public and it is reminiscent of the primitive system of police and administration.

11. Remedial Measures

The National Police Commission in its First Report expressed that "an institutional arrangement should be made by the Government not only to include internal checks and balance to minimise the scope for such misconduct but also to ensure an effective enquiry into any specific complaint of an alleged excess or omission and expose it promptly for corrective as well as for penal action. This is specially necessary in the police who have vast scope for exercise of powers by a large number of personnel affecting the rights and liberty of individual citizens in daily life."

12. Constitutional Safeguards

The laws safeguarding against police excesses are: Article 21 of the Constitution and other fundamental rights and Sections 330 and 331 of the Indian Penal Code as well as Section 21 of the Police Act. In the event of death in custody, an enquiry by a Magistrate is mandatory under Section 176 of the Code of Criminal Procedure. The right to enforce human rights in the Constitution is itself constitutionally protected. Article 226 empowers the High Courts to issue writs for the enforcement of such rights, including "*habeas corpus*". Article 32 of the Constitution grants the same powers to the Supreme Court. According to Article 22 of the Constitution when a person is arrested, he must be produced before a Magistrate within 24 hours. But not infrequently prisoners are kept in police custody for several hours more than the stipulated 24 hours and they manage their records accordingly. The Magistrate before whom the prisoner is produced has to satisfy himself that the prisoner was not subjected to ill-treatment by the police and accordingly he has to issue a certificate, or otherwise he has to institute an enquiry against the police officer allegedly having mal-treated the prisoner. With all those safeguards, police manage to torture for extorting confessions in order to clinch guilt on the accused. There are also known and proved instances in which hardcore criminals inflict injuries on their persons and complain against the police that the injuries were a sequel to police torture, but factually the prisoners were not subjected to torture. They do so to prevent the Magistrate in granting their police custody for the purposes of further investigation. This clever ruse is usually adopted by them making the police unable to proceed with the investigation, and in consequence they are set at liberty and continue to harass the society by their criminal adventures.

The first requisite for any meaningful redress is to establish the truth about what happened through an effective and prompt enquiry into specific complaints of custodial violence, often that does not happen, and reasons are many. Hardly five per cent of cases are properly and promptly enquired into and the allegations against police are substantiated. Senior police officers have been reluctant and slow to investigate because of fear of publicity and an illusion that if they do so they would lose public confidence generally or fear of exposure of their own corrupt practices through the defaulting officers. It has to be fully understood and realised by senior police officers that when the defaulting policeman is unchecked, he can do more harm than good in the long run. It is vital for the police themselves that every allegation is cleared up promptly and satisfactorily and the guilty policeman is punished resolutely and for that the supervisory officers should not have a dubious character, they should be of the strictest rectitude, and probity, and then alone they will be able to muster courage to take exemplary action against the defaulting policeman. It should be borne in mind that the maintenance of police morale depends not on white-wash, but on a satisfying conception of the policemen's place in the society. In law enforcement ends do not justify dubious means, and this holds good for all down from a police constable to the Government *vis-a-vis* minister in charge of police administration. Only the will of the Government, and its involvement are capable to eventuate abnegation of torture by police.

13. Corruption in Police

Corruption in police, as in any other branch of public administration, is closely linked with the scope of exercise of power to the advantage or, disadvantages of some one or the other. It is, however, qualitatively different in police because of the predominance of extortion or harassment as compared to collusive corruption that prevails now in almost all the departments, judiciary not excluded. Further, because of the large spread of police personnel and their day-to-day interaction with the general population with a variety of situations, their malpractices and corruption vividly attract immediate notice and draws mounting criticism from different sections of the society.

14. Police Commissions

The Police Commissions of 1860-61, 1902-03 have to remark about the revealing picture of corruption as noticed by them:

> "The forms of this corruption are very numerous. It manifests itself in every stage of the work of the police station. The police officer may levy a fee or receive a present for every duty he performs. The complainant has often to pay a fee for having his complaint recorded. He has to give the investigating officer a present to secure his prompt and earnest attention to the case. More money is extorted as the investigation proceeds. When the officer goes down to the spot to make investigation, he is a burden not only to the complainant but to his witnesses, and often to the whole village. People are harassed sometimes by being compelled to hug about the police officer for days, sometimes by having to accompany him from place to place, sometimes by attendance at the police station, sometimes by having him and his satellites quartered on them for days, sometimes by threats of evil consequences to themselves or their friends or relatives, if they do not fall in with his view of the case, sometimes by invading their houses for search of property (of any kind including contraband articles and narcotics) sometimes by unnecessarily severe and degrading measures of restraint. From all this deliverance is often to be "BOUGHT" only by payment of fees or presents in cash (or kind)."

15. Post-Independence Development

Corruption in public services touched the high watermark during the period of Second World War of 1939-1945. The enormous spurt in government expenditure on war efforts including supplies and contracts of large value processed on an emergency basis without the thoroughness of peace time supervision and check created unprecedented opportunities for corruption and acquisition of wealth by doubtful means at all levels including the higher ranks. Police kept pace and their corruption spread wider and higher. Several Police Commissions appointed in almost all the States, and the National Police Commissions found unmistakable evidence of corruption in police everywhere. What the Police Commission of 1902-03 had said would more or less apply fully even to the present situation and the position has considerably worsened with more rampant corruption in police today with active connivance of numerous local *Dadas*, unprincipled men in public life and equally corrupt supervisory officers who are on the payroll of the police station either in cash or kind. Obviously, there are hopeless sign of abetment.

16. Scope for Corruption

A few typical situations giving scope for corruption are listed below:

1. Bribery in registration and investigation of cases.
2. Bribe connected with arrest or non-arrest of accused and release or non-release on bail.
3. Bribe for providing unauthorised facilities for persons in custody.
4. Extorting money by threatening persons with conduct of searches, arrests and prosecution in court on some charge or the other.
5. Unauthorised interference in civil matters between two parties and securing a disposal favourable to one party by threatening the other party with violence and involvement in a criminal case. Fabricating evidence during investigation of cases and implicating innocent persons, or releasing out the guilty persons on "*malafide* considerations".
6. Extortion of periodic payments "HAPTA" from shop-keepers, platform vendors, brothel keepers, prostitutes, promoters, gambling dens, satta betting, bootleggers, narcotic dealers, drug-peddlers, keepers of vicious trades *etc*. A substantial portion of the money collected in this pool is made available to supervisory officers, as per their requirements, either in cash or kind, and wet parties.
7. Obtaining free entertainment from hotels, cinema houses, drama theatres, shops, transport services on threat of prosecution for infringement of variety of rules and regulations.
8. Collusion with hoarders, black marketeers, and smugglers and tipping them with advance information about any intended raids or searches.

9. Extortion of bribe while verifying character and antecedents in connection with service, passport, government appointment any enquiry report of police *etc.*
10. Demand and acceptance of bribe for dropping action against violation of traffic rules and regulations and allied statutory provisions.
11. Bribery at the stage of recruitment in police.
12. The most abominable form of bribe is when holding inquest over the dead body, sending or not sending dead body for autopsy, handing the dead body to relatives for cremation or other rituals as permitted by the religion of the deceased.
13. Police prowl like a hawk and invent opportunities to extract money from any source that comes into contact with their working.
14. Use or non-use of handcuffs is a positive source and means of bribery, which is readily paid to avoid humiliation.
15. In order to meet with the camp expenses of supervisory officers contributions are collected from public as well as anti-social elements of the society.

17. How to Handle Problem of Corruptions

This is a question which has been eluding answer since several years, and post-Independence corruption increased by leaps and bounds. Prior to Independence mostly junior ranks of the force were affected by corrupt practices, but the post-Independence picture has completely changed, officers of the rank of Director General/Inspector General are involved in corruption. It is significant to note that such a high-ranking officer, who has put is minimum 26 years of service prior to his promotion to the elevated position does not become corrupt all of a sudden. It is obvious that he has practised corruption even as Superintendent or Deputy Inspector General of Police. When the head of a district or range is corrupt, how can he inspires his subordinates to remain aloof from corruption. On the contrary, he becomes the fountain-head of corruption, which flourishes in all the ranks of his charge.

Those junior officers who try to remain honest are unable to meet the financial demands of the superiors. "Annual Confidential Report (ACR)" is the dominant tool in the hands of supervisory officers and under the fear of receiving a bad ACR, the junior officers yield to corruption, initially, for the benefit of their bosses, and later for themselves too. Currently, corruption has not only become all pervasive, but also co-operative and collective. But inversely, while distributing the money collectively pooled through corrupt practices impeccable honesty is observed. Each gets his regular share according to his status in the police hierarchy, whether he is on leave or on duty. Inspections of supervisory officers too require that the expenditure of the entire camp is borne by the members of the police unit under inspection. Generally, a trend has developed in which good inspection note and ACR are bought by police officers, and the more is the purchasing power, the better will be the inspection note and the ACR. Promotional prospects entirely depend on these notes. One should not be surprised if he finds that a scrupulously honest policeman has been branded as dishonest for his failure to provide the unlawful demands of his superior officer and contrarily a dishonest policeman is elevated to honesty through his purchasing capability and power. To whom the complaint is to be made? Even the watchdog Anti-corruption Bureau or Vigilance Committee have not escaped from the virus of corruption. The tentacles of corruption have spread so wide that no escape route is in sight, they have become all pervasive!

It is manifest that the reward and punishment mechanism of the various political parties in different types of elections necessarily forges link between political parties and sources of money in different sections of the society. This nexus between money power and political power generates unhealthy contacts down the Line between different levels of administration on one side, and political party functionaries on the other. "*Malafide*" exercise of power at different levels in the police is induced by such links. The problem of corruption cannot be satisfactorily tackled unless these links are broken. At the same time, it is necessary to emphasise the most important principle that the basic responsibility for maintaining the honesty of the force, checking and finally weeding out corruption rest on the supervisory levels in the force, and they should be enabled to discharge their responsibility effectively, provided they themselves are scrupulously honest in their character and professional integrity and environments and do not become victims of any kind of allurement, which, by the nature of their service, is easily made available to them. In this context, their capacity to punish the dishonest personnel should not be diluted in any manner, and likewise their capacity to place honest officers in important and sensitive posts should not also be interfered with. It is common knowledge that transfers, postings, like recruitment, are purchased, and in many cases they are auctioned. The highest bidder gets the posting of his choice, but not before he doles out the price. This is the saddest commentary generally heard and applicable to any government department, and police cannot remain aloof. If such postings are not possible or feasible at the district level, pecuniary or other leverages at the state level are applied. In several cases, Home Ministers/Chief Ministers have issued posting orders in supersession or cancellation of the departmental orders. Such orders have been issued for any rank down from a constable to the Deputy Inspector general of police conveniently sidetracking the authority of the head of the police department. How can the honesty and integrity for the police system as a whole be secured under such circumstances? And the result is that some officers acquire a reputation of corruption by their continued dishonest practices over a long time and when they escape punishment for one reason or the other, their fellow officers are not only contaminated but encouraged to simulate, and perhaps excel in their corrupt practices. Instead of weeding out such corrupt officers, corruption is allowed to thrive unbridled.

18. Acquisition of Property

Money obtained through corrupt practices is never kept in any open account of a bank and in the name of the concerned officer. Such ill-gained money sometimes is kept in the locker, mostly not ostensibly operated by him. Either it is done in the name of another person of confidence and with the precise knowledge or guarantee that he will not dupe the officer concerned, or under a pseudonym. Clever devices are brought into operation to conceal graft money. Officers and their families spend lavishly, become addict to drinking and other vices for they have to find ways and means of extravagant expenditure, and they finally become spend-thrifts. A cursory look at the family members of an officer can conclusively establish if he is honest or corrupt. Another subterfuge that is commonly adopted is to show income from hereditary holding of lands or houses and alike properties, or investment in precious metals or stones. Demanding of a periodic or surprise statement of the assets, moveable or immoveable, either owned in his name or in the name of any member of his family, either acquired from his own resources or the resources of his family members is suggested, and often used as a method to check corruption. Section 16(5) of the Conduct Rules empowers the head of the department to demand from the suspect officer such a statement.

19. Integrity Certificate

The formats in vogue at present for the recording of annual confidential reports on the work and conduct of personnel in the Government departments contain a separate column under the caption, "Integrity" against which the reporting officer has to record a positive opinion one way or the other about the integrity of the officer reported on and also certify to his honesty and integrity if there is nothing in which a contrary opinion may be held. This system of recording the necessary certificate has actually become a farce, and many officers, who are notorious for corruption and dishonesty continue to get annual confidential reports favourable to them including the certificates of integrity. Obviously, they are managed — purchased or otherwise through the adoption of corrupt practices.

A certificate of honesty enables the concerned officer to stand on the threshold of promotion in due course of time, and as such utmost efforts are made to procure such a certificate by dishonest officers. Here again, if an officer is scrupulously honest and he is unable to cope up with the demands of his corrupt reporting officer, naturally his annual confidential report is spoiled, and he is forbidden his due promotional prospects. Instances are known, and those too in large numbers, that a corrupt officer was certified honest by the reporting officer who was hand-in-glove in corruption. Then the only remedy is pervation of honesty at all levels from top to bottom, and not the other way. The Vigilance Committees and Anti-corruption Bureaus could do precious little to check corruption which has permeated all levels of police administration and Criminal Justice System, and it is nobody's guess when and how it would decrease. There is no thought whatsoever of its repudiation by the police who are in the mire of corruption on account of individual, professional, administrative and political causes. Unless each and every factor is not only neutralised, but also eliminated and finally eradicated, corruption is bound to occupy a predominant position in the police by the "beat of a drum-stick". At least what can be done, is to protect an honest officer by all the public, press, politicians and the department from the mechanisations of the corrupt elements within the system and outside, who find such personnel a hindrance to their way of life and from malicious involvement in some manoeuvred entanglements. It is this honest officer, who needs steadfast support and appreciation from all, and it is he, who is responsible for the maintenance of the fragmentary good reputation of police, at least occasionally, though it may be symbolic. He alone bears out courageously all the privations and satires from everybody, including his own family.

20. Vohra Committee Report

How else does one react to the Vohra Committee Report on which the former Prime Minister P.V. Narasimharao, sat for about two years without any indication of action? It is the severest and damnest indictment ever of any Government, polity or society. Indeed, the worst anywhere, any time of a system that "allows *mafia* to run a parallel government" pushing the State into "irrelevance"; of a political chaos that permits the scum of society to ride piggy-back on politicians till they reach political puberty. From criminalisation of politics to politicisation of criminals, it is a full vicious circle and permitted the devil taking the honest.

Prominent scams like Sugar, Telecommunications, Animal husbandry, Urea import and others, big or small, by some political leaders in the Government made the country suffer unprecedented and fabulous losses to the tune of several thousand crores of rupees. On the top of it, these leaders had indulged in fabrication of evidence to defend themselves. The Central Bureau of Investigation (CBI) was not allowed to function and when public approached the High Court or Supreme Court for obtaining justice, the latter were forced to direct and monitor the investigations in order to truthfully find out the perpetrators. The *Hawala Kand* is one of the glaring and the most scandalous instance of such *malafide* motivations of these leaders, who brazenly went to the extent of purchasing some MPs of Jharkhand region to secure a majority vote in the Parliament. The CBI in order to bail out the culprits filed the diluted First Information Report (FIR) and the Delhi High Court had to order the CBI to file the correct FIR as ordained in the relevant Sections of the Code of Criminal Procedure. Paradoxically, these leaders criticised the 'Judicial activism', as an encroachment upon their so-called democratic privileges.

Is it good for our democracy to have people like this to represent us? When those who are supposed to lead us become saboteurs, then it is time for the people to assert themselves, as their syndicates have successfully corrupted the government machinery up to the marrow at all levels and wield enough influence to make the task of investigating and prosecuting agencies extremely difficult. So is the case with judiciary.

The cost of contesting elections and the craze to remain perpetually in power have thrown these politicians into the lap of these elements and led to a grave compromise by officials of the preventive/detective systems. So vitiated is the system that one considers how the perpetrators will be able to take action against the dishonest elements in administrative machinery, and in consequence "Corruption" will be allowed to thrive and flourish with immunity and impunity until each and every one becomes corrupt, and then in the total absence of "Honest" officials, no one would talk of corruption; cancerous malady of corruption will procreate its own species with greater intensity and potency.

35
Discipline and Police Strikes

1. Discipline

In the training of young policemen, high or low, discipline is of particular importance, because it is the adhesive that holds the police force together. Police task is to watch out for criminal behaviour on the part of their fellow citizens and hence the police personnel must themselves be above suspicion. There are two kinds of discipline — (1) self-imposed, and (2) enforced. Self-imposed discipline is the kind of discipline which the normal person imposes on him for rigid obedience. Enforced discipline is imposed upon a person by some authority, other than his conscious. Self-discipline stems from within, whereas enforced discipline is sought by rules and regulation framed by other authority. "No one is compelled to choose the profession of a police officer, but having chosen it, everyone is obliged to perform its duties and live up to high standards of its requirements. Compromise, personal feelings, animosities and prejudices have no place in professional police service. Honesty, integrity and discipline must ride in every cruiser, walk every beat, influence every command and answer every roll call. Good ethics and high standard of discipline must be in evidence whenever and whatever duty calls, every minute of every date" (John Edger Hoover, Director Federal Bureau of Investigations, U.S.A.). These concepts define a true policeman.

A uniform system of disciplinary control was brought about by the enactment of All India Police Act, 1861. Under Section 29 of this Act the punishments that can be inflicted on a police officer found guilty of any violation of duty or willful breach of neglect of any rule or regulation or lawful order made by a competent authority or who shall withdraw from the duties of his office without permission, or without having given previous notice for the period of two months, or who being absent on leave, shall fail without reasonable cause, to report himself for duty on the expiration of such leave, or who shall engage without authority in any employment other than his police duties, or who shall be guilty of cowardice, or shall offer any unwarrantable personal violence to any person in custody. Immediately, after the revolt of 1857, the then British Government of India found: "That Police Force is far from satisfactory, it is defective in training and organisation, it is inadequately staffed and supervised, it is generally regarded inefficient, corrupt and oppressive, and finally it has utterly failed to secure the confidence and cordial co-operation of the people for whom it seldom works with honesty and sincerity of purpose." Such a state of affairs led the British Government to appoint the All India Police Commission in 1860, and on the basis of its recommendations the All India Police Act of 1861 was enacted. This Act streamlined the Police Force considerably, and even today it is the foundation of the Police Force. Rules and regulations for the control of the conduct of the members of the police force were framed and incorporated in police manuals. Between 1861 and 1902 the character and performance of the police force did not exhibit signal improvement and, therefore, All India Police Commission was formulated in 1902 to extensively enquire into the affairs of the police force under the chairmanship of Fraser and its recommendations were, more or less, the same as were made in 1860. The Fraser Commission was emphatic on the point that discipline should be left entirely to the officers of the force, and not even the District Magistrate should interfere and no officer below the rank of Superintendent of Police should be empowered to inflict major punishments. Major and minor offences have been specified in the Police manual. Major punishments are those which involve stoppage of increment, reduction in rank or pay, dismissal from service, whereas minor punishments are confined to extra duty, censure, warning *etc.*

Against attempts that had been made (a) by means of the threats, intimidation, or otherwise to induce members of the police force to refrain from doing their duty, and (b) to spread disaffection among them, the Government of India enacted the Police (Incitement to Disaffection) Act XXII of 1922. Obviously, these measures were taken to checkmate the growing popular support to the Congress Movement with a view to destabilising the British Rule in the country. The Police personnel were covertly influenced by this movement, which assumed national form and significance year by year with increased popularity and velocity.

The Delhi Police Revolt led to the passing of the Police Forces (Restrictions of Rights) Act in 1966, providing restriction of certain rights conferred by Part III of the Constitution of India in their application to the members of the Police Forces charged with the maintenance of public order so as to ensure the proper discharge of their duties and maintenance of discipline among them. This Act provides that no member of a police force shall, without the express sanction of the Central Government or the State Government, be a member of, or be associated in any way with, any trade union, political association or with any class of trade unions, labour unions, or political associations, or communicate with the press or publish, or cause to be published, any book, letter or other documents except where such communication is of a purely literary, artistic or scientific character or is of a prescribed nature. Section 4 of the Act made the offence punishable with imprisonment for a term which may extend to two years or with a fine which may extend to Rs. 2,000 or both.

The present scheme of disciplinary control is based on the Civil Services (Classification, Control and Appeal) Rules, 1930 brought up-to-date in 1937, and later in accordance with the provisions of Article 309 of the Constitution of India. These rules prescribe the scales of punishment and the procedure that should be adopted for imposing a punishment and the redress that may be sought through appeal. Chapter XIV of the Constitution of India deals with the services under the Union and States and Article 311 makes it obligatory that no public servant (Inclusive of Police) can be dismissed or removed by an authority subordinate to that by which he was appointed and that reasonable opportunity must be furnished for showing cause against the action proposed to be taken. The basic rules of disciplinary control are amplified in Police Manuals, Police Regulations and police orders in various States and Central police organisations.

There has been a steady erosion of discipline in the rank and file of the police during the post-Independence era. Many factors are responsible for the growth of indiscipline, political patronage and partisan politics have proved to be the greatest handicaps. Politics, communalism, casteism and regionalism, colour the tenor of all life in India today. Police could not remain aloof from this national epidemic. The general climate of indiscipline prevailing in the country has its effect on the discipline and the morale of the police personnel. We have reached the stage where the rank and file have become uncontrollable and defied the supervisory ranks. The most dominant concern has been the infiltration of political party cadres within the ranks of the police. The Governments packed the police force with party cadres ignoring all rules of recruitment. They cannot be disciplined due to their close association with the party in power, to which they depended for their advancement rather than to the police hierarchy. All these ominous systems are serious threat to discipline within the force, more particularly because there are multi-party governments in the country. All the police forces of the country, whether belonging to Central Government or the State Governments, have to enforce the same laws of the land without any favour, fear and discrimination. Unless the police force is freed from political patronage and partisan politics and enforce effective disciplinary actions against indisciplined policemen sheltering behind political patrons, proper discipline cannot be maintained, and that would cumulatively result in the inaction, apathy or lethargy of the policemen having certain political leaning if situations demand of them to take actions against the protagonists of that party. The supervisory officers have to show a stricter observance of the norms which they expect from their subordinates. Divided loyalty has already imperilled the security of the nation.

2. Police Associations and Unions

Collective bargaining through the Trade Union rights have not been granted to all categories of workers. Police is one of them. Policemen cannot be conceded the right to go on strike and take recourse to any other coercive methods in a collective manner. This does not, however, mean that Police Forces numbering over 2.20 millions will be denied the rights to articulate their grievances when the industrial workers, civilian employees, railway men, teachers, and almost all kinds of employees are permitted to form unions or associations to promote and improve their economic and working conditions. It cannot, however, be denied that an international machinery for ventilating and redressing the grievances of policemen, with special reference to its impact on police discipline and efficiency will provide a safety valve to the present unrest among policemen, who are restive all over the world. Several foreign countries have such associations, and they are not analogous to Trade Unions, but they are strong negotiating machinery which deal with the Government directly.

3. Pre-Independence Period

Institutions of orderly Rooms and *darbars*, inherited from the Army, held at regular intervals, mostly weekly, helped to redress minor grievances such as fixation of pay, non-payment of travelling bills, grant of leave, allotment of quarters, education of children, medical facilities, and several others of individual policeman. These institutions could not have been designed to respond to what may be called the collective or corporate grievances of the police personnel, on the loyal support of which, the British could rule the country for over 150 years in continuation — the first ever foreign power succeeding to keep India a united and fully integrated territory. Therefore, no permission was given by the Government to form such association or unions.

The oldest staff and association of police personnel in India is the Bengal Police Association, which came into being as early as 1921 and was accorded recognition by the Government in 1923; which was, however, withdrawn soon. The membership included from constables to the Deputy Superintendent of Police, who belonged to the State Service Cadre.

Twenty-four years later in 1946, the Bihar Policemen's Association having inspectors, sub-inspectors and assistant sub-inspectors of police, was formed. It remained unrecognised till 1967, when the Government of Independent India granted recognition. The Indian Police Association, a central organisation, with branches in different provinces, was granted recognition and functioned during the British Rule. Subsequently, after Independence it was changed to Indian Police Service Association. It is recognised and still functioning.

The disability to form unions or associations was not statutorily enforced during the British period, but was imposed on policemen as part of executive policy. The Police (Incitement to Disaffection) Act, 1922 was put on the statute book. This legislation, still in force, forbids any external agency to do anything by way of spreading disaffection among the police, and, besides it puts the latter also under a stern injunction not to form, or associate itself with any association. The timing of this legislation is significant. The British Raj was evidently feeling concerned in the twenties over the rising tide of the Freedom Movement, and was determined not to let it dilute the administrative system of the land. It, therefore, lost no time in passing a legislation to penalise "whoever intentionally causes or attempts to cause, or does any act which he knows likely to cause, disaffection amongst the members of a police force, or induces or attempts to induce, or does any act which he knows or likely to induce, any member of a police force to withhold his services or to commit a breach of discipline....". The procedure regulating it was that if policemen wanted to form an association, they had to take the prior sanction or approval of the appropriate authority, which was not less than the Government. Under the Colonial rule even the people enjoyed hardly any rights, and the question of the police being allowed the right to form an association never allowed to become an issue. But the position underwent a basic change with coming into force in 1950 of the present Constitution.

4. Post-Independence Period

The Constitution of India abolished the distinction between policemen and other civil servants in the matter of protection of Constitutional Guarantees. The recruitment and conditions of service of all persons serving the Union Government or various State Governments are now governed by Article 309 of the Constitution. By Article 311 the protection guaranteed under the Clauses (2) and (3) of Section 240 of the Government of India Act, 1935, is extended to the members of the Police Force as well. Police Regulations were modified consistent with the provisions of Article 311 of the Constitution.

Part III of the Constitution confers fundamental rights. Article 19 which forms an integral part of Part III of the Constitution confers on all citizens of India the rights: (1) freedom of speech and expression, (2) to assemble peacefully and without arms, (3) to form associations and unions, (4) to move freely throughout the territory of India, (5) to reside and settle in any part of India, (6) to acquire, hold or dispose of property, and (7) to practice any profession, or to carry on any occupation, trade or business. Since policemen are the citizens of India, nothing will prevent them to exercise these Constitutional rights. Article 19 has also imposed certain restrictions on the people while they enjoy these rights, and this restriction is that people should not do any act that would tend to jeopardise the interests of the sovereignty of India, of public or morality. As such right to form association or union by policemen has also been restricted by executive instructions till 1959. The Central Government formed the Central Civil Services (Recognition of Service Associations) Rules in 1959, and imposed the following conditions on forming associations or unions: (1) no person who is not a government servant shall be connected with the affairs of the association, (2) the executive of the association is appointed from among the members only, (3) the association will not response or support the cause of individual government servant, and (4) it shall not maintain any political fund or lend itself to the propagation of the views of any political party or politician. Though the policemen were not prevented from forming associations, they were not specifically covered under the rules of 1959. The police being the state subject it was left to the State Government to formulate rules on such matters. Several State Governments formed the required rules.

5. Police Forces Restrictions Act, 1966

Since Parliament did not enact any law until 1966, the police personnel could not invoke the right to form associations and policemen did not agitate over this. The Government of India kept quiet until 1966 when the non-gazetted ranks of the Delhi Police set about to get their grievances redressed in organised agitation, which assumed a very serious turn, and in a bid to diffuse the situations, the Central Government rushed to enact the Police Forces (Restriction of Rights) Act, 1966. This Act, has six sections and Section 3 is its soul:

> "(1) No member of the police force shall, without the express sanction of the Central Government or of the prescribed authority (a) be a member of, or be associated in any way with, any trade union, labour union, political association, or with any class of trade unions, labour unions, or political associations, (b) be a member of, or be associated with, any other society, institution, association, or organisation that is not recognised as part of the force of which he is a member, or is not of a purely social, recreational or religious nature, or (c) communicates with the press or publishes or cause to be published any book, letter, or other document except where such communication or publication is in the "bonafide" discharge of his duties or is of purely literally, artistic or scientific character or is of prescribed nature, (2) no member of the police force shall participate in, or address any meeting or take part in any demonstration organised by any body of persons for any political purposes or for such other purposes as may be prescribed."

On 12th December 1966, the Central Government in the exercise of the powers conferred by this Act made Rules prohibiting a member of the police force from participating in or addressing any meeting or taking part in any demonstration organised by anybody of persons for protesting against the provisions of this Act, or with any matter pertaining to the conditions of service. On 19th December 1970, the Government relaxed certain conditions of these rules. Within the terms of the new Rules, members of a police force belonging to the same rank and desiring to form an association have to make an application for granting it recognition, and the Articles of Associations were also required to be brought in conformity with these rules.

Thus, the legal position is that:

(a) Policemen can form associations and such associations have to be granted recognition by the Government for continuation,

(b) The association is to work for certain specific purposes which are required to be incorporated in the Article of the

Association seeking recognition of the Government. No deviation from the contents of the Article is permitted.

(c) Minutes of the proceedings of each meeting are required to be sent to the head of the police force.

(d) Different ranks have to form their own associations, obviously, these rules prohibited co-operative organised agitation by the entire rank and file of the police force.

6. Police Commissions, Recommendations

This subject of forming associations was deliberated by the various Police Commissions of the States. The consensus was that the Government should normally accord permission and necessary recognition to form associations subject to the condition that under no circumstances the discipline of the force should be allowed to be impaired, as without discipline the force will be a total nullity. The National Police Commission also gave considerable thought to the right of policemen to form association with a view to redress their grievances, and made the following recommendations:

1. Government should have authority to impose such conditions as may be deemed fit to ensure the proper discharge of police duties and the maintenance of discipline among policemen before granting sanction to any proposed association.
2. Government should form the guidelines for the working of the associations namely:
   (a) Membership should be restricted to serving policemen only and no outsider shall be entitled to membership or function as an office-bearer of the association be connected with it in any advisory or other capacity.
   (b) Members shall not have the right to strike work or withdraw from their services or otherwise delay the performance of their duties in any manner.
   (c) The association shall not resort to any coercive method of agitation for obtaining redressal of their grievances.

(d) The association shall not do anything which may affect the efficiency of the force or undermine its discipline.

(e) The association shall be absolutely non-political in character and shall not be connected directly or indirectly with political activity of any kind, and in the application, seeking recognition, such an undertaking by the members has to be given to the Government.

(f) There should be one association for each rank of the force, such as, association for constables and head constables, association for sub-inspectors and inspectors, association for the officers of State Police Service up to the rank of Deputy Superintendent of Police.

(g) The existing Indian Police Service Association will cover all IPS officers.

7. Police Strikes

The loyalty of the police had generally been taken for granted although a couple of strikes in different parts of the country had put the authorities on warning that all was not well. To men who complained of long hours of duty, no weekly rest day, no national holiday, no festival holiday, poor pay, lack of housing, inadequate promotional opportunities, political interference in their day-to-day work by politicians and party cadres, political victimisation, harsh discipline, hazardous duties, no family life, the language of militants, trade unionism and incitement of political policemen, and subservient political elements, had an insidious appeal.

Every civilised society must be policed to ensure proper compliance with the law and harmonise the citizens' rights and fulfil its obligation. This is a minimum condition for ordered progress and civil tranquillity. Whatever lessening of standards may be acceptable in other works of life, in the police it is of paramount importance that they should be maintained as high a level as possible, for the peace and happiness of the country depend to a very large extent on the type of police it has and how they do their work. It becomes a matter of grave concern for all the public, the Government and the Chiefs of Police Forces when the police — the Law Enforcement Machinery breaks down.

Indiscipline and defiance of authority in the police must be neither encouraged, nor tolerated, otherwise no Government worth the name can hope to discharge its primary responsibility of maintaining law and order. The maintenance of an efficient, impartial, fully staffed, loyal and adequately remunerated, and incorruptible police is an essential condition for good law enforcement at a time when other public servants including the judges can go on strike, anywhere, any time, to demand "more and more benefits" in a ceaseless quest for security. Even the public utility private professionals like doctors, advocates of all courts, including the Supreme Court, for one reason or the other, have gone on strike. Only the Army and the Police did not so far adopt strike to be the medium for the redressal of their grievances as the law prohibited them to do so. Police are very much restive, and their simmering wrath was bound to erupt one day or the other.

(i) Pre-Independence Period: The first violent agitation by the police was in September 1942 when the police in Bihar revolted. Ramanand Tiwari (MP), then working as a Constable and 33 policemen were arrested. All of them were convicted and dismissed from service. Ramanand Tiwari had formed the *Inqualabi Sipah Dal* (Revolutionary Policemen's Association), and had enrolled 300 members, all drawn from constables and head constables. This association made in all 18 demands including the fixation of the minimum salary of Rs. 100 for a constable, better treatment by senior officers, *etc*. This agitation was suppressed with the help of the Army.

On March 18, 1946 the policemen in Allahabad went on a hunger strike in protest against reduction of their rations. It was quickly suppressed. On March 21, 1946 the policemen in Delhi resorted to hunger strike and went in procession to the town-hall demanding better conditions of service. The agitation was suppressed with the help of Army.

On April 16, 1946 the Malabar Special Police (MSP) then under Madras, finding no redressal of grievances relating to their conditions of service, struck work. It continued till April 24 and had to be quelled with the help of the Army, 926 policemen were arrested, and all of them dismissed from service.

In the latter half of March 1947 constables and head constables of Bihar Police resorted to a strike, which was suppressed with the help of the Army. Four policemen were killed and several of them were injured in Army action. The strike ended a few days after on Gandhiji's call.

(ii) Post-Independence Period: After Independence the first police agitation took place in Madras on January 6, 1953, when policemen in a few districts revolted demanding better service conditions. The agitation continued till January 9 and had to be suppressed with the help of the Army.

On February 2, 1955 police constables in Calcutta walked out of the examination hall in protest against the stiffness of the question papers in the departmental test.

In November 1957 the police of Lucknow district revolted in protest against the ill-treatment by superior officers. They were quickly disarmed by the Provincial Armed Constabulary (PAC).

For over three years prior to 1966 the non-gazetted policemen of Delhi had been agitating for removal of their grievances and none listened to them. They had put up posters, organised public meetings, refused to take their pay once, and had shouted slogans. All because their Union was not recognised and no redress could be secured. At last in 1966 the *Police Karmachari Sangh* was recognised, but having done that the Government felt all that was necessary for them was to refer the grievances which required immediate redress to the Khosla Commission. But the policemen could never forget that Government appointed the Khosla Commission to redress their grievances and hurriedly shelved the Report.

On March 28, 1967 over 7,000 policemen of Delhi out of a total force of 16,000 came out in their uniform to attend a meeting organised by the *Delhi Police Karmachari Sangh*. The congregation lasted for about four hours. The union leaders' principal demands included interim relief, abrogation of police rules of 1934, allotment of family quarters and an eight-hour working day. The agitation continued and the show down came on April 15 when 680 of the agitating policemen were arrested, no less than 2,500 of them had to be disarmed by the CRPF and the BSF, and well over 40 dismissed from service. Hundreds of them languished in jail till a new Government came and released them.

On 14th April 1967 an ugly situation was created by the determined call given by the lower ranks of the Delhi Police to observe a strike under the aegis of unrecognised Delhi Police Union. The striking policemen organised a long march of recruits under training and younger elements of the force from the Delhi Armed Police Lines to the residence of the Home Minister — a distance of more than 12 kms. The guidance to strikers came also from a committed band of junior Civil Police officers. In order to prevent any untoward incident the armoury of the Delhi Armed Police was taken over by the para-military forces of the Government of India. This action infuriated the striking policemen and made the non-striking policemen to join the strike and the long march in sympathy with their colleagues. The long march started at 10 a.m. from the Delhi Armed Police lines and without any interruption was allowed to go to the Home Minister's residence by passing the Rashtrapati Bahawan. The situation was so grave that the Director General of Border Security Force (K.F. Rustamji) had to rush to deal with it at 3 p.m. The strikers squatted outside the residence of the Home Minister and a few of them even intruded into the compound. They ostensibly had a design to go to the nearby residence of the Prime Minister, but they were not allowed to succeed in their mission by the police functioning under the direction of the D.G. BSF. The Prime Minister, Indira Gandhi was very much annoyed, and she asked the police chiefs, "How has all this happened and why were the striking policemen not kept away from the present location?" Obviously, she was upset, but eventually calmed down and regained her usual composure when she learnt that K.F. Rustamji was handling the situation after 3 p.m. of that day. The squatters were dispersed, but not before the necessary force was used. This incident had amply established that the policemen were required to take this last and vulnerable step as nobody cared to listen to their genuine grievances, there was no intention to redress their grievances as if policemen are robots

— inanimate beings! What an irony that a disciplined force was compelled to take recourse to trade union methods, because of callous indifference of the men at the top. Even then the way the agitation was conducted for almost one year without a single ugly incident in the city or a case of misdemeanour speaks volumes of their deft handling of the agitation. General dismissals and prosecutions of the striking policemen followed, and unlike the trade union workers no sympathy was shown to them. A Police Commission was announced to go into their grievances and suggest ways and means to redress them. And that was the end of it. The service and living conditions of policemen continued to remain as unsatisfactory as ever.

On July 31, 1969 during the United Front Ministry, in West Bengal, the killing of a constable by some CPI(M) workers gravely infuriated the policemen in Calcutta city. They quickly organised themselves, took out a procession carrying the dead body of the police constable and entered the Legislative Assembly Chamber to confront ultimately Jyoti Basu, the then Home Minister with a demand for action.

The greatest of the police agitations was of the PAC (Provincial Armed Constabulary) in Uttar Pradesh in May 1973 commonly known as PAC Mutiny. There was a danger of a collapse of the entire police administration in a large State like Uttar Pradesh. It took about five days to quell the revolt with the help of the Army, who took control of the armouries belonging to the PAC in different districts, and by the time the revolt was suppressed about thirty policemen had been killed and hundreds of them arrested. 795 policemen of the PAC were prosecuted in 65 cases. 148 of them were sentenced to terms ranging from two years to life imprisonment. 500 men who had fired upon the Army were dismissed. The original proposal to dismiss a few thousands failed because some legal experts opined that it would make Article 311 of the Constitution look ridiculous, the causes of the revolt amongst others were:

(i) unsatisfactory service conditions,
(ii) wrong selection of officers for posting in the PAC,
(iii) misuse of the PAC men by officers for personal and private purposes.
(iv) defective organisation of the PAC battalions.

(v) insensitivity of the political leadership as well as the secretariat towards policemen's problems and difficulties; and

(vi) inadequate housing and welfare arrangements.

After normalcy was restored, a number of concessions, totally more than a crore of rupees, were given to them to forget all the mistakes that had been committed. Would this not give the impression to all ranks in the police that it is only when you agitate and face firing from Government that any change for betterment can be achieved?

In August, 1977 in Bihar the policemen of the State Reserve Police (known as Bihar Military Police) went on a hunger strike in protest against the rude behaviour of a senior police officer.

On September 4 and 5, 1977 there was police unrest in Uttar Pradesh. It was alleged that two persons including a worker belonging to the Janata Party were beaten up by the Police in Varanasi, and this led to vociferous protests from the local Janata Party workers. Bowing to political pressure the city police authorities first suspended a sub-inspector and a constable, and later put them under arrest. On September 4, seventy' local policemen boycotted their meals and a number of them even refused to perform their regular duties in protest against the politically motivated arrests of their colleagues. The protest ended on September 6, only when the police authorities agreed to their demand for recording a complaint against the youth workers allegedly involved in demonstrations before the police station.

On September 19, 1977 police agitation, equally spontaneous in origin and style, occurred in Dhanbad (Bihar) when some policemen went on a hunger strike to mark their indignation against the beating of one of their colleagues by a MLA.

In Punjab, the rumblings of a revolt amongst the constabulary started in March 1978 at Patiala when the 1st and the 2nd Reserve Police refused to take their food in protest against the behaviour of a local police officer. A series of incidents were reported from Amritsar and Bhatinda districts in the months of September and October 1978. Posters appeared in several districts spelling out various demands of the constabulary such as eight-hour day schedule, overtime payment, revision of pay scales and residential accommodation. The poster campaign spread all over Punjab by the end of the year and posters demanding a police trade union appeared in the most of the important towns.

On April 6, 1979, *Baisakhi* day, a constable recited a poem highlighting the police demand at Ludhiana. So far, the main cause of police frustration, and anger had been their own officers and poor working conditions, but the assault of a constable by the close relatives of an Akali MLA in Patiala on April 14 gave a new colour to the situation. It was alleged that the constable was beaten up by the relatives of the MLA at the instance of a drunken friend who had picked up a quarrel with the constable when he tried to sort out a quarrel between the MLA's friend and a rickshaw-puller. The assault immediately sparked off great resentment among the local constabulary, who held a demonstration in front of the Deputy Commissioner's office. The Deputy Commissioner relayed to Government at Chandigarh, the State headquarters, the disaffection in the police but little was done about it. In fact, the Government later even denied that a police demonstration had taken place.

On May 7, 1979 an Akali MLA was passing through Mandi Govindgarh in Patiala. Finding that a constable on traffic point duty did not salute him, he slapped the constable and pronounced that the constable was "dead-drunk". On the direction of the MLA the constable was sent for a medical examination in spite of his protests. His medical examination revealed that he was running a high fever and was certainly not drunk. Further inquiry disclosed that the constable had a good service record and that had come to duty in spite of being ill. This was the last straw for the Patiala constabulary.

The same night they held a meeting and decided to go on a protest demonstration the next day. They also painted slogans against the Punjab Government and their own officers for not taking action against the erring MLA, and protecting the honour of the constable. On the morning of May 8 about 200 policemen marched down the main Mall Road shouting slogans against the Government and their officers. Many of them carried *lathis* and were in uniform. The Deputy Commissioner brought the matter to the notice of the Inspector General of Police, B.S. Dhanewalia, who reached Patiala within a few hours. Dhanewalia's arrival, instead of improving the situation, worsened it considerably. It was alleged that Dhanewalia was not liked by the rank and file for his rough and haughty nature. His shouts asking them to line up fell on deaf ears. The demonstrators ignored him and continued shouting slogans. No sooner Dhanewalia snatched away the mike from one of the leaders of the demonstration situation deteriorated. He was pushed around and showered with filthiest of abuses. Finding that no policemen were there to protect him, he hastily left the post. The demonstration continued till 5 p.m. when it dispersed after getting an assurance from the Deputy Commissioner that he would look into the matter.

News of Patiala spread like wildfire all over Punjab. Policemen took out processions and shouted slogans against the Government in Bhatinda, Sangrur and Sunam districts. Within 24 hours, the agitation had crossed Punjab border into Haryana where more than 500 Haryana armed Policemen shouted slogans squatting on the Grand Trunk Road blocking traffic for more than three hours. Rumblings were heard from Himachal Pradesh that the constabulary were also dissatisfied, and a statesman extended full support to the Punjab policemen on strike. The constabulary of the Union Territory of Chandigarh also staged a demonstration in full uniform in the city at night.

On May 11, the police unrest assumed ominous proportions and panic struck the Punjab Government. Army was alerted to standby and the BSF units moved into different districts. In a pre-dawn swoop, on May 12 about 100 striking policemen were arrested from various districts in Punjab and demonstrations at Muktsar in Faridkot were dispersed by force. The Government, however, ran into a major problem. Of the 28,000 police force in Punjab, while only a few thousands were actually taking to the streets, more than 30 per cent were silent sympathisers who refused to take action against the agitating policemen. The attitude of most of the so-called loyalist policemen was unanimous in support of the agitating policemen.

In Punjab the repression aggravated the situation and a giant rally was held at Sangrur where nearly 4,000 constables from all over the State attended. Demonstrations were also held in various towns in districts. At midnight, in a top-secret operation, the Army took over the armouries of the Punjab State Reserve Police at Bahadurgarh and Jullundur. Meanwhile, there was serious division of opinion in the bureaucracy itself on how to deal with the situation. While the Home Commissioner R.C. Kapila urged that the Government try and win over as many policemen as possible, the Inspector General of Police, Dhanewalia, insisted that a tough line be taken and no concession made to the agitators. However, within a few days the Punjab Government climbed down and raised the pay of a constable to Rs. 527 per month which was Rs. 85 more than what the Pay Commission had recommended and announced various other benefits.

The agitation spread to Haryana, Madhya Pradesh, Rajasthan, Kerala, Maharashtra, Gujarat, Tamil Nadu, Delhi, Andhra Pradesh, Bihar and Orissa States between the 10th and 26th May, 1979 (in Andhra Pradesh and Tamil Nadu the 2nd phase of the agitation started in October 1979), Para-military forces, namely, CRPF (Central Reserve Police Force) and CISF (Central Industrial Security Force) were badly affected. In most of the states where agitations took place they were confined to strikes, demonstrations and *gheraos* of senior police officers and were withdrawn only after the Government conceded to some of their demands. Their main grievances were inadequate emoluments, lack of housing, long hours of duty, use of policemen for personal work by officers, harsh treatment, inadequate promotional opportunities and absence of institutional machinery for the redressal of grievances.

The tragic loss of 23 lives in Bokaro, which included 19 Central Industrial Security Force (CISF) personnel and a home-guard in a three hours gun battle with the Army and the CISF personnel due to the former's move to disarm CISF personnel and take over the armoury in the early hours of June 25, 1979 must be viewed with disgrace. The CISF agitation was not unexpected. Since the beginning of 1979 the members of this force were agitating for better emolument, service conditions, promotional prospects, and eight hours working day and stoppage of the practice of inducting police personnel of high rank on deputation to CISF. Distribution of leaflets containing the above-mentioned demands started in Cochin and spread over the country wherever CISF units were deployed. CISF has a strength of about 50,000 although they are armed with guns, they cannot use them unless specifically ordered.

The Punjab police agitation gave the police personnel of the country necessary inspiration and also the lead they were looking for. The CISF thought that if the Punjab Police could do, why couldn't they ? On May 27, 1979 they demonstrated at the Steel Plant of Bokaro where they were posted on duty, and demanded interim relief in their pay. Their request was turned down by the Government.

On May 28, 1979 the CISF men went in a procession to the Bihar Military Police unit stationed at Bokaro to enlist their support. They raised slogans against their top officers who made the Government aware of this degenerating situation, without any heed by the government.

On 14 June 1979, at Delhi the representatives of the CISF demonstrated on their way to the Home Minister in a truck hired by them. En route the truck was stopped by the police deployed to deal with the agitation.

CISF representatives were arrested under Section 18 of the CISF Act and Section 7 of the Criminal Law (Amendment) Act. A senior official of the CISF at Bokaro had commented, "I really don't understand why these arrests were made."

Back at Bokaro the Secretary of the unrecognised CISF association, who had managed to evade his arrest in Delhi informed about the arrest of their colleagues of the CISF jawans. The latter felt betrayed by their officers and decided to go on *dharna* from June 16. On June 20 the DIG B.R. Sur was *gheraoed* for about 7 hours and the following day the Commandant A.K. Singh was *gheraoed* demanding the release of their colleagues arrested in Delhi. The officers dared not give orders and the jawans refused to accept them. There was a total breakdown of communication between the officers and the force. It is interesting to note that the men did not neglect their duties. They distributed guard duties amongst themselves.

The Army arrived on June 24 on the direction of the Central Government for the purpose of disarming the CISF jawans and taking over the armoury. On June 15 the Army and the agitating jawans of the CISF fought a pitched battle in the darkness of the night.

In Durgapur Steel Plant an Assistant Sub-inspector of the CISF was severely assaulted by some jawans of the force on June 23 for refusing to join the CISF association/agitation. The previous day about 1,000 jawans of the CISF employed in the steel plant took out a procession in uniform and shouted slogans against the Commandant and the DIG, CISF. Jawans entered the office of the Assistant Commandant and kept him *gheraoed* for several hours. It was only when the West Bengal Government issued firm orders to take legal action against the agitating jawans that demonstrations were called off.

The Jawans of CISF units at other places demonstrated in support of their charter of demands but there was no incident of violence.

The unrest of the CRPF (Central Reserve Police Force) was started at Trivandrum (Kerala) on June 21, 1979. In Trivandrum, Delhi and Bhubaneswar the Army had to be called to disarm them and take charge of the CRPF armouries.

The agitation at Jharoda Kalan CRPF Centre, New Delhi started on June 19 after a telegram was received from Trivandrum. The main leadership of the strike at Jharoda Kalan, significantly, was in the hands of Keralites, who comprised over 30 per cent of the total garrison strength and most of them were educated. In the confrontation between the Army and CRPF here the death toll of CRPF personnel rose to three besides a woman who was injured and died subsequently. A large number of CRPF personnel were arrested and dismissed from service.

In Bhubaneswar, the first signs of CRPF agitation had become apparent on June 22 when the Orissa Government requisitioned the service of the CRPF to maintain law and order for the cart festival of Lord Jagannath on June 26. With the civil police threatening to go on strike from June 26 for an indefinite period, the State Government was forced to ask for the assistance of the CRPF. This gave the CRPF an opportunity to re-group and the men of the CRPF started voicing their demands. They insulted their senior officers and refused to surrender their armoury when asked to do so. At this the officers of the CRPF and the Orissa Government panicked. The Army was called in to take over the armoury, which was peaceful.

Apart from unsatisfactory service and working conditions the CRPF jawans complained of ill-treatment by their officers, use of jawans for domestic work of the officers, favouritism in the grant of leave and distribution of duties, *etc*. According to them, there had been a number of suicides by the CRPF jawans in the past. They talked of the case of a young jawan of the CRPF, who had applied for leave to get married and after great difficulty he got the leave. Just the day before he was to avail of the leave, the leave order was cancelled. The desperate jawan committed suicide a day later. It was also alleged that one aggrieved jawan in the 25th battalion shot an officer and then killed himself.

The CRPF has a total strength of about 58 battalions comprising 75,000 men. It is a descendant of the Crown Representative's Police of the British era, then a small force maintained for dealing with possible recalcitrance in the former Princely States, but now greatly expanded and used to restore law and order in States where help is sought or Central intervention is deemed necessary, as also dealing with armed insurgency in border States. The CRPF, therefore, has a multi-purpose role.

Rumblings of discontent spread also to the IB (Intelligence Bureau) under the Government of India ever since the revolt of the Punjab Police in May 1979. On June 23 a secret meeting was held at which sort of trade union was formed by the IB personnel. Their grievances were inadequate pay and unsatisfactory service conditions, including absence of promotional opportunities, long period of deputation to areas with hilly terrain and unhealthy climate. They demanded that deputation by officers from States should be stopped and the organisation should have a separate cadre of its own which will open up avenues for promotion within the organisation itself.

Following the policemen's revolt, Chief Ministers of all States were summoned to a conference in Delhi by the Union Home Minister in June 1979. The major steps agreed at the conference were: (i) policemen should be permitted to form associations subject to restrictions specified by the interim report of the National Police Commission, (ii) machinery to be set up at district and State levels for quick redressal of grievances, (iii) orderly system to be abolished, (iv) pay scales of policemen to be raised, (v) the working hours of policemen to be rationalised and special pay for extra hours of duty to be given, (vi) housing facilities to be improved, and (vii) political interferences in police administration should be checked.

During the discussions one thing strikingly stands out, namely the violent opposition by a number of Chief Ministers to the formation of police associations and incurring extra expenditure on the police, as if, policemen are not men. While it has been said many times, it is necessary to reiterate that politicians are, by and large, more concerned with votes rather than to look to the welfare of the police, because there does not seem to be many votes in the redressal of grievances of policemen. No wonder these people seem to be entirely indifferent.

The second phase of the Police unrest started in Andhra Pradesh and Tamil Nadu in October 1979. Policemen's unrest in the southern and western districts in Tamil Nadu from October 15 affected the working of several police stations. Out of the five battalions of the Tamil Nadu Special Police, two battalions, one at Koval Pudur, near Coimbatore and the other at Mantmuthar in Tirunelveli district were on strike. Groups of district armed police were also on strike. The fact that 3,200 policemen were arrested and Government began recruitment of retired police constables and head-constables and unemployed young men as Special Police to replace the striking policemen, the CRPF and BSF were guarding vital installations, and the Army was alerted shows the gravity of the situations. The grievances regarding their general economic plight and unsatisfactory service conditions on which they had revolted earlier were there but the immediate cause for the large number of policemen going off work related to the formation of a police association which the Government refused to recognise on the ground that it was initiated by a suspended Sub-inspector of police.

While extremist activities have assumed serious proportions in Manipur, the police force is in total disarray. No district police headquarters in the State has its own police lines. Policemen live in rented houses scattered all over the town. Most policemen are unhappy about their working and service conditions. Here is an example: a Deputy Superintendent of Police in Imphal was reportedly promoted to the post of Deputy Commandant of the Manipur Rifles, superceding 25 colleagues because of his "political connections." On the other hand, some Inspectors who were promoted to the rank of Deputy Superintendents of Police on an *ad hoc* basis in February 1970, could not have their appointment regulated for few years. It was reported that the members of the IPS, DSPS and non-gazetted police officers associations had jointly submitted a memorandum to the Adviser to the Governor, Harminder Singh.

Policemen of Gonda (Uttar Pradesh) went on strike on December 15, 1979 alleging that "inhuman treatment" to one of their colleagues had resulted in his death. The strikers alleged that a constable, who had come to Gonda from Nawa Ganj on emergency duty was kicked and ordered to run by an officer when he expressed his inability to participate in the parade-because he was ill. The constable obeyed the order but died after a while.

During the last 35 years beginning from 1953, the first police revolt after the Independence, policemen in hundreds have been killed and thousands of them were arrested and languished in jail. The undertrial status conferred on them for nearly five years in many cases must have had almost the same deterrent effect not only on them but on their families as well. Thousands of them were dismissed and were never returned to duty. The jawans of the CISF, who were arrested in Delhi on June 14, 1979, had perhaps, violated discipline but had not, even going by the official version, committed so serious an offence as to justify detention without trial.

A section of the *Maharashtra Police Karmachari Sanghatana* (MPKS) first flaunted its belief in violent and mutinous methods in September 1981. Constables came out into the streets, deflated the tyres of police vehicles, obstructed the car of a Magistrate and assaulted the Deputy Commissioner of Police (Traffic). The Government in its wisdom decided to forget and forgive all this. The weakened police chiefs, who warned the chairs during this period turned a blind eye to the incident. During the two months that followed, the agitators intimidated those members of the working committee who had opposed the agitation. MPKS is an association of 96,000 policemen, of whom 22,000 are posted in Bombay.

On December 29, 1981, the MPKS men allegedly invaded the Matunga police station, damaged window panes, the glass tops of office desks. A number of them had arrived in a drunken state in a truck and roughed up officers who happened to be present. The officers' demand that the Government take action against the offenders went unheeded. There was utter chaos at some police stations. Striking policemen were joined by hoodlums, and held the city to ransom. Riots, arson, looting, firings and unprecedented hardship of millions of citizens followed. The Army had to be called out. Within a few hours four lay dead and scores injured by bullets.

The new Government and new Police Commissioner, J.F. Ribeiro who took over in February 1982, had a strike of the textile workers on their hands. Under the circumstances, they were simply forced to let sleeping dogs lie until the fateful week in August. On 16th August, the Government decided to suspend recognition of the MPKS (invoking Rule of the Police Forces Restriction of Rights Amendment Rules, 1970), arrest the incorrigible leaders of the *Sanghatana* (organisation) and dismiss their more lawless henchmen. Notwithstanding the instigation by the opposition parties the agitation was smashed with the help of para-military forces, and companies of SRP from Gujarat and Karnataka flown into Bombay in the dark of the night.

In the process of suppressing labour agitations over the years, Bombay's policemen could not be expected to remain untainted by the workers' indiscipline and militancy. Also, for more than a decade, a large majority of Bombay constabulary had been living in the hotbed of the most militant elements in Shiv Sena, and the *Dalit Panthers*, the Worli BDD chawls. These chawls have witnessed some of Bombay's most violent and pernicious riots.

The MPKS agitation was attributed to the erstwhile Chief Minister, A.R. Antulay, his supporters in Delhi and the men who headed the police force in the city and the State during his tenure. Rowdy and refractory MPKS agitators had been given complete freedom from accountability. Even as they indulged in acts of insubordination, Antulay built up their president, head constable writer S.D. Mohite, as their leader.

On 24th July 1988, Gujarat policemen belonging to four police unions from Constables to Inspectors launched a strike and left their posts after the State Government acted against the convener of the police union. It was alleged that the leaders of the unions had criticised the President of India, organised parallel flag hoisting ceremonies on National Days, made fun of Prime Minister of India's re-enactment of the "*Dandi March*" and had even had the temerity to incite the SRP jawans not to proceed to Punjab for performing duties there. Rowdyism seems to have become an intrinsic feature of police behaviour in Gujarat. The occasions of indiscipline are numerous. In 1980 non-gazetted policemen wrote vitriolic letter to the government condemning IPS officers. In 1981 when a police constable was fatally injured while on duty, a large group of constables marched to the V.S. Hospital in Ahmedabad and manhandled the Police Commissioner, and other senior officers who had gone there to pay homage to the deceased. In 1987, even while negotiations were going on with the Home Secretary regarding the strike they had called just prior to *Rathayatra*, the police set fire to two petrol pumps. The Chief Minister was forced to succumb to their demands.

Not only on this occasion but earlier too Army had to be called out to suppress the police strike, turned into a revolt. Only a few years ago policemen attacked newspaper officers and beat up the journalists in Ahmedabad. Past experience would show that such revolts had taken place earlier in States where politicisation of police, over the years, has encouraged indiscipline within the ranks and weak and incompetent Government reluctant or incapable to handle the problem firmly from the beginning.

Gujarat's 59,000 strong police force is grouped on caste and party lines and policemen are known to have disobeyed orders. On the present occasion the Inspectors and Sub-inspectors did not join. This had been a cause of friction within the ranks, for many constables felt that while they had gone on strike in protest against the arrest of their superiors, the superiors did not join them. Moreover, Bhatt, the general secretary of the association with BJP links, had alienated the minority section from the association. He had also increasingly become identified with the upper caste policemen's lobby. Though the unions have been derecognised and no longer exist legally, the police still look upon themselves as a powerful body. Throughout the period of unionisation in the 1980s the leaders behaved like politicians. They were rarely performing their duties but moved about the State soliciting support and threatening mass withdrawal from work every time there was a crisis. Gujarat is a communally sensitive place and unless the police are kept under strict discipline and control they can create a lot of mischief when law and order problem arises in future.

More or less similar conditions exist in almost all the states of the country, Central Government forces not excluded.

Senior police officials, by and large, are responsible for the sorry state of affairs since police indiscipline flows from decayed hierarchical control. There have been cases where shrewd police officials volunteered to oblige the political bosses and their mentors for personal gain. For them, main concerns are fast promotions and to avoid inconvenient postings. The general tendency is to take very few decisions and to get someone else higher up to take all decisions. There is the feeling that they may be thrown to the wolves when the new Government takes over. And when an emergency arises, disastrous consequences become inevitable. Leaders of this type can, neither enforce discipline, nor safeguard public interest. The moment the subordinates come to know of it, they refuse to give their chief the respect and loyalty he deserves.

8. Why Strikes Take Place

Obviously, the pay structure and other amenities given to policemen of all the ranks are much lower than the skilled workers, bank employees, and the civil servants of all categories who are not required to work like policemen continuously for several hours a day and night. Their rest is certain and regulated, whereas the word rest is anathema to a policeman. He is liable to be called to duty at anytime, and anywhere, in shivering cold, torrential rains and scorching heat. He has no holiday whatsoever. Festivals and festivities make him work more strenuously and with greater strain on his physical capabilities. He has practically no time to attend to his domestic needs, family life, education of children and sick relatives. His duties are hazardous and his very existence in the world is vulnerable. In view of all these rigours he is paid much less, because generally it is contended that a policeman makes some extra money during the course of his police functions. They forget that other workers are more corrupt that the police. The Prime Minister too is alleged of corruption. It is not an universal fact that all workers are corrupt, so also all policemen are not corrupt. Intrinsically they are honest, but they are made corrupt by the public and politicians and their partisan politics. They are not allowed to form unions like other workers and press their demands for the redressal of their grievances. The deterrent notions of discipline compel policemen to bear all these anomalies and privations without murmur. But they are human beings and there is nothing wrong if they expect the public and the Government to treat them as such — on par with others and without any disparity. Their profession is such that they cannot please anybody, the complainant, the accused, the public, the press, the superior officers, the family, the children and above all themselves, for, like others, they cannot enjoy life, and the company of the community and society. They are disowned by all. Working under such extraordinary adverse circumstances and service conditions a stage comes in their life when they become frustrated, more so when they find that the emoluments of MPs., MLAs., and for that matter any insignificant elected representative of the *gram panchayat* are increased from time to time and in an *ad hoc* manner and their continuous fervent appeals to raise their emoluments are patently time and again brushed aside by the Government for want of funds. This inequity in justice given to them by all from year after year breaks their self-control, restraint, and all barriers of discipline and the accumulated simmering wrath erupts like a volcano akin to the strikes of the past. This phenomenon is all over the world. The police in India have shown considerable restraint. Generations of policemen passed without getting any relief. It is usually forgotten that police is a public utility service, though it does not generate finances for the Government, but it is that agency which enforces the laws of the land, maintains peace and tranquillity and public order and fights incessant battles against crime, criminals and anti-socials. It is that agency which provides stable conditions conducive to the prosperity of the Nation. It is the policeman who walks on the street anytime of the day and night and renders safety and security to the people and comfortable sleep anytime they feel doing so. His is the most genuine case for enhanced emoluments. These are the various extenuating circumstances where he is impelled to strike work, for no mother will milk her child unless it cries for it. Perhaps, strikes of greater dimensions and potency in the near future may awaken the Government at least to look into their demands, and till then policemen will have to slog in the prevalent wretched conditions!

36

Welfare Measures for Policemen

No Government worth the name throughout the world can have to discharge its primary responsibility of maintaining law and order and public peace and tranquillity without the help of the Police — the only law enforcement machinery in any country. What infuriates policemen most is that while there is ceaseless multiplication of their duties, and more and more fringe benefits to those whose weapons are strike and trade union, there is nothing about improving their service and living conditions. Peoples' possessions, and lives are "Secure" as long as the policeman is on duty. If he is present he irritates, if he is absent there a temporary anarchy. There is no way we can afford him; perhaps, we do not even deserve him! It is not denied that over two million policemen in the country today are, by and large, understaffed, under-paid, over-worked, inadequately housed, demoralised, corrupted and subjected to political influence and public humiliation.

With the deteriorating conditions of law and order and multiplication of social legislations which the police are required to enforce, a policeman has practically no time to attend to his domestic needs. In police profession more than 25 per cent of their men in service are either killed or injured in the line of duty. Look at the States of Jammu and Kashmir, Punjab, all the States of the Northeastern Regions only to find large casualties among the Police forces deployed on duty. In Punjab even the family members of policemen are killed by terrorists. Their work in containing the worst type of fanaticism; and in fighting espionage, terrorism, insurgency, and even their loyalty, endurance and steadfastness, when every one is losing his head in strikes and uprisings, are rarely remembered. Gratitude or sympathy rarely comes to a policeman, no homage is paid to those killed in action while saving the life of others. India is the only country in the world claiming to be civilised in which more is expected of the police and less is given to them in the way of encouragement and material advantages. Police Commissions of 1861 and 1902-03 did not at all consider their welfare. The Government periodically hands out a string of decorations and indigenous titles or issues an official eulogy of the work of the police, but the rank and file still find themselves handicapped in the struggle for existence by inadequate emoluments and wretched housing-cum-living conditions. Incidentally, the emoluments in Japan of a policeman are almost 50 per cent more than any industrial worker in his country.

1. Pay Structure

The First (1946); Second (1959) and Third (1973) Pay Commissions upgraded the status of the constabulary by taking them out of class IV category and fixed their pay scales at a slightly higher level, but at the same time it refrained from specifically expressing an opinion that a constable should be rated as a skilled worker, who gets much more emoluments than the former. However, they acknowledged the importance of a constable:

> "From the standpoint of authority and personal responsibility, the police personnel stand apart from the other Government employees. Considerable authority, including arrest without warrant has been vested in the lowest rank of a constable. Wide powers are given to police for the prevention of crime and maintenance of public peace and tranquillity. Their duties are hazardous. The standards of discipline required of the police necessarily have to be high. The social and family life of a policeman is always disturbed and he cannot pay attention to the education of his children. They are not able to participate fully in the social and other activities of the community due to the peculiar nature of their work. Uncertainty of working hours, liability to work at night and on gazetted holidays, are all inseparable features of police work. In combination, they result in a degree of social segregation. Since the Independence certain fundamental changes have taken place in the role and functions of policemen. In the investigation of crime, there has been a significant

change. Besides the increase in the volume of crime, the nature of offences have undergone a qualitative change with industrialisation, urbanisation, increase in economic activity and proliferation of controls and licences. There is now greater need and scope for application of scientific techniques in the detection of crime and maintenance of security. It also calls for a higher degree of intelligence to comprehend the *modus oprandi* of sophisticated criminals, to thwart their designs, or to bring them to book, specially where economic offences are involved."

Despite these favourable observations the pay structure ultimately fixed for the constabulary did not secure for them a satisfactory relative position *vis-a-vis* other employees in public services. The pay structure of a constable varies from State to State. The Central Government Police Forces get a marginally higher pay, but still less then a skilled worker by almost 50 per cent.

2. Constable to be Rated as Skilled Worker

The minimum qualification for recruitment of a constable in many states is now fixed as matriculation. Recruitment is followed by a period of intensive training in specialised skills, including a course in law which is very important for a police functionary. The duties on which a constable is employed call for considerable initiative and exercise of judgement in dealing with public situations, in most of them he has to function by himself and in accordance with the various laws which he has been asked to enforce. A thorough knowledge of law on the part of every constable is now required. The base of all progress in a country is peaceful existence of law and order and no country can afford to ignore the needs of the Police machinery and personal responsibility for the maintenance of law and order for orderly progress. Police personnel function openly very much in public view and constantly vulnerable to criticism by the public, judiciary, press and even their supervisory officers. Therefore, they have to act with full awareness and care that they do not err and eventually this circumstance places a far greater restraint on police action which is almost throughout the 24 hours a day during the entire period of service. Having due regard to these considerations the Government now rated a police constable as "skilled worker" for determining his pay structure *vis-a-vis* other public services.

3. Compensations for Additional Demands of Duty

A constable's work stands out prominently when compared with other services and, therefore, he is entitled to some compensation for the handicaps and privations suffered by him on account of the following distinctive factors:

1. An obligation to work even on Sundays and other gazetted holidays; festival holidays, which are usually occasions for enjoyment and rest by the community. Such occasions invariably call for additional deployment of policemen for law and order duties for containing the exuberance of the holidaying public.
2. Inability to avail the normal entitlement of leave every year being called on to remain on duty to meet the ever-increasing demands on manpower for incessant law and order duties.
3. Long and arduous hours of work on every day of duty, very much in excess of the normal eight hours prescribed for other workers.
4. Physical hazards and risks involved in the performance of his duties, the enormous degree of mental stress and strain under which he functions, the nature of responsibility that devolves on his job and the manner in which he deals with the public in any given situation, the constant exposure to criticism and a very strict evaluation of his performance by the public and the consequent social degradation which his family suffers in the estimate of people in the neighbourhood *etc.*

The lost Sunday holiday should be compensated by giving an extra holiday during the week concerned, and the inability to avail the normal entitlement of leave and the gazetted holidays every year should be compensated by the grant of additional 15 days leave to all the members of the constabulary. This system sounds good on paper only as in practice it is found that the constabulary is never at rest and always on the move, being deployed on one duty or the other. The duty-requirements are never fixed; they are as diverse as erratic and unpredictable as the monsoon weather. Similar is the case with overtime allowance, because almost throughout the career of the member of the constabulary they have to work at least 15 hours a day. Many time during nights, and this continuous strain and stress cause their physical capability to break, and lose their initiative and interest in police work.

4. Special Qualification Pay

The constables have been provided with financial incentives of acquiring special qualifications as they progress in service, they are:

(a) Proficiency in driving and motor mechanism.
(b) Proficiency in handling wireless equipment for transmitting and receiving massages.
(c) Proficiency in handling computers and electronic data processing machinery.
(d) Acquiring University degree, higher than what he had already secured at the time of his recruitment in such a subject as would be of professional use to him.

The quantum of special pay payable to each of these categories is slightly less than drawn by similarly qualified personnel working in other services or the private sectors.

5. Housing

Ever since 1861, when the police system was created provision of free housing to non-gazetted police personnel has been recognised as the responsibility of the State, for the simple reason that the police personnel have to live in their quarters for attending to the call of duty at any hour of day or night, and such calls are unpredictable. It is always necessary to pool together the available manpower to deal with a situation and unless all the police functionaries of the police station do stay within the precincts of the police station, bringing them together is not possible. Most valuable time would be lost in mustering the required strength eventuating in the worsening of the situation. For this very reason the police station and all its staff members have been given residential accommodation within the police station premises. During the British Rule large areas were acquired and occupied for this purpose and the required houses constructed. Post-Independence era witnesses large-scale augmentation in the Police Force, new branches have been created for meeting with the expediency and exigencies of Police service. As against the general principle enunciated over 100 years ago providing 100 per cent accommodation (barracks or family type) to the non-gazetted police personnel, the actual position in the field today is that more than 50 per cent of the non-gazetted police ranks all over the country have not been provided with government accommodation of any kind whatsoever. Even among those provided with the government accommodation a very small percentage alone has family accommodation and the rest are lodged in barracks. The overall picture that emerges is that the percentage of family accommodation provided for police personnel is very low, and lowest in the rank of constables. The position with regard to other ranks is marginally better, but on the poorer side. Securing of private accommodation has become increasingly difficult over the years. Payment of house rent allowance operates under very restrictive reels and procedures which do not take a realistic account of the existing high rentals. The deficiency in housing and increasing hardships in paying house rents for private accommodation, secured with great difficulty, operate as the largest single factor responsible for grievous loss of morale in police ranks. Government has done precious little to improve this existing and deplorable condition. House rent allowance paid by the government for hiring private accommodation is hardly 12 to 15 per cent of the basic pay of the incumbent which is almost 50 per cent less than what he is required to pay. The government accommodation is not roomy enough and is unhygienic at many places. There is generally scarcity of water. Roofs leak during rainy season. Door and window panes are generally broken, so also the floor. Wall plaster has peeled of at many places and whitewash is not done for several years at stretch. Drainage system is generally impaired, electricity is not always provided. Generally there is a stinking smell in the police compound. Occupants make some makeshift arrangement for whatever convenience they might yield and pay for it from their own sources — lawful or unlawful. Even stables are better than such quarters. Each year the Police Department comes up with certain proposals for the construction of quarters, and each year they are turned down by the Government, reason being insufficiency of funds, when the financial requirements of other departments are fulfilled. In the line of priority police has been rated the last. This is the fate of the police personnel who are bound to be on 24 hours duty and this special priority has been given by the Government to them! How can the efficiency be improved, and sagging morale of the force sustained? Recently Police Housing Corporations have been formed in most States and they still continue to ride in the first gear as in inertia. The progress of construction of quarters is going with snail's speed — the major impediment being failure of the Government to release the required funds.

6. Other Welfare Measures

In the recent past the following welfare measures have been introduced:

1. Supply of essential commodities at slightly less rate than the market price on account of exemption of certain government taxes.
2. School grants, for purchase of books, a paltry sum of Rs. 50 per annum for one child. If there are more than two children to an incumbent the available facility is withdrawn.
3. Free medical treatment.
4. Departmental scholarships to brilliant children.
5. Group insurance.
6. Police welfare fund.
7. Benevolent fund to the widow of an incumbent died while in service.
8. Resettlement of retired policemen. There is a Welfare Officer for the whole state. He has practically done nothing mostly due to the stigma attached to police service. The retired personnel on their own, run from pillar to post, in order to find out a job for supplementing their depleted income through pension. Even their

children are not considered for enrolment as a matter of right and they have to compete with other candidates according to the available Reservation Category/ quota. No special weightage is given to them for their relationship with a policeman.

9. Other benefits are so marginal that they do not deserve any mention here.

By the reason of his employment, a policeman should have the facility of taking sustaining food, which he cannot afford to do. The expense over house keeping is increased not only by the irregularity of hours at which he has to take his meals, but also due to the fact that generally a constable has to maintain two establishments. He is not able to look after the education of his children and attend to sickness in the family. Service in the Police makes the demands of the physical and moral qualities of the individual such as are made on the members of no other public service. Since these demands have increased in severity and versatility as the years rolled by, the present welfare measures are very scanty and do not attract better candidates for recruitment in the Force, the members of which are not at all satisfied with the working conditions. Naturally, no improvement in the quality of the work could be expected, and they would continue to serve merely as mercenaries. A policeman is in a peculiar position — a position of renunciation by all, his family, the public and the Government. He is the neglected child of all, and yet, he has not usually played truant. His apathy and lethargy are forced on him due to negligible attention paid towards him by all. Before the members of the constabulary become frustrated and take to action, which they did in the past by striking work, the Government should improve their pay structure, give them sufficient amenities and good service conditions. A constable is the foundation stone of a nation. The Fifth Pay Commission may present them some benefits.

7. Police Athletics and Sport Meets

It was the initiative of the then Director Intelligence Bureau (B.N. Mullik) the formation of the All India Police Athletics and Sports Meet took place and first meet was held in Cuttack (Orissa) in February 1951. Since then it is a regular annual feature, the venue is being changed from State to State. This competition is of the same standard as that of the Olympics and all field events/ games are open for competitions. The Police Games and Sports Meets are controlled by the All India Police Sports Council Board (AIPSCB) whose membership is open to all the police forces of India and all centrally administered forces and units. This Board is affiliated to the Amateur Athletics Federation of India, and the Swimming Federation of India. For its participation in the inter-departmental national volleyball championship, the Volley Ball Federation of India has granted the necessary permission of the Board. These police meet help to improve the '*esprit-de-corps*' and morale of the police forces in the country and to establish better relations between the police and the people. A General Fund through contributions from each state/ unit, at the present fixed rate of Re. 1 per policeman per annum has been created, so that the burden of expenditure is equally shared by all the members of the forces of the country. The Government of India also helps financially to some extent.

In 1989, for the first time the Indian Police teams contested in international meets. They distinguished themselves in the process and brought honour to the country.

During the period of these meets various Police Officers from all over the country come together, and they discuss professional problems common to them all and put their heads together to find solutions for them. A seminar on Police Welfare is also held.

Besides the field games, competition is held in First-Aid and Ambulance Drill; Scientific Aids to Investigation, Police Photography, Rifle and Revolver Shooting, and Motor Transport. There is also Prime Minister's Police Medal for life saving. Many Police athletes, and players of various games have played in the national teams.

37

Spurious Notions of Police Reforms

1. Law Commission on Police

The first Law Commission of India (LCI) was appointed in August 1955 and up to 1988 there were 20 such Commissions. One hundred and thirty eight reports have been submitted to the Government while dealing with "normative law reforms". The LCI, has on a number of occasions, examined the powers and functions, the emerging role and the operational problem of police, and made a number of valuable recommendations.

2. Investigation of Crimes

Investigation of crime and prevention of crime are extremely difficult and delicate exercises for the police in its capacity of the Law Enforcement Agency of the country. This is more so in an accusatorial system of criminal justice as ours in which the whole burden of providing proof rests upon the prosecution while the accused is presumed to be innocent until his guilt is proved beyond any reasonable doubt. Therefore, the durability and credibility of the Criminal Justice System depends to a great extent on police response to crime, which is directed and regulated by the procedural laws of India. It was the Code of Criminal Procedure of 1898 that spelt out the framework of investigational procedures which have remained more or less unaltered to this day as far as the police are concerned, as is embodied in the revised Code of Criminal Procedure, 1973, which came into force on 1st April 1974. The LCI has dealt with certain aspects of procedural reforms in Criminal Code in some of its reports. The revised Code of Criminal Procedure is based on the recommendation of the LCI.

Procedural reforms apart, the LCI dealt with other aspects of investigation, namely interference by writs with investigation of economic offences, concentration by police on investigations, association of women social workers with investigation of sexual offences against women, extension of the jurisdiction of the Central Bureau of Investigation (CBI) to make investigation of certain specified offences relating to the Union List, powers of the police to take coercive measures in investigation. Throughout the prolonged period of 33 years from 1955 to 1988, the LCI members found that the calibre of the persons who are in the police has not improved and malpractices in police investigations continued to exist. It is precisely for this reason that the LCI adopted a cautious approach while dealing with the discretionary powers of the police in the conduct of investigation and had sought to improve certain legal obligations on their part in such matters as procedures for recording the statement of witnesses and sending copies of such statements to the concerned Magistrate. Suitable amendments of Sections 160 to 163 of the Code of Criminal Procedure, 1898 were suggested, but surprisingly, these valuable recommendations found no place in the amended Code of Criminal Procedure. The LCI suggested the following remedial measures to remove the defects in the investigation of offences and they are non-legislative and fully departmental:

1. As far as possible the investigation of an offence should be conducted by a single police officer, preferably a senior officer, with the assistance of junior officers.
2. The investigating wing should be separated from that dealing with law and order.
3. Systematised training for police officers in proper methods of investigations should be urgently given.
4. Necessary legal assistance should be provided to investigating officer.
5. It is necessary to ensure strict and effective supervision over investigation by special officers of the rank of a Deputy Superintendent of Police.
6. Attempts should be made to resume greater public co-operation.
7. Association of women social workers in investigations of crimes involving women, both as a complainant or

accused should be secured; and as far as possible such cases should be investigated by women police officers.

8. Coercive measures for taking measurements and photographs, finger impressions, foot impressions may be permitted in certain specified offences which are of greater common interest of the society for the protection and punishment of crime. Offences like robbery, *dacoity*, trafficking in drugs *etc.*, have been included in this category.
9. The question of admissibility of confession made to a Senior Police Officer in evidence had been stalled by the LCI. However, it adopted a cautious but rational and balanced approach and contended that without sacrificing the essential elementary requirement of 'voluntariness' it would be possible to improve upon the existing rigid rules by adding certain safeguards in Sections 162 and 163 of the Code of Criminal Procedure. It is hoped that if these amendments are made, the danger of extorted or fabricated confessions will be considerably reduced without unduly hampering investigation of crime.

3. A Helpless Investigating Officer

The following are the amended provisions of the Code of Criminal Procedure, 1973 relating to Sections 160-167, and they are capable of giving a general idea to the people about the handicaps fined by the police during the investigation of cases.

Section 160. Police Officer's power to require attendance of witnesses

1. Any police officer making an investigation under this Chapter may, by order in writing, require the attendance before himself of any person being within the limits of his own or any adjoining station who, from the information given or otherwise, appears to be acquainted with the facts and circumstances of the case; and such person shall attend as so required:

   Provided that no male person under the age of fifteen years or woman shall be required to attend at any place other than the place in which such male person or woman resides.

2. The State Government may, by rules made in this behalf, provide for the payment by the police officer of the reasonable expenses of every person, attending under sub-Section (1) at any place other than his residence.

Section 161. Examination of witnesses by police

1. Any police officer making an investigation under this Chapter, or any police officer not below such rank as the State Government may, by general or special order, prescribe in this behalf, acting on the requisition of such officer, may examine orally any person supposed to be acquainted with the facts and circumstances of the case.
2. Such person shall be bound to answer truly all questions relating to such case put to him by such officer, other than questions the answer to which would have a tendency to expose him to a criminal charge or to a penalty or forfeiture.
3. The police officer may reduce into writing any statement made to him in the course of an examination under this section; and if he does so, he shall make a separate and true record of the statement of each such person whose statement he records.

Section 162. Statements to police not to be signed — Use of statements in evidence

1. No statement made by any person to a police officer in the course of an investigation under this Chapter, shall, if reduced to writing, be signed by the person making it; nor shall any such statement or any record thereof, whether in a police diary or otherwise, or any part of such statement or record, be used for any purpose, save as hereinafter provided, at any inquiry or trial in respect of any offence under investigation at the time when such statement was made:

   Provided that when any witness is called for the prosecution in such inquiry or trial whose statement has been reduced into writing as aforesaid any part of his statement, if duly proved, may be used by accused, and with the permission of the Court, by the prosecution, to contradict such witness in the manner provided by Section 145 of the Indian Evidence Act, 1872 (1 of 1872), and when any part of such statement is so used, any part thereof may also be used in the re-examination of such witness, but for the purpose only of explaining any matter referred to in his cross-examination.

2. Nothing in this Section shall be deemed to apply to any statement falling within the provisions of the Clause (1) of Section 32 of the Indian Evidence Act, 1872 (1 of 1872), or to affect the provisions of Section 27 of that Act.

Explanation: An omission to state a fact or circumstance in the statement referred to in sub-Section (1) may amount to contradiction if the same appears to be significant and otherwise relevant having regard to the context in which such omission occurs and whether any omission amounts to a contradiction in the particular context shall be a question of fact.

Section 163. No inducement to be offered

1. No police officer or other person in authority shall offer or make, or cause to be offered or made, any such inducement, threat or promise as is mentioned in Section 24 of the Indian Evidence Act, 1872 (1 of 1872).
2. But no police officer or other person shall prevent, by any caution or otherwise, any person from making in the course of any investigation under this Chapter any statement which he may be disposed to make of his own free will:

   Provided that nothing in this sub-Section shall affect the provisions of sub-Section (4) of Section 164.

Section 164. Recording of confession and statements

1. Any Metropolitan Magistrate or Judicial Magistrate may, whether or not he has jurisdiction in the case, record any confession or statement made to him in the course of an investigation under this Chapter or under any other law for the time being in force, or at any time afterwards before the commencement of the inquiry or trial:

Provided that no confession shall be recorded by a police officer on whom any power of a Magistrate has been conferred under any law for the time being in force.

2. The Magistrate shall, before recording any such confession, explain to the person making it that he is not bound to make a confession and that, if he does so, it may be used as evidence against him; and the Magistrate shall not record any such confession unless, upon questioning the person making it, he has reason to believe that it is being made voluntarily.
3. If at any time before the confession is recorded, the person appearing before the Magistrate states that he is not willing to make the confession, the Magistrate shall not authorise the detention of such person in police custody.
4. Any such confession shall be recorded in the manner provided in Section 281 for recording the examination of an accused person, and shall be signed by the person making the confession; and the Magistrate shall make a memorandum at the foot of such record to the following effect:

   "I have explained to (name) that he is not bound to make a confession and that, if he does so, any confession he may make may be used as evidence against him and I believe that this confession was voluntarily made. It was taken in my presence and hearing, and was read over to the person making it and admitted by him to be correct, and it contains a full and true account of the statement made by him.

   (Signed) "A.B. Magistrate"
5. Any statement (other than a confession) made under sub-Section (1) shall be recorded in such manner hereinafter provided for the recording of evidence as is, in the opinion of the Magistrate, best fitted to the circumstances of the case; and the Magistrate shall have power to administer oath to the person whose statement is so recorded.

6. The Magistrate recording a confession or statement under this Section shall forward it to the Magistrate by whom the case is to be inquired into or tried.

Section 165. Search by police officer

1. Whenever an officer in charge of a police station or a police officer making an investigation has reasonable grounds for believing that anything necessary for the purposes of an investigation into any offence which he is authorised to investigate may be found in any place within the limits of the police station of which he is in charge, or to which he is attached, and that such thing cannot in his opinion be otherwise obtained without undue delay, such officer may, after recording in writing the grounds of his belief and specifying in such writing, so far as possible, the thing for which search is to be made, search, or cause search to be made, for such thing in any place within the limits of such station.
2. A police officer proceeding under sub-Section (1), shall, if practicable, conduct the search in person.
3. If he is unable to conduct the search in person, and there is no other person competent to make the search present at the time, he may, after recording in writing his reasons for so doing, require any officer subordinate to him to make the search, and he shall deliver to such subordinate officer an order in writing, specifying the place to be searched, and so far as possible, the thing for which search is to be made; and such subordinate officer may thereupon search for such thing in such place.
4. The provisions of this Code as to search-warrants and the general provisions as to searches contained in Section 100 shall, so far as may be, apply to a search made under this Section.
5. Copies of any record made under sub-Section (1) or sub-Section (3) shall forthwith be sent to the nearest Magistrate empowered to take cognizance of the offence, and the owner or occupier of the place searched shall, on application, be furnished, free of cost, with a copy of the same by the Magistrate.

Section 166. When officer in-charge of police station may require another to issue search-warrant

1. An officer in-charge of a police station or a police officer not being below the rank of sub-inspector making an investigation may require an officer in-charge of another police station, whether in the same or a different district, to cause a search to be made in airy place, in any case in which the former officer might cause such search to be matte, within the limits of his own station.
2. Such officer, on being so required, shall proceed according to the provisions of Section 165, and shall forward the thing found, if any, to the officer at whose request the search was made.
3. Whenever there is reason to believe that the delay occasioned by requiring an officer in charge of another police station to cause a search to be made under sub-Section (1) might result in evidence of the commission of an offence being concealed or destroyed, it shall be lawful for an officer in-charge of a police station or a police officer making any investigation under this Chapter to search, or cause to be searched, any place in the limits of another police station in accordance with the provisions of Section 165, as if such place were within the limits of his own police station.
4. Any officer conducting a search under sub-Section (3) shall forthwith send notice of the search to the officer in-charge of the police station within the limits of which such place is situate, and shall also send with such notice a copy of the list (if any) prepared under Section 100, and shall also send to the nearest Magistrate empowered to take cognizance of the offence, copies of the records referred to in sub-Sections (1) and (3) of Section 165.
5. The owner or occupier of the place searched shall, on application, be furnished free of cost with a copy of any record sent to the Magistrate under sub-Section (4).

Section 167. Procedure when investigation cannot be completed in 24 hours

1. Whenever any person is arrested and detained in custody, and it appears that the investigation cannot

be completed within the period of 24 hours fixed by Section 57, and there are grounds for believing that the accusation or information is well-founded, the officer in-charge of the police station or the police officer making the investigation, if he is not below the rank of sub-inspector shall forthwith transmit to the nearest Judicial Magistrate a copy of the entries in the diary hereinafter prescribed relating to the case, and shall at the same time forward the accused to such Magistrate.

2. The Magistrate to whom an accused person is forwarded under this Section may, whether he has not jurisdiction to try the case, from time to time authorise the detention of the accused in such custody as such Magistrate thinks fit, for a term not exceeding 15 days in the whole; and if he has no jurisdiction to try the case or commit it for trial, and considers further detention unnecessary, he may order the accused to be forwarded to a Magistrate having such jurisdiction:

Provided that

(a) the Magistrate may authorise the detention of the accused person, otherwise than in the custody of the police, beyond the period of 15 days, if he is satisfied that adequate grounds exist for doing so, but no Magistrate shall authorise the detention of the accused person in custody under this paragraph for a total period exceeding,

   (i) ninety days, where the investigation related to an offence punishable with death, imprisonment for life or imprisonment for a term of not less than 10 years;

   (ii) sixty days, where the investigation related to any other offence, and on the expiry of the said period of 90 days, or 60 days, as the case may be, the accused person shall be released on bail if he is prepared to and does furnish bail, and every person released on bail under this sub-Section shall be deemed to be so released under the provisions of Chapter XXXIII for the purposes of that Chapter;

(b) no Magistrate shall authorise detention in any custody under this Section unless the accused is produced before him;

(c) no Magistrate of the second class, not specially empowered in this behalf by the High Court, shall authorise detention in the custody of the police.

[1][Explanation I — For the avoidance of doubts, it is hereby declared that, notwithstanding the expiry of the period specified in paragraph (a), the accused shall be detained in custody so long as he does not furnish bail].

[2][Explanation II — If any question arises whether an accused person was produced before the Magistrate as required under paragraph (b), the production of the accused person may be proved by his signature on the order authorising detention.]

[3][(2-A) Notwithstanding anything contained in sub-Section (1) or sub-Section (2), the officer in-charge of the police station or the police officer making the investigation, if he is not below the rank of a sub-inspector, may, where a Judicial Magistrate is not available, transmit to the nearest Executive Magistrate, on whom the powers of a Judicial Magistrate or Metropolitan Magistrate have been conferred, a copy of the entry in the diary hereinafter prescribed relating to the case, and shall, at the same time, forward the accused to such Executive Magistrate, and thereupon such Executive Magistrate, may, for reasons to be recorded in writing, authorise the detention of the accused person in such custody as he may think fit for a term not exceeding seven days in the aggregate; and on the expiry of the period of detention so authorised, the accused person shall be released on bail except where an order for further detention of the accused person has been made by a Magistrate competent to make such order; and, where an order for such further detention is made, the period during which the accused person was detained in custody under the orders made by an Executive Magistrate under this sub-Section shall be taken into account in

1. Explanation I ins. by Act No. 45 of 1978, Section 13(b).
2. Renumbered by *ibid*.
3. Ins. by *ibid*. Section 13(c).

computing the period specified in paragraph (a) of the proviso to sub-Section (2):

Provided that before the expiry of the period aforesaid, the Executive Magistrate shall transmit to the nearest Judicial Magistrate the records of the case together with a copy of the entries in the diary relating to the case which was transmitted to him by the officer in-charge of the police station or the police officer making the investigation, as the case may be.

3. A Magistrate authorising under this Section detention in the custody of the police shall record his reasons for so doing.
4. Any Magistrate other than the Chief Judicial Magistrate making such order shall forward a copy of his order, with his reason for making it, to the Chief Judicial Magistrate.
5. If in any case triable by a Magistrate as a summons-case, the investigation is not concluded within a period of six months from the date on which the accused was arrested, the Magistrate shall make an order stopping further investigation into the offence unless the officer making the investigation satisfies the Magistrate that for special reasons and in the interests of justice the continuation of the investigation beyond the period of six months is necessary.
6. Where any order stopping further investigation into an offence has been made under sub-Section (5), the Sessions Judge may, if he is satisfied, on an application made to him or otherwise, that further investigation into the offence ought to be made, vacate the order made under sub-Section (5), and direct further investigation to be made into the offence subject to such directions with regard to bail and other matters as he may specify.

The offender is given so much liberty and latitude and contrarily the law enforcement agency considerably constraints. In cases of contraband drugs, narcotics illicit distillation and possession of liquor, gambling, *satta*, betting and alike anti-social offences, normally no witness of the locality is prepared to come as a witness for the search. Considerable valuable time is lost in procuring the witnesses with the result that by the time the witnesses are available the articles in evidence are either destroyed or dispossessed. In consequence, the search party returns empty handed. This legal procedure is redundant in practice. Normally, these directions of search are flouted flagrantly, police conduct the search without the presence of the witnesses, arrest the offender and seize the property in the offence. The memorandum — the seizure memo and other legal procedures are reduced to writing at the police station, and witnesses under the control of the police are made to sign. The status of these witnesses is such that they are reduced to the level of irrespectability by the judiciary and the usual fate of the case is 'clean acquittal'. In most of the cases these witnesses are bought over by the accused, or they depose the truth that they were not present during the search procedure, and in consequence the accused is set at liberty to carry on his anti-social activities unhampered. This is the basic reason why such offences cannot be checked, besides delayed trials due to overburden work for the judiciary.

4. Admissibility of Evidence

The following Sections of the Indian Evidence Act, 1872, as they stand today (Sections 24 to 31) are also of equal interest to the public for knowing and understanding the insurmountable difficulties faced by the police in controlling crime and criminals.

Section 21. *Proof of admissions against persons making them, and by or on their behalf*: Admissions are relevant and may be proved as against the person who makes them, or his representative in interest; but they cannot be proved by or on behalf of the person, who makes them or by his representative in interest, except in the following cases:

1. An admission may be proved by or on behalf of the person making it, when it is of such a nature that, if the person making it were dead, it would be relevant as between third persons under Section 32.
2. An admission may be proved by or on behalf of the person making it, when it consists of a statement of the existence of any state of mind or body existed; and is accompanied by conduct rendering its falsehood improbable.

Comments

There is neither any rule of law nor of prudence that evidence furnished by extra judicial confession cannot be relied upon unless corroborated by some other credible evidence — *State of U.P. Vs. M.K. Anthony*, AIR 1985 SC 48.

Section 26. *Confession by accused while in custody of police not to be proved against him*: No confession made by any person whilst he is in the custody of a police officer, unless it be made in the immediate presence of a Magistrate shall be proved as against such person.

Section 27. *How much of information received from accused may be proved*: Provided that, when any fact is deposed to as discovered in consequence of information received from a person accused of any offence, in the custody of a police officer, so much of such information, whether it amounts to a confession or not, as related distinctly to the fact thereby discovered, may be proved.

Section 28. *Confession made after removal of impression caused by inducement threat or promise, relevant*: If such a confession as is referred to in Section 24 is made after the impression caused by any such inducement, threat or promise has, in the opinion of the Court, been fully removed, it is relevant.

Section 29. *Confession otherwise relevant not to become irrelevant because of promise of secrecy, etc.*: If such a confession is otherwise relevant, it does not become irrelevant merely because it was made under a promise of secrecy, or in consequence of a deception practised on the accused person for the purpose of obtaining it, or when he was drunk, or because it was made in answer to questions which he needs not have answered, whatever may have been the form of these questions, or because he was not warned that he was not bound to make such confession, and that evidence of it might be given against him.

Section 30. *Consideration of proved confession affecting person making it and others jointly under trial for same offence*: When more persons than one are being tried jointly for the same offence, and a confession made by one of such persons affecting himself and some other of such persons is proved, the Court may take into consideration such confession as against such other person as well as against the person who makes such confession.

Section 31. *Admissions not conclusive proofs but may estop*: Admissions are not conclusive proof of the matters admitted but they may operate as estoppels under the provisions hereinafter contained.

Statements reduced to writing are not to be signed by the deponent. Witnesses are examined in the trial court on oath, binding them to depose truth and alone truth. Such a degradation of today in the moral standards of the society was not prevalent in 1872, when the laws were passed. In those days it was said that nobody lied even at the cost of his life. After fifties the degradation of the society has gathered faster pace and after eighties it is fastest. Reasons are many, but the most dominant and pervading reason is the partisan politics, political interference and corruption at all levels, the greed for acquiring fast wealth is uncontrollable, the means do not matter. Society is divided into various political groups, which support the complainant or the accused with the result that evidence is either exaggerated or tarnished. These versions are reduced to writing by the investigating officer, who cannot ask them to sign. There is no binding on the witnesses, who retract their statements or give a go by to valuable piece of evidence in their statements. May be on account of the dexterity of the defence council! Result — acquittal of the case.

If Section 162 of the Code of Criminal Procedure and Sections 24 to 27 of the Indian Evidence Act are juxtaposed the anomaly will be clearly understood. On one hand admission before a police officer is inadmissible, and on the other it has been admissible — only that part of the admission leading to the discovery of incriminating article in relation to the crime under investigation, and that too during the police custody. Here again some memoranda are to be reduced to writing and attested by two or more respectable witnesses; and the same disobedience of the statutory provisions by the police occurs. Actually, and for all practical purposes, the investigating officer is so helpless that many a times circumstances compel him to commit such violation. In practice these rules of laws are rarely observed — may be in 5 per cent of the cases and the remaining 95 per cent cases are the flagrant violations of the law. Now the change in social behavioural pattern necessitates, never than before, that such impractical provisions of law should be deleted from the Statute Book and only such provisions should be formulated as could be honestly, truthfully and universally obeyed. What is intended to convey could be best understood when the provisions of Motor Vehicle Act are taken into consideration. Under this Act to carry more than one person on the pillion seat of a two wheeler is an offence. What is the normal practice and sight? Minimum four persons are carried. Do the drivers not know that what they are doing is an offence? Or do they do so purposely, innocently or compelled by circumstances? Although these restrictions are to the good of the people, the general public are practically unable to obey them. Because every family cannot afford to own or hire a four-wheeler on account of the prohibitive costs and their need is to carry at least four persons on a two wheelers. This is the universal and popular practice adopted by the public. A policeman stands as a mute spectator. If each and every such violation is taken note of, then the judiciary will be only trying cases under the Motor Vehicle Act. As it is, the Judiciary is so much understaffed and so much over-burdened that trial procedure is not completed before five years even in offences like murder and *dacoity*. Justice delayed is justice denied. Laws which people normally tend to disobey are redundant in the socio-economic complexion of the existing society. It is better that such laws are honoured by their abrogation from the Statute Book. What is intended to emphasise is that the role of the police in the enforcement of laws is akin to their colleagues of the Western countries, but the Indian Police are not treated with the same quantum of honour by the public and the Government. This basic distrust has to be removed and let them function in a manner full of trust. Once they realise that the trust is reposed in them, scarcely they will betray it.

5. Difficulty in Getting Witnesses During Search

Search of a place during the investigation of a crime is the most important medium to discover evidence against the offenders. The restricted authority of the investigating officer has been amply manifested in Sections 100 to 103 of the amended Code of Criminal Procedure, 1973 which have been reproduced below. Likewise an inquest over a dead body is also required to be conducted in the presence of two or more witnesses of the respectable category of the society, some of them necessarily of the locality.

General Provisions Relating to Searches

Section 99. *Direction, etc., of search warrants*: The provisions of Sections 38, 70, 72, 74, 77, 78 and 79 shall, so far as may apply to all search-warrants issued under Section 93, Section 94, Section 95 or Section 97.

Section 100. *Persons in-charge of closed place to allow search*

1. Whenever any place liable to search or inspection under this chapter is closed, any person residing in, or being in-charge of, such place, shall, on demand of the officer or other person executing the warrant, and on production of the warrant, allow him free ingress thereto, and afford all reasonable facilities for a search therein.
2. If ingress into such place cannot be so obtained, the officer or other person executing the warrant may proceed in the manner provided by sub-Section (2) of Section 47.
3. Where any person in or about such place is reasonably suspected concealing about his person any article for which search should be made, such person may be searched and if such person is a woman, the search shall be made by another woman with strict regard to decency.
4. Before making a search under this Chapter, the officer or other person about to make it shall call upon two or more independent and respectable inhabitants of the locality in which the place to be searched is situate or of any other locality if no such inhabitant of the said locality is available or is willing to be a witness to the search, to attend and witness the search and may issue an order in writing to them or any of them to do so.
5. The search shall be made in their presence, and a list of all things seized in the course of such search, and of the places in which they are respectively found shall be

prepared by such officer or other person and signed by such witnesses; but no person witnessing a search under this Section shall be required to attend the Court as a witness of the search unless specially summoned by it.

6. The occupant of the place searched, or some person on his behalf shall, in every instance, be permitted to attend during the search, and a copy of the list prepared under this Section, signed by the said witnesses, shall be delivered to such occupant or person.
7. When any person is searched under sub-Section (3), a list of all things taken possession of, shall be prepared, and a copy thereof shall be delivered to such person.
8. Any person who, without reasonable cause, refuses or neglects to attend and witness a search under this Section, when called upon to do so by an order in writing delivered or tendered to him, shall be deemed to have committed an offence under Section 187 of the Indian Penal Code (45 of 1860).

Section 102. *Power of Police Officer to seize certain property*

1. Any police officer may seize any property which may be alleged or suspected to have been stolen, or which may be found under circumstances which create suspicion of the commission of any offence.
2. Such police officer, if subordinate to the officer in-charge of a police station, shall forthwith report the seizure to that officer.
3. Every police officer acting under sub-Section (1) shall forthwith report the seizure to the Magistrate having jurisdiction, and where the property seized is such that it cannot be conveniently transported to the Court, he may give custody thereof to any person on his executing a bond undertaking to produce the property before the Court as and when required and to give effect to the further orders of the Court as to the disposal of the same.

From what have been dilated earlier it will be apparent that the investigating officer has to face several inhibitions when he conducts an investigation into crime. While on one hand it is advocated that these inhibitions are safeguards or safety valves to impel the police to confine to the legal provisions in the interest of the public, it is not realised that these safety measures considerably help the criminals, who manage through various dubious methods to escape punishment and remain free to menace the society with their acts of criminality. The general population has suffered, as police have become apathetic/lethargic, if not remiss in the discharge of their duties in view of the dishonour foisted on them by branding them to be untrustworthy without even giving them a chance to prove their trustworthiness. The police have been rated worse than accused who is given every opportunity to prove his innocence, nay he is deemed to be innocent unless the prosecution, by leading incontrovertible evidence, proves that he has committed the offence. An agency, that has been given the power to arrest without a warrant should be considered so degraded by the Government is the unique feature of our Criminal Justice System, which has utterly failed to contain crime and criminality in the country. Instead of giving the necessary protection to the complainant and assuring of action against the person who has offended him, he is subjected to harassment by making him prove the allegation. This is the justice, which is being meted to a law abiding citizen, and inversely, the criminal is indirectly helped to remain free as honourable member of the society. For this very reason people refrain from lodging their complaints to the police, who try to burke the registration of the complaint as far as possible, and after registration their involvement in the investigation is very sketchy and devoid of interest, rarely it is painstaking.

6. Legal Inhibitions and Effects

These legal inhibitions on the investigating officer have been imposed primarily because it is always presumed, now, and in the past, that a police officer is not worthy of any trust and confidence, and he is always mischievous in thinking, acting and prone to criminal propensities. He has even been rated below a confirmed criminal, who has spent the prime of his life languishing in jail for committing crimes. Even a statement before him is admissible. The judiciary expects that there should be an eyewitness, to every fact — every ingredient constituting the offence defined in the various Penal Codes of the country such as the Indian Penal Code, as if criminals commit offences after public announcement of their intention to do so. Perhaps, the judiciary also expects that the criminal would go to the police station *suo motu* and confess to the crime committed by him and police should only work as the forwarding agency to the court of the complaint, the evidence and the accused and await the judicial verdict. With this basic concept of the police — a concept of distrust and dishonesty and abettor of crime these provisions have, obviously been incorporated in the Statute Book, as if magistrates and judges are always of pristine purity, being superhuman, they have not at all indulged in mal and corrupt practices. Even the judges of the Supreme Court and the Prime Ministers in this country have been accused of corruption. If that be the case, on the assumption that all are corrupt without any streak of honesty, police should be divested of their powers of law enforcement, and they should be given to the magistrates or judges, police will only help in any manner prescribed by them. Let the Police only maintain law and order. For the benefit of the society and the country, a dishonest and corrupt government functionary should be immediately displaced from the good offices and replaced by persons whose conduct and honesty are beyond impeachment. Those, who have taken oath as ordained in the Constitution, betrayed the Constitution for having failed to implement its Directive Principles. The present and well-debated example — the failure of the Government to endeavour the implementation of Article 44 relating to 'uniform civil code' is sufficient enough to establish such aberrations. Neither the Government, nor the Parliament has been dissolved; and those found guilty may never await their punishment. There is no rationale in saying or feeling that the entire Police Forces of the country are corrupt and conducive to malpractices, which do exist in some of them. The remedy would not lie in totally condemning them, but in finding out what the causative factors responsible for this behaviour and to remove that malady. Those proved to be guilty should be ruthlessly dealt with so that policemen sitting on the fence would improve their conduct. While trying to correct others the beginning should be made by the Government. Trust begets trust. Without giving any chance to improve those aberrants outright branding of the whole police personnel is not at all justified and cause great injustice and humiliation to those who have reputation of the strictest rectitude. After giving a fair chance as a trial, if it is still felt or experienced that the police personnel conducting the investigations are not worthy of the trust reposed in them, the legal privileges given to them can be withdrawn at any hour of the day.

7. Attitude Towards Police

After 48 years of Independence the Police of this country are despised as the most untrustworthy and corrupt institution without any legal assistance as elaborated earlier. Who has suffered? It is the poor person who has knocked the door of the administrative machinery to secure justice for the wrong done to him, and in return he finds that the wrong doer could not be punished as evidence, sufficient enough to convict him, could not be adduced by the Police. The Police advocate their own failure and helplessness due to these existing provisions of law. What the law has stipulated is not practicable today, though in the twenties it was convenient to all — the public, police and the Government. Since then the total picture *vis-a-vis* the moral standards of the society has undergone a sea change. Terrorism, insurgency, anti-social and anti-national crimes have stupendously increased since the last two decades. People who have witnessed these ghastly crimes run away from their obligation, and fake either ignorance or their inability to depose against the criminals. The number of prosecution of cases has deplorably fallen and hardly 3 to 5 per cent of the cases put up for trial end in conviction.

Such witnesses are from all categories of the society, even the magistrates, judges, advocates, doctors, engineers, academicians and all the elite are not excluded from this leeward behaviour. The police and the complainant are the lone two-some, who meet the challenge of the criminal. Invariably the complainant also renounces the policeman, who has taken up his cause, and ultimately, he is the only sentinel who fights crime and criminals. The laws meant for the betterment of the society are being flouted with impunity and in some cases with immunity. The Penal Codes *vis-a-vis* the sentencing machinery and the provisions of the

Indian Evidence Act being intricate and obsolete are now unable to restrain the vaulting crimes and criminal propensities. At least they can be contained by making suitable changes in the present systems. Harsh punishments which could assure lasting effect on the criminals, and easy and speedy justice would be the only saviours of the society and its poor masses. In other countries policemen are always confided. There are some provisions in the Police Act of 1861 that the crime, if committed within the view of a Police Constable, can be taken cognizance of, and in the past, on the lone testimony of that witnessing constable the offender used to be fined. These offences mostly deal with public nuisances. (Section 34 of the Police Act, 1861).

8. Revised Classification of Offences

It is felt that today there is an ardent need to classify the offences in various categories of evidential standards *inter alia* the onus of proof. Offences, which affect the moral standards of the society, which threaten harm to the solidarity and integrity of the Nation, which if not checked tend to increase criminality and which by their commission erode the social and communal fabric, should be treated first in order of priority during all the stages and in these crimes the burden of proof should not lie on the prosecution. The accused will have to prove that he did not commit the offence. The fear of quick and rigourous punishments, coupled with the liability of proving innocence is bound to thwart the existing criminality in this country. The people through the Government can meet this challenge of the day provided they have will to do it. Any number of such Law Commissions would not be able to ameliorate the pitiable conditions prevailing in the administration of Criminal Justice System which is currently in total disarray.

9. Police Commissions

The present police system in India was devised by the British with the enactment of the Police Act, 1861. This legislation was largely based upon the Reports of the first Police Commission of 1860 presided by M.H. Court. It was this Commission which projected the idea of a uniformed civil police, as distinct from the military police to be deployed on civil duties, for the preservation of public peace and prevention and detection of crime. This Commission was of the view, "The Police should not be used as an agency for the record of any evidence, confession, inquest or the like, but a system of keeping faithful, accurate and minute diaries should be maintained. These diaries should specify, concisely but in detail, all duties in which every Police Officer may have been engaged and every occurrence and information that may have required the attention of the police within their respective ranges. All Police Officers in specific detective duties should keep an accurate and minute diary of every step taken, and every information obtained in following up the clues of evidence, such diaries should be police document only, and be sent to the District Superintendent of Police, but should be open to the inspection of District Officer" (District Magistrate). This is the genesis of the Station General Diary.

It is most unfortunate that the First Police Commission did not recognise any meaningful and responsible role for the police for recording evidence of any kind. The denial of this role for the police in the documentation of evidence has had long range repercussion on the entire police psyche in the long years that followed. The Code of Criminal Procedure (1898), and the Indian Evidence Act (1872) naturally reflected the same attitude to the Police regarding documentation of evidence. It turned out in practice that the police record of investigation, if at all used in courts, would not be in aid of prosecution, but could be used by the defence counsel to point out inconsistencies between the police record, and the evidence recorded during the trial in a court, the latter process starts after several months; and as such these inconsistencies are bound to take place due to the human nature of the witness who is prone to forget. The mere existence of such contradiction is cited to demolish the prosecution case, so assiduously built by the police. No one bothers to examine the causative factors leading to such contradictions and whether the police record is to be rejected. *Per se* as untruthful and unworthy of reliance for convicting the offender. This disdainful treatment even to a Police Officer of the highest rank — the Chief of the Force still continues after 48 years of the Independence. No step, worth any result, has been taken till date. India is the lone country in the world where policemen receive such contemptuous treatment.

Thereafter several Police Commissions, both of the States and Nation, were appointed and they deliberated on such issues, as would improve the working standard of the police, their efficiency and competency, the public co-operation and finally their image. Instead of improvement, there has been consistent deterioration in all these spheres. The most discordant fact is that, neither the Government nor the public, are courteous enough to take out their law enforcement machinery from this disdainful atmosphere of distrust by making suitable changes in the law and it has adversely affected the society because due to this handicap. Police find itself incapacitated to effectively checkmate the rising tide of criminality and anti-social and anti-national activities.

10. National Police Commissions

1. In 1902 Police Commission headed by A.H.L. Fraser, Chief Commissioner of the then, Central Province and Berrar was formed. Besides him there were six other members, including a judge.
2. *Police Commission, 1977-81*: It was set up in 1977 by the Janata Government which came to power in 1977 for the first-time after trouncing the Congress which had uninterrupted 30 years of rule in the country. At this period of time the Police image touched the bottom rock, may be due to the excesses committed by the members of the force at various places during the Emergency imposed on the Nation by the then Prime Minister Indira Gandhi. This Commission worked up to 1981. The Chairman of the Commission was Dharma Vira ICS (retd.) and several outstanding Police Chiefs, Judges and Social Workers, whose high capabilities could not be questioned.

The Commission made a comprehensive review of the police system at the national level, having regard to far-reaching changes that had taken place in the country after the enactment of Police Act of 1861, and the Report of the Police Commission 1902. This Commission was given wide ranging terms of reference covering the entire gamut of Police functioning. Only a few of the recommendations of the Commission found support with the Government which took some sketchy steps.

Several recommendations have yet to cross the stage of consideration. The most important among them is the amendments in the sections relating to the documentation of evidence during Police investigation conforming to the compulsion of reality in crime situation. Fourteen years is a short period for the Government of India to consider those recommendations when a generation of policemen passed in oblivion!

11. State Police Commissions

After the Independence several State Governments appointed Police Commissions to look into the performance of the State Police and recommend only the organisational changes for improving their efficiency. These recommendations were mainly confined to the details of the administrative set-up, the strength of the police force in different wings of the system, the relationship between the police and the District Magistrate, pay and allowance for the police in the different ranks, qualification for recruitment, set-up of training centres and the like. The terms of reference of these Commissions were more or less restricted to secure efficiency within the broad outline of the police system brought about by the Police Act of 1861. These Commissions did not address themselves (rather allowed to address) to fundamental changes in law to enable the police to discover their proper identity as imperial agents of law in a vibrant socialist democracy. Consequently, the recommendations made by these Commissions had only a marginal effect on improving the overall police image in the country.

In four decades of Independence the country witnessed progressively unbridled exercise of power by ruling political parties at the Centre as well as in the States. The police, that had faithfully served the British Raj and sustained it with their devotion to duty and loyalty to the Government, continued to serve with greater devotion to duty; loyalty and zeal the National Government of democratic India. But the political parties failed to recognise their role as an impartial agents of law with unavoidable consequence that the police image continued to be dishonourable and maligned. The various State Police Commissions were:

1. Kerala Police Reorganisation Committee 1959.
2. Bihar Police Commission 1961.
3. Punjab Police Commission 1961-62.
4. Maharashtra State Police Commission 1964.
5. Madhya Pradesh Police Commission 1965-66.
6. Delhi Police Commission 1968.
7. Uttar Pradesh Police Commission 1970-71.
8. Assam Police Commission 1971.
9. Tamil Nadu Police Commission 1971.
10. Andhra Pradesh Police Commission 1983-84.

The recommendations of these Commissions are almost akin to one another. Their marginal implementation did not improve the situation, and the Police Force is still reeling under public malignity. The National Police Commission, and the State Police Commissions failed in their missions to induce the Government to amend the relevant provisions of law regarding the documentation of evidence, and its admissibility during a court trial. These are futile exercises to hoodwink the public, and the police by the Government of India, mostly of Congress, who is mostly concerned to sustain its prolonged existence. The result: "The euthanasia-mercy killing of Good Police Image."

38

Woes of Police

1. Role of Honour

The King's Police Medal was introduced by the British Government on 7th July 1909, as an award for gallantry or distinguished service on the part of the members of the Police Forces throughout the world-wide British Empire. In course of time, the need was felt for wider recognition of Police Services in India, which though meritorious, were not given due recognition. On the contrary, police faced humiliation from all — the public, judiciary and the Government in view of the rising tide of the Freedom Struggle launched by the Congress, and its related organisations. The services rendered by the police in maintaining law and order and communal harmony during the First World War period of 1914-18 were also without the semblance of any appreciation. Police personnel openly started ventilating this grief and compared the awards given to the personnel of the Army. In order to do some justice, in February 1932, the INDIAN POLICE MEDAL was instituted as an award for police services in India, which though worthy of recognition, was not sufficiently distinguished to justify the grant of the King's Police Medal. Obviously, it was a racial bias on the part of the British, that the Indian Police personnel were debarred from seeking the honour. The Indian Police Medal subsequently came to be granted either for gallantry or meritorious service. After the Independence the above two awards were replaced by the President Police and Fire Services Medal, and the Police Medal under the Government of India notification dated 15th March 1951.

The awards of gallantry carried monthly allowance; the amount varies with different rank. When an individual is in receipt of the allowance at the time of his death, it is continued for life or till remarriage of his widow.

The "Gallantry" exhibited by a police constable and also by the Police Chief does not change the complexion and importance of the valour. The gallantry shown by a Police Constable in arresting a notorious criminal can, by no stretch of imagination, be less or of inferior quality than the gallantry exhibited by the topmost Police-Chief in arresting a criminal of equal notoriety. But a disparity was made, and the anomaly was corrected in November 1987 by giving uniformly the allowance of Rs. 100 per mensem. In view of the present inflationary rate the amount of this allowance has not been proportionately increased. Moreover, it is almost .01 per cent of policemen receive these awards, as if other members of the force do not contribute to the meritorious acts of the recipient. In the Army for each deployment, even in peace time, a medal is awarded, and by the time a military man puts 20 years' service he has at least 10 medals to decorate his chest; contrarily a policeman of the same standing has nothing. If the services of both are analysed, a policeman's job is more hazardous and full of stress and strain, and except to continue the tradition of the British to consider army man superior to policeman, there does not seen any rationale behind this discriminatory attitude, with which the police are deeply concerned and grieved. In 1988 (394); in 1992 (808) and in 1995 (approximately over 2,000) police personnel belonging to the States and the Union Territories were killed while dealing with criminals. Similarly, in 1988 (284); in 1992 (419) police personnel belonging to Central Police Organisations such as Border Security Force, Central Reserve Police Force, Indo-Tibetan Border Police Force, Railway Protection Police Force, Central Industrial Security Force, *etc.*, have been killed mostly by terrorist and insurgent outfits. In 1995 this figure may be over 1,000. Injuries sustained during police operations by police personnel run in to several thousands. During 1994-95 police opened fire on more than 5,000 occasions resulting in the death of about 5,000 anti-socials. If not actually a war of international standard, the police are perpetually embattled with anti-socials, terrorists, insurgents and drug *mafias*, and the casualties suffered by them in a single year amply justify their pressing demand for better emoluments, conditions of service and recognition of their work, which is more hazardous, stupendous and vulnerable than that of the Army. Even during an active war so many casualties are not the result of direct confrontation with the enemy forces. Who, other than the people, would wipe off the tears of the police, whom they themselves appointed for their own security, safety and protection from crime and criminals?

Another sad appendage to this lamentable story is generally the partisan attitude of the Police Chiefs in submitting recommendations for these awards to the Government. A really honest, trustworthy, conscious hard-worker renowned for his strictest rectitude, is generally denied his due award, because he has refused to be in line with those who are quite opposite to his qualities and followed the unlawful or illegal orders of the superior and political bosses. Political patronage is always required for obtaining an award; or else the award can be bought at some high price; unfortunately instances cannot be quoted.

2. Crime Situation

Crime situation in the country is alarming. About 50 per cent of cases are not registered in police records. The departmental figures are a mockery of the real incidence of crime in the country; may be they satisfy the higher echelons, please the Government and cheat the people! The country's population has touched 95 crore marks. The density of population per square mile is 290. The annual incidence of total crime in India is about 1,000 in one lakh of population for which the police strength is 12 for every 100 square km. There are about 15-20 policemen of all categories and rank and file in a *Tahsil* Police Station. The police strength for 1,000 population is less than 1.4. The police strength is never utilised fully for the prevention of crime and detection of offences and offenders as for majority of the annual hours it is engaged or involved in giving security to elected representatives, and such other sundries, besides the maintenance of law and order. In 1953 (6,01,964) and in 1995 (approximately 20,00,000) cognizable offences were reported to various police stations in the country and of them there were over 20 per cent of violent crimes, 40 per cent property crimes, and 5 per cent white-collar crimes. Almost 80 per cent of the cases are investigated, and 70 per cent are charge-sheeted in various law courts. Figures of crimes reported under the local and special laws render a colossal figure. Percentage of conviction or acquittal cannot be given as only in the various High Courts and Supreme Court there were 28,51,238 cases, as on September 30, 1994, pending final verdict (Parliament was informed about this in September 1994 by the Minister concerned). The pendency of cases in courts, lower than these superior courts, is beyond the contemplation of citizens. This is the Criminal Justice System of India! Percentage of conviction in property offences has not crossed the five marks ever since several years, whereas up to 1955, an officer who could secure 33 per cent conviction was considered as a mediocre officer for his promotional prospects. The old generation of policemen wails at such a damnable situation. Inadequacy of Police strength is one of the dominant factors for such a state of "Inefficiency", and it is all pervasive. These are the grouses; and even then, "Untrustworthy Police" is the public verdict.

3. Intelligence a Severely Damaged Instrument

The intelligence gathering in India is structurally monolithic, and is conspicuously missing by a strong and trustworthy organisation, which is leak-proof. Never before the organisation was tested by problems created by insurgent and terrorist outfits, it being mostly confined to the collection of political intelligence. The Police Station bear the responsibility of collection of intelligence, but they do not know, who are the anti-social and criminals though they form their inseparable company. The ground level intelligence is never collected correctly. The penetrative capacity of the organisation has come to a dead end; and instead of acquiring intelligence, foretelling and fore-warning the course of events, *post facto* information supported by press gossips is made available for analysis and eventual actions. Proper sources are rarely tapped or planted deep into the underworld.

Once a highly dependable instrument of the Government, by correct and timely warning, had saved the country from many disasters and pitfalls. It is now in a total mess. Nothing could be more disastrous than using the intelligence machinery for the purpose of internal political espionage; it never functions impartially, intelligence reports arc manipulated, and tailor-made and misused to please the politicians in power. It has over the years, frittered away its resources in chasing political rivals. Could there have been a more pathetic state of our internal security apparatus than the assassinations of Prime Ministers Indira Gandhi, Rajiv Gandhi and Chief Minister Beant Singh? The major reason as to why our intelligence apparatus became useless is the misuse of its crack intelligence officers. For no fault of theirs, a number of them got labelled as belonging to this or that group and their expertise could no longer be utilised. Since the last three decades Intelligence Organisation has taken the back seat. Maintenance of dossiers of political rivals, keeping surveillance over them and their illegal phone-tapping took most of their time in preference to collection of intelligence, against crime and criminals, and the national enemies. The Ayodhya incident, followed by large-scale communal riots engulfing the entire Nation and the high explosive blasts at Bombay, Calcutta, Madras, Hyderabad, trains occasionally; and almost daily in Jammu and Kashmir speak of the peak inefficiency of the organisation. Like law and order, politicians in power have made a mess of the Intelligence Machinery and eventually destroyed it. Analyse any communal, caste, regional, linguistic or for that matter any other riot or law and order situation and follow the chain, and one will find a politician at each end. But the entire blame is foisted on the police.

4. Politicisation of Police

In the first-place politicisation, and the takeover of the police force by political bosses must be ruthlessly eliminated. Nothing has contributed more to the demoralisation of the Police Force than its manipulation by politicians and the power-wielders. Nothing has shattered the fair name and credibility of the police more than its subservient and willingness to carry out illegal orders. Nothing has emboldened the police to violate the Rule of Law and indulge in lawlessness as the assurances of official patronage and political protection. It must be drilled into every policeman, even of the lowest and highest rank that primary loyalty is to the Constitution, and the laws whose obedient servant he must be at all times. There is little realisation among the police that not only are they entitled to disregard illegal orders, but they could be held criminally liable if they executed an order which was patiently illegal and criminal in nature.

5. Service Conditions

There should be radical improvement in the service conditions of the police force and the treatment meted out to them by the establishment, public and Government. Urgent attention is required to better their working and living conditions which are very unsatisfactory. Do not expect the police to be incorruptible and law-abiding in the prevalent vicious environments, and if their pay and benefits are woefully inadequate to make both ends meet? It is extremely difficult for the police to be civil or civilised if they are ill-treated. There must be public acknowledgement of honesty and devotion to service whenever one comes across it, but unfortunately it is never done.

The workload of the police has increased substantially, thanks to the added burden of providing security to thousands of elected representatives of no significance, and coping with demonstrations and agitations, all of which are not non-violent. It is never realised that the police have been over-stretched to the point of breaking, and unfortunately there is a growing tendency to take the police for granted till the occurrence of a serious police unrest or a mini-mutiny.

The crying need is for proper, comprehensive education of the police personnel at all levels, knowledge of the various sections of the laws is not sufficient. Nor a nodding acquaintance with Constitutional provisions designed to guarantee and protect fundamental rights is adequate. It is essential that the police are taught, and are made to understand the rationale and the philosophy underlying the various Constitutional provisions meant for the protection of fundamental freedoms of the individuals. Every police person must be made to grasp the basic principle that ends do not justify means. Unless these measures are implemented it will not be possible to humanise the Criminal Justice System and secure respect for and observe human rights.

At any one point of time, Rule of Law, should be the governing principle. Failure to appreciate this leads to confrontation. But at the same time the police have to face the fact that the issue is most often complicated by political decisions and interference. In the result, in many such contexts, the performance of the police role of enforcement in public order situation is surely "tight-rope walking". If he does too little, he is found fault with; if he does too much he is arraigned. This brings to the fore the need for political executives to be clear in their own minds on the standards they want the police to keep and the people themselves to willingly co-operate with the police in performing their difficult task, with due regards to the observance of human rights.

Human situations and mode of operations are never static, and they require constant reviews, the prevention of crime has always been recognised as one of the prime functions of the police, who is generally the first group of people to notice persons, situations and conditions that lead to crime and they continue to be the only body which has the necessary organisational base to tackle the criminal problems effectively. If the police do not take the steps to neutralise the criminogenic potential and attempt to keep people out of penal institutions, it is doubtful whether other agencies, which do not have the resources of the police will be able to take on this job. There is need for establishment of specialised units, augmentation and provision of viable organisational structure and network of communication to these units and initiation of motivation to attract deserving personnel, review of functions in terms of local needs and positive response to higher echelons in the police.

6. Police-Press Relations

Relations between the police-press, and the public in India have been a love-hate one, more of the latter. The citizens view the police as the strong arm of the State that harasses and not befriends them, the police are feared by the common man, misused by the powerful, the monied, the politically supported and the criminal-political nexus, and above all the Government, for their selfish ends, pilloried by the press and made a scapegoat by the party in power. Cordial police-public relationship despite some successful experiments here and there, is nothing unprecedented in India, and has yet to be attempted in a sincere and serious manner. Today, there has been ceaseless expansion of their functions, which have given them more and more duties and added power. The police have to enforce many regulations, orders, and laws, with the public life at a number of points and have nothing to do with criminals and criminal activities. An alert and conscious "Press" is able to build-up or destroy their good image. In a stable developed society where the Parliament and State Legislatures and the Executive are healthy and vibrant, the functioning of the press is largely confined to its traditional role of reporting and interpreting events. But when these institutions are ineffective or on the decline, greater responsibility devolves on an independent press to critically examine the deeds of the police.

Unfortunately in India, Parliament and State Legislatures are packed with people of lesser integrity. Nexus between politicians and criminal gangs has come to stay, corruption in the bureaucracy, and even the judiciary is frequently reported, and they have become ineffective, police brutality is considered passe and politics is sordid. In such a situation an independent press plays a vital role of keeping India an open society, which is the only way it can be governed. Police have to constantly realise this situation and take such action, as is not open to public criticism.

7. Police-Public Relationship

Relations between the public and police are by no means cordial, much less ideal. Police should be aware of this shortcoming and make continuous efforts to improve the situation by better training and supervision. There has been a serious setback by new developments in the political scene of the country. Criminalisation of politics has introduced a new dimension in police-public relations. Persons involved in crime get elected on party tickets, and even become ministers and members of Cabinet. Co-operation of the people towards such a government and police which is the visible arm of the Government, can hardly be forthcoming. Again political parties organise demonstrations, many times in violation of laws, adopt illegal means or expose illegal cause resulting in discomfort and inconveniences to the law abiding citizens. Police normally adopt soft approach to such demonstrations. Can the police be blamed for this ineffectiveness? Are not the anti-Sikhs riots of 1984, the cumulative results of Government attitude and policy to support Congress protagonists? Party in power promoted the political careers of such criminals. Such an attitude has always its impact on police-public relation. Such ineffectiveness of the police can never draw any public sympathy or co-operation. This is a serious situation getting more serious day-by-day. Police will have to redraw their priorities if they want to serve the people and their nation, and in the eventual process improve police-public relations.

Police should always note and act that, their authority under the law is strictly defined and they are personally liable for consequences whenever they invoke it. They play no part in determining guilt or punishment and their accountability to courts, both criminal and civil, to local police authorities, to Parliament and to public opinion is unsurpassed anywhere else in the world. In the legal and Constitutional framework in which the society requires them to enforce the laws enacted by its elected representatives, the most essential weapons in their armoury are not fire-arms, water-cannons, tear gas or rubber bullets but the confidence and support of the people on whose behalf they act. That confidence and support depend on their personal and collective integrity, and in particular to the long tradition of Constitutional freedom from political interference in their operational role. Police are not the servants of the Government at any level. They do not act at the behest of a minister or political party, and not even the party in the Government. They act on behalf of the people as a whole, and the powers they exercise cannot be restricted or widened by anyone, save Parliament alone. All these have been denied to the police. The observance of these ethical concepts by the police will alone determine police-public relationship, especially in relation to the maintenance of public order and prevention and detection of crime and criminals. Woefully, the image of the police is that they are mercenaries to establish perpetually the party in power and their criminal colleagues, and not to help the common man, the poor, the needy and the oppressed!

8. Police Tradition

The recommendations made by the All India Police Commission 1860 and 1902 formed the foundation of the existing police system of the country. But everybody failed to realise that the Police system was organised by the Britishers for the perpetuation of their rule in India, and most of the principles enunciated by them for guidance of the Police are fundamentally at variance with those prevalent in free countries. The greatest drawback was the insufficient appreciation of the status-cum-role of a Police constable, and his consequent relegation at least in the matter of pay, to the rank of ordinary class four workers or unskilled labourers. It is always forgotten that no citizen in the country, other than a Police Constable is vested with the wide power to arrest an offender; he is sufficiently educated and trained for that purpose, and without his faithfulness, trustworthiness, initiative, zeal and energy no work in a police set-up can be carried out with the expected efficiency and competency. The result is that persons with higher educational calibre desist from joining the police service. The separation of the Judicial functions from the Executive was given effect from 1st May 1960, bringing profound influence on the working of the police. In the matters of trial, conviction, bail concerning the offenders, more particularly the hardened and habitual criminals, the police could no longer look to the District Magistrate for support. Creation of too many superior ranks and Government policy of rushing them to enquire into the most ordinary complaint of a politician have diluted the interest in work of the subordinate police officers, who have lost their initiative and the confidence to deal with a situation with the help of the available resources at their command. They have developed inertia and a resolute practice to pass on the information about a matter either to be tense or likely to degenerate the peace to senior police officer and await their arrival with additional police contingent and deal with the situation as ordered. Courage is the foremost qualification required of a good policeman, and these days that is conspicuously missing. The cumulative effect is that a good tradition of service could not be built up after the Independence and policemen are becoming increasingly mercenaries. The sense of individual responsibility, and its legitimate and truthful discharge have totally vanished. Hardly 2 per cent of police personnel still remain responsive, and that is not sufficient enough to deal efficiently with the ever-increasing degenerated law and order and crime situations.

9. Incomplete Records

It is well-established and recognised that the primary objective of any police organisation is the prevention and detection of crime. But it is common knowledge that, over the years, police duties have grown both in volume and complexity. The maintenance of law and order, performing of security and associated duties, and meeting the numerous situations arising out of communal tensions *etc.*, have and will take a very heavy toll of police resources and time. The consequences of these developments, however, have been quite disastrous, for the efficiency and competency of the police specially in the fields of prevention and detection of crimes, the systematic collection of criminal intelligence, and the maintenance of criminal records have all been relegated to the background. One clear fallout of this is the near collapse of the system of collection and dissemination of information on crime and criminals at all levels. As a consequence of these there is a very poor quality of police data that had and being fed in the computers all over the country. If this sorry situation is to be retrieved and improved, crime investigation and maintenance of crime records will need to be given much higher priority.

10. Effect of Reservations

The Constitution envisaged the phenomenon of reservation only as a transitional measure, but each time the period has been extended. Now a stage has come when Reservation Category for Scheduled Castes, Scheduled Tribes and Other Backward Classes have more or less become permanent. This decision is politically motivated, but it impregnated seeds of dissension in the solidarity of the Force, which is now divided on caste, class and religion. It has ceased to function as a homogeneous unit. It has already eroded the cohesive band which once led them with the motto — one for all and all for one, and created more acute problems. Obviously, placing a person, who has just completed his probation, over the heads of a set of efficient officers awaiting promotion after completing long years of service, is scarcely the right way to ensure efficiency and contentment in the organisation. The very concept that a particular incumbent belongs to the reservation category and bearing special status drove a wedge in the '*esprit-de-corps*' tradition of the police belonging to the previous generation. If not on face, clandestinely disrespect or abuses are hurled at each other and tendency to form groups has increased. There is covert contemptuous behaviour of either group — the reservationists, and the non-reservationists. Discipline has been greatly damaged. As in the Army, police should have been excluded by the Government from the mire of reservation. Frustration, indiscipline and fall in standards have become unavoidable in such a context. In due course of time this practice is likely to spell disaster when groupism based on political ideologies is likely to be the order of the day. Actually, seeds of caste-class conflicts have started germinating. It is the consensus that candidates from weaker sections for whom reservations have been made, may be considered for such promotions only after they have become eligible according to the time-frame and efficiency, probity, integrity and honesty. On this analogy the recruitment system is also faulty. The best candidates though available, cannot be drafted into the police service. The standard norms of recruitment have been considerably down stepped to the detriment of the police force.

The under-manned, over-worked and ill-equipped police organisations in India have done reasonably well in the conduct of ten massive general elections during which, each time over 70 crores of people moved about freely to cast their votes. Several hundred elections of various local bodies and *Gram Panchayats* have also been creditably conducted by the police, who were literally driven to this work for maintaining the essence of public peace and order and in ensuring reasonable justice delivery. But still their image is not good at all. A perceptible attitude of groupism politics is taking hold in the rank and file of the force; low as well as high police personnel have already been affected by this partisan behaviour. The strength of cohesive identity, and function with singular unity has now become questionable. Group reliance has become an order of the day.

11. Judiciary

Delay in trial, easy bail to repeaters, acquittals, imposition of punishment not commensurate with the offence committed and wrong exercise of discretion by courts make the task of law enforcement difficult. Court evaluation of evidence is not realistic, and the aggrieved runs in search of justice from pillar to post. Contrast the situation of a policeman with that of a presiding officer of court, which takes his own time to come to a decision, whereas the policeman has to decide on the spur of the moment whether to take action or not and face the consequences of his actions, and at times perhaps, violence and riot. If a Magistrate makes a mistake, it is construed an error of judgment. He does not lose his job. If a policeman makes a mistake, woe betied him. If he fails to make an arrest when he should make one, he is liable to disciplinary action involving even possible dismissal from the force. If he makes an arrest without sufficient cause he is liable not only to departmental action, but also to a civil suit for damages which may run him financially and beggar his family. The unfortunate policeman is, after all a convenient scapegoat between the devil and the deep sea. Obviously, there is no question that the police on occasion make error. But should a criminal go free because, policeman has blundered? If the police function in a utopian world, in which all policemen were infallible, there would be little, if any, need for courts.

Lakhs of cases are pending in courts, some more than three to five years, if not more. Acquittals are high and bail for repeaters is easy. Criminals are let loose to prey upon the society. The public are demanding from the police to use rough and ready methods to curtail crime and violence in the streets. A major part of the misuse and abuse of discretionary power is based on the ineptitude of our legal institutions in fulfilling the elementary end of any legal order — to keep the peace.

12. Poor Leadership

Frequent failure of police during a crisis in many parts of the country has demonstrated that leadership in the Police Force is the greatest single factor for efficient performance of duties. In the handling of disturbances a leadership of high order is needed. Such a leadership as would inspire the confidence of the subordinates and redouble their courage, and capable of taking versatile action. Such a leadership as would extricate the subordinates from distress and look after their comforts more than its. On the achievement of Independence the Colonial system was interjected by a new element — politicians and political parties. The concept of neutrality and impartial functioning became the first victim. Senior police officers got increasingly aligned with politicians. Alternatively, they withdrew into a shell and did the minimum expected of them.

Over the last 48 years the police have received much buffeting at the hands of politicians. The police leadership has ceased to function effectively due to day-to-day political interference, political control in the police functioning, corruption and indiscipline within the rank and file. Officers rarely lead the men from the front, on many occasions they flee away leaving their subordinates to deal with an ugly situation. When results are good, they do not fail to boast that the action was directed by them, but when results are bad they do not fail to condemn the subordinate and award as serious a punishment as possible. Senior officers generally exercise power by lobbying, by string pulling, by insinuating, by forming cliques and secret intrigues. Feeling of jealousy towards colleagues or superiors in office to rise to a higher rank are then encountered. Management requires that while efficient and impartial officers should be given adequate protection, there should be no hesitation to discipline the wayward, and the intransigent. But the greatest handicaps faced by the police today are political patronage and partisan politics. There are regrettably high promotions of delinquents. Policemen who have been dismissed are reinstated and even promoted under political pressure. Police recruitment, discipline and promotion are subjected to various external influences, mostly political. All these things have neutralised the efficiency of police leadership. It is absolutely necessary to remove the police from the control of politicians and as soon as it is done many of the shortcomings, of the police force would disappear and relations between police and public vastly improved. Leadership, management and morale are interdependent but without good leadership there cannot be high morale or good management.

A lament increasingly heard throughout the country, is the poverty of our leadership, at times bankruptcy, at every level of administration, national leadership not excluded. Service pride and self-discipline nurtured over the years are no longer valid. This has deeply affected the police administration and struck at the very root of the police leadership.

Where senior police hierarchy is motivated solely by consideration of personal agrandisement and habituated to take shelter behind politicians for self-interest sacrificing the interest of the force, loyalty of men towards their superiors has taken a back seat. Frequent police strikes assaults and manhandling of Senior Police Officers by their subordinates in the midst of riots, refusal to open fire on the rampaging armed mob engaged in looting and arson or refusal to make arrests when directed to do so, favouring one party against another in a conflict situation *etc*., have crippled the police administration.

Mushroom growth of senior assignments in recent years have subverted command control and discipline. Infighting between senior police officers, for power and pelf, has grown rapidly and have spilled from the police corridors into the streets. The nexus between politicians, gangsters and the police is the most formidable law enforcement problems of the future. It is difficult to say what can be done to bring into being an impartial and efficient police force out of the chaos in existence. But the most intractable, and from the police point of view, the most damaging factor is the complete failure of police leadership. The police leadership has deserted their rank and file, and unless they stand-up manfully and fight every adverse influence, political or executive, the Police Force would accelerate its downward trend and efficiency, discipline, honesty, probity and integrity would be on the verge of disappearance.

13. Final Analysis

We have a turn down in the economy, we have increasingly high rates of unemployment. We see a resurgence of Naxalites and rapid increase in insurgency and terrorism. We see crimes of violence increasing faster than our population. We see hostilities between landowners and landless peasants, between Hindus and Muslims, between class and castes, between Hindus and

Scheduled Castes, *Harijans* and other backward classes, between tribals and non-tribals and growing rivalries between political parties and groups. We see corruption, indiscipline, various malpractices and growing discontent in the Police Force. We are aware of criminalisation of politics, and the political criminal nexus, and we have a Criminal Justice System that people perceive is not working at all and failed to provide protection to life and property and we see the growth of the parallel extra-legal, if not actually illegal, system of grievance redressal through the *mafia* hierarchy growing rapidly in connivance with politicians and police, from year to year. There has been a steady increase in smuggling and gun-running across the borders and illegal manufacturing of fire-arms and bombs, mushrooming as a cottage industry, in different parts of the country. We see the volume of public complaints against the police is increasing steadily and relations between the police and public worsening almost every day.

Full enforcement of our present laws is physically impossible and as a result police have developed a discretion in the registration and investigation of cases and prosecution of offenders. This discretion formed an era of great power, and has contributed to abuse of power and corruption.

The police have a right to demand that the path they must tread should be clearly redesigned to lead to a just result for the community, for whom they act, as well as for the accused. The distance between the crime, and the courts is often the distance between law and justice. Therefore, prompt and painstaking investigation by police and prosecution is the only befitting answer to the existing malady.

The police has failed to think about the future in terms of social equity and justice. Their thinking would profit if they came out of their shell and concerned themselves with their essential role and human relations. Continued deprivation amidst plenty of failures in the redressal of grievance breeds widespread militancy and belligerence. A police administration that has so far failed in its task to ensure justice has been bypassed. Policemen failed to be stern and authoritative to the criminals and anti-social elements. The police have to retrace, and once again achieve their reputation — criminals and anti socials are their rank enemies needing judicious eliminations from the society infested and menaced by them.

Today the greatest source of friction between the police and the public arises from law enforcement. People, by and large, feel no obligation to respect the law and no legal responsibility to obey it. Multiplication of legislation, rules, regulations has far-reaching consequences in law enforcement. The terribly understaffed police often find this task extremely difficult. As the new laws have poured out, police face the problem to draw the line in each case between what the police must do, ought to do, can ignore and those they must not do. Police discretion has now become a major source of corruption, and strained its relationship with the public, politicians and the judiciary. Today enormous range of discretion exercised by the police has contributed to criticism of the police, both for enforcing laws and for failing to enforce them. The Police failed to strike a balance between excesses and inaction. However, no Police Force in the entire world can carry out duties, without the help of the public, who must be perceptibly satisfied that the police are acting impartially, within the powers conferred on them by the law of the land.

Our society is like a molecule full of internal tensions held in a precarious balance by a criss-cross of group alignment. In consequence, the function of the police are expanding and growing in importance. As an instrument of social defence, no society can dissolve its police or to do without them. The nexus between the *mafia* hierarchy, politicians, and the police is the most formidable of the law enforcement problems of the future. Indeed, the point has been reached in which the underworld can commit crime with ease anywhere, anytime and buy immunity from police action. Policemen are passing through a disturbing phase and time. Ethical and political mandates run counter to each other, and this resultant situation has undermined the established tradition — old honesty and loyalty. For all that, policemen rightly feel they have been mucked about a lot. A partisan and demoralised police administration cannot work as the bulwark of law and order and social stability. In a rapidly changing society it is of paramount importance that the standards of the police service must be maintained at as high a level as possible, because police service is one of the dominant organisations of the civil administration which can sustain or destroy the happiness of the community, and integration and stability of the nation.

14. Peoples' Police

Coolly, calmly, collectively, and partial introspectively, a policeman muses and wails his woes:

> "In the police station, I meet the complainant, the suspect and the hardened criminal. In the hospital, I meet the victim of rape; the person fighting for life after being grievously injured by a criminal; the person who attempted to commit suicide; the doctor and the nurse charged with kidnapping of a new-born baby. In brothels, I find teenage girls brought after kidnapping, and sold for prostitutions. In hotels, I meet call girls and occasionally sodomists. In the university campus, I meet students on rampage. In factories I meet workers and management fighting for their mutual rights. In courts, I meet magistrates, judges and lawyers, much more educated and talented than me and who by and large are very critical of the police and believe they are corrupt, brutal and untrustworthy. In the underworld, I meet criminals and gangsters and all vicious persons not caring for my life and those evading the law under political cover. I seldom meet the public at their best and they seldom welcome me — many times abhore my sight. To them, I am the law, the interfering, dangerous and a source of trouble. I find my children are teased in schools and wife heckled by the society because I am in police service. In spite of my ostensible functioning as protector, I meet only those I am protecting them from, and for me they have no good word, appreciation, sympathy. To think of sympathy, affection, love and regard for me is anathema I have failed to acquire the goodwill of the people and retrieve my good image."

But the public use a policeman as scapegoat for its neurotic attitude towards crime and always turned two faces towards a policeman. They expect him to be human. They employ him to administer the law, and yet ask him to waive it. They resent him when he enforces the law in their own case; yet demand his dismissal when he does not elsewhere. They offer him bribes, yet denounce his corruption. They admire violence even against the society itself but condemn force by the police on their behalf. They ask crime to be eradicated, but only by the use of "sporting methods".

Inversely, unlike in the past, people have segregated themselves from rendering the necessary assistance to the police in their already difficult battle against crime and criminals, anti-socials and anti-nationals, and this isolation left the police all alone to accomplish their service goal — "The maintenance of law and order and detection of crime and criminals."

Bibliography

A Concise Encyclopaedia of Indian History — M.B. Chande.

A Philosophy for the Police — B.N. Mulik.

Administrative Reforms Commission 1967.

Amnesty International Report (India) 1992.

Betrayal of the Police — S.K. Ghosh.

Civil Disturbances — B.N. Mulik.

Code of Criminal Procedure.

Communal Riots in India — Jitendra Narayan.

Communal Riots in India — S.K. Ghosh.

Constitution of India.

Crime, Criminal and Cops — R.S. Kulkarni.

Crime in India, Probation — R.R. Bhatnagar.

Crime in India, Problems and Policy — R.R. Bhatnagar.

Crime Statistics Published by Bureau of Police Research and Development—Ministry of Home Affairs, Government of India.

Criminology — Ahmad Siddique.

Criminology — H.R. Mukhi.

Crisis of Credibility — Press Council of India, New Delhi.

Encyclopaedia of Police in India — Three volumes — S.K. Ghosh and K.F. Rustamji.

First to Fifth United Nations Congress on Prevention of Crime and Treatment of Offenders, New York.

Freedom of Speech and Assembly — S.K. Ghosh.

Image of the Police — Shrivastava Saraswathi.

Indian Evidence Act.

Indian Penal Code.

Indian Police Act 1861 and Police Acts of Several States.

Indian Police Journal — Various Volumes — Ministry of Home Affairs, Government of India.

Juvenile Delinquency and Justice System — B.N. Mishra.

Juvenile Delinquency and the Role of the Family — Social Wealth — S.K. Bhattacharya.

Kautilya Arthashastra — 3 volumes — R.P. Kangale.

Keeping the Peace; For Whom the Bell tolls; Police Then and Now — S.K. Ghosh.

Law Enforcement in Tribal Areas — S.K. Ghosh.

Muslim Politics in India — S.K. Ghosh.

Police and Law Enforcement — R. Deb.

Police and Social Changes in India — Rashmi Mishra and Samrendra Mohanty.

Police Today—Shankar Sen.

Politics of Violence — S.K. Ghosh.

Reflection on Police, Society and Allied Subjects — D.N. Kaul.

Several Social Legislations.

Social Defence — An Indian Perspective — S.K. Bhattacharya.

Social Order in India — S.K. Ghosh.

Social Problems and Welfare in India — Jogan Shankar.

Sociology — Dr. G. Das.

State Police Organisation in India — S.C. Misra.

The Crisis of Indian Legal System — Upendra Baxi.

The Indian Mafia — S.K. Ghosh.

The Police and Human Rights — Sali J. Sorabjee.

Traffic in Narcotics and Drugs Addiction — S.K. Ghosh.

United Nations Declaration on Justice to Victims 1985.

United Nations Organisation — various publications on Human Rights; Police; Crime; Juvenile Delinquency; Drugs; Weaker Sections of Society and Co-related Issues.

Universal Charters of Children's Rights 1966.

Unquiet Border — S.K. Ghosh.

Various Criminal Law Amendment Laws.

Various Enquiry Reports on disturbances including communal riots.

Various Newspapers, Periodicals and Magazines and Publications on the Subjects.

Various Reports of Law Commissions.

Various Reports of National Police Commissions and State Police Commissions.

Women and Crime — S.K. Ghosh.

Woman Police and Social Change — Shamim Allem.

Index